A Journal of
Nonfiction Narrative

THE RIVER
TEETH READER

Volume 10 · Numbers 1–2
Fall 2008/Spring 2009

Published by the
University of Nebraska Press

Ohio Arts Council *River Teeth* is grateful for funding from
A STATE AGENCY the Ohio Arts Council, which helps
THAT SUPPORTS PUBLIC to make this journal possible.
PROGRAMS IN THE ARTS

SUBMISSIONS

River Teeth invites submissions of creative nonfiction, including narrative reportage, essays, and memoirs, as well as critical essays that examine the emerging genre and that explore the impact of nonfiction narrative on the lives of its writers, subjects, and readers.

All articles must be prepared in accordance with the most recent edition of the *MLA Style Manual* and submitted electronically, double-spaced (including quotations and end-notes), with 1-inch margins and 12-point font size. Individuals whose works are accepted for publication must supply a final copy in both paper and electronic form (RTF, Microsoft Word, or WordPerfect). Please include a one-sentence personal bio.

River Teeth uses an online submission manager to read and track your submissions. In order to use the Submission Manager, you will need to set up an account online at http://apps.ashland.edu/submanager/. Please note that your contact information will only be used to communicate news and events about *River Teeth* and to respond to your submissions.

Writers are strongly urged to use the Submission Manager to submit essays. Mailed sub-missions will take lower priority and will take many months longer to receive a response, but if this is the only means available, submissions should be sent to

> *River Teeth*
> Ashland University
> 401 College Avenue
> Ashland, OH 44805
> www.ashland.edu/riverteeth

SUBSCRIPTIONS

River Teeth: A Journal of Nonfiction Narrative (ISSN 1544-1849) is published semiannually at $25 for individuals, $65 for institutions, and $16 for single issues by Ashland University. For subscriptions outside the United States, please add $16 for postage and handling. Canadian subscribers please add appropriate GST or HST. Payment must accompany order. Make checks payable to River Teeth and mail to:

> River Teeth
> Subscriptions
> Ashland University
> 401 College Avenue
> Ashland, OH 44805
>
> (419) 289-5110
> www.ashland.edu/riverteeth

Contents

Editors' Notes

Ten years ago we penned the first editors' notes to our readers. At this point ten years later, we should be writing at length about our humble beginnings and singing of the heights we've reached. Our words should reveal just the right amount of nostalgia, pride, and just a hint of self-congratulation. But there is no time for that; or rather, no space.

We have to keep this note short. In the ten years *River Teeth: A Journal of Nonfiction Narrative* has been around, we have received over twenty thousand submissions, and we've published about three hundred of those twenty thousand. Most of what we reject is the work of fine writers. And now we've had to reject the work of writers whose work we've previously accepted. Worse than that—we've had to reject the very same pieces we once accepted! We had to choose the best forty or so pieces of the three hundred we've published. To make matters worse, we've had to divide the pieces up into four categories: Essay, Memoir, Literary Journalism, and Craft and Criticism. If there were no space concerns, we'd write a few sentences about how difficult it can be to say, for instance, where memoir ends and a kind of literary journalism begins, and how much we like pieces that flirt with those boundaries. If we had more space, we'd brag about our Pushcart Prize and our Best American Essays. We'd love to pat ourselves on the back and tell you how many Pulitzer Prize winners we've published—and with even more pride—shine a light on the people whose *River Teeth* publication was their first.

Saying no to our own writers was the hardest thing we've had to do as editors. We hate to reject a piece we love because there's simply no more space. So the best thing we can do right now is to shut up, and thank you for reading.

—JM and DWL

THE
RIVER TEETH
READER

A Special Issue Celebrating the
Tenth Anniversary of *River Teeth*

VOLUME 10, NUMBERS 1–2
FALL 2008/SPRING 2009

Nancy Mairs

Sex and the Gimpy Girl

The other day I went into a tizzy. As a rule I avoid this state, not merely because it violates the reticent courtesy demanded by my Yankee upbringing but because it reinforces the misperception that people with disabilities are difficult to deal with. But to be honest sometimes I get sick of acting the Girl Scout of cripples, and I fall out of (or perhaps into my true) character.

On this day I had scheduled a Pap smear at a clinic new to me, on the eighth floor of the hospital at the center of the Arizona Health Sciences Center. In this building I can't reach higher than "3" on the elevator buttons, so I must make sure someone else gets on with me. When I arrived at the clinic the doors weren't automated: another wait till some other woman came along. The counter was too high for me to reach the sign-in sheet—so high, in fact, that I couldn't see the receptionist to ask for her help. After a thirty-five-minute wait a nurse escorted me into a windowless cubicle with a standard examining table, although I had specified when booking the appointment that I required a model that can be lowered and tilted.

"I can't use that," I said.

"You can't?" She sounded skeptical and slightly aggrieved.

"No, my legs are too weak to climb up. That's why I use a wheelchair. Surely I'm not the only woman ever to have come in here in a wheelchair."

"Well, we don't get many."

"I don't wonder," I said with an asperity I now regret, "if this is the kind of treatment they receive."

She skedaddled, sending back the head nurse, who assured me that they had one of the tables I needed, though it was being used and wouldn't be available for some time. So I settled down with the book I'd brought, took my turn, and left, pretty well exhausted. The ten-minute procedure had consumed two hours, but I'd survived a classic example of the reproductive "care" women with disabilities are all too apt to receive.

Although, when I first consulted Harvey W. Buchsbaum, MD, in 1972 I hadn't yet presented the symptoms "disseminated in space and time" necessary for a diagnosis of multiple sclerosis, he had no doubt that my body had gone neurologically awry. "Not to get pregnant," he scribbled in my chart. "Not to take birth control pills." He did not, of course, suggest how I was to accomplish the former without resorting to the latter. He was a neurologist. Modern doctors chop their patients into pieces and parcel them out like so many cuts of beef, and this one wasn't about to have anything to do with my reproductive system.

I betook myself to a gynecologist, who suggested that I have my uterus removed. Uh-uh, said Dr. Buchsbaum: all my innards should remain in place, a decision with which I rather concurred. I consulted another gynecologist, who recommended tubal ligation. Nope, said Dr. Buchsbaum: I ought to avoid anesthesia. If any tubules were to be prevented from transporting their reproductive cargo, they ought to reside in George's simpler anatomy. A little xylocaine, a couple of snips, and our worries would be over. This didn't strike me as a fair bargain. Although, owing to Rh incompatibility we had decided not to produce more children, he was only in his early thirties; if anything happened to me he would almost certainly marry again; and he might well want to have children with his new wife. So we resorted to barriers until, after a pregnancy scare a few years later, he decided that he really didn't want more children with anyone and elected a vasectomy.

It didn't strike me as odd, in those days, to have a bunch of guys dictating orders about my reproductive system. As I recall one of them was female, so I'm using the word "guys" loosely. But since some medical schools continue to pride themselves upon inculcating traditionally masculine attitudes and behaviors in their students—the problematic ones like arrogance and competitiveness right along with the noble ones like bravery and self-discipline—a good many of the doctors I have met have been "real men" regardless of gender. And I was reared a good girl, deferential to authority and expertise. Even though my docility had made my son's early life as an anti-Rh baby into something of a tragedy, since I accepted their decrees instead of following my instincts, I continued to do as I was told.

Nor did it occur to me until some years later that my experience might be generalizable in any way. I had a habit of assuming that whatever happened in my life happened to me alone rather than that my experiences might typify those of other women in similar circumstances. I didn't much think of myself (or think much of myself) as a woman then, and I didn't think of myself as a disabled woman at all, since early on my multiple sclerosis (MS) was more a nuisance than a handicap, and I seldom encountered others like me. As I worked my way into graduate studies, and particularly into feminist theory, my perspective began to shift until I came to recognize not merely that I was far from unique but that there wasn't an original word in my life-story. The details were distinctive, of course, or else I wouldn't be myself and not some other woman of my age and heritage, but the structure recapitulated many of the features that had marked females as "women" from time immemorial.

Despite the real progress generated by feminists, female and male, over the past century or so, for example, our society persists in construing women as commodities. In this we are hardly singular. Several years ago, when I visited my daughter in Zaire, I was entertained by Tata Nzulu, a farmer of about sixty. Over a dinner of mfumbwa (peanut-flavored grass clippings) and tilapia freshly harvested from his pond, he counseled me to accept in exchange for Anne's hand in marriage nothing less than a cow, a Coleman lantern, and ten thousand zaires (worth about three hundred dollars at the time). He was not trying to mock or offend me. On the contrary, he was trying to convey just what a treasure this young Peace Corps worker was to the village of Mfuatu. I was flattered.

Nevertheless, upon her return to the States, I didn't ask a bride price for my daughter. We don't do that here. Perhaps we ought. If all those pregnant fourteen-year-olds at the alternative school where my husband teaches had believed themselves to have some authentic value (though I don't think being traded for a cow would do the trick), maybe they'd have thought again before hopping into the backs of pickup trucks with one acned lothario or another swearing love for all eternity or at least until orgasm, whichever comes first. As it is, we commodify women—the models, the movie stars, the pretty little girls in beauty pageants, and the millions who, willingly or unwillingly, are held to their standards—without investing them with any specific worth. In the information age ours is an economy of images, not of substance, and a woman's situation may be worse—or at least no better—than it was in the days when she could feel certain that, as long as she behaved herself, her price would be far above rubies.

If you view women as commodities (and as social products, none of us can altogether escape such an unconscious assumption) then a disabled woman must inevitably be damaged goods. How many people do you know who would willingly take home a television set that displayed only snow or a loaf of bread that had fallen from a shelf under the wheels of a shopping cart? Interestingly, my son would do so on the grounds that a little tinkering might restore at least a moderately visible image to the screen and the nutritional value of bread remains the same whether the loaf is six inches or pita-flat. His partners have been similarly the worse for wear—one, obsessed by the certainty that she had a brain tumor, so agoraphobic that she couldn't leave the house, another a heroin-addicted prostitute, now on methadone—and I have often wondered to what extent his choices have resulted from being reared by a disabled mother.

Unlike Matthew, most people would send the broken television or the spoiled loaf straight to the dump, an outcome that may help explain the high level of anxiety triggered in people with disabilities by the question of physician-assisted suicide. And indeed, many disabled women might have an easier time finding someone to help them end their lives, assumed by their very nature to lack quality, than enlisting the corps of medical personnel required to resolve my daughter's infertility. Anne is an ideal matrix—doesn't drink, doesn't smoke, eats little fat and lots of complex carbohydrates—and no one could figure out why she didn't get pregnant. She just didn't. Finally, on the second try, intrauterine insemination did the trick, and soon we were all awaiting the birth of Colin James Mairs Peterson, who has burgeoned from the cutest little fetus in the world into the cutest little toddler in the world and doubtless will become, before we know it, the cutest little college graduate in the world.

No one ever questioned the appropriateness of Anne's desire for a baby. In fact, she'd have raised more eyebrows had she elected not to reproduce. Suppose, however, that she'd been exactly the same woman except that she had cerebral palsy. Would the nurse practitioners and doctors, who considered Anne's inability to conceive a treatable problem and mustered their arsenal of scopes and dyes and hormones and catheters, be just as eager to rush to her aid? I have my doubts. Her infertility might even be viewed as a blessing. If such a woman—Chloe, let's call her—insisted, health professionals might try to reason with her. How can you change an infant's diaper with so little control of your hands? they might ask. How will you chase down a toddler with your unsteady gait? How can your child acquire normal language skills listening to your slurred speech? I don't mean to suggest that hard questions ought not to be asked of a disabled woman. In fact, I think one of the deepest troubles of our society is that we don't ask enough questions, hard enough, of everybody. But those asked of Chloe are less authentic questions than veiled judgments—not so much "how can you . . .?" as "you can't possibly . . . ."—and as such they reveal not merely medical caution but some dubious premises about disability.

Medical professionals tend to pathologize disability, assuming that people whose bodies or minds function in abnormal ways have something "wrong" with them. People with disabilities certainly do have *something*— demyelination of the single nervous system, seizures, a severed spinal cord, inflamed joints, an extra chromosome, the possibilities seem endless and pretty unpleasant—but the "wrongness" of that something depends on one's point of view. From a doctor's perspective a disability is wrong because it deviates from the ideal norm built up during years of training and practice. But for the patient, disability simply *is* the norm. There is nothing wrong with me. In fact, for a fifty-five-year-old woman with multiple sclerosis, I'm just about right. I am occasionally ill, of course, being a mere mortal, but my disability itself is not a sickness. It's part of who I am. And I'm far more likely to thrive if you don't regard me as sick at my very core.

In another misconception society as a whole tends to infantilize those with physical or mental limitations, and none do so more readily than doctors and their adjuncts. To some extent paternalism infects their relations with all their patients—a word that doesn't share its root with "passive" by accident—because their apparent (and often real) power over life and death reduces us all to a childlike dependency on their superior knowledge. We reinforce their dominance through our docility. My father-in-law swallowed blood-pressure medication for years, never knowing—indeed, refusing to ask—what his blood pressure actually was. If I were a doctor I think that sort of quiescence would drive me nuts, but I can also see its allure. Not only does it endow the practitioner with an almost shamanistic force but it also makes treatment much more efficient. Patients who demand explanations for every detail of their care eat up time; and time, as HMOs know only too well, is money.

The tendency for doctor and patient to slip into a parent-child relationship is exacerbated in the case of people with disabilities by the fact that they are usually, in some way, genuinely helpless. In my case, for instance, I can no longer walk or even crawl; I must be dressed and undressed; I manipulate eating utensils with an overhand grasp; when the sole of my foot is scratched, instead of curling under, my toes flare in the Babinski response characteristic of newborns. In short my central nervous system is, quite literally, regressing toward its infantile state. Understandably others may have trouble remembering that these neurological deficits are not accompanied by spiritual, emotional, or intellectual regression. Even if they were—as they appear to be in Alzheimer's, for example—the end product would not be an infant but an adult, damaged, to be sure, but fully mature.

In no area of human experience does it better suit the general population to think of the disabled as children than the sexual. On the whole we are a society fixated upon sexual images and issues without ever feeling quite at ease with them. Shortly before a melanoma was discovered in his small bowel, my husband became impotent—a word I have never heard uttered in ordinary social discourse even though the condition is shared by a good ten million men in this country. When George mentioned his state to his oncologist, Dr. Ralph waved it off as the least of our worries. Only after George raised the matter, though not the penis, over a period of months did Dr. Ralph finally refer him to a urologist.

One day, I mentioned George's persistent impotence to my mother. "Good heavens," she said briskly, "you can live without *that!*"

"I know I can," I replied. "I just don't *want* to." She shrugged. What else could she do? As her response and Dr. Ralph's suggest plenty of people dismiss sexual enthusiasm in fifty-year-olds as at least a little silly. Perhaps the only person who can truly sympathize is my eighty-six-year-old mother-in-law. Her libido continues to flourish, and she has the boyfriend to prove it.

When it comes to sexuality in the disabled dismissal is apt to turn into outright repression. Made uncomfortable, even to the point of excrucia-tion, by the thought of maimed bodies (or, for that matter, minds) engaged in erotic fantasy or action, many deny the very possibility by ascribing to them the "innocence" of the very young. (In this of course, they are as wildly mistaken about immature as about adult sexuality.) Perhaps this disgust and denial stem, as the sociobiologists would probably have it, from the fact that such bodies are clearly less than ideal vehicles for the propagation of the species. Whatever its origin the repulsion lies buried so deeply in consciousness as to *seem* natural rather than constructed. As a result even someone with the best intentions in the world may fail to see a disabled woman whole. The parents of a congenitally disabled daughter may rear her to believe that she will never enter a sexually intimate rela-tionship like the one that they enjoy themselves, withhold information about reproductive inevitabilities like menstruation, perhaps punish her for the sexual acting out that adolescence brings. Those responsible for her health may "forget" that she requires reproductive care or provide it in a manner so cursory that she is left baffled and ashamed.

All the same, in most cases she will long for intimacy, since desire arises not "down there," in an area that may possibly be numb, but "up here," in the libidinous brain. If she is heterosexual, she will likely discover that, although she may make close male friends, most men will not think of her as a romantic object. I am fortunate in having found a partner before I became disabled who has elected to remain with me for thirty-five years. Nevertheless, I can speak with some authority here, because in order to prepare an article for *Glamour*, I read several hundred letters from read-ers with disabilities. I can't report as confidently about lesbian women with disabilities because they didn't write in, although several respondents naively contemplated trying lesbianism as a solution to their sexual frus-tration. Anyone who cannot accept as normal both a disabled woman's desire and the grief she feels when it is thwarted will never see her as fully human.

In condemning some of the social attitudes toward women with dis-abilities that may increase their difficulty in receiving optimal care, I don't propose that such a woman ought instead to be treated just like a non-disabled woman. To do so would be neither practical nor ethical. Dis-ability does set one apart from the general population, impinging upon every decision. Only when we define these differences frankly, instead of politely ignoring them, can we discern the ways in which they do—and do not—matter.

When a young friend of mine, already blinded and crippled by juvenile rheumatoid arthritis, suffered a stroke, she was found to be eight weeks pregnant. Although she and her husband, also severely disabled, wanted nothing more dearly than a baby, she bravely underwent an abortion and a tubal ligation knowing that her future health would never be certain enough for the long-term commitment child-rearing requires. Those in charge of her care botched the emotional dimension of her case, I think, brushing aside her desolation at the loss of this baby and the hope of any others, although I do not doubt that they did what her circumstances required them to do. They simply could not see her whole. They grasped the medical fact that her disability prevented her from bearing a child without acknowledging the emotional fact that, like ordinary women throughout the world, she wanted to do just that.

I'll concede the strain involved in balancing a disabled woman's significant differences with her equally significant similarities to the general female population—in the reproductive sphere as in all areas of human experience—but I also believe, true to my Yankee roots, in the virtue of hard work. Women with every kind of disability must learn to speak forthrightly about their needs and appetites even when society appears to ignore or repudiate their feelings. The nondisabled must accustom themselves to hearing their utterances without judging the "rightness" or "wrongness" of their realities. I am always dismayed when a parent snatches a curious child away from my wheelchair or shushes her when she asks, "Why do you use that?" I see in the making yet another adult who will, in the name of politeness, pretend there is nothing the matter with me while simultaneously but surreptitiously regarding me as an escapee from "The X-Files." Neither of these views is accurate, but she'll never find that out unless we talk.

Tracy Daugherty

Bakersfield

The longest oil pipeline in the United States runs from Kern County, California, where thousands of hungry Okies decamped in the '30s seeking redemption, to my home desert in West Texas where, when I was a child, no shelter could spare you from the dust in the air, no meals came without slabs of fatty meat, and the only redemption possible, if you believed the Holy Rollers, was loud, fast, and painful. My Okie parents, who'd followed the smell of oil to Texas's tumbleweed flats, cursed the dust, scarfed the meat, and feared the wrath of God.

That's life in Kern County even now. Though I've never been here before, this is home, as surely as if the All-American Pipeline pumped values, manners, and taste in tons of raw crude through its 1,223-mile artery.

At full production the pipeline carries 300,000 barrels of oil a day. It was built in the mid-'80s at a cost of $1.4 billion and is operated now by a Houston-based company whose biggest storage facility sprawls across the grassy plains of Oklahoma.

Fifty years earlier another artery linked the folks of Texas, Oklahoma, and California. Route 66 bore tons of tacky bedding, overalls and faded print dresses, jalopies shedding parts like pelts, across the deserts and the mountains and into the hard-labor towns of the West. Kern County, rich in crops and oil, became Little Oklahoma. By the late '30s, plains migrants had swelled the county's population by over sixty percent.

They dug in, stubbornly, picking cotton, pumping oil, plucking grapes. They built shelters out of strawberry crates, cardboard boxes, old tin cans. They cursed the dust and raised their kids to fear the wrath of God.

That's why, today, walking the back streets of Bakersfield, passing a barbershop and hearing the nasal twangs of fellows being buzz-cut, I'm home, though I'm a first-timer here. There's a lilt of the gospel and the swing of country music in their talk.

An old joke still makes the rounds here: "What are the first words an Okie kid learns? Mama, Papa, and Bakersfield."

A few miles north, moseying down an unpaved block of McCord Street in Oildale, Merle Haggard's childhood home, I glimpse skinny boys in front of rusty trailers. Instantly I know I'm among the children and grand-children of Okies. Once crate and cardboard hovels trembled in the wind here.

I've found where I might have lived if my grandfather hadn't stuck it out in Oklahoma at the height of the Dust Bowl drought; where I might have grown up if my father, an oil man all his life, had been transferred here from Texas.

I've come to the end of the road, the source of the pipeline, three years after the Oklahoma City bombing—another brutal scattering of folks like my own—to see what might have been and to witness what remains.

"I'll be everywhere," Tom Joad said, "wherever you can look. Wherever there's a fight so hungry people can eat, I'll be there. I'll be in the way guys yell when they're mad. I'll be in the way kids laugh when they're hungry and they know supper's ready."

Lately I've seen him in dreams standing by the house where I was born, by the banks of the Kern, by the fence around the Murrah site.

Today, in Oildale, in the Happy Acres Trailer Park, a man in jeans and a white T-shirt stands on a wooden stoop in front of his tiny mobile home scratching his belly. He squints at the haze in the air, a fume of valley dust and refinery steam. He's middle-aged, tired. Querulous and slow. He appears to be confused about something. He drops his gaze, sees me, and nods, both wary and open, noting my strangeness as well as my dim familiarity.

I nod back.

I might be looking at myself.

Later, I stop at a barbershop called "Oakie Ray's" near the Bakersfield air-port. Saddles, lanterns, farm tools, and saw blades line the walls of the one-room shop, along with 1930s California license plates, a 1902 Sears catalog cover, and an "Oklahoma Welcomes You" postcard.

Ray, a paunchy, jowly man in a pillowy shirt, is giving a kid a crew-cut when I walk in. The child's mother, a bleached blonde, sits in a white plastic chair by the front door.

"Ow!" the boy chirps. "Ow!"

"Sorry, boy," Ray says. "You keep yelling out like that, I'ma jump outta my skin."

"He just got over the chickenpox and he's still got some scabs on his head," the woman says.

"Is *that* what I keep hitting?" Ray runs the electric shears behind the boy's ears.

I relax and settle into my chair. In their talk are the rhythms of home: a bitten-off, aggressive friendliness, a politeness, a competitive humor. "The migrant people, scuttling for work, scrabbling to live, looked always for pleasure, dug for pleasure, manufactured pleasure, and they were hungry for amusement. Sometimes amusement lay in speech," Steinbeck explains in *The Grapes of Wrath*.

"Ow!"

"You keep saying that, I'll sick my dog on you."

"I'd kick him in the *whey*-vos." The boy grins, showing off crooked brown teeth. "That means 'balls.'"

"I *know* what it means," Ray says. "My wife's Spanish. Cojones, eh? You got cojones, boy?"

"Oh Lord, all my boys, they got cojones running out their ears," the woman groans. "This morning, Clint busted his lip on the trampoline— Rusty's riding him like a old horse."

"Least they ain't in no gangs," Ray says.

"That's right. Their old man, he tells them they get mixed up in gangs, if they don't die on the streets, they'll die in the back shed from a whupping."

"Fifteen, sixteen. Rough age. Gotta watch 'em."

"They're into sports."

"*I'm* into sports!" the kid pipes up: the great-grandchild of Winfield Joad.

"*What* sports?" Ray says. "How fast you can grab the TV *ree*-mote?"

"Ol' what's-her-name head back to Oklahoma?" the woman asks now, flipping through a *Car and Driver* magazine.

"Yeah."

"I knew she's wanting to."

"That ol' gal don't know *what* she wants."

"She's a nervous wreck, wudn't she?"

"That fella she's with—"

"*Young* fella."

"Yeah. Real joker."

Petering out the conversation turns naturally, now, to the weather and the recent flooding. "Ain't the rain bothers me so much," Ray says. "It's the dadburn wind."

All this time a teenaged boy has been patching a flat bicycle tire for Ray in a weedy yard next to the shop. When he tells Ray he's finished the job, poking his head through a narrow back door, Ray switches off the shears. "Okay, you've worked off your haircut now. But call your daddy and see can you keep your haircut money." I try to remember, and can't, the last time I witnessed this kind of even-up trade among people with only their labor to share.

We all listen to the young man hem and haw on the phone to his father, apparently too scared to come to the point. "Goldurn!" Ray yells over his shoulder into the receiver. "He wants to know, can he keep the money?"

"He said yes," the boy says quietly, hanging up. He disappears again into the yard.

A wide Latina steps sideways through the back door, gripping a raggedy broom. "Spaghetti's ready, Ray, when you get a chance to get to it."

"Ow!" the kid in the chair shouts one last time, and Ray declares him done.

He turns to me.

"I don't want to keep you from your spaghetti," I say.

"It'll be there. Just let me grab a quick smoke."

I take a seat in the barber chair. A big gold dog chases another pooch past the front door.

"You from Oklahoma?" I ask when Ray snaps the drape across my body.

"Naw, I grew up in the desert here, but I been around these damned ol' Okies so long, I'm one of them now."

"I'm a desert kid myself," I tell him.

"Whereabouts?"

"Midland, Texas."

"Shit. Oildale East."

"Right."

He laughs at a memory of riding his bike in the desert as a child. "When you punctured a tire, you put evaporated milk in it and kept on going. The milk kept it solid, but eventually it ruined the rubber." He seems to be talking to himself more than to me. The electric shears skim the tops of my ears.

He asks me what I do for a living.

"Man, our Oildale boys can't read a lick coming out of school," he says when I tell him I teach in a university up in Oregon. "Hell, the other day, I saw three Oildale High boys sitting on the curb. I asked the first one, I said, 'What's three times three?' '156,' he said. I asked the second one, 'What's three times three?' 'Tuesday,' he said. So I turned to the third one. 'What's three times three?' I asked him. 'Nine.' 'Well now, how'd you arrive at that?' 'Easy,' he said. 'I subtracted 156 from Tuesday.' That's our Oildale boys for you." He trims my sideburns. "These days all the boys want to do is get the girls pregnant, and the girls, they *want* to get pregnant and get the taxpayers to pay for 'em. Good thing I'm not running the country. If you weren't productive, I'd shoot you. That's how I'd run it." He clicks off the shears and picks up a pair of scissors. "You married?"

"Divorced."

"Shoot yes, I know *that* tune. I thought I's married for thirteen years, first time around. Turns out, I's just in *counseling* thirteen years."

"It's hard work," I agree.

"Worked *me* to the bone."

A young Mexican couple walks in with two long-haired boys, about six and seven, and a baby in a stroller.

"Howdy, girls," Ray says to the boys.

Their father frowns. He looks like any number of guys I went to junior high and high school with in Midland, Mexicans from the "other side of town" whose houses I never saw.

"Be right with you," Ray says. "Y'all from Oildale?"

"Just moved here," says the young mother.

"You *like* it?"

"Better'n where we were."

"Where's that?"

"East Bakersfield."

"God a'mighty. Lotsa gangs there."

"Why we left," the woman says. "Three men was shot on our block and two stabbed, just this year."

"When they robbed our landlord, we decided to move," the young father says, still checking Ray out, wary, but clearly looking for an ally in his new neighborhood. "He was putting in a security light out back, middle of the day. Some guy pulled a pistol on him and shot him for his money. He had three dollars."

We're all quiet. The boys look at their father as if to measure the tone of what he's said. Is he making a joke? "It's even worse up in Fresno," Ray says finally. He slides a soft brush across the back of my neck, then tugs the drape off my legs, spilling curly hair to the floor. "Thanks, *Pro*-fessor."

I hand him twelve bucks. "Sorry about your spaghetti," I say.

He shrugs. "Ought to get yourself out to the Raceway while you're in town. Everybody goes out there on the weekends. They put on a good show. Lotsa crashes and stuff."

Afterwards I go to a store for a local map and a newspaper (yesterday, Niki Deutchman, the forewoman of the Terry Nichols jury "criticized the government's case against Nichols, saying too much of the evidence was vague and circumstantial and too little effort was spent pursuing other [bombing] suspects . . . 'I think that the government perhaps really dropped the ball,' Deutchman said.")

I set the paper aside and unfold the map. Like a trip to a neighborhood barbershop even a casual glimpse at a map of Kern County shows why anyone interested in the secrets of America—in the social ferment behind a mess like the Murrah bombing—needs to see this place.

It's not the tourist's California. No pristine beaches, redwoods, or towering bridges. A few days before arriving here I landed in the tourist's California, at the John Wayne Airport in Orange County, south of Los Angeles Orange County, a stronghold of the John Birch Society, is a consumer's paradise of tanning salons, stretch limos, and malls. America the Prosperous.

In the airport a larger-than-life statue of the Duke hovers mid-stride over travelers struggling with their bags. For decades, in the movies, he portrayed men who cleared the path for America's greatness. Standing in his path, though, were the dark-skinned peoples of the likes of Kern County: Yokuts and Yauelamni Indians, Mexican migrants.

In Los Angeles the self-proclaimed "capital for the twenty-first century," birthplace of the Internet, I toured the brand new Getty Museum, an architectural marvel of travertine limestone, metal, and glass, with twenty galleries for paintings and a lovely collection of impressionist masterpieces.

The stone for the Getty was quarried in Bagni di Tivoli, near Rome, but the sweat and labor on which the Getty fortune was founded you'll find in Kern County, in the Happy Acres Trailer Park, among drilling rigs and pools of chemical stink.

The most beautiful museum in America rests on the wretched scaffolding of cokers, cat crackers, distillation towers. The twenty-first century may be blooming down the road, but here in Kern County, most people still live in cramped quarters reminiscent of the twentieth century's hardest times.

On a Kern County map Interstate 40 skirts the old Route 66. Running north and south, Highway 99 cuts Bakersfield in half. To the west big green patches: "Sundale Country Club," "Stockdale Country Club," "Patriots Park," "Green Acres," "Seven Oaks Golf Club."

White Lane, right down the middle.

East of 99, the streets are called Panama, Casa Loma; the major park is named for Martin Luther King.

The patches here are labeled "Department of Water Resources Waste Treatment Plant," "Mount Vernon Sewer Treatment Plant," and "County of Kern Sewer Farm."

North of the Kern River, fed by snowmelt from the Sierra Nevadas east of town, its banks now scraggly, trampled, yellowed, and denuded (agribusiness tells the water where to go, diverting the snowmelt all over the county and beyond), Oildale is blotted with petroleum tanks, vast refinery compounds.

Near the bottom of the map, south of Bakersfield, Kern County goes nearly blank with only a few signs of human activity—Aqueduct, Pumping Plant, Oil Field—scattered among the natural landmarks of Bear Mountain, the Tejon Hills, and the Tehachapi Mountains. Only by actually going there will you discover Weedpatch, the labor camp made famous by Steinbeck in *The Grapes of Wrath*, and see that what the map doesn't show is a swarm of seasonal laborers.

Nowhere in America are class and race divisions more readily apparent than they are here.

Supplementing the map with the newspaper I piece together a vivid narrative, a story of contemporary America in miniature. On one side of Bakersfield affluent whites enjoy the fruits of development, new houses, strip shopping centers, chain stores. Chevron, Arco, and Smith-Barney do their business here, next to the offices of the U.S. Border Patrol. On the other side of town live most of the dark-skinned folks (Latinos make up twenty-five percent of the population). Their neighborhoods are crumbling. The city dumps its sewage in them. Shootings are a nightly occurrence.

To the north, in Oildale, poor whites, many of them descendants of Depression-era Okies, struggle to keep what little they own as a result of their blue collar jobs. They live in trailers or box houses tucked among smelly oil derricks, one generation—or one layoff—removed from fieldwork.

This is where Timothy McVeigh would live, if he lived here, hustling from one lousy day job to another, hanging out at gun shows on the weekends.

Good thing I'm not running the country.

And to the south, the poorest of the poor, migrant laborers, cluster in dirt-colored housing units, all but invisible behind chain link fences guarded by nervous German shepherds.

In the '30s, jobless peoples from all parts of the nation believed the riches of Kern County would sweep them into the American Dream: opportunity, social mobility, comfort. In the '90s, when any day now despair might take the shape of a bomb blast, the dream's limitations are clear.

"This land," writes the California novelist James D. Houston, whose folks were born in Duncan, Oklahoma, "could torture you for years without ever quite killing you."

"Bakersfield's rash of bank robberies continues," said the headlines, the day I arrived here, a dusty traveler looking for traces of home. You'd think Pretty Boy Floyd was on the loose. Three banks had been picked off this month.

Bakersfield's City Manager was "gunning for a raise," according to another Old West headline.

"Flat oil prices" was the other big news. The local energy giants, Chevron, Tosco, Texaco, EOTT, Mobil, and Shell, were all hurting because crude was down to $7.25 a barrel (though in a smaller article inside the paper company spokespeople admitted their profits were still up nearly forty percent because of "streamlined operating practices"—namely, layoffs).

The paper devotes more space to oil field news than to anything else. Its regular oil columnist, Bill Rintoul, writes in highly technical language, which still, somehow, manages to sound as thrilling as a sports event: "[Occidental] spudded in Friday evening to drill its first well . . . the target is the Shallow Oil Zone at the N. 152-36R in the N. E. quarter of Sec. 36, 30S-23E."

Shades of my father's supper talk, in Texas.

The Classifieds: "Laborers needed, roustabouts, backhoe operators. Hazardous materials and confined space work."

Pepsi-Cola's huge local manufacturing plant needs production line technicians, floor managers, warehouse loaders.

The Okies brought to California a love of honky tonk music and rigid Baptist churches. Sin and redemption. That legacy spices the back pages, still: an ad for "George Strait tickets (8th row, make an offer)" borders a box declaring, "Take a wonderful trip to the Holy Land—retrace the steps of Paul."

Of the thirty-eight bookstores listed in the Yellow Pages here, eighteen of them specialize in Christian material (seven others sell only technical manuals).

"Divorce hurts," said a billboard for a law firm next to my motel, just off Highway 99. I could see it from my window. "When you've taken all you can, call the Divorce Experts."

Over storms of drizzly static on KUZZ, Bakersfield's best-known country music station, Merle sang softly, one dusk, "Tonight, your memory found me much too sober."

Mornings I ate in a place called Maggie's Cafe in Oildale, just around the corner from the Gettin' Hitched Wedding Chapel and Sam's Auto Repair. The restaurant baked in the shade of a billboard: two cowboys sitting, chatting on their horses against a red and yellow sunset—a deliberate echo of the old Marlboro cigarette ads.

Said the caption: "I miss my lung, Bob."

Hash browns, biscuits and gravy, chicken fried steak. Rusty washboards cluttered Maggie's walls.

"Sorry, I served my last biscuits an hour ago," a waitress told a noisy family in a booth as I walked in one day. Her dyed red hair was heavily teased; her body was shaped like a kite, broad in the shoulders, then tapering off, drastically, down to her toes. "My regulars didn't even get none."

One of the boys in the booth had lost his wristwatch in a crack in the cottony seat. "Where's it at?" his mother asked him irritably.

The waitress reached down and found it. "Next time I'm keeping it," she said. "You ain't big enough to fight me for it."

I picked a jelly-stained newspaper off a table, *The Arvin Tiller*, established in 1939 ("Garden in the Sun's Hometown Paper"). An editorial said, "Government in America has become like an overblown fat cow trampling anything that gets in its way."

A man on crutches took a seat with his wife. I overheard him tell the waitress he was a stock car driver at the Raceway. Recently he'd been in a crash. "It'uz a freak accident," he said.

"Them's the worst kind. You look good, though."

In fact, he looked like hell, yellowed, thin, and bruised. "Lost 16 pounds in four days. Hospital food."

The father of the noisy children said he'd been "out to the Raceway on Saturday."

"How's the track?" asked the battered man, perking up.

"Heatin' up, heatin' up."

"That's good," said the driver, plainly proud of his ties to the place despite its terrible risks for him. His color improved right away and he eagerly scanned the menu.

"I take a lot of pride in what I am," Merle used to sing.

In frontier towns like Bakersfield, Oildale, and Weedpatch—even in Oklahoma City—where life is hard and most folks don't own much, where the raceway's the biggest draw around for its promise of freedom and speed, pride's at a premium.

A cynic might say pride, like Heaven and the assurance of an afterlife, is easy to grant to the poor.

It doesn't cost anything.

It makes families happy and keeps them in line.

If pride is all you have you cling to it fiercely; you brag about it to noisy families in run-down cafes.

Clearly some fellows are so proud to be plain-spoken, beer-drinking good ol' boys, they view with suspicion any chance to improve themselves.

So. Sure. The poor can have their pride. Why not?

One day I saw painted on a tan stucco wall at Bakersfield High School a hard-hatted roughneck sneering and gripping a big red wrench. "Driller Pride" said the slogan at his feet.

On the outskirts of Lamont, a sign declares, "Lamont—With Pride and With a Future."

This struck me as an awfully tepid community motto.

Not a bright future, necessarily. Nothing bold or special. Just a future—as if to say, Whatever the hell happens, we'll grit our teeth and take it, like we always have. And by god, we'll do it with pride.

This weekend Merle was in town for a pair of sold-out concerts at Buck Owens' Crystal Palace, a bright red, white, and blue country music mecca in the middle of Bakersfield. "So much has changed here," Merle told a newspaper reporter. "The neighborhood I grew up in was . . . a quiet, elderly, peaceful place but now it's something other than that."

If he'd searched Chester Avenue looking for the Blackboard Cafe, he'd be flat out of luck. For decades, the Blackboard gave country singers a place to hone their acts. Bill Woods and the Orange Blossom Playboys used to jump-start the place while people tore into chicken fried steaks. The Playboys have passed beyond memory now.

One afternoon I ate a bland cheeseburger at a joint called Frosty King a block from the Blackboard's old spot. That's as close as I could get.

Tall grass nettled with thistles ringed Oildale's Standard Elementary, Merle's first school, the morning I dropped by. "Candy Sale/Winning at Parenting," said a sign out front. "Please Come." Across the street, railroad cars rusted behind a chain link fence, next to a row of oil tanks.

That night, in the Crystal Palace, Merle, now a wealthy elder statesman, a graybeard in glitter, a man who'd like to be honored, he said, by having the Bakersfield airport or a train station named for him, sang nostalgic songs about growing up poor.

Each night, while an older generation of wildcatters and drillers still gathers in the honky tonks of Oildale to listen to Merle's records, to the grits-and-gravy of pure country music, Bakersfield's teenagers, unaware of the history of their town, its hidden life, cruise sparkling new shopping centers, past Blockbuster video stores, United Artists cineplexes, Pizza Huts. As rap tunes thud incessantly from their state-of-the-art radios, they zip past the old Fox Theater downtown, which used to post a sign in its lobby: "No Niggers or Okies in the Balcony."

An old Bakersfield story: a little boy, passing a dusty field with his dad, sees a bunch of Okies picking cotton. "Look, Daddy," says the boy. "Them things almost look like people when they stand on their legs, don't they?"

Joe McCourn, CPA, born February 12, 1911 in Coalgate, Oklahoma.
    Charles "Chuck" Day, plumber and miner: Ponca City, Oklahoma.
    Bessie Beatrice Weeks, a Sunday school teacher and Kern County resident for over fifty years; born in Oklahoma on August 14, 1917.
    In yesterday's obits there was even a notice for a Mexican man who'd died in Midland, Texas, and whose relatives all live in Bakersfield. For fifteen years he worked as a chef in Midland's Petroleum Club, where my father often ate lunch and went to meetings.
    A whole generation passing quietly into shades within shades within shades.

In a dream I had, my last night in Kern County, I was sitting in a porch swing of an old wooden house, a house similar to my grandparents' Oklahoma home, rocking back and forth. A sloping lawn spread before me; each time I swung high, I could see, beyond the lawn, a vast landscape, changing with each new arc I made. Now a forested valley, then a sunny canyon, now a desert, then a spring-fed meadow. Fireflies and constellations swirled in the sky, now dawn, then dusk. *Where am I?* I thought, the age-old migrant lament. Then: *It doesn't matter. I can take it all inside me.* I opened my mouth for a pleasurable scream.
    At that moment I awoke, feeling happy, comforted, expansive. Through my motel window a big Western sun hung in the east. By the road below an old mattress lay in a ditch and a glut of cardboard boxes, as if Tom Joad had just clattered by in his truck, spilling junk.

Ted Kooser

Small Rooms in Time

Several years ago, a fifteen-year-old boy answered the side door of a house where I once lived, and was murdered, shot twice by one of five people—two women and three men—who had gone there to steal a pound of cocaine. The boy died just inside the door, at the top of a staircase that led to the cellar where I once had set up my easel and painted. The robbers—all but one still in their teens—stepped over the body, rushed down the steps, and shot three people there, a woman and two men.

Somebody called the police, perhaps the people who rented the apartment on the second floor. The next day's front-page story reported that the three in the basement were expected to survive. The boy's father, who was somewhere on the first floor and out of the line of fire, had not been injured.

It's taken me a long time to try to set down my feelings about this incident. At the time, it felt as if somebody had punched me in the stomach, and in ways it has taken me until now to get my breath back. I'm ashamed to say that it wasn't the boy's death that so disturbed me, but the fact that it happened in a place where my family and I had once been safe.

I recently spent most of a month building a Christmas surprise for my wife, a one-inch to one-foot scale replica of her ancestral home in the Nebraska sandhills. The original, no longer owned by her family, was a sprawling fourteen-room, two-story frame house built in 1884. Her great grandparents and grandparents lived there. Her great aunt, still living and 108 years old at the time I am writing this, was born there. Her father and his brothers and sister chased through those rooms as small children, and as a girl my wife and her younger sister spent summers there, taking care of their invalid grandmother.

Day after day as I worked on this dollhouse, pasting up wallpaper, gluing in baseboards and flooring, I would feel my imagination fitting itself into the little rooms. At times I lost all sense of scale and began to feel grit from the sandhills under my feet on the kitchen linoleum, to smell the summer sun on the porch roof shingles. I had never lived in that house, but I lived there during those moments, and as I worked, the shadows of wind-tossed trees played over the dusty glass of the windows. Now and then I would hear footsteps on the porch, approaching the door.

Immediately upon seeing the dollhouse on Christmas Eve, my wife began to recall the way it had been furnished when she was a girl, to talk about this piece of furniture being here and that one there. I watched her feed the goldfish in the dirty aquarium and sit down on the stiff, cold leather of the Mission sofa. I saw her stroke-damaged grandmother propped in her painted iron bed under the eaves. Listening to my wife, watching her open the tiny doors and peer into the tiny closets, I began to think about the way in which the rooms we inhabit, if only for a time, become unchanging places within us, complete in detail.

I clipped the article about the shooting and must have read it a hundred times those first few days. In a front-on photograph, like a mug shot, there stood the house, sealed off by yellow police tape, looking baffled, cold, and vacant. Next to the picture was a row of slack-faced mug shots of the five arrested. They looked as empty as the house.

I mailed a copy of the article to my first wife. I wanted her to share the shock that I was suffering, like a distant explosion whose concussion had taken years to reach across a galaxy of intervening happenstance. At the site where only the most common, most ordinary unhappiness had come to us—misunderstandings, miscommunications, a broken marriage like thousands and thousands of others—there had been a murder, three people had been wounded, and five were on their way through the courts and into prison, all for the want of a pound of cocaine that the article reported had never been there.

For several years in the early 1960s we'd rented the first floor, which included the use of the cellar that I used as a study. We'd been married for three years and were then in our early twenties. Diana was a schoolteacher in a nearby town, and I worked as a clerk at an insurance company. While we lived there, Diana became pregnant, our son was born, and when we brought him home from the hospital we carried him in through that same side door where the murder took place.

I remember matted orange shag carpet inside the door and continuing down the steps to the cellar, and more of the same carpet on the damp concrete floor and glued to the walls. (I can't think of it now without seeing bloodstains.) At the foot of the stairs, in a mildewed, overstuffed chair I'd bought at a thrift shop, I studied for night classes at the university. In that room I painted a few amateur pictures by bad basement light, one of a towering grain elevator that I thought was pretty good but which I mislaid long ago. A life-sized nude of Diana disappeared while we were packing to leave that house for another across town. I wonder if someone doesn't have it nailed up over their basement bar. Perhaps over cocktails on football Saturdays their guests try to guess who that pretty young woman might have been.

Two quiet, Latvian women rented the upstairs apartment. They had emigrated from Europe during the Second World War and spent spring, summer, and autumn on their knees beside beds of annual flowers they'd put in along the driveway. Olga was the older, then I suppose in her sixties. She had a badly curved spine, a shy smile, and from a forest near Dresden had seen wave after wave of Allied bombers. She told me that a thousand feet over the city the atmosphere stood in red columns of flame. Alida was handsome, dark-eyed, dark-haired, younger than Olga. Of the two, she was the less approving of the young couple who lived downstairs, who drank too much, who had a very barky dog.

When I think of the exterior of that house, their flowers are always in bloom—petunias, asters, pansies, bachelor buttons, phlox—but when I remember Diana and me living there, it is always winter and we are closed in by heavy snow. The side door where the boy was killed opened onto the driveway, and the first thing I did on those blizzardy winter mornings was to open it to let out our black Schipperke, Hagen, and watch him wade through the snow to pee and then turn back, a miserable look on his sharp little face. It was a cheap, aluminum storm door with loose glass panes, icy to the touch. As I waited there I could hear the kitchen radio behind me, turned up loud so that Diana, who dreaded the twenty-mile drive when the roads were bad, could catch the list of schools that were to be closed for the day.

In a few weeks time I could build a miniature version of that house, using the approximate measurements of memory, and as I worked with plywood and paper and glue I would be able to gradually remember almost everything about it. But I won't need to do that; since the murder I have often peered into those little rooms where things went good for us at times and bad at times. I have looked into the miniature house and seen us there as a young couple, coming and going, carrying groceries in and out, hats on, hats off, happy and sad.

As I stared at the article, every piece of our furniture took its place in the rooms. I could have reached in through the door of that photograph and with the tip of a finger roll our antique dental chair over the floor. A friend's big painting of the Rolling Stones hung on the opposite wall. On the living room floor was the plush, white carpet I bought with money from a literary prize. It was always dirty. Down the hall and through a door to the left, our bed, rumpled and unmade, stood right where it stood when we were young parents, with Jeffrey's crib nearby, and by leaning a little forward I could hear the soft, reassuring sound of his breath.

It has been more than thirty years since we lived at 2820 "R" Street, Lincoln, Nebraska. I write out the full address as if to fasten it down with stakes and ropes against the violence of time. I hadn't thought about it often, maybe a few times a year. But it was our house again the minute I opened the paper that morning and saw its picture and the faces of the people who had struck it with terrible violence. They didn't look sorry, they looked like they'd do it again if they could.

Now and then since the murder I find myself turning into that decaying neighborhood and down that street, slowing to look at our house. The window shades are drawn on what were once such bright, welcoming rooms. Nobody lives there now, as far as I can tell. On snowy days there are no tracks up the drive to that flimsy side door.

I lean down, I try to fit myself inside. Even after thirty years there still might be the smell of Olga and Alida's salt herring being cooked upstairs, and on the first floor the fragrance of phlox, a few stalks in a water glass. For thirty years I had put it all firmly behind me, but like a perfect miniature it had waited in a corner of my heart, its rooms packed with memories. The murder brought it forward and made me hold it under the light again. Of course I hadn't really forgotten, nor could I ever forget how it feels to be a young father, frightened by an enormous and threatening world, wondering what might become of him, what might become of his wife and son.

Only a year after Diana, Jeff, and I moved away and into another house across town, our marriage came apart, and I began to learn to be a single father. From time to time Jeff came to visit me at the home of friends who had taken me in. The dead boy, too, had gone to visit his father.

If my luck in this life had been worse I might have been that other father, occupied by some mundane task, perhaps fixing a leaky faucet when my son went to answer the door. But I was lucky, and my son was lucky, and today, long after the murder, finding myself imagining that damp cellar room, peering down into it as if looking into a miniature cellar, I don't hear shots or see blood on the steps. I hear only soft sounds: my breath as I sit with my book, Diana's stocking feet as she pads along the hall above me, and water running into the bathtub as she gets ready to give our baby a bath.

The landlord, who owned a little doughnut shop, died many years ago. They had once lived in that house. His wife had Alzheimer's disease and sometimes arrived bewildered at our door, wanting us to let her in. She too is gone. If I were building a miniature of that house I would stand her at the door, clenching her purse in both hands, her hat on crooked.

The flowers that grew along the driveway are thirty years past their season and their beds are only dust today. My friend who painted the Rolling Stones has died. Olga and Alida, having survived the horrors of war to come to the new world and take a little pleasure in simple flowers, they too are gone. I've noticed lately when I've driven past that the porch has begun to slope toward the street as if to pour our ghosts out the front door and onto the buckled sidewalk. And I am not that young father any more, but a man in his sixties who is slowly becoming a baffled old woman who hammers and hammers at a door, wanting to be let in again, knowing by instinct that something good must still be waiting just inside.

Sam Pickering

Dog Days

An aging man should not own an old dog. George turned thirteen in July.
His dog days foreshadowed the doldrums into which I am slowly nodding. In past summers George loped down the lane behind the barn, air
currents spinning salty fragrances around him, pulling his nose right and
left. This summer George wallowed through troughs of grass, his hull slipping warped, no longer scudding in the bright sun. His head hung down,
and the skin under his jaw looked like a flying jib stripped of wings.
During days he wandered without purpose, one moment hunching by
the steps leading to the backhouse, appearing to want to go outside, the
next scratching the screen door on the porch asking to come in. Time
has swept his helmsman overboard, and his tiller swung directionless.
When not pitching and yawing, he clung to me, seeming to need assurance and affection. Occasionally I became exasperated and shouted, "Go
to your bed." Immediately thereafter I imagined myself tottering toward
the kitchen in slippers and bathrobe, weary children saying, "Go back to
bed, Dad." At nine o'clock every night I carried George upstairs. I set him
atop a pillow on the floor next to my bed, then I covered him with a blanket. At a quarter after eleven I lugged him back downstairs and took him
outside so he could pump himself dry for the voyage through the night.
Afterward I carted him back upstairs. Shortly before six in the morning,
he stood and flapped his ears to awaken me. I took him back outside, after
which I built a fire in the kitchen stove and he fell asleep on a pad beside
my rocking chair.

"You live a dog's life," Vicki said one night.

"Not yet," I answered, "not quite yet."

In the past George resembled a trim bark. This summer he became a
lugger. Heavily laden and lumbering, he bolted meals and lived, Vicki

said, to eat. "Like me," I thought. Once a week I went to Tim Hortons, a doughnut shop in Yarmouth. I drank a medium-sized cup of coffee, always in a ceramic cup, and ate a Dutchie, a rectangular wad of glazed dough, spotted with raisins and fat. Trips to Tim Hortons were the high points of weeks in Nova Scotia, and I looked forward to them eagerly. One Wednesday an old man sat across the aisle from me, a worn version of myself, I thought. The man's back curled like the upper half of a question mark. He wore a green and white checkered shirt, a red baseball cap, Canadian Tire sewed above the bill, boots, and dark khaki trousers held up by red suspenders. Time had shrunk the man's hips into coat hangers, and the trousers hung loosely from his waist, wrinkled like laundry bags. His two middle-aged daughters accompanied him, one sitting on his right, the other on the left. That morning they signed him out of "the home" for an outing and for a treat brought him to Tim Hortons. The man was deaf, and while he ate a sugar doughnut, the women leaned toward each other and talked over his shoulders. The man paid no attention to them and concentrated on eating. He held the doughnut tightly in both hands, head pushed up looking like that of a turtle sticking out of its shell. His eyes gleamed alertly, as if he thought someone might snatch the treat away. "No more Dutchies for me," I resolved. The resolution lasted only until the following week.

July was flush with beginnings. Four newly-hatched red-bellied snakes lay under a slab of plywood near the bluff overlooking the Gulf of Maine. Tadpoles, big as thumbs, roiled the cow pond. A young muskrat swirled through rushes growing beside the bridge spanning the Beaver River outlet. Seventy yards above the bridge six ermine bundled across the gravel road. A robin lured a fledgling from its nest in the golden elder behind the backhouse. Hares no bigger than fists crouched under canes of rugosa roses. Some mornings I got up at three thirty and, after brewing a pot of tea, wrote in the study, sitting at the desk in the bay window. One morning I watched a young hare thrust through periwinkle under the window. On reaching the front entrance, he tried to hop up the steps. The hare was so young that he moved awkwardly. Instead of forward its big feet pushed its body sideways, and the hare tumbled over four times before he reached the top step.

Often while the green extravagance of summer nourished my eyes, my thoughts drifted to endings. Two days before watching the hare climb steps, I'd found tufts of brown fur on the headland, sweepings from the meal of a marsh hawk. I chased the hare off the porch into roses bearded with ferns. "Stay there," I said, "and maybe the hawk won't get you." Life, alas, is beaked. That morning I received a letter informing me that two days before his retirement party, a friend died in a car wreck. That night cirrus clouds curled fruity overhead, orange then pink and purple. Instead of imagining fair seedtimes, I thought about sad old women, dyeing and baking thin locks in hopes of disguising age, hiding not so much from others but from the people who stared at them from mirrors.

"More than two score years and ten have come and gone since that day when I, Benjamin Lathrop, put out from Salem harbor, a green hand on the ship *Island Princess*," Charles Boardman Hawes wrote at the beginning of *The Mutineers* (1920). Almost as much time had passed since I read such books. Late in life, though, a man returns to childhood reading, tales of butchery and cowardice on the high seas, of bravery and the improbable survival of virtue appealing more than great books in which meaning gapes like a bog, pages scratchy with leatherleaf. After dinner between journeying up and downstairs with George, I read three of Hawes's books: *The Mutineers*, *The Great Quest*, and *The Dark Frigate*. No matter the guttural cough of the foghorn at Port Maitland, I steered a straight course under blue skies to enjoyment.

"What do those books make you think about?" Vicki asked.

"Nothing," I said, "just the subject people my age should think about."

Returning to Nova Scotia every summer contributes to the illusion of smooth continuance, each summer not the first thread in a new fabric but another button on a cardigan, perhaps looser than buttons below but still familiar and comfortable. Every summer the songs of white-throated sparrows bounce from scrub like novelty tunes from the fifties. Early in the morning ravens grind woodenly. In the evening verries perch in damp ruffs of spruce, their songs refracting and piercing the fog in beams of color, blue, green, and pale pink. Every summer I scythe Japanese knotweed growing at the edge of the side meadow. In the barn I split firewood. Early in July Vicki buys beet greens and strawberries at roadside stands. After a flick of time she buys potatoes, peas, raspberries, and Swiss chard. No matter how slowly I jog, on the headland butterflies spring from my feet in clumps, first azures and orange crescents, then wood nymphs, and finally, over the lowlands near the outlet, cabbage whites spiraling, dizzy with mating. Although the children now spend summers far from Beaver River and the arms that carried them down the sharp headland to the beach, occasionally a child telephones and memory lifts me. Late in July Eliza called from Minnesota where she was teaching Russian. She was weeping. Francis sent her an e-mail from Storrs. He said Harvard had written her. Because of an unanticipated high rate of acceptance, some freshmen, including Eliza, would have to live off campus.

"The university," Francis wrote, "will help you find an apartment."

"Daddy," Eliza sobbed, "I want to meet other freshmen. I have been so lonely in high school. I want to make friends and be part of college."

Francis's e-mail was a joke. "I must have forgotten to write 'ha, ha' at the end," he said. I explained that good jokes did not upset or create anxiety. Instead they provoked warm laughter, making people appreciate life.

Vicki and I do not agree on humor; the disagreement, however, long standing. This summer we didn't watch television. Instead we listened to the radio, on Saturday nights tuning in the CBC and "Finkleman's 45s." For two hours Danny Finkleman played pop songs from the '50s, '60s, and '70s, lining each record with quirky commentary, suggesting, for example, that the CBC construct a bowling alley in the basement of its building in Toronto. One Saturday while Vicki was outside emptying the slop dish, Finkleman told a joke. Normally I don't like jokes, but I enjoyed this one so much I was gasping for breath when Vicki returned from the compost pile. Golf provided the frame for the joke, any discussion of which makes me dream of holing out. Moreover the pesticides and weed killers slathered over courses have turned fairways into toxic dumps.

"The poisons pit even steel-plated shoes," my friend Josh told me, stepping forward to address an idea. "The only safe way to indulge in golf is on stilts. Even so, eighteen holes can reduce a pair of sixteen-foot titanium stilts to six inches."

"If sprays shrink stilts that much," I said, swinging my niblick at the idea, "a real sportsman would need several bags of clubs for a single round, the lengths of the clubs in one bag different from those in another. Caddy fees would be enormous. The game is doomed."

"No," Josh said, always up for the short game, "all a duffer needs is a set of clubs with adjustable shafts, the length of a driver at the top end, say, twenty-one feet. Of course bags would be expensive, and giants could charge monstrous fees for caddying."

Finkleman's joke hooked less than Josh's musings. At the bar on the nineteenth hole, a man described his new golf ball to a friend. "If topped into water, the ball floats," he said. "If sliced out of sight into deep rough, it beeps, and at dusk a light beneath the gutta-percha blinks automatically." "Good-bye double bogies," the friend exclaimed. "That's fabulous. Where did you get the ball?" "I found it," the man said. I laughed uncontrollably after telling the story, belly rising like a bunker then sinking into a divot. Vicki looked, as scratch narrators put it, teed off, her expression grittier than a sand wedge.

I expected silence, that being par for a 7,200-yard course of marriage. Often I don't respond to Vicki's remarks, and if I answer, frequently I chip only a word or two her way. Unlike Vicki I eschew fashionable discussion on the radio, particularly boutique programs that pander to the salacious. One chilly, July afternoon Vicki sat in the rocking chair by the stove, sipping Earl Grey tea, feet raised, resting on the seat of a kitchen chair. From the radio atop the table to her right a feline voice purred.

"Do you think," Vicki said as I strolled into the room, "our marriage could survive a sex change?"

"Yes," I said and striding into the barn split wood.

Next spring Michigan will publish two books I wrote. "I wonder if I will make a half million on the books," I said in the kitchen that night.

"I want to win the lottery," Vicki replied.

"I'm talking about the sales of my books," I said.

"I prefer to talk about something more realistic," Vicki said, "like winning the lottery." Years ago, Vicki would have allowed me a handicap and not responded to my musings. The most any of my books has earned is four thousand dollars, the half million simply the dream of a buccaneering reader.

Not all summer's doings dragged like anchors, stirring silt. I thought of titles for two essays, both from songs, the first, "Precious Memories," susceptible, I am afraid, to waterlogged melancholy. The second song, "Give My Love to Nell," told a story. Two close friends, Jack and Bill, left home arm in arm and sailed across the ocean seeking to better their lots in life. Besides home and family, Bill left his girlfriend, Nell. Jack made his fortune first. "Give my love to Nell," Bill requested before Jack returned home. Jack obeyed his friend, and later when Bill arrived home, he discovered that Nell and Jack had married. Instead of pinning or behaving badly, as characters often do in sentimental songs, Bill wished the couple well and got on with living. Rather than mulling connection or opportunity missed, my essay would celebrate actual happenings. "In other words," Vicki said, "whatever is, is," adding, "that's a wallet stuffer."

Although the titles now look hackneyed, other summer doings seemed practically new. A boreal chickadee foraged alders around the cow pond, the second boreal chickadee I've seen. At my age sights and sounds are suspect. Not until a second sighting confirms the first do I claim seeing a bird. At the Beaver River outlet I found a dead loon. Salt had cured and sun dried the body. The loon died during winter, the feathers on top of its head dark gray and a white patch under its bill. I snapped the loon's spine at the base of the neck. The neck was long, resembling the butt of a pistol. When school starts in August, I'll take the head to class and use it as a pointer. "Students will think you insane," Vicki said.

"Exactly," I said, "a lunatic."

"Is everything a joke with you?" Vicki asked.

"Very little," I said, lifting George into my lap and rubbing him behind the ears.

Not every animal I held was dead or declining. "What's that?" Vicki said one night, switching on the lamp sitting on her bedside table. A little brown bat whirled overhead then, swooping low, flew out of the bedroom into the upstairs hall. The house resembles a barn. Ceilings are high, that of Vicki's and my bedroom being the highest, beyond my fingertips even if I stand on a stool. I closed the bedroom door so the bat could not return and hang himself high above my reach.

"I will find him in the morning," I told Vicki.

"I hope so," she said. "I'd feel terrible if the bat starved to death." Before breakfast the next morning I searched the house. I began upstairs, scouring the long hall and the other four bedrooms. I peered under beds and looked behind headboards. I pushed chests away from walls and shifted clothes in closets. Downstairs I searched the hall and the study. I lay on the floor trying to spot droppings. I almost gave up and told Vicki the bat must have flown into the chimney in the study and escaped. But then I found it behind the door to the front parlor. The bat looked like a furry Mars bar. While Vicki peeled the bat's legs off the top of the door, I held a butterfly net over and below the animal. The bat clicked then slipped into the net. I carried the bat into the barn and set it atop the old sleigh, placing it on the rear seat, making sure it couldn't slip off. Eight minutes later when I returned to the barn, the bat was gone.

"We should have named it," Vicki said.

"Yes," I said, "it is our first house bat. What a thrill!"

This summer I spent more time than ever before stirring about purposelessly. "Like George," Vicki said. I wandered outside throughout the day hoping to glimpse an unfamiliar insect. I had spent fourteen summers in Beaver River. The chances of my spotting a creature not seen before were small, and so like those of George, my excursions were short, and I quickly returned to the kitchen and munched on cheese and crackers, prunes and peanut butter, muffins, and rhubarb flummery, in the middle of this last a mound of whipped cream as alluring as Treasure Island.

To prevent myself from dozing the summer away, I did things I had not done before. The first Saturday in August Vicki and I went to the Quilt Show and Tea sponsored by the Patchwork Pals Quilters Guild and held at Beacon United Church in Yarmouth. Over 150 quilts hung from railings or draped over the backs of chairs. The chairs stood in double rows on the tops of tables, eight, six, four, or two chairs to a table. For an hour and a half I roamed the hall studying patterns: bow tie, double wedding ring, flying geese, Dresden plate, city streets, winning hand, postage stamp, Ohio rose, Lady of the Lake, and Bargello rippling in waves. Color spilled from vases of Trapunto flowers. From the center of a radiant star, eleven pink and red eight-pointed stars shimmered outward. My favorite quilts were old, in particular grandmother's flower garden, its bright bouquets washed into pale delicacy. The three-dollar ticket not only admitted me to the show but it also let me drink tea or coffee and eat as many homemade confections as I wanted. I sampled six. Culinary memory deteriorating almost as fast as nominal, I recall only two, a devil's food cake muddy with icing and cheese cake, a bush laden with blueberries drooping over the top. Few men attended the exhibition. On entering the auditorium I counted six men and forty-four women; on leaving, seven men, and seventy-four women.

Pasted to a wall in the men's lavatory was a yellow sign, black letters printed upon it. "Please wrap your gum in a piece of paper towel and throw it in the garbage not in the urinal." Under the request, someone scribbled, "as it tastes bad then." The impulse toward disorder runs deep in me, as in society itself, and I admired the person who wrote on the sign, in the act not marring cardboard but making it reflect human nature. In contrast the quilts fostered the pleasant falsehood that life radiated design or at least that order could be imposed upon living, transforming chaos into the beautiful and the functional. In the house at Beaver River clocks tick like balm, generating the illusion that time is regular. In the attempt to control living, man created time. Now man deludes himself into believing he controls time when the truth is that man never masters his creations. Instead they master him, binding him and his offspring like serfs to ways of living. Studying the quilts led me to ponder education. Instead of attending university for four years and coming to believe that learning prepares people for life, wouldn't children fare better, I thought, if they mastered quilting? Although sewing might foster wrong-headed ideas about order and disorder, at least the children would belong to a community. Society has accepted the exaggerated claims of education for so long that place and family no longer provide identity. Instead schools furnish pedigrees, the bluer the educational lines the more admirable the person. Rarely do people mention family or birthplace when they introduce me. Instead they cite the schools I attended, almost never referring to Sewanee but not failing to mention Cambridge and Princeton.

Such ponderings are not for young but old dogs who have ground teeth away chewing at life. That aside, one Sunday Vicki and I drove to Salmon River and watched the stock car races at Lake Doucette, a clay triangle sunk into a hilltop and bound on three sides by spruce. Berms, buttressed curbs of tires, and wire fences surrounded the track. We sat at the base of the triangle just beyond the end of the straightaway below the start. Protection seemed flimsy.

"That fence couldn't restrain a sleepy cow much less an automobile," Vicki said after a car cartwheeled toward the grandstand, trunk over engine at the start of the first race.

"Right," I said, brushing clods of dirt from my shirt and trousers. Throughout the afternoon dirt rained upon us. When Vicki bit into a slice of pizza, she got "the works." Gravel had drizzled over us and covered her pizza, resembling nubs of hamburger. The cars looked like boxes wrapped in crumpled foil. Trucks towed them into the infield: dump, pickup, tow, and a pink and white Firestone repair truck. During races people sat in white plastic chairs on the roof of the Firestone truck. Throughout the afternoon tires smashed into berms, and the cars themselves whirled about like water beetles. I scanned the infield looking for an ambulance but did not discover one.

"What happens if someone in the stands is hurt?" Vicki asked.

"I don't know," I said. "The best you can do is learn from that woman in front of us," I said, pointing down to the right. Tattooed on the woman's left shoulder were two hands, palms pressed together in prayer.

Just after the start of the first race, three cars flipped. At the first turn following the restart, five cars spun out, smacking the berm beneath us. "Oh, shit!" Vicki said when a tire flew over the grandstand. Vicki said the word so many times during the first three races that I suggested she emend her exclamations.

"*Sugar* would sound more like a lady."

"Fudge you," she said.

The cars raced in categories: those with four cylinder engines, six cylinders, then eights, followed by cars whose eight-cylinder engines had been modified. To muffle the storm of noise we stuffed cotton balls into our ears. Still, by afternoon's end, I recognized categories by the noises engines made: the heavy thrum of modifieds and the thin popping of four cylinders. Individual cars stood out, one with "Welcome to the Swamp" printed on a mud flap, and a 1989 Volkswagen Fox painted white and black like a Holstein. Rubber udders hung beneath rear doors on both sides of the car. Unfortunately the car needed freshening and did not finish a single race. Local businesses sponsored racers, and their names appeared on doors and hoods, often sprayed on: Nightime Auto Salvage, Howard Andrews Electrical, S&H Newell Trucking & Bait, Bishara's Garage, Waterview Machine Works, Andrew LeBlanc's Excavating, and D. J.'s Corner Store, this last in Salmon River where we bought newspapers and ice cream cones. Between races the Water Buffalo, an old tanker that once hauled milk, sprinkled water over the track. The announcer discussed cars and drivers. Sometimes he addressed the crowd, wishing Gerald and Christine a happy anniversary. At the entrance to the track, the Lions Club sold tickets for the half and half. Tickets cost a dollar, fifty cents going to the Lions, fifty cents to a winner-take-all pot. I bought three tickets, and we stayed until the draw. We arrived at the track at eleven twenty; the drawing took place at three fifteen, the winner receiving $954. "We must go now," I said to Vicki. "I have to let George out."

"I know. I know," Vicki said. "But we are coming back next week. This is the real stuff."

"Perhaps," I said, "but maybe you have been brainwashed."

"Washed!" Vicki exclaimed, brushing off her trousers; "I look like I have spent the day on my hands and knees in a garden."

"I read an article that accused the government of experimenting with mind control," I continued, ignoring the interruption.

"What proof did the article cite?" Vicki asked.

"The number of yellow cars in New York City," I said. "Mind control provides the only reasonable explanation for so many people driving yellow cars."

"Sugar," Vicki said.

On the way home Vicki didn't talk. Instead she stared at the dunes behind Bartlett's Beach. George moved so slowly when I let him out that I picked him up and carried him into the yard. "You're a good old fellow, my good old fellow," I said, suddenly unutterably sad.

David James Duncan

Valmiki's Palm

"In the beginning," say the *Upanisads*—a scripture composed, according to the rishis of ancient India, by no one; a scripture self-created, found floating like mist, or the bands of a rainbow, in the primordial forest air,

> there was nothing here at all . . . Death alone covered this completely, as did hunger, for what is hunger but death? Then Death made up his mind: "Let me equip myself with a body" (Sanskrit: atma). So he undertook a liturgical recitation (arc), and as he was reciting, water (ka) suddenly sprang from him. Amazed, Death thought: "Recitation caused water to spring from me!" This is what gave the name to and discloses the hidden nature of recitation (arc-ka). Truly, water springs up for he or she who knows the secret of recitation. Recitation is running water.

I. ADORATION OF A HOSE

I was born in a hospital located on the flanks of a volcanic cone. This cone, named Mount Tabor, looks innocent as an over-turned teacup as it rises over densely populated southeast Portland, Oregon. Decades before my birth, scientists had declared the cone unimpeachably extinct. The hospital, however, afforded a nice view of another cone, thirty-five miles away in the same volcanic system, also declared extinct in those days: Mount St. Helens. Forgive my suspicion of certain unimpeachable declarations of science.

My birth cone's slopes were drained by tiny seasonal streams that, like most creeks in that industrialized quadrant of Portland, were buried in underground pipes long before I arrived on the scene. There were also three small reservoirs on Tabor's slopes, containing the water that bathed me at birth, water I'd drink for eighteen years, water that gave me life. But this water didn't come from Mount Tabor, nor from the surrounding hills, nor even from the aquifer beneath: it came, via manmade flumes, from the Bull Run River, which drains the slopes of the Cascade Mountains forty miles away.

I was born, then, without a watershed. On a planet held together by gravity and fed by rain, a planet whose every creature depends on water and whose every slope works full-time, for eternity, to create creeks and rivers, I was born with neither. The creeks of my birth-cone were invisible, the river from somewhere else entirely. Of course millions of Americans are now born this way; some of them grow up without creeks, live lives lacking intimacy with rivers, and become well-adjusted, healthy, productive citizens even so.

Not me. The dehydrated suburbs of my boyhood felt as alien to me as Mars. The arid industrial life into which I was being prodded looked to me like the life of a Martian. What *is* a Martian? Could Mars support intelligent life? I had no idea. My early impression of the burgeoning burbs around me was of internally-combusting hordes of dehydrated beings manufacturing and moving unnecessary objects from one place to another in order to finance the rapid manufacture and transport of more unnecessary objects. Running water, on the other hand, felt as necessary to me as food, sleep, parents, and air. And on the cone of my birth, the running waters had been eliminated.

I didn't rebel against the situation. Little kids don't rebel. That comes later, along with the hormones. What I did was hand-build my own rivers, breaking all neighborhood records, in the process, for amount of time spent running a garden hose. . . .

In the beginning in Southeast Portland, there was nothing much there at all. Dehydrated Martians seemed to run the place completely. So my *atma* and I fastened the family garden hose to an azalea bush at the uphill end of one of my mother's sloping flowerbeds, turned the faucet on as hard as Mom would allow, and watched hijacked Bull Run River water spring forth in an *arc* and start cutting a miniscule, audible river (*ka*) down through the bed. I then camped by this river all day.

As the Hose River ran and ran the thing my mother understandably hated and my *atma* and I loved began to happen: *creation*. The flowerbed topsoil washed away and a streambed of tiny colored pebbles appeared—

a bed that eventually looked like that of any genuine river, complete with tiny point bars and cutbanks, meanders and eddies, fishy-looking riffles, slow pools. It was a nativity scene, really: the entire physics and fluvial genius of Gravity-Meets-Water-Meets-Earth incarnating in perfect miniature before me. I built matchbook-sized hazelnut rafts and cigarette-butt-sized elderberry canoes, launched them on my river, let them ride down to the gargantuan driveway puddle that served as my Pacific. I stole a two-inch tall blue plastic cavalry soldier from my brother's Fort Apache set, cut the stock off his upraised rifle so that only the long, flexible barrel remained, tied thread to the end of the barrel to serve as fly-line, and sent the soldier fishing. I'd then lie flat on my belly, one cheek to the ground, and stare at this U.S. Cavalry drop-out, thigh-deep in his river, rifle-rod high in the air, line quavering in the current; stare till I became him; stare till, in the sunlit riffle, we actually hooked and landed tiny sun-glint fish. "Shut off that hose!" my mother would eventually shout out the kitchen window. "You've turned the whole driveway into a mud-hole!"

Poor woman, I'd think. *It's not a mud-hole. It's a tide flat . . .*

I'd gladly turn the hose off, though: that's how I got the tide to go out. I'd then march my river soldier out onto the flat, to dig for clams.

II. WOE V. WADE

The undisputed matriarch of my large suburban family was my maternal grandmother, Ethel Rowe. Gramma Rowe was four feet eleven but insisted with such vehemence that she was five foot one that most of the family felt her missing two inches were an oversight on the Lord's part and should be imagined as real. For my part I wished Gramma Rowe was three feet eleven or even two foot eleven, since at four feet eleven she was overwhelming. In those days we called people like her "firecrackers," but firecrackers explode once and that's it. Gramma Rowe could just keep exploding. She was more like a four feet eleven Uzi. When a young nephew who had trouble with "R" sounds one day referred to our matriarch as "Gwamma Woe," it was too perfect. I called her nothing else ever after.

Gwamma Woe's lovingly despotic rule, like her mystical Five-Foot-Oneness, was based on an interpretation of scripture that corrected countless oversights on the part of the bible's authors. All this "*God works in mysterious ways*" stuff, for starters, was hooey. Gwamma Woe knew *exactly* how God worked, exactly how humans should work in response, and *atmas*, garden hoses, rivers and U.S. Cavalry drop-outs had nothing to do with it thank-you-very-much. A fiercely devout Seventh-Day Adventist, Gwamma Woe had, per her self-bowdlerized bible's instructions, turned herself into a crackerjack real estate sales lady the better to serve the Lord: she was now spending her life getting rich by the sweat of her brow and enjoying all but a tithe of those riches, just as God ordered, after which she might agree to die, or at least briefly slumber, until such time as Jesus woke her, gave her body the complete rebuild that would make her a true five foot one and whisked her up to the gold mansions and permanent riches of heaven forever.

I had only one objection to Gwamma Woe's Gold-Mansion-Track plan for her life: it was her plan for *my* life too. There were just two incarnation-al options for a Woe grandchild. You either: 1) became a staunch Adventist like Gwamma, spent your life pursuing wealth like Gwamma, and later retired for eternity to the even greater wealth of heaven with Gwamma, or, 2) surprise, surprise: *YOU BURNED IN HELL FOREVER!!!*

Ah, Gwamma Woe! If only I'd been able to embrace her plan for my life, I'd have saved myself a lot of heartbreak. Capitalist fundamentalism, I still believe, is the perfect Techno-Industrial religion, its goal being a plan-et upon which we've nothing left to worship, read, eat, or love but dollar bills and bibles. My boyhood worry, though, was that this world might not *be* techno-industrial. Maybe only the *human* world is techno-industri-al. Maybe the world God made is *natural*, its "industry" a bunch of forces like gravitation, solar rays, equinoctial tilt, wind, tides, photosynthesis, sexuality, migration. And if the world *is* natural, I'd fret, if it was the *natural* world God loved enough to send His son to die for it, then it might not be such a God-pleasing thing to spend my life converting that world into industrial waste-products, dollar bills, and bibles.

Needless to say my matriarch disagreed with every iota of this. She rec-ognized natural beauty in a way: a "beautiful day," for instance, increased the likelihood of selling a house. But the word "nature," to Gwamma, had an unwashed unsaved ring to it. Wild Nature, she believed, was basically a bunch of naked, dirty, heathenish creatures having sex with, stalking and devouring each other—more or less like realtors, she admitted, only in Nature's case there was no post-prandial Gold Mansion to give purpose to the earthly gizm and gore. The Natural World's duty, Gwamma Woe was certain, was to be knocked down, processed, and converted ASAP into Industrial Christian World. And she was a force: I was convinced by age six that I'd eventually become a well-heeled Adventist doctor or lawyer not because I wanted to but because a less highly paid, more nature-loving career would result in that formidable annoyance: eternal agony in hell.

One day when I was still six, though, my religious advisor committed a fatal tactical blunder. Everybody likes doing what they do best. Gwamma Woe also liked showing off while she did it. As a combination matriarch/ real estate whiz, she had an exhibitionistic love for hauling my siblings and me to "Open Houses" at various properties she had listed for sale and letting us eavesdrop while she hooked and played prospective buyers like fish. Between clients she delivered impassioned sermonettes on Salesmanship, a biblical virtue that ranked right in there with Cleanliness and Godliness in its power to convert penniless wretches like us kids into Gold-Mansion-Track sales experts like her. No matter how many times she explained the key concepts, though—terms like "earnest money," "commandment," "mortgage," "Holy Ghost," "immaculate interior," "redemption," "FHA-approval"—I couldn't wrap my nature-smitten mind around them. After a single open house spent cross-eyed with boredom, I became an extremely reluctant companion.

Like I said, though, Gwamma Woe was a great saleslady. One day in October she drove her snappy red Rambler convertible down our driveway, spotted me merged with my garden hose river and fishing soldier, but instantly conjured three words that made me leap into the car's Immaculate White Interior with pure anticipation. The words were: "*Creek-front property!*"

I don't remember a thing about the drive, the sermonette en route, the layout of the home. All I remember is hearing—the instant Gwamma parked beside a For Sale sign and shut off her engine—the unfamiliar song of unpiped, non-hosed water flowing somewhere behind the house. In the lost Celtic recesses of my bloodstream a bagpipe and drum immediately answered. I told Gwamma to holler when she needed me, shot round the house, scrambled down a riprapped embankment into a ribbon of ancient fir and alder—and the world of mortgages and immaculate interiors vanished as a remnant slice of green and ancient world suddenly shimmered on all sides.

It was just one of Portland's dying creeks, really. One with a much needed but long-lost Indian name. "Johnson Creek" was now its anemic title. But it was twenty-six miles long, hence a little too big to bury. And when you fail to bury Northwest creeks, or to poison them quite to death, a few of them, even now, receive unimaginably non-Adventistic visitors from wild and distant realms. Gwamma Woe had not foreseen this.

I found a walking stick. I began walking and wading a stone stream-bed for the first time in my life. Because of what ensued, thirty or so pairs of wading boots later I'm walking them still. Love, it turns out, is for me something slippery, arrived at on foot, via lots of splashing.

Kids tend to befriend creeks the way adults befriend each other: start shallow and slowly work your way deeper. So: skippers; water-striders. That's what I noticed first. Inch-long, spraddle-legged, white-walled black-topped creatures embarrassing Gwamma Woe's man, St. Peter, by demonstrating that mere bugs not only walk on water, they *run*. Next, deeper down: caddis fly larva. Driving their glued-gravel RV's back an' forth, back an' forth all day across the bottom like it was Arizona down there an' they were sick o' golf, dang it, an' maybe shouldn'a took early retirement after all. Deeper yet (I had to turn submerged stones to flush these) crawdads: designed right there in the '50s by staunch war hawks, it seemed, judging by their attraction to bomb-proof rock shelters, their preference for traveling backasswards, their armor, Cold War antennae, and over-sized Pentagon-budget claws.

Then I came to water too deep to wade, or to even see bottom: a shady black pool, surface-foam eddying like stars in a nebula. And though I wanted to keep exploring, the big pool proved a psychic magnet . . .

Its surface was a night sky in broad daylight. Its depths were another world within this one. The entire frenetic creek stopped here to rest. I was seventy-eight percent water myself. I felt physically ordered to crawl out on a cantilevered log, settle belly-down, and watch the pool gyre directly beneath me, the foam-starred surface eddying, eddying, till it became a vision of night; water-skipper meteors; sun-glint novas. The creek would not stop singing. I spun and spiraled, grew foam-dazed and gyre-headed. Pieces of the mental equipment I'd been taught to think I needed began falling into the pool and dissolving: my preference of light to darkness; sense of rightsideup and upsidedownness; sense of surfaces and edges, sense of where I end and other things or elements begin. The pool taught nothing but mystery and depth. An increasingly dissolved "I" followed the first verb, gravity, down, and found that depth, as a dissolved "I" sees it, is also height:

Up from the sunless depths, or down from foam-starred heavens, a totem-red tartan-green impossibility descended or arose, its body so massive and shining, visage so travel-scarred and ancient, that I was swallowed like Jonah by the sight. I know no better way to invoke the being's presence than to state the naked name: *Coho.* An old male coho, *arc*ing up not to eat, as trout do, but just to submarine along without effort or wings; just to move, who knows why, through a space and time it created for itself as it glided. And as it eased past my face not a body's length away, the coho gazed—with one lidless, primordial eye—clean into the suspended heart of me: gazed not like a salmon struggling up from an ocean to die but like a Gaelic or Kwakiutl messenger dropped down from a realm of gods, *Tír na nóg*, world of deathlessness, world of *Ka*, to convey, via the pure fact of its existence, a timeless message of sacrifice and hope. The creek would not stop singing. My bagpipe heart could not stop answering. When you see a magnificent ocean fish confined in small, fresh water, it is always like a dream. And in our dreams every object, place, and being is something *inside* us. Despite my smallness, ignorance, inexperience, I felt a sudden immense entitlement: this creek and its music, secret world and its messenger, belonged to me completely. Or I to them.

The coho vanished as serenely as it had come, back into depth. But not before its shining eye changed the way I see out of my own. I'd glimpsed a way into a Vast Inside. A primordial traveler through water and time had said, *Come.*

So now I had an interior coho compass. *Find water*, it told me daily. But mine were not a culture, church, and family whose members employ salmon as compasses by which to direct their lives. A salmon, in my culture's view, was a "resource" placed on earth by God, so that human beings (which in our suburbs meant white folks) could "convert the resource"—via a process of commercial fishing, cooking, chewing, and swallowing—into ever-larger and more numerous white folks. To admire the flavor of the "resource" was allowable. But *to revere it? To believe the resource in some sense lived inside us? To fuel this belief by worshipping the waters that spawned both the belief and its salmon?* This was all a lot of unsaved unwashed heathen nonsense. Yet Gwamma Woe's grandson was suddenly full of just that.

I became the Hamlet of the Adventist church, lurking in back pews, haunted by a suspicion that something was rotten in the State of Rote Worship. I managed not to blame the followers on the Leader: I saw Jesus as an expert fisherman and non-Christian, same as I longed to be. But I did notice, as a born river-lover and tree-hugger, how Christ never really got cracking till John the Baptist dunked Him in a river, and never saved the world till He died on a tree. Jesus, as I saw it, needed Christianity and churches the way an ocean needs sailors and ships: i.e. not at all. It made no sense to me to demote the Cause (Jesus, or the Ocean) of an effect (churches, or ships) to the level of a mere occupant of the effect (Christians, or sailors). So I didn't.

And with that conclusion, church became a stagnant pool in which I waited for rain, fresh flow, and escape. The real sacrificial dramas of the Northwest, the truly Christlike activity as I saw it, were taking place not in the buildings where Christians so brackishly tried to worship but in the lives of the wild salmon I spontaneously *did* worship, for the way they poured in from the sea in defiance of every threat, predator, and pharisee, climbed increasingly troubled mountain streams, nailed their beautiful bodies to lonely beds of gravel, and died there not for anything they stood to gain but for the sake of tiny silver offspring.

Longing to bust out of burbs and churches into the natural, God-given world that helped me explore the world within me, I realized: *I need to fish.* And not just in the River Hose. My intuition blasted me daily with the sense that real rivers contained living denizens of fluid darks and deeps: I needed to lay literal hands on the life of these deeps.

III. THE TROLL BOY'S SECRET

My family moved twice during my boyhood. The first time was from the foot of the volcanic cone to a country lane nine miles east of Portland, called Rockwood Road. We had a huge garden there, a cherry, apple, and peach orchard, eight long rows of three kinds of berries, fifty chickens, a yard big enough for baseball if it hadn't been for windows and foul balls, a rose garden, a thick laurel hedge between us and the quiet road, and a row of stately maples just inside the hedge. Several neighbors owned little

Jeffersonian farms and a fourth owned two hundred acres of ancient fir forest, which I roamed freely. Our front window faced Mount Hood and the sunrise. It took no effort on my part to consider our home an earthly paradise and me the luckiest bounder alive.

Then, one calm country morning, a chunk of basalt the size of a football crashed through the front window and landed on the couch. Blown there by the dynamite of a new kind of creature called "a developer." I marveled at the rock on the couch, not yet knowing what a metaphor was. Over the next few months I found out.

First, we learned that federal highway planners had designated Rockwood Road as the main artery connecting Interstate 84 and U.S. Highway 26. Next, our country road's name was changed to NE 181st. Next, the highway department cut down our maples, tore out the sheltering laurel hedge, widened the road to four lanes, ran a concrete sidewalk through our rose garden, traffic increased a hundredfold, and a car ran over my dog, Hunter. My parents got me another dog. I named it Hunter the Second. Two weeks later a bus ran over Hunter the Second. The Jeffersonian farms vanished beneath a multicolored acne of the dynamite developer's housing. Another developer snuck up from behind, converting the two-hundred-acre forest into another vast housing tract. There was suddenly no woods to wander, no dog to wander with, and we no longer knew our neighbors. Bikes began to be stolen, homes robbed or vandalized, the words "rape" and "abduction" entered our vocabularies. A sicko in an old Pontiac tried one day to steal me out of our hedgeless, unprotected yard. Another jolly old soul wagged his penis at my little sister while she stood waiting for the school bus. We learned never to leave the yard, never to talk to strangers, never to go anywhere alone, always to lock doors.

In recognition of our changed circumstances, my father bought my brothers and me boxing gloves. First time I tried them I was still just gawking at the bizarre look of them on my hands when a sizable new neighbor kid hit me flush on the jaw, I fell to a concrete floor, hit my head, and was knocked out cold. When I awoke, I no longer wanted to box again, ever: what I wanted was our country road, dog, trees, gardens, forest, knowable neighbors, farms, and freedom back.

Amazingly, I got them. When I was eight my parents moved us to a fir-tree-lined street twelve miles east of Portland. One June day, riding my bike to the general store in the postage-stamp-sized town of Fairview, I purchased my vices of the era—one cent Bazooka bubblegum and five cents bags of sunflower seeds—jammed my face full of this chaw, and set out for home when I heard, seemingly under the pavement of the street, a gruff voice yell, "*Son of a bitch! Gotcha! Ow! You shit!*"

I stopped for several reasons. One: I didn't cuss (yet) so the dialect interested me. Two: the voice was a boy's. Three: the boy was invisible. Four: despite his choice of words he sounded unusually happy.

Further oaths drew me to a barn-red barbershop. "You *bastard!*" yelled the boy from nowhere. "*Come 'ere ya lil' fuck! Ha! Gotcha!*" I followed these sounds to a cavelike opening in the briars covering the west wall of the barbershop. I peered in and under. There in the dim light stood a rough-looking lout about my age, holding a galvanized bucket in one hand and a coat hanger spear in the other, surrounded by the source of his happiness: he was standing knee-deep in clear, lively creek water.

"Wanna see?" the troll asked me, holding up his bucket.

Without a thought of shoes or clothes, I waded in beside him and saw that his bucket was crawling with speared and dying crawdads. The troll boy informed me (as I contemplated multicolored skeins of intestine trailing out of shattered shells) that their tails and claws, once shelled, boiled, and dipped in French's Mustard, were delicious. I laughed. Yeah right.

Then I heard splashing downstream of us and was alarmed to see a bigger, wilier-looking troll boy, who in one hand held not a spear but a fishing pole and in the other held not crayfish but a fresh-caught, still flopping trout. No Christmas or birthday moment had ever compared: a mile from my house, beneath a magic barbershop, True North on my coho compass: *a secret trout stream.*

I tore back home, grabbed a pole, hooks and split-shot, rode back to the creek, caught crawdads barehanded, crushed the life out of them without compunction, used the tails and claw meat for bait, and by suppertime had caught my first two wild cutthroat trout.

IV. NATIVE TEACHER

Fairview Creek, it turned out, was five miles long, two-thirds wild, and amazingly full of life. Over the next six years I probed it from the gravel pit source to the Mud Lake mouth, catching hundreds of its cutthroat. In the gravel pits at the headwaters I caught stocked rainbow trout. Near the greyhound racetrack in Fairview, in a pond hidden by a raspberry farm, I plunked for bullhead catfish. In the plunge-pool below the Interstate 84 culvert I caught a thirteen-inch Pacific giant salamander that flared and hissed at me like something out of Gwamma Woe's hell till I apologized, cut my line, and freed it. In the cottonwood-lined meanders down near Mud Lake I moved aside the sheep herds and caught channel cats, enormous carp, bluegill, crappie, perch, bass, and a cutthroat approaching two pounds.

Giving way to full obsession I fished the creek an easy fifty or sixty times a year. There were interesting problems to work out. I was chased by police many times at the gravel pit ponds, arrested for trespass near the Mud Lake mouth, and run out of yards and off farms by irate landowners, teen bullies and a variety of militant dogs. Did these chasings and arrests combine to "teach me a lesson?" Absolutely. I learned to be *much* sneakier. The moral ambiguities of private property issues, though, were resolved for me in a 1964 publication called *Trout Fishing in America*, in which Justice Richard Brautigan gave this verdict:

No Trespassing
4/17 of a haiku

My fishing koan, ever since, has not been whether to trespass but how not to get caught.

I learned to fish the gravel pit ponds on moonlit nights to avoid watchmen and cops. I learned to clean up a pile of creekside garbage and hold it under one arm before knocking on the porch of a landowner to ask permission to fish. I used the mailman's trick—a pocketful of milkbones—to tame the dogs. I learned to drift a worm and bobber down into the backyards of those who forbade trespass, skiing fish back up to where I legally stood (which twice so amazed people who had no idea their creek held trout that they gave me permission to trespass for life.)

I grew wily as a fisherman. I worked the creek's skinny headwaters in April and May, before buttercups closed over the surface and plied the Mud Lake terminus in summer heat, when trout had gone into hiding but big warm water fish, especially carp, were on the prowl. I took pruning shears to impassable tunnels of briars, cutting my way back into sunless holes from where I snaked nearly black cutthroat. I learned an array of lessons from the creek's confounded wild and "civilized" worlds: learned, for instance, via a few terrifying encounters, not only to spot and duck hoodlums before they cornered me but also learned to build lean-tos in a rainstorm, to forage hazelnuts, apples, and berries in tossed Dairy Queen cups, or to make small smokeless fires and cook fare found along and in the creek (my best such meal ever a borscht of filched corn, green beans, onion, and catfish simmered in a tossed Van Camps bean can).

To spend so much time on a single small stream is to encounter every life-form it sustains. My presence in marshes and thickets untrod by humans enabled me to catch baby killdeer, baby mallards, and baby cot-tontails in my hands. I stood face-to-face with one of the last black-tailed deer ever sighted in East Multnomah County and glimpsed perhaps the very last fox, which a teen idiot named Booth, no doubt related to John Wilkes, soon after shot. I stumbled onto wood ducks, raccoons, ring-neck pheasants, possums, turtles, horned owls, and herons, and once, via an accident that soon became nonaccidental, a pair of joyously fucking teen-agers. I once lay so quiet on a low wooden sheep bridge that a musk-rat swam into my monofilament. Thinking myself hilarious I lunged for-ward and went BOO!, inspiring a lightning quick flip-ass dive that drove a quart or so of muddy water under my eyelids. I bewildered my father, every April Opening Day for six years in a row, by refusing his invita-tions to the famed Deschutes River. I then dissipated his bewilderment, six years in a row, by bringing home ten-fish limits of Fairview Creek cut-throats while he often returned home skunked.

In this era of rapid-fire unconsidered change I suppose anyone older than five or six is the relic of some sort of "lost era." For my part I'm one of the last Americans raised on the edge of a major city who knows what he knows not just from desks in eight successive classrooms or from tough night streets or from TV screens but from six years as the Huck Finn-style lover and terror of a five-mile long ribbon of life. I stuck my hands, feet, nose, eyeballs, tongue, ears, and body into a thousand places they did and didn't belong. I learned by poking at things and gathering, stalking, killing, cleaning, cooking, and eating things; I learned by letting things mesmerize, dazzle, and hypnotize me, forming the million impressions that, when I'd collapse in bed at night, became an equally informative scramble of impression and nightmare and vision and dream and prayer. I learned from Tri-Met bus exhaust and Union Pacific locomotive smoke,

from Crown Zellerbach paper-mill stench and Reynolds Aluminum efflu-
ent, from cottonwood fluff on May pools, tractor dust in July bean fields,
October cricket songs waning and geese songs waxing. For six rich years
the living *ka* that was Fairview Creek flowed unmediated through my
brain-halves and heart-valves, teaching me that this world is peaceful and
dangerous, wild and artificial, beautiful and wounded, obscene and sublime. For six years, in other words, I studied with the most perfect teacher
I can imagine for life in the America I've inhabited ever since.

V. BODIES OF BLOOD AND WATER

Two weeks before my fourth consecutive Fairview Creek Opening Day,
my eldest brother died, at seventeen, of a series of failed open heart surgeries. The little creek's presence, its flow, its ability to keep generating
life, helped me a little with this grief. The ten Opening Day trout I caught
that year felt different than any I'd caught before: their deaths especially
felt different: the concept of sacrifice had begun to invade my fishing. I
could articulate nothing but big feelings swept over me as I snapped each
neck—and what an eerie version of fisherman pride I felt when my family
and I, we "survivors," sat down to eat the little bodies whose lives I'd tak-
en. Men, women, and children, I suddenly realized, were dying, and no
one seemed to notice but the funeral parlors who'd turned death into an
industry. But each time I bloodied my hands, killing a trout as innocent as
my dead brother, I noticed. Each time I killed a trout the pain would ease
for a time inside me. Why? Christ. You tell me. I sensed a depth, in the act
of killing fish, that spoke to my grief. A consciously snapped trout-neck
was like a blues-string consciously bent against the day-to-day industrial
harmonies. And a bent note, in the ears of the sorrow-bent, rings truer
than a note clean-struck. Nothing soothes quite like the blues. A little
trout stream, if played for keeps, can be a miles-long blues tune.

By my seventh Fairview Creek Opening Day I'd grown so confident in my
abilities and creek that I bet a high school pal five bucks I'd take a seventh
straight ten-fish limit. My five-mile teacher had a strange lesson for me.

   At 6:30 on a rainy April morning I crept up to a favorite hole, thread-
ed a worm on a hook, prepared to cast—then noticed something impossible: there was no water in the creek. I gaped at mud and exposed rock,

then up at the falling rain. The sky was doing its job, had been doing it all April. How could this be?

I began hiking, stunned, downstream. The aquatic insects were gone, barbershop crawdads gone, catfish, carp, perch, crappie, bass, and sacrificial cutthroats not just dying but completely vanished. Feeling sick, I headed the opposite way, hiking the emptied creek-bed all the way to the source, where I found the eminently rational cause of the mass killing. Development needs roads and drain fields. Roads and drain fields need gravel. Up in the gravel pits at the Glisan Street headwaters, the creek's entire flow had been diverted for months to fill two gigantic new settling ponds.

My native teacher was dead.

I was sixteen and drove a car now. I didn't know enough to grieve. I felt so panic-stricken by Fairview Creek's death that I tried, as if keeping a stranded fish alive in a bucket, to transfer my need for water to the other stream within easy driving distance: Johnson Creek—source of my first glimpse of a coho and an inner realm. But ten years and fifty thousand industrious new human inhabitants had been murder on this friend too. I encountered none of the magic of Fairview Creek, little wildlife, no native fish, and few birds. Johnson Creek's trout were now drab hatchery rainbows, planted in March by Fish and Wildlife to entertain local yokels on Opening Day. By May no one fished for them because the same Fish and Wildlife department pronounced them too toxic to eat.

I kept after them, though. I was old enough, now, to know a metaphor when I hooked one: I was fascinated by the trout's growing discoloration, growing scarcity, and growing weakness. I entered a zone, fished Johnson Creek hard. By June it was low, warm, filmy, and the trouts' living skins had burst out in a pox of strange clear bubbles. By mid-month the rainbows stopped taking any kind of bait or fly, but I'd still see one drift past now and then, in a sudsy foam-line, sometimes belly-up, sometimes weakly finning. One hot June day I managed to catch a few suckers near the creek's terminus with the Willamette: they were on a spawning run, hadn't been in the creek long enough to be dead yet. One July day, near the 55th Street bridge, my catch was a discarded car radio and a woman's dress (red, with small white polka dots; short; sexy; poisonously sopped). Another day it was twenty bags of rotten meat and vegetables floating along in zip-lock bags, looking like twenty disembodied stomachs still trying to digest their meals. By August, and drought, my new native teacher was an oil-scummed, fetid, foam-flecked sewer, there were warnings posted on phone poles telling kids not to swim, and even the hatchery trout of June seemed like a comparatively beautiful vision. The last day I fished Johnson Creek I waded into a nice-looking run, knelt low, cast a fly up into the riffle, noticed a more-offensive-than-usual stench coming from the creekbank behind me, turned—and started gagging at the sight of the crawling, maggot-filled head of a horse.

VI. CRASH-TEST DUMMY

My two boyhood mentors were a brother and a creek, both now dead. My coho compass seemed to die with Johnson Creek. I still loved rivers. But river don't come with you to school or ball games, don't brother you when you're haunted, don't speak English, don't intellectualize. So—linguistically, socially, fraternally, intellectually—I felt alone and unguided. The fishing talk of the best anglers I knew—honest working stiffs, men I guardedly liked—was a lingo of technique, conquest, and gloat. The rivers within driving distance—the Columbia, Clackamas, Sandy—were the domain of fishermen who on their work days helped destroy rivers and on their off days plundered them. There was no one to whom I could even mention such perceptions. Love for animals, birds, and wilderness led to no A's on report cards. If Henry Thoreau or Gary Snyder had attended my giant high school they'd have dropped out if they hadn't been expelled. If they'd taught there they would definitely have been fired. There would be no coho questions on my SAT exams. Free-flowing streams made no campaign contributions to senators—and look what happened to them as a result. A big trout sipping a mayfly may be a veritable hymn to the health of a watershed, but no TV or newspaper covered that hymn. On TV and in the papers I watched businessmen, economists, and politicians place a dollar value on everything on earth and discount anything that lacked such a value. I knew this was wrong—knew that if everything was material then everything was negotiable and one's body, home, friendships, honesty, honor, could all be bought or sold. I then watched democracy itself be bought and sold; watched the TV war escalate in Asia, the campus and race riots escalate at home; watched a patriotic foster brother die almost the day he set foot in Vietnam; watched Martin Luther King and Bobby Kennedy die in the midst of expressing compassion and love of justice; watched people who define things in the crassest, most material way get what they wanted over and over; watched evil, mortality, and stupidity win and win and win.

There came a time, in adolescence, when I questioned every last thing my heart had intimated to me since childhood. All this "nature stuff" suddenly felt too hard to articulate to bosses, teachers, parents, too airy-fairy to share with red-blooded three-sport pals. My unchecked river-love suddenly struck me as a way to achieve numb-nutted poverty, cultural irrelevancy, and maybe a stint in Vietnam. I began to want to get what I wanted. And what I'd begun to want, I came to believe, was not richness, not meaning, not interior truth or depth: I wanted a skin so thick this world couldn't hurt me. A skin I'd open, now and then, if the right looking kind of girl wanted in. But only briefly.

Hoping to create such a skin I began to crash-test everything I'd ever loved or trusted, then pick through the wreckage to see what survived. I crash-tested my connection to creeks and rivers in the simplest way possible: I abandoned them. Quit seeking wild water. Quit yearning for it. I even quit crying, for any reason, since tears too are a bit wild and all too wet.

Taking aim at nothing I couldn't eat, feel, fool, fuck, or buy, I became a pathologically common brand of high school student, landed a series of the best-paying jobs I could find, became a cog in the purposeless box of industrial gears that had appalled me as a child, and "repaid myself" for this purposelessness by granting myself every pleasure I could grasp.

I began to grow that thick skin. The sensation scared me for a bit. But life, as I was living it, thickened me so fast that I was soon unable to feel even my fear.

VII. VALMIKI'S PALM

At seventeen I took a full-time summer job at a plastics factory in the industrial heart of Portland. I then began, after work, to wander the city in the company of my fine new principle of depravity, seeking whatever pleasures I could physically grasp.

One day I dropped into a disheveled little used bookstore: the cram-packed, cigarette-singed '69 vintage Powell's Books, as it happens. I read books as a hedonist in those days, read them to trip. Looking for the wildest but least expensive possible ride, I impulse-purchased a musty verse translation of the *Ramayana* and headed home.

I knew, from having read *The Odyssey*, that epics were a trip. I knew, from reading a remark made by Snyder or Tolkien or somebody, that the *Ramayana*—story of the prehistoric king, Rama—was India's greatest epic. But the translation I'd purchased in a post-work stupor told King Rama's story in wrenched, rhyming Victorian couplets that made even epic battles and ancient wisdom sound like the chuggity-chugging sentiments of an interminable Hallmark card. I soon threw the book away. Before I did, however, I took one small wonder to heart:

The *Ramayana's* author—the forest poet, Valmiki—states in his opening verses that he did not use his imagination while composing King Rama's story. He didn't need imagination, he said, because at dawn each day he took an urn to the nearby river, filled it, carried it to his hut, sat down on an eastward-facing mat, then scooped a little river water into his palm: in this tiny body of water Valmiki saw first Rama, then Queen Sita, then every god, demon, and hero, every love dalliance and bloody battle, in his epic. Fragrances and sounds, too, rose from the water: the smoke of brahmanic sacrifices, stench of demons, cries of warriors and victims, hissing flight of arrows, blood-burst of every wound. The poet then sang what he saw. All twenty-five thousand *Ramayana* couplets were born in the water pooled daily in Valmiki's palm.

I was smitten by this. That an epic could spring from a palmful of river brought a jolt of the liturgical joys a garden-hose river and two-inch fishing soldier once gave me. Thanks to the Victorian prosody and my cynical teen self, this joy didn't blossom into anything life-changing. In honor of Valmiki, though, I did develop an odd tic: I took to glancing at my own palms, dozens of times a day, as if at a watch I expected to tell me more than the time. Just a nervous habit I suppose. Because of it, though, I came to see that palms have skin like no other part of the body: the moisture; visible texture; almost legible-looking lines. I learned the palms' topography—four ominous little canyons in which palm-readers claim to see secrets of the head, heart, fate, and lifespan. I saw that palms, compared to fists or fingers, have no agenda: they're not a weapon, a tool, a talon: they're just a handy portable shelf revealing exactly what they hold.

I soon tossed the *Ramayana* and wandered off in search of more sensual or phantasmagoric trips. But I couldn't shake that little palm-reading tic.

The plastics factory that employed me produced a tough red polyurethane, dubbed "Redskin," from which we made indescribable geometrical gizmos we simply called "parts." These parts were shipped to other factories to be attached to larger indescribable gizmos, which were shipped to still other factories and attached to indescribable machines which were in turn shipped and affixed to larger machines. Five or six removes from us, rumor had it, our Redskin gizmos became part of something you could actually name: a raspberry-picking machine. We had no way to verify this, but our bosses told us so and we believed them. We were Americans after all. What could be more American than manufacturing plastic crap called Redskin to produce a machine that put the real, destitute, flesh-and-blood "redskins" who in those days picked Oregon's raspberries, out of work?

I lived next door to a raspberry farm harvested, for the most part, by impoverished Indians. I liked those Indians when I worked with them. But I didn't feel sorry for those our Redskin helped put out of work. The reason I didn't was that we were being killed for our crime; management had deemed the slow killing of workers an acceptable cost of the Redskin manufacturing process. What better revenge could the real Indians want?

The murder weapon was not an object but a lack of objects. In the time I worked at Redskin I saw no blue-collar employee spend a single hour working with materials that weren't toxic, yet I never saw a respirator, an exhaust fan, a gauze mask, never heard or read a single warning. We spent every day stoned on carcinogenic fumes. Yet no one complained. In fact, plant morale was high. I think it had to do with Vietnam, which in turn had to do with childhoods in rowed houses in suburbs, rowed pews, rowed desks in classrooms, immaculate interiors, fake democracies, every thing and everyone destined to be packaged, boxed, sold, and shipped out. Every Redskin worker had an *America: Love It Or Leave It* bumper sticker on their vehicle and seemed genuinely grateful to be spending their health and allotment of heartbeats making incomprehensible polyurethane gizmos. The typical Redskin Plant attitude was, "I'm non-union, I'm underpaid, I'm making nothing I understand, I'm breathing shit, I'll be dying young—and I'm *proud of it!*"

My job as plant lackey was of a janitorial nature. I cleaned up spills mostly. Redskin started out as a stew of toxic liquids which were mixed together in vats, poured into molds, placed on racks, rolled into a huge walk-in oven, baked to hardness, rolled back out, and removed as hardened "parts." There were spills at every fluid stage of this process, and spilled polyurethane quickly fuses with anything it touches. Once hardened the only way to remove the stuff is with an acetone solvent—also toxic. I spent my Redskin career blitzed on solvent.

One of my daily tasks took place in Dumpster bins. Even after they'd been emptied into garbage trucks, the sides and bottom of our bins remained caked with enormous slabs of waste Redskin. It was my job to climb in the Dumpster, pour solvent on the slabs, let it work awhile, then attack the now-gooey Redskin with a giant C-clamp. The clamp was hooked to a steel cable that attached to the overhead hydraulic lift. Blinded by tears from solvent fumes, terrifically stoned by them, I'd screw my C-clamp to the biggest meanest flap of Redskin I could find, hit the "Up" button on the hydraulic lift's remote, and hope the weight of the Dumpster and me would together tear the slab free while I was still fairly close to the ground. When the slab didn't tear I'd just continue toward the ceiling, too fume-ripped to tell the "Up" button from the "Down." It was a thirty-foot ceiling. I don't recall dropping a Dumpster from the top— management really didn't like that. But when a Redskin slab tore loose even at eight or ten feet, the Dumpster crashed to the floor with a force that brought a roar of laughter from the other workers, knowing I lay in a swamp of half-dissolved plastics inside. I laughed too, if brokenly, to show the world I was tough.

Another job was cleaning the walk-in oven. Every time a rack of fresh-filled molds was rolled in, liquid Redskin dripped onto the oven floor. These drips built up after each firing creating bumps that caused more spillage. My task was to pour solvent on the bumps then hack them free with a garden hoe. Since "time is money," though, and cooling and reheating the oven took time, the plant foreman considered 140 degrees Fahrenheit "Can Do" cleaning conditions. At 140 degrees my solvent vaporized the instant it touched the floor, turning the oven into a blinding, brain-fogging sweat lodge. The foreman would stand by the open oven door, watching me scamper into the lodge, throw solvent on bumps, run back out, take a breath, run back in, hoe bumps, run back out, take a breath, run in, hoe, run out, till the floor was smooth. His vigilance was not a kindness. Dead workers waste time, which is money.

Most Redskin parts had thin, sloppy edges created by a skin of plastic that had overflowed the mold. We removed this skin by hand with X-Acto knives. Six weeks into my job, after yet another toxic sweat and hoe in the oven, I sat down at my work station, fetched my X-Acto, and began trimming sloppy edges from a box of Redskin parts, feeling as if time and space were drunk and my mind was dipped in plastic and indispensible parts of me were dying and so the fuck what. I was making eight hundred dollars a month to feel this way. I was tough.

I fetched another part, trimmed away another edge. Fetched another. Trimmed. Then something happened: feeling a faint swirl in my left palm, I glanced down—and saw a silver fin crease the surface of my skin.

"Trout," I murmured, too oven-stoned for surprise.

A trout had risen in my left palm. Hmm. My Valmikian tic was producing the goods. The trout's dorsal lazed up into sight and stayed there; broke the surface, making no ripples, and stayed there. I'd seen a lot of fish in my day but never one rising from inside me. Half-forgotten river thoughts began to swim through me. *How did a trout get inside my hand? What did it do in there all day? Had it risen to sip some kind or fly or just to move, who knows why, through a space and time it created for itself as it glided?*

I had no idea. But a second wave of notions slopped through me. That something as fragile as a trout could survive inside the Redskin Plant seemed even more unlikely than that one was living inside my hand. Which led me to ask: what were my hand and I doing in the Redskin Plant? I grew vaguely aware of a throbbing that never left my body, realized it was the dark digestive rumbling of the entire unventilated building, felt the plant sucking at my limbs, my lungs, my life—and grew less vaguely aware. I looked at the men with whom I worked and joked all day, saw the black rings beneath their eyes, the lethargic movements, the dissolved plastics slopped on clothes and skin. Then a third wave struck:

Turning back to my own palm, I began to gasp. Like a fresh-beached salmon I began gasping for life, my entire body needing clear running water, moss-trimmed cedars, clean-pebbled streambeds, the vast, preacherless church of the wild so badly that my eyes filled not with fume-tears but with real tears and my palm—*could this be happening?*—began to bleed, right from the rise. I watched blood stream down my fate-line like water down a riparian, watched it fall, then pool, on the factory floor.

It took me the longest time to realize I'd stuck the X-Acto through my hand from the opposite side and was staring at the tip of its blade in my palm. It took so long that, in the end, I reacted not to a blade but to a trout's rise—and began trying to rise myself.

Taking fresh aim at life and water I told my Redskin cohorts that we were dying and quit my job that day. I stopped at an Army Navy surplus store on the way home, bought a box of thirty-nine cents trout flies, an inexpensive fly rod kit, and a stack of wilderness maps. I embraced poverty—and the freedom it buys. I built the fly rod. I then began, like a blind man with a nine-foot cane, to feel my way back toward things I once fully loved and trusted.

The palm of a hand is impassive. Fists and fingers have their agendas but what rests in a palm is free to tell its silent truth. In the years since a steel dorsal rose in my fate-line I have waded hundreds of wild streams, held thousands of trout and salmon in my hands, and watched a million silver rises. To this day I sometimes cup a little river in my pierced palm, flood the tiny scar, and check for signs of life there. To this day I keep thanking Valmiki.

Sophie Beck

Monster Trucks and the White Bellaire

We sang the national anthem. Then they shot the buxom blonde out of a cannon. Naturally there was a great pop—a breathy, explosive punch of sound. The white sparks of the fireworks traveled out with the Cannon Lady, and she sailed high above the red, white, and blue Buicks and Caddies in her shiny red suit and crash helmet. She was free, though she had only a fraction of a second to consider the fact before turning her mind to the rotation she needed to achieve before landing. Or perhaps she was always thinking of the rotation—never thinking of the flight so much as the requirements she must meet to carefully end it. In her instant of travel we were hushed, wondering at the sensation that she must have, waiting for her safe return to our more ordinary, ground-bound existence. Fireworks. Air rushing past a small body encased in a tight and iridescent red suit. Flight and descent. Once she'd plopped into the net, we clapped encouragement. A man near me yelled, "Whew!" Another whistled—a long and warbling streak of sound traveling alone above the applause.

She strode across the arena then, popped off her cherry red helmet, shook out her mane of curls, and revealed herself to be somewhat shy, though she'd undoubtedly been confronted with that microphone in many cities before ours. Not the exuberant gunpowder traveler that we might have expected, she was a bit quieter, a bit more serious than we might have imagined the Cannon Lady would be. They shoot her so fast that the first few times she did it, she was a good fifteen feet out of the barrel before she had the awareness that her journey had even begun. She told us this and then the announcer told us that she came from a family of cannonballers—her father and brother both holders of assorted cannon-balling records, having been shot distances exceeding two hundred feet. And then we seemed to understand that she came to her profession by the complex familial ties that shape us all as much as by any compulsive need to descend that dark barrel in order to achieve an instant of exhilarating, unfettered flight. "Whew!" the man yelled again. Then they drove her cannon away and turned to the serious business of vehicular competition.

Grave Digger is the most popular monster truck in the world. This is according to the Grave Digger Web site. While the other trucks were gathering and circling, Grave Digger remained tucked away beneath an *inconspicuous* fifty-foot tower of cardboard boxes right in the middle of the arena, only to come careening out at the last minute to *surprise* us. The men in the row in front of me yelled "Donuts!" and swung their hats over their heads, then giggled and settled in to watch quietly as the various competitors drove over the red, white, and blue Buicks and Caddies. Grave Digger is painted with a death motif of gravestones, ghosts, bones, and the inky blackness of an uncertain eternity. Jurassic Attack, High Roller, and Obsession were also in attendance. Not present but discussed in my program were Cyborg, Captain America, Backdraft, Live Wire, and Reptoid. And lest you question the potential for mayhem, other truck names include Destroyer, Devastator, Equalizer, Eradicator, King Krunch, Thrasher, Maniac, and Godzilla.

I'm not so very certain that there really is anything that is actually mindless about mindless entertainment. We throw ourselves into this extravagant display of gears and wreckage, but it can't engage us unless it summons or suggests the greater forces of uncertainty and damage against which we shake our small flesh fists. Why watch an exercise of power if not to quell fears of powerlessness? To what dire battle do we summon Eradicator and Destroyer? What greater work do we have at hand for the Equalizer? To the darkly moving unknown monsters we reply, "monster truck."

They crunched their way over the row of old cars, sprinting into the air and descending again in a great roar of pure engine power. And after the second time or so, I suppose we were all wondering what was next because we'd become aware that driving over cars loses a bit of flavor with every repetition. The men in front of me again cry for donuts, but none are offered.

In this sparkly new sports arena with thousands of seats, expensive boxes, and legions of beer vendors, any event can be manufactured. Tonight they have brought in dirt and old cars. Tonight the sponsors make motor oil. Tonight there are vendors selling bright-yellow earplugs because the trucks promise to be so very loud—crazy and churning and growling and eardrum-rupturingly loud! Who wants those plugs? We've come for the dirt and grease and noise. Moms buy them for kids who won't wear them. No one in my section is plugged.

Teams of quad racers careen around the outer perimeter periodically, and then the respective team captains approach the microphone for the opportunity to revile one another with that variety of florid insults cultivated in professional wrestling. A quad, it turns out, is a small and rather stable-looking beast that is perhaps fun to race but not much fun to watch racing because it appears impossible to overturn. Unlike motocross bikes that can careen out from under the driver on a bit of loose dirt or a hard turn, quads are squat and grounded; they hiccup over the ridges in the track and then settle back down to the business of yet another revolution. We cannot cheer heartily for the quad racers. We see little skill in their scooting along, and we cannot believe them to be courting death and danger. Flip it! Fall down! Skid perilously close to the Penzoil board and nearly snap your neck! If someone would tumble, we would muster our investment. We want someone's life in the balance—or at least his good health, and at minimum, his dignity. We want those revolutions to have consequence—push to win, put up a meaningful stake to do it.

It wouldn't take so much to find a bit of danger, after all. The quads resemble the four-wheelers my cousins drove around in backwoods Louisiana when I was small and we would visit and they would call me the Yankee because I lived substantially north. When I was fifteen I ran one into a ditch, overturned it, and bent the fender. But someone is always overturning a vehicle somewhere down there and this is where the good yarns come from. It is by the grace of breakneck speeds and roaring motors that we so often find narrative—narrative with that raw appeal of life and death and rushing air, mixed with good luck, bad luck, and speed, speed, speed. Risk is a story as nothing else can be.

Months before the Monster Jam, I'd gotten an unshakeable bee in my bonnet about the prospect of getting a custom paint job for my car. It isn't common for most girls, I suppose, but I was possessed with the idea of tricking my ride out like a rally car, with a giant number on the roof and whatever other regalia I could think up. I'd gone to get an estimate from a custom paint shop and found myself surrounded by examples of the kind of vehicular artistry you are undoubtedly envisioning right now—American flags and bald eagles, howling wolves and spiky, intertwining abstract patterns that suggest a kind of angry Celtic inspiration. Plus flames. Great, lapping, multicolored flames. There are any number of ways to suggest that your car has just driven through a wall of fire or that, by traveling the city streets at warp speed, the friction generated at the grill causes a conflagration that laps at the hood and fenders, only dissipating somewhere about halfway down the flanks of the vehicle.

The guys at the shop offered to place rippling checkered flags on my car door. They were ready to work with my rally car theme. Were I another customer, they might have suggested the airbrushed curves of that cartoonish pinup girl I saw, who offers the viewer her thonged derrière for inspection as she turns around to wink. Or the devilish girl with the wry smile who provides an only-just-obstructed view of her Brazilian wax, with the furry little landing strip. The girls on cars are never sweet, but naughty. The girls on cars want *it*. Naturally, when one is dealing with speed and risk and power and the dark forces of fortune, sex is the next logical addition. The pretty Cannon Lady descends the long, dark barrel.

The girls on cars promise not just the sex but the wanting. They have glistening breasts and butts, certainly, but the eye is drawn to their expressions—to the wink. The promise is not mechanical but spiritual—sex with desire and creativity and abandon. Sex with the enthusiasm of joy and erasure. Sex that is naughty and loaded and consequential. Sex that risks damnation or domination or capture or exposure.

In the bedroom and at the wheel, we're seeking that intensity that feels like *real life*. Real life, as in that elusive feeling that we *are* alive and not simply going through the motions of being alive. Real life, like those great thumps that you hear when you place your ear to your lover's chest and listen. Real life, as the promise that comes with consciousness but slips away from time to time. And when we find it, it's a story, though we hardly have the words with which to catch it.

At the Monster Jam I drink a beer and consider whether I might want to paint a giant, snarling animal mouth on the front of my car, extending the grill into a slobbery, fanged chasm that would chomp at the rushing air as I sped down the freeway as fast as I dared. Maybe go careening around some narrow mountain pass curve, considering that rail-less shoulder and wondering what it would feel like to just not turn the wheel and rocket off the edge. Then feel my heart race simply because that thought had welled up from some dark eddy in my own psyche, at odds with the far stronger self-protective will. If I could *think* of driving right off of the edge, could I ever accidentally act on it?

Meanwhile an eight-year-old boy in my row whips off his shirt and, exuberantly baring his naked little belly to the arena, swings the shirt high over his head in a grand arc. He is yelling, "Donuts!" We are all slightly dissatisfied with the Monster Jam. The cheering is anemic. The great promise of spectacle that was initiated with a burst of sparks and a blonde woman shooting through the atmosphere has not been sufficiently met. Grave Digger charges the Buicks and Caddies and rears up, with front wheels suspended in the air for an instant like a massive, challenging grizzly, belly of rods and pipes exposed, before crashing down again, gas tanks sloshing in the back. The most popular monster truck in the world then crunches over a red van, and the girl to my right with the tattoo on her lower back stifles a yawn. Riskless. Let's go home, go to bed. But in that instant when the vulnerable belly was exposed it seemed just possible to rear up too far, to fall backward instead of forward and lie helpless in the arena, with wheels churning in the air like the legs of an upended beetle.

We want donuts. We want them to commit two wheels to a single space of dirt and then go spinning round and round that little space in a great roar of engine labor, faster and faster until the driver vomits all over the cab. We want g-force. Harnessed physics. Someone has to get dizzy. Don't stop. Don't stop. Just don't goddamn stop. Heady stuff. Hot, really, in some hard-to-identify way. You don't need a pinup girl to associate cars and fooling around.

The cars don't have bench seats anymore, so you can't be a freshman dating the junior with the giant white Bellaire. He picked you up before school in the mornings and played Led Zeppelin and laid an arm across your shoulders and you sailed along, untethered, floating over the roadways on cold fall mornings. Broken seatbelts mashed deep in the crack, and the bench seat was a sea of mighty, undulating springs. And though he didn't press too much, he wanted things from you that you didn't really understand just yet, even as you pretended not to be so very naïve. He wanted to do *it*. There was a time when *it* was a strange and secret promise—a dark barrel that you peered down. Even now, Led Zeppelin and Levis and fuzzy dice remind you of *it* as it was when it was purely metaphorical because it was not yet mechanical. At least, not for you. It was the winking girl on the cab of the truck—all promise, all dangerous, all possibility, and so, so *fast*.

Barbara Hurd

Stones

Turning Points

> Who placed us with eyes between a microscopic and a telescopic
> world?
>
> Henry David Thoreau

The shore was my mother's favorite subject, but in the foreground of her
paintings I can't recall a single object—never a boat or bird, not even a
rock or shell. If my mother were here on the Maine coast with me this
afternoon, easel in the sand, she'd be painting the wild skies and disheveled ocean, but there'd be no broken oar in the foreground of her canvas, no daughter rearranging stones on the beach. Even the grasses would
seem less like singular blades, more like elongated blurs—inconsequential, a means of getting to what preoccupied her more: what was above or
behind, even beyond.

In one of her paintings, the sea seems to be rising into the sky, an uplift
of metal, lit up from within, reaching into the clouds' swirling grains. I
used to wonder how she achieved that combustion of platinum and silver and how old she was when she discovered which compelled her more:
water and fog or the people and things that traveled through them. Were
there failed seascapes somewhere in the attic, their foregrounds littered
with spars and brown kelp, the handle of a child's broken shovel, maybe
even a clam digger bent over his bucket? Or did she know from the start it
was distant possibilities that commanded her attention?

Without her on this mid-July late afternoon, surprisingly cool and
storm-imminent, I pile rocks on top of rocks with the intention of watching them fall down. I haven't consulted a chart but know from the narrowing exposed mud that the tide is on its way in. I figure I have a couple

of hours. Working without a plan, I stack and ring, balance and wedge, glancing now and then at the water, which eases toward me almost imperceptibly. The stones take on personalities—one so quirkily jagged and unstackable it needs to be its own monument. Another just right for a rampart; a few flat ones, perfectly shaped for a threshold. In the spaces between large, lined-up stones, I press pebbles into mud, like cobbles in an alley. On the tops of flat rocks, I steady smaller ones, and on top of those, even tinier ones. When I stand back to study what I've done, the array resembles a foot-high city of alleyways and towers, nothing my mother would ever have assembled.

*   *   *

The Pueblos believed the sun wouldn't rise if they weren't there to watch it, and though I know better, it seems suddenly crucial to stay here and see the exact moment this tide turns. It should be easy; I know tidal charts are marked in minutes: high tide, say, at 11:43 or 4:16. Even without a watch, isn't that an observable moment? The water will approach and approach and then, as if there were some lever pulled, some click that reverses the direction, the water will halt, begin to recede. I'll know it will come up no farther. I'll be able to mark the line of high water with a stick, do what I've never been able to do in my life—say, here, *this* is the turning point. Things—my routines, work, relationships, whatever seemed unsatisfying—would be different from then on. How many times have I made that pledge? Here at least there's a chance, and I can hype the symbolism for a little pleasure. A small pine branch from just up the bank serves well; I study high-water marks on the shore, make a guess, and lay it parallel to the shoreline, fifteen feet inland from where the water now sloshes.

Meanwhile, in my hand: a chunk of granite the size of a chicken egg. Formed over three hundred million years ago from magma in the volcanic hotbed that ringed what's now the Maine coast, it cooled below the surface for millions of years—cooled unevenly, spottily, certain minerals crystallizing first, others intruding later, speckling the molten rock with black mica, feldspar, and quartz. When the last glaciers retreated and the land rebounded, the overlying rock eroded until that granite, now hard and cold, lay exposed, susceptible to fracture or quarrying, worn by wind and water and more ice. And now, after thousands of years, this piece has tumbled to this beach where I can pick it up and place it on my palm. I can still see the pink feldspar, shiny bits of mica and quartz, the concoction of some stonemason and a Fabergé egg designer with a pointillist bent, though there's nothing delicate about it. The granite from this part of Maine underlies Manhattan bridges and clads the Museum of Fine Arts in Boston. It holds up the New York County Courthouse and graces the JFK Memorial in Arlington National Cemetery. This stone, I decide, belongs on top of the largest one I've found so far. I try perching it there, like an oblong lookout, but can't decide which way it should lean: toward the cobbled land or the oncoming tide? Which requires more vigilance? My mother would have said the sea; I decide on the land.

I like the way stone feels so solid. And even though I know its history and probable future, I like, for now, the pleasure of lifting a single one. When I touch it, I can say, with a certain degree of confidence, *this is a stone*. I can run my fingers over its edges, lick its contours. I can't do that with water, my mother's element. I can see it, swim in it, cup a handful. But it's not possible to touch the sea. It's too amorphous, too vast, and, like too much thought of the formless spiritual, it finally numbs me, splatters my attention. At the edge of the ocean, it's the stones now that ground me. And because they make my back ache and my fingers raw, I'm learning which ones I can lift and which must remain where they are—a necessary lesson in limitations I hope will help me watch the stones—and perhaps my own too-precious ideas—collapse.

*   *   *

"A thing of beauty is a joy forever," John Keats once said. I doubt that anyone who messes around with stones on the beach would agree with him. I'm thinking especially of that master tidal cairn builder Andy Goldsworthy, who arranges and balances big stones between tides. His work compels because, in many ways, it quarrels with Keats's long-revered notion of beauty's permanence. Goldsworthy isn't interested in forever and he isn't interested in joy. What he is interested in, however, is paradox, those yoked contradictions that sometimes hold elusive truths. In fact the genius of Goldsworthy's work, for me, is his ability to make paradox so aesthetically pleasing.

Goldsworthy, of course, makes his art at the edge of the sea because he needs the incoming tide to undermine his cairns. But I'm also inclined to think that his work compels not just because of what the tide does but because the inevitable backdrop of the sea forces us to consider the cairn, which is discrete and well shaped, in juxtaposition with the sea, which is fluid and formless, behind it. The contrast is sharp: the amorphousness of the ocean emphasizes the concreteness of the cairn and vice versa.

And because the cairn is egg shaped, it provides visual closure: our eye travels around its edges and arrives back at the beginning, perhaps imagines what's inside. The visual movement is one of convergence. If Goldsworthy were building here on the beach with me, I would be able to see his entire structure, could even circle it, examine it from all angles, have some confidence that there's nothing, visually at least, that's eluding me.

But he's not here and what most of us know of his work is through photographs. In them the sea stretches the eye sideways, up, and out toward the horizon. Its invitation is to distance, expansion, which reminds us how limited our vision is, how vast the sea and sky are, how impossible it is, as my mother might have said, to know even a fraction of them.

To see Goldsworthy's cairn at the tidal edge, then, is to have one's eye pulled simultaneously in and down in some satisfying visual closure *and* out and up in some unsettling, open-ended expansiveness. It isn't just the work itself, in other words, but the work in its carefully chosen setting that heightens the simultaneous experience of both form and formlessness, intimacy and distance.

My city needs an arena, I decide, a coliseum where opposing forces could battle it out. I'll try for arched doorways and tiered bleachers. Though it rarely happens, doesn't the conflict of certain ideas deserve dedicated spaces and audiences who know when to cheer? I roll a few big stones in a circle, ring the inside with smaller ones.

One of the most poignant paradoxes of Goldsworthy's sculptures is their relentless reminder that nothing lasts. That is their beauty, too, which, as Albert Camus says, is unbearable because it offers us "for a minute the glimpse of an eternity." It's only a matter of time before the water softens the sand beneath the stones—his and mine—rises over and destabilizes their bases, slides one stone and then another into the sea. I wonder if Goldsworthy knows Robert Frost's description of a poem as "a momentary stay against confusion." Perhaps he thinks of his outdoor work that way too—as structures on the sinking, sliding edge of the sea that for a moment constitute a figure, a form, *made* things that last a few hours, a reminder both of the great wash of the tides and our own mute and futile attempts to pause the inevitable. But I think there's something else. If, as Goldsworthy says, "the beach is a great teacher," what is it we learn here? There's no news in the tide's return. If a tidal chart can tell us exactly when the agent of destruction will arrive and we build anyway, it doesn't seem like risk so much as a wish for timed transformation. We're in cahoots with the sea, not creating in defiance of its destruction. Every tidal sculpture is doomed; Goldsworthy knows it and so do I. The making is done with an eye on the waves, which come up, sure enough, right on schedule. Constructing it there, it seems, must enact what we all do and don't want to know: that beauty built on the edge of the beach—maybe everywhere?—is in part beautiful because it cannot endure.

And look what guarantees its end: water—formless, transparent, one of the softest substances in the world. That's what will destroy the cairn and ultimately the stones themselves, which are nothing more than remnants of mountains we think of as stable, enduring. "Under heaven," the *Tao Te Ching* says, "nothing is more soft and yielding than water. / Yet for attacking the solid and strong, nothing is better; / It has no equal."

I toy with stones and memories and the lessons of paradox. Goldsworthy toys with ideas of stability and completion. He is, in fact, counting on a natural law: matter changes constantly, erodes, disintegrates, transforms into something else. If, as he reminds us, we live in a world where things are constantly evolving or devolving, metamorphosing, might that not be true of us too?

Watching the top rock on one of my towers topple, I think of another line by Keats: "'Beauty is truth, truth beauty,'—that is all / Ye know on earth, and all ye need to know." I doubt Goldsworthy would argue with that one. There's beauty in his work not only because it's aesthetically pleasing but also because it seems paradoxically true, meaning accurate, the way things are, how we really live our lives. We hover between form and formlessness. On some level we know nothing lasts, yet we cling to things as if they will. We pretend we don't need what we long for.

An hour later the water begins to threaten my entire city. It inches quietly forward, no gush, no current I can see, just a small rising so gentle it doesn't seem to be coming from an oceanic tidal rhythm, but from an underwater spring inside this cove. The stones grow darker, wetter; they seem to stick their heads above the water. On the north side of the array, all the top rocks slip off their bases and disappear. But on the south they remain, better balanced, perhaps, or their bases more firmly pushed into mud. Gray granite, I see now, works better as a base than flint does. Pink granite has more ledges for pebbles. And mica-speckled granite is wasted on foundations—too soon covered by water. Sometimes when a thing collapses, I realize now, I have a chance to get to know it better.

* * *

Years ago my mother painted on the Jersey shore while my siblings and I built elaborate, moat-ringed castles with turrets and arched doorways. She loved the morning light gold-leafing the water; we loved the moment incoming tides spilled into our moat. She was thoughtful; we were happily frenzied, redirecting the water with plastic shovels and hastily dug channels, full of shrieks when the sea encircled. There was something graceful and noble about that destruction—the castle hand-patted into place and then softened into the sea—and about the way she'd turn and watch us then. What kept her from joining us? What, seeing us there, was she thinking? What we knew was the best sand was close to the water, that the tide would have its way, and we'd build regardless, as if part of the pleasure were seeing the ruin, which didn't feel aggressive, of course, but rhythmic: first you build it and then you tend its demolition. For us, fun. But as an adult, she would have felt the weight of such a rhythm. Was that what she couldn't—or wouldn't—find words to say?

* * *

On the wall of our foyer is a photograph of a sand sculpture—a naked man and woman. The artist evidently began by digging a pit at the edge of the ocean. On its longer sloped side, he sculpted their two reclining bodies, feet down toward the center of the pit, torsos up the inclined edge. The woman is pressed up against the man's back. Her hand lies over his left shoulder. The rest of her body is invisible, behind his. From calves down, his legs are buried in sand. The work is finely wrought; it's easy to imagine touching the ribs, earlobes, toes, the folds of the cloth draped over his groin. I swear if I were there on that beach with them I could lift her finger.

The artist has fashioned their faces to make them look oblivious to the trough he's obviously dug to channel the sea across their heads and down around their torsos. Already the tide is coming in. They lie with their gaze upward, their backs slightly arched, the way one might in pleasure, submitting to the touch of another as the sea funnels under them. Or they look as if they've willingly crawled onto some sacrificial table, but instead of fire or knife, it's water that will do them in. Their bodies will dissolve, be taken back into the sea.

What did the artist want us to imagine they were feeling? Rapture? Some kind of sublime resignation? I think we, viewing it, are supposed to feel a sweet inexorability. Yes, my enigmatic mother might agree: nobody can stop the tide from coming in, but the artist can heighten that exquisite pressure by building something beautiful just moments before it has to disappear.

*   *   *

I watch the Maine tide for what seems like hours. The water rises and rises and every time I think it's halted, is about to recede, it slides up another inch, drowns another tower. Again and again I have to move my pine branch inland, sure each time that the water will advance no farther. It laps against it. Laps against it again and then three more times at the exact same point and then ten and then doesn't touch it on the next creep up and there! I think, that's the pivot point. I've marked it, seen it, can say with confidence it will come up no farther today, that I've been here to witness the turning point. And then the water laps over the stick and lifts it, floats it a little farther inland.

For my mother, the tumultuous sky and sea—and not any small figures she might sketch into the foreground—were characters to be reckoned with. She was the one who showed me in her paintings what she couldn't say in conversation: pay attention to what looms all around, however formless and blurred. For a long time I understood her focus as tutelage, spent years myself absorbed by landscapes blurred by ambiguity and mindscapes fogged by abstract notions of the spiritual. I seldom felt ungrounded, though one of the hazards of being engrossed by the groundless is that it's hard to tell when it's time to put more concrete and dirt—or stone—beneath the feet.

But there's a point—isn't there?—in most of our lives when we sense we've gone far enough and need to change direction. For so long I wanted the boundless out-there, wanted to lose myself in its mystery. And now, the opposite: absorption in these objects that litter the shore, ones I can rearrange or stash inside my pockets. Perhaps someday I'll know I don't have to choose between them, that it's possible to study the sea and the sky *and* to have a hand in arranging things, whether they're under the surface or exposed on top. Isn't this what Goldsworthy's paradoxes suggest? The tide's ancient rhythm, after all, is first to conceal and then to reveal.

And this one, it seems, hasn't turned yet. About so many things in our lives—obsessions, dogma, a daughter's unkind boyfriend—maybe the opposite of the Pueblos' belief is sometimes truer: if you scrutinize them, they won't change. Pivotal points might need a little darkness. In the house just up the bank, my husband and friends by now have probably lit the candles, poured the wine, begun to wonder if I'll come in in time for dinner. At my feet the stick twirls again, but this time, I swear, the water doesn't quite cover it.

Teddy Macker

On Dusk

Dusk does not expect of you an identity. No longer do you have to be Charles, Samantha. Dusk is a time for self-naughting.

The only wisdom we can hope to acquire, says Mr. T. S. Eliot, is the wisdom of humility: humility is endless.

Dusk presents to you little information. And won't just unbosom itself to any old Joe. Still you strain to listen for profundities not yet sounded.

Dusk does not seek to make friends and yet is the friendliest time of all.

Why is the sight of sunlight setting between two houses on a neighborhood block so heartbreaking?

Right before dusk, in the surprisingly vivid parlance of the moviemakers, is "the magic hour."

Dusk's antonym is cataclysm.

And at dusk there is no need for the messiah.

How does one touch it? And if it were a body part what would it be? The flat back of a thigh? A work-thickened shoulder? The web of flesh between thumb and index finger?

This is not a dream, says dusk.

Dawn, to use a phrase of James Wright's, is "suicidally beautiful." It goes for the jugular, is an agony of light, enmightier of the blood. It resists the moment of its making. Mongrel energy, wild spleenful horses. An enormous rusting ship sinking with a cargo of fabulous chandeliers. Dusk conversely is resistless. Is the sum of silence. And seeks wildness's perfect opposite.

Dusk, to quote the Taoists, is as selfless as melting ice.

During dusk you let go of the constant need to handle the world.

At dusk you may come to understand that the essential underpassion of your life is ambition. And then one of two things happens. Either you feel liberated by this epiphany and go on listening to the crickets, or the terrible hollowness of your existence swings through your soul like a wrecking ball.

On the other side of dusk, just beyond what we can see, fly the birds of dark water.

In the evening, sings Leroy Carr, in the evening,
momma when that sun goes down.
In the evening, momma when that sun goes down. . . .

Dusk makes young poets and middle-aged businesswomen feel something acute and lonely along the tops of their foreheads.

Dusk, to use a phrase of T. S. Eliot's, is "the still point of the turning world."

In the hospice of dusk even the countries of crows flying across the sky aren't threatening. In fact when you hear them pass overhead their faint wingbeats sound like the prayers of sand.

During dusk nothing obtrudes from the background, yet everything is noticeable.

There is another world, says Paul Éluard, and it is in this one.

There are mountains, says Dōgen, hidden in mountains.

If you handle the world gently, says dusk, it will anoint you.

Here is a poem by James Wright called "Trying to Pray":

> This time, I have left my body behind me, crying
> In its dark thorns.
> Still,
> There are good things in this world.
> It is dusk.
> It is the good darkness
> Of women's hands that touch loaves.
> The spirit of a tree begins to move.
> I touch leaves.
> I close my eyes, and think of water.

Dusk is not a wonder worker, refuses to partake of miracles, and under no circumstances will dusk marshal an army.

Dusk is the gentlest creed of all.

Dusk makes everything weep a little with the tears of things. If while driving through Austin, Texas, of a summer dusk with your younger brother, for example, and you see advertising in the left field of a neighborhood baseball diamond, advertising for Jerry's Fire-Alarm Installing, that ad— and you think of the man who ordered it, this Jerry, the man who one Tuesday morning decided it would be financially advantageous to pick up the phone and place the ad; and you think of his life installing fire alarms, how you never really knew such a vocation existed, how perhaps he's the best at what he does in the city—will spark in you a sudden inrush of sadness, and you will look upon everything, for a few moments at least, with nothing but love and compassion.

The greatest gift of dusk is its unassailable mildness.

And if there was a language called dusk every word would be marvelous and unpronounceable.

Dusk cocoons the mailbox on your lawn in a finely spun strangeness.

Dusk has no address, though it feels most at home in backyards (especially across Maryland) and threading its way through an aisle of cypress trees.

What image is more vivid than a long line of sunset-colored brake lights on a highway at dusk?

If, as William James says, wisdom is learning what to overlook, then dusk is perhaps the wisest of all, because dusk overlooks everything.

Michelle Herman

Idolatry

I was feverish, the first time—in bed under two down comforters and still shivering. It was midsummer; I had the flu. Too glassy-eyed and dizzy, too flat-out miserable for once in my life to read (although I'd piled a hopeful foot-high stack of books on my night table, right next to the bottle of Smart Water the doctor had recommended to combat the dehydration that left me feeling drunk every time I stood up, sat up, or closed my eyes) and sick to death of sleeping, I was flipping channels on the little bedside TV my husband watches sports on. I started with HBO—the several channels' worth our cable company provides "as a courtesy" to the customers it overcharges anyway for just the one channel of HBO—and moved through Showtime (ditto), grumbling all the while about how it can be, *how is it possible*, that they broadcast movies twenty-four hours a day and yet never show anything I want to watch, before grimly beginning the round of the single digits: 4, 6, 8 . . . and stopped, stopped dead, at Channel 8, where a nervous-looking, bizarrely overdressed young woman was belting the hell out of a song from the forties—a fragment of a song, cut off after just a few bars and replaced by a clip of a young man, equally self-conscious, his tie untied in the style of Rat Pack-era Sinatra, stumbling through *his* song fragment. A talent show?

A talent show! I nearly clapped my hands in pleasure (no doubt I would have, if I'd had the energy—if I hadn't been afraid that clapping, that *pleasure,* would have sent me over the edge, into the freefall of another dizzy spell) as I settled back on my pillows to watch. I *love* a talent show.

That first night, I was so transfixed I didn't even think to call downstairs to my daughter, then nine years old—though if I'd stopped to think, as I did the next day, I would have realized that she'd be at least as interested as I. She's a sucker for talent, too, and for pop songs of all kinds—not to mention the sort of human interest story I'd already sniffed out here. That first night, I just lay back on my pillows (a stack taller even than the stack of brand-new books I'd told myself I'd "use this time" to read after I'd been ordered to my bed), the two down comforters pulled up to my neck, and watched—with deep and growing pleasure—as the parade of awkward, unpolished, variously handsome young people, all of them groomed in an approximation of TV stardom (too much makeup, complicatedly styled and colored hair, wacky "glamorous" outfits that were clearly supposed to represent the look of the thirties and forties but didn't quite), sang and fidgeted and then stood tense and panting as they listened to the judgments passed on them by a panel of music industry professionals who seemed only slightly less self-conscious than they did.

All the singers looked frightened. Even the ones who looked cocky also looked frightened. I understood why, too, after only a few minutes. This was the "results show," broadcasting the highlights of the actual competition that had been on TV the night before—I groaned, as this became clear to me (how I wished I hadn't missed it!)—but already I saw how it worked. The judges could say anything they wanted—they could be downright vicious if they felt like it ("That was just awful. Honestly, that was possibly the worst singing I have ever heard") or utterly opaque (one judge, it seemed, did little more than sigh and shake his head and mutter the contestant's name again and again)—and there was entertainment value in their pronouncements. A viewer could (and inevitably did) judge the judgments just as she judged the singing. The judges competed—with one another, with the singers—for attention; they were showing off.

But in fact what the show-off judges said didn't matter, the show's hosts reminded us. "It was up to you, America." It was? It was! One could weigh in on the singing, via phone call. How I wished I'd had the chance! "Last night, America voted"—oh, how I wished *I* had!—and we'll find out what America had to say . . . "after the break."

I didn't change channels. What if I missed the news of how America had voted?

I already knew how *I* would have voted. Based on nothing but a fragment of a song I'd never heard before—"Stuff Like That There"—I'd picked out a favorite, falling in love the way I'll start to fall in love with a book thanks to a single gorgeous sentence. I'd picked a second favorite, too. I'd even dismissed a couple of the singers—and why not? A few bad notes, a delivery unhooked from emotion, an obvious misreading of a song I knew too well—it didn't take much more than that.

I've slammed books shut, after all, after just one ungainly phrase or a show-off, impenetrable opening. Or a sprinkling of clichés. Hell, a handful of misplaced commas will do it if I'm in a black mood.

I actually held my breath during the show's final moments, and then I watched open-mouthed as sweet-faced Christina, who had gamely sung "The Glory of Love"—not very well, I'd noted as I watched her clip, but not *badly*, either; certainly not as badly as others had sung *their* songs— was eliminated from the competition. Her cohorts wept in sympathy and relief. And poor Christina wasn't even present except in videotaped footage (a chunk of sentimental back story about how her parents had insisted she go to college even though she wasn't sure she wanted to, and how she worked part-time in a bank to put herself through school—with a voice-over by Christina herself about how she was sure fame wouldn't change her, and how her family still treated her as if she were "just a regular person" despite her being on the show) and a somber report of her removal to a hospital "only hours ago" to be treated for "exhaustion and stress." Our thoughts were with her, said the show's hosts. We sent our love.

This show has everything, I thought. I was enraptured.

"What can you possibly be enraptured by?" my husband asked the next day. He is a serious person, an artist, whose only idle activities are watching the Dallas Cowboys or Ohio State play football and just about anyone play basketball. But even then, watching the game, he isn't really idle. He draws while he watches, exactly the way other people eat pretzels and drink beer. Half-filled sketchbooks and drawing pads and black, fine-line markers are scattered all over the house.

Before I could answer him, he asked another question, sounding hopeful: "Is this a hobby?" *His* hobbies are practicing playing the bass guitar for an hour a day and painstakingly designing houses on graph paper, one of which (the best one, the perfect one he has yet to draw) he hopes to build for us eventually. I always tell him I have no time for hobbies; *I'm* too busy running the household. When I'm not writing or teaching, I'm cooking or shopping for groceries or balancing the checkbook or digging through our daughter's dresser drawers to weed out the clothes that don't fit her anymore or shopping for *new* clothes for her. Unlike him, I say pointedly—and meanly, I realize (but I get tired, and when I'm tired,

I tend to slide toward meanness; I turn bitterly jealous of the sixteen-hour days he spends painting—even though I could never put in those kinds of hours at my own work; I *like* to have lots of different things to do, and I like running the household)—unlike him, I say, I *have* no leisure time.

Well, you can't call it a hobby exactly, but I've made time for the talent show. For three seasons of it now I've managed to make time for it—for every episode after that first one I caught, that first summer, and for the two, four-month long seasons in the two years since. Twice a week, I have dropped everything—student stories, my own new book in progress, laundry, dishes, stacking books and papers on chairs and around the edges of the dining room table to keep the chaos at bay—and sat myself down in front of the TV set. And my daughter, Grace, is right there with me—sitting beside me on the couch we bought her father for his fortieth birthday, along with cable we installed so he could watch ESPN. Grace has been watching the show with me ever since the episode after the first one I caught by accident. On "results night," Wednesdays, we hold hands.

And the answer to her father's question is that I am enraptured by practically *everything* about the show. I love the striving and the hope of it, I love the singing (I am *crazy* about singing, always; I'm crazy about it whether I'm doing it myself or listening to someone else do it), and of course I love the songs themselves. I don't even care *what* songs. I don't care if they're dopey songs—songs by Barry Manilow, disco songs, unbelievably stupid songs made famous by Whitney Houston. Because the truth is, there's hardly anything I like better than songs—any and all kinds of songs. I like standards and show tunes and rock and roll and R&B and folk songs (real ones, "roots music," as well as the early Dylan/Joan Baez variety) and seventies singer-songwriters' songs and rap songs and lullabies and protest songs and witty, newish (as in merely forty years old) jazz songs like "Peel Me A Grape" and songs by Willie Nelson and Dolly Parton and corny turn-of-the-century songs like "By the Light of the Silvery Moon." There are days when it seems to me that I love songs even more than I love books.

But you can hear songs anywhere. And better singing, too. So I admit it: there's lots more to the talent show than singer and song. I could see that from my first encounter with it. That first night, I was already hooked on the *story*—hooked without any idea what I was watching, without the least notion that what I'd happened upon, mid-song clip, mid-summer-replacement-season, was a certified television phenomenon. How would I have known? I don't know anything. Sometimes—or so I've been told—it seems I hardly live in the world at all.

It's true. Most of the time, the world is too much for me. I read the *New York Times* cover to cover every Sunday, but *between* Sundays— unless there's an ongoing emergency that makes it impossible for me to think about anything else—I do my best to ignore everything in the world except my own work and the immediate or potential needs of my family, my students, and the ever-growing collection of pets living under my roof. I read novels; I listen to music. I even read magazines. But the newspaper is just too distracting, especially first thing in the morning. If I read it, I can't write afterwards—I'm too jittery and upset—and it's too hard to ignore it if I see it sitting there. Thus, six days a week, I don't even bring the paper into the house.

Sundays, however, I take a deep breath and let it in. I let it *all* in—even Sports and Business, and I have no interest in sports or business (I actually actively dislike sports and business, but on Sunday it doesn't matter, because I like *reading* about almost anything). I read the Travel section even though I never go anywhere, and the Style section even though I can't afford to buy anything and almost never have any idea who they're talking about in the columns. I read Arts & Leisure despite the fact that I can't remember the last time I went to a movie, or that when I go home to New York, I never go to the theater (all I ever do is visit with family and friends, eat lox and whitefish and sable and *much* better Chinese food than I can get in Columbus, Ohio, and take long walks feeling sorry for myself because I don't live there anymore. If Glen's with me, I go to art museums, but we always skip the mega-shows covered by the *Times*).

And I know next to nothing about television. Until the talent show came into my life three TV seasons ago, the only show I watched was *Sex and the City* (which was why we *got* HBO, a couple of years into our contract with the cable company). For years—for years and years—I didn't even own a TV set: a neighbor had to bang on the door of my apartment in Greenwich Village in December of 1980 to tell me about John Lennon, and when the *Challenger* exploded, six years later, while I was in graduate school in Iowa, I didn't hear about it until the next day, from someone in workshop.

This is all by way of saying that I came to the talent show an almost complete innocent.

My daughter did, too. Chip off the old block, until she was three, Grace had no idea there was anything *on* TV except sports. Dutifully, when she was three, I introduced her to *Sesame Street*, but she found it irritating. "It's so *jumpy*," she said (putting her finger on one of the reasons I so dislike the news on TV, and have never been able to get myself to watch it). Then, when someone told me that Shari Lewis—the woman I had loved most, after my grandmother, in my early childhood—was still (or again?) on TV, I sat Grace down in front of the set for the pleasures of Lamb Chop and Charley Horse, and she was delighted—for a week or two, before she lost interest. I concluded then that it was genetic, that she must have inherited from me the inability to sit still and watch anything. Because it's not—or not *just*—snobbery that keeps me away from TV. I've never even cared for *public* television, which my daughter's godfather, our beloved friend Michael, insists has taught him much of what he knows about the world. I don't have the patience for it. Reading keeps me still; writing keeps me still. Otherwise I need to be active, although not necessarily (well, never) vigorously so. I don't jog or play tennis. I cook, I walk the dog, I sort laundry, I *talk*. I don't sleep (I'd like to, but I can't—because, I suspect, it requires too much stillness, and I've used up my stillness allotment during the day).

The weekly half-hour I devoted to *Sex and the City* several months a year for six years, I've always thought, was the exception that proved the rule. People who knew about my affection for that show would always urge me to try *The Sopranos*, too, and I did try, but I couldn't tolerate the subject matter. The *surface* subject matter, friends pointed out (condescendingly, I thought). But what else is subject matter *but* surface? One has to be able to tolerate the surface to appreciate what lies below, and I couldn't stand being asked to empathize with the worries of a murderous protagonist.

This was the problem, I decided, in a little flash of TV insight, with most of television for me: it wasn't just that I hated sitting still and watching (almost) anything; it was also that TV lacked subject matter in which I had any interest. I can *read* my way through subject-matter apathy or even outright antipathy if the writing's good enough. But I can't *watch* my way through it. It feels like a waste of time.

This goes a long way toward explaining my affection for the talent show, since *its* subject matter—all of its subject matter—is right up my alley.

The songs, the singers, the stories. There's the business of character—the almost insane focus on character at the expense of story, as if "story" were about nothing *but* character. But that's the way I like it, always. I *loved* the "stories," that first night: the story of wan, pretty, exhausted Christina (who, we were assured, was "watching the show from her hospital bed"); of plucky, multipierced, kooky, single-mother Nikki and her sweet, young son; of Justin with his showbiz relatives and his job as "party starter," getting the kids up and dancing at bar mitzvahs. My two favorites had stories, too: adorable, innocent-yet-sassy, sturdy, *happy* Kelly the "cock-tail waitress"; savvy, serious, no-nonsense Tamyra, who'd pulled off the "hi-de-hi-de-ho"s of "Minnie the Moocher" with admirable, if amused, poise. They both had good voices, better than the rest. They could be singers; why not? What was to stop them?

Oh, even without the next episode—and the next, and the next—I knew the answer to that. Even without any understanding of television itself, or any knowledge of what the prize was or how it would be award-ed, I knew. That was part of what hooked me: the judgments to come, the potential for *mis*judgment, the missteps, the arbitrariness, the importance of a single moment, the way one good performance would matter more than it should, or one bad one. The sudden shifting of the tides. Luck, mood, happenstance. The subjectivity, the vagaries, the up-and-down, the why-now, why-me, why-*her* of it. The *mysteries*. It would be like watch-ing the start of a writing career—or a romance. That was what I thought, shivering under my comforters, propped up on my pillows. It would be like *life*.

There would be triumphs, justice, miscarriages of justice, beauty, pity, shame, despair, pride, self-delusion, tawdry misbegotten glamour (which I love, even more than non-misbegotten glamour), innocence, and expe-rience.

And I was right—I was right about all of it.

But really the true subject of the talent show, which in the finale of the season that just ended drew *sixty-five million votes*—considerably more than half as many votes, I feel obliged to point out, than the presidential elec-tion of 2000 (though cast, in the case of the show, by just under twenty-nine million voters, for unlike presidential elections, the talent show "elec-tions" allow more than one vote per person; allow, in fact, as many votes as any one voter has the patience to cast—and patience is required: the phone lines, even when the network allots three lines per contestant, as they did for this final showdown of the 2004 season, are relentlessly busy)—seems to me to be the blurring of the line between "professional" and "amateur": the implicit recognition of how porous these categories are.

This may be what I like best about the show. It's as interesting to me (and more interesting, I'm sure, to almost everyone else watching) that the line that's being blurred is the line between "pop star" and "non- [or not yet] pop star" as it would be if there were a way to dramatize the blurring of the line between "artist" and "non-artist." For years I have told the students in my introductory creative writing classes that one of the most pressing reasons for them to try to make stories themselves is to gain understanding in a visceral way (the only way that will mean anything to them) that literature doesn't fall from the sky, that it isn't made by gods, that it's the product, always, of a single person's heart and mind, of someone's imagination and painstaking, exhausting work. That even the mysteries of talent— even the mysteries of *genius*—cannot be properly appreciated until one has wriggled inside the process of making art itself, has had a go at what it feels and looks like. That patience, hard work, seriousness of purpose, effort, time, energy, and mastery of craft can be managed by anyone willing to give it a shot. That with a lot of "talent" and a little hard work—or a little talent and a lot of hard work—miraculous things can happen.

What pleases me most about the show, then, is seeing the veil that separates "legitimate" pop singers—those with recording contracts and concert stages to perform on and devoted fans and a publicity machine to fan the flames of those fans—from "ordinary people" who like to sing, and who *can* sing, begin to fall away.

The display of "raw" talent—pure talent, talent without *finish*— reminds me of the one or two undergraduates I see every year in my writing classes who don't know what they're doing yet but manage to write a single perfect sentence, even a whole paragraph, that will be as good in its own way as anything I have *ever* read. This past quarter alone, as Fantasia and La Toya and Jennifer and Diana sang—from time to time—so beautifully it made my heart constrict with joy, I read perfect sentences by Lindsay, Joe, Mike, Marcy, Alex, Keith, Melissa.

If my first encounter with the talent show had also been my last—if that had been the end of it and I had blamed the flu, as Glen tried to do when

I first spoke of it to him—then I could stop right here, and we could all have a laugh (a gentle, indulgent laugh, yes?) about my absorption in, my *rapture* over, the show. But for the rest of that summer and all last spring and all *this* spring, on Wednesday nights, as Glen passes through the family room and sees Grace and me on the couch, clutching each other's hands, waiting to see who's been eliminated on the "results show," he shakes his head. "Great example you're setting there," he tells me before he ducks out the back door again to hole up in his studio until the coast is clear.

"*Hush*," I hiss. "They're about to announce the top two."

You call yourself an intellectual. You call yourself a feminist.

He hasn't said it. It's what he's thinking, though—I know it.

I don't, in point of fact, call myself either of those things. The only names I ever call myself are *writer, mother, teacher*, and *New Yorker*—not necessarily in that order. But I know what he means (or I know what *I* mean). I write books. I'm a tenured college professor. An *English* professor. I own the complete New York edition of Henry James. I've had dinner—vegan (Columbus, oddly enough, which can't manage decent Chinese, has a fine gourmet vegan restaurant)—with J. M. Coetzee, who is one of my heroes. Coetzee, Bellow—Tolstoy! George Eliot!—*those* are my heroes. Not pop stars.

And yet . . . here I am, biting my nails over Clay-versus-Ruben (and still mourning Kimberly, who I preferred). Booing the TV set when Jennifer is eliminated in favor of breathy, chronically off-key Jasmine. Calling, again and again, and cursing the busy signal, to cast my vote for Fantasia, week after week. I'm the *mother*. It's one thing for Grace to pump her fist and cry *yes*! when John Stevens is eliminated; it's another altogether if it's me. But there I am, cackling and muttering, "For godsakes, it's about time. Send that boy *home*."

I'm the mother, all right: a devoted, overbearing, lavishly affectionate, occasionally intrusive, *Jewish* mother—and above all a Mother Who Thinks (*à la* Salon.com). What the hell am I thinking?

I'll tell you what I'm thinking. I'm thinking about whether Fantasia might be able to take it to the top this year. I'm thinking that I *love* Fantasia. I love her powerhouse, raucous, dirty-sounding voice. I'm thinking that I sort of love Camille too—but only, I have to confess, because she's so heartbreakingly beautiful, and so young, and because her hoarse, whispery voice makes me want to stroke her hair and tell her everything is going to be all right.

I'm thinking about how awful it is that Lisa didn't make it, that "America voted" and Matt the football player made it to the next round instead of Lisa, who has a terrific voice. Matt is likable—a likable lug—but Lisa can really sing. That's what I'm thinking.

But I'm also thinking about how, *last* spring, when she was in the fourth grade, Grace went to school with something she could talk to the other kids about for the first time in her life. *All* the girls in the fourth grade—the ones who used to ignore or avoid her because she's such an oddball (bookworm, leftist, dreamer, Child Who Thinks)—it turned out, were watching the show, too.

"And this is good?" That's my husband speaking, asking the question he's always asking.

I think about a number of possible answers, but all I say is, "She's stopped dreading recess."

When I mentioned to a friend—a smart friend, an excellent poet, and at least as much of a snob as I (she doesn't even *have* cable, so her TV set, in a small Ohio town, shows nothing but snow), not to mention another Mother Who Thinks—that I was trying to write an essay about the pleasures of watching the TV show *American Idol*, she suggested that I title it "American Idle." Then she added, sweetly, "Oh, but I suppose if you're trying to *justify* the time you spend watching it, and that you let Grace watch it with you, I guess not."

Maybe I have no business celebrating my daughter's (partial, and no doubt grudging) acceptance by the hoi polloi thanks to a TV show. Maybe it means I ought to be drummed out of the Mothers Who Think Club. But we're having such a good time! During the commercials we talk about the performances and *tsk tsk* about the judges' harshness. "It wasn't that bad, was it?" we ask each other. And even when it *was* that bad, and sometimes—often—it is, we murmur, "Must Simon say that *quite* so meanly?" The judges—all of them—get crueler every year. Randy no longer obfuscates: he comes out and says, "That just wasn't any good at all, man." Even Paula, "the nice judge"—the former cheerleader and former pop star, as improvidently dressed and coiffed as any of the female contestants—winces now and says, "Well, honey, you gave it your all, and that's what counts. You look beautiful, by the way." From her, that's as good as saying, "America, vote her *out!*"

But even as I complain about the meanness of the judges, I think about what Flannery O'Connor said when she was asked if courses in creative writing don't stifle young writers: that the fact is they don't stifle enough of them.

We mute the TV during commercials. Besides judging the judges, we talk about the contestants. Not their singing, necessarily, or not just their singing. Both Grace and I love back story (the kind of thing Glen tells us has ruined the TV broadcast of the Olympics, which he used to enjoy "before those cheesy human interest stories took it over").

Last year, during *Idol*'s second season, Grace picked her favorite singer early on, during auditions, based almost entirely (the "almost" is a gift to Grace, since she *still* insists that Julia had a good voice) on the story that unspooled around her, the kind of story that appeals most to my daughter: a story of triumph (talent and hard work) over adversity (in the form of lazy, less gifted, mean-spirited other girls). During stage two or three of the auditions, the other young women with whom Julia had been matched for the traditional group performance treated her badly. They were dismissive and contemptuous. But Julia the hairdresser persevered and made it! Grace was beside herself with delight. And when Julia was finally eliminated, quite late in the competition, Grace wept, and I wept along with her—but for *her*, because she was so disappointed, not for Julia, who'd stayed in against all odds and good sense.

Even more than the back story, Grace and I get swept up in the ongoing story of the relationships between the characters, the contestants— "the idols," Grace casually calls them—that play out week by week. I like seeing the characters themselves change as the weeks pass. You can actually see them changing, see it in the way they carry themselves (Fantasia softened; Diana grew up), the way they treat one another, and of course in their singing. "Of course," I say, as if this were the whole point of the show. But it isn't, *of course*, not entirely. The point *is* the story: it's watching the characters change as they must in any good story: characters wanting something and changing as they strive for it, fail to get it, begin *to* get it, slip and fall and pick themselves up again. The protagonists change, the relationships change, the story unspools.

And then there are the songs. Thanks to three seasons' worth of *American Idol*, my daughter now knows Al Green, Janis Joplin, and Bonnie Raitt. It's thanks to *American Idol* that when I pop in a tape in the morning on our way to school, Grace in the backseat sings along with "Respect" and "Chain of Fools." It's thanks to *American Idol* that she knows both Aretha's version of "Natural Woman" *and* Carole King's—because one thing leads to another, and every Tuesday night, Grace turns to me and asks, "Whose song is this one?" and, "Do we have that on a record?" And we nearly always do.

I don't even mind that some of the "idols" screw up (dumb down, misunderstand, flatten, shriek, or over-sing) some of my all-time favorite songs, because my favorite songs are being sung on TV, and after the show, Grace and I will listen to the originals. I hear her playing them all week long, teaching herself the words. Mornings, I can hear her in the shower singing "How Can You Mend A Broken Heart?"

And the girls in her class who used to give her (the one who doesn't play soccer, who uses what her fourth grade teacher derisively called "fifty-dollar words") such a wide berth are duly impressed both by her command of song lyrics and her familiarity with "the originals" of the songs they hear each week on the show. "Oh," I've heard Grace say, "I loved Trenyce's cover of 'Proud Mary,' too. But really you should hear Tina Turner's. And then if you hear the Creedence version, well, you can hardly believe it's the same song."

It's thanks to *American Idol* that my daughter has learned to work the turntable, so she can play the records in my collection whenever she wants to, whether I'm around or not. The other kids think she's a technological wizard *and* a musical genius.

There's another aspect of our watching *American Idol* that I had no way of knowing would figure in when we first started, the summer she was nine. By our third *American Idol* season, January through May 2004, it was the only thing she'd let me do with her anymore. The little girl who came to sit on the edge of my bed and hold my hand when I had the flu that first summer is gone forever, replaced by a "preteen" who will ask me to take her ice skating but forbid me to skate anywhere near her, who will not allow me to touch her in public (and even in private, kissing is now out of the question, except at bedtime). We use the walkie-talkies she got for Christmas—from her father, clever man—to keep tabs on each other when we go shoe-shopping, rather than her having to endure the humiliation (she shudders, and doesn't bother pretending she's cold) of shopping with her *mother*. But week after week, all this spring, she sat beside me on Tuesday and Wednesday nights, and we talked our way through the commercials, and afterwards I dug out the records she'd requested.

But here's something funny. Just as *American Idol* has brought us together at a moment when she's otherwise drifting off, and at the same time gained her a measure of acceptance and even respect within the circles she travels every day, it has set me apart from the world *I* have to live in daily. Almost everyone I know either thinks I'm being *camp* when I mention how much I enjoy the show, or—if they take me seriously— they get worked up over it. *That garbage! The worst sort of trash!* I understand their reaction, of course—I mean, in general, I understand anger about the silliness and ugliness and shallowness of popular culture. It's been known to upset me, too. It *still* upsets me. But have they actually seen *this* show? I ask timidly. It's, you know, a talent show. My husband at least has forced himself to watch it, a few minutes at a time, once or twice each season, trying to participate in something his wife and daughter are enjoying—trying to be a good sport. But he can't take it. "This is *horrible*," he says. "How can you stand it?" But then he can't stand *any* pop music, he has to admit. (He doesn't consider this an "admission." It's a point of pride. And he doesn't count Hendrix, heavy metal, punk rock, or blues as "pop." Pop means *pap,* to him.) He says the same thing when I put Norah Jones on the stereo; or Anita Baker, Grace's latest favorite; or Sinatra, for that matter.

The very name of the show, I can tell, irritates people—the idea that "America" is willing to *idolize* the winner of a talent show (indeed, that "America idolizes" its celebrities in the first place). Well—as my daughter would say—*duh. She* knows better. She says equably, with just the slightest rolling of her eyes, "They don't mean 'idol' *literally.* They mean 'idol' as, like, a synonym for 'star,' that they're *making* the person a star." She pauses. "That's what's cool about it. That it's possible to do that."

That's what I said, isn't it? It's such a porous category: *star.*

I should confess that not everyone gets angry or imagines irony as the default. Some people express sympathy or empathy—they know how it is to have to sit beside a child and endure kiddie entertainment—a Disney cartoon, *Spy Kids*. But *I* don't know. Grace hates going to the movies, especially kids' movies. She always has. She hates the noise and the giant faces, the trumped-up anxiety designed to satisfy a kid's supposed need for stimulation and excitement, the frantic pace that's tailor-made for her supposedly short attention span. She doesn't like action or thrills or suspense any more than I do.

Except for the kind of suspense offered by *Idol*—the human drama of striving and disappointment: who will make it and who won't? And on *American Idol* nobody (except Christina Christian, that one time) is ever in physical peril. Don't tell Grace and me that no one *really* gets hurt in a movie, that it's "just a movie." We are in absolute agreement about this: if you're aware the whole time that it's "just" a movie—aware enough to keep what happens from being upsetting or scary—then you can't possibly live in the dream of it. You can't possibly enjoy it the way we enjoy our episodes of *American Idol*, recklessly and wholeheartedly.

We love that dream, the dream that's so much like real life they call it "reality television." It's real life but with focused, specific, concentrated drama, *high* drama packed into an hour—much less than an hour, once you take out all the commercials, of which there are a staggering number (but Grace and I don't mind, because that's when we get the chance to talk about what we've just seen and heard; it's better this way, not having to store up all that conversation until the end).

The spectacle of untrained, "pure" talent—and the spectacle of its absence, or the presence of too little of it to overcome the odds against it becoming manifest, becoming *viable* (because the odds are *always* against it)—is pure pleasure for us both. And so we watch and listen together, week after week, clapping and laughing and groaning and shrieking and falling back on the couch cushions in dismay or joy.

And we're both aware, always, that the show has given us a whole new angle in dealing with the people who surround us when we go out into the world—each of our worlds. It's never a bad thing, I've told my daughter, who believes me—who still believes everything I tell her, although perhaps not for much longer—to try a new angle, to get a glimpse of what it's like on the other side. To surprise oneself. To surprise others. To take pleasure in something that others take pleasure in. To take pleasure in something that almost no one else in one's own world takes pleasure in.

To *take* pleasure.

To listen to voices lifted in hope, however misplaced or futile.

To hope. To celebrate hope.

To keep one's mind and heart open to the possibility, always, of celebration—of pure, unadulterated, screaming, clapping, confetti-throwing, tearful, goofy, glorious *rapture*.

Lee Martin

A Backward Spring

It's mid-September in Texas, and I'm stripping the dead leaves from our Caddo maple. I close my hand around the whippet branches and pull toward the tips; dry, coppery leaves crumble and fall to the ground. I keep their dust on my skin.

The Caddo maple, according to our local horticulturalist, is an ideal, much under-used tree for North Texas, but ours, planted in February, has yet to take hold. In spring, the buds swelled and green leaves opened but never matured. They drooped from the branches, tiny and wrinkled, like babies' hands. Now the nursery owner has nicked a branch with a pocketknife and showed me the green heartwood. "There's plenty of moisture in it," he's said. He's told me to strip away the dead leaves so the tree won't concentrate its energy on feeding them. "Water it a couple of times a week," he's said. "If it's going to make it, we'll know soon."

My wife, Deb, tells this story to her mother the next time they talk on the phone even though she knows her mother won't be able to recall it. My mother-in-law is losing threads of memory. People, places, episodes all of them slip away from her as soon as they occur. She no longer has the ability to retrieve them. She's sixty-four, and her neurologist suspects the onset of Alzheimer's, a suspicion that so far we've kept secret from her. Already naturally prone to depression, she's the sort that worries something to death. We're afraid that if we told her about the illness, her condition would deteriorate more quickly than it will if she doesn't know about it. "Do you know the date?" the neurologist asked her at their first meeting. "The day of the week? The president of the United States?"

"Al Gore," she said.

The neurologist chuckled. "You're a very smart lady, Mrs. Goss. You may know something we don't."

The first time Deb took me home to meet her mother it was eleven o'clock at night, and after an exchange of strained pleasantries, my future mother-in-law excused herself, went down the hallway to her bedroom, and locked the door. It would be years before she would finally decide that I was a decent sort and not the bogeyman she had feared that first evening.

Now her illness has accentuated her natural inclination toward paranoia. She draws the drapes around the corners of the rods and pins them to the wall; she makes sure the panels overlap in the middle, which she also pins together. She wants no gaps, no slivers of space where someone might be able to see into her house. She refuses to pick up the phone until she hears a familiar voice on the answering machine. If she's alone in her house, all the windows and doors locked, and she wants to tell someone something private, she'll come close and whisper, afraid someone might be lurking outside, trying to eavesdrop.

Deb tells me that she always remembers her mother being afraid, and there are hints of this in a few letters my mother-in-law wrote to Deb's father when he was in the Army. My mother-in-law would have been nineteen at the time, working in town at the Weber Medical Clinic and living with her parents out in the country. "The folks are going to town for a little while," she says in one letter, "and I don't want to stay home by myself, but I haven't told them yet." In another letter, she talks about coming home from work one evening when she knew her parents had gone to visit friends. "I got the car in the garage," she says, "and locked the doors." Like now, she didn't want anyone to know she was there.

Since my father-in-law's death six years ago, she's been lonely and eager for company. She has a few friends with whom she goes shopping, or out to dinner, or to singles' dances, but most evenings she's in her house, crocheting, the television on for the noise. Some nights, late, she calls us in Texas and talks about how depressed she is. Other widows snap up boyfriends at the singles' dances, she says, but not her. "I don't know what's wrong with me," she says.

In all honesty, even before her problems with memory, she's always been a difficult woman to tolerate. She's often too forward, quick to comment on other people's flaws. If she's in a public place and she sees someone she considers too thin, too fat, too overdressed, too—you fill in the blank—she makes no effort to hide her disapproval. "Look at that," she'll say in a too-loud voice. "What a sight." Privacy, which she values so much for herself, doesn't seem to be a concern when she speaks of others. Even her own family isn't safe. She once told a near stranger that her brother-in-law's testicles had swollen to the size of grapefruits. Another time, on an Amtrak train, she announced that Deb was in the lavatory "washing her privates."

Still, there are times when my mother-in-law is sweet and playful and generous. She gets a kick out of a good joke; she loves to make Christmas candies and give them to people. She often goes out of her way to be friendly to her neighbors, to help other widows with their shopping, to prepare hot dishes for church suppers. Still, if we weren't family, it's doubtful that we'd be friends. She's obsessively neat, bundling garbage in layers of paper towel, plastic wrap, paper bags before tossing it in the trash can. She's judgmental, quick to condemn people who differ from her own sense of moral behavior. She gossips about the divorcee who lives across the street, pointing out over and over that a certain gentleman's car was in front of the house until three o'clock in the morning. "Isn't that terrible?" she says, anxious for someone to agree.

I have to admit that over the years I've often been glad to live at some distance from her and her outrageous behavior while at the same time knowing that in some ways we're alike—both of us anxious for order, both of us afraid of being alone. I don't know exactly when she decided that I was a decent sort, someone to love and trust, but I'm determined now to be kind to her, to be tolerant and understanding and helpful. My own mother suffered from senile dementia as a result of a series of small strokes, and I know the frustrations and sorrows of watching someone you love disappear.

It's been seventeen years since Deb and I lived close to our families. We've lived in Arkansas, Ohio, Tennessee, Nebraska, Virginia, and now in Texas, as we've pursued graduate degrees and teaching positions. Last spring, when the opportunity to return to the Midwest presented itself, a chance to be a mere three hour-drive from my mother-in-law, it seemed at first so simple to say yes. But forces of time and circumstance conspired to make the decision a difficult one. We had just begun to notice my mother-in-law's memory lapses and hadn't wanted to consider that they might be a sign of Alzheimer's. Therefore, the fact that she might be ill didn't occur to us and didn't enter into our decision making process as it surely would have had we known. Deb and I, in the end, decided to stay in Texas. We had become disgusted with moving. We had had our fill of boxes and packing tape and change of address cards and trusting our possessions to moving companies.

For those of us who have long wished for a permanent home, a place can tie us to it in short order. We can invest so much in the effort that we find it difficult to leave. When we finally settled in Texas, Deb and I gave thanks. We bought a house that had been somewhat neglected and set out to revive it. We landscaped and nurtured the lawn, put up rain gutters, and painted. This is it, we thought. This is home. This is where we stay.

Once at a rest stop along Interstate 55 in Arkansas, a man asked me how to get to Illinois. It was the day before Thanksgiving, late afternoon, and my wife and I were on our way from Memphis, where we lived at the time, to her parents' home in southern Illinois, a part of the state known as "Egypt."

The man's question surprised me. He wasn't just asking how to locate a town, a neighborhood, a street, an address; he wanted to know how to find a state. He was putting down the hood on his car, an old station wagon with Texas plates. How could anyone, I wondered, set out from home on a journey of any length without knowing exactly how to reach his destination? What was I to tell this man? "When you get to Missouri, turn right?" He was wide-eyed and boyish, his face reddened by the cold. He had no coat and stood on the concrete walkway stamping his feet. His shirt cuffs, unbuttoned, flapped around his bony wrists. He needed information, and I was the one he was trusting to give it.

So I stuck to the facts. "Stay on 55," I told him, "until you hit I-57. You'll cross the river at Cairo, and you'll be in Illinois. That's where I'm headed, too."

Did I add the last part, the fact of my own destination, because I wished to chide him by pointing out that I knew my route and implying that he should, too? Or did I sense a similarity, a shared longing for home, I couldn't have then articulated? Was I telling him we were both in the same boat?

"Do you know Willow Hill?" he asked.

As a matter of fact, I did. It was a small town no more than twenty miles north of where I was going. I had passed through Willow Hill countless times during the six years my parents and I had lived in Oak Forest, a suburb of Chicago. We had made the five-hour trip back to our farm on weekends and holidays, and Willow Hill had been one of the towns I had always eagerly awaited since it signaled that our journey was almost at an end. That it should be the town where this man was going amazed me.

"I know it," I told him. "Sure. Willow Hill."

"I got a wife there I ain't seen in thirteen years." He smiled a big old cat-that-ate-the-canary grin. Then he shook his head, and his grin turned a bit sheepish as if he were thinking, my, oh my, won't she be surprised.

Although ten years have passed since that day, I still wonder what happened that night when he finally got to Willow Hill. Did he find his wife? Did she let him into her house? Or did she shut the door in his face, leave him scratching his head, feeling like a dope, wondering what he could have been thinking to have travelled so far?

In Genesis, when "famine was over all the face of the earth," Jacob sent his sons from their home in the land of Canaan, down into Egypt to buy corn. They had no way of knowing that the brother they had sold into slavery, Joseph, was now the governor of the land and that he was the one who had directed the storing-up of grain from seven years of abundant harvest. When he finally revealed himself to his brothers, they were ashamed, but he told them not to grieve; his presence in Egypt, though it had resulted from their own cruelty, had turned out to be necessary to their survival. If he hadn't come to Egypt, become governor, and had the wisdom to store the grain, what would they do now for food? "So now it was not you that sent me hither," he said, "but God" (Genesis 45:8).

I spent the first twenty-five years of my life in Illinois, most of them in "Egypt" where my father owned an eighty-acre farm. Although I've lived many places since, I've usually managed to find something to keep me connected to home: snow and ice, apple orchards and strawberry farms, corn fields and forests of oak, maple, hickory, beech, and sweetgum. But in north Texas weeks can pass in the summer without rain; temperatures in the mid-nineties signal a cool spell. The heat lasts deep into October, and the autumn colors of the trees are drab in comparison with the brilliant woodlands of the Midwest. A Texas winter is really not a winter at all. Perhaps one or two days will bring a dusting of snow that melts away in quick order or an ice storm that slicks things up for an hour or two. It's not uncommon for the temperatures to reach the sixties, even the seventies. For a native Midwesterner, it seems like cheating to live here during the winter. I watch The Weather Channel for video of blizzards, and I feel nostalgia and longing and guilt and relief.

Story has it that southern Illinois became known as "Egypt" after the harsh winter of 1830–31 during which snow to the depth of three feet covered the northern part of the state and frost lasted well into May. It was, as one source puts it, "a very backward spring." The killing frost came again on September 10, ruining the unripened corn. The only ears to mature properly were in the fields of southern Illinois. Folks from the north drove their wagons south to buy corn, claiming that, like the sons of Jacob, they were going down to Egypt.

Whenever I return to that part of the country now, no matter the season, I know immediately the way grass greens in the spring and how the earth smells as it thaws. I know the humid days of summer, the air dusted with corn pollen, the rich scent of autumn, leaves firing red and yellow and orange, and then dying away and falling to rot on the ground. I know the snows of winter and the wind screaming across the flat prairie.

I am the one who renounced this land, went away to college—the first Martin to do so—and became a teacher and a writer instead of working the family farm. After my parents were dead, I leased those eighty acres and finally sold them the year I came to Texas. There are times here when I feel my life is blessed. Each spring, I plant onions and radishes and lettuce and potatoes. Later I set out tomato plants and cucumber vines. My garden is a raised bed nine feet by twelve feet, a mere sliver when compared to the large gardens my parents used to tend. Still, when I press my hands into the soil—when I water and hoe and harvest—I feel a kinship with all the Martins who were at one time farmers in southern Illinois, in that land of "Egypt" where my mother-in-law, day by day, forgets. Each time we speak on the phone, I feel guilty because Deb and I aren't there.

By October, the Caddo maple is still leafless. In our garden, our pole beans—Kentucky Wonders—have wrapped their tendrils around the twine supports Deb has draped over a ridge pole and stretched taut to stakes in the ground. She's built the skeleton of a house in our garden—an A-frame formed by two sets of crossing poles, one set at each end of the garden, and a long pole laid into the crotches. The twine ribbons down on both sides. Soon this will be a house of green, the palm-like leaves of the Kentucky Wonders bushing out and then setting the long, narrow fingers of beans.

The evening I helped Deb build this frame, I thought of the way my own parents had spent years working side by side in their garden. I remembered the way my father, ordinarily a gruff man, would sometimes come in from hoeing and say to my mother in a soft voice, heavy with sorrow and regret, "I cut down a bean plant. You ought to shoot me. That's how worthless I am."

To me, when I was a teenager, my parents' garden was the place where I had to work when I would rather have been somewhere else. I cursed the roto-tiller that jarred me, the weeds that grew up and had to be cut down, the hoe handle that left blisters on my palms. But despite my aversion to this plot of ground and the work that tied me to it, I was learning, through my parents' reverence, a respect for everything that grew and the seasons that dictated the time allowed each living thing.

It pains me, then, to see the Caddo maple, bare-branched, here at the beginning of fall when its leaves should just be starting to yellow and become glorious with color. And when my mother-in-law phones and tells the same stories barely minutes apart or fails to remember episodes from our visit in the summer, I mourn the fact that neurofibrils are tangling in her brain, pairs of filaments wrapping around each other to form helixes. I grieve for everything that my mother-in-law doesn't know she's forgotten: the tomatoes she bought at the farmers' market, how to balance a checkbook, the needlework of crochet, its weaving of looped stitches from a single thread.

In my garden, the tendrils of the Kentucky Wonders snake up the twine supports, and their steady advance—the fresh growth of leaves come from seed—renews my faith in the value of all our days. In the sixteenth and seventeenth century English Renaissance, knot gardens were popular— herb gardens planted in an interlocking design to signify infinity. The knot motif had been used in the decorative arts of Rome, Islam, and Medieval Europe. The traditional Islamic garden was meant to be a safe and sacred place, designed to reflect universal unity and order. Imagine the herbs woven together—lavenders and basils, rues and thymes—looping and threading a single line that seems to have no beginning or end.

From my parents, I have inherited a penchant for straight rows. My father marked off his with strings stretched between two sticks; he followed that string with the blade of an old-fashioned single-shear cultivator, leaving a shallow furrow for the seeds we would plant. I can still hear the singing click of the cultivator's wheel, and the evening birdsong that serenaded us as we worked. I can feel the cool air of early spring, can see the dazzling green of the grass.

I remember all this because accetylcholine in the limbic system of my brain has carried the memory—visual, auditory, and kinesthetic—from short-term memory to long-term storage in my temporal lobe. The image of my parents and I working in the garden is there—the sights, the sounds, the muscular movement—in a vast chain of brain cells that neurologists call memory traces. Each cell in the chain holds only a small portion of the complete memory.

Alzheimer's patients suffer from a shortage of acetylcholine. Even though a portion of a memory trace may still be intact within a neuron, it may be unable to connect with other bits of the same memory because not enough acetylcholine exists to transport it. Migration, then, is short-circuited by the tangled filaments in the hippocampus. People like my mother-in-law lack the biological ability to send memories to long-term storage and, over time, become unable to retrieve the memory traces that already exist.

One winter evening in Arkansas, where my wife and I, on our way to Illinois, had stopped for the night, I went running in a thick fog. The vapor lights in the parking lots of the motels and restaurants were dim and fuzzy. Suddenly, I heard the honk of geese and raised my head just in time to see the skein passing over, each goose a black silhouette against the gray fog. Although I was delighted by their appearance, I was also swayed by their confident navigation through the fog. I was in a place I didn't know, trying to keep my bearings. My wife was waiting for me in our motel room, already having told me to be careful not to get lost.

My mother-in-law, from time to time, forgets where she lives. Her friends have told stories about being in the car with her on occasions when she stopped in the middle of the street and said, "I can't remember how to get home." Once she and a friend were travelling down a highway talking about the corn fields they were passing, when the car started to veer off the road. My mother-in-law's friend shouted at her, and after the car was back on course, my mother-in-law said, "I forgot I was driving. My word."

It's unsettling, of course, to hear stories like these, not only because they signal a need for intervention, but also because we don't like to think of our loved ones losing a steady foothold on the earth. We like to believe we're all anchored and capable of choosing navigation, that visible proof of our control over space, that movement which allows us, even if it is an illusion, to believe we can conquer time. Why else do we marvel over the migrations of birds, butterflies, sea animals—those instinctual journeys sometimes over thousands of miles, such efforts of faith? A Ruby-throated hummingbird, a mere sixth of an ounce in weight, flies from New Hampshire forests to Costa Rica. Painted lady butterflies leave the Sahara Desert and cross the Mediterranean Sea on the power of their dainty wings. Humpback whales swim through oceans following the geomagnetic field of the Earth even when that field fluctuates and draws them to land. Often, a beached whale, when towed back to the sea, will again swim to shore, convinced that it's moving in the right direction.

At the edge of our neighborhood, developers are clearing twenty-three acres of pasture land to make room for houses and apartment buildings. Where once there were mesquite trees and cacti and yucca, where each spring wildflowers bloomed—bluebonnets and Indian paintbrushes and primrose—there are now backhoes and bulldozers and dump trucks. The bulldozers are scraping the land clean. Already they have filled in a livestock pond. Already wildlife has fled. People have seen coyotes crossing busy streets in the middle of the day, found snakes on patios.

Mornings, when I run, I scan the sky for the blue heron who used to soar overhead, swooping down to drink from the pond which is now a mound of dirt. Coyotes, snakes, herons—all of them on the move and looking now for refuge.

Often, in the early evening, when I go to our garden to look at the Kentucky Wonders vining and leafing, I imagine my life is sweet and in its proper order. Our rose bushes are still in bloom, the air fragrant with their splendid attar. I check on the blackberry vines we've trained along a trellis of chicken wire stretched along our fence, the wax myrtle that grows at the corner of our house, the lantanna with its lacy yellow flowers. We have planted these along with snowball bushes and peonies, marigolds and zinnias, all of which I remember from my father's farm. I watch them grow, and I think back to the way our lot looked when we bought the house—the grass ragged with weeds, the ground splitting open from lack of water, only a few scraggly shrubs along the foundation in front, a gaping wound in the backyard where a satellite dish, anchored in concrete, had been ripped out. Now I fertilize the lawn and mow the grass and weed the flower-erbeds, and when night comes and the gaslight burns with such a warm glow on our front lawn, I think, this is enough.

Then there are other times when I think I'm the most selfish man alive to be here, content, during the season of my mother-in-law's decline.

In "Egypt," trappers rig up drowning sets along creeks and streams. They chain a steel trap to a wire stretched taut from a stake on the bank to a sandbag anchored along the bed. Once caught, a muskrat dives and follows the wire into the water. He thinks he's escaping. Instinct tells him he's doing the right thing. But when he tries to swim back to the surface, his own motion trips a stop-slide L bracket that crimps against the wire and holds him underwater where he drowns. What he never knows is that once the trap closed, any direction he moved—up or down—it was all the same.

I imagine my mother-in-law driving the streets of her town, so far away from us in southern Illinois, in a place called "Egypt." It's nearly dark, and she's driving slowly, looking at all the houses where lights are on, where drapes are yet to be drawn. She can see through the windows. She can see sofas and paintings and book shelves. From time to time, she glimpses people: a woman sitting near a lamp reading the evening newspaper, a man home from work lifting his arms above his head to stretch his back, a child running through an archway and disappearing into another room.

The one time she visited us in Texas, my mother-in-law walked through our house, slowly taking in each room. "This is all yours?" she finally said, delight and awe mingling in her voice. "Oh, I'm so happy for both of you."

Now in my dream of her, she keeps driving past the lighted houses, leaving the people there to go on with their lives, understanding, somewhere in a place more deeply etched than memory, that these houses aren't hers, that she lives alone and has some distance yet to go.

I have no idea whether the Caddo maple in our front yard will survive and leaf out next spring, nor how long it will take for my mother-in-law's illness to progress. In the final stage of Alzheimer's, which may take over fifteen years to develop and another seven years to complete itself, the brain's cerebellum eventually ceases to function. The patient loses motor skills, is unable to walk, to sit upright, and exists in a grim twilight where whatever spirit that remains is trapped in a body barely alive.

I think of winter, of lakes and rivers freezing. I imagine mink, muskrats, otters, hibernating below the surface, dark animals curled asleep in those pockets of air between water and ice. I remember a story I read about the horrible southern Illinois winter of 1830–31. One afternoon the temperatures dropped so severely that a woman, slogging through mud to fetch water from a well, suddenly found the ground frozen around her feet, and there she was, unable to move. She must have been drawing the water, thinking how cold it was getting, imagining the warmth of the fire back at her cabin, not knowing she would soon try to take a step and find herself caught, mud frozen around her ankles. How long did she stand there, freezing to death? The rest of her family had gone to town. The thin trail of smoke from her chimney faded away to a ghostly wisp as the fire went cold and the only sounds left were the rattle of sleet and the bare tree branches, coated with ice, clacking together in the wind.

Tom Feeney

Hairdo

Mrs. Eleanor Venesky was of the opinion in January 1995 that she was about to die, although she had no hard medical evidence to suggest it. She had been of that opinion for some years and was still of that opinion when I met her seven months later. Some days the weight of the notion pinned her to the davenport; she would spend long afternoons there, stretched out beneath a thin cotton blanket, listening to her music box and nursing her discontent. Other days, the notion had no weight at all. In fact, it was lighter than air. It lifted her up and carried her into battle.

So it was on January 17, a wintry Senior Discount Day. Her husband, Bernard, sat at the kitchen table drinking coffee and reading the morning paper. Mrs. Venesky stood on the other side of the swinging white louvered doors, in front of a mirror in the living room, making a careful study of her hairdo. She twirled a few slack curls between her fingers. She picked at the strands of bang that had fallen down across her forehead. She ran her palms along the side of her head and down the back to the base of her skull. She clucked her tongue. "Let me get a perm," she called through the door to Bernard, "so at least I look decent in the box." The fellow who normally did her hair could not fit her in on such short notice. She found a number in the phone book for Summa's Beauty Salon and called for an appointment. Sure, they told her, come on in. She hung up the phone and went to get dressed.

Mrs. Venesky lived with Bernard in a drowsy subdivision twenty miles west of Philadelphia, in a split-level home at the foot of a slope of well-barbered lawn. They raised a daughter in the house and kept company with a succession of fat, flatulent dogs. Their daughter married and moved out, and the last of their dogs had been dead five years. "God has not been with us," Mrs. Venesky said of the years she and Bernard had been alone, years that had been marked by declining vitality and a gathering sense of doom. A church-going neighbor brought Mrs. Venesky a few lengths of blessed palm during the Easter season. She wasn't much for church herself, but she folded the fronds in half and tucked them behind the mirror on her living room wall. There they hung—brittle and brown and curled at the tips—like a light left burning in case He returned.

The ride to Summa's took ten minutes. Bernard dropped Mrs. Venesky off at the front door. She hung up her coat and hat and took a seat. She was flipping through a magazine when a young woman invited her to step back to the shampoo station. She had her hair washed and then, with a wet towel draped around her stooped shoulders, she was introduced to her beautician.

This was not Mrs. Venesky's first trip to Summa's. She had been there two haircuts before. "That's a darn good perm," Bernard told her when she climbed back into the car that first visit. The nurse in her doctor's office, a woman who worked behind the counter at the post office, the neighbor lady who used to stop to chat late in the afternoon while her dog peed on a tree at the top of Mrs. Venesky's driveway—they all commented on how nice that perm looked. It made her feel pretty indeed.

The woman who had cut her hair the first time was not in the shop this day, so the job of satisfying her demands fell to Dina Summa, the daughter of the proprietor. Make it short, but not too short, Mrs. Venesky told her, curled but not too tightly. Use the little pin curlers around the base of the skull but something bigger on the top. Make the bangs fluffy and keep them off the forehead.

For her entire stay in Dina Summa's chair, Mrs. Venesky was kept facing away from the mirror, and that troubled her. She liked to keep a close eye on the progress. Her natural inclination is to raise hell about such matters. But there was something about being in a beauty salon, something about the smells of solution and mousse, about the whoosh of the dryers and the crinkle of the smocks, about the way a new hairdo offers the promise of something better. Her concern about the imminence of her demise notwithstanding, Mrs. Venesky was feeling generous, trustful, even buoyant that day. She let down her guard. She offered no complaint about facing away from the mirror. Soon she would wish she had.

When Dina Summa was through, Mrs. Venesky paid her forty-three dollars at the counter, pulled on her hat and coat, and walked outside.

Bernard, back from his errands, was sitting in the car, behind the wheel. As Mrs. Venesky took her seat, she pulled down the passenger's side visor to have a look in the mirror. She removed her hat. "That's a bad perm," Bernard told her. "Oh, my God!" Mrs. Venesky screamed when she saw for herself. "Boy, she really made a monkey of me." The bangs, she thought, looked like cotton candy. The curls were tiny—and not just around the base of the skull, like she wanted, but all over her head. "I told her 'shorter,'" Mrs. Venesky said. "Not 'short.' 'Shorter.' There's an 'er' on the end there." Some strands of black hair were standing up like antennae along her part. Had Dina Summa washed out the second solution? Mrs. Venesky didn't think so. Had the dryer setting been too high? "I think they ruined the pigments," Mrs. Venesky said. At one point during her stay, Mrs. Venesky noticed Dina Summa scratching at a small patch of dry skin and recommend she treat the spot with A&D Ointment. Now she wished she had said nothing. "She could itch all day for all I care," she told Bernard.

Bernard drove her home, and from there she placed a telephone call to the Minshall-Shropshire Funeral Home. The perm had left her hair short and brittle, she told the funeral director. She asked him if he would be able to do anything to pretty her up if she were to pass before it grew out. No, he certainly wouldn't be able to use a curling iron if it were too short, he told her, because it might burn her scalp. And if it were too brittle . . . well, he just wouldn't even want to touch it, for fear it would break off in his hands. "We would have to use a wig," the funeral director told her. A wig? That was not what Mrs. Venesky had envisioned, not what she had envisioned at all, and she did not plan to sit still for it.

The seven months that passed between that day and the first time I met Mrs. Venesky had not quieted her disgruntlement, nor had the entreaties from Bernard to let bygones be bygones, nor had the ruling of the Honorable William J. Dittert Jr. in the matter of Venesky v. Summa. And so she turned to her local newspaper, her theory being that the adverse publicity might serve to teach the ladies down at Summa's that you don't take advantage of Mrs. Eleanor Venesky without suffering recriminations. *The Delaware County Daily and Sunday Times* does not make a practice of writing stories about hairdos, good or bad, and I told Mrs. Venesky when she called the newsroom that morning. "I seen some of that other stuff you print," she said. I conceded the point.

The front door was open when I arrived that afternoon. Mrs. Venesky was sitting on the davenport in loose attire, a concession to the heat. The crescent-shaped splotches of baby powder under her arms looked like perfect quarter moons setting into her tank top. We could hear Bernard clanking around in the kitchen cupboards, preparing himself a late lunch.

On the floor at opposite ends of the parlor, two box fans were panting like dogs, and, from time to time, a bit of the manufactured breeze would lift up the cover on a brown file folder and rustle the papers inside. These folders were stacked everywhere in the living room—on an end table, on the coffee table, on an oak-veneer cabinet, on the floor. There were maybe three or four folders to a stack, all carefully labeled, maybe twelve stacks in all.

I stepped around one of the box fans, over a short stack of files, past two shrimp-colored arm chairs draped in bed sheets to protect the slipcovers. I sat down at the far end of the davenport. On the cushion between us, Mrs. Venesky placed one of her folders. It was labeled, "Hair." I told Mrs. Venesky before we got started that I wasn't sure I would be able to put anything in the paper about her hairdo, since so much time had elapsed since the perm. She elected to tell me her story just the same.

If not for some bad fortune sixty years or so ago, Mrs. Venesky might have spent her life on the other side of the clippers and curlers. There was a school of beauty culture in Shamokin, Pennsylvania, the Central Pennsylvania coal-mining town where she grew up, and Mrs. Venesky spent many Saturday mornings there. Although she was too young to enroll herself, she sat and watched as the students in their pale blue aprons washed, trimmed, and set the hair of the budget-conscious women who were willing to submit themselves as training models in exchange for rates lower than they would have paid in professional salons. Mrs. Venesky studied the students and the modern techniques they used, and she quietly planned one day to matriculate herself.

Before she was of age, though, the school moved from Shamokin to the state capital, Harrisburg, a good sixty miles away. Mrs. Venesky was not from a wealthy family. Her father, who worked hard days in the mines, enjoyed his beer and cigarettes, and she would not have dared to ask him to forgo those simple pleasures. The family's disposable income was thoroughly disposed of before her plans were addressed. Attending school in Harrisburg was out of the question. She settled, instead, for a job as an instructor with the Singer Co. She traveled by foot all over town to teach women who could not stitch a seam as neatly as she how to use their new-fangled sewing machines.

When Bernard finished his lunch, he joined us in the parlor. He was wearing a white T-shirt and slacks. A hearing aid dangled from a cord around his neck. He sat down in one of the shrimp-colored arm chairs, on top of the protective bed sheet. The box fan on the floor next to him was beating its futile circles at the stultifying heat and making enough noise in the effort that Bernard struggled to keep up with the conversation. "Bernard went to Bucknell," Mrs. Venesky said. "What's that?" Bernard asked. "I said you went to Bucknell," Mrs. Venesky repeated, not trying to disguise her exasperation. The cuffs of Bernard's slacks were fluttering in the breeze of the fan.

Despite a recent heart surgery, Bernard, a retired aeronautical engineer, had been keeping himself plenty busy around the house. He groomed the sloped lawn with his riding mower and gas-powered trimmer, controlled the population of ants and bumble bees with a home-made squirt bottle filled with Malathion 50 and tinkered with any mechanical contraption he thought might benefit from the attention. (On the day of my visit, his thumb was wrapped heavily in gauze because of an injury he had sustained while paying attention to the hot water heater.)

Mrs. Venesky was less active. She spent most of her time on the davenport. Behind her, the picture window was covered with a bed sheet. The curtains that once hung there had been cleaned and pressed and were folded neatly away in cardboard boxes, where they would remain until Mrs. Venesky felt well enough to hang them back up, which, she allowed, would not be any day soon. Without getting up from the davenport, she could lift a corner of the sheet and look out to the spot on the front walk where Bernard was emptying the contents of his squeeze bottle on an ant trail.

Mrs. Venesky kept a medical encyclopedia beneath an end table. The "doctor's book," she called it. She used it to match up symptoms (chest pains one day, perhaps, maybe a rash on her buttocks the next) with potential ailments (heart disease and various types of cancer were her primary concerns). She once left most of this diagnostic work to her family physician, but he has asked her not to call on him quite so often. Once or twice a week would be fine, he told her, even three times in a pinch, but no more four, five, or six. Mrs. Venesky filled that void first by frequenting the emergency rooms at two suburban hospitals near her home, but because her concern about the fragility of her physical state tends to manifest itself in churlishness ("You are the dumbest doctor I ever met," she told one physician whose opinion about her prognosis did not match her own), she was not long welcome there. She then took to traveling into the city, to the teaching hospitals downtown, where the anonymous young doctors with cold, pink hands tended not to show much interest in the diagnoses she cooked up on the couch.

Many of the brown file folders scattered around her parlor are stuffed with papers that document these experiences with doctors and hospitals. Mrs. Venesky believes these papers tell a powerful story about Medicare and fraud, although she has some difficulty articulating that story, and she intends some day to invite a crew from *60 Minutes* out to the house to look them over. She asked me if I could put her in touch with Mike Wallace and was suspicious of my credentials when I told her we were not acquainted.

The papers in the rest of the brown file folders tell stories not unlike the one about her hairdo. A hopeful Mrs. Venesky would set out to acquire some routine good or service. Then, a suspicious Mrs. Venesky would come to believe she'd been fleeced. Finally, an aggrieved Mrs. Venesky would hunger for her pound of flesh. "You have to be pushy, as long as you know you're right," she told me.

Bernard doesn't always share his wife's enthusiasm for the fight. This often was a source of tension in their marriage. Once, after the Veneskys had a minor automobile accident, the insurance company investigated the circumstances and agreed to pay their claim. Mrs. Venesky was not happy with the settlement, though, so she had the company send her the form she would need to appeal it. Her church-going neighbor had given her a vial of holy water, and she splashed a small quantity across the form to bring luck on the appeal. She then turned the form over to Bernard for processing, but he was satisfied with the initial award and so never took the trouble to fill out the form. "I could kill him sometimes," she said. "You could cut off his nose, and he wouldn't do a damn thing about it."

Bernard played a different role in the matter of Venesky v. Summa. Mrs. Venesky had dropped by the Brookhaven Regional Court sometime after her conversation with the funeral director to pick up the papers she would need to file a civil action against Summa's. She took the papers home and put them in the brown file folder labeled "Hair." There they remained for two or three weeks until Bernard told her if she was going to do something with them she might just as well go ahead and do it. With an ink pen, in an unsteady script, Mrs. Venesky filled out her complaint that very day. Bernard drove her down to the court. She paid the $49.75 filing fee. And the legal battle was on.

Her complaint listed seven counts. The most particular among them involved accusations that the beautician over-processed and burned her hair, neglected to rinse out the second solution, and employed the wrong type of curlers. Two of the counts—the second and seventh—involved more sweeping charges: "They gave me a terrible haircut" and "My hair is still falling out." The lawsuit sought two thousand dollars in damages to compensate for the aggravation and a wig to cover up the perm.

The case was slow to move to a hearing, too slow to suit Mrs. Venesky. Twice, it was scheduled by the court, and twice, the defendant hairdresser was granted a continuance. Mrs. Venesky used the time to make herself a familiar figure in the offices of the court. She called frequently to make angry denunciations of both the American system of jurisprudence and her hairstylist. "I guess she made a pest of herself down there," said Dittert, the judge.

The hearing finally went off at 3 p.m. on June 1. Dittert was on the bench. He had retired from another regional court in the county and was in Brookhaven to fill in for the regular district justice, C. Walter McCray Jr., who was ill. Dittert had never before handled a case involving a hairdo.

Mrs. Venesky represented herself in court. Bernard was her only witness. Despite his considerable mastery of mathematics and the physical sciences and despite a stint he did as an apprentice barber as a teenager in Shamokin, Bernard had no expertise in women's hair styling. He testified that the perm was the worst his wife had received in their forty years of marriage. Beyond that, he had little to offer the plaintiff's case.

Mrs. Venesky had gone around to other beauty parlors in the area asking the stylists to evaluate her perm. None agreed to accompany her to court. Two, however, did write notes for her, and Mrs. Venesky brought them along as evidence. (The stronger of the two notes said her perm had been wrapped with uneven tension and cut asymmetrically.) Mrs. Venesky brought a third note along to court, too. That one she had written herself as sort of a "memo to file" after a consultation with her family physician. The note read, "Dr. Thompson said his wife would be furious if she got a terrible perm like I got."

The defense presented testimony that Mrs. Venesky's hair had not been over-processed, that the temperature setting on the dryer was just right, that the curlers used were of the appropriate size and style. It presented testimony, too, that the Summas were reputable hairstylists who had had enough advanced training to be considered expert in some of the techniques they employed on Mrs. Venesky. It entered into evidence the curlers Dina Summa had used for Mrs. Venesky's perm. Several women who were in the shop that January day took the stand to say Mrs. Venesky's hair looked just fine when she left. (Mrs. Venesky was none too impressed with these defense witnesses: "Two of them didn't even have perms," she told me. "One of them needed a shampoo. The other one looked like a fried chicken. A fried chicken. That was a bad haircut. I could have told her that. But I kept my mouth shut.")

During his cross-examination of Mrs. Venesky, the defense attorney asked her if she had any medical problems. She mentioned something about a heart ailment and let it go at that. When he returned to the subject later, he dropped the word "medical" and simply asked if she had any "problems." She told him no, but he revisited the topic two or three more times, as she recalls it. I asked her why she thought he had done that. "He wanted to see if maybe I was nuts," she said. "I wasn't going to give him the satisfaction."

In the end Dittert found in favor of Summa's. He ruled inadmissible the notes Mrs. Venesky had hoped to get into evidence. He told her the expert hairstylists needed to be present in court so the defense would have the opportunity to cross-examine them. He advised her of her right to appeal his decision to the Common Pleas Court of Delaware County within thirty days, and he suggested she get herself a lawyer if she intended to do so. Mrs. Venesky does not think much of lawyers; she did not take an appeal.

If Judge McCray had been in court that day, Mrs. Venesky told me, the outcome would have been different. He would have thought about his own wife and how he might have reacted had she come home from the beauty shop with a similar perm. Dittert, well, him she held in low esteem. She doubted his fitness to decide any matter involving a perm, and she believed firmly that his own hair could have been better styled.

Mrs. Venesky believed in the proposition that a newspaper ought to comfort the afflicted and afflict the comfortable, and she had not a whisper of doubt as to which role she had played in the matter of Venesky v. Summa. She saw the newspaper story as her last best chance at justice.

Dittert wasn't the only one who had disappointed her. After her civil case had been adjudicated, she filed a complaint against the Summas with the Prosecution Office of the Pennsylvania Bureau of Professional and Occupational Affairs, hoping the hairdressers would be fined or have their licenses revoked. She included a few strands of her hair in the envelope with the complaint form before she sent it off to Harrisburg. A few weeks later, an attorney for the board—"some asinine lawyer," is how Mrs. Venesky described her to me—contacted her by phone to say the office would not pursue the case. Mrs. Venesky was thinking about filing a complaint with the state bar association against that attorney, but, if the truth be told, she was not hopeful. So that left her with me.

When Mrs. Venesky was through with her story, more or less, she went to the kitchen to pour me an iced tea, leaving Bernard and me alone in the living room. I already knew that the story I wrote would not be the one Mrs. Venesky had in mind as she was dialing the newsroom that morning. The truth was, even though she had led me on an exhaustive tour of her cranium and had schooled me on the significance of every feature of the topography, I could still not say with confidence whether the Summas had done anything worse than wander unbeknownst into the field of fire. It was true that Mrs. Venesky's hair did not look good, but I knew I would not be able to determine who was to blame for that. For one thing, the photographic record she produced to prove to me that her hair had looked much better before her January visit to Summas was unconvincing. One of her claims was that the pigment damage caused by the blast-furnace hairdryer had caused her hair to turn from gray to white. Maybe it was the poor quality of the snapshots, but as I studied her before and after photos, I was unable to discern the difference. Another barrier to determining who was to blame involved the chain of custody of the primary piece of evidence in the case, to wit, the perm. Mrs. Venesky had been alone with her hair for seven months and had had ample opportunity to do with it what she pleased. Who was to say she had not inflicted some of the damage herself? She admitted to having clipped her hair over the bathroom sink after her day in court. How could I know she had not fouled it up for dramatic effect? I knew, even as I sat there in the parlor with Bernard, that I would not be writing a story that cast the Summas in the role of villains.

"Why write a story if the judge already made his decision?" Bernard was leaning forward in the shrimp-colored arm chair when he asked me the question. Mrs. Venesky might have considered this a betrayal if she had been in the room to hear it. "I don't see any point," he said.

I did, and I said so. I told Bernard his wife was an irresistibly colorful character, and I told him I admired her moxie. What I didn't tell him— maybe because I didn't fully understand it yet myself, maybe because I didn't want to offend him—was that the story I planned to write would not focus on the particulars of the lawsuit but on the anger that propelled it. I saw Mrs. Venesky as an old woman who was anxious for death because life had so disappointed her. She feared death, of course, and searched frantically for its antidote in the dog-eared pages of her doctor's book and on the examination tables of the teaching hospitals downtown. But only death could resolve her disappointments. The friends who called on her so infrequently, the relatives who never appreciated the meticulous work that had gone into the garments she had sewn for their children, the claims man from the insurance company, all those damn doctors, the asinine lawyer from the Prosecution Office of the Pennsylvania Bureau of Professional and Occupational Affairs, the Honorable William J. Dittert Jr., and countless other boobs and nincompoops, stooges and fried chickens, even the imperturbable husband who had never bothered to help her clean up around the house—all of them would gather around her coffin and feel the weight of her passing settling down around their shoulders, and they would understand, finally, they would understand, and they would miss her and they would weep and they would remark to one another in somber, almost reverential, voices, "Boy, that's a darn good perm." That's the story I wanted to write.

Had I said so to Bernard, he might have asked me how I figured to get that kind of flapdoodle in the newspaper. He would have had a point there. We don't mind righteous indignation in our stories, but we insist that it be wielded with care and true to its mark. Mrs. Venesky, disappointed by forces of either such moment or such inconsequence as to defy detection, fires on any source of heat or movement and so tends from time to time to wing an innocent passerby. That makes newspaper editors nervous. Had I thought about that as I sat there in the parlor with Bernard, I might have told him I wouldn't be able to get the story in the newspaper after all. By saying so then, I might have spared his wife yet another disappointment.

Mrs. Venesky pushed through the white louvered doors and rejoined us in the parlor. As she crossed the carpeted floor, she stirred angrily at the undissolved powder in the iced tea she had made me. She put the glass on the coffee table and settled back into her spot at the end of the gold davenport. Bernard tried to continue the conversation about whether we ought to just scrub the entire story, but Mrs. Venesky shushed him.

A copy of the complaint she had filed with the licensing agency was the last scrap of paper in the brown file folder labeled "Hair." The rest of the contents were scattered around her on the table and the couch. She gathered them up and tucked them back in the folder as I drank down the last of my tepid tea. Was I going to be able to do a story, she wanted to know. I assured her I had every intention of writing it, but I warned her it might not make the Summas look as bad as she hoped. "So long as it's in the paper," she said. I told her I had to do a couple of other interviews. I said I might need to stop back to see her once or twice again before I wrote the story, too, and I told her I needed to schedule a time for a photographer to stop by to get a picture of the perm. What I told her, as I was leaving, was that she could expect to see the story in the paper in two weeks or so.

Of course, it never made it. I did the interviews. The Summas expressed pain at the prospect of reading the Venesky saga in the newspaper, and they decided they would rather not discuss the matter with me. They referred me to their attorney. He suggested the best approach for me might be to use the hairdo suit as an example in a larger piece on frivolous legal actions. The lawsuit was without legal merit, but frivolous? I didn't think so. I thanked him for the idea just the same. When I talked to Dittert, I mentioned that Mrs. Venesky had said some unflattering things about his hairstyle, namely that she had studied it during the hearing and concluded he combed it forward to cover up a bald spot. I told him she had also raised some questions about whether the color was natural. "I tried to be nice to her," Dittert said, rather nicely, "but with some people you just can't." I sent a photographer out to the Veneskys' house, and he came back to the office with a haunting picture of Mrs. Venesky standing in the living room, grabbing at a hank of gray hair. All of her disappointments seemed to be accumulated in the dark, dramatic bags beneath her eyes. The photographer came back to the office with a diagnosis, too, which, despite a lack of formal mental health training, he delivered with some conviction: "She's crazy," he said, punctuating the comment with an expletive.

I finished up my story on a Sunday. The decision to kill it was made Tuesday. One of the editors said the story warranted no more than a couple of paragraphs deep inside the paper, somewhere between the obituaries and the comic strips, perhaps. On Wednesday, at a staff meeting, the editor in chief, trying to explain why the story had been killed, offered an unflattering assessment of Mrs. Venesky's status in the community ("the village idiot") and expressed some concern that the story might have done irreparable and, more importantly, actionable damage to the Summas' reputation.

When I called Mrs. Venesky with the news, she did not take it well. She said she thought maybe the Summas had "gotten" to me, the same way they had gotten to Dittert and that attorney from the state licensing bureau, but I assured her that was not the case. I told her the decision to kill the story had been made by the editor in chief, after consultation with an attorney, and she said she thought maybe the Summas had gotten to them, too.

Over the next three or four weeks, Mrs. Venesky called the newsroom with some regularity to denounce not only her beautician and the American system of jurisprudence but also the lap-dog local press. She would ask for me, but she would tell her story in as much detail as she was permitted to whoever happened to answer the telephone. I did talk to her a few times myself but our conversations were not constructive, so I eventually stopped taking her calls. The last word I had from her was a note written by a colleague on a slip of pink paper and propped up on the keyboard of my computer.

"Mrs. Venesky called," the note read. "She's mad as hell."

And she's not going to take it anymore.

Steven Harvey

Laying on of Hands

A dark slick rising and falling in silky waves—that caught my eye. Some dusky residue of night. The sun had just risen above the Gulf, igniting the sky momentarily in pinks and reds and giving definition to the dunes and sea oats all about me while the house, the wooden walkway, even my arms turned golden in the glow. The water, which lay placid and still against the bowed horizon, culminated along the beach in a hush of long, perfect waves. I had been sitting in a beach chair strumming a ukulele when a black shape appeared—materialized, it seemed, in folds of blue—undulating with the water. I set my instrument down and stood to get a better look, shading my eyes. Suddenly a shape like a wind-lifted lapel emerged briefly out of the spray, and I knew that the darkness I saw could not be a shadow, but an object of some kind, though the movement seemed involuntary, more the rocking of the lovely and indifferent semitropical waters than a thing alive.

In *Moby Dick* Herman Melville compares a morning like this one to the morning after the nuptial night when formality and romance have given way to the act of engendering. The air, he writes, is "pensive" and "transparently pure and soft, with a woman's look" while "man-like" the sea heaves with "long, strong, lingering swells." The gulls, he imagines, float like the winking and fluttering thoughts of the woman roused from sleep, so different from the dark and "murderous" underwater creatures slithering through the man's mind, and the horizon trembles with passion, "the fond, throbbing trust, the loving alarms, with which the poor bride gave her bosom away." I often think of Melville on sunlit mornings at the beach when the sea takes the sky, the combination of elements creating life and offering it as a gift to the planet. It is a lovely metaphor.

But *this* gift, this offering to the dawn, I wondered, looking at the black shape in the breakers. What have we here? Rarely is it delivered so literally.

And a leviathan, to boot. I did not realize at first that the shape rolling in the water was a whale—a baby sperm whale to be exact—but I did walk down to the water's edge and on closer look saw that it was a large sea creature. Most of the enormous body lay hidden under water that was slowly turning azure in the morning sun, but I saw the tail clearly—the black lapel—that roiled with the waters and, when a breaker tumbled in, rose out of the wave with a gush and slapped back at the sea. We had often seen dolphins play here—St. George Island is famous for them—so I thought it might be a dolphin though it looked far too large. Recently we had heard reports of sharks attacking children at the water's edge so that thought glided ominously through my mind. I kept my distance. I'm pretty sure that I was the first on the scene since I had watched the shape emerge out of the night with no one else around. After a long look—in which the body rose and fell with the swelling of the waves—I went back to my ukulele and sat in the sand, wondering what is done when an enormous, dead sea creature washes up on the beach.

But it was not dead. I walked back to the beach house. Louisa, whose family shared the St. George house with ours, was pouring coffee and blinking her eyes to wake up. Louisa is usually game for anything, even the sight of a whale at the crack of dawn, so soon she and I were headed down the beach, holding coffee mugs in front of us as we tried to negotiate the tricky sand, making our way to the spot where the whale had washed up. It still looked lifeless and out of place, like a sofa rolling on the waves, but two plucky volunteers who were in the water, their shorts wet at the hem, assured us that it was alive, breathing through its blowhole.

A small crowd had gathered by now and no one, it seemed, knew what to do. A day earlier this same whale had washed up further down the beach and locals had guided it back into deeper water. Some suggested that we should try to do that. Others thought that the whale was too weak to survive at sea, that it had come here to die and we should let it. Someone said that we should call the aquatic center in Clearwater. Louisa and I were about ready to head back to our house, put off by all the squabbling, when one of the women in the water shouted. "We need some help here," and we saw that she and her friend were trying to turn the whale and lift its head out of the water. "I think it's drowning!"

Not long after that I found myself in the water with twenty or thirty other people. They had turned the whale so that it faced the shore and were holding it in their arms to keep its blowhole out of the water. Others had taken positions along the whale's body and passing blankets, towels, and T-shirts underneath created a makeshift sling in order to keep the whale up out of the surf. I found a spot about halfway down the whale's body and the dark-haired man across from me passed the tail of a shirt underwater. Grabbing my end, I leaned back, hoisting the whale up a bit. I secured the T-shirt, wrapping it tightly in my fingers—my knuckles turning white—and with my free hand spread water as the others were doing over the exposed hide of the whale.

How many people ever get to touch a whale! The breathing animal lay docile in the midst of all of us holding it in our hands and arms. The hide felt cold and stiff and hard like a car tire but beneath it beat the heart of a mammal that, if it lived, would grow to be one of the most magnificent creatures on earth. I twisted the T-shirt tighter in my fingers, pulled hard, and, amid the newly formed team of volunteers, waited.

From the time that Captain John Smith acquired a crown permit for whaling in 1614 until 1924 when the sinking of the *Wanderer* off Cuttyhunk put an end to the U.S. whaling industry, the history of humans and whales along the American coast was bloody. Whalers tracked down and killed sperm whales with alarming efficiency. The whaler, in fact, was more than just a killing machine, it housed a floating processing factory as well. After the main ship tracked the whale down, sailors in smaller whaleboats harpooned and killed it and brought it alongside the mother ship. Standing on the carcass, they secured the whale with chains, cut away the jaw in order to remove the ivory, and sliced off flesh in strips to be tried into blubber while sharks swarmed below. Meanwhile the case, taken from the whale's head and hauled on deck, was bailed for its precious oil. The sperm whale may be, as Melville wrote, "the largest inhabitant of the globe; the most formidable of all whales to encounter; the most magestic in aspect," but it was also "the most valuable in commerce; being the only creature from which the valuable substance, spermaceti, is obtained."

Whaling was dangerous business, as John B. Putnam reminds us in his essay "Whaling and Whalecraft" that comes with my edition of *Moby Dick*. Once the harpoon dug into the whale's hump, getting fast, the whale would breach, run, or sound, taking the whaleboat on a "Nantucket sleighride" at great speeds. Occasionally, the whale would turn on the small boats, attacking them, and we have contemporary engravings that show whales striking boats with their tails, capsizing them by rising out of the water, and snapping them in two with their powerful jaws. In all of these engravings the men appear to be small and helpless once the whale attacks, bobbing in the water and clearly out of their element. The whale can also attack the main ship, sometimes resulting in catastrophe, which is what happened to the *Essex*, the inspiration for Melville's book. The whale's "forehead smote the ship's starboard bow, till men and timbers reeled. Some fell flat upon their faces . . . Through the breach they heard the waters pour, as mountain torrents down a flume." In Melville's story, all but one drowned.

Much of the majesty of sperm whales comes from their sheer size. The largest of the toothed whales, they can live seventy years, grow to be sixty feet long, and weigh fifty tons. The heart alone usually weighs 275 pounds, about the same weight as two human beings. "You definitely feel puny," one diver wrote after swimming with a whale, "when thirty tons of flesh swims by." The whale that had beached with us was a baby—only eleven feet long—but already it was larger than any animal I had ever touched. It took about twenty of us, in shifts, just to hold the body up in the water, the simple bulk of the creature making it seem alien and strange to us.

And yet it was not alien or strange. After all, when the woman in the water called for help for the drowning whale most of us rushed in and when we lifted it in our shirts and towels and rubbed water over its hump most of us felt a mammalian kinship. The mother sperm whale nurses young calves like the one we were helping. While males roam wide across the seas of the planet, females and the young stay behind to form a kind of nursery. Mothers are loyal to their young but often depend on the group to protect them while they gather food. They sing to the calves—a form of echolocation—in order to keep track of them. When the males return during mating season, they dance in the water for the females as part of the courtship ritual in a kind of large-scale aquatic barn dance and chant songs they have learned from their adventures far away. All of that sounds pretty familiar to me.

But the strongest bond—the one I at least felt strongest—was the reason that we had to help: whales breathe air. They breathe through a blowhole located near the top of their heads and can go underwater for several hours at a time, diving deep in a single breath in pursuit of their favorite food, the bottom-dwelling giant squid. When they emerge they blow in a burst that can often be heard nearly a mile away. Once I was stationed near the head of our stranded whale, right by the blowhole—a small S-shaped lip of flesh that opened and closed every three or four minutes—and I felt the warm, musty breath on my face. "Watch out for whale snot," some kid said as a joke, but the joke died among us. "Baby's breath"—that is what I thought, remembering the sweet stale odor of my own children's breath when they were nursing. Baby sperm whales drink milk, warm blood floods the chambers of their hearts, and they breathe the air. They may grow to weigh as much as a tractor trailer rig, but they are one of us.

We dubbed the whale George Barry: George for St. George Island where he had washed up and Barry for the hurricane that had drenched the area with rain the day before and had forced us all to evacuate the island. Eventually a large crowd gathered with many vacationers in swimsuits and large hats taking a turn holding the makeshift sling of blankets, towels, and T-shirts. All in my family helped and so did our friends. Many vacationers who took a turn beside the whale came from far off—Canada and the northeast as well as the south—and Louisa and her husband, David, who teach with me met some former students, too. An *ad hoc* community was beginning to form. Those who did not actually hold the whale brought sunscreen and water and later pizza for the group that had gathered. It was nearly dusk before experts from the Clearwater marina arrived with a crane, so we had to stay with the task all day.

The hardest part for me was keeping my footing. Occasionally George grew restless and shifted in the water. Sometimes big breakers would crash in on us causing George—and all of his helpers—to slide to one side. Then children who were helping caught a face full of water and all of us had to reposition our feet and tug on the towels and T-shirts that suspended George to keep from tipping over. My hands got stiff from holding the T-shirts tightly, and when other helpers were relieved of their posts I noticed that they would shake their hands as they walked to the beach trying to get some life back into them.

But the work never seemed hard. Soon the curiosity wore off and the drudgery of holding a position set in, but I noticed as the day wore on that the crowd grew bigger—not just the crowd of onlookers but the group of helpers as well. My friends and family and I could go back to our beach house for lunch and return a few hours later and the group with their hands on the whale never diminished. When I took a spot I joined a team bound by nothing other than a desire to help. I remember the faces: the man with dark hair and authoritative eyes, the red-haired teenage girl with beads of water on her cheek and a dab of white sunblock on her nose, the little boy who kept getting waves in his face. Often we had to lean back, fighting the natural drift toward the beach, and at one point the woman ahead of me was nearly in my lap—her leg against my thigh—in order to keep her towel end up high enough. We didn't talk much, I remember, just a few barked commands about our positions, but we did look into each other's eyes to keep our actions in sync—more by intuition than plan—and moved together as the waves rolled in.

Most of all I remember the hands gripping the sling and gently rubbing the whale. Our task was to keep the whale body low enough in the water that it would not be burned or dried out by the sun and yet high enough so that the blowhole was free to breathe. Any exposed hide had to be covered by wet towels. Our hands kept the skin moist and towels in place, but there was more to the gesture of rubbing the whale's back than mere utilitarian need. Our hands kept the whale alive for a while, yes, but they also gave—and received—comfort. We caressed the animal, our eyes opening wide with affection and awe as we rubbed. It was, in the fundamental sense, a laying on of hands.

Many of the churches where I live believe in the power of the laying on of hands. I once visited one of the churches—a friend of mine goes there—a small chapel beyond the little town of Hiawassee. After a Sunday school class with a video on the end of the world when the souls of the faithful would be "raptured" into heaven while the rest of us poor suckers would get blown away by Armageddon, we attended the service itself. At first it seemed much like Sunday morning at the Methodist church with several announcements by the pastor and the youth leader and a few prayers, but when we got to the songs, hell, to be frank, broke loose.

Most of the members of the congregation put one or two arms in the air and began to sway. Occasionally a voice would float above the other singers in a kind of shout—an incomprehensible phrase that exploded across the room. A few of the women in different parts of the church fell where they stood—one in the center aisle—and began shivering and shaking uncontrollably in their Sunday dresses. Most of us kept on singing—though I must say that I had trouble following the tune amid the pandemonium—but I did watch a few members of the congregation gather around the nearest writhing woman and put a hand on her, still holding the free hand in the air, and praying aloud as the song continued. The gesture was meant as comfort, yes, but also as a weird drawing on the power of her spirit as well, perhaps to free it or purge it as a kind of contagious enthusiasm passed from one soul to another.

The Bible—especially parts about the ministry of Jesus and the early church—offers examples of the power of touch to transform. In Mark, a leper beseeches Jesus to make him "clean" of his disease. "Moved with pity," Jesus touched him and willed the man to "be clean," and "immediately the leprosy left him" and the man was cleansed of his disease. After the death of Jesus, his disciples, who had few rituals or sacraments other than baptism by water and communion, would often as part of their ministry place hands on others to bring comfort or give thanks. The spirit, it seems, is weak until the flesh is willing.

I believe in the transforming power of touch. The face of a lover in our hands confirms our humanity. Another's hand in mine calms me. I can't buy most of the pseudoscientific explanations of this power, especially "touch therapy" which holds that the balance in fields of energy around our bodies can be restored by the touch of a trained therapist. The inventor of this particular form of charlatanism was a theosophist named Dolores Krieger who relied heavily on language about energy fields from quantum physics, but some of the scientific lingo is taken out of context and other phrases, such as the exchange of "qualities of energy," are suspect. Studies by scientists offer no evidence that touch therapy works.

But touching does. Who would deny this? My wife worked for a while in an elementary school in a poor rural area of North Carolina. Every afternoon when she came home from work her clothes looked bedraggled and she looked worn down, as if she had been carrying heavy packages for miles. From the beginning of the school day to the end her students held her hand or pulled her blouse or played with her hair. By the end of the year she felt like a teddy bear with all the fur rubbed off. The kids, she said, are hungry for human touch.

When my dad was dying he was confined to a hospital bed and for hours on end I would hold his hand. We had never been particularly physical in our affections before that, but he wanted to hold my hand. We talked. We watched TV. All the while he held my hand. At times, when I thought he was sleeping, I would rise to go and he would grip my hand hard. "Stay here," he said. So we sat, mostly in silence, with me holding his hand while eternity closed in on him from all sides. I feel it now as I type, his grip on my fingers—a kind of afterimage for the hand—though he has been dead many years. Perhaps that is the point.

Last year my daughter Alice took confirmation vows with the Methodist church, and her mother and I stood behind her as her sponsors. Others were confirmed that day—about ten in all I guess—and their proud parents stood with us. At one point the minister asked us to put our hands on our children's shoulders or head. Since grandparents and aunts and uncles were among us, the crowd at the altar rail was large, so she said that if we could not put our hands directly on our children to put them on the shoulders of the person in front of us. I put my hands on my daughter and felt someone behind me put a hand on my shoulder. The service lasted only a few minutes. Words, which I don't recall now, were spoken. We said the Lord's Prayer in unison, but the rest is a blur. What I do remember is the crowd of us, so different in the course of our lives—a banker, a teacher, a U.S. Senator, a housewife—connected for a moment by our touch. Even I—an interloper on this scene—felt, as the minister liked to say, "lifted up" at the hands of others.

It was the touch—I believe—that confirmed what we could not see, Alice's spirit among us. I am baffled by those who argue that without a church people would become callous and uncaring and that their hands would turn to the devil's business. Touch is primary, not the church. The church insists on stewardship—requires its members to protect the planet and the people and inhabitants of it—but this urge to take care of what is around us, as well as the complementary urge to destroy, is surely more basic than any church credo or religious command. Curiosity may have called us to the dying whale at the water's edge that morning at St. George, but some quality far more profound than that led us into the water and kept us there as the day dragged on. Some of us hesitated—I know I did—but we got in anyway, overcoming inconvenience and fear to lay our hands on a beast.

The universe has no other hands as far as I know. Sometimes when Madge, our dog, watches me pick a pretzel out of a bag my wife vocalizes her canine thoughts: "Oh, Lord, for opposable thumbs!" And I wonder, if whales are as intelligent as some scientists claim, what George thought of the human hand. Had George heard songs in the ocean nursery warning against humans? What fears did those hands on his hide raise? And how much of that fear was allayed when the hands moved gently, bringing the kind of solace that only hands can?

My doctor has wonderful hands. When two of his patients meet and talk about him that invariably is the first comment they make. When he faces me and places the hands along the back of my neck all of my muscles immediately relax—my body feels suddenly suspended as if in buoyant water—and when he touches my forearms or chest any tightening just disappears. Of course, hands can rip and tear and destroy. I know a man whose hands are like two slabs of meat, and he can use them as weapons. But in the end destruction seems contrary to the subtle rotary capabilities of thumbs and the fine movements of fingers. Think of any simple act of the hands—popping open a beer, for instance—and consider the myriad muscle movements involved. The strength of bone, the flexibility of tendons, and the softness and toughness of flesh are all brought to bear on the aluminum tab.

Most of our taboos involve touch. Touch this sign, kiss this stone, or prick your finger on this spindle and tremendous energy for good or ill fills the room. Ring this doorbell and an entirely new future opens before you. Why? Why is touch the focus of these archetypal taboos? I suspect that the delicacy of the hand invites the idea. It is at the fingertips that the bulk of our body culminates in the tenderest motions. We throw our weight around, toss elbows, and stand our ground but when we want to see an object for what it really is we hold it in our palm or lift it to our eyes held only by the fingertips. It is that delicacy of motion that defines the hand. When we are powerless to change the world by brute strength it is the fingertip, our weakest link to the world, that taps into energy that lies dormant beyond us.

In the mountains where I live the grand musical tradition was transmitted by people watching each other's hands. Hedy West, the singer who grew up in Carrolton, Georgia, used to visit her grandmother in Blairsville, where I live, and learned banjo by watching the old woman's hand motion. That's the mountain way. The hands of old-time players are lovely to watch because they seem to produce so much sound with so little effort. You have to train the muscles you don't use to relax—that is the way one musician put it. You can't think about it, he said. You have to watch and do. The hand will teach you what you need to know. I, too, learned banjo by watching hands and once even apologized to the husband of a musician for staring so hard at his wife. I was watching her hands, I explained lamely. He seemed to understand. "They *are* beautiful," he said with a smile.

If the deity is pure spirit, then it lacks more than a face, a frown, and a mighty forearm. God also lacks opposable thumbs and is best understood as power without hands. Hands are *our* tools and our responsibility—there are no others available in the universe. They can be fitted with harpoons, it is true, but, based on their toughness, flexibility, and fineness, their true calling seems to be to caress, not hurt. To heal. We do not need a church to remind us to be stewards of our world. We simply need to look hard at our hands before we use them. They will teach us what to do.

After our vacation was over and we had settled back to work, Louisa, whose office is next to mine, had exciting news. George was still alive! She found his story on the Clearwater Marine Aquarium Internet site. We had seen the crew from the aquarium lift George from the beach with a crane and set him in a large truck for the three-hour trip. Online we learned that the whale weighed one thousand pounds when it arrived on August 9 and had large, infected wounds in its left tail fluke. The aquarium team lowered George into a stranding pool, but the whale seemed listless, could not swim, and had to be suspended in a stretcher held in place by volunteers. They did not expect it to live.

Slowly, though, George began to revive and Louisa and I followed the story on our computers. He drank formula at a rate of five gallons a day and after two weeks had gained 115 pounds. His formula consisted of milk matrix, esbilac, salt, sunflower oil, and vitamins blended together and served in gallon milk jugs at a cost of about one hundred dollars a day. By August 30 he could swim "like a champ." One of the volunteers said "that at times there was an actual wake behind him with whitecaps!" The enthusiasm of the Clearwater team filled us with excitement too. "Wow!" they wrote after this initial swim. "What a great day! We expect him to be very hungry after expending all this energy."

The *Today* show did a segment—"The lights and cameras didn't bother George"—and he was drinking up to nine gallons of formula per day by August 25. "His will to live has surprised us all," the team leader said on September 10, "and made us actually think he just might make it." Over the course of his stay at the Marina he gained more than two hundred pounds, and as late as August 18 George was still showing signs of progress. "It is so nice to see George moving around a little more. "George began to talk to his volunteers. When they would prepare the stretcher in order to weigh him he made a distinctive clicking: "We have come to call the sound 'stretcher noise.'" George was still very sick, though, and in September began to weaken. "Lymphatic swelling at the lower end of his gastrointestinal tract" led to difficulty in digesting food and the infection from his wounds began to worsen. Around midnight of September 21, 2001, George died. He had spent forty-three days under treatment and was "the longest-lived sperm whale in captivity." On the Internet site the leader of the Clearwater team mentioned that scientists would be able to use the information gathered on George to help whales in the future but added "I am equally impressed with the impact George had on us. He brought out the best in all of us." On the page he listed the names of the 104 volunteers in Clearwater who answered the call to save George. All of them—all of us—had a hand in helping George.

The morning after the whale had landed on our beach I took the ukulele back down to the spot in the sand and just watched the waves as they rolled in—a perfect, unbroken blue. At that time I did not know if the whale was still alive, though we had heard early reports on the news that he was taken to the Clearwater marina. As the sun rose above the waters to my left I thought once again of Melville's vision of the sea at dawn: the sky as a man tense with passion and the water as a new bride just awakening under his steady gaze. The "girdling line" of the horizon shivers with "a soft and tremulous motion." It is, Melville writes, a "throbbing trust."

I took up my uke and slowly strummed. Not a song, just a few chords played slowly, solemnly. It was a hymn really. Life begins here, I thought, looking at the sea, and so does death. The rest is up to us. Suddenly the picture of the rescuers on the beach the day before flooded my mind, and I remembered, with a chuckle, the way the whole crowd, with its precious cargo, lurched to one side as a breaker came in, trying always to stay upright and keep the whale safely in place at the water's edge. I liked Melville's phrase, "throbbing trust." For him it is that sexual moment when the bride will "give her bosom away," the point in her life where desire and love intersect. If we don't feel it we become unresponsive—irresponsible—but when we do we cannot hold back. We are entrusted with all that desires quicken. The swell of the sea, the rise and fall of our songs, and the curve of our fingers serve as reminders.

Rebecca McClanahan

Signs and Wonders

Artillery sounds wake me: car alarms screeching, honking, beeping—you know the drill—and a jackhammer breaking open the sidewalk outside our window. No, not our window, I remind myself. The window of the apartment we've been subletting these past four years—and the lease is almost up again. Another two years? My husband's leaving it up to me. He could live anywhere, he's that kind of guy. Easy, adaptable, like the ducks in the park. Things just roll right off his back.

When we first moved to the city, we couldn't believe how cheap the flowers were. "What a city," we said. "We can buy flowers every week, fill the apartment with them, the bathtub. What a city!" Then we went to the grocery store, and when I saw the prices I started to cry. "How can we possibly afford . . . we'll have to give up . . . oh my God," I shrieked, "what will we eat?"

"We'll just have to eat flowers," he said.

Last week I would have signed a hundred-year lease. After all this *is* the best city in the world, and I was just coming off one of my New York highs, the kind that hits when you least expect it and suddenly it's like first love again, first lust, and you wonder how you could possibly live any-where else. Then a steam pipe bursts, the couple in the apartment above you straps their steel-toed boots back on, you step in a puddle of urine on the subway platform, and some guy with three rings in his nose calls you Bitch and spits on you because—who knows?—you look like his second grade teacher, or some president's wife, or his mother, and you think, *Live another two years in this jackhammering, siren-screaming, piss-puddling city? In someone else's apartment—because who can afford their own? Someone else's bed, plates, forks, spoons?*

Maybe it's the wrong day to decide. Maybe I need some air. Maybe I need a sign. So I go where I always go when I need a sign—the park, and oh look, a day so beautiful you'd gladly pay the universe if it were charging. The leaves on the gingkos are falling as I speak, gold coins upon gold coins. And there in the pond are my geese, my ducks; how I admire them. Look, one is passing up bread crumbs to catch a blossom. He's eating flowers.

Along the promenade are the skaters in their T-shirts: *KickimusMaximus Assimus. Are you talking to me? Fun loving criminal.* One guy's skating backward, a small compact black man so graceful he doesn't need skates, his hip joints are on ball bearings, rolling in one smooth movement. But I know it's harder than it looks; isn't everything? Even for the ducks. If you peek just beneath the surface of the water, you can see their little paddle-wheel feet working, churning. It breaks your heart: little New York ducks have to keep moving all the time.

I stop at a bench beside a ragged guy in a black hat. His shopping cart is plastered with handmade signs. New York is a city of signs: Curb your dog. Curb your dogma. Love your neighbor, your neighbor's dog. His signs are bright red painted on cardboard: *Society of Jesus Christ. Society of Disabled Artists. Call me Ray.*

"So, Ray," I say, "you're an artist?"

He rummages in his cart and pulls out a painting of a bonfire, flames breaking into bloom.

I ask if he's ever seen a flame like that, or is it imagination.

"I like to think about Moses," he says. "I was seeing the burning bush."

My Bible knowledge is rusty, but I'm hungry for a sign. "God spoke to him in the fire, right?"

"That's right."

"In words?" I ask.

"*Through* him. Spirit."

I tell him I used to be in a black gospel choir, but I was only a lowly backup singer.

"Never call yourself lowly," he says.

Closer now, I can see his face beneath the hat: almost handsome. But the smell is ripe, and I won't be staying. Anyway, it's his bench; I'm just subletting. A lowly subletter, I think for an instant, then stop myself. But it *is* his bench, and I should respect that. I don't like it when people come to my gazebo. It took me months to find it, the most beautiful place in the park. There's even a place to fish. I can lean my back against the wooden slats, put my feet up, watch the geese form their predictable patterns. A limited vocabulary can be a good thing: that V, I mean. It's a comfort knowing you can always count on the geese. They won't slip into some ragged U or split into individual I's. It's good to have something to count on, like the gondola that glides through about this time of day, sliding under the bow bridge, the gondolier always singing badly *O Sole Mio*, which is the perfect song for New York, right? O sole mio, oh my sun, my ducks, my forks, oh my anything. Crazy, isn't it? When so much of New York is about we: *O sole wio*.

Still, it's a beautiful spot, my gazebo, and I'd tell you where it is, but what if word got out? A few weeks ago, on my birthday, no less, I couldn't even get a seat. It hadn't been a good week, the odometer of my life was clicking too fast, too many zeros stacking up. Birthdays can do that to you, especially in the city. Especially when you do what we did—wait until middle age to move here. "Like, isn't that backward?" my niece had said. "I mean, like, don't most people go to New York when they're young?"

So I really needed my gazebo that day, but some homeless guy was stretched out the whole length of it, beside a grocery cart with a handmade sign sticking out of the top: *I'm at the peak of my life*. I wondered if the sign was meant for me, if it was trying to tell me something. Because the homeless guy seemed fine with his life, more than fine, actually, lying there in my gazebo, one hand on top of the blanket, the other beneath, and, well, how do I put this delicately? Pleasuring himself. While looking directly into my eyes. Later, walking home, I had to laugh. Maybe at my age I should take it as a compliment, that I could inspire such . . . peaks. How much longer do I have on that meter? A few more clicks, and I'll look like those two ancient women over there, sharing a bag of peanuts like an old married couple.

Ah, the partners we make, the families we create in this city of strangers. Like that big guy on Ninth Avenue—big as a truck, I know you've seen him, he rides that little bike everywhere, with the little basket on the front. In it is one of those Cabbage Patch dolls that were popular a decade or so ago. He dresses her for the weather, secures her in with a seat belt, places a helmet on her head. Such care. And yesterday, beside the carousel, a teenage boy was strapped into a wheelchair, his head lolling, large brown eyes rolling up to the sky, his mouth opening, like a bird's, on a spoon lifted by a large, dark Hispanic woman. Caretakers, they call these women, or caregivers: give, take. You see them all over the city. The two were facing each other—he in his wheelchair, she on the green bench, their knees touching. Steam was rising from the thermos of soup. First she dipped the spoon in the thermos, blowing on it to cool it. Then she put it to her mouth and tested to be sure the soup was safe, that it wouldn't burn him.

When you see things like that you just want to break into lullaby. Sing someone to sleep in this town that never sleeps. Adopt an artist, a duck, a whole Cabbage Patch family. Look, here's a family now, spilling out of my gazebo, with their fishing poles, their buckets and bait, their beautiful children—black eyes, black hair, dimpled hands—the kind of children you want to touch but you can't of course, especially in New York. The little boy is wrestling a bright red carp the color of the fire in Ray's painting, and now his sister is catching the carp in a net. Don't they know it's against the rules posted all over the park? *Catch and release*. Yes, that's it. Catch and release. Look but don't touch. Enjoy for the moment, then let it go—the fiery carp, the brilliant day, the black-eyed children with the dimpled hands, the coins on the gingko trees swirling down, down. Our lives are sublets anyway, and too quickly gone at that. And what better place to live out our leases. Curb your dog, your dogma, love your neighbor, your neighbor's dog. We're at the peak of our lives. O Sole Wio. Catch and release.

Amy Morgenstern

The Etiquette of Being a Breast

You see it is not a matter of doing what is right or seemly; I can assure
you that I am not concerned with the etiquette of being a breast.

Philip Roth, The Breast

A funny thing happened on the way to my breast reduction surgery. I
grew fond of my 32DDs. Not *that* fond, mind you. But fond enough to
memorialize them by parading in pasties for a homemade holiday card:
Season's Greetings from Santa and her Helpers. I have never before sent
out Season's Greeting cards. I have never before worn pasties. I don't even
believe in The Season. But strangely—maybe because it was during The
Season—I felt that the DDs needed to be given their due. Strike up the
band! My hangdog breasts were going down in a blaze of glory. They were
going to be famous, find their way onto mantels and refrigerator doors all
around the country.

"Bend over. Lift them up," my photographer directed me in my red
pumps and itchy, royal blue sequined stars that refused to stick to my
nipples (chewed gum works best), red satin panties, and let's not forget
the Santa hat. Never mind that earlier in the day I had lectured authorita-
tively on Aristotle's ethics or that I had handed back exams graded in my
no-nonsense, stern-professor way. Ivory tower be damned, I was going to
look and behave like a freak show act for thirty minutes of my life! How
else is one to deal with the knowledge that in just twelve hours a relatively small but significant portion of my God-given body was going to
be carted off in plastic sour cream containers to the incinerator? That my
nipple area would be cut out from the surrounding skin, downsized, and
sewn back (with a possible loss of sensation)? That by not loving my body

as it is, I was committing a feminist faux pas? That I would soon be free, free, free of the DDs! How is one to confront the cacophony of excitement, anxiety, and guilt that results from knowing too much, from feeling too many different feelings? My solution: be giddy, and when that runs out, be gaudy. I was going to wear those contradictions on the surface of my skin and record the moment for posterity. For the truth was I did not love my body exactly as it was given to me. And the fact is we do have the technology to change our bodies. Besides, I have always wanted to wear strappy and strapless slinky summer dresses.

Why was I only able to celebrate my breasts by memorializing them? I certainly would not have been so free and flamboyant with the bad boys were they not about to be excised and turned into carbon. On the contrary, ever since the age of ten, I have done my best to hide them under oversized sweaters and T-shirts, to corset them with the world's best bras, to exercise them out of my life. I have done everything I can to ignore them.

Whether on a date or just going about my daily business, the DDs made a regular habit of busting out and taking over. No matter what the venue or situation, they could not help calling attention to themselves in the tackiest ways. They were the obnoxious guys in polyester leisure suits, they were walking disco balls, they were the royal blue sequined stars screaming, "Hey, over here! Watch out, zaftig woman in the house! Got milk?"

I will not miss walking on the beach in a bathing suit four times my normal size. I will not miss having my breasts referred to as "those bad boys" by a young and earnest massage therapist charged with treating my bad-boy induced upper back pain. And I will most certainly be able to live without the uncomfortable experience of first-time intimacy during which each new lover unfailingly reacted with shock and surprise upon the unveiling of the abundance that constituted my entire upper torso. Imagine, one minute the guy is fondling my minimizer-clad body, assuming that he is about to feel his way around an average-proportioned woman, and in the next moment, out pops the Venus of Willendorf. "Wow," he would cry or sigh, sounding out whatever particular mixture of delight and trepidation he felt upon realizing that he was about to have sex with a fertility figure. Damn, I would think, here they go again stealing the show, transporting us from a small Midwestern city to Mesopotamia.

The meaning Freud would have attached to my knockers! As Freud saw it, when a guy wants a woman it is because she reminds him in some way of the breast from which he was weaned too early (for it is *always* too early). This means that a man's erotic journey is really a quest to come home to Mama. Great. But even more frightening to me is Freud's analysis that before being weaned a baby has ambivalent feelings towards his mother; for all he knows, that approaching breast could be nourishing, or it could be poisonous. It's a toss-up, and he has no way of calculating the odds. So the foghorn-sounding signal would go off in his head: pleasure, danger, pleasure, danger! Well if anything could evoke the fear-fantasy of being engorged by womanliness, it was sex with me on top. There I would be, riding my pony while my breasts flailed about, practically smothering the man just as he climaxed (when they weren't smacking against my torso). Pleasure, danger! Shit, if he could just put things into reverse, get off the ride and have the bra back in place, the blouse on, then he would not have to revisit the infantile scenario of loving and loathing his mother. All this Oedipal crap could have been avoided altogether if he had just stuck to porn.

If Freud was right about the psychic power of breasts then I was in big trouble. Of course my breasts did not really *do* anything except show up (and up, and then down, down). No, the problem was the psychic power of my breasts in a culture that confuses *having* breasts with *being* breasts. But fleshy glandular tissue does not a person make. Unless, of course, you are David Kepesh, novelist Philip Roth's protagonist, the poor soul who one day finds himself strung out on a hammock in a hospital because he has been transformed into a 155-pound female breast. In Kepesh's case, however, the confusion between having a breast and being a breast is *not* a mistake; as far as the story is concerned, he really is a breast. Even so, David Kepesh finds his new appearance maddening. For in addition to all of the medical and technical difficulties his new bodily form presents, and besides the fact that he is "no longer the easiest person to buy a present for," his life is now marred by the fact that no one can get past his mammariness and simply see him as a person. No one—not his analyst, his father, his girlfriend, and certainly not his doctors—now gives a shit about the fact that he was (is?) a professor of literature, a lover, a son, a friend, a neighbor, a customer, a client. He is now just a breast.

I could relate to David Kepesh's frustration. From early adolescence on I have been suffering the feeling that despite my preferences, talents, and annoying qualities, I was being perceived by those outside of my immediate social circle as one big breast. "Here she comes, The Body," the boys in summer camp were rumored to have said about me. Me? The Body? At that age I was worrying about algebra, reading like there was no tomorrow, suffering from migraine headaches (yes, at the age of fourteen), watching *General Hospital,* and fighting off the bad hair days that afflicted my curly mop. What did The Body have to do with me? I had no idea. To me, I was a person—a subject seeing into the world, not an object of desire. And yet from the moment I developed breasts it could have been me, and not David Kepesh, whom his shrink addresses in the effort to counter incredulity at his new, uninvited identity. "You are not mad," states Dr. Klinger, "You are not suffering from a delusion—or certainly haven't been, up till now. You are a breast of sorts." Dr. Klinger was right. No David Kepesh, no Kafkaesque pretense, and yet I was yoked into the etiquette of being a breast. Of sorts.

When Kepesh announces to the reader that he is not concerned with the etiquette of being a breast, he is telling us that he is going to fight the acute case of femininity he is afflicted with and hold onto his identity as a person. I call his affliction "femininity" because in the end, and notwithstanding its charms (the best of which is the license to shop unremittingly for shoes), femininity is not about whether you wear lipstick or how you dress or whether you have breasts or a vagina or a uterus. It is not about how you look on the outside or on the inside. It is about having your identity usurped by a body part, by an attribute, in such a way that your dignity is ripped from you as well. Femininity is metonymic logic gone too far.

In his effort to fight for his dignity despite the overwhelming pressures of femininity, David Kepesh reminded me of the character, Saga, in the Swedish coming-of-age film, *My Life as a Dog,* who notes with regret that her budding breasts are beginning to show. "Look, I'm getting breasts," she says to her new friend Ingemar, the film's charmingly mischievous young male protagonist. "It's awful. Jesus, they're really swelling out. Can you see? I'll be kicked off the team. I know I will." Saga first appears in the film as she sideswipes Ingemar on the soccer field and steals the ball. She next appears as a fierce boxer among the village kids. Along with the viewer, Ingemar is not even initially aware that Saga is a girl; she is simply a venerable rival. Her personality, her possibilities, are open. But Saga knows that once her breasts are "sighted" she will be viewed not as the star athlete of the all-boys village soccer team but as a spectacle—as the cool teammate who was thought to be a boy but instead has tits. Saga is acutely aware that her world is about to shrink, dramatically. In one scene she is shown avoiding a ritual public shirt exchange between teams. Shoving off a boy attempting to take off her shirt—furious and vulnerable—she refuses to relinquish what she knows she will inevitably lose: the freedom to be competitive and surly, to showcase her talent without apology. Once "outed" as a girl, Saga's rigor and egoistic intensity will count against her. So when she laments out loud that her burgeoning bosom will radically alter the terms of her life as *she* has thus far chosen to live it, the sympathetic Ingemar suggests she find a way to hide them. They proceed to bind them with a scarf. "Can you see them?" Saga asks. "No, they're invisible," Ingemar replies. Saga looks at herself in the mirror and takes a boxer stance. The problem is solved, at least temporarily.

When I watched Saga bind her breasts I felt that she and I saw things in the same way. I understood her fear. Watching Saga I was brought back to seventh-grade science class and the bizarrely wrathful humor of John Hassler, the popular naughty boy of our grade. We could be at the Bunsen burner, learning about the law of thermodynamics or anxiously awaiting an exam; it did not matter. Everything reminded him of my tits, and he made these associations—no matter how far-fetched—loud and clear. John Hassler had brown straight hair with natural golden highlights that feathered back perfectly. Aside from appearing a little lanky in his Levi's and flannel shirts, he was beautiful. At least that is what I thought every night as I lay in bed fantasizing about that feathered hair burrowing into my afro, those lanky fingers latched onto my belt loops as he kissed me on the lips, darting his tongue right into my braces, not giving a damn. In my dreams, all he cared about was my forgiving him for wondering out loud in class about such things as how it would look if my tits were squashed or stretched or wrapped around my neck. The entire class would laugh. And then I—feeling that the only other alternative was to cry—would laugh too. I didn't know what else to do. I remember feeling like a mink caught in a trap, betrayed by everyone and everything in my immediate environment. I remember feeling my skin crawl in hot humiliation.

At any rate, Saga and I knew each other. We imagined our sprouting bodies being sucked into the vortex of femininity, swirling and swirling amid *Seventeen* magazines, low-fat foods, bikini line depilatories, pink puffy bridesmaid dresses, birds of prey. We saw breasts as barriers to pursuing the fullest range of human possibilities. Breasts spelled some pending sacrifice for another: of smarts for desirability, pleasure for respectability, ambition for children, meals for the little black dress, of breathing space. Saga and I suspected that once betraying the slightest hint of womanhood, our bodies (and our souls) might be spun into a galaxy of endless French gardens featuring grid after topiary grid of tame bush. But we were not ready to enter into a world uncarved by us, a world in which too many important decisions had already been made. We were digging our heels in at the threshold, like ancient women warriors did long before our time.

Ancient chroniclers such as Herodotus and Plutarch tell of Amazon warriors living during the Bronze Age near the Black Sea who were legendary for searing off the right breast to better aim a bow and arrow. Skilled equestrians, these women could shoot arrows on horseback as easily and accurately as on foot. If need be they could spin around and shoot while riding backward. They could vault themselves onto their horses with their spears. They chose and discarded lovers as they pleased, procreated when they needed to. They exiled or crippled unruly boys. They were cool and beautiful, disarmingly so. Lore has it that when the ancient Greek "hero" Bellerophon bombarded them with arrows and boulders from his flying horse (a significant advantage, the ancient equivalent of a B-52 bomber), they resisted him for eight days. When Heracles attacks Amazonia in order to steal Queen Hippolyte's golden girdle, they mercilessly slayed many of his soldiers on the beach before capitulating. And when they found themselves prisoners of war on a Greek ship they took it over. So what if they had no seafaring skills? So resourceful were they that when the ship drifted into the shores of foreign Scythia, they found the local men, fucked them, and then ran off with these men (and their inheritances!). When Theseus showed up in Amazonia, seduced Queen Antiope, and whisked her away to patriarchal Athens, her sisters threw a fit and laid siege on Athens for a solid four months. The Amazons lost, but not without heavy Athenian casualties, not without honor, and not without the story of this battle— so significant was it to the Greek imagination, as significant as the Persian War—being etched into the Parthenon walls.

Perhaps the most impressive and saddest story of an Amazon warrior is that of Penthesilea. In the tenth year of the Trojan War, Penthesilea showed up miraculously to help Troy. This was Troy's darkest hour, as Hektor had just been killed by Achilles. Penthesilea was lauded and celebrated as a savior, and she played the part well. A big talker, she vowed to drive the Greeks back, to challenge Achilles to single combat, and to "leave him groveling in his own entrails." She warmed up by slaying a bunch of Greek soldiers, disemboweling some, pinning others to the earth with her spear, trampling others with her horse. She was hell-bent on *winning*. But Achilles' shield deflected her blows; he managed to strike her in the breast and pin her to her horse—then fell in love with her once she was dead. Penthesilea lost (Achilles did, too, in a way), but she went down as a worthy opponent, not a victim.

The Amazon warrior was my kind of woman. She knew how to go for what she wanted, directly, without any manipulative, she-devil crap. She did not accept loss. There are conflicting versions about how and why Amazonian society arose. Some say the original Amazons killed their husbands for repeatedly raping them and thereafter excluded men from the fold. Some say they took up arms to avenge the treacherous deaths of their husbands at the hands of enemies. Others think they fought off foreign men who tried to move in when their husbands went off to war and failed to return. Still others think the Amazons are pure myth, that they are a fabrication of the ancient Greek imagination serving two purposes: to scare Greek women into remaining barefoot and pregnant and to provide a way for men to get off on outlaw women. But whether fact or fantasy, and whether a breast was really seared off or not, the message of the Amazon body is clear: big breasts get in the way of a good fight. Just look at the statues of the Amazon patron goddess Artemis. No larger than a B-cup. Now if Amazon warriors shaped their bodies for the sake of their freedom, why couldn't I?

My breasts were a part of my body, a part of me. And yet I felt they betrayed me at almost every turn. They broke up the unity of *my* fantasy about myself. In my mind I was a compact locus of force dashing around on horseback, bow and arrow on hand, fighting off pigs like Hercules. I was supposed to shield the honor of my warrior-harlot sisters, defend territory whenever territory needed to be defended. In the fashion of Penthesilea, I was supposed to be a worthy *opponent*, not a victim. I was not supposed to be perceived as a diabolical temptress like Helen whose loyalty to men more powerful than she is never certain, nor as the mother Mary whose loyalty to a man more powerful than she borders, quite frankly, on the canine. In fact, of all the archetypes available, the suffering maternal figure is exactly what I want my body to defy. For this reason I do not want my relations with men, with anyone for that matter, to be arbitrated by how emphatically my body announces its capacity to lactate. Which is why I frown upon breast augmentation. Not that silicone implants have anything to do with the capacity to lactate. But they do enhance the *announcement* of this capacity. And that announcement invites all sorts of other assumptions—such as my innate nurturing, or of all things, my virginity. (Whoever thought of that winning combination, the virgin mother, really should be sued.)

Besides, I am just not a suckling kind of woman. Other than being slightly persuaded by the high it is supposed to provide, I can think of few things less appealing than having a babe chomping away at my teat for months, or years. I know: breast-feeding is natural and beautiful. It is an all-around organic experience. Well, some of us like McDonald's French fries and fake fur and all sorts of artificial stuff. And some of us think that more lip service than honor is accorded mothers, even in this modern age. When I think about the fact, for example, that Andrea Yates's history of hallucinations, postpartum psychoses, and suicide attempts did not deter her husband from impregnating her a *fifth* time—against their doctor's recommendation—nor from insisting that she home school their children, I want to let out a thunderous warrior cry: We are not in Bethlehem! There are no more mangers! Nor are we in seventeenth-century Amsterdam, the time during which the tasks of motherhood and home schooling were sealed together in images of maternal, domestic piety. From art to literature, images abound of Dutch women sitting by the hearth and not only suckling their young but also educating them in the ways of virtue and modesty. It is a wonder that Rusty Yates did not have Andrea churning butter, frying herring, and trotting around in wooden shoes. For it is this idealized and sentimentalized model of motherhood that Rusty Yates pressed upon Andrea, and it was in the name of this model that a Texas jury thought to demonize her rather than to question how she was set up to fail miserably at motherhood.

This idealized and sentimentalized model of motherhood was enough to drive even someone as sane as author Adrienne Rich to record her feelings of "murderous alternation" between love and violence as a young, full-time mother. Which is why I fear breast-feeding. For no matter how irrational and exaggerated my feelings may be, this is the sequence of events as I see them: I'll have a baby. I will breast-feed. The next thing I know I'll be home schooling. Then I'll find myself understanding the feelings that coursed through the defeated and demented soul of Andrea Yates, and soon after I'll be herding the kids into the bathtub. As far as I can tell, in a society that denies the despair that lurks at the heart of full-time motherhood, breast-feeding could very well lead to jail. So until our mainstream vision of motherhood—of *parenting*, really—leaps out of a time warp and into the twenty-first century, I'll stick with the bow and arrow.

I recognize that the problem of protruding organs is not limited to women. I ran into a former lover a few months ago who, upon learning of my breast reduction surgery, confessed that he was contemplating a penis reduction because his large member hindered his lap swimming. "It's like a rudder," he proclaimed. "It steers me this way, it steers me that way, it slows me down." I swear this story is true. And I can believe that in certain situations his penis does act like a rudder propelling him toward all sorts of odd corners of the universe. Now mind you, this guy is weird. And truth be told, my primary motivation for sleeping with him was that he reminded me of Mickey Rourke's rendition of Charles Bukowski in *Barfly*. Why I was living out a fantasy of sleeping with a guy who recalled an aggressive, childish actor portraying a talented but self-destructive drunk is the subject of yet another essay. The moral of *this* story, however, is that, rare as it may occur, even big dicks can get in the way.

In one way "Mickey" and I were in a similar situation. We were both willing to trade the social clout our physique granted for some personal, physical freedom. But the similarity ends there. Mickey's grand member did nothing but open things up for him, so to speak. Getting a penis reduction would have been like a rich person throwing away money. My grand mammaries, on the other hand, were like counterfeit cash in a world of real currency. They got me appreciative looks, they got me dates (*first* dates). But once it was discovered that real, live cognition came with the cleavage (Pleasure! Danger!), more often than not my play money was handed back, and the aura of Eros dissipated into thin, thin air. For it turns out that he wanted to fuck Pamela Anderson while I was planning the seduction scene by whipping out my dissertation's table of contents.

My experience is that it is a rare man who gets beyond my boobs and wraps his brain around my mind, the part of my body *I* find most sexy.

Whether we like it or not, and unless we self-consciously use our bodies to question and resist these stories, they will not escape the dominant narrative flow. This is because a body houses meanings that predate its particular existence. Bodies speak. From a historical standpoint. As Aristotle writes, we are *zoon logon echon*, life with language. We reflect ourselves to ourselves through language in a variety of ways in order to give meaning to our existence. The Odyssey is such a story. The Book of Genesis is such a story. Femininity is such a story. Our bodies by default repeat these stories, if only for the reason that these narratives predate and loom larger than our particular existence. My large breasts, for example, repeated the story about womanhood that happened to gain political power and historical prominence: that a woman's value lies in the capacity to bear children and that this capacity is not very valuable. My surgery was one way to resist, to reposition my body so that it became an active interlocutor of, and not merely a passive vessel for, the grip of femininity, the vise of compulsory reproduction. This was a drastic move (although it could have been more drastic; had I persisted in finding a willing surgeon, and had I thought that I might still have a chance at getting a date, I would have eliminated them altogether). It is, however, by no means the only path of resistance. Wearing baby doll dresses and combat boots is one way. Dressing in drag or wearing men's cologne is another. Not giving a shit (if you really *don't* give a shit) is yet one more option. The possibilities for creating new bodily truths are endless.

The artist Orlan understands well the need for new bodily truths. Since 1987 she has undergone a series of cosmetic surgery procedures, all of which have been videotaped or broadcast live, each deliberately staged with a unique theme and accompanying props. When she alters her face, it is to resemble mythical beauties; she has sought, for example, the forehead of the Mona Lisa and the mouth of Boucher's Europa. She costumes herself, her assistants, her surgeon, and the surgical team. During the procedure, while under local anesthesia, she reads philosophical and literary texts, converses with cohorts or audience members, laughs while her surgeon slices open her lips or removes an ear. At every stage Orlan is in control. In Orlan's world the operating room has become a theatrical laboratory for testing the boundaries of personal identity. As she sees it, if used imaginatively and artfully as a way of questioning and altering the ordinary, cosmetic surgery can move beyond a force for social control into a powerful form of self-portraiture. In such a world my decision to have cosmetic surgery need not be caught at the crossroads between the feminist mandate to love my body and the mainstream pressure to loathe my body, a crude dichotomy that leaves little leeway for forging new forms of identity and beauty.

I have seen a short clip of Orlan's ninth operation. In this scene she receives injections of local anesthesia followed by incisions of the surgeon's knife into the skin between her left ear and cheekbone. We see the surgeon's scissors cutting underneath the cheek skin, scraping vigorously from the inside, poking the skin into the air. We can hear what is going on; if we close our eyes, it sounds like hedges being clipped. Orlan hears, too, yet she lies there in peace. As far as she is concerned the discomfort felt upon witnessing her performance is *our* problem, not hers. The last thing Orlan does is show us what we want or expect to see. So she takes us into a medical operating room—a space where technology blurs the borders between mind, body, artifice, and nature—to get us to confront the fact that a face is fragmented and flayed before it is reconfigured, that beauty touches the grotesque. Orlan knows that the border between beauty and monstrosity is the true source of imagination. By bringing us to this border, she intends to force our fantasies onto new paths. The experience of viewing her art is therefore not meant to comfort or entertain. It is meant to fascinate and disgust.

Orlan's art is warrior-art because through it she gives us a worthy opponent dispatched to challenge norms that no longer make sense to her—like the mandate not to tamper with our God-given bodies, or the assumption that this tampering is always aimed at a feminine (and not an individual woman's) ideal, or the idea that beauty and identity depend on stasis. Orlan knows that the source of beauty is difference, and it is for this reason that she positions herself as a self-promoting, self-mutating monstrosity. Orlan is always changing in ways neither we nor she can foresee, always leaping into new territory. And she asks us to come with her to the frontier. She knows that her personality, her possibilities, are open, and she wears this knowledge flamboyantly on her skin. Although small fry compared to hers, my Season's Greeting stunt was nonetheless a way of saying that I was not only at the brink of an important transformation, I was at the helm. For the first time I was in charge of the story of my breasts. I chose the setting and the costume. I was aware of the irony involved in celebrating my breasts just before they were about to be fragmented, flayed, and reconfigured. I knew how silly and potentially risky it was for a Jewish philosophy professor at a Catholic university to pose in a cream puff picture. It was a pleasure/danger scenario of my own devising.

When I returned from surgery I immediately looked in the mirror and made a major discovery: I have ribs. Next I saw my stitched and stapled Raggedy Ann breasts and thought: freedom. I wanted to find my surgeon and hug him. I don't know if it was due to my post-anesthetic haze or not, but during my recovery I frequently entertained the idea of asking him out on a date, just for the Pygmalion thrill. Now fully recovered, scars have replaced the staples and stitches. I balk at the suggestion of having these scars removed. They are indications that my body has its own complex history in relation to the larger narratives of gender. Strange as it may seem, I would feel more comfortable parading naked among strangers with my smaller, scarred breasts than with the uncut DDs.

Better poised to dispense with the etiquette of being a breast, I can now simply enjoy having breasts. I can enjoy unfettered, unfloppy, on-top sex (on the rare occasions that I actually get laid), I am an easier person to buy a present for, and most important, I can frolic about without a bra. Whether this thirty-six-year-old, perimenopausal body looks good in a halter-top is beside the point. The point is that I *feel* good in a halter-top. Wearing strappy and strapless summer dresses gives *me* pleasure. It reminds me of when I first switched my bed sheets from the crisp polyester blend ones to the soft, T-shirt material ones. When I go braless, I feel the breezy caress of silk, of worn-washed cotton, of cashmere—of fabric unfurling itself on my skin, over my still sensitive nipples.

Kim Barnes

The Clearwater

I take the river a step at a time. My feet slide from the shoulders of rock; my toes wedge between boulders. I am timid about this, moving out toward center, where the water is deepest, where the big fish might lie.

Here, at Lenore, the Clearwater is not easy. Too wide to cast from shore, too swift, too pocked with hidden currents and sudden holes. I go at it anyway, still without waders, determined to find my place of stability, the water at my belly, my thighs numbing with cold.

My husband fishes below me. On shore, our daughter and son dig pools in the sand. I watch as they flash in the sun, and I feel a rush of gratitude, the joy of living only minutes from water, the same water my brother and I played in as children. It is as though I am reliving my own young life, there on the banks of the Clearwater, as though I exist in two dimensions and know the pleasure of each—the child's pure delight in the moment; the woman's recognition of continuance, of nostalgia, of the water around her and the sun on her face.

I choose a fly I think the fish might favor, its color the color of the day's light and leaves and wings. I praise its tufts and feathers, its hackle and tail. I load the line, thinking not of the S I must make through air but of the place above and where the water eddies, the V above whitecaps, the purl below stone.

I do not think of the line or the fly or the fish as much as I think about the water moving against and around me, how the sky fills my eyes and the noise-that-isn't fills my ears—the movement of everything around me like the hum of just-waking or sleep, blood-rush, dream-rush, the darkness coming on, air.

I forget to watch for the fish to strike, forget to note the catch, the spin, the sinking. I pull the line in, let it loop at my waist, sing it out again, and again. The trout will rise, or they won't. The nubbin of fur and thread will turn to caddis, black any, stone fly, bee, or it will simply settle on the water and remain a human's fancy. Either way, it's magic to me, and so I stay until my feet are no longer my own but part of the river's bed. How can I move them? How can I feel my way back to shore, where my family is calling that it's time to go home? They are hungry, and the shadows have taken the canyon. They are cold.

From my place in the water, they seem distant to me. I must seem like a fool, numb to my ribcage, no fish to show. But I am here in the river, half-in, half-out, a wader of two worlds. I smile. I wave. I am where nothing can reach me.

North Fork, Middle Fork, South Fork, Main: see how the flow of the sounds is smooth, so lovely. The rivers themselves flow together this way, spilling down from the mountains. They drain the north Idaho land my father and others like him logged and loved so easily in the years before it seemed to matter.

And now it matters and we all know it, though we may come to our understanding in different ways. The timber companies worry about access and shareholders' profit; the mills worry about viability and foreign markets; the loggers worry about the land and life they know and ways to feed their families; the foresters worry about the politicians; the politicians worry about the timber companies; the environmentalists, some more, some less than radical, worry about the whole of it. Meanwhile, while the sales are being staked and the trees are being spiked, the land slumps from beneath its covering of burned slash and razored stumps, slides off the hills and down the draws, sloughs off its dying skin like an animal readying itself for another season.

And all of it moves toward water. Always, the run-off of rain, the soil it carries, the ash and cinder, the dry bones of trees. Maybe this is why I think of water as woman: it takes what it can, takes the land in its lap, holds the eggs in its belly.

Here, where I live with my husband and children above the Main Clearwater at Lenore, twelve miles from where the forks have all come together, we see the movement of land in the water's flow. Spring thaw, and the trees come fully rooted, ungrounded by the wash of high current. Old log jams from previous floods break loose; new ones pile against the bridge footings and small islands. Each becomes a nest of lost things: fishing lures, loops of rope, men's undershirts, women's shoes.

I wonder, sometimes, if my own life's mementos are contained in those tangles, perhaps a hair barrette I lost while fishing Reeds Creek, or one of my mother's pie tins that my brother and I used to pan for gold. Or the tree itself fallen from the riverbank I sat on as a child, searching for the mussel shells we called angel's wings, though they were mahogany brown and often broken.

What the river takes, the river gives, and so it is with my life here. Each hour I spend with my feet near water, I feel more deeply rooted; the further I get away, the less sure I am of my place in the world. For each of us, there must be this one thing, and for me it is the river. Not just the river, but the composition that begins as the North Fork and flows into the Main. I have known this river from its feeding waters to its mouth where it meets and becomes the Snake. I have known it before the dams, and after. I have known it as a child knows water, have known it as a lover knows water, and now as a mother knows and recognizes water as she watches her own children who are bent at the waist, leaning forward to bring up the sandy wings.

I am closest to the Clearwater when I am closest to its origins, and to my own. Reeds Creek, Orofino Creek, Weitas Creek, Deer Creek, the Musselshell—they feed the river as the river feeds me. It has taken me longer to feel intimate with the stretch of river that curves into *omega* below our house. I watch it each day, uneasy with its width and deep holes. I realize, too, that I distrust this length of the river because it no longer moves of its own volition: Dworshak Dam controls a great part of it now. The North Fork, the river I once knew as a tree-lined stream the color of turquoise, now ends in a man-made reservoir covering over fifty miles of land that was first logged for its timber before being flooded. The river bulges at its base, its narrower neck seemingly unaffected by the distant, concrete obstruction. People drive northeast for hours to reach the Bungalow, Aquarius—places where the water remains swift and the fish are often native.

But I know better. The river's betrayal sometimes shames me, the way it carries on as though what it travels toward is not a state of near stasis, depositing sludge along miles of rip-rap dikes, piling its dross against the pylons and locks and turbines. It cannot rid itself of what it is given, cannot carry its silt and timber and ash to the mouth of the ocean where it can be broken down, taken to great depths, washed and sifted into sand and dirt. Instead, the silt falls from the slow current, depositing itself in great layers, narrowing the river's channel. The river becomes murky, the flat color of pewter. The trout are replaced by bottom-feeders, lovers of warm water. Every year, the Corps of Engineers sponsors a trash-fish derby, paying the fishermen to catch and kill what their dams have spawned.

Like so many others who love this land, it has taken me some time to understand that the place—the rivers and streams, the forests and mountains and high meadows—does not absorb but reflects what we bring to it. Perhaps what I see in the river is some mirror of the contradictions that make up my own life—the calm surface, the seeming freedom. Certainly, the river is a metaphor for memory. "I am everywhere I ever was," Stegner wrote, and so it is with the river—water and rock, metal and mineral, stick and bone, trout-flash and deer-lick. Perpetual, even in the face of destruction, I think, even as I read the sad stories of pollution and poisoning, fish-kill and disease. Perpetual because the rain must fall and the mountains must accept and the water must run toward oceans. A comfort, knowing that the amount of water in our world never changes, that there is never any more nor any less, only the same and in various forms: ice, liquid, steam. I trust that water will withstand, given its basic demands— to fall, to move, to rise, to fall again.

This, then, may be my final recognition: the inevitability of movement. We slow, we go forward. We age. We rise to greet each morning. We fall into sleep each night. Constant as rain, perpetuated in death and birth and rebirth.

It has taken me time to understand the need I feel to be consumed by the river. Raised a stoic, I am seldom given to need. Need is a weakness, a loss of control, the Achilles' heel of human existence. My connection to the river is complicated by its pull; I resent the power it possesses to draw me. Yet I want its sound in my ears, its smell, its taste. I want to be immersed—my hands, my feet, my hips. Like all seductions, it necessitates surrender.

I am learning to let go.

I bring to the river my love and those that I choose to love. I bring to it my child's memories and my woman's life. I bring to it hunger but always joy, for whatever it is that weighs on me dissipates in those few miles between our house in the canyon and the water's edge.

I understand how water can become something grim, how it can rise and take and swirl and drown. How it can become something to fight against, something to resist. The dam on the North Fork, the largest of its kind, was not built for electricity or simple recreation, they say, but for flood control in Portland, four hundred miles west.

There's less flooding now, although three springs ago, in 1996, not even the dams could keep pace when the temperatures rose and the snowmelt came down with rain. We watched from our house above the river, stranded between washed-out roads, watched the roofs and porches, the dead cows and refrigerators and lawn chairs, the still-intact trailer house that slammed against the Lenore Bridge.

How can I cheer such destruction? For that is what I felt, an overwhelming sense of boosterism. I wanted the river to win in some essential way, wanted to see it rise up and lash out, pull down the dams and drain the reservoirs, ferry away the docks and cleanse itself of silt. I wanted it to show a god's righteous anger, a larger reflection of my own frustration and resentment.

I didn't mind then, that we couldn't get out. My husband had made a last, grand effort to snatch our children from their school in Orofino twenty miles east, hauling them back over bench roads not yet torn away by the massive run-off, roads that crumbled and disappeared behind them. Other rural parents with children in school were not so lucky; it would be a week before any travel was allowed in or out, except by helicopter. Our family was together, protected by our place high on the canyon wall. We had food, water, wood. We had days ahead of us without school or teaching, weeks before the roads would be cleared, and now the sun that had started the rain was back out and warming the air into spring.

We packed sandwiches and cookies, cheese and crackers and a fine bottle of red wine. We hiked to where we could watch Big Eddy, the place where the river curled against itself and created an enormous back current that caught and held the debris. While the river ran thick with trees and fence posts, goat huts and wallpapered sheeting, we ate and drank and gathered ladybugs for our garden. Certain logs were red with their hatching, their coming out of hibernation. We scooped them up in handfuls and carried them in bundles made of paper towels and candy wrappers. Their odor was strong, dry, astringent—a promise of summer.

We watched a jetboat make its way down the river. Foolish, we thought, for risking such danger. The river was running at a near-record high; the water was choked with flotsam, some larger than the boat itself. The two men inside were not wearing life jackets, and I shook my head. What were they thinking?

The boat pulled in at a smaller eddy downstream, and there we saw what they followed: a large raft of finished lumber, floated loose from the mill at Orofino. Scavengers' rights. If they were willing to risk for it, the lumber was theirs.

One man kept the helm while the other bent over the gunnels to grab the wood. They pulled it onto the boat's bow one plank at a time until the craft sat low in the already threatening water. We held our breath, knowing that if they went over or capsized, we could do nothing but watch.

They loaded the wood. They let the current swing them about, turn them upstream. They made their way slowly, navigating through tangles of barbed wire still stapled to barn doors, past trees three times the length of their boat. They had the booty. They were gone.

I couldn't imagine such nonsense, such greed. What desperation could bring on the willingness to risk so much for so little? I felt content, driven by nothing other than the warmth on my shoulders and the love I felt for this land and my husband and daughter and son, who gathered around me to show what they had found: a mantid's egg case, triangular and strangely textured, like meringue hardened and fired to a ceramic glaze. We would take it home as well and put it in the garden, where it would hatch its eaters of grasshoppers and aphids.

I must have believed, then, that it was love that would see me through the long hours of darkness, that would keep me grounded during the wild summer heat. I must have believed that, like the river, what we love may surge and wane but remains nonetheless constant, giving, taking, carrying on.

And doesn't it? Perhaps it is we who fail love, refusing to allow its seduction, its pull and sway. Love is a river we stop into, like the waters of baptismal rebirth. We close our eyes. We bow our heads. We allow ourselves to be taken as the water closes over our heads. For that moment, we must believe.

"I don't think we can make it." I looked at what was left of the road, stretching down before me into a dusk of low tress.

My daughter and son moaned. After a day of writing, I had picked them up from the sitter's in Orofino, promising a late afternoon along the river. My husband was in the mountains near McCall, hiking the upper lakes, safe with friends he'd known since high school. There was a place I'd heard of, just down some side road, where Ford's Creek met the river, a place with sand and stiller water, where Jordan and Jace could swim and I could spread my blanket and think. The stretch of river we were after mattered to me: it was a section of the last few miles of the Main Clearwater, the last free-flowing water between the headwaters and the ocean.

I needed the river in a way I had not only hours before. It wasn't fishing I was after. I was sour with bad news, begrudging even the rod, line and fly their pacification. That afternoon, I'd gotten a phone call from across the country and learned that our close friends' marriage was in sudden and serious peril, rocked by confession of a particularly insidious spate of infidelity. The levels of betrayal had shocked me, and the narrative of contentment and ongoing friendship that I had trusted was suddenly gone.

The anger that I felt surprised me. I am not comfortable with anger, having been taught from the cradle that anger, like other unmanageable emotions, is best kept under lock and key, somewhere in the heart's deepest chamber. The river would help, sweep away the confusion of emotions with its own ordered chaos. The river would help me find my footing, my point of rest.

But now this: I'd chosen the wrong road. Even after having made the decision to put the car into reverse and back our way out of the ravine, we were going nowhere. The tires of the front-wheel drive Toyota spun and chattered in the gravel, unable to push the weight of the car up such a steep incline. The dirt and basalt-studded bank rose close on my left; the road crumbled away on my right, slumping into a gully of black locust, poison ivy, blackberry brambles thick with thorns.

"*Now* what." I said it in the way my mother always had. Fatalism. Tired resignation.

I eased the clutch, tried again. Nothing but smoke and the bitter smell of burning rubber.

"I think we'd better get out of the car," Jace said. At seven, he's the cautious one, always sensing the adult's boundless capacity for error.

"No," I said. "It's okay. Let's just go on down. We can turn around at the bottom." I had no idea if this were true, but my choice was to keep going or for us all to begin the long walk back to town for a tow-truck. I also felt a kind of apathy: what was the worst that could happen? The river was only five hundred yards away. We'd find our way out.

What we found instead was an increasingly narrow once-road. I saw that, for years, the rain had washed down the path scraped from the hillside, taking what dirt remained with it to the river. What was left was a deep schism that forked and meandered its way around rocks too large to be moved. I concentrated on riding the ruts' shoulders until there was no rut to straddle but only a series of woven ditches. I kept thinking it would get better, that the road would even out. That *someone* had made it down here because the vegetation was scraped from the center. I kept wishing for the Suburban with its high clearance and granny gear, but I doubted that the path we traveled would have allowed its girth.

We bounced over boulders the size of basketballs. The skidplate caught and dragged. Jordan and Jace whimpered in the backseat. I tried to act as though this were nearly normal, to be expected. If I stayed calm, in control, they would feel safe.

"Mom, please." Jordan had her hand on the door handle, as though she meant to jump.

"We're almost there," I said. "We'll get to the river and be glad." We were far into the darkness of trees now, the yellow pine and locust, the dense undergrowth of vine maple. I jostled the car around a corner, then stopped. I could see ahead to where the road leveled off, where sunlight broke through. Between us and that point of flat ground was a final pitch downward, where the road hooked a ninety-degree right angle. The bigger problem was that the trail became narrower still, hedged in by the bank on the left and, on the right, an old tanker truck settled into a bog of brambles.

I examined my passage. A boulder twice the size of our car protruded like a tumor from the eight-foot dirt bank. The abandoned tanker, its red paint faded to rust, was just as intractable: steel and stone, and only the space of a small car between them.

If I stop here, I thought, the tow-truck might be able to reach us. But I had begun to doubt the plausibility of such a rescue, given the right turns and narrow corridor down which we had traveled.

I thought cable, winch, but could not imagine the logistics of being dragged backwards from the ravine without damaging the car beyond repair.

"Mom?" my son's voice quavered.

"What?" I was snappish, weighing our chances, calculating the risk.

"Can't we just walk from here?"

I thought of the brambles, the probability of rattlesnakes, what unseen dangers might wait around the corner.

"Just hang on." I inched the car toward the passage, like Odysseus steering his ship through the straits. I sucked in and held my breath, giving the air what room I could. One scrape and we were through and bumped into the clearing.

Whoops and hollers from the backseat. "We made it!" Jace shouted. Jordan crowed. I stopped the car, got out and circled it twice, looking for damage. Nothing but a few shallow scratches. No dripping oil. The muffler remained miraculously intact.

"Watch for snakes. Wait for me." I gathered our water bottles and bag of sandwiches, taking in the lay of the land. Between us and the river was the railroad track, built high on its ridge of rock. To the left, I saw remnants of a gold mine, its entryway framed in old timbers. To my right was a settling pond, green with algae. As we began our short walk, two blue herons rose from the still water, awkward on their wings.

There was a game trail that we followed to the tracks and over. What we found was a long beach of rocks and a smaller one of sand. The children had all but forgotten the trauma of our trip and stripped themselves of shoes and socks before wading in. I felt the heat, then, the sweat gone sticky at my collar and waist.

I walked a few yards upstream, found a rock close to water, where I could dangle my feet and keep an eye on my son and daughter. I tried not to think of the sun's low slant, the hard way out. I tried not to hear what I was thinking: there *is* no way out of here except to leave the car and walk. No way I could make that first climb and twist between the rock and truck.

I closed my eyes. The river filled my ears, and I began to float with the sound. I needed to find something to dislodge the fear—not only of the trek ahead of us, but the fear that had come while listening to my friend's grieving. It could happen, any time, any place, to anyone. One minute, you're on solid ground, the next moment the earth has cracked open beneath you. You get up in the morning and look in the mirror and tell yourself what the day will consist of, and then the light jerks sideways and you are left falling through the dark.

Behind me, a dog barked. I came back to my vision slowly, not willing to give up the cool place behind my eyes, the blindness, the deafness of water.

I turned to see a large yellow Lab, and then an older man walking the tracks. He stopped and raised his hand in acknowledgment of our presence. I hesitated, suddenly aware of another danger: a woman, two children, alone.

He could help us, I thought. He might live close by, have a tractor or winch. I thought, I can't let him know we're stuck here, can't let him see how vulnerable we are.

"How's it going?" he yelled.

I nodded and gave him a thumb's up. He stood for a long time, and I thought he might decide to walk toward us. And then what? For all I knew he was one of my father's old logging friends. For all I knew, he was a transient bent on some evil.

He stayed on the track, and I watched him disappear around the bend. There was too much to be afraid of, too much to fear. I rose and waded the rocks toward my children, suddenly distrusting even the river, its currents here strange and unpredictable.

They were making a catch basin for the small minnows they caught in the net of their hands. They hardly noticed my presence. I should have them gather their things, I thought, hustle them toward the car, or herd them in front of me up the rag of road, where we could walk the asphalt into town. It would take hours, I knew, hours into dusk, a woman and two children on a rural road where few cars traveled after dinner. I could hear my mother's scolding voice, the one I have known all my life, consistent through all my unwomanly adventures and forays: "What in the world were you thinking? What could have made you take such a risk?"

Risk. I looked across the river, where Highway 12 tied east to west. Cars flicked through the trees, distant and quick. I knew the benefits of being where I was: the water comforted me, the sand and rock and cottonwood leaves turning golden in the last rays of the sun. I needed this, often and sometimes desperately. I believed, too, that my children were made better by such a landscape, that every handful of water they dipped from the river was an hour they would later remember as good.

But why here? Why hadn't I been content to take the easy way, pull off the road and find the familiar beaches and banks: Pink House Hole or Big Eddy, Myrtle or Home Beach?

I looked up, then down the far bank. This part of the Clearwater was different than farther downriver. Not so big. The rocks on the other side seemed still part of the canyon wall, huge and jagged from the blasts of road-making. Maybe it was good to be in a place I had not memorized, to be surprised by stone and current. I ran my hand through the water, patted the back of my neck. I needed to remember what I believed in, remember that things might just as easily go good as bad.

I called my children in. They refused to be hurried, reluctant as I to face the trip out, though it would be much easier, I had cozily assured them, going up than down.

Mosquitoes clouded around us as we walked from the river toward the pond. My daughter swatted frantically: they are drawn to her especially, and their bites leave her swollen and miserable.

"Hurry," I said. "It's getting dark. We need to get out while there's still light."

We crowded in, full of sand and river smells. I made a last check of the ground beneath the car: no oil or other inappropriate leakage. We made a tight turn, and I sighed as we faced the hill. What was it worth to attempt the ascent, lose the muffler, bash in the doors? We wouldn't be killed. What were my chances? It seemed an impossible decision.

I thought of the mosquitoes, the long walk out with two tired children, our feet rubbed raw by wet stones and sand. I said, "Buckle your seatbelts and lock your doors." I gave the engine more gas than usual.

The first pitch was not dirt and rock but a click of muddy clay beneath a thick layer of pine needles. We spun, then began sliding backwards, back into the long thorns of locust, over boulders and humps because the car could not be steered in such muck.

When we came to a stop, I leaned forward, rested my forehead against the wheel. I thought I might cry.

"Mom?" My son's voice was high, nearly shrill.

"Yes, Jace."

"I'm out of here."

He opened the door before I could stop him, slammed it shut and ran for the railroad tracks. Jordan was fast behind.

I rolled down my window. "Okay," I said. "You stay right there, this side of the tracks. Don't you move. If I can get past this first pitch, we'll make it. When you hear me honk, come running." They nodded, miserable among the mosquitoes, shaking in the suddenly cool air.

I backed up as far as I could, put the car in first, gunned the engine and popped the clutch. I hit the hill with my tires screaming, went up, careened sideways, bounced off the boulder, lost traction and stalled, then slid all the way back down, cringing with the screech of metal against rock, wood against metal.

I need to focus on the initial few yards instead of the dog-leg corner at its summit, I thought—the boulder bulging from the hillside, the tanker truck with its sharp edges. If things went well, we could get out with minimal damage. If things went bad, I might slide down into the gully with the truck, be swallowed by blackberries, have to fight my way out of thorns and lord knew what else.

I got out of the car, tried to pull some of the larger rocks off the road, broke off what branches I could. I scuffed at the pine needles, realizing the uselessness of it: the ground underneath was saturated with moisture. I backed up, got a stronger run. Black smoke clouded around me. I got a foot farther before sliding back down.

I went at it hard then, again and again, as the sun settled lower in the west and the sky darkened. I was still afraid, still fearing too much power, too much speed. It was best to keep control, stay steady. But I got no farther. Always, almost to the top, and then the sudden spin and slide.

How many times? Twenty? Thirty? I didn't care about the car anymore, hardly heard the worried cries of my children. I was feeling something building inside me, something I hadn't felt for a long time. It was hard and headlong, heedless in a way that might be brave. I'd felt it often before, when I was younger and wildly free. No husband. No children. Only my own life in my hands. I'd felt little fear of anything then, and it was a comfort. Now, with so much to love and lose, I'd come to cherish the expected, easy ways. Risk came in larger increments: sickness, infidelity, divorce, death. I'd begun to live my life as though, by giving up the smaller risks, I could somehow balance out the larger, keep the big ones at bay with a juju bargain—the sacrifice of whatever independence and strength such risks brought me.

Sitting there, the car smelling of rubber and fire, the heat and the mosquitoes and darkness coming on, I felt something else, and it was anger. Anger at what I feared and must fear, anger that I was where I was and in possible danger.

I felt suddenly and awfully alone, not because of the isolation, but because I was a woman where I should not be, having risked too much for the river.

The car idled. I hit the dash with the heel of my hand. I let all of it come into me, then—the anger I felt at love and death, at men who might hurt me and the men who would never, at the car and the land in its obstinacy. I felt the quiver in my belly and the rush of heat that filled my ears. I needed speed, momentum to carry me through.

I revved the engine, popped the clutch. I made the turn and didn't slow down. I kept it floored. I hit the boulder, jerked the wheel hard to the left, hit the truck. The tires spun. I didn't know what was behind me now, what I might slide into. I turned the wheel this way, then that, seeking purchase. I yelled at the top of my lungs, "You son-of-a-bitch, go!" And then I was up that first pitch and breathing.

The kids came running, screaming, shouting. They piled gleefully into the car. We were going to make it. Everything was okay.

But it wasn't, because now there was another pitch, and then another. We spun. We stalled.

They got out. They ran all the way back to the railroad tracks.

I rocked the car back against the tanker. Bounce, spin, back. Bounce, spin, back. Each time a little farther, and when I found my ground and started careening up, I didn't stop. I bounced the car out of the canyon, figuring the exhaust system was already gone, figuring it had all been decided hours ago and this was the final scene.

When I got the highway, I set the emergency brake and jogged back down. Jace and Jordan were coming to meet me, exhausted and still frightened. I batted at the mosquitoes and hurried us all up the hill. I was laughing, giddy with adrenaline. They were weepy, a little confused by my gaiety. They never wanted to do it again.

"It was an adventure," I told them. "And see? We are fine."

As we drove the highway home, I felt vibrant, exhilarated. The moon rising was the most beautiful thing, the wind through the windows a gift. I'd check the car for damage tomorrow, but for now nothing could touch us.

My children would sleep well, and I knew that in years to come, they would tell this story and the story would change and remain the same. Always, there would be the road we traveled, the rocks, the ruts, the mine to the east, the tanker to the west. There would be the night and mosquitoes, the smoke as they watched the car beat its way out of the canyon. There would be their mother's foolishness or her bravery, her stubborn refusals. The words might change, and maybe their fear. But always, there would be the river. It would run cold and loud beside them, the water they cupped in their hands and held above the sand to be sieved and drained and cupped again.

It will keep them near me. It will carry them away.

Jessie Harriman

Among Women

Women breathe questions into one another. They question with their hands, with their fingers, slipping in and out of jeans pockets. A woman tosses her hair back over one shoulder as if to ask the other at the table, *Am I alluring? Should I braid it? Color it?* The woman at the table hums a quiet song and nudges the Mason jar by her plate, posing the cut daffodils in the light: *Will I always set just one place for supper? Will he come?* A daffodil bends left. This is how she asks for comfort, and her song grows softer.

I live with three other women, all of us breathing young and inquisitively. Our questions whiz past each other as we hurry off to work or class. We leave mixtapes and clementines as little presents for each other. We leave phone messages in blue on the dry-erase board, maybe in red if it was a boy who called. We leave our bedrooms cluttered with the day's assignments, with dirty laundry crumpled in a heap: a pair of jeans sprawled into a question mark on the floor. We sometimes hold our breath when the phone rings.

I have always lived in a community of women, watching them closely, sometimes even trying to shut them out. In my girlhood I lived in the Whetsell Settlement where women warmed their homes just over the ridge or across the fence row from mine. Most of them seemed ancient to me. Many lived alone, widowed. I grew up in oversized T-shirts, grew up plump with the love of those widow women all around me in workdresses. I suppose I come from a sad place, from a community of mourning. But that's not how I remember it. The widows didn't wear their losses on their dress sleeves where I could see them. They gave me kisses and yogurt candies and red apples. My mouth dripped with the sweet milk they offered, as though they lived lives of plenty. How could they have had any milk left in their jugs for me? How much had they given, how much had they lost? Why did they hold my plump face in their dishpan hands and tilt me to see that love in their eyes instead of the weary redness? These are the questions that I ask with raspy breath.

I am slimmer now, not gaunt with age like some of them, but more aware of my waistline. I cook for myself and have to think twice before stuffing yogurt-dipped malt balls in my mouth. I am older. And my face has turned blue with questions. I remember the plump T-shirted girl who took eggs to the woman at the crest of the hill. I remember the things I saw in the company of widow women. And I need to look again. And to ask, as though breathing hot breath onto the glass of their portraits and wiping them clear.

I remember staring at black butter. It scared me over there in the dark of the Jeffers' kitchen. A warm lump, black with coal stove dust under the porcelain lid of the butter dish. I didn't know if it was real. I had only known fresh pats of salty butter. I helped churn our cow's milk during Saturday morning cartoons, pressed it in the butter mold, and ran it under a cold faucet till it was firm enough to wrap in freezer paper. I knew butter that went limp on hot biscuits on clean plates. But black butter was hard. Mom took me with her to help clean Don and Eliza Jeffers' place, and on the way over, in the cab of the truck, she told me that Eliza had once been a pristine housekeeper. I just stared and sniffed back my fear as Eliza drew me to her and kissed me somewhere between my neck and my jaw, wherever she could reach.

Don had had a severe ear infection as a boy, so severe it had seeped into his mind and speech. I was afraid of Don. He shuffled into Beatty Church in his only brown suit coat on Sundays, his wife, Eliza, tucked by his side. When I or another kid passed him, he poked our toes with the rubber tip of his cane and laughed, saying something in words all mushed up together. We just had to smile and sweat and nod till he unpinned our toes, and we could bolt out the door to play freeze tag or to pick up chestnuts. Sometimes Mom and Dad were the ones to give the Jeffers a ride to church. When Don got sick and had to labor getting out of the truck, Mom said low, "Isn't it hard, Eliza? Isn't this almost impossible for you?" But the weary woman just answered, "Not when you love him."

The house slumped into the hillside on Butch Mayfield's property.

As Mom and I passed Butch's trailer on the way, we saw his son Wayne tinkering with a tractor, and I waved with my mop handle. Mom and I couldn't carry our buckets, mops, and jugs up the front steps because the whole front of the Jeffers' house had sagged and threatened to give under our weight. Sometimes Don spit his tobacco juice onto the floor, and I wondered if it just sat there till Mom and I came. Several rooms in the house were curtained off, and I was afraid of rats scurrying behind the threadbare-sheet doors. Cold air leaked out from under the hem. Mom said that all Don's mother's things were piled up in there, dressers and newspapers and plastic flowers.

Mom cleaned up the commode that sat behind a curtain in the bedroom, while I stayed at the kitchen table, fiddling with the lid of that butter dish. When I saw the black mush, I wondered right away how the coal dust that had seeped into Don and Eliza's clothes and crept up the walls, how it could have gotten under that lid onto the butter. But I didn't ask. Instead I asked if I could bring in some wood. I asked if I could take the stove ashes outside and dump them. I lifted the latch of the door that opened out to the wood stack, I lifted as if to ask, *Is this it, Eliza? Is this how love is?* My stomach coiled while my voice offered up the little girl questions. The old couple just smiled and nodded.

Eliza said Don died of a broken heart. The doctors wouldn't let him come home, and he died longing for company. Eliza listened to the local news program on WFSP so that voices filled the kitchen. I wondered if she sang to the radio songs when she was alone, like I did. She did dishes sometimes, at the sink where a framed sketch of the biblical Ruth hung duct-taped on the wall, Ruth the Moabite woman whose husband up and died. Up and died. Every time I came to help Mom clean, to bring in some wood or coal for the kitchen stove, Eliza drew me to her and untucked another kiss for me.

Now I live with these three women. Now I keep margarine wrapped neatly in the Blue Bonnet box in the refrigerator door. The yellow sticks stay pale and rigid till I unwrap them for baking, or till I cut off slivers for our hot dinner rolls. None of us have yet tucked ourselves by a man's side for good. In my mind I see black butter and I get scared. "For rich or for poor. Till death do us part." Give all, lose all. Just lay the butter out in the coal-dusty kitchen and expect it to go black. Or expect the tobacco juice to brown the floor because you love him. That kind of love sops up the heart like a dish rag. I don't want to wax hard and cold with fear. I don't want to wrap butter in freezer paper and tuck it away in a cool corner, never tasting, never being tasted.

I remember dirty leather. The dirty leather of an old baseball I found in my brothers' closet. I handled it like an orange ripe for peeling. I put it to my lips like a malt candy shell, fingering its red stitches. And then I saw that floppy worn mitt shoved back behind worn-out sneakers and I yanked it out. The mitt stank. It had "MACE" in game-worn ink along the inside. It had once belonged to my uncle. It was a glove flimsy from boys' punches. I loved it.

The ball glove gave me power and spunk. I struck out this boy Matthew in fifth grade gym class, my left palm sweating inside that mitt. I flung the ball, then clasped it with the glove, flung, and nabbed. Matthew asked me to "go with him." To hold hands. Up and asked me outright. I struck him out. I didn't put his name next to mine in my notebook: "Matthew loves Jessie, together forever," in ink. I kept my name covered with my hand.

I got my name from Jessie Beatty Shaffer who lived within hearing distance down over the hill. She must have heard us kids when we hollered "Red Rover!" or punched our mitts or pummeled each other in a game of longtown-shorttown, our two-base version of whiffle ball. Jessie was seventy-nine when I was born.

Hers was the name on the front flap of my journal, and on her own journals, shelved together on a bookcase after she died. "Sam came today," I read in one short entry. Sam and Budz were the boys who had squeezed out of her womb, who came to see her and drive her to town. Her husband, Rufus, was long dead.

Jessie asked me once to read her a poem from my journal. I read her one about moonbeams that danced, and another about a boy who kissed a girl behind a big oak tree. She was nearly ninety then, and I wanted to ask her, *Who were you as a young "Jessie"? Who kissed you?* But I didn't ask. I kissed her. I asked her for milk. I asked her who permed her hair. She lived alone with her feather white hair and that womb there: like a floppy mitt.

I made butter deliveries to Jessie Shaffer. I tucked the cool, wrapped package under my arm and walked down to her white gate and lifted the lever. She usually had an ironstone bowl of scraps set out for Jack, her slow beagle. She was the widow who kept a glass Christmas-tree candy jar filled with yogurt-covered malt balls and raisins, stuck together mostly. Jessie insisted I pluck one from the gummy mass each time I offered up the butter. The candy was stale and tough to chew. I loved it. I loved her for it. And for her powdery smell, for her white kitchen sink and her garden so soft and rockless she might've tilled it with a comb. For her advice to my mom on late Saturday nights when Dad called for her to come home and his voice carried down clear to Jessie's and the women kept talking till four in the morning. For the daffodils she planted around the flat rock for Mom in May. For every time she patted her Queen-Anne's-Lace hair when my stringy, darkening hair was pulled up wet.

For never forgetting my name when I visited, all the way up till she died like a whisper after ninety-eight years: a name on the palm of the inside of a mitt, ink thin, but clear. For the malt oozing into my spit, so sweet down the back of my throat.

I want to savor it now, tonight. I and the three women living here with me splash sweetness on our arms and necks, none allowed inside us. Skim milk like water, reduced fat peanut butter, sugar-free tea in the fridge. One woman squirts on cucumber-melon body fragrance, one smoothes sunflower silk lotion over the cuts on her shaven legs. One candies her cheeks with blush. I smear on vanilla lip balm just to taste it. We gloss ourselves up. Up and down.

With these gestures we ask each other, *Are we alluring?* As we ask, another woman-friend comes to visit. She is older, but not old. She's come for a glass of watery milk and to share a secret about "allure." I smooth my hair that can't be smoothed and listen as she flips through pages of her Bible. She points in Hosea's Book and reads what God has whispered of His people: "I will allure her, will bring her into the wilderness and speak comfort to her. I will give her her vineyards from there, and the Valley of Achor as a door of hope; she shall sing there, as in the days of her youth." My friend smiles at my expression, as if she knows that I have been remembering my youth, as if she knows that I, at twenty, am not young and not old. She reads the rest of God's promise: "I will betroth you to Me forever." I admire the beauty in Hosea, but I still feel my hand struggle from my jeans pocket to touch my hair. I work loose a tangle. My friend has scribbled a holy epigraph for my list of questions, as though I'll understand when I'm older.

I remember the spokes. The spokes with fluorescent plastic decorators snapped on. When I rode my bike I "click-clacked," a steady bike chatter, all the way down the road as the plastic slid up and down the spokes in bright whorls. A yellow bike with a banana seat, a basket attached with sandal straps. Wind lifted the straw hair off my neck and the shirt off my hot skin. I was a girl on a chattery bike like a fast ball, shedding the spit of a pitch, feeling flung. But the seat, even a stretched out banana seat, accommodated just one, a detail youth wouldn't notice. The singleness was simply necessary for a steady ride and a clear vision of the road. To be alone was necessary.

Mary Jane was a woman down the road whose driveway gate I passed on my bike. Mary Jane who had lain alone with tuberculosis as a high school girl, who had lost a baby daughter from the curve of her arm, who had lost George Schmidle from her bed, from her grove of pines. Pieces of her life had been erased before I ever knew her, or blew past on my bike, clacking.

Once I skidded to a stop in the gravel and leaned my bike against the fence along the road by Mary Jane's house. I pushed through the gate, with her mail under my arm, and walked up to her porch. She thanked me and held back her little dog from biting my leg. I wondered if that poodle was her only company. I asked if she wanted me to bring the mail again the next day. I waved and walked to the gate, pushed back through to the road. I eagerly picked up my bike, as though to ask my widow friend, *Did you spend years alone and clear on a bike out here, in the wind, like me? Were those the best years?*

Twice, when I was an older girl, I rode on a motorbike behind a kind boy named Billy. We were not in love, and the wind slapped in between us even though we pressed together, pressed hard when the street curved. "Lean into the curves," he told me over the bike's unsteady roar, drowning out the simple clack of my banana bike, so I shut my eyes and let my body sink left with his.

George had been the Gum Man, passing out bubble gum to kids in the Whetsell Settlement on his way home from work. I was too young to remember that, but I'd heard about it, and it was the only thing I could say about Mr. Schmidle. I knew Mary Jane. She did everything on her own. She drove her corn-yellow car to town, sometimes dropping a birthday card or money for eggs and butter in our mailbox. She drove herself even after she'd had one of her legs amputated. She mowed her grass on a lawn tractor, and she crinkled her face into a perpetual smile. I always kept my eyes on Mary Jane's smile from my seat up front in the youth choir at Beatty, as I sang with the other squeaky sopranos. "Praise the Lord," she said for our singing. "Praise the Lord," she said for an early Sabbath morning, for an early evening, for light, for the wilt of the world in rain. For the brain tumor that massed under her bob of gray hair. One Sunday she told the whole congregation about those festering cells in her head. She said she would have to cut her hair when they operated. It was necessary for the removal of the tumor. We all bit our lips and cried and prayed in a circle. I tugged my fingers through my own straw-shade locks. "Praise the Lord."

"Bless your heart," Mary Jane said, when I brushed up against her polyester salmon suit or took in her mail or grabbed a Milky Way from her paper sack on Halloween. "Bless your heart." One Sunday morning, our choir sang "The Beatitudes" straight from the King James Version: Matthew, chapter 5. I don't remember where the melody came from, but we sang the "blesseds" of the Sermon on the Mount, word for word. "Blessed are the poor in spirit: for theirs is the kingdom of heaven." Blessed are the meek. The merciful. The persecuted. And then right out into Mary Jane's smiling face, I sang, "Blessed are those who mourn: for they shall be comforted." I sang it to every widow in the oak pews, while I shifted weight on loafers and didn't see their tears. I tugged at my jumper for the end of the worship hour, for the bike ride waiting for me in the wind.

I pedaled past, streamer tassels added to my handlebars. I waved to the widow whose tendency it was to weep through a smile, and I never feared wrecking in a ditch or gravel patch.

But I'm afraid now. I know gravel hurts. Blessed are those who mourn. I am not as sure of Christ's promise as I was in my youth. I don't sing it as loudly. But my widow friend is sure somehow, and she wants my heart to be plump with faith and with blessing, for the day when I will need it. From this aging evening, I hear a whisper from my lips follow into the dip in the road in front of Mary Jane's: "I love you," I say to her. I love you as best I can. And it is raspy, almost a whisper, deflating as it trails the gravel and potholes. I'm not sure what's necessary for those words.

The women I live with are too old to whorl clackers into the town streets. And we are too nervous to hitch a ride on a roaring motorbike that leans us down. So we make noise with the key in the car ignition, with the knob on the tape deck turned up full blast. A mixtape flings a song to the wind out the window, and a somber girl sings to a steady guitar riff: "Now I am sitting here on the best years of my life, wondering where I'm going next and who's coming along, singing a song of a summer night." I rewind and play it again.

I remember watching Gladys scratch in the dust. She was our prize hen before she died. She laid eggs with tough olive-green shells that stuck out from the other freckled brown ones in the cartons my mom filled to sell. Gladys cocked her head around the corner of the house whenever she flapped over the rusted wire of the chicken coop fence or squeezed through the space between the coop door and the cinder block that held it shut. Gladys and her chicken sisters scared me from the other side of that fence, with the constant garble in the back of their throats, the putrid yellow eyes and jerky motions. Still, when I sneaked past their stares the day I got engaged, they kept my secret. We were five-and-a-half, Timmy and I, and we raced to the woods behind the chicken coop, making up engagement vows. He slipped a Mayapple-stem ring on my finger and kissed my hand, because I had told him I was not allowed to kiss boys on the mouth, not till I was a woman. I lost the ring somewhere on the race back to the house.

I sometimes had pity on the hens and fed them grass over the fence because their scaly toes had scratched the coop floor to gray dirt and rock, with only the occasional orange peel to offer any color. The hens fed me, too. Their warm eggs swirled into the bowl of flour and sugar for a chocolate cake or banana bread. "Girls," my mom always called the hens. "My girls." Girls losing eggs that I took and juggled around inside me, their yolk-and-white working into my body. Maybe into the secret parts of my own girlness, harboring a nest of tiny eggs, sealed off, waiting.

When our bird dog Gabe killed Naomi Close's best setting hen, Naomi didn't get angry at us. She didn't really let her loss show. Even when her husband, Toots, began losing limbs. It wasn't all at once. First there were the weekly drives to the hospital for dialysis, then the darkening of the foot, the leg. When he died, the big gray farmhouse down the gravelly road from mine looked so big all of a sudden, so big and stark on the ridge, with Mrs. Close hidden inside.

The Closes had a long, trailing driveway and a mud-caked cattle bridge without a gate. With my delivery in my sack, I played back and forth on the iron ridges until my sole almost got stuck in the dip between them, and I pressed on up the drive. A breeze always blew through Naomi's kitchen when I stood there and handed her the sack, asking if that was all she needed. Asking if that was all I could give her, as if to ask, *Can a girl really give anything to a woman, can I offer any secrets? How much am I like you, if I am like you at all?* If I delivered a jar of elderberry jam or apple butter, I expected a similar jar to turn up in our mailbox a few days later. Sometimes she filled it with jam, too, or cracked walnuts for cakes. She slipped us her special recipes for treats, like lemon sugar cookies the size of quarters. I had a sweet every time I stopped by. I stood in the breezy kitchen and Toots's enormous voice boomed from the living room, "Give that girl something from the freezer." I licked my lips all the way home. I didn't know Toots very well, but I knew Naomi, and I knew he left her alone in that kitchen for good.

I loved to say Naomi's name. It sounded secret. "Ny-oma" is how I said it. The only other place I heard that name was in Sunday school, when they told the story of Ruth the Moabite woman whose husband died. Naomi was Ruth's mother-in-law, and Naomi lost her husband first. Ruth clung to her for breath and promised, "Wherever you go, I will go." She sweated in the sun and gathered strands of barley in bundles for Naomi, for their small company of two. I just whispered that name and watched for jars of jam in the mailbox. "Ny-oma."

When I buy eggs at the store I split the cost with the women I live with. The eggshells are pale and colorless, except for the veiny web of cracks in a few of them. They sit right beside the Blue Bonnet. There's no way to tell whether the chickens that laid that dozen eggs were prize setting hens. But

I have my doubts. I just spill the store-bought eggs down into the ridges of flour and sugar, swirl, and wait.

But what do I wait for? For company? For another widow woman to draw me to her? These women seem to surround me like a great cloud of witnesses, and they breathe love into me like I'm worthy of it. I want to sit with them again, tuck myself into the folds of their work dresses and breathe back. To say something of blessed comfort for their mourning. To eagerly hold my youth open, like a puckered jeans pocket: They can slip secrets in that I won't forget.

What am I holding breath for? I push "Play," and my mixtape fills the stifling quiet kitchen, and I turn it up loud and sing alongside the woman's vulnerable voice: "In the thick of the night, get me out of the cold, let me sing inside like a radio. In the thick of the night, before we grow too old, let me sing inside like a radio." The other women in the house can hear me when I sing it at the sink, loud, with Eliza Jeffers. With a whole chorus of women singing inside with me, as in the days of our youth, the days of our betrothal.

I live among women. I go to their doors, out of breath from climbing the hill, and I offer up my cool, wrapped package, as though asking: *Is this all we need?*

R. Glendon Brunk

The Rage of Men

A WAR STORY

A true war story is never moral. It does not instruct, nor encourage
virtue, nor suggest models of proper human behavior, nor restrain
men from doing things men have always done. If a story seems moral, do not believe it. . . . As a first rule of thumb, therefore, you can
tell a true war story by its absolute and uncompromising allegiance
to obscenity and evil.

Tim O'Brien, "The Things They Carried"

I resist writing about my father. A part of me feels that in exposing his
human frailty I somehow betray him, belittle his memory. What once
seemed so unforgivable has been forgiven, so why bring it up again? Also,
I am reluctant to acknowledge that he passed on the imperfections of his
father and grandfather and great grandfather before him, that for all the
ways I resisted him, damn it, I, too, took them on. I know these are not
reasonable, objective emotions, particularly given that I now have some
perspective on my life. They are, though, what I have. And they are, I
know, the very place I must begin if I want to speak of men's ways in the
world; I must start with the men who taught me.

Mennonites came to America in the late seventeen and early eighteen
hundreds from Germany, Switzerland, Holland, and, later, from Russia.
They brought with them a determination to live quietly—safe, they
hoped, from Catholic persecution. How is it, though, that those who flee
oppression so often turn to some form of it again in their own communities? I know much has changed for the Mennonite church these last
years. There has been some self-examination. But when I was a boy, to

live in a Mennonite community was to live in a tight circle of control and judgment. It was rarely said, though inherently understood, that one must always be aware of what others might think of one's actions. There was an overriding dictate of simplicity expected in every act. It was not a simplicity born of thoughtful choice derived from a spiritual center, but one dictated by a rigid code of "shoulds" and "should-nots." These dicta were interpreted from the scriptures of a judgmental male God by a male, pastoral hierarchy that, it was just understood, had an inside track on God's desires. These elders expected that in all matters one should be humble. One should not associate with sinful people. One should tithe all income. One should not smoke, drink, dance, go to movies, or fornicate. One should practice stewardship in worldly affairs, but one should *not* derive satisfaction from worldly things. One should honor one's father and mother. To live in a Mennonite community was in many ways to live in a community of eyes.

My father was a good Mennonite, an obedient man, a servant of authority. He voted Republican, not because he had a logical affinity for the party, but because he detested Franklin Roosevelt. "He was a sinful man, the one who let Communism into America," he said on several occasions. That perception of Roosevelt and the Democrats pandering to the godless Communists was reason enough to vote Republican. My father would not dance, drink, smoke, swear, or fornicate. As were all good Mennonite men, he was a pacifist. He refused to go to war, would not take human life, would not raise his hand against another man in any way. He would, though, strike his own children. He did so often, impulsively, a hard knot of anger twisting his handsome face. I know now that he struck his children not because he thought it was the right thing to do, but because he knew no way not to. Easiest said, unexamined anger owned by my father, turned him against himself and those he loved. Of my childhood memories, too many of them are of my father striking out in impulsive and unpredictable ways.

There's one memory in particular that holds a lot of meaning for me. Once we had a dog that came to us as a stray, a simple-minded cocker spaniel that cowered and peed at the slightest hint of conflict. One summer day it crawled up on an old couch in our basement. I watched, horrified, as my father swung a claw hammer full arc against the dog's head, driving it to the floor.

"Why'd you do that?" I yelled.

My father bristled. "Don't raise your voice to me." He turned away from me. "You know that dog should not be on that couch. Get it out of here."

I carried the dog up the stairs and out into the backyard to my favorite spot under a spreading Siberian elm and sat with it in my arms. With my shirtsleeve I blotted blood oozing from an ear, convinced the dog was dead. Eventually, I felt it stir, watched it dazedly shake its head and come to life. As it did, my own rage grew, turned inward and festered against all authority, against a God who would make men in the form of my father, a God who was the center of a religion that held him so.

My father was a product of his own father: a rageful, Bible-toting, hell-fire and brimstone preacher, who thought it his God-given duty to level harsh judgment on his family and anyone else who he deemed deserved it. In his old age his bitter ire had grown so large that he could no longer find a Mennonite church to minister to. Rejecting the Mennonites as too meek and biblically cautious, he joined a more fundamentalist faith. From that pulpit he railed against any who were vain enough to doubt his God of judgment and vengeance.

My father cowered in his father's shadow and suffered serious self-doubt from his endless criticism. All others in the family were expected to cower as well, but my steadfast mother resisted. For this she paid a heavy toll. My grandfather was open in his disregard of her. "She should obey you," I once heard him say to my father. "She took the vows to do so, and she should obey you." My father said nothing to my grandfather in return.

Contrary to what one might expect, my father seemed not relieved by my grandfather's death, but lost. He struck more and criticized harder, as if afraid in some way he was not living up to his father's expectations. He labored under a visible conflict between his anger and another part of him that I know longed to prevail. As I say this I hear the sound of my own judgment, what could be taken as a condemnation of him. In no way is this my intention. In all fairness I must say that anger and frustration were not all there was to him. Oddly close to these emotions was an infectiously charming humor.

Perhaps for people filled with rage, to maintain some semblance of sanity, humor has to be the counterbalance, the balm that keeps the fire of rage from consuming all. My father could come up with the unexpected and laugh like no one I've ever known. Certainly, though, his humor could take some odd turns.

Once, before we moved to Indiana, I traveled with him from Michigan, just the two of us in a dark blue Oldsmobile. We were going to investigate our prospective new home in Indiana. Pre-interstate, we followed a two-lane road that ran straight south through miles of empty winter fields and the little look-alike main streets of the central Midwest. In a small town close to the Indiana border my father slowed and pulled left into the parking lot of a Dairy Queen, the new choice in Midwestern dining, the first of the fast-food, fast-life franchises that would before long alter the character of American communities.

I was interested in what my father might be up to but not willing to believe that I might truly be getting a treat without asking. He looked over at me. "What'll you have?"

"You mean an ice-cream cone?"

"Anything you want."

"Anything?"

"Anything," he said. "A cone, a malted. How about a fudge sundae?"

I was astounded. This was not my father. The best strategy for living with him was to not hope for anything too good. This way anything above disappointment was a bonus. But this was too good to pass up. I gave it some thought. "I'll have a large cone," I said, "dipped in chocolate."

My father got out and returned shortly with two large, chocolate-dipped cones. He handed mine through the window on my side, then stepped around the rear of the car and slipped in behind the steering wheel. We ate in silence. Ice cream and chocolate dripped down my chin, over my hands and arms.

I finished, secretly pleased with my good fortune. My father looked over at me, eyes twinkling. "Want another one?" he asked.

This was beyond understanding. "Another?" I replied weakly.

"Another," he nodded.

I was convinced there had to be a major hitch somewhere, but I also didn't want to blow it if there wasn't. "OK," I said.

He got out again, this time returned with just one cone. He slid in on his side and handed it across to me. I began again. My father just watched.

This is turning out OK, I thought to myself. If it was possible, I relished the second cone even more than the first, taking it slower, getting into the gestalt of licking and dripping. By the time I finished I was my mother's worst nightmare; I had Dairy Queen armpits, and my T-shirt was no longer Christian white. I could tell my father was trying not to laugh. And I was trying to decide if that was good or bad. Am I the dunce, or have I done something right?

"You want another?" he asked.

I was too far gone to be astounded. I really didn't want one. I felt terminally full and on the edge of nausea but with instincts honed by five years of scarcity, I agreed.

"Large with chocolate?" he asked.

"No, maybe a medium," I said.

"OK." He got out and shortly returned with the third cone.

I began slowly this time, took a couple of licks, then rested. I was clearly not going to be fast enough; gravity was going to be the winner on this one. The cone and its contents slid down my arms, spread an abstract, expressionist splay of vanilla and Hershey across the front of my white T-shirt and into my lap. My father began to laugh, full and out of control. He slumped forward and banged his head on the steering wheel. He struggled for breath. Tears came to his eyes. I had been a big hit, and I didn't have a clue why. Between gasps he turned to me. "You've had enough?"

"I have," I said.

"You sure?"

"I'm sure."

It was weeks before I could bear the thought of vanilla ice cream again and months before the word "chocolate" ceased to set off Pavlovian eruptions in my stomach. On the surface my father possessed a charming rascality, but beneath it, I think now, was a certain maliciousness. I say this, and yet I know at a most essential level, maliciousness would not have been what he wanted for himself.

My father did not go to World War II. He was given a deferment because he was a farmer. Thus his own pacifism was not tested. I suspect he suffered more self-doubt because of this, because a part of him thought that his faith, his pacifism, *should* be tested. But a bigger part, the part that ruled him, must have been terrified that it might be. Of course, as I write these words, I'm aware of how little I actually know of my father's inner life, how little he revealed of himself. I'm aware, also, that my experience is the same as most other men I know. Men in our culture, perhaps in most modern cultures, suffer from a misguided set of perceptions that rule our lives. Even in our play we are so often destructive. Fathers and sons are too often not connected in positive ways. There is little open, honest emotion shared.

Years after I'd left home and was living in Alaska, my father, recently retired, came north with my mother to visit me and my family in Fairbanks. We were fishing together, just him and me. The only activity we ever really shared. We were talking about what it was like to live in Alaska. My father acknowledged how much he liked the place, how he wished he'd been able to come up when he was young. I said something to him about how determined I was not to give in to a predictable life, saying something, I'm sure, that was unintentionally critical of him. My father was quiet for a moment. His big hands gripped the bail of his spinning rod and turned it down for the next cast. Then it rushed out of him. "I hated farming, hated the confinement of it. Hated milking a dozen cows morning and evening, hated fifteen years of working nights in the Oldsmobile plant in Lancing, just to make ends meet." He held his case, stared straight ahead out over the water. "But there I was with a wife and kids. What choice did I have?"

I don't recall exactly what I said to him then, though I know it was most likely not as understanding as I now wish it could have been.

"You don't know what it was like to live through the Depression," he went on. "You can't imagine what it felt like to be without a job for months at a time. After the Depression ended I vowed I'd never be without a job again. That's why I took up farming. I figured I'd always have work. It's why I took up working nights at the Oldsmobile plant." He put his rod down on the edge of the boat. "One night, though, I was working the assembly line, putting front bumpers on, one after the next. I'd never liked working there. But that night it just hit me, my whole life I might do nothing but put bumpers on cars." He stared at the water a moment, then turned and looked directly at me. "That was one of the worst feelings I ever remember having. I came home and told your mother I couldn't do it any longer. We had to find another way."

The solution to my father's Michigan despair was to pick up and take his family to Indiana, where he again took on a long line of jobs that brought him little satisfaction. My father's story is a familiar one: men and women trapped by their circumstances, or at least by what they perceive as their circumstances: clear out and create the same circumstances elsewhere. My father tried; he did his best to create a new life. But the weight of the same fearful perceptions kept him trapped. I know his father's criticism hung over his head like a guillotine. Out of deep-seated self-doubt he held on to ways of being and living that were wrong for him, ways that denied his true spirit. Whatever his circumstances, whatever his fears, they kept him from doing what he most wanted with his life. This I know, because he told me.

It hurts to admit this, but for a long time I felt ashamed of my father. I resented his caution, the fear of life I saw in him. Why, I wondered, couldn't I have a father who accomplished something significant? Why not a father who lived an adventure? By extension, the shame I felt for him, I felt for myself. This is why I had to act and act big, because he never did. I was determined that I would not become like him. In this unintended way he gave me a gift, painful but still a gift, one I'm thankful for.

I know my father was no different from millions of other men and women, who, as Thoreau said, live lives of quiet desperation. I'm not so sure about the word "quiet" though. Perhaps quiet in one way, that of not rocking the collective boat. But in another way, the anger and the emotional numbness that accompanies desperation is anything but quiet. It's more like a silent roar that in time spills out into loud acts of violence and confusion that affect families and children. Quiet desperation, too, can underlie lives that appear entirely on track. The most fundamental tragedy of it all is that whatever the circumstances, desperation gets handed on generation to generation, father to son, mother to daughter. It does unless someone along the line decides enough's enough and determines to break the chain. What I know, also, is that breaking the chain is never an easy task.

During the early sixties and my adolescent years, lurking like a thief in the shadows of my awareness was always the reality of war. Those were the first vainglory days of the so-called conflict in Vietnam. Feelings ran high in favor of kicking some Communist butt in some obscure little country in Southeast Asia. Get over there and get it over with was the way the talk went. The grasping hand of American imperialism was yet to be questioned by the masses, and it was every young man's duty to march off in lockstep to war, no questions asked.

Ironically enough, given my resistance to my father's direction, at age eighteen I chose pacifism. It was not an easy decision. I agonized long and hard over the idea. I knew I would not make a good soldier; I doubted I was capable of following someone else's orders. But, given my determination and a sense of my own anger, I imagined that I might make a fairly tenacious warrior. In the end, mine was not a religious decision, though certainly my religious background influenced me, at least introduced me to the possibility of an alternative. My decision to resist military service was not based on my father's obedient pacifism. It was more about resistance to the authority of central government and an unwillingness to give my life to some ideology that even then made no sense. I decided there was no way I was going to Vietnam.

I was still in high school when I stood for the first time in front of my draft board and declared my pacifist intentions. The board was made up of World War II veterans. The board chairman was a dark man with a permanent scowl etched on his face, the shop teacher in my high school. He had spent most of World War II as a German prisoner, and he publicly made no bones about the fact that he had little use for conscientious objectors.

I was scared. I waited in a poorly lit antechamber with several other young men. A clerk called my name. I entered a large, dim, windowless room that smelled of cigar smoke and cheap aftershave. Four board members sat unsmiling behind a long wooden table. One of the members motioned for me to move to the middle of the room. I stepped forward and waited. Finally the chairman looked up from some papers he'd been studying and addressed me. "So it says here you're afraid to go to war. Is that right?"

I had carefully rehearsed responses to anticipated questions. I took a deep breath and did my best to reply as articulately as I could. "No," I said, "I'm not afraid to go to war. I object for other reasons."

"What makes you think you know enough to refuse to serve your country?"

He had a point. Although I had thought a lot about the issue and had memorized the literature provided by various pacifist organizations, truthfully, what does any eighteen-year-old know of the philosophical and ethical implications of war? On the other hand, who better to send off to the battlefields than the young, who don't know enough to resist?

I delivered the lines that I'd practiced. "I was brought up in a Mennonite home," I said. "This background has led me to consider the moral and ethical implications of war."

"And what might those moral and ethical implications be?" the chairman asked.

"I have moral objections to taking human life under any circumstances. I also consider modern war a tool of the military-industrial complex, a tool that serves the wealthy and victimizes the poor. I believe it is not a rational or moral alternative in this nuclear age, nor do we have the right to impose our political agendas on other people." I took a deep breath. "I will not go to war."

There was a long silence. The chairman's scowl deepened. Finally, one of the other members, a gray-haired man with a cigar clamped between his stubby fingers, asked me what I'd do if a Communist came into my house and tried to rape my mother. "Would you let him do that?" he asked. "You wouldn't resist?" "I don't know what I'd do," I said. And I didn't. The question seemed to have so little relevance to what I saw as the issue. I repeated the answer that the pacifist literature had suggested. "It's a hypothetical question that I find impossible to answer."

They never asked me if I actually considered myself a Mennonite; I suppose they just assumed that I was. If they had asked, I would have been caught in a quandary, a choice to lie and take the easy way out or be honest and answer that I no longer considered myself a Mennonite, really never had, that truth be told I had developed a quickening aversion to religion.

The board members conferred among themselves, then the chairman spoke. "I hope you know what you're getting into here, young man. Prison is not a nice way to spend your youth. Do you hear what I'm saying to you?"

"I do," I said, and was dismissed.

A month after my hearing I got a notice to report for my physical. This was routine procedure. All males of draft age, pacifist or not, had to take a preliminary examination to see if there was any physical reason they were unfit to serve. In the half-light of dawn, a Saturday morning in April, several dozen of the country's brightest and best gathered beneath newly budding maple trees on the courthouse square. The draft board clerk called our names, handed each of us a folder of papers, then told us to board a bus. I took a seat in the rear. Even though I had yet to be given conscientious objector status, stamped on the outside of my folder, in black, were the letters C-O, for conscientious objector. *Chicken, coward, traitor,* the letters seemed to say. I knew it was going to be a long day at the army induction center in Chicago.

That day there were probably a dozen Mennonite and Amish boys on the bus with C-O stamped on their folders. The soldiers at the Chicago center had a field day with us. Clad only in our underwear, we shuffled from station to station. The soldiers would send us to the back, over and over, until all the non-C-Os had made it through. It was late in the evening before the C-Os were done. The other inductees stared coldly at us as we boarded the bus. I remember thinking at the time that some of them were already well on their way to becoming good and obedient soldiers.

If ever I had any notion of letting go of my pacifist stance, the bullying and taunts at the induction center that day sealed my determination not to go into the army. Once again I came up against the smug, self-righteousness of assumed authority. Fundamentalist Christian or military, they both simply seemed opposite ends of the same spectrum. Both relied on a sheep-like willingness of people to follow, to not ask questions.

For some reason, an accident of birth I guess, it was my nature to ask questions. From an early age I *had* to think about things, to consider questions that most of my peers seemed uninterested in. For me, growing up Mennonite intensified this tendency. I understand now that beneath the surface dogma of the religion there was a vital connection to a history of serious contemplation; the essential reasoning of the Mennonite faith was underlaid by some highly ethical principles. We were encouraged to live a life of social service, of simplicity, of peace and quietness. In what might seem a contradiction, we were told how to believe, yet those beliefs dictated that we live and think outside the norm. Of course, living outside the norm, for one inclined to ask questions, can take one to unintended places. As far as my pacifism went, the contradiction of my father's professed pacifism and his private violence pushed me into going beyond the rhetoric of pacifism to examine what it actually meant. I know this: my choice to resist the military was my choice, not my father's.

Saying this, I also reveal the ultimate paradox of my resistance. I resisted the military, an institution entirely dependent upon the manufacture and manipulation of men's fear and rage. Yet it was my own rage—rage passed from my father, my grandfather, and generations of fathers before them—that ultimately pushed me up against the institution of the military. My rehearsed performance in front of the draft board was a patina over the hard shell of my own anger. In some ways those hardened surfaces meant survival. In other ways they would haunt me, distract me for a long time from truly living from my inner voice, armor me against so much of what I actually desired to experience. If I were asked to define the most essential contradiction in my life, it would be my professed pacifism and all the ways that I have subsequently made war.

DOG MAN

> I thought my whole life had changed, and my basic understanding
> of values had changed, that I wasn't sure if I would ever recover, that
> I had seen god and he was a dog-man and that nothing, ever, would
> be the same for me again.

Gary Paulsen, "Winter Dance"

Life on the Tanana River outside Fairbanks, Alaska, quickly took on seasonal rhythms. One day it was fall, and the next winter, that time of long, dark, brutally cold nights when the air stabs at your face and the northern lights dance holy across the sky. We settled in.

I had come to Alaska after two years working at the Colorado Psychiatric Hospital in Denver for my alternative civilian service in lieu of the military and Vietnam. On long weekends during those two years, I would head up into the Rockies to camp and fish. In the autumn, with yellow aspen leaves spiraling to the ground, I had hunted and killed my first deer. But the Rockies proved to be just a temporary respite. They weren't enough. I laid awake many nights thinking of Alaska, vowing that as soon as I was discharged I would head north.

It was in Denver that I first began to think about the contrasts between the natural world, the cool peace of it that pulled at me so, and what I began to call the manufactured world. There was some quality in the natural world, a neutral receptiveness, a spiritual energy, that was the antithesis of the frantic, dominating energy that I felt around me in the city, the creeping anxiety that I daily witnessed in the mental hospital. I had begun to see Colorado Psychiatric Hospital as a place that took in only a few of the most acute victims of a modern war being waged on many fronts. It was a war that resided in attitudes and perceptions that were distorted and inaccurate, that were built on a single insane idea: that by making war we can somehow save peace. Ultimately, I was just beginning to see that battlefields the world over, large and small, begin and end in the human heart.

In Alaska there was a little community of dog mushers who lived in the vicinity of the Tanana River, most of them up along the Alaska Highway, six or seven couples total, all of us in our mid- to late-twenties by then. With so much work to do in the summer, there was little time for us to socialize then. But winter, that was our time to come together. Many nights we would hook dog teams or take skis and travel moonlit trails to gather in one cabin or another for potlucks and saunas.

All of us, I believe, were imagining another time, a time of our great-grandparents. The women would gather in their own corner and talk recipes and baking, canning meat, summer gardens, children. We men, holding to the roles we had defined for ourselves, would talk of our own things: hunting, fishing, log building, boats. Whatever our conversation was, though, without exception it would always eventually turn to dogs. Dogs ruled us.

Once, our first winter, my wife B suggested that she and I begin socializing with a new couple she'd met in Fairbanks. "Do they talk dogs?" I asked her.

"They don't have any dogs," she said. "They're just normal people."

"I'm not interested in normal people," I said. "I've got nothing to talk about with them." And that was it for me and any socializing with regular people.

Outside our dog circle, ruled by the single-mindedness of the born-again zealot, what a bore I must have been. Even before coming to the river, dogs had become my identity. We talked and talked and talked. Of sleds and gear, of the right kind of food, of medicines and veterinarians, of breeding, of lead dogs. We talked about what it took to make a top dog, that certain combination of desire, athletic ability, and speed that showed up in maybe one out of ten, or twenty, or even a hundred of the very best. I suppose I had the dog disease worse than others. There was something about the sport that seemed to meet so much of me. I took it on like a noble cause. There was something deep and crazy in it, the mystical pull of addiction. A couple of months ago, I read Gary Paulsen's wonderful book, *Winter Dance*, about his experience running the Iditarod. Even though, like the recovering alcoholic, I know it's something I can never do again, I caught myself scheming how I might be able to put together another dog team and run that race. Just once more, I told myself. Then you can let it go. It took a week or two after finishing the book for my dreams to quit being about dogs.

We talked of "jumps," the way a good one strides full out and eats up the distance. That long, loose-jointed, almost reckless reach. It's a way of moving that no other animal on earth can duplicate over distance. None. A cheetah, the fastest animal living, could outdistance a top dog team three-to-one for the first hundred yards or so but be left behind, exhausted, in a half mile. A fast thoroughbred horse might stay with a sprint team two miles, at the best three. Six or seven miles and everything in the animal world is left behind, and that's just when racing huskies are warming up, settling into their full stride, down into that rhythmic, hypnotic pace that's like poetry. I can think of few things more beautiful. It's still that way for me, and it's been twenty years now since I drove that last fine team, the one Jenny led.

We talked of the whip too. How to put the edge of fear into a good dog, that extra drive that's instilled by pain. Beyond the quality of the individual dog, beyond the point of desire and toughness, it gets down to who's driving them. Good dogs can be made either better or worse by the musher. It's a delicate balance. The highest compliment you could pay someone then was to say he was a good dog man, even if that someone was a she. A good dog man meant that the musher could communicate with dogs, could get all they had to give. In those days, at least that's what I told myself, it usually meant the person had learned to use the whip efficiently. I suppose it's still that way for some driving dogs. But I'm glad to hear some things have changed. People who win, now, I'm told, have figured out another way.

It was that first winter on the river that I learned the fine points of whipping from Denis. Denis started driving dogs when he lived in Minnesota. But like most mushers outside, he knew Alaska was the center of the universe, the place with the best dogs and dog men. So shortly after getting out of the army he came north. Those of us in our community were all fairly accomplished Alaskans, experienced at a lot of things that had to do with living in the bush. Denis, though, the youngest of us all, was the resident expert on everything; he worked hard at out-manning us. In just a few years in Alaska he had gained a reputation as a tough dog man. But then Denis was good at most anything he undertook. Anything, that is, except holding a job. He hated working for anybody else, so he schemed every possible way to avoid it. Dogs were one of his schemes. Raise a lot of pups. Cull ruthlessly. Prove out the best ones and sell them for big money. No attachment. No sentimentality.

It was just the two of us in his cabin that night. The propane lights cast a soft yellow glow against the log walls. Denis sat in his big red recliner chair, in a green plaid shirt, down vest, red wool stocking cap, and Sorels. He stood up. As he strode to the center of the room he reached into his vest pocket and pulled out a shot-loaded whip made of braided kangaroo hide. A signal whip it was called. "I'm never without this," he said. "I'd feel undressed without it." He balanced the whip in the palm of his hand for a second. "A three-footer like this is best; you can work them over close." He took hold of the butt end, circled it once at his side, then with a quick flick of his wrist he cracked it. It sounded like a rifle shot. "You got to put the fear into 'em." As he spoke he reached down and panto-mimed the act. "Pull 'em to you by their backlines with one hand and jerk hard. As you jerk, whip 'em with the other till they scream and struggle to get away." He put it to his imaginary dog a few strokes, then straight-ened and looked at me hard-eyed. "If they lie down and give up, then you know they haven't got it; they're bullet bait. You want the ones that'll go through the front of the harness to get away from you.

Denis was harder than most; he drove dogs with the cold intensity of a samurai, like they were the enemy. He had a reputation for producing tough-minded dogs. They had to be tough to survive his training. Maybe they weren't all that happy—"sour" we called them—but as Bernie Turner, a dog sage who lived up the highway said, "Those sons-a-bitches that old Denis turns out can sure eat up the ground when you pull the leather."

The next day after Denis's demonstration, I took a ten-dog team out on a training run, a bunch I'd picked out that I thought needed a tune-up. I drove them past the turn-around and headed for home. A couple of miles to go, I called for more speed, the coming home drive that a good dog team needed to have. They gave me a little, but I wanted more. I stopped them, drove the snow hook in where I knew it would hold well, pulled the whip from the pocket of my parka and moved quickly. I grabbed the backlines and jerked each dog to me, working my way from the wheel dogs to the leaders, cutting each one rhythmically with the whip, hollering loud at the same time "Aw right!" in what we called a fear voice. The whole team began screaming and lunging just like Denis said they should. I ran back to the sled and pulled the hook and hollered "Aw right!" The whole team put their heads down and ran hard for home.

I'd whipped before but had never given much attention to the fine points of it, to the psychology of twisting a dog's mind into terror. In societies of wealth, where we have the luxury of owning animals as pets or competitive objects, I believe dogs and horses reflect back to us some primary and instinctual world that we yearn to connect with again. In our hyper-domestication we turn to domestic animals for a way back to something. They offer us a reciprocal relationship. A cooperative kinship. We humans, though, rarely honor the reciprocity of that agreement. Instead we often demand that they give us more and more. And most of the time they oblige. When they don't, they usually pay a grim price.

Denis also instructed me on how to kill what we called culls, the ones that were too slow or stubborn, or had some defect like not being able to handle what we asked of them. "Hold them headfirst between your legs," he said. "Draw an imaginary X between their eyes and their ears, put the muzzle right there where the X crosses, and pull the trigger. They never know what hit 'em."

One out of four pups made it for him. The rest he killed and piled on the river ice in front of his cabin to wait for spring breakup to sweep them away. Sometimes I would think of Denis's pile, imagine it spinning on an ice cake after spring breakup, passing Indian villages along the way, twisting and tumbling along the Tanana, out to the Yukon, and along the Yukon until it entered the Bering Sea. There some Eskimo in a kayak would spot it on an ice flow, a gruesome testimony to some human run amok.

Those first years on the river I raised my own pups and acquired more adult dogs, and I made my own pile. The ones I deemed not good enough, I drew the imaginary Xs on their heads and pulled the trigger and watched them quiver into death. If a pup showed a weakness of any kind, I killed it.

If killing and whipping were any measure of a dog man, by that first spring on the river I was a card-carrying member. I too had begun to learn how to turn out tough-minded dogs. I learned to strike and yell and flail until they pulled away from me in open-eyed terror, until sometimes flecks of blood spit like fire from their nostrils. I could holler a command and watch fourteen dogs drop their heads and tails, bow their backs, and scramble for life. There was something so powerful, so addictive, about the feel of the driving bow jerking alive in my hands.

How easily we take on the sins of our fathers. I know as a young man I carried a hard anger, though I know, too, that anger did not always define me. I've thought about it a great deal, and I can say now that the violence of whipping dogs was not my instinctual way. It was my inordinate desire to succeed at the sport, my early frustration of falling short, which too often spilled over into rage. It was then, particularly my first years driving dogs, that my animals suffered the most. Most of all it was the ego-driven part of me that was willing to do whatever I perceived was needed to win.

These things I've just written about I'm not proud to recount. Will someone judge me harshly today for the things I did then? I find it easier to recall a gentler part of my life on the river. In my memory certain things from those days hold as much sway now as dogs did then. Like Christmas. A week or so before the big day I would hook a few dogs to a freight sled and take my daughter Cara out along the river sloughs to look for a tree. "That one, Dad." She'd point at the first big one we'd come to.

"No," I cautioned her, "let's keep looking. You never know what you might find if you keep looking."

"That one." She'd repeat it a dozen times before we'd finally make a selection. I would saw down the tree and tie it on the sled. B would be waiting with hot chocolate when we got back, and of course she'd make a big fuss over the tree, even though the trees we cut were always sparsely branched, typical subarctic spruce.

But I had a solution to a thin tree. Once I got it inside the cabin I would take a hand drill and bore holes in the trunk, then add branches from another tree until it looked as full as any commercial tree you could buy off a lot in town. We would make ornaments and string popcorn, and once we had it decorated I would add a set of tin candleholders that had come from Germany. Neighbors would come from all over for our can-dle-lighting ceremony. I would play guitar and we would all sing carols. Denis, who would never sing, who could be counted on to say "Games are for cripples and old people," would sit close to the tree with a fire extinguisher at hand. "Can't be too careful with fire in the bush," he'd always say. "Nothing worse than getting burned out the middle of winter."

We made presents for one another. One Christmas, Cara, taken by my carpentry skills, wanted a toolbox. I made her a wooden one with her name burned in the side and filled it full of tools. Another Christmas I made her a little scaled-down racing sled. We had an old, retired leader named Bubbles, a tub of a dog who had charmed her way into living in the house. Bubbles loved heat. Once the weather turned even slightly bitter, she would install herself so close to the woodstove that every now and then we'd get a whiff of her hair scorching. When we told her to move, Bubbles would look at us in disgust, then reluctantly drag her body only a foot or two away from the stove. She hated going outside under any circumstances. Her only legitimate sled-dog job was to take Cara up to the school bus, which stopped a mile from the house up at the boat landing.

School mornings in the winter I would drag Bubbles out of the house and hook her up to Cara's little sled. Cara would come out of the house all bundled up in her green winter parka, wolf ruff up around her face, with mittens that a neighbor had knitted for her, the right one with "gee" (for turn right) embroidered on it, the left one with "haw" (for turn left). She would step on the sled. "Don't let this dog buffalo you," I'd say to her.

In her tiny voice she'd yell, "Get up, Bubbles!" Bubbles would make a big show of pulling her down the trail and out of my sight. At which point, too often, she would try to turn around and make a run back to the stove. But Cara, true to her training, would hop off the sled and smack her on the nose and pull her around. "No, Bubbles!" Eventually Bubbles would get Cara to the bus stop. There they would both wait. When the bus came, Cara would turn Bubbles and the sled loose, and Bubbles would double-time it for home, eager to get back to the fire, the little sled careening along behind.

THE RACING GAME

Tell me, what else should I have done?
Doesn't everything die at last and too soon?
Tell me, what is it you plan to do
with your one wild and precious life?

Mary Oliver, "The Summer Day"

You're a full-fledged dog man now. The first winter racing in the lower 48 you win a few races, never place out of the money in any one you enter, outside or in Canada, or back in Alaska in the spring. By the end of the season you've accumulated enough points to win the International Sled Dog Racing Association bronze medal for the season—the third highest ranking of all sprint racers. You're making good money at it now: race winnings, breeding fees, selling the dogs that are a notch or two off. And the dog food you designed and market is selling well, bringing in more money, essentially feeding your own dogs for free. You're in the chips.

You bring them back to Alaska in late February, and you start training for the North American Championship in Fairbanks. Through the winter you've discovered that of the twenty-eight dogs you had on the truck when you left, ten of them are super dogs, the "tens" you call them. They've made every heat of every race you've run. If only you could get twenty as good, you'd win every race you entered. Instead, each race you sort through the other fourteen left, looking for the strongest, the most rested, the healthiest six to go with your ten all-stars.

It's fascinating stuff. The strategy, training, breeding, it's so all-consuming. The racing, though, that's where it gets intense. The championship races—they can take you into another dimension.

Imagine it. Race time. The city's hauled in truckload after truckload of snow to cover Second Avenue in downtown Fairbanks. The sidewalks are filled to overflowing—Indians and Eskimos in from the villages, homesteaders from the bush, locals of all descriptions—with everyone milling around, greeting each other, going in and out of bars, some holding children over their heads for a better view of the dogs. It's winter festival time, a celebration of the cold dark time waning and spring just beginning to knock at the door. The dog race is the main event, the dog men the heroes of the day. Photographers everywhere. At the start/finish line, TV cameras. You're part of it, one of the top contenders.

At race time the temperature is a sunny ten above zero, marginally warm for sled dog racing. But the trail's bullet hard; it's going to be a fast race. You tell yourself, be careful out there. If you're not smart you'll use them up this first day, hammer them with crippling speed and not have anything left for the other two heats. This first heat is a twenty-miler, tomorrow another twenty, the third day, the killer, those left standing go thirty.

You're starting with sixteen dogs. Maybe tomorrow you'll have to drop down to twelve, if you're lucky, fourteen. The third day, who knows how many you'll have left? Most likely you'll be down to ten, the same ten that always make it all three heats. Whatever the number, though, they'll be tired, and then you throw an extra ten miles at them. It takes a good dog team to do that third day. It takes a good dog man, too, to get all you can, to push them to the limit without blowing them up.

The teams leave at three-minute intervals. You've drawn the sixth start position. The sixth team of twenty-two. It's a great draw. Just far enough back to run your kind of race; a few teams to chase, but not too many to pass. The trail won't be torn up. Tomorrow you figure you'll be starting higher up.

Your sled is tied to the front bumper of your pickup. The dogs are harnessed and ready, picketed on short chains around the truck. After the second team leaves, you begin to hitch. You've got twenty minutes. You work calmly, methodically, careful not to betray any nervousness or haste. Your handlers work with nervous dogs, keep the lines straight. One holds out the main line. But you do all the hooking. You want the contact, the constant reminder of who's in charge here. You want to touch each dog, to feel their energy, to have them feel yours. A dog every forty seconds, that's the plan. Fourteen dogs, 9 1/2 minutes. The fifth team left the starting line thirty seconds ago.

Your two leaders go in last. The idea is to give them the least time on the line. Keep the pressure off them as long as you can. You bring them up together, hook them in, then trot easily back to the sled.

These dogs of yours are eager to go, lunging and barking, just crazy to run. Your handlers grab the gangline. You stand on the brake and release the tie-up rope. The dogs surge forward. You've got the brake dragging, scraping through snow down onto hard pavement. Your handlers pull back on the gangline, all four of them doing their best, and still you're careening down the street; there's just so much damn power out in front of the sled. The sled handlers at the start line are ready for you. They step up and grab the sled, stop it, and hold on for all their worth.

You step off the runners and walk up along the team, checking back-lines and necklines, looking close for any signal in a dog that might indicate a weakness, a hesitation, something you hadn't seen back at the truck. You pick up one dog that has gotten over on the left side but runs best on the right, and you drop him over on the right side of the gangline. All the dogs have a paint strip on their right shoulder to indicate they've been signed into this heat. The race marshal paints them just prior to the start, a different spot for each team, so you can't add new dogs tomorrow or switch dogs with another musher. Over the three days you can drop dogs, but you can't add any.

"Thirty seconds!" the announcer calls over the public address system. You move up to your leaders, stand in front of them. They're screaming to go, lunging, making a big show of it. You call them by name. "Jenny. Heidi." They each acknowledge you with quick flashes of their eyes, then go back to barking, looking straight down the street. "Fifteen seconds!"

On the way back to the sled you plug the earphone in, the one connected to the little portable radio you're carrying in your parka pocket. Halfway there—"Five! Four! Three!"—You run—"Two!"—Swing onto the runners—"One!"

"All right!" you shout. The sled handlers step back, and you're off, down the middle of Second Avenue, downtown Fairbanks. In your earphone you can hear the radio announcer: "A fine start for the young up-and-coming musher from the Thirty-Mile area out on the Tanana. He leaves today with sixteen . . . "

They start fast. They're stretched out full in front of you, eight tandem pairs, seventy-five feet from where you stand on the sled to the noses of your lead dogs. They're all digging except for a red dog named Rosie, who runs in the middle of the team, and the sour old veteran you bought from Denis, Chicken, who runs in wheel. Both of them bob up high-headed and reluctant, their backlines flopping slack. But you know all there is to know about those two. They always hesitate at the start. That's just the way they are, slow to get into it. You know, also, how the two of them will scramble when you call for it, know how hard they'll come home once you make the turn for the finish.

You can put up with a couple like Rosie and Chicken in a team. Too many like them, though, and you'd never make it off the line. Not making it off the line happens often enough to some of the hard drivers.

You make the end of Second Avenue—twenty-eight seconds running time—and drop down on the Chena River. Ahead there's a short stretch of river, followed by a cut into Noyes Slough, then up over a high bank into a parking lot that leads to the tricky crossing over College Road.

They do it all flawlessly. Jenny bumping Heidi into the turns. At College Road the crossing guards have the traffic stopped. Your two leaders take it effortlessly, blast over the berm on the far side, onto the trail paralleling the railroad tracks. Two hundred yards of railroad right-of-way, then it's a sharp left turn into the bush. Once you make the bush you can all start breathing a little easier.

They take the left turn, their heads down, all of them running hard, even Chicken and Rosie are starting to get into it—get over there and get it over with. They're all striding, reaching, punishing the distance. A backline or two bob here and there, but mostly those back lines are tight as guitar strings. Yes, that's it, music, all harmony and expression of emotion, sixteen dogs working together, reaching for more ground.

They're all bone-light animals, tucked up in the gut, moving with the grace of harriers. On a good hard-packed trail they'll average twenty miles an hour. Twenty miles in sixty minutes. Places on this trail you'll hit close to thirty miles an hour.

The sled runners have little pads where you plant your feet. You ride with your knees flexed and loose, like a skier. The race sled you ride is twenty-five pounds of bent ash and rawhide, flexible as green willow, half the weight of your biggest dog. On the straight-aways your hands grip the driving bow easy. Other times, on the tight corners, it's all white knuckles, a matter of just hanging on and surviving.

You wear a marten fur hat with the earflaps tied up behind. And a light, powder blue down parka with a wolf ruff on the hood, your racing number over the top, black ski pants, and beaded beaver mitts. Your feet are cased in mukluks made by an old Indian woman you know, light as ballet slippers, smoked moosehide soles, hair-out caribou, bands of red and blue beaded trim at the tops. In the tricky places those mukluks frisk over the trail, skitter quick little steps, then leap for the runners again.

Riding a sled is all about balance and grace, about doing your best not to make your dogs work any harder than they have to. When you steer the sharp curves, you tip the sled up hard, ride it on one runner, so you don't pound your wheel dogs. In the long straight-aways and the hills, you stand on one foot and kick with the other. "Pumping," it's called. When you pump you strive for rhythm, for matching the lope of your dogs. Kick. Your leg flies up high and out behind. Kick. Your face frosts, a rime of white across your beard and back onto your parka hood. Kick. You can feel it now, what every dog man hopes for and few experience: each dog moving exactly the same way, all driving with the same long, easy, ground-consuming lope. "Cadence," it's called: a melodic or harmonic progression, that rhythm where sixteen individuals become one thing. No, where all seventeen of you become one thing.

It's taken you ten years of breeding and culling, buying and selling, wheeling and dealing, conniving and cajoling, to get dogs this good. Super sled dogs are no different from superhuman athletes. There's something born into them that sets them apart from the average racing husky. The physical ability is a given; they can run faster, jump farther. But it's more than physical; just like in a superhuman athlete, it's some quality of mind. That's what mushers call it, "a good mind." Which means there's no quit in that dog. None, even given the very worst of circumstances. The good minds possess a determination that supersedes any other possibility; it's not a reasonable thing. "Toughness" is another word. So tough that pain, real agony, appears to be only a background noise to them—a nuisance, not a hindrance. The other word used a lot is "desire": a bred-in willingness to succeed, to compete. An unequaled obsession for running.

You have nothing but words to keep your leaders honest, no reins, no physical control, only "gee" for right turn and "haw" for left, and simple "all rights" and sharp little whistles for more speed, and "easy" and "whoa" for slowing. Not that the good ones are much for whoa; they're bred to run, not to stop.

You don't say much. Driving good dogs means mostly keeping quiet, saying only what needs to be said. Because they're tuned to hair trigger, and talking can just push them over the edge. Your job is to be back there on the sled, shut up and ride as gracefully as possible. Study them, watch for weaknesses, be ready to load a dog if one goes down.

You don't want one to go down though. Today you're racing the big time. It's what you've trained and raced all year to do. One going down complicates things. You lose time stopping, not to mention the extra weight hauling a dog. No, you just keep quiet, keep pumping, and listen close to the radio announcer for the checkpoint times—both yours and the other teams'. You need to know how you're stacking up with the rest of them. Keep your eyes on your dogs.

You look up along your team and here's what you see. In the wheel, closest to the sled, there's Chicken and Felix. Chicken's a brown dog, the oldest one on the truck. She's the only certified lazy in the bunch, a dog who puts the lie to the notion that the good ones do it all on their own. Anywhere but wheel, Chicken will slack off, screw around, drive you half crazy. She needs to be close to you, close enough so she knows you can get to her quick and put the leather on her if need be. You run her today because she's tough as barbed wire; you know she'll never, ever go down, and that she'll make all three days. Certified tough by Denis. They don't get any tougher than that. And you know, too, when you turn the corner for home, or when you need all you can get and you pull the whip, Chicken will scream once, then put her head down and roll; she can move a sled all by herself when she digs in. She's in this race because it's an important one; you know you may need that kind of coming home on the third day.

The other wheeler, Felix, is all toughness too. That's why he's in the wheel, that and he handles it so well. He anticipates the turns, throws himself against the lines, literally looks like he's on wheels when you take the tight corners. He's totally honest, willing to work, will never try to cheat on you—the antithesis of Chicken. And he glides when he runs, smooth as water-polished stone, a total ten.

In front of the wheelers is where you've put your weakest dogs, the question marks. Front of wheel is the position of least stress, the place for the unproven ones, maybe a new dog you don't know that well, or one coming back from an injury, or a young dog. Today it's a white dog named Frog, a new dog you paid nine hundred dollars for from a guy in Knik, Alaska, and the black dog named Mary. Mary's young, only a year and a half, too young, really, to be running in a big team. But she's got a special edge for a young dog, a total willingness to be there. She's a leader in the making. Even now you know you can move her up front in lead if you have to. But you don't want to have to. You don't want to put that much pressure on her yet. Next year that's where she'll run, up there with Jenny.

The team dogs are next, the reliables, the pick-up-the-lunch-bucket-and-go-to-work-every-day kind of dogs. Six of them, back to front. You try to match them for gait and compatibility. Alex and Coolie run together. One's brown, the other red. They're brothers out of the same litter. They love each other, travel together in the same box, just dig being together. They're the kind of dogs you don't notice that much because they're always doing exactly what they're supposed to be doing; they're not making a big production out of any of it. They're not tens, though, because they come up sore sometimes; they just don't do the speed as easy as they need to. They're what you call two-day dogs; you know they'll make two heats, but are not likely to make a third.

The next two are both tens. Doofus is a big rangy black dog that barks the first three or four miles out of the chutes, just for the sheer joy of running. He's with his son, Jake, out of Chicken, the only male Doofus won't fight with. Jake's a good one, steady, not showy, though he'll lead in a pinch. Doofus and Jake are sired and grandsired by a dog named Junior, owned by a top musher by the name of Harvey Drake. Junior was bred by Steve and Rosie Lasonsky. Drake's whole breeding program turned around when he bought Junior from them. Junior's so crazy to run that when he's left behind in the kennel, sometimes he gets so upset, so screaming crazy and wild about it that he literally has fits. That's the kind of dog you like to breed, not for the hits but for that kind of desire.

And then there's Adam and Rosie (named for Rosie Lasonsky), both tens. Adam's an entirely consistent gray male, a no-nonsense worker. Rosie goes out slow, her backline flopping. But you know this dog; you know how she performs. There seems to be no limit to her speed, or at least you've never seen her look like whatever's happening is anything but entirely easy. You can move her up in lead on the way home if you have to. She's what's called a "coming home dog," one that just pours on the coal after the turnaround. Then you'll never see her backside bobble. She's also out of Chicken, the certified lazy in wheel.

Next up there're the two pairs of swings. All four are tens. They're all dogs unwilling to lead but eager to run just behind the leaders. Swing dogs are the ultimate athletes, combination gymnasts and long-distance track stars. They never tangle, handle the lines like magicians. If the leaders slack off and drop their backlines, the swings will spread instantly to stay out of the way. The leaders pick up their lines, the swings automatically move back in close so they can get the most power on their own backlines. Something goes wrong on the trail, the team starts to ball up, the swings will jitter-step over the lines, like football players running tire drills. If it's really bad, they'll twist, dive and hit the ground, roll back up on their feet, all in one easy motion, just to stay out of a tangle.

Your four swings are all flawless, interchangeable animals, really. Not one of them has ever had an off day that you can remember. None of them has ever crippled or even come up sore. They're "easy keepers," which means they utilize food efficiently, and they never get sick. Lisa and Otter (another dog from Denis) are a matched female pair, both coal black and absolutely perfectly gaited. Lisa's blue-eyed. Otter brown. Both work so hard they have permanent calluses on their hips where their harnesses have rubbed the hair off down to the skin. The other swing pair—Knight, gray and white, and Jasper, black and white—are both males you bought as young dogs. Both were surprises, really. You don't expect dogs to turn out so good that you bought so cheap. Some of it was just luck. That, and you had a hunch.

Last, the farthest out there, are the leaders. Without the leaders all the dog power and talent in the world is not going to matter one iota. Leaders make a dog team, take what all the other dogs have to offer individually and turn it into teamwork. There are plenty of dogs that will run lead, but there are few real leaders. Real leaders, super leaders, just demand to run up there. They'll pout if they don't get to. They're competitors.

Heidi, a little blond dog, is a leader, but she's not a dominant dog. She's really as good as she is only because of the dog next to her. Jenny is beyond description. She's the best there is, the one you dreamed about, the one most mushers never get to experience. You platoon other leaders to run with her, a different partner for every heat. You have to, because they can't take the pressure that Jenny puts on. How much do animals understand? You know this: Jenny understands winning. She gloats when you finish first. For her, it's all about overtaking teams and passing them, about the giddy joy of racing. Contrary to the romanticized notions of the sled-dog leader, she's not aggressive with other dogs. No, she has a way about her that's not quite aloof, but not familiar either. Her talent lies in leading by example, in her complete enthusiasm for running and focused selflessness that somehow instills in the other dogs the same desire. That deed red color of hers has to signify heart. In every heat of every race Jenny is up in the front. She's that good.

At the fourteen-mile marker the radio says you're running a tag over forty-three minutes. That's just under twenty miles an hour average. A good fourteen-mile time, but probably not good enough for a first-place finish today. More like third or fourth. But don't think of the finish. Pay attention to this very moment. Not too fast, not too slow, just try to stay in there with the best of them, and hope you have something left for the third day when the chips are down. Just keep quiet and let them do what they're trained to do.

Sometimes all of them look fine, they're settled in and you're gaining on the finish, then all of a sudden one goes down. This time you've just passed the sixteen-mile marker and you're headed into the homestretch. You're pumping hard, picking them up a little at the end. Suddenly, it's Frog, the new dog in front of wheel who starts to wobble. Just a little hesitation at first, then he takes on the motion of a blown tire, wobbling big time. The next thing you know he's down, dragging on his side like he's been hit in the back of the head with a ball-peen hammer. You drag him on his neckline a ways, just to make sure he's all the way out, so he won't struggle much when you load him.

It's all about speed now.

You hit the brake and in the same motion set the snow hook. You're off the sled running, your knife in your teeth. The dogs still standing start lunging against their lines, thinking they're in trouble. You reach the downed dog. He's trying to stand again, trying to get back on his feet, not wanting to quit, not wanting to risk quitting. You grab your knife, cut the backline, cut the neckline, pick him up, and run for the sled. In one connected motion you throw Frog in the basket, reach down and pull the snow hook, holler "All right," pivot and hit the runners. If you've done it right, it's all fluid, fifteen seconds for the whole operation, start to finish.

The team's slow to gain speed at first, they're tired, and their concentration, the trance of distance, has been broken by the stop. But Jenny's working hard at getting things moving again. She winds them up like a locomotive, climbs up into that rhythm again and settles down. Your only desire now is that you make the finish without any other distractions.

You keep an eye on them as you reach over the driving bow and tie in Frog. There was no quit in him, no give up, he just pushed himself past the point of no return. He wasn't in the shape that the rest of them are, didn't have the miles on him. You made a mistake taking him, a new dog, one you didn't know that much about. The guy you bought him from said he was good, and you watched him run in the guy's team. He looked good, in your mind the best one in there. But you should have known better than to trust a new dog in an important race. It's always ultimately all about you and the decisions you make. It always seems to get down to the old saying, "Races are won by the dogs you leave at home."

Your policy is if they go down once, that's it for them, they're sold as soon as you get back to the truck. It's a policy that has its flaws. In early January a little black female, a hell of a hard-working dog, went down in the second heat. You were mad, driving way too hard. But it was only a fourteen-miler, a short race, and the black female went down like a stone in water, a half mile from the finish. You had your policy. You sold the black female to a fellow from Alberta who had said to you before the race that he'd take anything you wanted to get rid of.

You can't win them all. The fellow from Alberta called you two months after you sold the black bitch to him, said that she'd been carrying pups. She had three healthy ones four days after he bought her from you. "She's the best dog I ever drove," he said. "The pups look good too."

That's just how hard and tucked in the belly she was, how willing she was to run, how tough she was. You lost a good dog that time, sold her way too cheap. She was a ten, but you couldn't see it.

If you're driving top dogs, though, and you know them, they don't often go down. To win you have to count on the flawless run. If it's all working the way it's supposed to, you the driver become part of it. You become the dogs and the dogs become you. You think something, more speed maybe, only think it, and the dog team thinks the same thing. You just know it because you experience it. Because you've put so much of your life into this game, so much energy, spent so much time in the kennel and on the back of a sled, you've become them and they've become you. It's spooky sometimes.

How much did loading Frog hurt you today? In sprint racing, seconds count. Loading and hauling one dog can mean dropping several places in the finishing order. Fifteen seconds it took to load him. But there's always the chance that one of the other front-runners will have trouble too. Never give up. Never. Just keep pumping, let those dogs of yours know you're working with them. There're still fifteen of them out in front of you, and they're all looking strong. Whistle to them, the sharp little signal for more gas: "Wheet!" That's all it takes. They respond, put their heads down and give you more.

You're closing in on the finish line. Keep kicking. The radio announcer says they have you in sight at the College Road crossing. Kick. You're headed home. Call to the leaders as they enter the crossing: "Straight ahead!" But Jenny doesn't need any command. She knows as much as you do.

You're off and running. They cross the street in fine shape. You leap for the runners. Kick. Down the steep bank, onto Noyes Slough. Kick. You notice Doofus falter on the downhill. He's looking tired. But Doofus always looks tired at the end, and he's never gone down. If he did, you would have to break your sell-if-they-go-down policy. If Doofus went down there would have to be something out of the ordinary happening. Speak quietly to him now, assure him: "It's all right, big fella, we're almost home."

You're on the river now, closing fast on the team that started in front of you. Whistle them up—Wheet!—ask them to finish hard. The musher in front is having trouble with one of his swings. It's trying to pull off the trail, a sure sign of a dog that can't take any more pressure. You come closer, and when your leaders are within twenty feet you call, "Trail!" The guy hits his brake, just like the rules call for. Jenny blasts by, passes the team like they're tied to a post. No looking back now, just keep pushing, keep kicking.

You're up the riverbank and making the turn onto Second Avenue. Way down at the end you can see the trucks lined up at the finish. The crowd behind the storm fences sees you and begins to cheer. Jenny picks it up; she loves the sound of that cheering. So do you. Kick. Let them know you're serious about this game. Kick. The finish is a hundred yards away.

Off and running, your lungs burn, but you can hear the announcer now: "And here he comes, ladies and gentlemen, a young musher from out there at Thirty Mile on the Tanana, starting in sixth place today, finishing with a fine time that puts him right up there among the leaders."

So you're a dog man now. You know the warm seduction of a crowd cheering. But that's not even close to the main thing you love about driving dogs. What you love is putting together so many disparate elements: diet, medicine, gear, dealing, breeding, developing pups. The psychology of training. You love shaping it all into one thing, the power of that many elements molded together into a single composition, the sheer enjoyment of being the key to the success of it. You're a hero in the making. You've played the game the way you thought it was supposed to be played. And you're so close now.

One of the peculiarities of the white race's presence in America is how little intention has been applied to it. . . . Once the unknown of geography was mapped, the industrial marketplace became the new frontier, and we continued, with largely the same motives and with increasing haste and anxiety, to displace ourselves—no longer with unity of direction, like a migrant flock, but like the refugees from a broken anthill.

Wendell Berry

We flew east and north. The country spread out below us, green and mottled with lakes and streams, miles and miles and miles of untracked wilderness. To the north, the southern foothills of the Brooks Range climbed up into what looked like an endless mass of high gray peaks. Even though I'd already flown over a lot of country in Alaska, I'd never felt anything like this before. It was as if we had penetrated another dimension, a step back into something entirely primal. Paul Shanahan, my bush pilot, looked over at me and he must have seen my awe. Over the clatter of the engine he yelled, "Ain't a bad piece of country, is it?" I nodded and felt such great joy for my life right then. Joy, because I was entering a wilder place than I'd ever been before. And because I was still caught in the fantasy that it was all out there just for me. At that moment I was not in an airplane flying through the twentieth century, but was eddying backward in time, seized by the sensual excitement of a man about to enter virgin territory.

We flew up into the southern foothills of the Brooks Range, banked, and twisted north into a narrow valley with a frothing stream plunging from it. As we broke over a low ridge, there below us was the lake, a long narrow jewel of water surrounded by steep mountains of gray talus and pale green tundra. Shanahan dropped quickly, nosed into the close end of the lake, and landed. We skimmed across the water's surface, slowed, and settled to a stop on the far end. "Here's where I leave you," he said. "Weather depending, I'll be back in a week."

My companion, Murry, and I waded ashore with our gear. We stood there and watched the Cessna take off. The engine's roar beat against the mountains. Water sprayed white and charged from its floats. It gained speed. One float tipped up, then the other, and then the plane was off, disappearing quickly over the ridge at the west end of the lake. I felt it then, and have many times since, the mix of joy and vulnerability of a bush pilot leaving you in some remote place. Your lifeline, the only person alive who knows for sure exactly where you are. Pray that nothing happens to the pilot. Pray for good weather the day of his scheduled return.

The next morning we got up early, ate a quick breakfast, then climbed a mountain at the head of a valley. Within a half hour of climbing we came up on a fine, full-curl ram. He stood staring at us less than a hundred yards away, white and muscular, horns perfectly formed and unbroomed. He was alert but not particularly afraid of us. Murry wanted to take only a record-book sheep; if he couldn't kill big, he said, he wouldn't kill at all. He told me to go ahead and shoot. I crept forward a few more yards, dropped down into a sitting position, and shot. The ram hunched then launched itself forward into space. He landed hard on rocks thirty feet below and tumbled sickeningly, over and over, down the mountain. I felt my stomach grip as we watched the fall, scared that I'd lose him in some crevice or his horns would be damaged. Finally his descent slowed, and he came to a shuddering stop on a rocky outcrop just above the valley floor.

Murry slapped me on the back. "Good job," he said. We climbed down to the ram and I touched him. He was a beautiful animal, his horns miraculously undamaged from the fall. I felt a wave of affection for the animal, an appreciation for it. I asked Murry to take the pictures, then we skinned and caped the sheep, cut it into quarters, and packed it back to camp.

That night we fried back-strap on the camp stove. There's no better wild meat that I know of. A fat bull caribou, taken before the run, is wonderful. A dry cow moose can be superb. Elk is almost always good. But a wild sheep, it's as if the essence of the mountains is concentrated in the flesh. On your tongue is the taste of pure wild.

The day that Shanahan was due to pick us up, the sun came out and the snow began to melt. Around noon we heard a plane approaching. The Cessna landed, taxied close to our pile of gear on the lakeshore. We loaded up and took off. I'll come back, I vowed, as we cleared the ridge and dropped down into the valley below. Little did I know what was in store for that country. Years later I ran into Shanahan up on the North Slope, and he told me that after he flew us in there the pilots up in that country had taken to calling the lake Brunk Lake, because as he said then, "No one else was ever crazy enough to want to go in there before you came along."

Several years later the state of Alaska pushed a haul road through the Brooks Range to the North Slope, the first road ever in those mountains. Today I'm not exactly sure where that lake is; I can't pinpoint it on a map. The best I can figure is that the haul road comes within a few miles of it. A year or so after the road was built, I talked to my friend at Alaska Fish and Game who had told me about the lake. I asked him if he knew anything about the sheep in those mountains. He told me that the road came close enough to the lake that hunters could pack into it fairly easily. He thought the sheep had mostly been shot out the years immediately following the road's construction. I felt something go cold inside me. I felt anger and regret. It was as if a sense of ownership had been violated; that was my country. I knew that my experience there was going to be difficult to have again—anywhere; Murry and I had experienced one of the last untouched places of the last frontier.

The construction of the road north through the Brooks Range—the Dalton Highway—was like a slash across the face of the Mona Lisa. I've seen it so many times since, how the promoters get their way and a road is pushed into a place, and as soon as it is something terribly vital is lost, a crucial spirit is sucked from the country. The sellers of Alaska, sellers the world over, push for more access, more roads, talk about the economic necessity of them. Beneath the obvious economic grab, I suppose some promoters and engineers and construction workers believe they're doing something useful and good, that somehow they're advancing the cause of mankind. But what they won't see, can't see in their blind greed, is that every mile built is one more nail in the heart of the natural world.

Today I'm well aware of the paradox of my own special privilege in entering that country when I did. I could afford to use an airplane, so the argument could be made, and is, that without roads, access into wild country is left to only an elite few. In the scheme of the American class system, though, I'm anything but elite. The point is, I made it my priority to go there, and I wouldn't today if I could access it by road because the place wouldn't be the same. The qualities I desire to experience would be gone. Certainly, though, I must take some responsibility for being part of the place's demise. It's not lost on me that my entry, to be the first to kill a sheep there, was a violation of sorts, a very small act, comparatively, in a much larger, destructive drama that's been going on for several centuries now. The central issue, then, is not about whether we arrive by road or air, but about all the destructive things and attitudes we bring with us, the mentality that builds roads and hunts areas to extinction. This is what's ultimately destroying the biosphere that we all depend on for life.

THE RAGE OF MEN

> The tragedy of the old rites of manhood is that they made so many of us morally tone-deaf. We have become so tough-minded and tough-hearted, such experts in control and command, that we can hardly hear the crying needs of our time or the first faint strand of melody the future is sounding. . . . The historical challenge for modern men is clear—to discover a peaceful form of virility and to create an ecological commonwealth, to become fierce gentlemen.
>
> Sam Keen, "Fire in the Belly"

Much later, a year after my own brush with death, I found myself at my father's bedside. He'd had a long history of small strokes, attacks to his brain that over a span of ten years had taken him deeper and deeper into a distant and agitated senility. After his final stroke he lay comatose in a Mennonite nursing center. "I'm here, Dad," I said, as I came to his bedside, knowing full well he could not reply, but hoping he could sense my presence. His eyes were strangely complicated, vacant, yet fearful at the same time. His barrel chest, now only ribs and soft folds of red, mottled skin, rose and fell with the slow effort of his breathing. His mouth hung agape, toothless. The skin of his face stretched like parchment over his cheekbones, so hot and dry that it looked as if it might split if touched.

I sat with him then, night and day, waiting for the inevitable. I held his hand, stroked his head, played a tape of his favorite hymns over and over. "It's OK to die," I said to him many times. "It's OK, you're loved." The sound of my voice, my presence, seemed to be a comfort to him. His breathing would slow and his face would settle into the most fragile countenance. In these moments I uncovered evidence of the progression of my own healing—I discovered that I loved my father, without embarrassment; I deeply loved him.

I left his side for only short periods of time to get some food or help my invalid mother come see him. When I returned each time he was agitated again, his eyes wide with fear. But as soon as I came into the room and spoke to him he visibly calmed.

He became weaker and weaker, yet he held on. I was astounded that he could continue to live without taking any water or food. Mid-morning of the third day I told him I needed to get something to eat, that I would be back soon. I left and was gone for no more than an hour. When I returned, something had changed in the room, not anything I can describe easily, more just a feeling that a decision had been made.

I sat beside him again, took his hand in mine, and said to him, "I'm back, Dad." He took one long shuddering breath. This is it, I thought to myself, he's actually going to die. But then he took another breath, and for an instant I thought he was going to hang on a while longer. Let go, I thought, just this once, let go.

His next breath ended differently, with a deep sigh at the end that seemed to say, "Enough, I've had enough."

I watched the blood drain from his face, the death mask, watched it fall like a curtain over his life. And then I tapped him gently on top of his head, signaling his soul that it was time to leave, a ritual carried from my Buddhist readings. Otherwise, the Buddhists say, the soul may stay with the body, confused about the departure time. I knew that my father had waited for me to return before he died. He waited, and as soon as he knew I was there by his side, he let go. This fact means a lot to me.

I sat quietly with him then, knowing I needed to mourn. I felt both sorrow and relief for his dying. A flood of memories rolled across my mind. I thought of all the ways he had pushed against life and against those who had tried to love him. I thought of the years he had come to Alaska, how he had seemed at peace there. I was glad he had those times. I began to cry. There was no apology to it. In my sorrow for his dying I uncovered further evidence of my own healing. For I knew that I loved my father. Despite all his sins against me, a man who had never once in his life said to me "I love you," still, I loved him, and I had told him so before he died.

Not long ago I came across a journal entry I wrote while my father was dying. "Being here is such a gift," the entry begins. "I watch him hold onto life out of the fear of death. I see it: underneath all his religious trappings is a deep mistrust of his God. And rightfully so, for who could ever be good enough to meet a God so full of judgment? Who would *want* to meet such a God? How lonely this time must be for him."

It was after the funeral that I asked my mother if he had ever talked of dying, ever mentioned his fears or his questions. She thought about it for some time before she replied. "No," she said, "in all the fifty-five years we were married he never once mentioned death."

"But why?" I asked.

"I think he was afraid of it," she said. "Your father did not like to admit his fears." I recalled a time six months earlier when I had visited my father. He sat essentially mute, hunched over in a wheelchair, food stains dribbled down his shirt front. I thought of my own near-death, the tunnel of white light, the voice. "Dad," I said. "I think there's nothing to fear. It's OK to die."

He turned his head haltingly and looked at me. Like a storm building in a distant sky, his eyes filled with the old rage. "What are you saying to me!" he shouted. "What kind of craziness are you talking about?" And then as quickly as it had built, his rage ended. He turned away from me, back into his private and lonely world.

Awareness is the first step toward change. I began to look seriously at my own anger, where it came from, where it had taken me, the things I desired that it kept from me. I saw my father. My grandfather. I began to address the hard ball of anger in my gut. It has not been an instant change. But the disease that I inherited from my father, my grandfather, a long line of men, began to soften and dissolve. Often now, I live free of it.

Rage acknowledged and turned outward toward some injustice is a great tool. Rage carried and turned inward, denied, becomes disease. In my pacifist father I saw elements of the same frustrations that turn men to war, to the obliteration of the earth. The rage of feeling inconsequential and impotent in the face of forces one cannot understand, the frustration of feeling something important and essential in one's life as being out of reach because of circumstances, the press of a judgmental God, all of these things gnawed at my father. I believe, too, that all these things gnaw at a lot of men, men in all walks of life, all levels of power.

My father was no different from most of us. We rage against the inevitability of our death, rage against the paltriness of our own existence. We fear the darkness. Against all of it we strive desperately for control, and in the pursuit of this illusion we subdue, conquer, manipulate, wage war, attempt to manage things from a myopic and limited perspective of how they need to be. Ravaged forests, rivers, farmlands, cultures, families, women, and children, all bear witness to our disease.

We have to find another way. We need to make amends. It's no exaggeration to say that if we don't change there's little hope for this earth. I'm here, as a witness, also to say that the rage we carry can be released. It's as simple and as difficult as that, *released,* like taking off a suit of armor or dropping a weapon. The world is crying for us to do so.

A couple of years after my near-death experiences, one fine, cloudless bluebird of a day my daughter Cara and I carried backpacks along the continental divide of the northern Rockies. We had left the Forest Service trail the day before and were now angling high along a ridgeline, through fields of dusty red boulders and carpets of yellow and deep purple alpine flowers. Once a band of bighorn sheep wheeled and ran away from us as we approached. Another time we stopped and watched a cow and calf moose break from the timber far below and move quickly across a meadow.

At the base of the tallest peak for miles around, we dropped our packs and began to climb. We climbed fast, both of us breathing hard. I reveled in the strength of my legs, my breath coming strong, the sheer joy of being alive in the wild.

We gained the peak and hunkered down out of the wind to take in the view—mountains stretching bold in all directions. It was some time before Cara broke the spell.

"Dad," she said.

"Uh-huh."

"Thanks for being here with me."

"Thanks back to you."

She turned and looked at me, her expression so kind. "Remember when you almost died?"

"How could I forget?"

"Well, if I haven't said so, I'm sure glad you didn't. Because I feel really lucky to have you as a dad."

"Thanks for saying so," I said.

"Sure," she said. "Anytime."

Brad K. Younkin

The Speed of Memory

The man who raped my mother may not have been from Indiana, and he may have never lived there, but he drove through there. He carried a switchblade knife in the front pocket of his jeans where he could access it easily. He drove a small red car. He had brown hair, a bit disheveled, but had nice-looking features and seemed nice. He wasn't very tall. He smiled. Sometimes he wore a red flannel shirt, or at least did so once, when he drove U.S. Highway 41 in southwestern Indiana toward Vincennes. He drove behind a black four-wheel-drive Chevrolet Blazer that was pulling a brown horse trailer. He followed the Blazer and drove into the lane beside it. His windows were down. It was summer, warm and clear, late morning. From the left lane he motioned and got the attention of the woman in the Blazer, and he was saying something to her and pointing toward the back of the horse trailer.

"Like there was something *wrong*," my mother said. My father, my sister, and I had met her in the kitchen; she had just returned home, it was evening, already dark. She had told us the trip was fine, and sat down at the table, still in her boots, her purse still on her arm. "There was something *weird* that happened, though. I mean *weird*. This guy in a little red car drove up beside me and started waving at me and he kept pointing at the back of the trailer, like there was something *wrong*."

"You didn't stop, though?" my father said.

"No. I wasn't going to stop, I just kept driving. But it was so weird. After that he dropped back for a while, and a few minutes later he drove up beside me again. It was scary. And it was so bizarre—the man didn't have any *pants* on." She soaked up our reactions and told us that she'd sped up, that she drove over ninety miles per hour, that the man in the little red car finally dropped back and took an exit, and that she didn't see him again.

I was eleven when my mother told this story, the first lie I remember her telling, and the first of many more she would have to tell to uphold it. I stood by her that night listening, confused about the man in the red car, his nakedness, about her awed and almost smiling disposition as she spoke. I couldn't understand—why a man would do that, what he felt he could gain by it, or why a woman would tell of it the way my mother did, her story hopelessly unfinished, her body language mismatching her words.

When my mother and father were children, they both loved horses without ever owning one, and both resolved to raise horses when they reached adulthood. My father was a self described "city boy," raised in small towns in southern Illinois by his father, a Pentecostal preacher, and a stern, often unfair stepmother. He enlisted for Vietnam so he could leave home, and after a year of duty he chose to stay six more months instead of returning to his family. My mother grew up on a farm in Massac County in southern Illinois, the youngest of four children. Most snapshots of her show her in the yard with animals: dogs, chickens, goats, a pet squirrel, a duckling. She was a tomboy, preferring to work outside with Grandpa, in the garden, with the cattle and hogs, than inside helping Grandma with household chores. She hunted and fished with Grandpa. One time she fired twice and shot four ducks flying from a pond. When she was twelve, one of her brothers saw her bathing in the metal tub in the shed and made fun of her to schoolmates and she hit him in the head with a brick; Grandpa gave her a spanking she still remembers. She was fourteen when they got indoor plumbing. Though she was an aggressive tomboy, she was also thin and sickly, with allergies and a picky appetite. High school classmates called her "Bones" for her skinny frame, and she finished school with a rather disinterested efficiency, earning good grades without much engagement, with an unlikely notion that she'd like to be a nurse someday, and after graduation she married the young man she'd dated for two years, a drummer in a country band, and wouldn't meet my father for another two years.

Her first marriage produced my sister, but otherwise failed. Just before the divorce was final, she met my father while selling lingerie at a Sears in Paducah, Kentucky. He worked across the aisle selling men's suits and soon synchronized his break schedule with hers. He used the time to get acquainted, angle for a date, deflect her insistence that she didn't want a date, that she instead wanted time for herself and her baby. He was undeterred, confident, charming, kind, and she gave in. No one support- ed their relationship: my father's Pentecostal family called her "the devil's daughter" for having divorced and for wearing long pants and makeup; Grandpa said my dad needed to be castrated. But two years into their marriage, I was born.

It would require many more years—switching jobs, relocating, visit- ing family, sending and receiving birthday and Christmas cards—until their parents' criticism abated and at last stopped. Any disapproval was pointless now. When I was six Dad took a job in Paducah and we moved to Massac County onto a hill on twenty acres of cow pasture, part of Grandpa's will intended for my mother, bequeathed early. They wheeled in and anchored down a double-wide mobile home amid cow paths and cow piles, built a barn, put up fences for horses, and settled down across the gravel road from my grandparents' farm where their cattle, displaced by our new home, stood grazing and flipping their tails.

On this horse farm, our lives were woven according to the needs of the horses, the needs of the farm, and we lived in a rhythm—daily, monthly, yearly—of work intended to keep the horses healthy and productive and marketable; and so when, in 1983, Mom came home the night after being raped and told us about her trip, business went on as usual. I don't remem- ber when she started to waver; the rhythm for a while held her up, kept her and everyone else busy, until she couldn't find a way to weave her life into it anymore, and her life, outside of that rhythm, began to unravel.

She had driven into Indiana, bound for Vincennes, to drop off a friend's stud for a surgery. She turned north onto Highway 41, a four-lane divided highway, around midmorning. After a while, the small red car drove up beside her with the man inside waving, motioning toward the trailer. She saw him and tried to ignore him. She shook her head, as if to say, no, I'm not stopping. He dropped back behind her and drove in that manner for a time, before driving up beside her again and continuing to motion. She was scared, both of this stranger, and of the idea that perhaps something *was* wrong, either with the trailer, or, worse, the horse inside. She slowed down and drove onto the shoulder and stopped.

She stayed in the driver's seat, the Blazer's engine running. She rolled down her window. In the side mirror she saw the man get out of his car. He put up a hand.

"Good morning," he said. "You got some trouble back here."

She stepped out. "Trouble?"

"Something's wrong here with this window. It's banging around."

She walked toward the trailer. She wondered how anything could be wrong with the back window; she tried to recall closing it. When she got to the back she looked at the window, which was closed, and then at the man. He raised his switchblade in one hand and drove his other forearm under her chin, pinning her against the trailer, the blade at her face.

"You'll be dead by morning," he said.

He opened the left side of the trailer, the vacant side, and pushed her down inside it. On his knees, he unclasped and pulled down her jeans and opened his own. An occasional car may or may not have passed by, but it's unlikely either of them knew for certain; they both struggled. When it was over he leaned back and sat just behind the trailer, facing her, and looked up at the sky. He may have been unguarded for only a second, maybe two. In this moment, with her jeans to her knees, she kicked the man in the crotch, pulled up her jeans, and ran.

He lay there for a moment, writhing, buckled, reaching out. The Blazer was still running and she climbed in. Before she could shift to drive, he had almost reached her. She pushed the button for the window to rise and pressed the accelerator, and as she pulled away his fingers were stuck in the window, and he dragged along a few feet, his fingers cracking, before he fell alongside and she drove away. In the side mirror she saw him climb to his feet and run stumbling to his car.

Perhaps a year or so later, but long before we knew the truth, Bobby Knight, basketball coach for the Indiana University Hoosiers, said: "If rape is so inevitable, why don't women sit back and enjoy it?" My family watched the story on the evening news. Bobby Knight didn't try to defend himself in a hastily arranged damage-control press conference; he apologized and pleaded that his words were out of context, although he didn't adequately explain what that context might have been.

"How could somebody say that?" Mom said.

"It's pretty stupid," Dad said.

"How could somebody even *think* that?" She shook her head, awed. "Rape is awful. It's a horrible thing, and to even think that is ridiculous, it's insane."

Dad and my sister and I agreed.

Mom said, "Remember last summer when that weird guy drove up beside me in Indiana and didn't have any pants on—that man could have raped *me*."

This was a stunning and perplexing possibility, and we were frightened and agreed that Bobby Knight was a fool. Connie Chung, while discussing the comment with a guest or with a co-anchor, said Knight's statement sounded like something an old grandfather would say, which further angered old grandfathers everywhere and which would lead her to publicly apologize for offending *them*. Mom said, "Grandpa would never, *ever*, say something like that. Would he?" We told her he would never say that.

It wasn't long after this that Mom became depressed periodically. She'd get sick. She wouldn't eat supper, but would instead stay in bed all night. When she left the bedroom late in the evening she'd wear her robe and move slowly down the hall. She'd move like a statue on wheels, across the kitchen floor to fill a glass of water. She'd step into the living room where we were watching television and wave to us sadly and say good night and go back to her bedroom. Her depression would last a couple weeks and subside.

One day Mom came home from shopping in Paducah.

"I just had the strangest experience," she said to me and my sister. "I was in Readmore, and this guy walked up to me; he was a young person, in his twenties, probably. He looked at me and said, 'Excuse me, ma'am. I just wanted to say that you look very . . . healthy. You really look healthy.' I didn't know what to say, so I just said, 'Thanks.' Isn't that weird? What does that mean—'You look healthy'? Healthy?"

We didn't know, but whatever it meant, or whatever the man and his strange compliment meant to our mother—it sent her falling, soon after, into another depression.

After my mother was raped, she sped away on Highway 41 with her left trailer door swinging and the rapist's red car trailing her, visible in the side mirror, moving closer. She drove faster. The Blazer had a full-size eight cylinder engine, and soon she approached one hundred miles per hour and the red car faded.

She didn't slow down, even after she couldn't see the red car and didn't know where it had driven to. Little time had passed when she drove by an Indiana State Police cruiser, which immediately chased her with full siren and lights.

She pulled over. After a few long moments, the police officer approached. He looked in her window and asked if she knew how fast she'd been going. Mom said, "I was raped back there. A man in a red car raped me. I got away from him and he's still out there chasing me. He's still on the road."

The police officer looked at her. He was silent for a moment, and no cars passed and nothing seemed to be happening. He looked up and then down the highway. It was bright and still and quiet.

"Look," he said. "Just slow it down, lady."

He turned and walked back to his patrol car; in a few seconds he turned off his pursuit lights and drove away easily.

During Mom's depressions, we were all confused, perhaps no one more than my father. He would spend long hours sitting at her bedside talking to her, whispering, trying to locate the problem, asking her why she was feeling so bad, hoping to hear it articulated. Their bedroom was adjacent to mine, and instead of sleeping I would often put my ear to the wall. Now and then I listened through a wet glass, which seemed to amplify tiny sounds more clearly. Sometimes, in the living room, Dad would tell me, "Your mother and I are going to talk," and he'd ask me to go to my room. I would crouch in the hallway and listen. He asked her many times, in many different phrases: Why? He didn't know that she saw the rapist's face in any place at any time: while driving, eating dinner, taking a bath, walking to the barn, glancing out a window or into a mirror. He didn't know what she had to ignore and overcome when they made love. He didn't know how fast her memory had to run to elude the rapist before she could settle her mind enough to fall into restless sleep. He didn't know how heavy a burden her guilt had become, that when she looked at her family she saw people she loved who were hurt by what she considered an inability on her part to cope with pain, which made her feel more guilty—

guilt on top of guilt—until the pain and inability shook her down and, indeed, coping became impossible.

For almost two years, she openly blamed money problems for her depression. The horses drained their budget, for certain. Other times she said she worried about my teenage sister, who had become disenchanted with many things and made it known through various means: lying, smoking pot, dodging family events, ignoring school work. Other times Mom simply said she was feeling sick, tired, or plain sick and tired, or worried about various friends who were having problems. Yet the extremity of her reaction, her depression, never seemed consistent with the causes she offered, and Dad couldn't understand and he finally told her so. I couldn't understand either. My sister was troubled by it and often displayed her confusion through harshness. "I don't know what her problem is," she said once. "Why does she act like that?" This was a question we all asked. Dad would tell us, "Mom is just worried—a lot of it has to do with money problems. She doesn't want you all to feel bad or have a hard time. She's a kind and caring person and she's worried about us. It's in her nature to worry. She feels things more deeply than most people." I couldn't make sense of it. All I could do was file the experiences away without examination, without processing them, without thinking about them productively at all. There were times I heard her say to Dad, "I just want to die," or "I wish I could die," and I wouldn't know what to feel, or what to do differently, and even today I can't remember what I felt, beyond an open emptiness or despair and an almost tangible frustration that made me want to go to her and touch her shoulder and ask her to tell me why she would rather die than be with us, with me—what was it that made her life with us worse than death?

Before she told us about the rape, we went to a weekend horse show in Louisville in early October. My fourteenth birthday fell on that Sunday. It was an important show, held for yearlings and two-year-olds. We hoped to show well and sell a horse. My sister stayed home. During the weekend there was an enormous flea market, and I slipped away now and then to buy baseball cards from the various dealers with tables there.

On Sunday morning before the show Mom started acting strangely. Her speech was slurred, her movements uncoordinated, her words seemed to make little sense. She said a man backed his horse into her and knocked her down on purpose. We knew this was ludicrous, but she cursed him, said he worked for Larry Watson, a horseman who they knew. She lay down in the backseat of the Blazer and we had to leave her there with the doors locked when it was time for our class. I had to go with Dad.

I don't remember if we won or lost, but afterward we went back to the trailer and Mom was gone. We took turns looking for her while the other waited at the Blazer. Three hours passed. At midafternoon, I was searching around the flea market, moving quickly from one building to the next. It was crowded. Over the intercom I heard, twice: *Terry Younkin and Brad Younkin please report to the nurse's office in Assembly Hall.* I learned where to go and ran there, expecting she might be dead, expecting at least an ambulance. I suppose my expression gave away these fears; the woman outside the nurse's office saw me and said, "Are you Brad? Your mother's okay. She's in the office with your dad."

Mom was lying down on a table in the office. She had been found by a guard in a golf cart; she had been rolling, crying, in the middle of one of the streets of the fairgrounds, saying that someone was trying to kill her. They determined she was incoherent and took her to the nurse, who gave her a mild tranquilizer and found out from her who to page to pick her up.

Back at the trailer Mom was insisting that a man with brown hair and a red shirt with a brown jacket who worked for Larry Watson backed his horse up and knocked her down on purpose. Dad said that was ridiculous, that no one would do that, that someone working for Larry wouldn't do that, but Mom shook her head and insisted. "He meant to *hurt* me," she said. "I want you to go to him and tell him he's a son of a bitch."

"There's no way I'm going to do that."

"Tell him he's a son of a bitch. If you don't do it I will. He is a son of a bitch."

"You're not going to do that," Dad said. "He didn't do it on purpose."

"I want you to tell him. If you don't do it I will."

They stared at each other. The trailer and Blazer by now had been packed and we were ready to leave. They looked like two gunfighters about to draw pistols.

Dad pointed at her. "I'll find Larry," he said, "and find out where this guy is, and I'm going to tell him he's a son of a bitch. It's not right, and you're crazy, you know that? I'm going to do this and we're leaving." Dad walked away. Mom went to the backseat of the Blazer and lay down. I sat in the passenger seat, with a sunken feeling, knowing, as Dad did, that there was no positive solution to this problem. If he didn't do what she insisted, she would implicate him, blame him for taking the wrong side, even though he knew it was wrong. Going along with her seemed to be the only path to choose.

In fifteen minutes, he came back, and we left. After a few minutes of not speaking, we were on the interstate toward home. Dad said, "I told that guy he was a son of a bitch, and he didn't know what I was talking about. He never did anything wrong." Dad's voice was weakening and now he was crying. "If I thought," he said, "that you did this on purpose—I'd want to kick your ass." Nothing more was said for the rest of the four hours home; Dad and I would try vainly to figure out what had made her behave as she did. We would not know for another year that the man wearing a red shirt and working for Larry Watson had simply buttoned up his own misfortune. He had reminded her of another man.

When the police officer drove away from Mom and left her on the shoulder of the road, she was left with an immediate and horrible fear that the rapist would return. She hurriedly got out and closed the trailer door and drove away. The environment in the Blazer offered a heinous sense of normalcy: a plastic cup of iced tea, directions to the vet in Vincennes, her purse, a cinnamon roll, a George Jones cassette. She drove, frantic and dismayed and scared to death. The idea of disease came to her. She stopped at a convenience store, pulled up and parked, afraid to get out, afraid that he would be there, working the counter, hiding in an aisle, hiding in the bathroom, afraid that he would appear out of nowhere. She got out, locked the doors, and inside the bathroom tried to clean herself. She hurried back to the Blazer, looked inside, looked in the trailer, and then drove away, constantly trying to compose herself, always checking the side mirrors and the opposite lanes, her heart leaping at that color of red, remembering the neat fingernails and wide knuckles of his fingers clutching her window as it tried to close on them, and when she arrived in Vincennes her eyes darted about the pedestrians in an ongoing search for a man in red flannel, a young man with nice features who seemed nice, and she pulled up at the veterinarian's and took a deep breath.

She told Dad about the rape three years after it happened, in their bedroom, around 11 p.m., a Friday night. I heard it through the wall. She said,

"I was raped." She told him it happened in Indiana. She told him she shouldn't have stopped, but she thought something was wrong with the horse. She said, "He had a switchblade knife, and he forced me into the trailer and raped me. He said I'd be dead by morning." She told him how she kicked him and escaped, and how she was pulled over, and how the police officer had said "Just slow it down, lady." She said later, "I couldn't tell you. I thought you would try to find him and you'd want to kill him. You'd have gone to jail. And I couldn't tell the kids. I just couldn't hurt them like that. I couldn't tell Daddy. I couldn't hurt him like that. He wouldn't understand." I listened longer, but I don't remember much more.

The next afternoon I was in the barn working and Dad said he needed to talk to me. He set up two folding chairs. I sat facing him; I was guilty for knowing the truth. He summarized her cycles of depression and suggested to me that there was a reason for them, and reminded me that Mom loved my sister and me very much and that she was a strong person, a good person, who never intended to hurt any of us or anyone else—I nodded and said that I agreed. He was crying. He said, "Three years ago, your mother was raped." He said the last word carefully. "It happened in Indiana." He asked if I understood, and I nodded that I did. He said it wasn't her fault. "She didn't do anything wrong. It was violent; it was wrong. And your mother tried to get over it on her own. She didn't want to hurt any of us. Your mother is a strong person, probably the strongest person I've ever known." He said a rape could happen to any person, that even a man can be raped, and that it can affect a person for years. He said that Mom would need our help, our support. The decision was made to not tell Grandpa, and to handle it ourselves.

After she told us the truth, things were better. There was a palpable sadness, but with it an understanding. We at least understood the facts, the reasons. We conducted ourselves with an optimism, probably unaware how overwhelmed we were by the truth, standing as if in the shadow of an enormous mountain, needing to climb it, our feet shackled. We knew why, when she again fell into a depression a few months later, but we knew of no means to help her through it, no words to say, no system to initiate to handle her particular needs. We let her know we understood, that it was okay, and that provided some comfort, but when she again became depressed, and then again after that, we grew tired of making the same appeals that didn't work well enough, and she likely tired of hearing them.

She became bitter. One night before supper, she and I were outside feeding the horses. In about thirty minutes she cussed twenty-one times, over anything: a horse, the barn door, the temperature, a bird on the rafter. When we were inside eating I was thinking, *twenty-one cuss words in thirty minutes.* Sometimes she would cry in the kitchen, behind the barn, sitting in her recliner, all evening, alone, in her bed; other times she would become nauseous and throw up. Viruses lasted for weeks. Arguments would flare up over small things: the way I said something, something my sister decided to do, some criticism Dad raised. She would sometimes stare at one of us for minutes on end without saying a word. Though I knew better, her expression looked like one of hatred. One time, I offended her—I don't remember how—and she demanded that I apologize. I knew I'd done nothing wrong, but as she stared with that look like hatred and disgust, I could think of nothing better to say.

"I'm sorry," I said.

"Do you mean that?" she said.

"Yes," I lied. It may well be that all of us—Mom, Dad, me, and my sister—looked at each other with some genuine resentment during this time. Everyone knew the truth and the reasons for Mom's behavior, and we tried to modify our actions around them without any sustainable success. There was no fine line between tough love on our part and soft compassion. Everything we tried didn't work in exactly the same way. She regarded us at times with love, with an apologetic and sorrowful sadness, but at other times with that look of disgust; we knew the truth, and confronting us meant confronting the truth that she was raped. It's no wonder that she resented such a regular threat, a regular reminder that, yes, she was raped, and no, she wasn't dealing with it. Our hopefulness for her recovery, probably visible on our faces, translated into something unrealistic and unfair. She was left more vulnerable yet, unable to appreciate anything we, or she, did to try to help, the chemicals in her mind swarming about in dangerous mixtures, stupefying her every three months or so, and for a couple weeks she behaved, as my sister pointed out, "like a zombie."

One summer, on a Saturday, she drove away in Dad's work truck to buy strawberries at a u-pick farm. She spun out of our driveway and down the hill and onto the road. After an hour or less, a strange car drove up and Mom got out of the passenger side. She was bruised on her face and her legs and arms were bleeding. She had driven too fast on a curve on a washboarded gravel road. The pickup was light in the rear and flipped easily; wearing no seat belt, she was tossed into dense weeds at the edge of a thicket. The truck was totaled and she was lucky not to have been killed. After being driven home, she walked from the car to the house without thanking the driver or speaking to anyone, stumbling, shrugging off the details of her accident, as if drunk, as if nothing was a big deal at all.

Something gave her the idea to drink vodka one afternoon in May while my sister and I were at school and Dad was working. She rarely drank, and I had never seen her drunk, but she found an old bottle of vodka and drove away in the Blazer.

She drank as she drove, turning down roads that seemed to suggest themselves. The roads she chose became progressively more rural, until she turned finally onto a tractor path that led into a farmer's field. It had rained recently, and she wound up in a low valley of heavy mud that stuck the Blazer.

I had gotten home from school, surprised to find Mom gone, but unaware of any problem until Dad came home and didn't know where she was. He made some calls but no one knew anything. Around 6:30 the Pope County sheriff 's office called. Mom was drunk, in jail in neighboring Pope County, charged with a DUI.

Her license was revoked for two months, and because the arrangement was so unusual and obvious, we had to tell Grandpa about the DUI. He was already aware of her depressions, probably more than we realized. We told him she was worried about money and about other things, but we said nothing of the rape. He seemed to take in the information quietly and sympathetically and without judgment.

I drove Mom around for the two months. She was ashamed, yet thankful for my understanding and help. We talked during the drives, and I learned the streets of Paducah quite well, and Mom seemed to enjoy the shared time. She had reached a low point, and seemed stoic about it; for those two months it seemed as if she might only go up from there.

Later that autumn, my sister's life, like my mother's, began to twist away from the rest of the family's. She had settled down and given up much of her teenage rebellion, and after graduating high school took a year and one-half of classes in a nursing program. She was working steady, studying well, and was in a two-year relationship with a likable young man. Over a two-month period beginning in October she inexplicably ended her relationship and began a new one, dropped out of college, quit her job, got married, and moved away to Chicago, leaving behind much of her belongings and a dumbfounded family.

It's unlikely that my sister's trouble was the ultimate cause of Mom's drifting back into periodic depression, but it didn't help. There was one less warm body in the house, one less person whose presence Mom could think about as she lay in bed in the evening, and one less person whose arrival she could anticipate during a long afternoon of worry and sadness.

My sister's problem, unavoidably, became the family's, but Mom had much more difficulty dealing with it. Because people tend to recall difficult times when difficult times are happening, Mom, depressed, began reliving pain, sorting through decisions she'd made that she wished to change, finding herself in the Blazer at one hundred miles per hour, sitting in the Pope County jail, hiding her face from her family, finding herself, like anyone depressed, wrestling with her memory and losing, wanting to find a kind thought, a soft hand, a hope to help her out of bed and elicit from her a smile, and finding herself without the energy or means to do so; depression made her thin, barely a thumbprint on an enormous pane of glass, an alien in her own body.

One afternoon Grandpa called Mom from his house across the road. He knew she was home, but there was no answer. After a few minutes, he called again without getting an answer, so he drove over. He found her in the backyard, lying on the ground, crying. She got up and insisted she was okay, only a little sad. He said it just wasn't right for a person to act that way, that she needed to get better or, if she couldn't get better, get help. There was no way for her to adequately explain her behavior without telling him of the rape, so he left after a while, not understanding his daughter, knowing something in her had spun out of control.

The next January was cold. Mom had been steadily feeling worse since the holidays. One night she was in her bed while Dad and I watched television in the living room. One of our mares was in the barn, due to bring a colt any day. At 7:30 Mom walked down the hall and stepped into the living room, wearing her long blue robe and slippers.

She said, "I'm going to go check on Amber." She waved to us weakly and stood for a moment, waving, and turned into the utility room. I heard the back door open and close.

Just before eight o'clock Dad got up. "It's been a while. I'm going to go check on Mom." He went down the hall and returned after a couple minutes, carrying a note. "Brad, come here." He put the note on the counter in the kitchen. "We have to go find Mom. She's taken sleeping pills and run off." He held up an empty prescription bottle. "Get your boots on."

He and I put on boots and coveralls, and he got two flashlights. "Put a watch on," he said.

"Mom didn't wear her boots," I said, and I pointed to her boots, still there. "She's out there in her house-shoes," I said. On our way to the barn I said, "That's a suicide note?" He said it was.

Outside was a damp cold and a coal black sky with a bright moon. The barn was still and lifeless except for Amber dozing in her stall, standing under the orange glow of her heat lamp. Asleep, her bottom lip hung down like a cup and her ears fell sideways. Dad flipped on the security light in front of the barn and it flickered to a steady hum.

Dad said, "You go check the back pasture and the back woods and I'll get the Blazer and drive into the front pasture and down by the road. Come back here in thirty minutes."

I went into the back pasture. I shone my light around and now and then I ran a few yards, particularly when the shadows of the moon tricked me, when I thought I saw something lying in the thick weeds and fescue of the pasture, something that made a shadow; but when I ran to it I saw that it had been nothing but pasture. I picked my way into the woods. I imagined her propped against or lying at the base of every tree, alongside every log, partly underneath every briar or bush. Many times in the silver light I was afraid that I had actually seen her, the patterns of the cold bark of a tree trunk suggesting her image, sitting with her eyes closed, wearing her blue robe, her arms hanging down and her mouth open, with pieces of leaves and grass caught in her hair. But when I held the light on the spot I only saw the blank face of a tree.

I was in the barn when the thirty minutes had passed. Dad had just driven back.

I said, "You didn't see anything?"

"No."

"I thought I did a few times but my eyes were playing tricks."

We split up again. I checked in the neighbor's pasture and Dad looked across the road on Grandpa's land. When this turned up nothing after thirty more minutes, Dad called for help from the police, who said they'd come out and bring the volunteer fire department.

"We're going to have to call Grandpa," Dad said.

He called Grandpa. I stood nearby in the tack room and looked at her note. It was scrawled in mostly heavy letters, sharp lines and long curves, literally tear-stained in places. It was a message of love and sorrow and pain; dying seemed to be the only good thing she had the courage to do, the only thing she could do to make our lives easier. She said I was her pride and joy, that Dad was a wonderful loving husband. References to my sister were scattered and confused, much like my sister herself— depression had gnarled my mother's life and rendered it unrecognizable.

I stepped out in front of the barn. I told Dad I was scared and I cried, uncontrollably for a moment. Grandpa's truck was moving down his hill. It turned onto the road and moved along slowly, like a knob, silently. Turning into and climbing our driveway, the lights of his truck sliced and cut a long arc out of the dark. Grandpa got out of his truck and approached us without speaking.

When he reached us, Grandpa said, "What's wrong?"

"Carol's taken a bottle of sleeping pills, and she's run off. We've got people coming to help us look for her. She left about 7:30."

"Taken off?"

"She was depressed."

"She's been that way."

"There's a good reason," Dad said, and he took one deep breath and told Grandpa everything. Grandpa watched Dad without judgment. His glasses were dark in the cold. He shook his head and looked down and then back at Dad. "Well—you tell me where to look and let's find her."

We went searching again a few minutes before help arrived. At least ten vehicles, and up to twenty men. The deputy sheriff came with a German shepherd search dog that responded to German commands. Everyone dispersed. There were walkie-talkies and orders made and received and thoughtful speculation over where she might be and many sympathetic and optimistic comments like: *I'm sure sorry we've got to do this*, and *Don't you worry, we're gonna find your Mom.* The night wore on and midnight approached and passed. Nearing three o'clock, Dad and I stopped in the kitchen to call the deputy. I got a glass of water and felt guilty and out of line for taking a sip of it. I told Dad there was one more place I wanted to look, though I doubted she could have gotten that far. The bridge over the creek, where I sometimes hiked to, where I liked to spend time alone; the water was heavy and dark under the bridge, with a false echo when a rock was flung into it. That was the last place I could think she might have reached, and beyond that I couldn't imagine any other possibilities; beyond the bridge the possibilities became too innumerable and daunting to know where to begin. Just as Dad and I were discussing this, the deputy called. They had found her lying in a ditch beside the bridge over the creek, alive, cold, and incoherent, wearing her robe and a jacket.

We got there as they loaded her in an ambulance on a stretcher. At the hospital they pumped her stomach and stabilized her. We were told she would be fine, and I went home for sleep.

I got to the hospital at nine o'clock in the morning. She had been moved to an open area behind a sliding curtain. Before I stepped around it, I was powerless to imagine what I would see or how it would affect me. Would she still be depressed, or ashamed of herself? Would she be incoherent? Would she be physically scarred, somehow damaged by pills or by the long night of cold? Would she be feeling okay or sick? Would she be able to speak? Would she recognize me, or even want to? I set my sights optimistically at okay. I hoped, realistically, for no change: nothing worse, certainly, but I could hope for nothing better, and I stepped around the curtain with my heart dangling.

She smiled.

I have tried, now and then over nearly fifteen years, to talk to my mother about her smile in the hospital that morning. My first attempt was when I went with her to Paducah for counseling after her suicide attempt. Her therapist, Bill Draper, asked me what I felt in the moment when I saw her smile.

"It was like the clouds moved away and the sun came shining through," I told him. He smiled too, as if he knew exactly what had happened. But he couldn't have known; neither could Mom have known, sitting in a chair beside mine, both of us facing Bill. If I could have known then what her smile meant to me, and had the words to describe it (I'm not sure I have them now), I might have added, *I felt as if we had reached bottom and were finally looking up, and we both knew it. We had nowhere to go but up, and, as hard as it might be, we could only move up, and we would be in control of things, and things would get better and easier.*

A week ago I visited Mom and Dad and my sister and her growing family, and while I was there I drove Mom to an acupuncture appointment. She wasn't scheduled for another week, but recently the pain from degeneration in her spine had flared up and she needed the needles. She and the doctor knew each other well, and he scolded her mildly and said to me, "She needs to stop pushing herself so hard and take it easy, doesn't she?"

She took her shoes and socks off and pulled up her pant legs and lay down on the examining table. The doctor opened a package of needles. Starting at her face, he tapped the needles in and gave each one a little twist and a push, finishing with several on her feet and toes. Over twenty in all. He picked up a handheld device that would send electricity through her body, and wired the machine to two needles on her neck, clamping onto them like tiny jumper cables. He turned it on and raised the electricity level until she said, "Okay. Let's try that." He turned off the light and left us alone. We would have about twenty minutes.

My eyes were adjusting to the dark. "Can you see this?" she said. "On my neck?" I stood up and saw the clamped needles. "Look at them twitch. I must really be hurting; it's usually not this bad."

She said after a few moments, "Brad, I've been thinking lately, and I want to tell you something: I'm sorry that things were hard for you growing up."

"You don't need to be sorry for anything," I said.

She said she was sorry anyway. "There's so much about what happened I'm not proud of." The needles on her neck were twitching. "It took so long," she said, "And it's been so long. I should have found help sooner. I wish I'd have told you all sooner."

I told her my childhood, in spite of anything, was wonderful.

"You know," she said, "one of the strangest things about it, and one of the hardest things, was the fear. I remember being so scared, sometimes for no reason at all. Even when I was working and things were going better, I used to have this irrational fear." She had gotten a job at the *Metropolis Planet* while going through counseling. She put together advertisements for local businesses and arranged her counseling sessions around her work schedule and volunteering for Rape Victims' Services in Paducah. After a couple years of working at the *Planet*, she went to school and received, as my sister had, an LPN license. "One night I got off work and walked to my car. It wasn't dark yet, and the parking lot was small and it wasn't far to walk, but on my way to the car I was absolutely terrified. I started walking faster, and when I finally got to the car I was so scared I actually jumped inside so fast I hit my head—right on the door frame, I hit my head. *Hard.*" The needles on her neck continued to twitch. Soon a nurse would return and remove them. "It took so long to get past it. There's a lot about it I'm not proud of." She lay in silence for a moment. "But the fear," she said. "I hit my head so hard that night it made a huge knot. There wasn't anything to be scared about but I was—I was scared to death. Some nights I would lie in bed, scared. I would think someone was outside in the yard, looking in the windows. It was hard. That fear really never went away." She was silent. She smiled. Lying flat, her body needled and unmoving, her eyes turned in my direction, she said, "But I don't get it as much anymore."

Shine On

When Beverly and I enter the nursing home, its doors always close behind us with a sigh. I know it's a good sound indicating regular maintenance and a firm seal against the weather. A facility in superb condition. But I hear it as a muffled gulp all around me, like being swallowed.

We sign in at the front desk, where the phone rings with a soft chirp and the receptionist whispers a greeting. As usual, a man named Clarence sits in his wheelchair before a bin of cookies, chewing solemnly. A middle-aged man wearing a wrinkled linen jacket stands beside his mother, patting her shoulder as she nods in sleep. We put on visitor tags and approach the locked doors of the Memory Impairment Unit to punch in the security code.

As soon as we enter the unit, we're swamped by a woman's high-pitched shrieks. "HELP ME! SOMEBODY HELP ME!" Without being able to see her yet, we know it's Charlotte, who sits in a recliner by the solarium's windows at the far end of the hall, footrest cranked up, hands gripping the armrests, eyes goggling in terror. Since she was admitted six months ago, Charlotte's cries have been a steady accompaniment to our visits with my mother.

At ninety-five, mind and memory destroyed by dementia, my mother has not seemed to notice the noise or the chaos it rained down around her. As never before in her life, she's calm. She doesn't lash out at Charlotte or try to drown her out with a blast from her own well-trained voice. There's usually a whimsical smile on my mother's face, the look of someone enchanted by an inner music and oblivious to distraction. As indeed she is. The only way she communicates now is through songs, a patchwork of tunes and fragmented lyrics that emerge in place of conversation or coherent thought. The former "Melody Girl of the Air," who had her own radio show in the 1930s Bronx, will croon a few phrases of an old standard, maybe a line or two stitched together with scat. But she won't be able to sustain the briefest conversation, or answer questions about the life she lived. She won't know who I am.

The last time we visited, her inner music was Jimmy Monaco's classic "You Made Me Love You." Over and over as we sat with her, my mother gazed in my direction and sang about how I made her love me, though she didn't wanna do it. Didn't wanna do it. Her song selections during these visits often have an eerie resonance, as though chosen to deliver a message to me. I know that can't be true, of course. Organic brain damage has left her incapable of such sophisticated cognition. She can't plan. She can't hold thoughts in mind or make the sort of fully conscious decisions that delivering such hurtful messages would involve. Her most commonly used phrase is *I don't know*, something she never would have admitted in her life. But given the rage, volatility, and cruelty that once dominated her intimate behavior, this woman was not only capable of, but often did say things like *I never loved you. I never wanted you.* So when she sings "You Made Me Love You," I am engulfed by a sudden sadness.

It's nuts for me to continue holding on to this outdated version of my mother. I'm fully aware of that. It's also nuts for me to impute meaning or intent to her choice of songs. But this is still her familiar voice, this is still the familiar delivery of a lyric snippet laced with meaning, and I react physically, react immediately and without logic. Just as I hear the soft sigh of a door's tight seal as the sound of being consumed.

Today, as we reach the solarium where my mother should be sitting, we can't find her. We've already looked in her room, so we know she's not there either. When we turn to retrace our steps, an aide appears from inside a resident's room. She greets us with a smile. "Your mother is in the toilet."

Suddenly Charlotte cranks down her recliner's legs and hurtles toward us as though propelled by the chair's action, arms reaching out, fingers flexing. As the aide intercepts her, Charlotte shrieks "IN THE TOILET! REMEMBER THAT! YOUR MOTHER'S IN THE TOILET!"

The two of them move past us as though signaling the end of the show's opening act, at which point my mother emerges from a door behind them, led onstage by another aide. They shuffle together, holding hands like dancers performing the world's slowest fox trot. The aide drifts backward one measured step at a time, easing my mother into the solarium's autumn light. From behind us now, fading as she heads toward her room, Charlotte calls out "MOTHER! MOTHER IN THE TOILET! REMEMBER THAT!"

The aide arranges my mother at her customary table just west of the door and waves us over. My mother's head droops. We sit beside her and, as though she'd simply been waiting for her audience to settle down, my mother looks up and begins to hum. It's just a brief repetitive phrase that circles back to the beginning before I can recognize it. *Name that tune, Floyd!* I study her face, trying to see her in this moment, to be with her here rather than allow the past to intrude as it often does. Her expression is vague, as in a fading snapshot, and I'm shocked to see how much she resembles her father. And my brother in the months before his death. It's as though she has begun passing over to the other side, right before my eyes, a passage that has radically changed the way she looks. But then I realize it's because of the missing teeth. A few weeks ago she lost her lower dentures, a common event on the Memory Impairment Unit. Since her diet consists exclusively of soft food, and the staff feels she's more comfortable without them and is likely to lose them again anyway, we've agreed for now not to replace the teeth.

"Hello, Mother. It's me." I pat her hands. She continues humming, nodding to the rhythm, and now I think I recognize the melody. She doesn't recognize me, though, and looks away. Maybe it's her vision, riddled and glazed by macular degeneration. So I say, "Floyd. Your son."

There's still no response. Without thinking about it and without giving them voice, I find myself filling in the lyrics of her song, "Shine On Harvest Moon."

"And I'm here too, Mother," Beverly says. "We're both here to visit you."

At that, my mother goes silent for a moment. She is mostly still, like a jukebox searching for its next record, then turns her head toward Beverly, smiles, and sings *Hey, good lookin', whatcha bah dee bah, something some something da dee dah for me?*

We sing along with her for a moment. At the same time, I hear Charlotte making her way back along the hall toward us, screaming "TOILET!" and I see a couple of my mother's fellow residents sidling up to our table to listen in on the concert. So I decide to introduce a topic for discussion, hoping to discourage the crowd by stopping the music.

"Tomorrow's Thanksgiving, Mother. Do you remember we used to have Thanksgiving at your brother's house in New York?"

She shakes her head. "I don't remember anything, so they say." Hearing her add "so they say" brings me to the edge of tears. She's so confused that she doesn't remember she can't remember, forgets her own forgetting, but somehow manages to remember that she's been told she forgets. Her tone is so soft and vulnerable, so unlike the way my mother would ever speak. If someone had the audacity to suggest that she didn't remember anything, she'd have turned on them viciously. *Don't you dare speak to me that way!* This simple openness, and this tone of benign acceptance are new to my ears.

"Yes," I tell her, "we always used to visit Al for the holiday."

She shrugs, unconvinced, perhaps uninterested, so Beverly adds, "You loved him very much. You used to call him Albie."

"I don't think so," she says, though Beverly is right. "It was Algae."

"Albie," I say. "Albie and Marge."

I'm always thinking of you, Margie! my mother sings in reply.

Most of her recent songs, I realize, emerge from the same specific moment in time. Can this, I wonder, truly be what's happening in her shattered mind? She's somehow living again in the fall of 1931? Or are her song selections random, plucked from a deep and still-preserved remnant of memory that just happens to hold a cluster of tunes made popular in the same year, the same season? During a visit a few weeks ago, my mother was singing a version of Herman Hupfeld's 1931 song, recorded that year by Rudy Vallee, "As Time Goes By." *I can't remember this*, she sang, *a kiss is just a kiss*. And "Margie" was a hit for Bix Beiderbecke in 1931, just before he died, and for Cab Calloway then as well. "You Made Me Love You" and "Shine On Harvest Moon" were both sung by Ruth Etting in *The Ziegfeld Follies of 1931*. This was the final *Ziegfeld Follies* show on Broadway, which ran for 164 performances between July and November, closing just before Thanksgiving. My mother told me many times that she used to see the *Follies* every year, intimating that Ziegfeld himself was grooming her to join the cast.

This period in late 1931 appears to be the moment my mother is locked into now, though it hardly seems possible for someone in her condition to be anywhere in time. In the fall of 1931 she was just turning twenty-one, just becoming an official adult. She lived with her parents in a New York

City apartment, longing to be a singing star and to be courted by celebrities or distinguished men of wealth and aristocratic bearing. She was then, as she remained for the next seventy-five years, obsessed by two themes embodied in these songs and their performance: the difficulties of finding and sustaining the sort of romantic love for which she yearned, and the horror of being ignored, of not being bathed in the brightest light of public or private attention.

It was still possible for her to believe she might have a career on stage, singing love songs as Ruth Etting sang them. To believe, I suppose, that potential loomed all around her despite the bank failures and food lines and grim prospects that defined the fall of 1931. Her stint as "The Melody Girl of the Air," a fifteen-minute program that would, in fact, air opposite Rudy Vallee(!), was three years in the future.

It was also still possible for her to imagine for herself the sort of love in which a boy sighs—as in "Shine On Harvest Moon"—because the girl he loves is by his side, the sort of love in which she would die—as in "You Made Me Love You"—for her sweetheart's brand of kisses. These were the hopes that fueled my mother's dreams as a young woman and her later fury as the housewife of a chicken butcher. She never let them go, hoarding and embellishing her youthful possibilities till they nestled like tinder in her emotional core.

For most of her life, my mother kept a box of photographs in the bottom of her lingerie drawer. Buried under the usual family snapshots, in a small and wrinkled manila envelope, were images of the suitors she rejected before marrying my father. After he died in 1961, she would often produce this collection as a kind of after-dinner entertainment, demanding that I look with her and listen to her lamentations. This one was now a famous attorney on the Upper East Side, Upper West Side, just off Central Park, and also in Boston and Hartford. Simultaneously, he was a judge in the Bronx and a European diplomat. This one was an actor, a novelist, a concert violinist and pianist, a conductor and producer. This one was an inventor who spoke eleven languages fluently and moved to both Greece and Spain the day after my mother turned down his proposal on the grounds that his parents had a terrible genetic disorder. Thereby saving my life. There was a prince in exile, a dentist whose patients were limited to royalty—perhaps she met him through the prince—and a man with such wealth that he didn't have to work, which is why she said no to his proposal, because who wanted a husband around the house all day. When I asked how she met my father and why she said yes to him, she shook her head. *God knows.* Love, I came to understand from these photographs and the phantasmagoria that accompanied their display, was a matter of unrequited yearning. It had no present moment, no actual existence, no fulfillment. In fact, its very unattainability, except perhaps in the dreamworld of old standard songs, was what made love so miraculous. Such an obsession for her.

I know that I'm still trying to find meaning, or order, in her dwindling stock of songs, in her fragmentary remarks, the "memories" I always hope she will offer. I want something from her that she can't possibly give, that she never could have given, a coherent life story, maybe even a love-centered life story. One that included my father, if for only a brief moment when they were first together. One that included me. But the truth is, she never had much enthusiasm for or commitment to her life or its accurate recollection after the 1930s.

Now, when she finishes singing about Margie, she closes her eyes as though thinking, and asks me, "Is it classy?"

Beverly and I look at each other. I'm not sure where this question came from, but despite what I know I'm still driven to treat it—like everything she says—as significant. My mother considered her brother and his wife, Albie and Marge, classy people. They were wealthy, had a Park Avenue apartment and also a home on a lake in upstate New York, attended cultural events. Perhaps my mother's statement was some sort of recollection triggered by our having mentioned them.

Into this brief, desperate silence comes a shout from the table behind us. "Hello!" It's Bessie, whose room is across the hall from my mother's. She is turning the pages of a magazine and greeting each face she sees there.

My mother begins to sing again, moving deeper into "Shine On Harvest Moon," complaining now about not having had any loving since January, February, June, or July. She abandons the melody and speaks the lines, with dramatic emphasis, as though relating her recent experience. *I have not had any loving since the beginning of the year!*

Beverly and I, singing as a duet, try to lead my mother back to the song. After another round of the chorus my mother leans back and asks, "Do you agree with everything?"

I have no idea what this question means. Actually, I doubt it means anything. But looking around the solarium, listening to my mother and Charlotte and the other residents of the Memory Impairment Unit, knowing all that is lost to time and illness, I know I must agree with everything. This is how it is.

Soon a cart laden with lunch trays begins to circulate through the room. Beverly and I, dazed by the repetition of lyrics, bizarre questions, and background cacophony, get up to leave. My mother doesn't notice, lost in her recapitulation of all the months that have gone by since she had any loving. As we exit the solarium, Charlotte returns to her recliner and screams "I FORGOT MY PURSE. HELP! I LOST MY FINGERS."

Exiting the nursing home's parking lot, I linger at the Stop sign, unable to remember which way I should turn. It's just a momentary confusion, hardly surprising in the aftermath of this visit, and Beverly doesn't even notice my hesitation. But as I make a left onto Boundary Avenue, I can feel my mother's presence in the car. *You should have turned right!*

It's as though I've contracted a touch of mother's confusions. *In my little deuce coupe, la da de da do dah.* Then I remember her driving the great white Plymouth Fury she owned, a machine she blamed for always getting her lost.

I haven't thought about my mother and cars in years. She didn't learn to drive until she was forty-eight. That was in 1958, the year after we moved from Brooklyn to Long Beach, an island off the south shore of Long Island, where there were no subways, the few buses stopped too many blocks from our house, and taxis had to be summoned by phone. Until then, living her entire life in various boroughs of New York City, she had no need to drive. No desire either: my mother aspired to being chauffeured. To sit in the back seat while a man in livery did her bidding. A chief complaint of her life with my father, the chicken butcher, was that he refused to hire a car when they went to visit such well-do-to relatives as Al and Marge on Park Avenue. Instead, he raced through city streets behind the wheel of a black Buick, ash flying off his cigar whenever they hit a bump.

Once we'd settled in Long Beach, with both my father and brother commuting daily to Manhattan, my mother felt stranded. As a ten year-old, I was of no use in transporting her. I can easily remember, forty-eight years later, the night she announced to the assembled family that she would learn to drive. It was a Friday because we were eating roast chicken and baked potato at the dining room table. When he heard what she said, my father stopped chewing and looked at each of us in turn, cheek bulging with meat. Then he finished chewing, crossed his fork and knife on the plate, and said, "Who's going to teach you?"

Even I knew what he meant. *I didn't wanna do it, I didn't wanna do it.*

My brother, now nineteen, said he'd teach her.

"You'll be sorry," my father said.

I don't remember how many evenings my brother took her out for lessons, but soon she was enrolled in driving school. She failed her first licensing test, but by late spring she'd passed. The first car she bought for herself, a few years later, was the Fury, a long vehicle whose grille looked like a frowning face. At just barely five feet tall, my mother seemed lost inside it. She had some trouble seeing beyond the edges when turning or parking and tended to scrape against parked cars, parking meters, lamp posts. The scratched surface would then canker and rust in the island's salt air. She also had some trouble with rules and procedures, unwilling to accept commands that she stop at the behest of silly red octagonal signs when it was obvious that no other cars were coming, to defer to arrows ordering her not to enter streets she wished to enter. She had no patience for traffic conditions intruding on her intentions.

As a driver, she routinely got lost. If a highway exit sign didn't specify the precise village she was looking for, she refused to take it. So unless her destination was a major town, she could travel for hours in the wrong direction before concluding that something was wrong. Driving from Long Beach north to nearby Baldwin, seeing only signs for Merrick or Freeport or New York, she would stay on the highway and cross from Long Island's south shore to its north shore before stopping to call home and complain.

"The stupid signs made me get lost."

"Where are you?"

"In a gas station."

"I mean in what town?"

She paused a moment, then said, "Shell."

Her wayward senses of direction, geography, and time didn't stop her from giving navigation advice when someone else was driving. *You should have turned right*! I always saw my mother's inability to find her way around as part of her disconnection from reality. The outside world never did matter much to her. Fantasy, fabricated memory, distortion: my mother seemed to live in another world entirely. It frustrated and often embarrassed me. I didn't see how lost she was in the world, as she is lost in it today, her mind swirling with confusions and retreating beyond dream, even beyond song.

As I drive west out of Portland, moving from Interstate 5 to 99W and on to state and county highways, traffic thins and each road is narrower the closer we get to home. My mother's directional commentary fades from mind, but not the image of her smiling vaguely, having no idea who I am, singing snatches of song from the 1930s. It's a long drive home, and whenever we return from these visits with my mother it feels as though I'm shedding the world as I move from city to town to village to the remote hillside where Beverly and I live in a small round house she built in the middle of twenty acres of oak, fir, maple, and wild cherry. It's a place my mother would have found deeply alien. The opposite of her aristocratic imaginings. But it has fulfilled my own longings—longings I didn't even know I had—for isolation and tranquility and quiet. *And I shall have some peace there, for peace comes dropping slow.* I see these visits as enacting my original escape west from my mother's place, from the noise and chaos of life in New York, life with her, to a space defined in part for me by its radical difference from all I grew up knowing.

Back home that afternoon, Beverly and I take a walk through the woods. This time of year, when the poison oak has died down, we like to follow deer trails that circle the landscape, clearing deadfall and dangling limbs as we go, making a viable path. Our kitten, Max, who is named after my mother's father, comes with us. He leaps from log to log or races ahead of us through the brush, his youthful energy a tonic after we've spent time at the nursing home.

Softly singing my mother's songs, we exchange scraps of lyric till I get stuck in the chorus of "Shine On Harvest Moon." How does that line about snowtime end? It's no time to stay outdoors and croon? To stay outdoors after noon? Neither of us can remember. But we laugh at ourselves, having brought home a part of my mother, her way of conversing through song. When Beverly scratches a small rash on her arm, I sing *I've got you under my skin*; when I tell her that Charlotte's screaming about my mother being in the toilet was unforgettable, she responds, in her lovely alto, *unforgettable, in every way.* When singing of romance, my theme seems to be astonishment at finding love and a place for it in the world. Every time I think of my mother and her obsessive songs of failed romance, I think of how fortunate I am. As Beverly and I come back out of the woods, I break into one of my favorite love songs, scaring away a pair of dark-eyed juncos at the bird feeder. *You are so beautiful to me.*

The next time we visit my mother, we stop in to visit with her nurse before entering the Memory Impairment Unit. Maureen has been caring for my mother since we brought her to the nursing home from New York in 2001. She smiles when I ask how things are going and tells me that my mother has been singing today because a guest pianist provided entertainment for the residents. But also that my mother is slowly, steadily fading away, sleeping more often during the afternoons, less and less able to summon up the will to move or to sing unless prompted.

"She's all right," Maureen says. "But she's leaving us."

This is something I've known for a while now. But as she has slowed down, lost weight, lost balance— she now uses a wheelchair—she has done so in gradual, barely noticeable ways. She may be in the right lane, but she still hasn't found the exit she's after. I tell myself that, despite what Ronnie says, despite how lost my mother is, the journey can go on for quite a while.

There is a sign posted on the door to the Memory Impairment Unit warning visitors to check before opening them, in case a resident is waiting on the other side. People with Alzheimer's are sometimes compelled to wander, and a few of my mother's companions do tend to hover by the door. Beverly and I peer through the crack and see a familiar face peering back at us. In a moment, Charlotte has turned away and is walking back toward the solarium. "HELP ME! SOMEBODY HELP ME!"

We punch in the security code and enter the unit, waiting till the door shuts behind us—in case Charlotte makes a dash for freedom—before moving down the hall. Again my mother is not in the solarium. The bathroom door is open, so we know she's not in there. She is, in fact, in her room, in her bed, asleep. She lies on her side, facing the wall, backed against a full-length body pillow. She is draped in orange and white alarm cords that will warn Maureen and the aides if my mother attempts to get out of bed, so they can rush to her and prevent her from falling.

Beverly and I look at each other, then back at my mother. We agree that we shouldn't wake her. Beverly gently covers my mother's exposed toes with the blanket that has slipped away. Before we leave, we lean over and kiss her.

Shine on!

Chris Offutt

The Best Cake Made Both of Us Sad

Last night's rain has drained the air of all but blue. I am outside listening to the singing of birds. The Daniel Boone National Forest begins at the tip of my fingertips, while civilization spreads the opposite way. My sons are in the house playing a board game, one I played with my brother as a child, but one of the boys gets mad and the laughter stops. As the sun rises high the heat douses the singing of the birds.

I am left soundless—feeling as if I should enter the house and settle the kids or enter the woods and revive the birds. Instead I remain marooned in the shade. Today is that rare day when I'm content to sit in the sun and straddle the boundaries of my life.

Earlier this morning I watched my children sleep. Their bodies lay in such abandon, sprawled across the sheet, a testament to the safety they feel at home. I kiss their cheeks knowing that they will never remember it but hoping that the ghost of my kiss will carry throughout their days. The children cheer me up and give me light. Sometimes I lie beside their warmth and worry about my future life after they leave home. Where will I find moments of joy? Who will make me smile and hug me tight? How will I live in a house with no laughter? Perhaps it will be like the woods in winter—occasional visits from the birds who sing briefly and alone.

Last night I talked to Arthur on the phone. He tells me he is lonely. His friends are dead; he's outlived them all. He is back-up man at his temple in order to make a quorum for a minyan, and he sees some people then. They are all retired. They look at their lives and examine what they've done with them. One man says, I've made a million dollars. Another says, I've made two. Someone else has a yacht and a place in Florida. Arthur claims none of these. He says that he is shrinking.

The cabinet doors of his kitchen no longer bang the top of his head.

He spent years walking into the doors from his blind side, then getting angry at his wife for leaving them open. At last, he says, old age has made him safe from himself in the kitchen. His body is drawing up, shriveling in advance of death. As he becomes smaller, so does his world, the places he goes—a deli, his backyard, a bakery.

Yesterday at the bakery a woman cut line in front of him, but he let it go. Another woman did the same thing, and he said that he was there first, and the worker apologized. She hadn't seen him standing there. Good thing Arthur says to me, that she didn't say I was short.

I laugh because this is a reference to his having once knocked a young man to the floor of a bank for calling him short. It occurred ten years ago, the day before a visit to Rita and me in Iowa. He was running late. He was nervous about the flight. He told the story with shame and humility but secret pride. At age seventy he could still take care of himself. Now, at eighty, he cannot. The last time he tried to kneel he was unable to rise. He cannot run and he cannot punch. His bowels treat him unfairly. Waw, he says, it's no fun, this getting old. No fun at all.

The key to understanding Arthur is knowing something of myself. I can never be truly happy because I mourn everything in advance—the wilting of flowers before they bloom, children leaving home, the end of each season while still at its apex. I enjoy the sunniest of days while bemoaning that there are not more of them. The same is true of food and sex. Every meal is the finest, which means there will never be another. The last time I made love was the best ever. All further sex will be downhill.

Arthur never thinks something is the best but that it might be a little better. If he brings home the finest cake from the bakery, he worries that there was one more tasty that he didn't get. I, on the other hand, worry that there will never be a cake as good. The best cake in the house always makes us sad.

Quite simply Arthur is adept at surviving rather than living. He knows how to get through a situation. He knows how to circumvent, to tolerate, to withstand, to compromise, to accept. He knows how to hope. He knows how to suffer. He knows how to try. It's the living that he has trouble with, the same as me.

He and I both live in the moment, but Arthur looks at the future and I at the past. Perhaps this is why we enjoy each other's company—an unlikely match surely—an eighty-year-old Polish Jew and a forty-year-old

Kentucky hillbilly. We recognize in each other what we crave for ourselves. My exuberance for the best is quickly replaced by a sense of loss. What he has lost makes him always on the lookout for what will be better.

On the phone last night he was lonely and tired. He is becoming one of the last survivors of his community of Holocaust survivors. One by one his extended family died. After sixty years he still misses his brother. Irene's condition requires his constant care. She cannot stand from a chair or roll over in bed without help. He has not made a million dollars, designed great buildings, and doesn't own a yacht. He's not sure what he's done with his life.

I get pissed—we are always getting pissed at each other—and I shout into the phone. You have a successful marriage to one woman all your life. You have two daughters who love you. Your sons-in-law work hard. You have three grandsons who adore you. That is the definition of success, Arthur. Most people don't have any of that. You have it all.

There is a silence on the other end of the phone. He is sitting in his chair in a dim room in Queens, a man who never in his life expected such an outcome—alive at eighty across the sea from home, listening to a gentile son-in-law shout praise in a foreign language. Before the war he was both a boxer and a pianist. His hands are enormous, and he dreamed of being an architect.

Into the silence I say, to hell with the yacht.

What's wrong with a yacht, he says immediately. You don't want a yacht? Take your family on the ocean. Hire a captain and a cook and lady to massage your back.

Look, I say, if I were you, I'd look back on your life with satisfaction. You've done a lot. You're an ethical man and your family loves you. All except one thing—you're short.

You had to say it! He yells. You son of a bitch, you had to say it.

But he is laughing, the first time in days, and I know that is partly why he called. I have done my duty. He now wants to hang up the phone, still chuckling. I have restored his dignity with a grave insult. He's still alive, one of the gang, able to take a good joke. Goodbye, sonny, he says. Goodbye.

The conversation has saddened me. I walk through the house to find my own family. My boys grin expectantly when I enter the room. I look at each face and wait for them to make me laugh.

Jill Christman

Paddling the Middle Fork

A Love Story in Low Water

In 1991 two summers after my fiancé was killed in a car accident, dead on the scene, I headed north into Idaho in a white Subaru wagon with two kayaks lashed to the top like fins. My companion was my wild-haired boyfriend, Stevie, blond curls sproinging out from every follicle (really, you've never seen such hair on a white guy)—frenetic energy bound in the form of man. They were his kayaks, I was in love with him, and this was his idea. I was twenty-one; he had two years on me. We had met a year and a half before at a kayak school in southern Oregon, where I seared salmon steaks and baked pies to feed the paying customers after he'd worked up their appetites teaching them to paddle, brace, and roll down on the river.

A recipe for romance, but we struggled. There were three of us in the relationship and one of us was dead—and perfect. Stevie once told me he felt as if we slept with a ghost between us, and I couldn't deny that I'd felt him there myself. Sometimes I wonder if the trip to Idaho wasn't some sort of exorcism: a trial by water. Colin had been dead only six months when we'd met, but what could I do? On my first morning in the riverhouse kitchen, this wood sprite of a man materialized by the sink as if out of some kind of never-never land, smiling impishly, and offered me this sweet welcome to the river: a bouquet of wildflowers and osprey feathers for the windowsill. And, I swear, watching him paddle a boat was like witnessing the dance of the loon. He and the boat were one body. While some of the other instructors, excellent paddlers, would muscle and jerk, he seemed to anticipate and understand every ripple, rock, and hole: swish, swish, swish. *Beauty*, Stevie would say—to describe me first thing in the morning, or a brimming, nutty bowl of homemade granola, or a drop in a river with the kind of decapitating water pressure that would make a normal person announce a portage. Danger made his blood pump. *Doesn't it make you feel alive?* he'd yell over the roaring water, grinning. And in the beginning of our relationship, emerging from the lock-in of numbing grief like a prisoner into the too bright light, I think perhaps his wild waters did just that. Before a drop, I'd tighten my hands around my paddle and set up my angle. In a kayak, I had no way to distinguish the sweat on my palms from the spray of the river. Wet is wet and alive is alive. *Beauty.*

So the Subaru was loaded down with everything we'd need to navigate down the Middle Fork of the Salmon River in late August—sleeping bags, tent, water filter, toilet paper, ground coffee, bag after bag of dried beans and rice, a single-flame stove, and a small blue pot. This journey is what I learned, in kayak dude lingo, was called "a seven-day, self-support," and I had been so involved in suiting up the gear, buying all those beans, and rolling every last item into neat plastic bags, that I'd forgotten to be afraid.

Or maybe, after Colin's death, I hadn't yet rediscovered fear. Fear is funny. I'm sure that there are psychologists who could explain this to us, or at least take a stab at it, but let me say simply that in those first months after Colin, I wanted to follow him. I would never have taken up a gun or a handful of pills, but if my foot had slipped on the edge of a cliff, or I'd gone under the water and failed to roll up, well, that would have been an accident. I remember a feeling of great and mournful recklessness.

Entering the Frank Church River of No Return Wilderness, that first incomparable Tracy Chapman album blaring in the tinny speakers of our own fast car, singing along over the road sounds, I was ready to wedge my hips into the plastic hull of a baby blue boat named Pegasus and point her down the Middle Fork of the Salmon River. I did it for love. I wanted Stevie to know I was tough, to see with his blue, blue eyes that I had the spirit of an adventurer. I wanted him to know that I was not a sissy girl.

Here's a river-running term that I didn't yet know as we drove north in the golden light of late summer: bony. A run is "bony" when the water is low. Imagine the water as the smooth flesh on the well-padded hips of a shapely woman; her hips will not jut out and poke you, her ribs will not be visible. She moves fast, sometimes too fast, but when she pulls you in, you feel such sweet, bosomy softness. Imagine this same woman down forty pounds. Her eyes stare gauntly from between sharp cheekbones, her hipbones are knife blades when you dance, her clavicle carves a precipitous ledge on which you knock your head. Here is a woman who could hurt you.

She is bony, like a northern river at the end of summer, rocks poking through on every bend, sharp places to scrape your hull, pin your nose. I had been kayaking for one year when we took this journey. I was competent: I could paddle in a straight line, set up my angle to ferry across a moving current, find an eddy and swivel my hips to change my edge when I tucked into it. I loved eddies, those small, still respites of the river. I knew the basics: speed, angle, edge. I could even do an Eskimo roll in moving water—a combat roll—that is, usually, and if a noseful of water hadn't signaled to my brain that I should panic. I had brought my nose plugs for this journey. They weren't attractive, but neither, I figured, was bare-nosed panic. I thought I was ready.

Then I learned the word "bony."

"Hmmm," Stevie said at the put-in, his eyes squinting, looking down the sparkling, jagged water to the first bend. "It's pretty bony."

Here's what I'm guessing. I'm guessing I had no business kayaking down that river in a loaded boat so late in the season. With basically one season of paddling experience sucked into my spray skirt, I'm guessing I had no business kayaking down that river at *any* water level—engorged by the melting snowpack in early summer, this river would have taken me and my blue boat onto her slick tongue like a breath mint and swallowed me down. This much I'd figured out before I started packing beans, and I'd been grateful for the low water, but nobody had said anything about bony. I'm guessing that my Class V–boater boyfriend, who sought out the unrunnable to show that it could be done, and who could not only roll a boat with no paddle but could do so holding a cup of coffee, passed hand to hand over the hull of the boat after he flipped, and not spill a drop (I know because I was the one who delivered the coffee for him to perform this trick before the unbelieving eyes of the clients)—remember, this boy and his boat were hard to distinguish once he slipped into that spray skirt—I'm guessing he looked down that glinting river and had a second thought or two about bringing a greenhorn such as myself on such an adventure. But he wanted to go, and he wanted to go with me, and he probably figured he could get me out of just about anything.

He took a photograph of me there at Boundary Creek before we started out. I'm suited up in my polypropylene undershirt and teal waterproof pants. Sitting on my dry-docked boat, I'm still helmetless and my long, chestnut hair is shining. The word "bony" has already been uttered so my chin is in my hands, on the edge of despondency, and my grin is more gritted than gleeful, but I look pretty. Hopeful. Definitely outdoorsy and adventurous. I am the very portrait of who I was trying to be.

But we're still in the parking lot at the launch. We haven't even made it into the water. Our paddles are dry and we have seven days to go. We're the only people putting in—I didn't make the necessary cognizant leap to wonder *why* we were the only people putting in—and gear spills out onto the gravel like the day after Christmas. Somehow all of that stuff has got to be squeezed into dry bags and crammed into our boats. We're going to be *riding heavy*. We're going to be *low in the water*.

Before lunch on Day One I learn another new kayaking term: tacoed.

We were at the top of a long rock garden called the Sulphur Slide, and Stevie was leading the way. Stroke, adjust, sweep. Remember the boat dancing? He made this look easy. For him, of course, this *was* easy.

Trying to cut through a narrow, rushing channel between two jutting rocks, I miscalculated and smacked the nose of my boat on the left rock and the fast-moving water wasted no time in swinging my rear end around and jamming my tail against the right rock. So there I was: bridged (this term I knew). But the water was pushing, pushing, pushing, and it was so shallow here that I could jam my paddle into the riverbed and arc my body and head out of the water. The bridged boat began to bend with me in the middle, just slightly, ever so slightly, and there you go: my boat was being bent like a taco and I was the meaty filling.

"Help!" I yelled to Stevie who was just a few strokes ahead of me in the rapid. "Help!" Have you ever yelled help when the word was really, *truly* in order? Then you'll know how pleased I was when I saw my sproingy-haired boy turn around and paddle against the current to come back to me. Here was my knight. Forget for this heroic moment that he got me into this in the first place. There I was: one cheek getting slapped by the water, lips barely above the surface, wondering just how tightly a girl could tuck her head in a bent-up boat, if it would be possible to avoid having my skull planted in the gravel like a fence post—that must be a river-running term, right? Jackhammered? To be jackhammered? As in to have one's head driven into the bottom of a river in a pounding, driving, violent way?—whatever the name, this was next for my head except that Stevie had *heard* my scream for help above the raucous, hungry water. He paddled up, leapt from his kayak like a goat, lifted the nose of my boat free and managed to keep me from going head-under all in one superstar moment. I hadn't *really* been tacoed, but I heard him utter the word as we scraped up onto the gravel bank. Maybe we could say I was somewhere between a tostada and a taco: bridged, but bending, and now I had this new possibility in my mind. I'd considered cracking my neck by smashing my hurdling head on a rock, or drowning in a whirling hole that wouldn't let me go ("Maytagged"), but now I had this new possibility to confront. I could be squeezed, bent, snapped in half. I was building a vocabulary for my returning fear.

Stevie returned from rescuing the only near-casualty of the incident, my shiny new Werner paddle, and we took a lunch break. In the next photo, my nose looks red from crying. I am eating a cookie bar under the protection of my bright pink helmet. Nose plugs hang on a black cord from a hole in the helmet near my ear. I must be sitting in my boat again because I'm leaning back on my zipped life jacket—time to get back out on the water. Two more miles and we'll be at Velvet Falls. Sexiness is no longer my concern. I need to make it out of this canyon alive. My eyes squint into the sky.

I imagine that I am scanning the treetops for helicopters, somebody to spin down out of the heavy clouds and whisk me away. Not quite two reckless years after Colin's death, and my capacity for fear was back, that much I knew.

Day One ended at mile thirteen in a moment that should have been idyllic. Stripped of our wet, freezing paddling clothes, we camped on a terrace with steaming hot springs, and as I soaked my anxious bones, a small herd of elk moved toward us through the mist. This kind of thing doesn't happen in places that are easy to reach, does it? My breath caught in my throat—not from fear now, but from the sheer magic. Stevie lifted his torso out of the water for a better look and steam rose from his chest, a vaporous nimbus coiling around his curls, and the river-running tough guy melted into the sweet, sweet boy I loved. I'm sure I wanted both men:

without the thrill seeking, the skill with the paddle, his gentleness might have seemed wimpy. And if I wanted him to be both manly man and angel boy, well then, I had to be more than one girl, didn't I? I could wear my lipstick and paint my toenails, but I had to throw my body down waterfalls too. I could keep photos of my dead lover close to the bed we shared, but I'd also have to prove to Stevie that I could learn to love the living best.

And what a magic kingdom he had led me into. In the River of No Return Wilderness we breathed air sweetened by ponderosa pines and sagebrush, bent our necks to see the tops of huge granite cliffs, and then rested on the sun-warmed stone benches at their feet. The place was wild and wildly beautiful. The August water was too low for rafts here at the top of the run, and our only company all day had been those light-footed elk, the otter family we'd seen sliding down the bank upstream, and a water rat foraging in our camp. As for humans, we were it. Let me tell you, if couples' counselors could send their struggling clients bobbing downriver in two plastic boats with just each other and seven days to make it through the canyon and work it all out—well, some would make it and some wouldn't, but as my ceramics professor remarked sagely when he came upon one of us holding the shards of a broken pot in our sorry hands: *You learned something, didn't you?* Stevie couldn't ditch me there on the bank with the river rat: I wouldn't make it out alive. And I certainly couldn't paddle off in a huff because he refused to listen to my fears, could I? That would have been impractical indeed. We were stuck with each other.

Even warming my frozen limbs in the steaming water, I was terrified of what lay ahead but wanted desperately to fake it. As for Stevie, he was stretching the boundaries of his empathy. For him, the only thing to be afraid of in this canyon was me—or possibly himself. He wanted to let me love him and to love me back, but for him that would be a greater risk than any mountain, trail, or drop. For the four years we were together, besieged but together, he would often tell me—when I begged him not to carry his boat down into the flooding creek or jump in the car on a skiing whim and head east through the snowy mountains in a blizzard—that he felt the most alive when death was near, when survival required his sharpest skills and concentration, when getting out alive meant thinking of nothing, and nobody, else.

I should have recognized that my fear that evening in our first camp was a good thing. Wedged between those rocks in that sulphur slide, I knew I did not want to die. My fear bound me to this earth. Colin was dead, but I was alive. I pledged not to spend the night feeling afraid. The elk drank from the creek and then moved back over the ridge, never spooked by our heads bobbing in the mist, and we dried off and bundled into our zip-together sleeping bags.

Fifteen years later I still have the pumpkin-colored map book printed by the Forest Service. Bent, water-stained, and ragged, it is also annotated rapid by rapid. Next to "Velvet Falls" I have written this: "Not so frightening after all! Like a water slide." Chalk one up for low water.

Farther down the river I am sitting on a ledge rock in camp clutching this guide and a mug of coffee. In a photo shot from behind my shoulder it appears I have forgotten my brave-face pledge because I am pouting and fear lines my face like a paddle blade mapping out a route in the sand.

Love is a rock planted hard in the bed of a river. Rushing toward a rock in a kayak, everything you've ever learned about processing environmental cues tells you that you're in serious danger, fight or flight, and how do you fight a rock? But you mustn't act on your visceral fear. Instead, as Stevie told me again and again, you must do the utterly counterintuitive: you must *lean into that rock*. On land, in a car, this action would be equivalent to turning the wheel *toward* the giant oak tree at the bend in the road—an act of lunacy or self-destruction. But on the water, so different from solid ground, that's just the thing to do. Lean in, relax onto the very thing that looks for all the world poised to split open your head. If you do this with just the right amount of edge, a yielding lean but not quite a surrender, you'll feel the push of a watery cushion. Turns out the rock you so fear has been upholstered in flowing water—this is called the *pillow*. The *worst* thing to do when approaching a river rock is to panic and lean away. You will flip—which means your upside-down head will now be both airless and next to that rock. Trust me, I know. I follow my gut. On our run down the Middle Fork, I tried to reprogram my pragmatic self with this mantra: *Lean into the rock. Lean into the rock. The rock is your friend.*

A rock is love planted hard in the bed of a river. Of course, it is possible to lean in too far.

From my near water-level perspective that summer on the river with the beautiful sproingy-haired boy, I never could have imagined the route that my life would take if I made it out alive. I never could have imagined that looking back to a week on a river could make a thirty-five-year-old woman feel so ancient. Before I tell you about my near miss on Day Six, I will tell you what I'm sure you already suspect: I am married now to a good man who is not the sproingy-haired boy. The sproingy-haired boy is married to a good woman who is not me. She didn't appreciate my insistence that I and the boy, now so obviously a man, were still friends, and the last time I sent a birthday present to their house in Oregon, he called me and asked that I not do that again. I was making trouble. I do not want to make trouble, make waves, and so it's been over two years since we last spoke.

Last summer the Ridgeback puppy we raised in our final year turned twelve, and then something went wrong in her blood and she died in the night. I thought that her death would be an exception to the moratorium, and I wrote him a letter with the sad news. I thought he would want to know. Once upon a time, he had loved her like a daughter; not long after I moved away, he had made her a food bowl out of clay to commemorate her first capture of an actual squirrel. In a hand-scrawled letter, he had recounted a dream in which I told him he could never see her again. He woke up crying, he wrote, and in the same letter he demanded that I take her somewhere to run in the woods without a leash. I promised I would, and I did. But nine years later when I sent my letter—*I am writing with the saddest of news . . .*—he did not respond.

There are so many different kinds of fear. I cannot possibly cover them all here.

Much of our journey on the Middle Fork is lost to the murky, mud-dwelling, bottom-feeding mouth of flawed memory. I remember more hot springs, a stop at a ranger station for a can of tuna fish and toilet paper, a screaming fight after he let me go through a rapid alone because he was fishing, two bald eagles running around on the riverbank looking more like barnyard chickens than national symbols, and strangely—or maybe not—near photographic moments from the scariest drops. My cerebral cortex retains the spray of white water, the pull of a hungry hole's gaping maw on the tail of my boat, the solid rush of an approaching cliff wall and no way to avoid it, *Lean in, lean in. . . .*

On Day Five, we stopped for lunch and never got back in our boats. Not long after the screaming fight—*You let me go through alone! Yeah, well, we live in this world alone! You need to learn to take care of yourself!*—I caught the biggest fish of the journey, a cutthroat, and we decided to pitch our tent by the Kimmel Creek waterfall at a place called Fly Camp, forgive each other for the hundredth time, and celebrate.

Our festivities were premature. That night, rats invaded our camp and polished off the cookies. By bailing out early we'd left about twenty miles to travel on Day Six, with a lot of big water. My own scribbled asterisks by the to-be-feared rapids on Day Six indicate that I thought I was through the hard stuff when the accident happened. I was ready to pop the cork on the bottle of wine in which we'd invested so much: hull space for five days and five nights, a safe ride at the center of a sleeping bag, the risk of a hard knock staining everything red and ruining the party.

The rapid was called House of Rocks, and sounding for all the world like a nightclub, dancing and drinks, rock 'n' roll, bourbon on ice, I didn't even have it circled in my book. That's another thing about fear: we're never afraid at the right moments, of the right things. When Colin was killed, he was in a company van on a five-minute drive back to his motel. He and his airship buddies had worked late at the hangar; they were probably hungry, maybe looking for a place to grab some pizza. Maybe that's the thing about Stevie and those like him: by pinpointing the loci of fear—*this* ski jump, *this* waterfall, *this* rock wall—their fear has somewhere to go. Fear is externalized. In regular life we're rarely afraid of what sneaks around to get us in the end.

The maneuvering at the top of House of Rocks wasn't that technical. It certainly wasn't the hardest thing we'd been through that day, but when things go wrong, they go wrong. This is why you hear stories of Class V boaters drowning in Class II rapids. Complacency. Lack of attention. Maybe I was just tired. I swung easily into the crucial eddy at the top, river left. The eddy was a tight fit, barely room for two boats, and so Stevie yelled the most basic instructions—*punch it and follow the tongue*—and then with a flash of blue, he was gone. The rocks on either side of the eddy were enormous, and once he was gone down the drop, I couldn't see anything. I was alone. I took a breath, pointed Pegasus toward the eddy line, and punched it. Except that I didn't. I didn't give her enough juice to get her nose through, the line was stronger than I'd realized, or I was less strong, and we bounced. The eddy line pushed us back, and not straight back. In one of those moments that happens too fast and can never be redone, I ended up pinned between the two giant rocks and slipping forward. My lessons failed me: there would be no leaning into either rock. There was only the space between them. This is how it looked to me: it looked to me like an impossible drop in an impossibly small space. If I flipped over in Pegasus, and that seemed likely, we could be jammed in that space. The drop was too steep and Stevie was way down at the bottom. He was too far away to help me, but now I could see the top of his body through the gap in the rocks, the one I was about to slip into, and I could tell he was scared. He was waving his arms and shouting, but his words were moving lips and nothing more.

There are so many different kinds of fear.

Fifteen years later mine is such a different geography. I live in Indiana, a professor, with my professor husband, in our comfortable, two-story house on a flat street with nice, big maple trees. We have a one-year-old daughter, which means, of course, that the circle of my fear has expanded like a lasso to hold this baby: cars, electrical outlets, staircases, bathtubs, any object small enough to slide through the center of a toilet paper tube or into a toddler's throat. I look around and see danger everywhere. I have so much more to lose than my own head.

Back on the river time shifted. I felt as if I had a lifetime to decide what to do, and this is what I chose: dry exit. I pulled the cord on my spray skirt and tried to scrabble out onto one of the big rocks, calculating in advance that the edge was too steep, I wouldn't make it, but at least my head would be up. I was right on both counts. I don't know which of us shot through that gap first—me or Pegasus—but I know I did what Stevie had taught me. I pointed my feet downriver, riding the furious current the same way I would sit in a recliner during a hair-raising movie, fingernails sinking into the armrests. White all around, a gulp of water, nothing that could be called cold: the perfect now of my terror. I had been told that drowning was not such a bad way to go, that after the struggle and before dying, there's a kind of peace. . . . Then I hit a rock. The sharp, submerged point caught me between my legs and sent me up in the air. But that was the worst of it. I was a bloody mess—scraped, smashed, the deeply bruised feeling of six days in the saddle—but that was the worst of it. I was breathing. Bleeding and breathing. At the end of the rapid, the river spit me out onto the bank to nurse my wounds and tell my story.

Stevie pulled Pegasus from the river, but my new paddle never came back up. He speculated that there was an underwater rock shelf just below the drop that held onto things like dropped paddles—or anything a boater failed to hold. *That could have been me*, I gasped. *If a paddle could be stuck, I could be stuck, right?* The fear was back.

Sure, he said. *Yup.* These were the risks he knew and accepted. He could point to them and maneuver around them. He didn't need to live inside of them.

That evening, in the long light after our rice and beans, and finally, that wonderful bottle of wine poured into our plastic mugs, orange and blue, the sproingy-haired boy held a you-made-it-down-the-river ceremony. He recorded the moment on film using the timer, so there we are, alone in the wilderness, together, as he presents me with a single wildflower.

My husband will read this essay and think I am not happy. He will say that I'm longing for the sproingy-haired boy, the uncertainty of the next drop, the always present sound of the rapids roaring in my ears. He will say that I think my life now is boring, but I will tell him that he is wrong. I will tell him I am done with that particular kind of going under.

Maybe, I will say, maybe I am writing a cautionary tale for our daughter, writing out of my past and into her future. Someday she will be looking for love, and if there are any constants in this world, she will try to change herself for love. She will try to be tougher or more gentle, thinner or quieter or less smart than she really is, and it won't work, the façade won't stick.

Or maybe, God forbid—but how can we stop it? how can we protect her?—she will suffer a great loss and give up her fear. Maybe she will need her mother, her much younger mother, to show her that some fears are worth getting back. But that's not exactly it either. I want my daughter to know what it is to choose love over fear. Maybe this younger me—the me holding the flower at the bottom of the last rapid, not the me she will know—can show her how fear and love can exist together, an unmovable rock in the dancing water.

Fifteen years off the river and leaning in no longer feels counterintuitive to me. Leaning in feels like what we do in love.

Diana Joseph

It's Me. It's Him. It's Them.

It may just be me.

I worry that my friend Andrew Boyle is a pervert even if he doesn't hang fuzzy dice from the rearview mirror of a sleekly black Pontiac Trans Am. Andrew doesn't own a Trans Am or a customized van all decked out with zebra skin rug, waterbed, and a sign that reads "If You See This Van A'Rockin' / Don't Come A'Knockin'." He doesn't linger in front of the Kwik-Trip where the troubled high school girls—the pukers, the cutters, the partiers, the sluts—like to hang out smoking cigarettes and drinking Diet Cokes after school. He doesn't unbutton his polyester shirt all the way down to his snakeskin belt. Andrew Boyle fusses over his appearance, he is always fashionably dressed, he purchases his clothes on eBay, designer brands so expensive I've never even heard of them. He doesn't wear polyester shirts. Andrew Boyle wouldn't be caught dead in polyester. Nor does he wear shiny shoes, like the ones the sleazy teacher at your school wore so he could stand close to a cheerleader and sneak peeks up her skirt in the reflection of his shoe. Though he lists *Lolita* as one of his favorite novels, Andrew does not leer at schoolyard nymphets, nor does he say *light of my life, fire of my loins* or *hey little girl, do you want some candy?* or *I'm gonna make a big star out of you* except, maybe, as a joke, something he might drunkenly say to a beautiful woman of appropriate age with the hope that she will model for him.

When I was first getting to know Andrew, I didn't think I would like him because he seemed arrogant and show-offy. And it would turn out that I was right: Andrew Boyle is arrogant and show-offy, but he is also witty and well read, environmentally conscious and politically aware, a person with whom you can have a smart and interesting conversation about Raymond Carver's short stories or Robert Altman's films or the

Canadian rock band Rush or Peter Singer's argument against speciesism. When I like Andrew Boyle, I like him a lot. He can be easily amused, easily entertained, his laugh is nice to hear.

A vegetarian except during Thanksgiving dinner, Andrew takes good care of himself. He doesn't smoke cigarettes or marijuana, he doesn't chew tobacco or gum or drink cheap domestic beer. He drinks grenache/shiraz/mourverde, vintage 2001. I've never heard of it, but he says it tastes like PBJ without the bread or the peanut butter. He doesn't mind when I call him a snob. He doesn't take offense.

He doesn't have a pierced ear or wear a gold medallion on a gold chain. He does have a gold watch that his parents gave him as a graduation present, an expensive gold watch from a fine watchmaker, but because gold jewelry is tacky, he doesn't wear it. When he thinks about his parents giving him this gift of a watch that he'll probably never wear, he feels guilty.

At some angles, Andrew is very handsome; at others, he's sort of funny-looking. Gawky. Geeky. He can look hip and cool and urbane, or he can also look like what he is: a dorky high school valedictorian who spent many a Friday night playing Dungeons and Dragons and secretly wishes he still did.

His undergraduate degrees are in math and music. He has a PhD in art history from a prestigious European university. Andrew can affect the world-weary, snobby, snotty, fashionably androgynous attitude of someone who's spent some time hobnobbing in Europe. A friend of mine, upon first meeting him, was surprised to learn that Andrew is not gay. "Of course he is," she said. "He's completely gay. He's totally gay." And when I told her no, he's just serious about the time he spent hobnobbing in Europe, she insisted, "That guy is so gay."

Lots of people assume Andrew Boyle is gay—probably because of his meticulous posture and graceful gesturing, his lack of interest in organized sports, and the jaunty gray scarf he wears indoors wrapped around his neck so the ends dangle over his shoulders and down his chest in a casually studied way. But he's not gay. Andrew Boyle is just the kind of guy who knows about girl stuff. What girls like. What it's like to be a girl. Sometimes the thought occurs to me that he knows more about being a girl than I do, that I've been doing it all wrong. Why don't I get my eyebrows plucked? Why do I still buy my clothes at JCPenney, and how can it be that I haven't ever heard of Marc Jacobs? Why was I so flattered when

Andrew Boyle told me he approved of my shoes, cork wedges that take me from barely five feet to five foot four?

"Those are great shoes," he said. Then he told me he loved what I'd been doing with my hair. "It looks good. Your hair looks like a shampoo commercial."

"Well, thank you, Andrew!" I said modestly. I was very flattered because usually I don't think about my hair unless it's to hate it. "I usually hate my hair!" I told Andrew Boyle. "It's so thick, it's hard to manage. It's hard to find something to do with it."

"You know what I like to do when a woman has thick hair?" Andrew asked.

"No. What? Tell me."

He slid his hand under my mop of big, thick hair, he grabbed a hunk of it, he yanked, snapping my head back, exposing my neck. "Sexy," he said.

I frowned, but I stayed calm. I took a deep breath, raised my eyebrows. "Well," I said.

But I was furious. Because when Andrew Boyle pulled my hair like that, it hurt like hell. But I was determined not to let him know that. Because I wondered if that's what he wanted. Because I think there's no way it's me: this guy is definitely a pervert. *I bet he's seen that move in a thousand and one pornos,* I thought. *He is such a fucking pervert.* But what made me angriest is at the time I couldn't think of what I could do back. What was some comparable physical action that's equal parts pain and humiliation?

What I came up with, of course, is that someday I will kick Andrew Boyle in the nuts. Hard. When he is least expecting it.

Currently, Andrew is an assistant professor of art history at a midsized state university. According to RateMyProfessors.com, a Web site that asks college students to comment on their teachers, Dr. Boyle is demanding; a real tough grader; very helpful; boring even though he doesn't think he is; an okay teacher; a great teacher; a total phony; an excellent teacher; hostile to Christianity; extremely open-minded; a guy who loves to hear himself talk; enthusiastic and laid back; someone who wants everyone to be his pal; and a blowhard who thinks he's better than everybody else.

Andrew Boyle is almost exactly two years older than me. Soon he will turn thirty-eight. To celebrate his birthday, he'd like his friends to join him for a night on the town. He'd like to have some fun. In the meantime he wanted to know if I was interested in going out for dinner and drinks with him one night this week. He seemed lonely, and I felt bad for him, but I had to say no. I had to remind him why I don't go out on weeknights. "I've got that kid at home," I told him. "I've got that husband."

"Oh, right," he said. "I forgot." He sighed, loud and sad. "Everybody has a kid at home. Everyone has a family. Everyone except me."

Andrew would like to have a kid at home someday. He'd like to have a wife—he's never had a wife—but right now he doesn't have a girlfriend or even prospects for a girlfriend. He doesn't have a dog or a cat or a houseplant or a house. He lives in a duplex. He says he doesn't have a reason to live. One night last March Andrew Boyle sat at my kitchen table where he ate five garlic-stuffed olives and drank half a Summit pale ale, then told me he'd been entertaining thoughts of jumping off a bridge. "Pretty much every day," he said. Six months later he's saying the same thing. In fact, just the day before yesterday he told me he doesn't know why he goes on living. "I have nothing to live for," he said.

What Andrew Boyle does have is a camera. He takes pictures with it, pictures of landscapes sometimes, but more often, when he can find willing models, he takes pictures of women, especially young women of appropriate age (which means they're at least eighteen) who also happen to be beautiful (which means they're thin and bosomy, or as my father would say, "built like a brick shithouse"). These women must also be interested in participating in what Andrew calls art photos (which means they disrobe). Andrew Boyle is always in search of beautiful young women willing to pose naked for him.

In his experience high-end hair salons are a good source of such young beautiful women. "Hairstylists tend to care about their appearance," he says. "They're interested in beauty. They keep themselves up." Hairstylists, according to Andrew, are frequently vain, a quality he very much approves of, because an appeal to a woman's vanity is often what finally convinces her to model for him. Because you look good, I imagine him saying, you're hot, you're sexy, and well, you know, you're not always going to look like this.

Andrew has also noticed that waitresses at bars in college towns are frequently young and beautiful. One Friday night I went out for dinner with Andrew, and afterward he suggested we have a drink at the Wooden

Nickel, a bar that's well known as a meat market for college kids, the place where after they get good and drunk on Jaegermeister and Red Bull, screaming orgasms, and six-dollar pitchers of Long Island iced teas, they hook up and have sex. Andrew said he knew a waitress there, a girl named Robyn, who was working that night. "I want to invite Robyn to my upcoming birthday festivities," he said. "I also want to ask her if she'll model for me."

Robyn had blonde pigtails, blue eyes, dimples, and long legs in knee-high socks. She was wearing shorts. She was wearing high-heeled boots. Her eyebrows were plucked to perfection, her nose was pierced, her ears were double pierced. She was cute as a pixie, and she knew Andrew by name and drink.

"Hi Andrew," she said. "Do you want a Summit?"

Andrew said, "Robyn, some friends and I will be celebrating my thirty-eighth birthday next week, and you are invited to join the festivities. My birthday is on a Wednesday night, but most people can't party with me in the middle of the week. So we are going to have the festivities on the weekend. Are you free on Friday night?"

Robyn said she thought she had to work on Friday night.

"Are you free on Saturday night?"

Robyn said she wasn't sure, but she thought she might have to work on Saturday night.

"Let me know," Andrew said.

Robyn told him she would let him know, then she glanced at me. We smiled at each other, tight-lipped smiles, and I understood that this girl may be cute as a pixie but she wasn't stupid, and I knew Robyn the Waitress at the Wooden Nickel would be posing for Andrew on the twelfth of never, and it's not just me. It's him. Other girls feel it, too. Andrew Boyle is most definitely a pervert.

On several occasions Andrew has sat at my kitchen table, opened up his leather satchel, and pulled out a leather-covered portfolio containing his art photos, pictures he took of a beautiful naked woman of appropriate age. Before seeing these pictures, I made fun of Andrew. I said oh yes, *art photos*. I said do you drive a Trans Am? Do you wear shiny shoes? Where is your gold medallion? Are you a pervert? No, really, are you?

However, after seeing the pictures, I had to agree that they were neither dirty nor pornographic. The pictures are beautiful. The woman in the pictures is always beautiful, her body the body of youth, her skin smooth skin, her body a firm but curvy body, nothing is fatty, nothing is drooping.

The woman in the pictures may change but what remains constant is that she is always someone Andrew had fucked or was fucking or wanted to fuck, and that's something that, for me, keeps them from being art photos, the work of an artist. That's something that turns them into booby pictures that Andrew took and pulled out of a leather satchel as we sat at my kitchen table, pictures that for reasons I haven't yet figured out, Andrew showed to me but not to my husband who wandered into the kitchen to fix a ham sandwich while Andrew and I flipped through his leather-covered portfolio, and I tried to think of things to say that weren't "How on earth did you ever talk this girl into doing this?"

Instead I commented on how many triangles I could find. The bend of a knee is a triangle, and the crook of an elbow. "There are so many triangles in these pictures!" I said. I wondered if it is just me. If I am too much of a prude to appreciate the human body, a woman's body, the beautiful thing that it is. I don't want to be a prude, but maybe I am.

One of the models looked just as good clothed and in person. I know because she ate Thanksgiving dinner at my house last year when she and Andrew were still a couple. Her name was Lauren, she was twenty-one years old, a college junior who had once been Andrew's student, and during the entire turkey celebration, Lauren hardly spoke. She sat at the table with the other guests, but she didn't contribute to any conversation unless a specific question was directed at her. She only spoke to Andrew, and she let Andrew speak for her. I didn't hold this against Lauren then or now— it probably was unnerving to have dinner at a stranger's house, it probably was intimidating, it probably was embarrassing that the person at Thanksgiving dinner closest to your age was the hostess's thirteen-year-old son. It probably took every bit of courage Lauren had to come up to me and say what she said.

What did she say?

I'm still not sure. It came out sounding a lot like chirping. Like tweet! tweet! tweet!

"What?" I asked her.

"Tweet! Tweet! Tweet!" Her voice was high pitched and squeaky. Like a little bird.

That night, she and Andrew went back to Andrew's duplex where a "photo shoot" took place.

In December Andrew spent hundreds of dollars buying her Christmas gifts—designer clothes, silk lingerie, high-heeled boots.

In January he was talking about marrying her.

By March it was over. Lauren—quite inexplicably, Andrew thought—broke things off. She wouldn't return his calls. She wasn't interested in his broken heart. She may or may not have been involved with someone else, and all Andrew had left was her image on black-and-white film. "I don't understand," he said. He was sitting at my kitchen table with his half a Summit and a jar of garlic-stuffed olives. He looked terrible, unshaven, unshowered, like he hadn't slept in days. I felt really bad for him.

"I'll tell you what I didn't understand," I said, and I did what I thought a friend should do: I badmouthed the person who caused him such pain. I told him about Lauren chirping at me on Thanksgiving. "Tweet! Tweet! Tweet! I didn't understand a word of it," I told him.

I thought it would make him feel better, but it didn't. "That's really mean," Andrew said. "You're really catty to talk about her like that. She thought you were so nice. I can't believe how cruel you can be. That's pretty shallow of you."

As a precelebration celebration of Andrew Boyle's thirty-eighth birthday, we went to the Wooden Nickel. Andrew and I sat at a table in Robyn's section, and as he watched the little pixie blonde waitress serve drinks, he sighed. He said he just knew that people think he's a dullard, that he comes off as a man with a very dull personality. He seemed sincere about this self-perception, he seemed glum. I told him I don't think he's a dullard, which is true, I don't. I said I thought he was a weirdo.

This perked him up. "Really?" he said. "Tell me why!"

I considered telling him I actually think he's more of a pervert than a weirdo, but he was smiling so nicely, expectantly, and I could see the boy in Andrew Boyle, the sweet, smiling kid in blue footy pajamas waking up happy on the morning of his birthday knowing that there will be a cake and lit candles and a chorus of loved ones singing him a birthday song. "The scarf!" I said.

"What scarf?"

"That gray scarf you wear. You take off your coat, but you keep that scarf wrapped around your neck. It's very jaunty. You wear a scarf indoors, Andrew. Where I come from, men don't do that. Men don't wear scarves in a blizzard, let alone indoors."

"I'd get beat up where you come from, wouldn't I?" said Andrew.

Yes, I told him, he would most definitely get beat up. He would get the shit kicked out of him.

He didn't seem insulted or displeased. In fact he took it more as a compliment. "I guess I'm not very manly," he said. He was scanning the crowd at the Wooden Nickel. He reminded me of myself, examining every chocolate in the box of Whitman samplers, wanting the one that was caramel but convinced someone else had gotten to it first. Andrew fixed his gaze on a beautiful, willowy blonde twenty-year-old. "I won't go talk to her," he said, "because I think she won't be interested in me. I mean, what could I say that won't sound like a line?" His shoulders slumped, and I resisted the urge to tell him sit up straight! Don't slouch! "I won't ask her for a date," he continued, "but maybe I can ask her to model for me. She won't be interested in dating me, but she might be interested in modeling for me. The point is, I got a girl to talk to me."

Whenever Andrew Boyle follows a woman's name with the words "model for me," I don't know how to feel. Maybe he's not a pervert, maybe he's just a lonely guy, full of self-doubt, worried that he's not good enough for a woman to love, worried that he'll never get married, have a kid, a family, and the camera is something for him to hide behind, that inviting a woman to model for him is a way to strike up a conversation with a woman he'd never dare speak to otherwise. Maybe the art photo booby pictures are just about his very human insecurities.

Or it could just be me. I've never hobnobbed in Europe, I've never been to Europe; the most international I've ever gone is the Canadian side of Niagara Falls. Maybe I am just a prude, an uptight American, sexually repressed, opposed to pleasures of the flesh, puritanical, and who am I to judge him? "You can't fault me for my social choices," he told me once. "I'm not breaking any laws. I'm not doing anything illegal or unethical. I'm not doing any harm."

Or maybe it is him, Andrew Boyle. Maybe it has to do with the way Andrew Boyle talks about women, their bodies, their faces, their hair, their clothes. When a woman walks by, he can't not comment on her appearance. He can't not judge her by what would appear to be a very narrow aesthetic. Sometimes his comments remind me of the bitchy things I've heard girls say to each other about other girls. When a blonde girl with big breasts and wide hips walked by, he said, "I'm not into dairy princesses."

When a chubby girl wearing too-tight clothes and whose hair was pulled back into a high, tight ponytail walked by, Andrew said, "That is international, my friends. The white trash high-and-tight ponytail. You don't just see that in America. I've also seen it in Britain and Spain."

When a skinny brunette with straight hips and perky boobs walked by, and Andrew said, "I'd love for her to model for me," I know there's no way a woman like me can talk to a man like Andrew about another woman's body without it sounding bitchy or insincere or prudish. I don't have to wonder why he's never asked me to model. I know why—I'm too old, too short, too soft—but I don't feel competitive or jealous or worry that my own body doesn't measure up. I stopped worrying about that the day I found a hair growing on my big toe.

The ickiness I feel when I'm around Andrew Boyle and he's looking at women and talking about their bodies is a very old feeling.

It goes back to the morning when I was twelve years old, the morning I woke up with a pair of D-cup breasts and a va-va-voom swing to my walk that horrified my mother and enchanted perverts. As a little girl with enormous boobs, I had a body that attracted attention: from boys my age, of course, who behaved in all the ways one would expect, immaturely and in song, Paul Searle revising the lyrics of the Manhattan Transfer classic "The Boy from New York City" to a version that included my name and the words "has got," "big," and "titty."

It was embarrassing but not nearly as strange and creepy and uncomfortable as the way grown men behaved. Carrie Laughlin's dad circled back around the block to offer me a ride home from school, and in the car, put his arm around me, rubbing my back and squeezing my shoulder. The custodian at John F. Kennedy Junior High suggested I come back to school a little later and "visit" with him a while. A man older than my dad asked me if I had some milk to go with that shake, did I have a porch to go with that swing. A very old man at the public library asked if I knew where they kept the Louis L'Amour books, then before I could say yes, I know exactly where the westerns are, he kissed me on the mouth, his breath smelling like a cherry cough drop, his tongue tasting like one.

It seemed to me all I was doing was walking down the hall, or down the street, or home from school, or I was looking for a book about magic tricks at the public library, but obviously, I was doing something more. I was doing something dirty and wrong. I've never quite gotten over the idea that the body I live in could invite such attention. That something about me—the way I walked, maybe, or the way I chewed gum, the way I dressed, or those really great high-heeled shoes, or that I was such a little girl with such an enormous chest—invited men into thinking it was okay to let me know they wanted something from me, something I didn't want to give them, but since I brought it on myself, maybe I had to.

Do I wear a shirt that's big, bulky, baggy, or do I wear a shirt that clings? Do I hide my body under sweaters and sweatshirts and jackets, or do I let the world know I'm female and as a female, I have breasts? Why do I feel so self-conscious anytime I wear a color other than black? Do I want to be looked at or not?

I don't know.

It's me. It's them. It's me. It's Andrew. It's me. It's you. It's any man with greedy eyes. I've never stopped wanting to kick you in the nuts. Hard. When you least expect it.

No

You are *not* a slut. At least this is what you've been telling yourself for the past eight months, but when the phone in your hotel room rings at 3:30 in the morning and the desk clerk asks if you're expecting a visitor, you feel like one. You hear the surprise in the clerk's voice, in his you-look-like-such-a-nice-girl tone, but maybe what you hear is concern, not judgment. After all, you're surprised and concerned yourself.

"What?" you say, throaty, half-awake, as if you didn't hear.

The man repeats himself. "Are you expecting a visitor?"

After you ask who it is, though you know, you listen for the name of the man who thinks it's acceptable to come to your hotel at 3:30 in the morning. When you hear his voice, your stomach flips in seventh-grade-crush style. Why does he have to have this effect on you? You're angry. You're hurt and angry and irrational (you're being irrational, he would say), but something is shifting. You're awake (and alert) enough to recognize that something is shifting.

Tonight at your friend Marina's reading—one of the reasons for which you have made this trip—he ignored you. Last night the two of you fucked the way you have always fucked each other, as if it might be the last time. And then tonight, after all that, he ignored you. Last night, you now have decided, *was* the last time. With a glass of red wine in hand, he moved about the crowd, working the room the way he does, the way they all do, yes, you included. You drink too much, laugh too loudly, kiss a friend on the lips a second too long, and wrap an arm tightly, possessively around a waist as if you are entitled. At their worst writers are bottomless pits of need and want. Pathetic. The man you wish you didn't love circled around, careful not to touch you, careful not to get too close to the slippery edge.

In the crowded room, happily married Marina (the only one who knows your secret) pressed her back against yours, which had a calming effect, but when you turned your neck (your beautiful neck, he would say) slightly, discreetly, you saw him leaning into her. The room went out of focus when he complimented her reading. That voice, that voice, that euphonious voice he had used on you eight months earlier, after your reading. While you both sat on the bench beside the fountain, he leaned into you with his warm mouth on the spot between your neck and your earlobe, and whispered how beautiful you were, how strong, how talented. And that was all it took for you to slip and tumble. No one has to tell you: pathetic. But here in this hotel room alone with yourself you know something is shifting.

The desk clerk is still there, waiting for you to respond, and when you do, you shock yourself. "No, I'm not." You say it again, louder, clearer, to convince yourself that you said it. "No." And you hang up the phone. You're awake now. You get up to pee. At the bathroom sink you splash cold water on your face. With your eyes closed you reach for the towel hanging on the back of the door. You open your eyes, look in the mirror. Yeah, you might be a slut.

For January this city is unseasonably warm, so before you get back into bed, you turn off the heat. You pull the sheet over your head, still thinking of him, of how you followed him all over New England, and then up to Montreal for the Jazz Festival, where, so close to home, where anyone could have seen you, you boldly held hands in the street. As if you are watching some artsy independent film in which someone is fated to lose everything, you watch the two of you at that rooftop café. Spread upon the table is wine, a crusty white baguette with a warm soft center, and a platter of assorted French cheeses. Music plays in the street below, while you hold hands, smiling at each other as if you have the right to be falling in love.

Cut to a beachside cottage where you lie on gritty, tousled sheets. He stands over you holding his camera and pretends to take a picture. "Do it," you say.

"Can I?"

You nod, propping yourself up on your elbows. He snaps a picture. You pinch your nipples to make them hard. He's still snapping. "Spread your legs," he says, taking one more picture before he puts the camera down and slides into you. These pictures, which he will save on his laptop to look at later, are not what might make you a slut. Nor is the fact that you liked posing for them. When have you felt freer, more alive, than with him beside you, on top of you, under you, behind you, inside you? You gladly, gleefully, give him anything he wants in bed, or in a car, an alley, darkened or brightly lit, the kitchen, standing over the table, in front of a mirror, on a wooded trail in a state park. Anywhere. Anything. For him. And you are not afraid to ask for what you want. You're not shy that way. Not with him. None of this, however, is what might make you a slut.

What might make you a slut is that this man, the man you avoided for a year because you feared the way he looked at you, feared the attraction, the energy that had passed between you, an unsettling familiarity, as if you had known and loved him your entire life, as if he knew the source of your brokenness and might heal it, this man, this man is married. And you struggle with the sin of it. You actually believe in God. You believe that people have souls. You fear for both yours and his. Ripping the sheet off your head, you get up again. More cold water on your face and an honest look into your own bottomless pit of need and want. Who do you see first? You know. You're not surprised. Your father and mother. Side by side. After all these years. (And who doesn't look into the pit and see their parents first?) How disappointed they would be in you. They didn't raise you for this. They did not raise you to be the other woman. You were raised to be the wife. You were raised to be the wife asleep at home while your husband was out doing whatever and whomever he pleased. You were raised to love someone who lied as deeply and as naturally as he breathed, to wait for the phone to ring, and when it did, to brace yourself for the news the other woman would deliver: your husband was with me tonight.

You have battled this woman all your life. Why would you want to become her?

If you, the sleeping wife, did wake up, because sometimes sleeping wives do just that, then you were to turn the proverbial cheek. Offer the other. You were to ignore the long blonde hair (you are the dark one) on a hunter-green sweater, ignore the faint scent of her on his shirt, his neck, his hands. Linger on this thought as if it were a kiss on an inner thigh. Feel the bite: maybe you were raised to be a slut. Alert. Receptive. Look at your pajamas: floral-printed bottoms and a long-sleeved pink top. Finger the pink ribbon tied in a bow at the neck. These are not the pajamas of a slut, are they? Another bite: sluts like you come in all kinds of pajamas.

It is hard to tell who would and who wouldn't cross that line between flirtation and full-blown affair. You did not think you would. Not once did you imagine yourself as an accomplice to adultery. You heard your mother crying. You, at almost four years old, stood in the crack of your bedroom door (a door your parents would never completely close), and watched your mother, nineteen and pregnant, drop to her knees and wrap her arms around your father's legs, tightly, possessively, begging, "Don't leave me for her."

Under the fluorescent light of the bathroom mirror, you see your mother, sad, tired, bewildered. Upon closer inspection you recognize your father's stare, haunted, restless, detached.

You tried to end this affair one Sunday in September, five months ago, after a particularly moving church sermon on forgiveness and healing, hours before you were meant to get into your car and drive four hours north to his town, check in a hotel around the corner from his house, and spend four days being available to him between his work and family obligations. You had been willing to do that, but something started to shift that Sunday. Enough, you said, enough. You did not make that drive and hadn't seen him since August. But when you saw him last night, your resolve weakened. You missed him so much. When he led you to his hotel room, it was not to talk, you knew that, yet you went, feeling the heat from his hand on the small of your back as he slid the key in the door.

Maybe you like being a slut. Like the ache. The warmth between your legs that pulls you toward him. Maybe you have never known such sexual pleasure. Maybe to protect yourself you chose for a husband a man so mean and ugly on the inside that no one else would want him. Maybe the meanness numbed you. Maybe you could only perform your "wifely duties" begrudgingly or drunkenly. Maybe you deserve to feel good after feeling bad for so long. Maybe you don't give a fuck who gets hurt.

But that's not quite true, is it? You do care who gets hurt. When the ugliness of your marriage began to hurt more than it protected, you left. Some lesson was learned from the mother who, after fifteen years, said "enough." Late, yes, but a lesson regardless, and that you can recognize it proves to you that something is shifting. You can't do this anymore. You won't. Something is shifting. Something inside you. Something beyond you. You see yourself clearly. Maybe for the first time. You are responsible for your actions. You will not avert your eyes. Look! Throw open your bedroom door. Watch your mother rise to her feet. Listen as she tells your father to go. Go!

Tonight you said no, no, he cannot have you whenever he wants you, no, he cannot expect this to be enough, no, you deserve more than this, and so does his wife, his children, so, no, you said, you were not expecting a visitor. You said no tonight, and it has made you stronger. Something has shifted. You can feel it. What is whole in you is bigger than the broken. You refuse to help this man hurt another woman, another child, for his wife and his children live inside you. They *are* you. And you love them more than you love him. And so, from the slut, from the sleeping wife, from the mother on her knees, from the father who goes and goes and goes, from the pajama-clad daughter watching from the doorway, you are going to save yourself one "no" at a time.

Ann M. Bauer

The Oil Man

Imagine a girl walking down a street in Paris. The Champs-Elysées. The Eiffel Tower rising, stretching its flexed frame to a golden tip, in the distance. No, it cannot be Paris. I've never been to Paris—which remains a dark bruise inside me because fifteen years ago my younger sister went to Paris with my parents and I was not allowed to go. My father had decreed that I had too much studying to do and couldn't take the time, and he didn't want the squabbling and hair dryer noise of two teenage girls in Paris with him anyway. So if it were Paris, the story I really want to tell would be crowded out by all those other things seeping in. My bitter jealousy and love for my sister; the fact that I, somehow, during adolescence, fell off the neat square of our family of four. Besides, Paris would require French, at least some French. And even after two years of high school French and one year in college, I remember nothing but a few verbs and the word for fish: *être, marcher, rirer, poisson.*

Imagine a girl walking down a street in New York City. Wall Street. The massive financial buildings made of stone and glass shining in the distance, rising like cliffs against a clear blue sky. No, it cannot be New York, either. Because, though I went there once when I was sixteen, I remember nothing except one street corner with two dumpsters and a battalion crowd thronging toward our car. Then, later, an evening with my uncle on Cape Cod: the long estranged brother of my father who had agreed, for just one night, to see my mother and my sister and me.

But that's not the story I want to tell, either.

It must be London. I've written this story before, always moving it somewhere else, changing the names, events, masking my identity. But this time it has to be London. Because it *was* London, and that may be the only way the story can be told.

So. Imagine a girl walking down a street in London. It is a Sunday. The streets are wide and empty. The caged steps leading to underground train stops empty now of the constant rush of people; they are scattered instead with cigarette butts and stray sheets of tabloid newspaper. The cars, driving on the left side of the road which looks wrong no matter how many times you see it, are sparse and slow-moving, powered by those small, growly English engines. The girl is walking alone in a soft, brown leather jacket, a black backpack slung over one shoulder, black boots. She is headed . . . No, the girl cannot be wearing those things. The leather jacket that I own now and wear almost every day. The black backpack and boots that would have been stylish and right for London. They would change the story entirely by making her more sophisticated, different than she really was back then. That would make what happened to her so much less possible.

The girl is walking. Baggy blue jeans, a hot pink sweat shirt with a hood. A huge neon green shoulder bag that says Ciao! in black letters across the side of it. She is walking toward a cathedral, because it is Sunday and there is nothing else to do. Her fellow student travelers are sleeping in because they were up drinking whiskey and bitters at a pub called the Gorgeous Goose until four this morning and she, in her little girl clothes, got lost in a crowd of toothless, whiskered Brits, but none of them offered to buy her a pint. So she went home. Went to bed early. Awoke at 8:00 a.m.

She is carrying a book, a chunky travel guide, open to the page that lists Catholic churches in the Kensington area. Mass time: 10:00. She checks her watch; she is an hour and five minutes early. The sky is open and clear and blue and looks exactly like the sky back home.

So she tries not to look up.

She stops in front of a newspaper kiosk. Considers buying a paper.

The words, when they come, drop suddenly into her solitude. "Hey, what time do you have?"

It is an American voice—a drawl. Not her America, but it reminds her of home anyway. The home she frantically wanted to leave. Needed to leave. The home she misses, calls every Sunday with a sticky puddle of tears in the back of her throat, but doesn't know how she will live in when she returns.

"Almost nine," she says, turning. And looks up into his face. He is tall and dark. Handsome, clean-shaven, blue-nearly-black eyes, an expensive-looking charcoal gray V-necked sweater.

Now, here's the thing. He must be tall and dark for the purpose of the story, because that's the sort of character he was. But even more to the point, because I do not remember faces. Ever. It's not just his face, because of what happened later, but any face. I remember places down to the finest details. Events are fuzzy, but I usually recall the high points: where they took place, what time of day, how I, myself, got from the beginning of whatever it was to the end. But people. Their clothes, their mannerisms, especially their faces: I have no memory for these things. Eyes and noses and lips all get muddled in my mind. Once I stood in line behind my cousin in the grocery store and because he was out of context—not at my aunt's house, attending a family function of some kind—I could not place him. I *knew* I knew him, but I was just stumped as to where I had met him and exactly who he was. This is a true story.

So the man in London is tall and dark now because it's easy and it works well and because that's the closest to what I might vaguely remember about him.

He starts walking next to the girl. Slowing his stride to match hers. He smiles. "Where are you from?"

"Minnesota," she answers. She shifts her bag to the outside shoulder so it is not between her and the man. And he moves a little closer. She is excited by him, by the fact that he has chosen to walk with her. "And you?"

She is trying very hard to sound older than eighteen. She wishes she had not worn her pink sweat shirt, at least not the one with the draw string hood.

"Texas!" He says it proudly, as if that's all one need say about so large an accomplishment. "I'm an oil man." And he winks.

They walk on, talking sparsely about England, about her studies, about the time he visited Minneapolis. Eventually they reach the steps of the cathedral. The one where mass will be held in fifty-seven minutes. But right now it is empty. The cement steps are at least ten yards wide. The man walks up to the doors, casually, without speaking. He is still with her. She doesn't know why he has stayed, but she is happy. Fantasies start unrolling in her head: the man taking her to dinner, leaning over the table to touch her hair, taking her home to Texas to meet his family. The oil people.

But here I'm not sure this is exactly what happened. I like to think there is a possibility that it was me, that I asked if he would like to go inside, look at the structure, admire its history, its architecture, its spiritual force. But I almost certainly did not. Because it would have been beyond me, then, to invite him anywhere. I suspect the truth is that I let myself be led from the beginning. Led wherever he wanted to go.

Well, almost.

The man turns to the girl, eyes snapping, crinkling at the corners in that way men's eyes do in their late 20's if they have worked out in the sun and aged particularly well. "Are you going to church?" he asks, laughing.

"Like a good Minnesota girl?"

"No," she lies. "Services don't start for an hour yet. I just wanted to see inside." So they walk in together, through the cottony quiet of polished pews, thirty-foot arched ceilings, the empty, waiting pipes of a massive organ with rows of shiny foot pedals. The air is clean and white, washed with piety.

Standing in the middle of the church, two insect-sized creatures in this house of a foreign God, he takes the girl's hand and strokes it idly with his thumb. She almost jerks her hand away, worried that he is making fun of her in a sly way she cannot detect.

"You are an ugly little baby," she imagines he would say. But he doesn't. He holds her hand and she feels his wide, warm palm against hers. She shivers inside her pink sweat shirt in the broad aisle of the silent church.

They walk up to the nave, still hand in hand, and climb four, no, just three, steps to the top. There is a thick, white cloth draped over the altar. A gold chalice on top, its globe as big as a mixing bowl. He lifts the chalice with his free hand and pretends to drink from it and the girl laughs out loud. The high-pitched sound bounces crazily off peaked ceiling, towering walls, stained-glass windows.

This scene in the church, I realize, must be in part a fiction. A marriage of what I remember and what I have dreamed. I know we went in. At least, I think we did. But the part about him lifting the chalice. . . . I'm just not sure. I am certain I saw the inside of the church while I was in London—felt that still, white air. Now it seems it must have been with him. But I cannot recall if it was there that he took my hand, there that I decided his touching me without yet knowing my name held a secret logic in this new, adult world of mine.

I do know that the next thing, the most unbelievable thing, was true. This is exactly the way it happened:

They leave the church together, without speaking. He has dropped her hand but walks very close to her now, bumping into her shoulder with the side of his arm in an intimate sort of way. He must be leading; she has no idea where they are going. But she keeps up with his long steps, doesn't ask any questions. She smells clean, citrusy aftershave and a sharp, slightly pickled odor coming off his clothes.

"Hey," he says suddenly. "Would y'all mind?"

"Y'all." She smiles, feeling warm inside. So charming. Of course, she won't mind. Whatever it is.

"My hotel is right there, across the street." He points. "And my contacts are killing me. I've had them in all night." They stop on the curb, in the block of shadow from his fourteen-story high-rise hotel. She looks into his eyes. They are clear, the whites clean without a single crack of red in them. But she nods anyway.

"Fine," she says.

They walk into the lobby of the hotel. It is hushed and thickly carpeted. All the men, but him, wearing suits. There are no women except the tall one behind the desk. The girl wants to hide her loud green bag that screams Ciao! at all the tweedy, somber men. She wants to look down and be surprised by the fact that her sweat shirt has turned into a sequined evening gown and her tennis shoes into delicate spindly heels, like Cinderella when the fairy godmother waved her wand. She walks quickly, between padded armchairs, past a roaring fire, down a wide corridor and into an elevator with the Texan.

They are in a room together. It happens to be rising, behind a wrought-iron cage and slick sliding doors, but it is the size of her kitchen in the flat she shares with two other girls from Minnesota. She leans against the upholstered chair rail on the wall and he leans against her body. Reaches out with one hand and runs his fingers through her hair, across her cheek, down the length of her neck and against her pink cotton-covered breasts.

Actually this scene in the elevator may or may not be true. I know the whole thing really started in his hotel, but I do not recall where. How he did it. What I thought. It is as if we entered the building together and my body went along with him but my mind stayed behind, out on the street, refusing even to step into the lobby. Too smart to go along on an adventure that could only end badly.

His touch does not feel as good as she had imagined it would. It is slightly rougher, faster, less loving, than she would like. The girl inches away from the man, crawling sideways against the rail, but does not say a word.

He laughs. "Don't know what you came here for. Do you, honey?" He pats her cheek. The same hand, but this time it feels brotherly, quick and sweet. Her fear stops cold in the middle of the road leading out of this place. Stops with a screech of its tires, turns around, and begins racing back toward adoration. Toward him.

The elevator's doors open on the fifth floor and she shuffles behind him to a white door that displays the room number in raised, bronze numerals. He opens the door. "You want to wait out here?" he asks. He's still walking, being swallowed up by the room, leaving her alone in the hall. She slips in behind him and shuts the door with a definite Chunk! Says, "No," in a voice even she can barely hear.

He is in the bathroom for ten minutes. She hears him juggle heavy objects, urinate, flush the toilet. Toilets sound different in London than they did back home—more muffled and genteel. When he comes out, he isn't wearing glasses. She was expecting him to be wearing glasses, but he's not. He's also not wearing a shirt. He has his pants on, but his belt is hanging open: loose, like a dead snake. He walks straight at her, bare chest out front, and she begins to back away.

This is interesting, because I know that he came out of that bathroom not wearing something and his shirt seems like the logical choice. In fact I'm fairly certain this was not the only time I was with a man who appeared, after leaving the room briefly, wearing only his pants. But now I'm not sure this *was* one of the times this happened. It could be he came out without his sweater—and without those glasses he should have had—and that was all. But I don't think so.

"I was hot," he says, irritation cutting like a razor blade on the edge of his voice. "I'm just getting a T-shirt. Christ, if you're going to be so jumpy maybe we ought to just call it a day."

The girl panics. He is going to make her leave. There will be no oil people in Texas, no sweet caresses, no long kisses. "I'm fine," she says. "I just . . . need to use your bathroom." She drops her bag. Goes into the bathroom where a pale blue plastic contact lens case is resting on the shelf next to the sink. In the mirror she watches her face redden with private embarrassment. For having suspected. For having thought he would want anything here except relief from his itching eyes. She locks the door, sits down, contracts her bladder so she will not urinate and make a noise that he can hear. She pulls the chain alongside the toilet and allows a few drops to squeeze out of her during the burst of flush.

When she re-enters the room it is dim, the curtains drawn. He is lying on the bed, T-shirt on, belt still hanging open, eyes closed. "Sorry," he mutters. He does not open his eyes. "I'm wiped out. It was a long night."

He pats the mattress next to him. She crosses the room. Sits where he wants her to sit. He runs his hand up and down her leg, rumpling the denim forward then back.

"Why don't you lay back with me for awhile?" His voice is like a slow song. She lowers herself, rests against him. His body is firm and unforgiving. When he begins kissing her neck, her ears, running his hands down her sides, easing off her sweat shirt, with a final tug at the pink hood, she wills herself to comply. She knows she will feel it, the joy, the beauty of his wonderful hands, if only she can make herself.

He has not opened his eyes. Though he has pulled off his T-shirt, the limp belt, the creased wool pants. Her loose jeans, fuzzy socks, white cotton bra. He is unseeing. Smiling faintly and humming a solid noise from somewhere deep inside him. She is watching it all. Feeling nothing, but seeing his long body turn firmly muscled like a snake's. She is cold. And now her body, too, has slipped away from her somehow.

Suddenly, without knowing she intended to do it, she screams. She realizes there is pain splitting her in two. Sharp and dry, echoing in stabs, as if broken tree branches were being forced into her. He opens his eyes and looks at her. Half amusement, half anger. A serpent with a charming tongue and dark, hypnotizing eyebrows. "A virgin?" He laughs an evil note. "Jesus Christ, honey. You shouldn't be here."

He observes her for a moment and she says nothing. Then, hands on her shoulders, he pushes her down. Steers her and slips her mouth over himself. Grabbing hands full of her hair, works her head like a machine and gags her over and over as his tight flesh batters the back of her throat. She is grateful. He has made this sacrifice for her benefit: offered her a less painful assignment. A far better deal. He is, in this way, very kind.

But once again, she fails him. After five minutes of her inadequate mouth, he pulls away, rolls over to face the wall on the other side of the bed. He touches himself, hard with quick, grabbing motions, and quickly accomplishes what she could not. Then he is silent. He sinks like liquid into the bed. Stillness shrouds the room.

The quality of the stillness: that, ultimately, is my most vivid memory. The light seeping in around the heavy curtains. The portrait of our clothes in separate pools all over the floor. The clock on the night table that said 11:09. (I do not recall the exact time, but I know there was a clock sitting there to prove that just a tiny segment of life actually had passed.) And the truth.

That even now I feel grateful for his leaving me intact. Indebted to this man for being human enough to pull away from evil.

The girl moves tentatively. A hand on his shoulder, not stroking but testing. To see if he is awake. To make sure he is there with her, that she is not truly all alone in this room. He does not move, does not respond with a ripple or a quick bite at her fingers. She rises. Limp and sorry. Begins to dress.

There is a groan from the bed. A thick, normal sound with words attached. "I'm getting up," he says. A slow shift in his body, one leg moving as if through water. "I'll get you to the tube stop, honey. It's the least I can do."

He moves like a drugged bear. Fastens his buttons, his zipper, his belt. He picks up a large brown hat, a Texan oil man's hat, from the dresser and puts it on. Pulls it down low over his eyes.

"Come on," he says. And they walk out the door together. A film in reverse: back down the hall, into the elevator. Silently, together, through the lobby and the wide doors into the sunny street outside. They walk with space between them. It is just a few blocks to the nearest station. To the red-painted rail around stairs, leading down, under the earth, to the caverns and roads below the city. He descends a few steps with her. Then stops. Leans one shoulder against the cement wall. The hat darkens his face with shadow.

"You can find your way from here." A question, but it doesn't sound like one. She nods. Turns away. Steps down. Again. And again. She feels it: that he is still there, watching her.

I ask myself now what I really thought, what I really wanted. Perhaps there was still some adolescent part of me that hoped to be lodged in his heart, causing him to watch with longing, making it possible that he would come after me and retrieve me. Then fold me into his arms. There was I am sure. Because this moment, above all, I remember clearly. I see the figure behind me on the stairs. The hat. I recall my desire to be forgiven by him.

The girl swivels to look back at him and he forms his hand into the shape of a pistol, with his index finger playing the part of the gun shaft, his thumb the mechanism that must be cocked to fire. "Hey," he calls down the stairs. "You watch out for us Texans!"

She can hear him laughing even as she reaches the bottom step and walks toward the turnstiles that separate her from the oncoming trains.

Steven Church

Danger Boys

Dad's rusty-red Ford station wagon—a family car, big and beefy—has a CB radio that looks like a telephone. His car is wired up to a switch-board at his office and a woman named Linda who connects him to the world if he wants. I tell the kids at school he has a car-phone. This is the seventies. Dad wears shirts with big collars, Highway Patrol sunglasses, and sideburns. He is huge to me in many ways—gigantic in both size and presence. He fills up spaces. In the car we eat from crisp plastic bags of fried pork skins and drink pony-bottles of Miller. We sing along to "Elvira" by the Oak Ridge Boys. Matt, the younger one, sits up front with Dad. I ride in the wide backseat—the orange vinyl rolled and glazed like a bread loaf—and I can't yet imagine that there is anything dangerous about two boys drinking beer with their father, listening to country music, and shooting guns on the weekends.

We ride the bus to elementary school like the other kids in the neighbor-hood. I guess I'm supposed to watch out for Matt. He's just a first grader, a year younger than I; but he doesn't seem like he needs much watching. So I bounce through the front door like any other day, wearing my blue Bruce Jenner shoes (the ones that come with a replica gold medal), and carry-ing my NFL lunch box. Mom asks me where is Matt. I just look around the room and shrug my shoulders. Was he on the bus with you? Yes. Well, where is he now? I don't know. Panic sets in. I can see it in her agitated hand movements. Did he get off at another stop? I don't know. Are you sure he was on the bus? I think so. Frantic phone calls are made to friends of parents, teachers, the principal, and the bus company. I'm not really worried; but Mom holds the phone in her lap and bites her lip while they search. Mom has a lot of fear. Slowly, she's teaching me to own mine. It's not a bad thing, really—just the development of an active imagination.

The phone rings. Nobody has seen Matt. They're pretty sure he boarded the bus after school. When the driver is located again, she has already dropped all the kids off and parked her bus in the lot. Are you sure he's not on the bus? Yes, but she will check again. We wait, my mother and I at home, my father at work. They find Matt sleeping beneath one of the green vinyl seats in the back of the bus. It is well after dark when my dad picks him up at the bus barn. When he arrives Matt is not sitting in an office whimpering into his fist. He does not run screaming into Dad's arms. He is playing cards with some of the drivers and mechanics, four or five of them sitting around a table in the garage. He doesn't want to leave. He's just made some friends.

Interstate-40 between Empire and Winter Park, Colorado is made for danger. A ribbon of asphalt clings to mountainsides and drops sheer cliffs down to rocky slopes. Every year, my family makes the trip up from Kansas. To us, sweltering in the flat humid days of summer, Colorado seems a promised-land of elevation and air. The drive up Berthoud Pass puts us out on the edge fast. There is no shoulder to speak of, nothing but space and gravity. Dad likes to nudge the right front tire just a hair off the pavement, just to frighten us. Even though I know it is coming, my heart still shudders when I hear the sound of gravel spitting up under the Ford and watch the car point off the edge, over the line, for just a split second. Dad smiles and chuckles at the white-knuckled grips Mom and I clamp down on door handles. Matt sits serene; but I can't help imagining what it would feel like to go over—all four of us rattling around like pebbles in a can, hoping to slam into a tree just to stop the roll. I can indulge in these imaginings only because my father is an excellent driver, only because I trust him completely. Matt seems incapable of or unwilling to imagine his own death. This fearlessness will later allow him to sit on the floor of our garage and pound .22 rifle shells with a hammer while I hover over him stammering out warnings, pleading with him, describing the ricochet of bullets, holes in skulls, our father's wrath, our mother's tears. I will wonder if he is doing it just to spite me, just to see the fear wash over me. Matt will claim this never happened, that I am lying just to make him seem foolish.

Dad always said Matt was better on wheels than either one of us. The implication here for me is that Matt always seemed better at living— more comfortable in his body. Dad said it's because Matt never thought about what he was doing. He just relaxed and rode out the bumps. He followed the spirit of my father's lessons. Crashing to Matt was something you allowed, even created, and not something that simply *happened*. He never crashed because he was never afraid. He was never afraid because he never imagined the possibility of crashing. Even at a young age, I believed crashing was inevitable. Wracked with illness, I suffered fevers that spiked at one hundred and five, apocalyptic hallucinations, and blackouts—my father holding me under a cold shower to wake me. In my fevers, I had seen the destruction of my family, my neighborhood, my town. I had imagined the apocalypse. If anyone needed Dad's lessons in fearlessness it was I. Scars show my healthy flinch of self-preservation. Stitches mark the tracks of my imagination. Sixteen sutures in my face at age four from a bike wreck; an amoeba of burn tissue on the inside of my thigh, a mottled continent of scar tissue on my shoulder; I never could ride a bike like Matt. Rushing down a dirt trail or driveway, flying off a jump, pushing myself over the line, I could never completely let go. I always imagined the crash. I always flinched; and I wonder if this is ultimately what defines the difference between Matt and me. I wonder if my flinch is what keeps me scarred but alive.

Dad has this way of demystifying danger. Several spots along the Berthoud Pass road are marked with yellow signs warning drivers to "Watch for Falling Rock." Every trip he tells a story we've heard before, one we've come to expect. You see, there was an Indian boy who wandered off from his parents and became lost in these mountains. His father, a wise old chief crippled with sorrow, painted up these signs, asking our help in looking for his lost boy, Falling Rock. Dad doesn't have to remind us. Matt and I peel our eyes for the yellow signs. We gaze out the windows of our car up into thick stands of lodge-pole pines, scanning ridgelines, looking for a little lost Indian boy wandering around in a loin-cloth. Maybe he carries a spear and walks with a pet squirrel on his shoulder? Maybe he can come live with us in Kansas and teach us how to skin a beaver? We never think to look for rocks falling from their perch, smashing through our car. We want to help the boy get back home safely, back to his father.

My brother speaks in tongues. It's a game he plays on road trips. I'll point to a billboard or a street sign and Matt will say the words backwards. He can do it almost instantly. *Marlboro* becomes *Oroblram*. Matt swaps *Budweiser* for *Resiewdub*. *Denver Nuggets* switches to *Revned Steggun*.

He can break down words into letters and rearrange them in his head as if he was tossing Scrabble tiles around. The whole family will get into the game sometimes, trying to stump him; but it's creepy what he can do with words. I still get snagged up on the power of individual words, wrapped up in their own unique personalities. I can't bend and twist them like Matt does. His habit unnerves me on some level because it suggests a disregard for authority, an elevation of himself above the rules of language. Maybe I'm just jealous. Maybe it's just another time when Matt steps over a line that I'm waiting at with everyone else.

Corona Pass is an old railroad line connecting Denver and the Fraser Valley. We've come to know this road—the old ghost town that's just a few buried stone foundations and a graveyard hidden in the trees. Riding the road here isn't much fun. There's traffic sometimes and railroad ties buried under the dirt will rattle the teeth out of your head. The switchbacks in the road are connected by trails. Matt and I stick mostly to these. This day we're on our motorcycles, coming down the pass into Winter Park. A light afternoon rain has begun to fall. Dad is driving his truck and will meet us back at the cabin. We see him once on the road and then lose sight of him. Matt crosses the road and I follow him down another trail. Looking back over my shoulder, I realize we're moving away from the road we need to follow. Matt has a good lead on me and is riding hard. Dad always tells us to never lose each other. Always stay together. I shift gears and speed up, bouncing over rocks and roots, trying to catch him or at least get his attention. Matt is fast and I follow him forever it seems. We stop the bikes, and I scream at him over the sputter of the engines. "We're going the wrong way. We'll be lost." He just waves me away, climbs back on his bike, and roars off. I have no choice but to follow.

As much as I want to turn around and leave him out here in the woods, I can't do it. We're deep into a part of the mountain we've never scouted before. What would Dad say if I came back without him? Would he paint yellow signs and pound them into the ground? Would he remember this like the time I left Matt on the bus? So I follow and curse Matt the whole time, convinced that by the time I get him to stop again, we will be so hopelessly lost that we'll never get back to the road. I catch up to him as we're coming down a muddy wooded hillside; but I slide out taking a turn and crumple my clutch pedal against an aspen tree. By the time I get it bent back out with a rock, Matt is well ahead of me, sitting on his bike atop a hill. I pull up beside him. I am seething under my helmet. He just grins and points to the town of Fraser in the distance, and below us the lodge for the small privately owned ski area, Idlewild. He rides off down the ski run beneath a dormant blue chairlift. I follow him down the grassy slope, across the lawn in front of the ski lodge, into their gravel parking lot, and out the road that leads into the heart of Winter Park, only two blocks from the cabin and our father. We are miles from the Corona Pass road and still I wonder if Matt knew all along, if he knew that all he had to do to get home was keep going, keep moving.

Once, when we are still living in our big house and I am wracked with a wicked case of hiccups, Dad sits down on my bed and says that if I hold my breath for an hour they will go away. I squeeze my mouth shut and count to thirteen in my head before I realize he is playing a joke on me, before I understand that to hold my breath for an hour is to kill myself. Dad laughs and points at me as I puff my breath out. And you might think this is one of those things only a child would do. But later in life, when I am thirteen or fourteen, I burn my leg on the tailpipe of my motorcycle. The flesh peels off in brown flakes. Little bits of skin stick to the metal. Dad calls the burn unit at the hospital. When he gets off the phone he says to keep an eye out for red streaks and swelling. "If you see that," he says, "they'll have to *amputate*." *AMPUTATE!* The word rattles around inside my skull. Dad leaves me alone for a couple of hours while he runs some errands—only that word to keep me company. When he returns I am in near hysterics, pointing at the redness in my leg, and crying for the limb I think I have already lost. Never, never again, will I wear shorts on a motorcycle. Dad laughs at me nervously and says that he is only kidding, that the nurse on the phone didn't mention a word about amputation. *It was just a joke,* he says. *I thought you knew. A joke.* But I didn't know. I believed.

Dad's hands look as big as sea monsters—five-fingered giant squid that can swallow you whole. When he wakes me up in the morning for school, sitting down on the edge of my bed and resting his hand on my back, it feels like a small warm creature sitting on my shoulders, squeezing my neck, pulling me out of the watery haze of sleep. It may sound strange, but sometimes I wonder what it's like for a big boy with small parents, his father with tiny hands. Does this boy have a different understanding of parental authority? Would he hold his breath for an hour just because his father said so?

My father's ears burn with my mother's worries. She knows about the beer and the pork skins and the guns, but I'm not sure she knows the thrill we find in dancing along the thin line between safety and danger, between right and wrong. Sure it is "wrong" to feed alcohol and pork by-products to an eight-year-old, perhaps "dangerous" to put a gun in his hands at that age, or give him a motorcycle when he's only eleven. But among friends—that's what we are to each other—these words don't seem to carry much weight when we have so much fun together. Besides, it's not like we get drunk and reckless. Mom knows my father. He's never out of control, even when he acts dangerous. Most times, he's responsible to a fault. Still, she's seen him push limits on family vacations, step ever-so-lightly across the line, carrying Matt and I with him. She has to wonder about the safety of her children. We'd stop the car at a roadside vista, the four of us standing at an iron railing, gazing out at some panoramic view of mountains. Dad lifts Matt and me up and holds each one of us out over the rails so we can look straight down at the rocks or river or highway below. Every single time, he loosens his grip just slightly, just enough to give us the sensation of falling, and then clamps back down again with his giant sea-monster hands. There is immortality in that instant of separation, a fearless weightless feeling I can enjoy only because Dad's hands are there to pull me back. Matt, I imagine, lives his whole life for that instant, that moment of separation.

We spend our weekends on wheels. The Toyota pickup becomes our project. We cut out a hole in the cab and install a sunroof one Saturday. Dad puts in a tachometer and a custom-made roll-bar welded at a local metal shop. The three of us dream of racing in the Baja Off-Road Race in the desert. Dad even orders racing harnesses that strap cross-wise over your chest. Buckled up, it's impossible to move. We buy ammo boxes from the surplus store downtown and bolt them into the bed of the truck. We drive to a junkyard in search of a bench seat for the back. We carry our tools into an old empty school bus buzzing with wasps, take a seat, and barely make it out without getting stung. We bolt the seat in the bed of the truck, up against the cab, and install seatbelts so Matt and I can ride back there together with Mom and Dad up front.

We carry the rifles behind the seat. No gun racks for us. Dad doesn't like to show off like that. Guns are not toys, not something to be waving around or propping up in your window. Guns are to be respected. I start shooting at seven and own my first .22-caliber rifle by the time I turn ten. Matt does all of this a year earlier than I. He does everything before I do. Both of us learn how to clean and oil a gun completely. We learn to shoot with the rifle Dad learned to shoot with. We take hunter's safety classes. There is this old pond we like to sneak off to—summer, winter, it doesn't matter. Out on the edge of town, hidden down some old rutted roads that twist past piles of junk people have dumped—refrigerators and mattresses, car batteries and a water heater peppered with rusting buckshot wounds. We back the Toyota up to the pond. Matt and I sit in the back with our rifles propped up on the tailgate. Dad tosses an empty soda can out on the water and watches proudly as we compete to see who can sink it the fastest. The air rings with the sharp crack of .22 rifle shots. Matt is a much better shot than I. He's calm, cool, and quick. He doesn't jerk the trigger, doesn't flinch. I've seen him pop poker chips from ridiculous distances. In the winter the pond freezes solid. Dad skims beer bottles on the ice, we try to shoot them dead, and the air is punctuated again by rifle shots and a new seasonal sound—the sweet hollow tinkling of an empty Miller bottle skipping across the frozen pond.

Dad's company buys a field of corn on the south side of town. He drives us out there in the Toyota. It has rained recently and the black soil sucks up to everything, clinging to shoes and tires. We drive down off the road up to the edge of the field. Matt and I are still not sure why we've come here, but we've grown used to this feeling of ignorance mixed with anticipation. We trust our father, even though it looks just like any other terraced field in Kansas—maybe a little smaller since it's surrounded by sub-developments. Dad leans up on the steering wheel and grins at us. He punches the accelerator. The truck spins sideways, fishtailing out, and shoots forward, plowing through rows of corn—the stalks whacking up against the hood of the trunk like a kettle drum. We launch off of a terrace and splash down in the mud and corn—all three of us screaming and yelling, getting bounced around inside the truck, slamming our heads on the roof. We mow down rows and rows, hitting the stalks just below the ears. They come flying up over the windshield and land in the bed of the truck. When we are finished, much of the field lays broken and muddied. The truck is caked brown and the bed is filled with husks of corn. We take it home, dry it out, grind it up in our electric flour-mill, and Mom makes homemade cornbread.

When I am in fifth grade, two years after my father's business fails and we move out of our big house into a duplex, my parents begin divorce proceedings. Lurking over us now is this new threat of courtrooms and lawyers and judges and family counselors. Public spectacle. A three-ring circus of our failure as a family. The TV show *Divorce Court* gives me fits because I can see us there now, when before I never imagined this reality as one remotely possible for our family. This is where I'll be dragged if my parents can't work things out like adults. Matt doesn't worry about these things. He still doesn't believe it's true, doesn't see the danger. He thinks our parents will still get back together. He can't imagine the crash. I, on the other hand, have little trouble believing that our family is finished. I believe because I've seen the absence in their eyes. It's easy for me to imagine my parents sitting at cold wooden tables flanked by lawyers, Matt and I propped up in the witness box getting badgered by a man wearing a yellow tie and shiny shoes. I imagine the judge, a black robed inquisitor with a wooden hammer—afraid he will make us tell the things we know, the things that might pull us away from our father. What would he say if we talked about the beer, the pork-skins, the guns? Would he make us choose between parents? Danger boys like us don't look good to outsiders.

Dad wakes us when the winter sky is still black. Put on your snowsuits, he says. We're going sledding. Bought at the JC Penney catalog store, our suits are blue with yellow and each one has a 1980 Lake Placid Winter Olympics patch Mom stitched to the left arm. Dad leaves a note for her, *Gone sledding. Back soon.* I am scar-faced already from my bike wreck five years earlier, black-toothed from a brick, still afraid of my fevers, and just last year Matt crashed his sled into a hedge thicket, punching a thorn right through his nose. At times even he has started to seem fragile. But still we drag ourselves down to the garage, stopping to slip on moon-boots in the mud-room. We all climb in the pickup. Dad has thrown the green Western Flyer saucer sled in the back—a solid steel sled, the kind they now make out of pink plastic—and a coil of nylon ski-rope. The snow is not heavy, maybe only a couple of inches that will melt for sure when the sun comes up. Time is wasting, and the way Dad bounces with energy makes me consider the possibility that he has been up all night watching the snow fall, waiting for this. We drive to a frozen terraced hayfield, land owned by the University and largely forgotten. We have come here before to four-wheel-drive on the rutted out dirt roads that wind around the property and up into a forested hillside just west of the Aerospace buildings on campus.

When Dad stops the truck all three of us climb out. Matt and I are still not completely sure why we have come to this field this morning. Why are we here? It's not an especially nice spot to sled. There's no hill to speak of, just a few gradual slopes and irrigation berms. We trust our father. When he gets this look in his eye we're rarely disappointed. So we just wait. On the eastern horizon, over the roof of the dormitories, the sun has just begun to pink the sky. The wooded hillside where they found a dead girl once is dappled in purple light. Dad beams and tosses the sled out onto the snow. It skims lightly across the surface, leaving a wide flattened trail, before getting hung up on broken stalks of hay-grass. He ties the ski rope to the bumper, lays it out on the ground, and ties the other end to the saucer sled. Matt and I shuffle around in the crisp snow, kicking dirt clods and snowballs. *Who's first?* Dad asks. It must be Matt who sits on the sled first, folds his legs under and wraps his fingers over the front lip. Matt is always going first.

Matt the second son, the little one. First to shoot and ride. First to lose the lines of language—speaking in tongues. First to win trophies too big for shelves. First to move away from home. First to skydive. First to wrap his car around a tree. First to die. Was it a final flinch, some tick of the imagination that pushed him over that line in Indianapolis? Or did he believe he could ride it out, will himself not to crash? Was it fear or fearlessness that killed him? When my father's voice—of course it's *his* voice I hear—comes to me over the telephone, I am asleep in Utah at a friend's house, one week into a West Coast road trip in my blue Subaru wagon. Half-conscious, I don't believe him at first, hoping instead that this is some sick joke—sort of like the burnt leg destined for amputation. Maybe if I hold my breath long enough it will all disappear? But I know he wouldn't joke about something like this. I fly home the next day for the funeral, spend a few days grieving with my family, and then fly back to Utah. I pick up my car and just keep moving. Moving like Matt might. Driving, driving, cutting through landscapes of memory in my blue Subaru. Blue Subaru named Stella. Slow and steady, we camp in sagebrush. We eat meals of canned ravioli cooked on a Coleman propane stove. We don't talk to people for days. We keep running, running, running with Kansas at our backs. And the desert lasts for years, the mountains hardly a distraction, and *Jesus* the ocean is so big and deep it won't let me forget.

In the final accounting what lives is what lingers in my mind; and this is it for me: we are together again, the three of us in a field of white snow, a saucer-sled tied to the truck. It's cold. Dad and I lock in the wheel-hubs and climb into the cab. Matt gives us the thumbs-up sign. Dad shifts into four-wheel-drive and starts out slow. The sled bogs down a little in the snow, catching on patches of tall grass, but soon flies along behind the truck, skimming out over the frozen field like a puck on ice. I glance at the speedometer. It reads twenty-five. Dad cranks the wheel and turns. The sled swings out wide, g-forces ripping at Matt's snowsuit and he actually lifts up off the ground. I look in the mirror and see this blue boy flying for a split second on rope just barely tied to us, stretched out along the line between earth and sky, suspended there—before he comes down hard, bounces, and goes sailing head-over-heels through the snow. He's a little slow to get up. It hurts to crash. Believe me, I know. But then he is all smiles, all action and buzz—that quick electric sensation of being separated from the earth, weightless like he's built with the hollow airy bones of a bird. Matt jumps up, runs over to the sled, and climbs back on. He's forgotten all about the ground. Dad smacks me on the knee and laughs, twisting his head back to see if he is ready behind us. He gives us the thumbs-up again. We drive fast over the terraces, whipping him out wide over the berms, and snapping the sled back hard, letting him zip through the air and smack down again and again. When Matt has finished, I will climb on the sled. I will do it because I want to, because it's expected of me, and because I trust my father. I will do it because I want to live like my brother lives, like Dad has taught us. I will do it because that's what danger boys do. There is no question, no blame, and no answer here. All that matters is the three of us burning tracks in the snow, tethered together, bound up in these moments.

For Albert, and Norma, too, lurking in the background

Stephen Gutierrez

At the Drive-In with My Brother

My brother and I used to go to the drive-in on weekends to get out of the house. Mostly it was after a long week of washing and caring for my father, on my brother's part, doing the dirty things that needed to be done to keep a convalescent man in a decent state of hygienic solvency, basic cleanliness, though my father was too far gone to be aware, howling, as he was, in his room at all hours, in bed, propped up on pillows with his mouth open and pajamas wet. But my brother took care of my father as best he could, as best as his condition allowed, which was pretty dismal. He was gone then, too, himself, my father, preceding my brother into that terrible gulf of pain and irredeemable hopelessness that is my family's legacy, that motherfucker, that bastard, that son of a bitch disease, called "*la cosa*" in my childhood, dictating everything.

The nature of it wasn't known yet, what it was, exactly, a mystery. Trips to the hospital misnamed it. Huntington's disease, Alzheimer's disease, pre-senile dementia came flying out of doctors' mouths, typed on to labels stuck on to folders, printed on letters forwarded to the Railroad Retirement Board to guarantee a pension. Before he could retire, he had to be disabled. Before he was certifiably incapacitated, he had to be diagnosed. But words got thrown around. Nobody knew. Only that the chart, tracing our family's history, smudged and barely decipherable on the tree, proved a rot, a blight in our genes, in our bones.

And it was horrible.

But my brother and I used to go out on Friday nights when the mood struck us; we wanted to get out of the house. It usually proceeded from his antsiness, sprawling in front of the TV with his head on a pillow, comfortably uncomfortable, becoming fretful and disillusioned with the bad Friday night offerings.

So he would say something like, "Let's go to the drive-in, Steve."

And I would say, "Okay, dude, let's go," not really caring if we went or not, too preoccupied with my own troubles—adolescent trials scorching me in their own right—besides my own immediate grappling with "the thing" in front of us, around us, all the time.

That thing was a beast, an unknown quality, a shadowy character I had heard referred to but never confronted head on until now, that dark and stealthy criminal robbing us of everything we knew, a mysterious, ugly stranger who was bound to show up in our lives, take over, by the earnest whisperings of my aunt and mom years before, for as long as I could remember.

They'd square off in a hall, across from each other, and talk, oblivious to all else around them, so important was the conversation they'd shoo us away from, my brother and sister and me, not wanting us to hear, I suppose, verification of those signs we knew meant something. We knew our father was different, but not how much.

His mental capacity, always disputed—he is slow, he is not—had become irreversibly damaged, so that any lingering doubts about his competence in the world had long been dispelled, shattered, vanquished. Banished from our own sense of security, which was real—we were a solid enough working class family—life seemed malign and at fault now. Even the damn TV, zigzagging in front of us, seemed a curse.

We had to get out, especially my brother. Perhaps some elemental sense of where he was heading urged him, though I doubt it. Maybe he knew he too was afflicted with the thing that drove us all nuts, scared us, ruined a normal childhood and life by its volume. It was bad, very, very bad.

And maybe his fleeing was from himself as well as my father in the bedroom. Maybe, but doubtful. I just think he wanted to get out, see some pussy, some tits and ass, as he called it, those soft-core flicks he took me to, being a celibate man himself, not out of choice, but out of necessity from the disease that governed him, himself. He was weird and unable to land a girlfriend.

So I would agree to go, and then go back to my Green Chip Stamp licking at the table, say, in the living room, which served as a focal point off to the side, the shallow area called the dining place in the master plan of our Commerce home.

And my brother, Albert, up and active in the house now, would be gathering stuff, keys and wallet and glasses and smokes, stopping in the hall to get a jacket if it was cold, asking me to call the Rosemead Drive-in or the Gage to find out what blue flick was playing, what big butted, heavy breasted rendering of girl meets guy with thick masculinity on the wanting island.

I always went along because I didn't know what else to do. I didn't have anywhere to go or goals to accomplish, school being a bust for me in those days, my father's screams, his head-above-bath-water frantic wailings (that was my brother's job, keeping him dipped while he scrubbed his back and shampooed his hair) and tendencies to whimper in the night filling my head with noises that distracted me. I had no concentrative powers, no attention span anymore. All I had was a willingness to get out, and I didn't care where.

So I would follow him out the front door to the show, as we said, to the drive-in.

"Dude, let's go to the show."

"All right."

And this night my mother was particularly beaten. She agreed to every-thing we wanted to do, not begrudging us the money she gave us to enjoy ourselves but nodding her head absently when my brother made known his plans.

"Okay, go," she said, almost a zombie.

She was sitting on the end of the couch in the living room, eyes fixed on a page, or gazing past the TV screen to the dusty plant in the corner, ready to say anything, to do anything, to keep us happy that night.

It was as if she paid my brother Albert with those trips to the drive in, knowing she couldn't afford to give him more and that what he did for my father was beyond recompense. She loved him, loved us all, my broth-er, my father, my sister, me, though that, as hard as it is to say, isn't easy to recognize in those days of stress and anger. She was often irritable and moody, downright bitchy and mean, but sometimes she was sweet and caring, generous, as when she gave my brother what he needed to save his own sanity, recognizing, perforce, the supreme burden put upon him by asking him to care for my father, an eighteen-year-old, out-of-work misfit nursing a forty-five year old man in full-blown dementia.

She asked a lot and got much in return, my brother's love and readiness to perform the tasks asked of him.

She handed him the money out of her purse, which was handy on her lap or in the kitchen, reproaching him, as she did, for leaving her. She changed her mind. "No, Albie, stay home with me, stay home tonight. We need you, Stevie and me and Dad."

My father was down in his room, and that was a moment to enjoy, to sink into, to breathe out heavily and suspirate in pure, simple freedom. But the hall was dark and ominous, the pilot light flickering in the furnace, the black-and-white TV fuzzy and those tits and asses waiting for us anyway.

So my brother said, "Aw, Mom, let me go," and she said sure, go.

"Okay then, go," she waved us off, settling herself on the end of the couch where she kept her vigil, watching the TV and listening for my dad, able, still, to muster the energy to quiet him if he woke up.

My sister was out at the drive-in herself that night, dating her boyfriend, a good guy who came over in a beanie (not *cholo* style, but just winter-cold-pulled-down-low-over-the-ears) these frosty nights. In L.A. anything that causes the breath to congeal is excuse for heavy coats and gloves. It was probably in the mid-fifties but severe enough for us to turn the heater on in the car and warm our hands before starting down the driveway.

A short history of the genre of tits and ass might start with the V of a woman's crotch, puffed out under her bikini bottom, just caught astride a hunk felled by her ferocious swing of a ball-and-chain across his face that was deadly enough to near kill him, but not without a smirk.

Tits and ass. I've seen it all. I've seen titties hanging from trees, squeezed under plumbing pipes, in love with the wind on motorcycles, in underwater shots making sharks look tame, on top of trains threatened by fire. I've seen them all, and butts, too, bending over every rail in the northern hemisphere and some south of the border or on a tropical island far, far away from civilization, those cheeky effronteries to everything ordered and well managed. I've seen them in conjunction with each other, zippers flying and buttons popping, great, mounded fleshinesses hard to tell apart in the sweaty moment. I've seen them escape every single predicament and create a few, too! Torturing the warden who had an insatiable need for domination and power by lustily turning the tables on him. I've seen them stride down halls in college professor's blouse and rumpled skirt, just the wink of a nylon askew behind the leg.

And I've seen them bore me and get my brother excited, cracking up with the good ones, at the best parts, leaning forward in his driver's seat at the drive-in, adjusting his glasses, asking, "Huh?"

He was a weird dude, my brother, a Waldo in a way, a complete misfit, who nevertheless hung around with what passed for hoods in our neighborhood, minor characters with no spark in them but the sarcasm and meanness of the knuckled under. He hung around with this losing set, and they called him The Goon, and the name stuck, following him everywhere he went ("Hey!" "Hey, Goon, you fucking asshole!" "You're fucking stupid, eh!"), which he answered to in his naiveté and kindness. Innocent, good, terribly troubled, afflicted early with the disease that was taking my father, uninhibited and strange, rare, he was a case to be around; harmlessly embarrassing at best, dangerously foolish at worst (he once picked up a graffitti-covered ball from a hardcore *cholo* and muttered, "What the fuck is this?" about that *vato's* ancient and deadly gang, and it was with a sly and slick maneuver that I got him away from the guy before he caught on; he might have knifed him or shot him), helpful and damned, he was my brother, The Goon, Albert.

He drove me to the drive-in this night for our usual tits and ass movie and laughs. More came with the package: a pizza, two Cokes and maybe popcorn and candy in between, my mom generous with her scant resources, always sending us off with the proviso to, "Buy a large pizza, so you don't come home hungry!"

We went off in our car, down the L.A. streets, past the warehouses and factories deadened for the night, into commercial zones, motel lights gleaming, liquor stores glowing. We drove on the shiny black streets into the great curving driveway, under palm trees, leading to the screen. We made jokes, ribbed each other, two boys in love, two brothers, Albert, myself, a date.

But things don't work out as easily as that. There were some difficulties that night. My brother didn't want to see the movie I wanted to see, *The Doberman Gang*. And so the motherfucker tricked me out of the house, promising my mother he was taking me to one I would enjoy, too, answering her warning with an indifferent lie.

"Not your usual smut, eh?" she shouted, enjoined us out the door, and my brother improvised with a forward grin and a hang of his shoulders, "Yeah, yeah, Mom, whatever he wants," my father waking up in his bedroom to his ongoing agony.

"Go, just go," my mother ridded herself of us.

She stood at the door, a lonesome figure, backdropped by the TV-thick night, her own living room, in silhouette. Then the noises started. You could hear him as we got in the car.

"Ah, ah, ah!" I have never heard anything more terrible since.

We drove away. My brother turned on the radio, R&B or soft-listening jazz, and started whistling and chuckling.

"What, man, what's so funny?"

"*The Doberman Gang*," he said. "What?"

"Yeah, man, let's go see *The Doberman Gang*," I said, reiterating my plan for the night. I wanted to see the movie about dogs, Dobermans, robbing a bank.

"Fuck you, dude," he said. "*Women in Chains*, man, that's where it's at." He laughed all the way to the drive-in, the motherfucker, the cock-sucker, the lying sack of shit, my brother. But just "fucker" escaped me.

He exploded in unbelief, pounding the dashboard, lighting a cigarette, blowing out smoke at the signal, "*The Doberman Gang*? You gotta be kidding, man. *Chichotas*! Titties! Pussy!" He pursed the ultimate thing. "That's where we're heading, man, not to your fucking dog show." In a blaze of older-than-me he had the last word.

I wanted to see that movie, too. Ever since catching the preview a few weeks before, it had intrigued me. How a pack of Dobermans could be trained to carry out a heist at a city bank was a question to be answered. Plus I liked Dobermans. The dogs were sleek and mean and arrogant. They trotted around on soft-padded paws, princes of the breeds. I knew "The Working Breeds." I was into dogs, then, devoured books on them by the dozens. As many as I could get my hands on, I read and studied. Perhaps it had something to do with breeding and the willful refusal to accept fate as the random shot in the dark it seemed, but to find in the preordained world of a select breed something like mind and design over-coming the terror of chaos.

I just wanted to see those fucking dogs.

I sulked and even sniffled against the door, staring out the window at the L.A. night, banging my head against the glass, softly, "Shit, man, you promised, fucker."

"Ah, man, shut up," he muttered, swinging into the big driveway that was the Rosemead Drive-in.

We paid the lady, my brother handing her the twenty with the confident air of a working man, which he was, cigarette dangling out of his mouth, pocketing the change quickly but then deciding better and wadding it in my lap. "Here, man, take care of it," he said, not giving a shit about money, as always. What was his was mine and what was mine was more than his, was ours.

We made our way into the drive-in; we found a spot, crunching past the other cars already parked, some *firme*, some bad—noses up, fog lamps on, *cholo* style, lowrider style, just showing off, guys and girls moving into the back seat *para la cosa*. Carloads got crazy around us. Horns honked, headlights flashed on the still-gray screen, and then the scene started.

Woman walking on a beach.

"Yeah!" Comes from three or four cars. Beep! Beep! Beep!

"Dude, want something to eat?!" He shouted over the noise.

"Sure," I said, getting out of the car already, watching him in profile absorb the action. "What?"

"Get whatever you want," he said. "Get me a Coke, a pizza. Hurry back, dude," he said. "It's started."

I came back with popcorn and Cokes, saving the pizza for intermission when we would be hungriest, with one more movie to go. I set the popcorn between us and started eating, laying a bunch of napkins on the dashboard and handing him his Coke. I drank mine stealthily and watched him, laboring to eat and watch the movie at the same time.

"What the fuck you looking at, dude?" he said.

"*Chichotas!*" Then we both started laughing, tossing popcorn across the seat at each other, cracking up and getting into the spirit of the thing, the damn movie in front of us, two broads already intertwined on the muddy hut floor, unbuttoning each other's blouses, kissing each other feverishly, entering the zone of forbidden desire.

"Nasty, eh," my brother said, and we cracked up some more, holding our mouths, not being able to contain the ridiculousness we felt watching this shit, this stuff, up on the big screen, just a night with my brother at the drive-in. Behind us, on screen number 2, the looming shadow of a Doberman, teeth bared, appeared.

Seth Sawyers

Fried Eggs

My lovers suffocate me,
Crowding my lips, thick in the pores of my skin
                              Walt Whitman, "Song of Myself"

Long before she turned out to be a plate of fried eggs, Sarah was a bagel. A toasted everything bagel with cream cheese and tomato. That's still my standard order. I've gotten it in Baltimore, DC, and now Norfolk. And it's not only the bagel itself, still warm from the toaster and wrapped in waxed paper, but the process too. The walk to the counter, the glance at the bins, the order that's simple and confident. Through the whole process, she's beside me, within, rolling her eyes at my jokes, holding my hand.

She was big on food. She loved the Philadelphia roll at the sushi place on Charles Street, was disconsolate for two full hours the time they were out of fresh salmon. I went out of my way to bring her the things she liked and smiled when I thought that her being an actor heightened her senses, made her more aware of what she ate and things like the way I stood when I was drunk (pelvis out and teetering backward). I remember once, after a silly fight about something I don't remember, she made me a dinner of pasta with fresh mozzarella. The noodles were overdone, the wine was cheap, and the tomatoes cut so strangely that they fell apart on the plate before I could get them to my mouth. But I smiled and said it was good and she was none the wiser. She ate everything on her plate, joyous and drunk on the burgundy I poured from an enormous handled jug.

It seems now that I was happy all the time then. We made dates for vegetarian subs without yellow peppers and ate on the bench outside the theater building at school where Sarah spent all her time. We skipped classes so we could lay naked in my bed, our legs entangled and our arms wrapped around each other's backs, lightly stroking, up and down.

One time I stopped by her place while her roommates were watching ER. I walked into the apartment and three girls pointed toward the hallway. "She's in her room," one said. None of them looked up from the television.

Sarah didn't hear the door open, so I eased my way in and saw a pack of Newports on her desk. She didn't smoke menthols. Didn't smoke anything before she started bumming my Camels. I crept along, listening to Sarah talk to herself. She laughed at one of her jokes that only she knew about. Then she turned and saw me. I folded her small, hard frame in my arms as she hit me on the chest, half-kidding.

Then she did her impression for me. It was for a project in theater class. The guy she chose smoked Newports, and I found out that he had a bad lisp. Or maybe Sarah wanted the guy to have a lisp. I never asked, just sat on her bed with my back against the wall and watched, laughing when she laughed, the tendons in her neck flaring when she squealed and got one just right.

She had a squeaky bed that year, so we made love on the floor of her room that night while her roommates watched TV a few steps down the hall. We moved with great intent but slowly, very slowly. We touched each other's fingers, hands, arms, shoulders, backs, and hips. My belt buckle didn't make any noise when she let it fall to the floor. We breathed quietly, and when I locked my eyes on hers it was the quietest thing I'd ever done. We dropped some pillows on the floor, and I reached up to the bed for a quilt her grandmother had made. I draped it across my back. After a while I pulled it over our heads.

"This is just for us," I whispered.

"I know," she said.

I could just make out her eyes in the dim light, steely blue but sparkling, looking back at me into something I knew only she could see. I noticed, without looking, her lips curled into a smile.

"No one's allowed in here with us," I said.

"I know."

"This is nice," I whispered.

"I know," she said.

Where before jangly nerves ate away at my stomach, everything turned warm and soft and I knew that I was home. I knew that I had nothing to worry or think about except what was underneath that quilt. My life was there on the floor of this girl's bedroom in the space between where she and I met, and nowhere else. Then I kissed her, and it was dark and warm inside the quilt. That was when I almost said I loved her and when, later, I really did say it, she told me she had guessed as much.

On the weekends, after I graduated, we got coffee and toasted everything bagels with cream cheese and tomato from Sam's in Catonsville. We'd take them back to the town house I shared with three other guys and eat in the living room. When the cream cheese squeezed out between the two halves of her sandwich, Sarah licked it like she would a melting ice cream cone. Then she'd burp and laugh, every time, as if she had never done it before. Afterward she bared her teeth and I checked for poppy seeds.

After a night of double tequila shots at the bar one time, we came back to my house and watched TV with my roommate. When it was time for bed, I gave Sarah a piggyback ride up the steep stairs to my room. She had trouble even hanging on.

"Goodnight, kid," I shouted to Dave, seated on the couch.

Sarah didn't miss a beat. "Goodnight, kid," she said, loud, giggly, and drunken. She laughed without a break until she fell asleep ten minutes later. I fed her Tylenol in the morning and told my boss I had a flat tire when I walked into work an hour late.

Another time that summer, she came in the front door minutes after I laid on the couch for a nap. She was ready to go, ready for a talk, or if I was up to it, a wrestling match. I could see it in her face. While I laid on my stomach, she climbed on my back and let her full weight rest on me. She wiggled around, grinding her hip bones into my butt. I groaned something about sleeping and she sat up so that she straddled me. I kept an eye open and watched her lean back. I felt her hands on my ankle and then she wrenched the sandal from my left foot. The laughter started right away.

"What are you doing?"

"Nothing," she said.

I faked lazy for a few seconds as she waved the sandal inches from my face. I smelled sweat and damp leather.

"Are you gonna put it back?"

"No." Steady giggling.

I kept my eyes closed and waited to see if she'd take the bait.

"Oh, come on. You're no fun," she said.

She got up and I heard her feet on the hardwood floor, so I pushed myself up from the couch and leapt at her in one motion, arms out. She started so fast that her bare feet slipped. She screamed something and ran through the dining room, through the kitchen, down the stairs, and out the basement door. She laughed her way three or four times around the house before I could tackle her to the grass and tickle her in the spot that let me get the sandal back.

She always said I was mad that time but it never seems that way. We remembered it differently, even back then when we were still together. Maybe she remembered some expression of mine that betrayed a frustration I didn't yet know I had. Maybe she knew somehow that it could never last, that we were in our early twenties and had no idea how perfect things can be so easily tossed aside like newspaper.

But I know what I remember. It was the look on *her* face, the sheer joy I saw when she glanced back and saw me chasing her around the town house on the outskirts of Baltimore, her look that was absolutely content with warm sun on her forehead and the breeze that lifted her shirt up an inch or two from her waist.

I still own the pair of sandals that lets me remember something sweet. Their soles are shot now, worn out, and the leather, like that of an old baseball glove, is stiff from sweat and rubs away at my feet, leaving little raw spots that turn smooth and pink by the end of the summer. Sometimes your stuff is so ripe that a kind of potential energy radiates out from its insides, into your hand and up your arm, and before you know it you're daydreaming. And when I pick up the sandals, I can't imagine buying a different pair, even if they make my feet hurt. I don't care if the history they tell is skewed either. If it's skewed it's because I want it that way. The sandals carry with them the kind of memories that nostalgia bends and shapes for me, and I don't mind.

And sometimes you pick up your histories at their most painful moments. You debate whether they should be left alone, to be buried in the back of the drawer, where you keep all the mementos too valuable to throw away and way too pungent to leave lying around. But then something inside wins out and you relent.

Like eggs, for example. They're common, a staple. If you can't get away from your history then you embrace it. You go to the door on the refrigerator, grab some eggs, and fry them the way you like them because that's the only thing that makes sense.

Because Sarah is in a plate of fried eggs too. Now, in my little kitchen, years after she moved away, I make a plate of them every few weeks, right after frying up a pan of bacon. Some people say it's comfort food, and I won't argue. I like the easy preparation, the steady sizzle, the pang that tells me I should substitute a bowl of oatmeal. So I pour the grease into the coffee can, leaving a little in the pan to coat the surface, working it into the scratches where knives and things have gotten to it. Then I crack two or three eggs, dump what's inside, and watch as the whites race around the edge of the pan until they seize up, whitened by the flame. Sometimes I toast a few slices of bread, you know, for a complete meal, but usually I just pile the bacon on the side of the plate so that there's room for the eggs. They're always over-easy now, ever since Sarah.

It took some convincing though. Every Sunday, the year after I got my degree, the year she was finishing hers, we walked to Leon's and ordered the breakfast special. Same thing every week, for $3.85: bacon, toast, coffee, and eggs, any way we wanted them. I ordered the kind with the hard, broken yolks. We called Leon's our place and sat there for hours talking about movies and what our kids would look like. Most Sundays we sat in the same booth next to the Keno machine and drank cups of bad coffee, filling the dark and forgotten diner with clouds of cigarette smoke that swirled up to the ceiling like dreams.

Then Leon's turned into something else, slowly, without either of us catching on. By the end, the diner changed so convincingly, so thoroughly, that I can't remember it any other way. One Sunday, a couple of months before she left for New York, I sat across from Sarah and watched her finish her breakfast. We hadn't been talking much lately and everything felt sad. We rarely had sex anymore. I could feel her drifting away, and I didn't know what to do about it. I don't think she knew either.

I grabbed a triangle of buttered toast from her plate and, without thinking, dragged it across the runny, bright-yellow yolk that had pooled next to the bacon.

"What are you doing?"

I tried to smile through a mouthful of toast. "What do you mean?"

"I mean, what do you think you're doing?"

I could tell she wasn't joking. "I just thought I'd try some of the yolk."

"Get your paws off my eggs," she said. "This is my breakfast."

Something was happening, but I wasn't sure what.

"The yolk's my favorite part," she said. "I can't believe you did that."

I was sure it didn't have anything to do with eggs. At some point we had decided that the distance thing wasn't going to work. I wasn't ready to move to New York, and she was set on making a go at real acting. I know now that I had no real understanding of her ambition. I knew she ached to make it on her own, in the only place where stage actors can, but I tried my best to ignore it. I only know now, years later, how blind I forced myself to be. And it wasn't until years later, too, that I found out how much she hurt when I never considered moving with her.

We broke up in February, over the phone, and by June she had an apartment in a Puerto Rican section of Brooklyn. I found out later that she was sleeping with one of my good friends in the time between when we broke up and before she left. After that I got drunk with my roommate a lot and it was half a year before I returned her calls.

Sometimes you can't even pick your stuff up it stings so much. The electric coffee grinder in my kitchen is all about Alexis. The first time I went to her parents' house, during the winter break of my third year of college, she asked if I wanted a mocha and I had to ask her what that was. She thought it was funny that I didn't know. Alexis wasn't bored with me yet, not after three dates, and she walked over to the kitchen table and kissed me long and hot, her tongue ring clanking against my teeth.

Then she loaded the beans in the top of the machine and hit the button. The noise made me jump in my seat and she laughed at that too. Minutes later the coffee tasted strong and thick with chocolate syrup. She had learned how to make them the summer before at the coffee shop in DC where she worked. One of the guys there played in an acid jazz band and wanted to sleep with her, she told me. I could tell it was something she wanted me to know, that she turned him down.

I thought about the first time we hung out, at the Denny's in LaVale, the week before. That was when Alexis fed me spoonfuls of apple pie à la mode. She was telling a story about how some guy had seen a poster or a picture in her bedroom, but I tried not to listen. Her friend Veronica, sitting across from us in the booth, interrupted her.

"But really, who hasn't seen your bedroom?" she said.

"Shut up!" Alexis said. "We didn't do anything!"

I caught Alexis looking at me to see what my reaction was. I laughed a little but mainly kept my eyes on the table. Then, a week later, as I was sitting in her parents' kitchen, I thought about how I didn't play acid jazz, or jazz, or even a few chords of acoustic guitar for that matter. I wondered, for the first time, what this girl was doing with me.

I still don't know really. What I suspect is that I stood in the way of loneliness and that she had—still does, I imagine—a thing for tall, skinny guys. The first time we did it was on the couch in my parents' basement. We tried to wait as long as we could—about two weeks—but there I was between her legs in the dark, with our clothes piled on the floor, and my dad watching TV upstairs. And then, right before, she said she loved me. I said that I loved her, too, but I was sure I didn't mean it.

And she was way cool, this girl, too cool. A closet full of Salvation Army stuff that fit her thin, curvy frame just right. Dark hair a little long down the back of the neck and cropped close everywhere else. She had tests to see where I ranked in her hierarchy too. Once she asked me how many CDs I owned. She laughed at my answer, ridiculous to her, and said she had five hundred. At *least* five hundred, she said, and then, just then, I felt as if I was in the sixth grade again, staying up late to hang out with my older brother and his friends, trying hard to laugh at their jokes about getting stoned and pretending to know what they were talking about. I felt small.

Alexis ran the coffee grinder a lot that winter. She liked making coffee for me, for a little while. We rested mugs of it on the back patio, watching the cups melt through the crusty January snow, chasing the last bitter swallows with Parliament Lights. But we mostly drank it in her bed, under the covers, with the window open just wide enough to let out the smoke.

Toward the end of break, before she went back to school, I mentioned that I had read a Graham Greene novel. She dug around in her bookcase and came up with his anthology. I could tell she was showing off, that she wanted to prove she had read important books too. Rotten with coffee, nervous from sex, I tried to read it in the bathroom. From my seat I heard the machine grinding, shattering a fresh batch of beans. I wondered what I was doing on this strange toilet, naked, trying to read a book that I was supposed to like in this bathroom decorated entirely in blue by someone's stepmother.

For months that next semester my stomach tightened every time the phone rang twice for an off-campus call. She called just once, to leave a message that she and her new Indonesian boyfriend were at my school. They needed help, she said, in finding their way around the library. I assume they found someone.

The last time I saw Alexis was the summer after she stopped calling, at one of those outdoor bars in Ocean City where the patio is covered in sand. I was with my brother and some of the guys he worked with at the restaurant, and when I walked over to say hello she kissed me on the lips and wondered aloud about my coming out of the woodwork. She and her friends were drinking beer from pitchers and eating from a huge plate of fries. Before she left she told me where she was staying and that I should stop by. The next morning, hung over but lucid, I sat in a lawn chair outside the condo and wrote her a letter. I asked her how she was doing. I asked her how she could have said she loved me and then not called. I asked her six months' worth of questions that I wasn't sure I wanted answered. She wasn't in when I went over, so I left the letter, tucked inside a nine-by-twelve manila envelope, with her roommate. I felt like a pitiful mess the next day when she didn't call, so I went out with my brother and did a bunch of tequila shots and threw up on the beach because it was what I thought a guy who didn't care about a girl would do.

How can I tell my mom, who bought me a coffee grinder for Christmas, that it's not a coffee grinder at all? How do I let on that the mere thought of it doing its job makes my guts pucker, makes me think of the girl who wanted a tall, skinny guy who played acid jazz? When she visits will she understand when she sees it tucked away beside the microwave, its cord still bundled? Will she have any idea how much power it has over me, even though it's been four years since I've seen the girl who has one like it?

Sometimes I wonder if I have a choice in the matter. My stuff breathes life. It breathes all my best moments, all my pain and nostalgia and silliness and every three-in-the-morning, drunk-on-cheap-red-wine revelation I've ever thought myself lucky to have. So sometimes I think I might as well get used to it, that it's just as well to sit in my living room, take a deep breath, let my eyes wander, and get busy remembering. Because it's not at all clear who owns whom, whether it's me or my stuff that's the master.

In my apartment in Norfolk I have a worn 1998 edition of Rand McNally's road atlas. I've always liked maps, with their gobs of yellowed cities that line the rivers and coasts. As a boy, studying maps highlighted with my parents' trips from Cheyenne to Preston, Idaho, and from Boise to Cumberland, Maryland, I liked how the plain, two-dimensional sheets transformed the wild into the definite. Each of the states had its own distinctive shape. Some were nervous and crowded with tiny place names. Others seemed indifferent that huge national parks lived inside them, marked by little green teepees that meant you could camp there.

Michelle and I took a map like the Rand McNally on our trip out West. I met her not long after Sarah left. I didn't mean to date someone so soon, but coffee turned into long nights talking on my bed, which turned into her staying over three times a week while she looked for an apartment, and pretty soon I had a new girlfriend. I helped her with the new job teaching middle school math, and she listened to my ideas for newspaper stories. We e-mailed each other all day, trading bad poetry, and pretty soon she had vacuum-packed tofu stashed in my freezer. I stopped cooking meat, except for when she wasn't there, which meant that I rarely cooked meat. We shunned our friends. I had someone new to go to the bagel shop with, and I tried not to think about Sarah.

That was when Michelle laughed a lot. When I went to her place she waited until she heard me coming up the steps, and then she hid in a closet or behind a door. I'd walk around the apartment, calling her name and guessing she was on the balcony smoking. Then she'd wait until I got near before she'd scream and laugh until her brown face turned red. Some nights when she'd been thinking about those days before I knew her, about the time her dad left bruises on her face for all the kids at school to see, I'd hold her in my arms until she stopped crying and fell asleep. And then, toward the end, when it felt like she didn't need me for anything at all, I missed the times when she used to hide in her apartment waiting to see if I'd fall for it again.

We spent months planning our trip. A map on her dining room wall, bright with plastic pushpins, marked our course: Baltimore to Wyoming, in a loping northern route. Then it was south through Utah to the Grand Canyon, then east through Utah to Colorado before heading home to Baltimore. I managed two straight weeks off from the newspaper, and we left with the sun on our necks one morning in early July.

It took us a day to get to Chicago. We crashed at her aunt's house, a mile from Lake Michigan, where we ordered a deep-dish pizza. It was our first real meal since we had left Maryland. Michelle was a vegan then and had them stuff it with spinach instead of cheese. It's a specialty, I said, and why would you have them change the ingredients in a specialty? But she was the one on the phone in her aunt's kitchen, and I was the one sitting at the table, and I never won those kinds of arguments with Michelle. She explained her order three times before the guy on the other end understood. When the pizza came it was no good at all.

We camped at Blue Mounds State Park in southern Minnesota where we used our gear for the first time. The day turned cold at night and we huddled together under a thick blanket my grandmother gave me for Christmas when I was in elementary school. We ate ecstasy in a hotel room in Gillette, Wyoming, and speed-read Hemingway to each other. Inside our tent at Utah's Dead Horse Point State Park, we drank from a pint bottle of Bacardi and put it down to make love halfway through a game of rummy, a thunderstorm charging the hot air outside. We saw a double rainbow the next day, and I called my parents to tell them about it.

But before Wyoming we spent two days in South Dakota hitting all the parks: the Badlands, Mount Rushmore, the Black Hills. From I-90 we watched as South Dakota changed west of the Missouri. At 75 mph prairie gives way to rolling hills and tall grass. After three days we felt like we were finally getting somewhere, the passenger's feet out the window, matching bandanas stretched tight over our heads. I was in charge of the music, and I played it loud: the Velvet Underground, Lenny Kravitz, mid-sixties Beatles. I asked her trivia questions, and she quizzed me with math problems. When I got one wrong on purpose, she explained the answer as if I was one of her seventh-graders. We saw storms far away to the north that looked like giant beams of dark light focused on the plains. And then the park's pinnacles rose on the left side, to the south, and we knew we were in the West. We pulled off at a rest stop to get a good look at the Badlands and didn't say anything at all for a long time.

After we camped for the night, we hiked for an entire day, the sun overhead and hot on my bare shoulders, the park's pulverized stone crumbling underneath. We hiked a huge, circuitous route and drank our water slowly on purpose. Michelle's skin shone brown and mine turned red. Halfway through I started thinking about the journal I was keeping. I wondered if it would make for any kind of story when we got back.

"You know, life is kind of like a hike," I said. "You're optimistic when you start out and it's really easy, but then, somewhere in the middle, you realize that it's a lot harder than that." I paused a few steps. "Know what I mean?"

Michelle had to stop walking, she was laughing so hard. She bent her hot forehead to the ground and braced herself on her knees while she snorted.

"That's the corniest thing I've ever heard," she said through her gasps. "Life is like a hike? Are you serious? Oh my god, and you want to be a writer?"

"No, it is," I said. "You know, you start out one way but it always ends up another way."

She was still laughing, but now she was sprawled on her back along the trail bed. I couldn't tell if she was squinting her eyes because of the sun or because she thought I was ridiculous.

"OK," I said. "Maybe it's a little corny, but I was just trying to think of similes." It *was* kind of funny, really. Life is like a hike.

I took pictures of everything: elk, bison, the mountains, the rivers, mountains reflected on rivers. In the plastic grocery bag in my closet I have at least thirty black-and-whites of Michelle driving. She looks the same in almost every one: dark sunglasses, bandana, left knee drawn up under her elbow, a dimple of a smile casting a shallow shadow on her cheek. I have a dozen shots of her eating a strawberry Popsicle. She ate them the whole trip, across several states, the pictures tell me, backgrounds through the driver's-side window different each time: grassland, high desert, brown desert.

I don't know why I'm surprised that Michelle is the map of an entire state, all seventy-six thousand square miles of it, with a giant river running through the middle, separating the bland from the striking, the calm from the angry. She's beautiful Wyoming, stark Utah, chilling Nevada. The only time I've been out west is with her. She's the entire map of South Dakota, and she's the goddamned Grand Canyon. And until I go back, she'll be the only one there.

But only one kind of Michelle lives in South Dakota. I can still look at that map and it tells a history that I like. I know that if you don't like the memories in your stuff you can throw most of it away. You can pile it in a barbecue and set fire, watching the flames work through years and years. Pictures, necklaces, used books, letters. Those are the easy ones. If you want to, and if you're lucky, you can avoid the others. You can, if you want, buy coffee that's already been ground.

Michelle loved her computer. Hated everything about sports, made fun of me on fall Sundays, but loved her laptop and everything she could make it do. But now she's the Super Bowl and the college basketball championship all rolled into a little hundred-pound half-Chinese package. Somewhere I lost ownership of the big games.

We stopped having sex that winter after the trip, and maybe she was right. Maybe we were two different kinds of people. Maybe she was right about all the things she said about me, and maybe I was right about some of the things I said about her.

She packed her things at my house a few hours before the Patriots-Rams game. That was when I tried to punch a hole in the kitchen wall. I can still see her crying, backing out of the screen door, struggling with the laundry bag that held pounds of her clothes. And yet, I wanted to give her a hand.

The second and last time we broke up was right before Maryland played Indiana for the national championship. I obsessed over Maryland's run, reading everything I could find on the Internet. That was their year and I wanted to make sure I'd have stories to tell when it came up in a bar later. But that Monday I watched the game at a friend's house, drunk, staring at a plate of buffalo wings and not caring if my team won. They did, as I recall.

They're in everything I do, these memories, these girls. Not that they're bad roommates. They don't make much of a mess, although they sometimes keep me up at night. We've had our run-ins, it's true, like any roommates, but we've got an agreement now. They stay in their part of the house, and we only run into each other occasionally. And since it is my place, and not theirs, in my own way I get to boss them around a little bit, when I'm in the right kind of mood.

Sometimes you tailor your life so that your history lives all around you.

Your memories live in a plate of eggs, and though it hurts, you fry them up anyway. Because some mornings when the floor is cold on your bare feet, and the apartment breathes silence, you almost convince yourself that fried eggs are all you have left.

Like on Sunday mornings when I fry up some eggs, over-easy, the way I like them now. I eat the whites first, with the bacon. At the end I'm left with the neat little centers. It's the part that, when you take a fork to it, opens up and bleeds all over the plate.

Diana Hume George

The Last of the Raccoon

I hit the raccoon on the road. Three decades ago I was driving home alone late at night in an old couch-like Buick or Pontiac or Oldsmobile, trying to make it to the off-reservation house where I had recently ended my marriage. We'd created a mutual myth—he was my primal man, I his white goddess. Lennie is a Seneca Indian of the Iroquois Nation, and I am a white Presbyterian minister's daughter. Neither of us had any idea who the other was or what we were doing. The marriage didn't work, nor could it have. When I saw that, I left him.

Ending us is still one of the hardest things I've ever done. I was very young, and marriage to an Indian man had been part of my lifeplan for almost a quarter of that life. Through intermarriage I thought I was fighting old racist traditions in both our families. My family had been appalled that I was crossing lines of race and culture. His family didn't like it any better—our child brought whiteness into the family bloodline—but my half-blood, two-heart baby was the only son in that generation, and once we were actually married, my Indian in-laws fell in love with him. Marrying into the family was something they could eventually accept, but never my divorcing out of it.

My husband's grandmother Elida was a reservation wise-woman, a canny combination of old ways and new, half protector of Seneca tradition, half bingo queen. Elida and her family were members of the Turtle Clan, so the turtle was their totem animal. Elida placed a curse on me for divorcing her grandson. She called me on the phone—on the phone—and shook turtle rattles through the lines, chanting in Seneca, then translating so I'd know what she'd done. Her curse was that I'd never be happy after leaving her grandson. Bad luck would follow me in everything I did, she said, but especially in love. I laughed and hung up on her, half charmed by her AT&T curse. Within an hour I had a flat tire.

I didn't believe in her curse, I claimed, but car trouble and love trouble came to me in the years after that. Somehow I wrecked the Pontiac my car-racer boyfriend gave me. My financial marital problems years before had begun with the purchase of another Pontiac, with its Indian chief profile on the blue high-beam button. That boyfriend accused me of cheating on him (I wasn't) and chased me around the house. I had to wall myself up in the bedroom and call the police, who had to call in their dogs, he was that crazy. Animals can help people. The turtles helped Elida curse me, and dogs saved me from that crazy man. Twenty years later my beloved collie died while trying to save my failed second marriage—we got back together for awhile when Alfie was ill, strewed roses on his grave together. But our problem with each other was too big even for Alfie.

Once, in the decade after Elida's call, I quietly asked an Indian friend if his own grandmother could take off the curse, which did seem to be working. She'd never liked Elida anyway—those reservation wise-women can get pretty competitive—so she lifted the curse with a counter-curse, but I don't think it worked. Elida had strong Love Medicine, stronger Hate Medicine.

Somewhere along in there, I hit a raccoon on the road, a woman driving home alone at night, always afraid that the old car would break down in the dark, almost smelling home in the far distance around an S-curve snaking through the reservation that was famous for killing drunk people in their cars at night. I was sober. Black eyes gleamed back at my car-eyes and then came that terrible thump, more like hitting a dog than a raccoon. I turned the car around to see how badly it was hurt. It was slowly crawling across the road. I couldn't get out and aid the raccoon or take it to a vet, so I would have to end its misery. But there were no houses nearby from which to seek help or the mercy of a tire iron. I decided to run over the raccoon again, as a way to take responsibility for what I'd done.

This was a big raccoon. My tires seemed to rise way too far off the ground, once, twice, front and back. When I turned the car around to look, it was still crawling. Bloodied, stunned, it heaved toward the weeds at the side of the road. So I did it again. This time it seemed flatter, less lumpy, and I was sure it must be dead. Spinning the car around, I said the word *No* out loud when my headlights hit the pavement—I had run over the back half of the raccoon three times and it was still crawling, its determined front legs hauling the flattened mass of the back half of its body, trailing blood and organs in its wake. I had missed each time because I'd been calculating where the raccoon had been, but it was steadily moving. As it crawled now, it looked back at me, its night-eyes shining at the car-eyes bearing down on it. I wanted one last chance to end its pain, but I was just in time to see its bloody mass disappear into the high grass. What could I do? Pound on the nearest farm door in the middle of the night and yell that someone must help me track a dying raccoon through the fields?

I drove home. The babysitter found me rummaging in the garage for a baseball bat or a tire iron and said she had to leave. I didn't own a gun. I told myself there was nothing I could do, I was helpless to stop its suffering now—and it was only a raccoon. But the truth is that I was afraid to do more, cowardly to the core. I did not sleep easy for the next few nights, so I went to the reservation to learn how to apologize to the animal soul I'd offended. The Seneca system of totem clans made me hope I might find someone with knowledge of a ceremony to perform. Indians are supposed to know this stuff, yes? I knew where I was going: to Elida.

Elida listened to my story with wry contempt and the merest shadow of that strange affection we two warring women shared in the final years of her life—she could not banish me utterly because I was her only great-grandson's mother, and I had custody, and my son's father seldom came to take him to the reservation. Elida had more contact with my child through me than through her grandson.

When I told her the story, she shook her head like I was too stupid for words. Stupid white girl, she always called me. *You better go talk to Albert*, she said. Albert was Elida's longtime companion and partner in life, ancient, wrinkled, quiet, observant, toothless. He never had much use for me, but I felt safe with him. Once during a traditional Longhouse funeral ceremony, I'd had to remain behind at someone's tarpaper shack. Albert was there with some men who were drinking beer. Albert himself didn't drink. A small black and white TV blared in the background, and I sat in a corner with my half-blood baby in my arms. Late at night they began speaking in Seneca, and I thought they were talking about me, the scrawny white girl my husband married. On the TV was an old Cowboy and Indian movie, and when the Hollywood Indians came screaming across the screen in war paint like right-proper savages, the air grew edgy. My fear was paranoid and white, but I knew I'd be OK. Even if Albert

George: The Last of the Raccoon   301

didn't like me much, I was a member of his family, and he would not let anything happen to me.

So now I went out to talk to Albert by the woodpile. His bulk and height made him seem sturdy, but his eyes were clouded and misty with age, and that made this tough old man look frail. *I need to talk to you*, I said. We'd never had a conversation. Without saying a word, he sat down on a stump and nodded, my signal to speak. He listened, not looking at me, his gauzy gaze scanning the horizon beyond me. I told him about hitting the raccoon, and what I'd tried to do, and how I'd failed. *I was just wondering*, I blathered, *if there was, you know, something I could do to, you know, um, make up for the thing I did? You know, like a kind of apology? a reparation? something?* I stopped talking. It had been hard to learn to do that but I'd gotten the hang of it over my years with these people. Shut up, already. The silence was long, long. And then Albert said, *No, there is nothing you can do*. Nothing? *No, nothing*, he said. And then he looked at me, his eyes as piercing as the raccoon's in the headlights, and he said, slowly, exactly, *You have not yet heard the last of that raccoon, white woman.* He actually said that.

I rolled my eyes and put my hands on my hips and leveled my gaze right at him for the first and last time in my life, and stalked off disgusted, convinced there was some ceremony he was withholding from me as a punishment for being white and female, for wrecking their precious bloodline, which was obviously not all that pure anyway—hell, I could see white in this family face, black in that one. I was mad. What was the matter with these people? Didn't they understand that I was trying to respect their own way of honoring animals? And pure Seneca like hell, with a name like George? I figure some Frenchman got his gonads into their DNA *way* back. And what's this crock about bloodline anyway? I don't care which side is saying it, it's wrong. And that toothless old ring-tailed son of a bitch Albert, what did he know?

Then I opined—I was warming to my subject—that these people have fallen so far from their own grace that they think playing bingo is spiritual. And then I thought, ring-tailed? Where did that expression come from? And what was Albert's clan? He wasn't turtle, was he? Could the raccoon be his totem? Was there a raccoon clan in the Senecas? I didn't know and the hell with it. (There isn't.) You have not yet heard the last of that raccoon, white woman? Pleeeze, Albert, you've been watching too much TV.

And there I thought I'd left the entire matter, even if the raccoon came back to me now and then in dreams, eyes in the headlights, guts on the road, front paws looking much like human hands dragging it off the berm. My luck with vehicles continued bad through my broke years, though I graduated from Pontiacs to VW Rabbits, vapor-locked in mountains and deserts. Finally my income rose and my cars improved, and as the years passed so did my luck in love. The curse seemed to have lifted, though whenever something went awry, my lover and I would joke that The Great Raccoon had returned. Then my dog died and that love died, too. Nothing to do with raccoons, just our own stupid selves. I made my peace with road-killed animals by doing what I've done for years now, ever since my friend Jill told me what someone else told her. I put my hand to my heart whenever I pass a dead animal, then hold out that hand toward the road in a ritual recognition. I am faithful about it. I do it for animals large and small. I do it for anything that looks like an animal from a distance. It is perhaps compulsive at this point. Now and then I find that I have heart-handed a chunk of road-rubber.

Several years ago I bought a stone cottage on the shale cliffs of Lake Erie in order to save my own spirit life, to find sanctuary, to escape untenable love and the hailstorm of responsibility that comes with the big career I apparently chose, while also playing my traditional role as matriarch of a multigenerational family that includes ailing elders, grown children who still need me, and grandchildren for whom I would like to be more than a shadow they will not remember. The cliffs are my refuge. When I run away to the cottage, musing over a sundown, I think of the irony that I am a role model for many young women, that they look at me as embodying a well-lived life, they think I am fully autonomous, graced, and happy. They're wrong. My life feels like it's out of control. My relationships with men and with women are usually a shambles of misunderstanding and betrayal. If I didn't have my cottage to run to, I'd feel like road kill.

But the raccoon has returned. The acres of waterfront at the cottage are owned more by animals than by me: bats, mice, and raccoons. Every dusk, clouds of bats spiral from under the eaves, flying free in the dark, frightening visitors, delighting me, returning at dawn. Mice make nests in my clothing drawers and I let them, much to the disgust of my half-blood, two-heart son, grown into a no-nonsense police officer who finds my notions of a peaceable interspecies kingdom very silly. And the raccoons are everywhere, although we seldom see them, for they are genuinely wild. I told myself that allowing them to run free is my way of making up for what I did those many years ago, but the truth is that once again I've been careless, and once again murderous. No, not once. Stop lying, stupid white woman: over and over.

It started right after I bought the place. In the cottage next to mine, my neighbor and I cleaned out his fireplace, preparing to light the first fire. As we cleared away years of debris we heard a *screeing. Bats*, I said to Karl. He looked skeptical. *No really, it's bats*, I said to him, absolutely certain I knew that subtle rustle of tissue-thin wing. *I'll light the fire*, I said, *and you'll see, they'll fly out and find a different place to nest*. The blaze came up fast. The screeing turned to screaming and over the next hour, long after we stopped the fire, raccoon babies dropped a plopping death-rain from the chimney. Burned and crazed, they tried to crawl out. Choking on smoke and guilt, I consigned them to the fire.

I turned to my favorite animal poet, Maxine Kumin, who told me that I must cap my chimney immediately because porcupines and raccoons would certainly make nests in mine, too. I was going to do it. I was. But there were no animals nesting in my chimney that spring, and some domestic disaster or other—another crazy-man, someone's abortion, another one's cancer, I don't remember what—made me postpone. I made a note to myself to do it the following spring, top priority during cottage opening. But while I was gone on a trip, my children decided to open the cottage for me early as a surprise for my return. They started a fire in the woodstove and by the time my granddaughters came running to tell their parents the stove was screaming, a raccoon was ablaze in there. Our friend Chip managed to drag the melting raccoon, still alive, from the stove. He killed it with a shovel and buried its smoking corpse. Burning with guilt, I performed my inadequate penance, capping the chimney myself when I got back, teetering on a ladder on the steep tile roof and trembling with shame.

The next season my makeshift cap was ripped off by a mother raccoon who nested her babies in the stovepipe. I did not kill them this time. My neighbor Karl and my friend Sharain and I lured mother and babies down the stovepipe and into cages, a delicate, slow, smelly procedure. The irate mother hated me as much as Elida did. She trembled with rage and stared straight at me through her mesh prison. *It's all right*, I told her in that sappy voice women save for animals and babies, *I won't let anyone hurt you*. She answered me with a quiet hiss, then shit through the cage onto my foot. An environmental control man from the county took the raccoons to be freed in the hills high above the lake.

It goes on. This spring, when my son and I opened up the cottage after a winter in which the dirt roadway was inaccessible for months, we rounded the lakefront side and stopped short. The picture window lay collapsed inward on the cottage floor, the interior a mass of diced glass, the rugs mold-encrusted. The chair cushions were wet with who knows how many days or weeks of wind and rain. I leafed through books with covers curled, pages water-rotted. How could this have happened? The window wasn't on the storm-side, and when my son did whatever kinds of checking cops do, he found no evidence of human violation—an errant checkbook lay unmolested on a table, and the wine supply was intact. I wasn't even surprised when I saw the claw marks on the window ledge and, later on, on almost every piece of wood in the place, including salad bowls. Piecing together the circumstantial case, Bernie said, *Raccoons broke in, they actually pushed in the window*. He shook his head. I righted an overturned lamp and wandered to the kitchen to check the cupboards. Bare, with food bags on the floor next to raccoon scat.

Most puzzling of all, the main room was covered not only with glass, but powdered with a fine, white substance. The place looked like an anteroom for a salt mine. We kept sampling between our thumbs and forefingers, rolling it back and forth, trying to identify what it could be—it was almost sticky, almost hard, pebbly but waxy. Oh! The candles! I smiled in wonderment, holding out my discovery to my son as if he didn't already have a handful. They'd chewed every candle to a fine grind. I always have dozens of white candles on hand at the lake. *Wow, I wonder why they do that*, I mused, my IQ pitching precipitously, as it always seems to when raccoons are at issue. My son was not as fascinated with the chewing ritual as I was. His crisp uniform rustled as he adjusted his holster.

Itching to execute perps? I asked brightly. Given the mess I was facing, I was in an unaccountably good mood.

Enough tree-hugging? Can I trap them now?

No, I sighed. I righted another lamp. Albert may not go for reparation, but raccoons clearly do. Bernie said something under his breath. I inquired.

I said, Mother, that you do not have any special relationship with raccoons. Special relationship was delivered in dulcet New-Age tones.

After cottage cleanup, which took a few days, I went home to the church building where we live, packed up, and left for a long summer trip in Europe. During my first phone call home from Italy, my stepson, who was staying with his mom but stopping by the vacant church regularly, said that everything was OK. Except for the raccoon. I thought I'd misheard him. This was such a loony thing to say. The church is in a town, for pity's sake. Raccoon?

Uncle Billy and I think there's a raccoon in here somewhere. Even a small old church is large enough that it could house a raccoon "somewhere" without much trouble, but how had it gotten in?

Through the cat doors. *And we can't close the cat doors or the cats can't get in and out.* Oh. *There may be an entire family, we're not sure.* Oh. *Billy's wiring the cupboard doors shut.* Thank Billy for me. *And it sort of smells like shit downstairs. Or musk or something weird.*

Back home weeks later, we knew that even if it (or they) had moved in for a few days, they were now gone. They'd used up all the edibles long ago, and the cat food was in the fridge while we were gone. We assumed that the house being occupied again would deter them. Long-term therapy for the cats would be the only concern. But raccoons are creatures of habit, and they'd gotten into a steady scavenging routine while we were gone. In the middle of the first night home, jet-lagged and slightly crazed, I stumbled down the stairs, tracking a considerable racket, and thinking they were now, damn their eyes, pushing their luck. We'd bought fresh cat food that day and locked it up in an industrial-sized pressure cooker almost two feet in diameter. We had not yet unwired Billy's animal-tight cupboard system, and it was a good thing, for when I turned on the kitchen light, a black-ringed tail disappeared out the first of my complicated cat doors. In its wake, I saw that one or more raccoons had dragged the thirty pound cooker across the floor a good ten feet to the doorway. Then they had somehow rotated the clamped lid and opened the latch with their prehensile hands. Cat food covered the floor. Why had they bothered to take it to the door? Were they planning to drag that sucker outside? What they'd already accomplished suggested the work of one large and ingenious raccoon, or a feat of teamwork to make you stand back in admiration. Or give you the creeps. I hauled out the plywood, and John nailed the cat door shut. I let the cats in and out myself, one of them perpetually pissed off, the other skittish and trembly.

But while I have my limits on raccoon-tolerance where I live, I figure I still owe them at the cottage. The chimney cap is secure. I tell myself I've done what I can. I won't use the woodstove until next fall, and I'll flush out any living creatures before I do. This season, like last year, they say that some of the wild raccoons are rabid, and warnings in the papers and on the radio tell locals to steer clear of them. I do, when they let me. I want to hear the last of the raccoon, but when I listen, I can still hear screaming in the woodstove, and when I look, I can see a vision of paws, hands that look human, burning as it drags itself out of the woodstove, onto the night highway, then off the berm into the far field.

Tough

It was the summer of John Fitzgerald Kennedy and Martin Luther King, of Allan Shepard and Yuri Gagarin. But most of all—for a ten-year-old kid—it was the summer of Roger Maris and Mickey Mantle, when they fought to beat Babe Ruth's record for most home runs in a season, a record that had stood since 1927. Maris was my man. Maris could do it; 61 in '61. The coincidence gave the event the aura of mystery, like Maris himself. The truth is, I didn't know much or care much about baseball. I was not a baseball fan. Not even, really, a Yankees fan. I was a Roger Maris fan. I preferred the dark brooder to Mickey Mantle's talky, cheerful I-can-'cuz-I-think-I-can. Maris was silent. Maris was deadly. Baseball's Montgomery Clift. You could never get under the rock of his mystery. He was like my dad that way.

My dad was a family legend, a navy frogman, a Raider who'd won a medal for "pre-assault hydrographic reconnaissance" at Inchon. And like all legends without a beach to hit or a harbor to clear, he was a little lost among the coffee cups and dirty socks of daily life.

Every time he'd come home on leave, he'd spend the first few days just staring at me as if he weren't quite sure what to make of me, the way you'd stare at a patch of ceiling mold. Now where in hell did *that* come from? I felt like the child of gypsies, spawn of the devil, my mother's dirty trick.

After awhile, he'd spend the days at the picture window, staring out at the mostly empty street. Eventually he always hauled down the brown leather case that held his great grandfather's Queen Anne box-lock. For a while he'd just sit there with the case in his lap, sometimes for hours. Then he'd lay it open, lifting the twelve-inch pistol from its compartment, disassembling it, cleaning and oiling each part, then reassembling it. Sometimes the process took days. When he'd finally fit it back together, if he was in a good mood, he'd show it to me, the inlaid silver scroll-work, the demon's face embossed on the butt. Once I looked up from my homework to find him sighting me along the twelve-inch barrel. He said, "Shoot she may but shine she must."

Some nights he woke me by tapping my shoulder with the butt, his words a sharp whisper between clenched teeth: "You're in deep ground, mister!" Other nights I'd wake up to him standing beside my bed, his dark eyes wet with tears. "Things just haven't went my way."

Toward the end of every leave, he'd start carrying the pistol everywhere he went, even to the bathroom, talking to himself, arguing. In Latin, I think.

When my mom complained, he said, "'Si vis pacem, para bellum.' 'If you want peace, prepare for war.' That's what the Romans believed. That's what I believe."

"But Les," she said, "what good did that do the Romans? They're gone, extinct, *fallen*."

"Makes no nevermind, Janice. I take my family's safety very seriously. You never know—any minute the Russians could come over the hill."

"What hill? We live in Indiana. It's flat as a frying pan around here."

He cradled the box-lock like an injured bird and shook his head as if she'd gone simple. "I just want to make sure nothing happens to my family is all."

My mom brought her hand to her forehead and squeezed her temples, closing her eyes as she spoke. "Les, *you're* what's happening to your family."

He noticed me then, watching from the dark hallway. "You get in the kitchen and take out that trash, swabbie, and no mistakes or you'll learn the meaning of hard duty." He led me with the barrel of the gun.

Mostly when my mom wanted me to do something, she just yelled. So the day she sat me on the sofa and held my hands, I knew something was terribly wrong.

She looked at me hard, her forehead ribbed with worry. Bouncing my hands nervously in hers, she spoke slowly, as if she were speaking in code. "Your father has had to go away."

"Back aboard ship?"

"No," she said, "a different place, a place where he can rest."

My legs felt as though they were made of sprung steel. It was all I could do to keep my feet on the floor. This was panic. I was afraid of my dad, but I didn't want this. "Well, can't he rest here at home?"

"Not the kind of rest he needs, no."

"So when's he coming home?"

"Honey—"

"—He's dead, isn't he."

"Now, honey, no, he isn't dead." She slowly bounced our hands, once for each word. "He isn't dead. But I wouldn't count on him coming home anytime soon. Maybe not for a long time. If ever."

"What'd I do?"

She squeezed my hands tightly. "You mustn't think that way. It isn't something you did." She leaned back and looked at the bright blur of light coming through the picture window. She said, "Maybe it's something we both did," and sighed. "Or maybe it was something we didn't do." She looked back at me. "I just don't know. It hurts my heart just thinking about it."

I looked around the room without turning my head too much. "OK," I said. My own heart was banging like a radiator. "OK. I see." But I didn't see. Not at all.

For a few months, things went along as if my dad was only overseas. I went to school every day and my mom went to work at Woolworth's, the dime store where she was a clerk. But things weren't the same. On the days she went to visit my dad at the VA hospital, she dressed up in the pink skirt suit that made her look like Mrs. Kennedy. When I asked to go, she said my dad didn't want me to see him in a place like that, but I think she was the one, really. I remember those days like I was in a contest to see how long I could hold my breath.

My dad scared me, it's true, but I wanted him back. Any way I could get him. He only did what I thought dads were supposed to do. Didn't every kid's dad walk the halls all night long and, once in a while, lock himself crying in the bathroom?

After awhile, my mom stopped dressing up to visit my father. And then she stopped visiting altogether. On visiting days, she didn't go out. She didn't do anything. She sat up in bed all day smoking cigarettes. Then she spent more and more days doing that.

The school year ended about the time she lost her job for missing too many days. I came home to find her in the kitchen, the table covered with open roadmaps and the air ropy and thick with cigarette smoke. She stood behind me and covered my eyes while I touched my finger to one of the maps. That was where we would move—Kingston, Pennsylvania, anthracite country, a coal town in the foothills of the Poconos.

For two days I didn't say much on the road. Stunned, I guess. I'd had to give up my go-cart, my marble collection, my bow and arrow, and my dad. It took a little getting used to. Sleeping in the car the second night was easier than the first. I was too tired to be uncomfortable. Too tired to worry about railroad bums murdering us in our sleep or about being sucked into the seat crack.

My mom didn't seem to sleep at all, not the whole three-and-a-half days of the trip. She sat up all night in the driver's seat drinking from a flat glass bottle that jingled wetly when she raised it to her mouth.

That second night I fell asleep quickly, as though I were plunging into deep water. Almost gone, I said, "How's Dad going to find us?"

My mother, who'd been drinking from the flat bottle for awhile, said, "Oh, honey, you'd best forget your father." When she looked away, her eyes kind of went out of focus. "They've taken a melonballer to his brain. I doubt that he can find his way to the bathroom these days."

That first day of our new life, my mom taught me how to lie. Before we'd even unpacked in our half of a shabby double-block on a quiet side street off a wide avenue, she walked me across the street to a neighbor's house where she'd seen a boy about my age.

Mrs. Kirschner was a young widow. Steve was her only kid. She had mahogany hair that she brushed up on the sides and forward into a kind of loose knot that always made her seem to be leaning over you. Steve was tall and rangy with a thick brush of red hair and pale, freckled skin. His Ivy-look shirt and chinos were too loose. He held his hand out to shake, but when I reached for it, he only slid his palm against mine and said, "Cool, daddyo." Steve, I would soon learn, was so cool that everything he said and did was in quotation marks, like Maynard G. Krebs in *Dobey Gillis*.

"Automobile mishap" were the words Mrs. Kirschner used to explain her husband's death. "Recent." She nodded her head slightly and closed her eyes. When she opened them, she said, "And *your* husband?"

We were standing on the walk in front of their porch. My mom's eyes dropped to the gray, peeling steps, as if they were a mountain she had to climb. She searched for words to explain what had happened to my dad, to us, then said, "Naval mishap."

Mrs. Kirschner, looking down from the porch, shook her head sadly and said, "You leave your boy here as long as you want. I'm sure he and Stevie will become fast friends."

From where she stood, she couldn't see Steve roll his eyes. When our moms left, we sat on the steps, not sure what we were supposed to be doing.

Before long, someone in the street yelled, "Look sharp, you fream, you cube, you dude!" And Steve looked up just in time to catch the football spinning neatly toward his chest.

He threw the ball back to a dark-haired kid coming up the walk. "You trying to kill a guy?"

"Ah, boohoo on you," the kid said, throwing the football again, harder this time and to me. I caught it, barely, my hands stinging. "Who's your hillbilly friend?" he said.

I could tell that Marchenko—the only name he gave me—was dangerous. A madman. All sweaty black hair, darting eyes, and a chin like a clenched fist. He was a couple of years older but seemed even older than that.

We threw the football around all afternoon, the perfect way to get to know each other. We didn't have to talk or think. We just had to throw and catch and run.

The game ended when Steve yelled "Go long!" and Marchenko ran straight into Schuyler Avenue without looking. Cars swerved, tires shrieked, horns blared. The football landed on a VW ragtop. It didn't bounce or anything. It just landed there like the car was a giant fielder's glove. The driver never even slowed down.

We watched the car drive off. "Your ball . . . ," I said to Marchenko.

"Wasn't mine anyway," he said spitting.

We sat on Steve's front porch steps while he showed us the new guitar his dad's life insurance money had bought. He lifted it reverently from its case. He treated it like a baby. A black '57 Fender Strat with hand-beveled pickup magnets, maple neck, and a scalloped fretboard. Not that I paid attention. Not that I gave a damn.

Marchenko let out a wolf whistle. "And you got that because your old man died?"

"I guess. Sort of." Steve slipped the strap over his head and cradled the guitar in his lap.

Marchenko shook his head slowly. "Lucky stiff. I wish my old man would die so I could get stuff."

"How'd he die?" I said to Steve.

Marchenko leaned out over the yard and spat into the grass. "Circus train bisected his Buick."

I laughed. "Good one!" I pictured a Broderick Crawford sermon at the end of *Highway Patrol*. I even said it out loud, raising my index finger like a teacher: "'Clowns in the circus are funny, but on the highway, they're murder.'"

Steve looked up from his guitar with a sick little smile. "Actually," he said, "that's what happened."

I felt bad, but before I could apologize, the screen door creaked open and slapped shut as Mrs. Kirschner came out with a tray of Steve's favorite drink, root beer mixed with orange drink.

"Ah, good ole swampwater," Steve said reaching for his glass.

Before she went back into the house, she took me aside and said, "You and Stevie have both lost your fathers. That's a special bond you share." She touched my hair lightly, like she thought I was sick.

When she was gone, Marchenko drained his glass and licked his lips. "Ahh, good ole panther piss!" He stood up and pretended to pee into the bushes. "You know about that Natalie Wood movie? I want to see it. I want to see it. I want to see that Natalie Wood spinning in that grass."

Steve laughed so hard swampwater came out of his nose. He had to hold his face away from his guitar so he wouldn't drip on it. "Dig, Melvin," he said. "It's *Splendor in the Grass*, not *Spin Her in the Grass*."

"Same dif'," Marchenko said. "Anyway, I'm going to see it."

"Like fun," I said. "My mom says it's too spicy."

Steve looked at me, rearing his head back like he was just now getting me in focus. "Spicy?" he sneered. "Spicy? Man, you really are a hillbilly, aren't you." Before I could answer, he added, "What about that new spy picture? Would you make that Ursula Undress? You say Dr. No, but I say Dr. Yes-Yes-Yes!"

Marchenko stiffened, gazing down the street. "Cruiser alert!" From down the street came a brand-new Plymouth Fury, red with black leather interior, its front fenders so arched they looked like a pair of raised eyebrows. Like Natalie Woods's eyebrows.

"Dang!" Marchenko said in a reverent whisper as it passed.

All three of us gazed after it. Then Steve said, "I'd kill Santa for a ride in that."

My stomach kind of dropped, it was so beautiful. "Dibs," I said. "Me want."

"There ain't no Santa Claus," Marchenko said, spitting into the grass again.

It turned out that all three of us loved cars, which Steve called "shorts," "rods," and "rockets." We loved dragsters, deuce coups, and wood-paneled daddy cars. We loved flip-tops and cherry chariots with bent 8s. We loved them dagoed, decked, hopped-up, jacked-up, souped-up, leaded, and lowered. Cars that weren't afraid to show their teeth.

"This is a good corner," Steve said. "You get to see a lot of people race for pinks. You can see some pretty cool stuff from here."

Marchenko paced nervously up and down the short, broken walk in front of the house. Without the football, he didn't know what to do with his hands. Steve sat on the top step, across from me, fingering the dead strings of his guitar. His mom had agreed to get it for him as long as he never plugged it in. So we listened to the dry *thup* of his fingers against the strings. When he really got going, he stuck his tongue out, the fat, pink tuber worming back and forth.

I sat there on the step feeling like a criminal getting used to the new life I had stolen, thinking of all I had given up. But not Maris. Never Maris. Maris needed me. And I needed him—Maris the brooder, Maris the shadow man.

Without provocation and before I could stop myself, I said, "Maris. No sweat."

Steve stayed hunched over his guitar, his eyes on his fingers playing, his tongue working away.

"No way," Marchenko said. "Mantle by a mile."

"Could be," I said. "Mantle's a great hitter."

"What do you mean?" Marchenko said. "Maris is no slouch. He could take it clean away!" That was Marchenko, ready to fight you at every turn.

"Down, boys," Steve said, "or I'll have to send you both back to the pound."

"I'm going home," Marchenko said.

"Which house is yours?" I said.

Steve stopped playing and began to wipe down his guitar with a piece of chamois. "His pad's the big naked house at the end of the street."

"Naked?" Marchenko said, stiffening. "There's nothing naked at my house."

Steve's voice came out thin with boredom. "Pick up the slack, daddyo. I mean the paint. It's all wore off. Naked."

"I ain't your damn daddy," Marchenko growled back.

I'd seen the house that morning, walked past it. It had gone without paint for so long that the weather had worn it down to the raw, gray wood. The place was full of people, more family than one house could hold. They overflowed into the yard, the street. In his backyard was a crumbling outhouse. Someone had slapped it together years ago with stray lumber. Now it was so old that one good push would bring it down.

"You live there?" I said to him. "At the end of the street? That's the place with the outhouse."

Marchenko stopped pacing, seemed to stop breathing. His smile fell back on itself.

I wasn't picking up on it. I kept talking. "I saw it this morning. It was the outhouse I noticed first."

His neck began to glow bright red, then more of his face. I couldn't help it. When I saw the outhouse, a strange joy swept over me. It grew stronger as I watched an old man step out of it stretching his suspenders back up over his shoulders. "Irina!" he shouted, and then something I couldn't understand. Somehow the sight of an outhouse in the city was oddly comforting, the first real sign of welcome I had seen. Back home everyone had an outhouse.

"That's a shed," Marchenko sputtered. "For tools and stuff. Not a damn outhouse."

"I know an outhouse when I see one," I said, still smiling, still not getting it. "There's a moon carved in the door and everything. We got a lot of them back home. My grandma has one."

Marchenko looked stricken. His voice quaked. His words came through clenched teeth: "Every dang shed you see isn't a dang outhouse, you dang *hill*billy."

"Hey, no offense," I said.

Marchenko stepped up close to me. "I know about your old man," he said. I thought of the picture my mom kept in her dresser, my dad in the white uniform, the squared-off Steve Canyon face under an officer's cap, its black brim shiny as a hearse. I felt a sudden stab of longing for him. I missed the stories he'd tell, about being a combat swimmer on a boomer, a ballistic missile submarine, and swimming through twenty-five-foot rip-tides and walking the beach so thick with gooney birds you couldn't find a place to put your foot. And then I thought of him toward the end, how once he locked us in the bathroom with him, how he kept us there for hours, talking at us in Latin, stuffing his shirt under the door to keep out the poison gas and the x-rays and every other thing.

Marchenko was standing in front of me now. He lowered his face to mine. "Your old man's dead." He said it like an insult. Like it was the worst thing in the world you could say about somebody.

Steve had gone back to playing his guitar, nodding over it, barely lis-tening to us, his tongue swelling as he snatched at the dead strings. Maybe he didn't hear. Or maybe he thought I was getting what I deserved for making fun of his dad dying, even though I didn't mean to.

"What'd you get, anyway?" Marchenko said to me, straightening.

"What? What do you mean?"

"Tell me what you got. You know . . . when *your* old man died."

I listened to Steve's fingers stumbling and squeaking on the strings. I looked down at the step the way my mom had. "Clothes," I said. "Mostly. School clothes. These shoes." I held a foot up in the air, showing off the brown oxfords my mom had bought me last week at Sears. "I got these shoes when he died."

Marchenko's eyes went shiny and hard. "Is this another so-called joke?"

I turned the shoe so we could see it better. It was scuffed from our game of street football but shiny enough to catch the light in a way I liked.

"No," I said, setting my foot back on the step. "No joke."

Marchenko looked at my shoes like they were a pair of dog turds. He said, "My dad was in the marines. He says the navy is for queers. And you didn't get those dang shoes when your old man died. My old lady got me a pair just like them last week at Sears. She brought the shittin' things home. I took one look at them, one look, and threw them away. I wouldn't have them shoes on my feet for anything. I wouldn't be caught dead in them shoes. That's just what I told her."

"I guess I was thinking of some other pair of shoes."

Marchenko huffed. "Yeah, sure. You know what I think? I think your old man didn't give you diddly-squat. I think my dad's right about navy men."

I flipped him the bird, holding my middle finger out longer than I had to. "Climb it, Tarzan," I said, which I thought would make Steve laugh, but he still wasn't paying attention.

Marchenko's face pinched in a little. "Climb?" he said. "Climb what? navy queer," he murmured. "You think you know so much. I wouldn't put shoes like that on a goddamn dead man." And then louder, "You think your old man was tough?" He stood with one foot on the porch step, the other on the sidewalk. He leaned forward at the waist.

Steve sat there hunching harder over his Strat, his wet tongue working like a shot snake.

"Was he?" Marchenko said, kicking his chin at me.

"Was who what?" I said.

He rolled his eyes, then made a face for Steve's benefit. "*Tough*. Was your old man tough?"

"Pretty tough," I said.

"Liar," he said quietly. "I'm here to tell you you're a goddamn dirty liar." Then he laughed, a dry laugh at the back of his throat. "I'm standing here calling you a liar and you do nothing. I'm here calling your old man a queer, and you do crap."

"I'm not going to fight you."

"A liar *and* a coward. I think you must be as queer as your old man."

I tried to catch Steve's eye. "'Meanwhile, back at the ranch . . .'" I wanted to give him the big tickle. I wanted to see that swampwater come gushing out of his nose again, wanted things the way they were, but he wasn't buying it.

"What ranch? What's that supposed to mean?" When he realized I wasn't going to answer, he turned his head to the side and spat again. To Steve he said, "You ever notice how this queer never spits? You ever *see* him spit? Ever?"

The only sound we heard from Steve was the sharp squeak of his calloused fingertips against the strings.

"Me neither," Marchenko said. "What does he do, you think? Just swallow it? If you ask me, that's queer."

"I'm not going to fight you."

He smiled and stepped in close to me. "No need for a fight. If your old man was tough, you should be able to take a punch. Simple." He balled up his right hand and snapped it against his open left a couple of times. "One punch. Just to see what you're made of. Or are you all show and no go?"

"It's stupid."

"Sure," he explained with exaggerated patience. "You think that because you're a queerbaby. You're queer as a two-dollar bill."

I was stunned. In my suitcase I had three two-dollar bills that my dad had once sent me. Sometimes the service paid him that way, he said. He told me to keep them, that someday they'd be worth a fortune to a collector. I was so ashamed I stood up, facing Marchenko.

Just then we heard another car coming toward us from the far end of the street, a T-bird with a muffler so loud Steve's living room window buzzed. The car was raked low. We stopped fighting, stopped arguing, stopped breathing, I think. Canary yellow, nosed, cherry beyond cherry. The car kept coming, then pulled over to the curb, miraculously, in front of my new house, the big engine grumbling.

"I'd love me a port holer like that," Marchenko said.

"Choice," Steve said.

I stepped away from them, toward the street. I couldn't help myself. I said, "That's my dad."

Marchenko's mouth went wide. "Your dad? Your dad? Your dad is *dead*."

I took another step down the walk, toward the street, toward my house, toward him, toward my dad. It took so little to believe it. Just saying the words. It had to be my dad. Who else would stop in front of our house like that? Why else would my mom buy me new shoes with school already over for the year? And then, because I wanted it to be true, because in some universe it might be true, I said, "He's not dead. That's the story we have to tell people. My name isn't really Spencer. It's Maris."

"What?" Steve said, looking up at last from his guitar.

"You got to be shittin' me," Marchenko said.

Almost as soon as I said it, as if he'd heard my lie, the driver goosed the gas, popped the clutch, and peeled out, charging right through the stop sign and across Schuyler, leaving a curtain of pale blue exhaust hanging in the air.

It might have been my dad. Back home I'd left a note in the hollow tree in our front yard. *Dear Dad, How are you? Better I hope? We are going to Kingston, Pennsylvania. Please find us.* And I signed it *Your son, Brent Spencer,* as if he might need to be reminded who I was. How I expected him to find the note in the tree, I'll never know. It seemed like a good idea at the time. But now it seemed like the dumbest of the dumb.

I turned to Marchenko. "Go ahead," I said, standing as solidly as I could. "Hit me."

He smiled, cocked his head, and wiped his mouth with the back of his hand. All his hard work had paid off. He stepped close, closer. "Yeah," he said. "Queer as a two-dollar bill."

Steve laid the guitar on the deck behind him. Something was happening, and whatever it was, he didn't want it happening to his Strat.

"You know what I think?" I said to Marchenko as he took his stance. "I think you never saw two dollars in your whole entire life. And furthermore, for your information, Roger Maris *is* my dad."

He swung hard, the punch landing solid and square in the middle of my stomach. I held my ground. I didn't back off an inch. I smiled tightly. It was the hardest thing I had ever done.

Marchenko just stared, his mouth hanging open.

I turned and walked away slowly, out of the yard, across the street, toward home. I knew they'd watch me all the way to my house. I went down the side yard, past the bay window, where I could see my mom watching television, her gaunt face flickering in the gray light. I walked past the back door and out into the backyard where no one could see me die. I fell to my knees. From the moment he'd hit me I hadn't been able to breathe. I thought my head would explode. I could feel my heartbeat in my eyes.

When I could finally breathe again, my gasps came with racking sobs. I fell onto my face, weeping into the freshly cut grass. I tried to picture my dad's face, but now all I could see was the face of Roger Maris. I had betrayed my dad. It was like I had killed him.

After what felt like a long while, I could breathe again, each breath a raw scraping convulsion.

When I was able to get my feet under me, I stood up and went in through the kitchen door. I could hear the TV in the parlor. My mom was half-sitting, half-sprawling on the couch, a cigarette in one hand, its thin flag of smoke trailing to the ceiling. She didn't look up from *Queen for a Day* when I passed the doorway or when I opened the cellar door and made my way down the dark, plank stairs. She probably thought I was going to practice with the furnace. The landlord had fired it up for us, showing me how to tend it, and the fire was still going.

It was a huge, cast iron monster, smoke leaking from under the rust-stained cement patches. I lifted the handle and pulled open the door to the firebox. Inside, the heaped coal glowed red. I shook down the ashes and stood back, feeling the waves of heat wash over my face. Then I pulled off both of my shoes and chucked them into the fire. With the poker I shoved them in among the bright fists of coal, where they stood out black against the flames. The laces caught, flaring up. The polish sucked off in a quick wisp of black smoke that also burned. Black smoke began to flow from the empty foot holes. The shoes began to look not like shoes. Then, as I watched, they began to clench slowly with the heat and flames, the air thick with the smell of burning leather. I heard my mom jump to her feet. She must have smelled it. But she would be too late. It was done. I would wear torn high-tops wrapped with duct tape and studded with bottlecap cleats, like Marchenko's, for the rest of my life.

LITERARY JOURNALISM

Tom French

The Exorcist in Love

Think of it as a love story like no other. What you are about to read can be described, without exaggeration, as an intragalactic, interstellar tale of reincarnated passion. A cosmic romance unfolding during the dusk of one age and the dawn of another. All of it taking place between real people. All set in Pasco County, Florida.

The basics: Boy meets girl. Girl is not like girls. Girl has unusual abilities and interests—this is putting it mildly—but opts for a conventional life, at least on the surface. Girl marries boy, has family, endeavors to be normal. Many years down the line, after multiple experiences purportedly involving demonic possession, lights in the sky and other phenomena not explained by science, girl abandons normal thing. Girl decides boy is wrong, all wrong, and that the forces of darkness have possibly replaced him with a copy of the husband. Girl divorces boy/dark copy of boy, descends into depression, and seeks solace in her career, which happens to be battling evil and channeling communications from what she believes to be a bevy of aliens. Alleged aliens, who apparently know a thing or two about the hell of modern romance, take pity on girl and set her up on a blind date with—

Wait. We're getting ahead of ourselves.

THE EXORCIST CONTEMPLATES THE MASTER PLAN, RIDES A HURRICANE, AND DEFIES HER MOTHER

When it started, the exorcist was still a child.

This was many years before she began talking to the dead and to those who were never alive. Before she figured out who she was and what she was and accepted that she did not fit.

It was also before she took her wedding vows and brought five children into the world and then stepped off the cliff of the edge of her life, before she opened herself to visions, before she confronted the entities with "No" and then cast them back into eternal darkness. Before she took dictation from another corner of the galaxy, before she brought her son to visit his grave from another lifetime, before she had any idea what to think about the face at the window or the dream of the baby in the woods, before she devoted years to pondering the mysteries of the universe only to discover that there was nothing more than her own heart.

For Laura Knight, it started long before any of these things.

It started several decades ago, when she was growing up on the west coast of Florida. Even then, she lived on curiosity. That is where it really began: with Laura's monstrous, breathtaking, epic curiosity. From early on, she refused to believe in randomness. She was sure there were cosmic blueprints, an underlying grid of meaning, and she wanted in on it. She devoured libraries of books. She immersed herself in particle physics. She pored over Freud and Jung. She studied Greek to aid her reading of the New Testament. She longed to understand the matrix of the tides, the language of the periodic table, the seductive progression of Beethoven's *Moonlight Sonata*.

But understanding these things was not enough. Laura hungered not just to comprehend, but to experience.

So one day she climbed into the storm.

It was 1966, and Hurricane Alma was spinning cartwheels in the Gulf of Mexico. At the time, Laura was fourteen years old and living with her family on a farm in northern Pasco County, outside Hudson, less than half a mile from the coast. She had heard on the radio that Alma was generating mountainous waves, and she wanted to behold their ferocity for herself. She asked her mother to take her to the beach, but the answer was no.

As Laura recalls it, she made her move late that afternoon. Her mother dozed off while working on a crossword puzzle—all these years later, Laura is still astonished that the woman actually labored over something so mundane in the middle of such a spectacular day—and Laura grabbed some binoculars and slipped outside. She was headed for her favorite tree, a towering camphor that she had often climbed to gaze out into the gulf and that was ideal for what she had in mind now. Slowly she fought her way toward the tree, leaning her body against the wind and the rain, walking drunkenly through a sea of mud and debris.

Around her she could smell the unmistakable ozone perfume—earthy, pungent, almost sulfurous—of Alma making her presence known.

When Laura finally made it to the tree, she climbed until she reached her usual vantage point, a three-branch fork that formed a natural cradle near the top, some thirty feet off the ground. Wedging herself in, she took her place in the heart of the maelstrom. The camphor pitched violently; the wind whistled and cried; the rain pounded into her, pushing against her eyelids and into her mouth.

Peering westward through the rain-splattered binoculars, she could just make out the black, seething expanse of the gulf.

Inside, Laura willed herself into stillness. When she had stepped out of the house, a part of her was afraid. But now she had ascended to a place above fear. As the hurricane rocked her in her cradle, engulfing her and the rest of the visible world, she was transported into a heightened state of both perfect calm and absolute exhilaration. She had become the eye of the storm, the consciousness inside the chaos. She was not afraid to die.

In that moment, the questions of Laura's life—questions that would run through all the years stretching before her—announced themselves once and for all. Was it brave of her to venture out into the hurricane? Or was it foolish? Was it proof of something wonderful inside her, or an early sign of something not quite right?

Laura had no time to contemplate such questions. She rode the storm in all its fury. She wiped the water from her eyes. She felt the ecstasy surging inside her. She turned her face to the dark skies, surrendering to the power and grace and glory of things beyond her control.

Another question: What happens to someone who is willing to ride the storm? Where does the wind take her? Does it tear her apart, or does it carry her someplace above the clouds? And what about the people who get close to her? Does the storm leave them untouched? Or are they swept away, too?

Laura has already found the answer. At least, she has found her answer. It is there in the details that make up the rest of her life. It is in the account I am about to share with you.

For the record, I have followed Laura, off and on, for five years. I met her in Clearwater at a meeting of a group of people who are interested in UFOs and alien encounters. I had spent the bulk of my career doing the kinds of stories that reporters are expected to do, writing about law-yers and teachers and police officers. I had gone to the meeting looking for a change of pace. I wanted to follow another kind of person, someone unusual, someone different. Perhaps he or she would be there.

I had never heard of Laura. As it happened, she was there as a guest speak-er. If I had gone to a different meeting, on a different afternoon, I would have never met her. I would call this a coincidence. Laura would not.

In front of the group, she laid out the basics of her story. She said she was a psychic, a channeler, and a hypnotherapist who had worked with people who had possibly been abducted by aliens; in passing, almost as an afterthought, she mentioned that she was also an exorcist. As if that weren't enough, she said that she and her children had once seen two UFOs gliding across the sky over their house in New Port Richey.

I sat in the audience, trying to fathom what I was hearing. To me, what stuck out the most was not her story but the woman herself. She was genuine, smart, and funny, immensely likable. She did not claim to understand everything she was describing; she admitted, without a trace of defensiveness, that she was way, way out there. She told us she was not even sure what to believe and not believe.

"I have been, and will continue to be, a skeptic in these matters," she told the audience. "Still, I feel we are on the right track."

In the years since that day, I have interviewed Laura repeatedly, fol-lowed her to UFO conventions, attended some of the channeling sessions where she attempted to communicate with entities from another part of the galaxy. Yet I still do not know what to make of her. Much of what Laura claims has happened to her is jarring, strange, beyond disturbing. And while I myself have witnessed some of the scenes that follow, the bulk of this account relies by necessity on Laura's memory, her word, her perceptions.

Virtually all of it, as you will see, is open to debate and interpretation.

I have no idea if Laura is truly psychic. I cannot begin to prove one way or the other if she ever really confronted a demon or talked with extra-terrestrial beings. In fact, I recognize that she could have made up many things she has told me about her life. Still, I don't believe that to be the case. I have spent enough time with Laura to trust her sincerity. I do not know that she really saw two UFOs flying over her house. I am convinced she thinks she did.

To me, though, this story was never about the spirits of the dead or demons or UFOs. From the start, I saw it as an account of one woman trying to come to terms with the unknowable, searching for something out of reach.

In our own way, many of us are on a similar quest. Physicists, for instance, labor to understand the origins of the cosmos. So far, the best they've come up with is that originally there was only a void, and then, in an instant, all the matter of the universe—all the matter that today makes up our bodies, our planet, our sun, every solar system and every galaxy in existence— suddenly sprang into being in a massive explosion. That's their theory: One moment nothing, the next everything.

Personally, I find it to be far-fetched and deeply unsatisfying. That does not necessarily mean it isn't true.

Millions of Americans go to church every Sunday and contemplate a story about a man who was born two thousand years ago, the son of a divine father and a human mother. This man, according to the story, grew up to raise the dead and perform other miracles until, at age thirty-three, he was tortured and killed and then rose from the tomb to rejoin his father in heaven. Ever since then, one of the most sacred rituals of this story's adherents is to symbolically drink the blood and consume the body of this son of God.

I intend no disrespect to those who have faith in this particular story. I grew up inside that faith myself; during the catechism classes of my Catholic childhood, I was taught that Communion is not symbolic at all, that every Sunday at Mass we truly do eat the body of Christ.

By any measure, that is a wild story. How much wilder are the possibilities that Laura has embraced? If you believe in the soul, how much more difficult is it to accept that spirits may roam among us? Knowing what we have learned about the evolution of life on Earth, how much of a leap is required to consider the notion of life springing up on other planets that revolve around other stars and that some of these life forms might actually wander into our neighborhoods?

Who can say?

All of us are drawn to the unknowable. Mysteries sustain us, just like food and water. They get us out of bed, give us something to do, provide our lives with depth, texture, meaning.

Obviously, Laura has taken this pursuit to a whole different level. Many people are willing to accept the possible existence of aliens; few would try, as Laura has, to chat with them during a makeshift seance in the living room.

Once I started spending time with her, I found myself wondering what her quest for answers meant for her and her family.

Whatever was happening to her, whatever she was experiencing or thought she was experiencing, where would it lead?

Doubt the things Laura believes she has seen, if you want. Doubt her conclusions, her logic, her state of mind. But know that Laura herself is real. She has a driver's license and pays taxes. She has a family.

And like many of us, she is simply trying to make sense of herself, her life, her place in the world.

This is her story.

The story of what happened after the exorcist came down from the tree.

LAURA WATERS HER ROSES, PONDERS THE FORCES OF DARKNESS, AND TALKS WITH GOD

Just before dawn, and a mockingbird already calling from the woods beyond the house. The smell of coffee, very strong, tons of cream, drifting upward from the cup in her hand. No sign yet, thank God, of the demented billy goat from next door.

Laura, seven months pregnant and feeling it, walked slowly through her garden. She was soaking up the early morning stillness, waiting for the sun, talking to her roses.

"Hello," she was saying to them now, speaking in her most gentle and soothing voice. "Did you miss me?"

Laura treasured these moments in her garden. Her husband, Lewis Martin, was busy getting ready for his job at the sawmill. Her four older children were still asleep in the house; her fifth was swimming quietly inside her womb. As for the neighbor's goat, a four-legged terrorist with huge horns and bloodshot eyes and a fondness for butting anything in his path, he usually waited until well after sunrise before launching one of his sneak attacks.

All of which meant that daybreak was Laura's best chance for grabbing a few moments to herself. So every morning, she would rouse herself at 5:30 or so and slip outside to tend the flowers, sip her coffee, and think.

It was the summer of 1989. Laura was living with her family outside Hudson, in a rural area not far from the house where she'd climbed into the tree as a little girl. She was thirty-seven now, with penetrating green eyes, thick brown hair that almost fell to her waist, and an open face that seemed to be perpetually searching for something more. She did not know what she was searching for exactly. All she knew was that she felt a desperate need inside her to understand, the same curiosity that had driven her as a little girl. Only now it was accompanied by an emptiness she could not name, a vague sense that something was not right in her life.

After years of marriage, Laura was sometimes plagued with a feeling that Lewis was not the one she was supposed to spend her life with, that there was someone else out there waiting for her. She told herself these feelings were ridiculous, the romantic fantasies of a schoolgirl. But the feelings persisted, nagging at her.

Laura was excited about the child growing inside her. It made her think that perhaps things would be all right after all. She told herself that she was not just pregnant with a baby. She was pregnant with a chance for a new life of her own.

So much had already happened to Laura. She grew up in Tampa and on her grandparents' farm, the one with the tree. Her father, who worked at a family drugstore, left before she was born, and her mother, a bookkeeper, did the best she could for Laura and her older brother. After the divorce the family moved around, sometimes staying with Laura's mother's parents or other members of the family; in the years that followed, her mother married and divorced four more times.

Laura struggled to find her place. She was sent to a psychiatrist. He met with her several times, gave her some tests, then delivered his conclusion to Laura, her mother, and a counselor from Laura's school.

"She's not the problem," Laura and her mother remember him saying. "The fact of the matter is that she's smarter than all of us in this room and smarter than all her teachers."

But there was more to it than that. From the time she was a little girl, Laura had felt that she was fundamentally different. She was sure she knew things she had no way of knowing. She could see inside people, feel the essence of them, read the patterns of energy playing out in their lives. She had strange dreams that seemed to come true; driving through neighborhoods, she sensed that she was seeing and hearing and smelling snippets of whatever was happening inside each house she passed.

Her mother, asked later about these things, would confirm that her daughter had a gift.

"She had what we called the premonitions," remembers Mrs. Knight. "She understood things about people."

But there were incidents that were inexplicable.

When she talked with her mother about these things, her mother said she was being foolish.

"You're just imagining it," Mrs. Knight said.

Laura wanted to believe that herself. As she grew older, she told herself that these moments were all just waking dreams, fantastic products of her imagination. She learned to stop talking about the incidents to anyone else, especially adults. But the episodes did not stop. They continued as she took classes at Hillsborough Community College, then met Lewis, married him, and began raising a family.

She was doing her best to be ordinary. She was having her babies, first two daughters, then a son, then another daughter, and working off and on at various jobs to help pay the bills. She was going to church— although Laura had been raised Methodist, she and Lewis now attended a Pentecostal church—and tending to her garden, and buying groceries, and worrying about the family finances just like everyone else.

No matter how hard she tried, though, Laura simply could not fit in. She still saw the world as differently as she did when she was a child; still read reams and reams on every subject from mythology to astronomy, looking for answers; was still haunted by mysterious, inexplicable experiences.

There were nights when Laura would wake in her bed and sense something there in the room with her and Lewis. Often, she would get sick after these incidents, developing ear infections and other ailments. Sometimes part of the house would grow strangely cold. Glass objects would break around her. They would break when she was upset or startled, and always when she wasn't touching them. Drinking glasses, a lamp, a window over her bed, even the window of a friend's brand-new BMW.

Then came the night when she woke beside her husband to find the house bathed in white light. Still half-asleep, she told herself it was nothing, just some people outside with pickup trucks, shining their headlights through the windows. She went back to sleep. But when she woke up, she was turned around, with her head at the foot of the bed and her feet up by the pillows. The bottom of her nightgown was soaking wet and soiled with weeds, as though she'd been walking outside.

Laura finally began to accept that she would never be anything remotely close to ordinary. Life would be so much simpler if she were like everyone else, but now she realized that such a wish was impossible.

That was when she opened herself up to new directions, when she began performing the spirit detachments and the exorcisms.

"Oh, is that a nasty bug on you?" Laura was saying now, peering at the leaves on another rose bush in her garden. "Let's get that off right away."

She liked being out here at dawn, when the glow of the new day was spreading through the trees and the dew was still on the grass and she could lose herself among the flowers. She would hear the bees zooming by and watch the hummingbirds poised in midair above the blossoms, and she would remember that there was balance in the world. She adored her lilies—lilies of the valley, day lilies, cups and saucers—and the marigolds that exploded in a stunning wall of yellow. But the roses were her favorites. They were so delicate, so demanding of her care and time, that she thought of them as her children. She grew them on the east side of the house, just outside her bedroom. At night, she would drift asleep to their scent.

Laura loved living in this house, surrounded by woods. Not long ago, though, she had received a surprising prediction. She had gotten out a Ouija board and was fooling around with it, asking questions about what to do with her grandparents' nearby farm, now that they had died. She would rest her fingers on the planchette, a small piece of plastic with felt slides under it, and then ask her questions and watch the planchette glide back and forth, moving through the letters of the alphabet laid out before her on the board. Letter by letter, the board would give her answers. It was telling her to sell her grandparents' property; also to prepare for another change in her life. She and her family were moving, the board said.

They were going to Montana.

Laura didn't understand. She had lived virtually her whole life in Florida. But the board was insistent.

"m-o-n-t-a-n-a," it spelled.

Laura wasn't necessarily opposed to the idea. Maybe Montana would be good. But she couldn't think about making such a drastic move at this point in her life, especially with a fifth child on the way. She walked through the garden, and felt the baby inside her, and thought about all that had happened to her, and tried to understand what it meant. She thought about all the things that lay ahead of her. There were so many possibilities, probabilities, ghost realities fighting their way into being.

Repeatedly she was struck with a sense that there was something more she was supposed to be doing.

Since childhood, she had felt there was a hidden meaning to everything that had happened to her, a plan that had been kept out of her view. Now she was sure of it. Inside, she felt a growing certainty that all her studies and all her experiences, even the frightening ones, had laid the groundwork for a role waiting to be fulfilled.

But what was that role? Not knowing was excruciating.

She tried to wheedle some answers out of God. Morning after morning, there among the roses, she asked God to please let her in on the plan. She promised not to let him down. If he would just give her some answers, she would make the most of it. She swore it. But she had to understand why she had been made the way she was made. Why was she so driven to learn? What exactly was she supposed to do with all of these things careening around inside of her? Why did she feel so empty? Was it her marriage?

Or was there something wrong with her?

Tell me, she would say. If you exist, and if there's a reason I am here, tell me what it is. Show me the path. Tell me where to place my foot next. Please.

The house was alive with Mozart. From the tape deck and out through the speakers he came, soaring, diving, teasing with the glee of a man who had been dead for two hundred years and did not care.

Laura listened to Wolfgang all the time now. She'd made a tape of her favorite pieces—*A Little Night Music*, excerpts from *The Magic Flute*—and she'd put it on the stereo in the afternoons while she worked, humming and singing as she made the beds, did the dishes, nursed her baby daughter.

Arielle, she was called.

Only a few months after the conversations with God in the garden, Laura was deliriously happy. The ghost realities were no longer ghosts. Now they were alive.

The first thing that happened was that Laura had reached an understanding with God. She had decided that there was no point in trying to pry answers out of him. Whatever God planned for her, he would show her when the time was right.

In the meantime, she had more than enough to keep her busy, caring for the new baby. Arielle had made a dramatic entrance into the world. Laura had gone into labor early one August evening and then struggled until just after midnight, when the doctor performed a c-section. But it had all been worth it.

Her daughter was beautiful, and Laura was holding her at last.

There was other work to do as well. With the arrival of a fifth child, Laura and Lewis had decided they needed a bigger house. Laura had found one in New Port Richey, not far from downtown. It was a wreck inside—"a handyman's special," the real estate ad had called it—but it had a big yard and five bedrooms.

Laura was thrilled. She had an intuition about the new house. This was where she was supposed to be, she told herself. This was where whatever was meant to happen to her would begin. She could feel it. There was just one thing. Something that did not even register with Laura when she first found the house. Something she didn't even think about until after she and Lewis had bought it. The house was on Montana Avenue.

NAZI SOLDIERS IN THE STREET, GIANT BOOMERANGS IN THE SKY

"I wish that damn light would change," said the woman on the couch.

Her eyes were shut, her body stretched out under a blanket. Her hands were folded above the blanket, making tiny movements. In her mind, she was still at the wheel.

Laura, sitting in her chair a few feet away, did not understand.

"What?"

"I'm just waiting for the light to turn green," the woman said. Suddenly her voice changed. "Oh my God, Patrick! What did you do?"

Something was wrong. They had gone through it all together, Laura and the woman. Laura had gotten her to close her eyes and slow her breathing, and then the woman had gone under and resurfaced back inside that night out on the turnpike. She had already told Laura what happened. Now, still under hypnosis, she was telling it again, letting it run in her head, like a scene in a movie.

She and her teenage son, Patrick, were returning from a funeral in Pittsburgh. It was snowing. There was fog and ice. They took a detour onto another highway, trying to find better weather. Then the woman sees the light in front of the billboard. The light is an iridescent blue, a pale oval of baby blue, and the oval is hanging there in front of the billboard. It makes no sense, and the woman thinks she is imagining it; she is rubbing her eyes, but it isn't working, the light doesn't go away, it just keeps getting bigger. She asks Patrick if he sees it, but he doesn't, only he does say something about electricity. Then she feels something taking control of the car; now she's not driving it anymore, something else is, and the light is still growing.

Then the skip.

Suddenly she and her son are somewhere down the road. Now they are in a little town called Waynesboro, off the highway, just north of the Maryland state line. Something has happened. Fifty miles have ticked by on the odometer, and they do not know where the miles have gone. All they know is that they are sitting at a traffic light in Waynesboro. The woman is at the wheel waiting for the light to change, and her son is beside her trying to open a tin of cookies someone gave them after the funeral.

But he can't open them, so she tells him to look in the glove box, there's a penknife. He gets the knife, he works at the cookie tin, and he cuts himself. Now he is bleeding. They are at the light, and Patrick's hand is bleeding.

"Oh my God, Patrick!" the woman was saying. "What did you do? There's a towel in the back seat. Get it."

Still in her chair, Laura studied the woman carefully. Freddie Irland, a friend of Laura's, was watching, too, videotaping the session from the corner.

By this point the woman had grown agitated. Something was upsetting her, and not just the cut on her son's hand. She was breathing faster. She had raised her arms to her chest and crossed them, as though she was trying to protect herself.

Laura told the woman everything was fine. She reminded her that she and her son were safe. But they needed to go back to the beginning, back to the turnpike, and start over.

"Let's go through it again," Laura said. "A little more slowly this time."

It was the night of Thursday, 15 April 1993. Laura and Freddie and their subject were working in Laura's living room in her home in New Port Richey, there on Montana Avenue. Outside it had been storming. Inside, all was quiet, except for the interplay between Laura's voice, soothing yet insistent, and the woman's voice, confused and edgy. Occasionally there were the chirping sounds of the family's cockatiels; there were also murmuring noises as Freddie whispered a few words to Laura.

More questions. Freddie wanted Laura to ask the woman many more questions. He was very excited, and when Freddie got excited, he could be a little pushy. Laura did not mind. She adored Freddie; besides, the unwritten contract of their relationship allowed great leeway for pushiness. The two of them were not just friends; they were cosmic explorers, trying to solve the mysteries of the universe. Timidity would get them nowhere.

That evening, they had the house to themselves. Laura's children—including Arielle, now three years old—were with Laura's mother. Lewis was working late. Laura still did not know what to think about her marriage. Lewis was a good man, decent and hard-working, and he did his best with the children. But to Laura, it seemed like he was growing increasingly removed. The two of them hardly talked anymore. Lewis did not seem to know what to make of Laura these days. He was there beside her, but also far away. Or maybe she was the one who was far away.

One night, Laura had a disturbing dream. She saw herself in another life, somewhere in Europe during World War II. In this dream, she was married to a different man, and her heart belonged to him in a way it did not belong to Lewis. They were happy, and their happiness came naturally, without effort. Still, it did not last. In the dream, she saw her husband being killed. She was standing on the balcony of their house, and there were Nazi soldiers in the street below, and as she watched, they seized her husband and shot him to death.

The dream haunted Laura. Not just because of its violent ending, but because of the depth of emotion she had for the man in the dream. Long after the dream, he stayed in her thoughts. She felt that the man was real, not a figment of her subconscious. To her, it seemed that she had truly known him and that he had known her and that the two of them had not only been married but had been meant for each other.

She decided that the dream had not been a dream at all, but a vision from a past life. She'd had other visions that she was convinced were from other lives—she had seen herself in ancient Egypt, in Paris during the French Revolution—and this one was the most powerful yet. It would not leave her.

Laura did her best to put such thoughts aside. What good did it do, dreaming her days away like that? She was married to Lewis, and they had these children, and it was far too late to change any of that. The kids were growing—Aletheia, her oldest daughter, was fourteen now—and Laura had decided to homeschool them. After her own experiences in the schools, Laura did not think highly of public education. She thought that the schools were not nearly demanding enough, that what they really taught children was to be quiet, to not ask questions, to conform and become complacent consumers who did what they were told and bought what they were told.

She had plenty of books on hand; the walls of the house were covered with shelf after shelf of them. When they were baking together, she would lecture on chemistry, explaining how all the ingredients bonded in a carrot cake.

"Their classroom," she would say, "is the world."

Laura wanted her children to bloom, wanted their imaginations to roam. She was with them almost constantly. After taking various jobs over the years, she no longer worked outside the home. She was not a fan of day care or baby-sitters.

"I don't believe in quality time," she said. "I believe in all the time."

The children weren't the only ones getting an education. Laura herself was learning at an exponential rate. In the last few years, she had given herself free rein to pursue all the questions inside her that she had spent so long trying to push down. She was studying astrology and making charts for herself and others.

She believed Freddie to be a talented medium in his own right. At first, when the two of them had gotten out the Ouija board, they'd been searching for lottery numbers, hoping to strike it rich. Now they were trying to speak to the dead and to spirits from what Laura and Freddie called "other realities."

Always, Laura looked for signs of deeper patterns. She studied the weather, scanned the newspaper, kept track of floods and earthquakes and even the movement of palmetto bugs inside her house, trying to find some way to tie it all together.

Sometimes, the kids would roll their eyes. "Mom," they would say, "get a grip."

Much of Laura's time was devoted now to the hypnosis sessions, which occasionally evolved into exorcisms. Laura had been interested in hypnosis for years; she had read exhaustively on the subject and taken classes. Using hypnosis, she had begun performing what she called "spirit detachments," where she would put a subject under and find what she thought to be spirits of the dead that had attached themselves to a living host. Once, as she would later explain, she went inside a subject and found the spirit of a man who had died in a house fire; another time, while performing a detachment on a young subject, she found the spirit of a boy who had been fatally hit by a car in a grocery store parking lot and was lonely for the company of another child.

Laura's techniques were straightforward. She would put her subjects under, locate the spirits and talk to them, find out what was bothering them, then tell them it was okay to let go and move into the light. Basically, she saw herself as a counselor to the dead.

The exorcisms were different. They involved entities—"dark entities," Laura called them—that had never had a life of their own. Some people would call them demons. She had done only a few exorcisms. Sometimes she worked with children who were behaving in disturbing ways; other times she worked with adults who were alarmed by their own destructive habits and wondered what was causing them.

Laura had prepared herself for the exorcisms as best she could. She had read everything she could find on demonic possession; she studied the literature on traditional exorcisms, as performed by the Catholic church. Her version of the ceremony was more informal. She would hypnotize her subjects, find her way to the entity, then send it away.

Talking to the entities sometimes left Laura feeling as though she needed a bath. They were slimy, disgusting, deceptive. They frightened her.

"What is your name?" she asked one of them.

"I never had a name," it answered.

"Who sent you?"

"My master sent me."

Whether Laura was truly confronting demonic beings, she had no idea. All she knew was that something—some form of negative energy—had found its way inside these people, and after these sessions that she chose to call exorcisms, the energy was gone.

She was thankful that the sessions were rare. The spirit detachments were much more common. Sometimes Laura was called upon to conduct them as often as once a week. She didn't mind; the detachments were not nearly as stressful and required far less of her emotional energy. She approached them like any ordinary counselor, on her way to just another therapy session.

"Talkin' to dead dudes," she called it.

Still, even after all these encounters, Laura had never come across anyone quite like the woman reclining on the couch before her this night.

"I wish that damn light would change," the woman was saying again.

As Laura would later tell it, she had met the woman a couple of weeks before. They had talked, and Laura had mentioned in passing that she did hypnotherapy, and the woman had told her about this strange experience, several years before, on the highway in Pennsylvania. Something had happened, and she didn't know what it was. But every time she thought about it, she said, she would grow extremely upset—upset to a degree that did not make sense. She wanted to know why. She wanted to understand what had occurred that night. When Laura offered to put her under and see what she could learn, the woman agreed.

Now here she was, lying in Laura's living room with her eyes closed, driving again through that night. Every time she replayed it for Laura, it came out the same. She and her son would be driving on the turnpike, and they would take the detour, and then she was seeing the blue light. Then the skip. The same skip, every time. Suddenly they would be at that traffic light in Waynesboro, fifty miles down the road, and her son was opening the tin of cookies with the knife and cutting his hand.

Laura was determined to find out what had happened during those fifty miles. Freddie, videotaping from the corner, already thought he knew. That was why he was so excited.

"This is an alien abduction," he told Laura.

Freddie was big on UFOs. He was well aware, as was Laura, that a growing number of Americans—the exact number remained unclear—had come forward in recent years with stories of disturbing encounters with creatures that had traveled here from other planets. Many of these people believed, or claimed to believe, that aliens had abducted them from their cars or bedrooms, somehow rendered them helpless, then taken them aboard a spacecraft of one kind or another, subjected them to medical or scientific experiments, then returned them to their lives with all memories of the abductions blocked from their minds. When these people would try to recall what had happened, they would simply draw a blank; their recollections of the aliens typically surfaced later, often under hypnosis.

Freddie believed these people's stories demanded attention. So did others who followed the phenomenon, including John Mack, a Harvard psychiatrist who had interviewed some of the alleged abductees.

Laura was not so sure. At Freddie's urging, she had been reading about the abduction accounts but had found them unconvincing. Laura was open to believing in many things; her whole life was devoted to considering possibilities in the universe that others found ludicrous. Still, she had trouble believing that little gray men were stealing people away by the hundreds or even thousands and playing doctor with all of them on some fancy mothership in the sky. If it was happening to so many, why was there no proof?

Why could no one produce a single indisputable snapshot of one of these aliens or even one of their ships? Where was the video? Why weren't these aliens appearing on *Geraldo*? Like many others, Laura found it far more likely that these people had undergone some serious trauma—possibly sexual abuse, suffered during childhood—and that now they were subconsciously transforming their buried memories of these experiences into encounters of another kind. Perhaps it was easier for them to imagine an alien illicitly entering their bedroom and violating them rather than confront the fact that it was really their stepfather or their mother's boyfriend.

Laura thought she detected an element of mass hysteria in the proliferation of abduction accounts. With the approach of the year 2000, maybe these people were simply going a little nuts. "Millennial disease," she called it.

All of which explained why Laura was taking such pains to find out precisely what had happened to the woman she was working with this night. Before hypnotizing her, Laura had asked the woman about her childhood, probing for any sign of abuse or family problems or anything suggesting emotional or mental instability. But she had found nothing to account for the missing time in the woman's story.

Laura was undeterred. She decided to take the woman under even deeper, getting her to slow her breathing even more and replay that night yet again. This time, the woman remembered a parking lot. She could see the blue light growing, and feel the car leaving the highway, and now she and her son were stopped in the parking lot of a diner, just off the road, not far from the billboard where she'd first seen the light.

"What happened next?" said Laura.

"I wish that damn light would change," said the woman. Back to the skip. Whatever it was, it had happened somewhere between the moment in the parking lot and the moment when her son cut his hand.

So Laura tried again, taking the woman as deep as she knew how. Speaking softly, she asked her subject to imagine herself sitting inside a favorite room. Maybe the family room at her home; maybe a study. Anyplace where the woman felt safe. Inside this room she was asked to imagine a recliner. She was sitting in the recliner, resting comfortably, and in front of her was a television. She was to project the scene from that night on that television and describe what she saw unfolding on the screen. Laura told the woman she had a remote in her hand and could manipulate the action before her. She could fast forward, rewind, turn it off. Whatever she needed to do to feel safe and in control.

Back onto the highway went the woman, her son at her side. They were taking the detour. The billboard was coming up. Slow it down, Laura told her. Use your remote, and hit pause, and let the tape advance one frame at a time.

The light. She saw the blue light. It was in front of the billboard. It was growing. She was losing control of the car. It was leaving the road. Then they were in the parking lot. They were in the lot, outside the diner. They did not know why. Wait. Someone was coming. Someone was approaching the car.

Laura asked her to describe who it was.

"I can't," said the woman. She was getting agitated again. She was hyperventilating; her upper arms were twitching; she was rubbing her hands, as though she were in pain.

"What do you mean, you can't?" said Laura.

"Because they won't let me."

Laura pressed the woman to tell her what was going on. Who was she talking about? Who was stopping her from saying?

The woman just shook her head.

"I can't tell," she said. "I can't."

That was the night when the other ghost realities began to tumble forward. Laura's understanding started to shift, and the universe shifted with it. It did not happen all at once, but slowly, in bits and pieces.

That evening, when the woman on the couch grew so upset, Laura decided to end the session. She wanted to keep probing, but for the moment it was too traumatic. So Laura brought the woman out of hypnosis and told her that they would try again, in another session. Laura was left to consider the implications of what her subject had revealed. Was Freddie right? Had this woman and her son been abducted by aliens?

At first, Laura remained skeptical. Then, in the weeks that followed, something happened that chipped away at her doubts. The newspaper and TV were reporting multiple sightings of UFOs in the area. From mid- to late April in 1993, more than a dozen people in Pasco, Hernando, and Pinellas counties said they had seen a large, boomerang-shaped craft moving across the sky. One of the witnesses, a Hernando County sheriff's deputy, said the craft carried no markings, was adorned with blue lights and had a wingspan of at least two hundred feet. He watched it for several minutes, he said, before it accelerated away from him at a speed that would have been impossible for any human-made craft.

"Based on what I know now, no, I don't think it's from this planet," the deputy told a *St. Petersburg Times* reporter. "Nothing on Earth could hover and haul ass like that."

Reading the accounts in the newspaper, Laura was startled to discover that the first alleged sighting of the boomerang-shaped object had been made in New Port Richey on the evening of Thursday, 15 April, the same night she was conducting her hypnosis session with the woman in her living room. The person who had seen the object that night lived only six blocks or so from Laura's house; she said she had seen the craft through her bedroom window after 10 p.m. that evening, after *L.A. Law* came on.

As Laura read the details of the account, she realized something else. The witness claimed that she had seen the giant boomerang at the exact time Laura was deep into her session; in fact, she said she'd seen it hovering over Laura's own neighborhood.

To Freddie, this was all more proof that the woman with the missing time had been telling them something dangerous that night, something the aliens didn't want her to share. That's why her memory block was so strong, he said; that explained what she'd meant when she said "they" wouldn't allow her to continue with the story.

Laura still was not ready to buy Freddie's theories. As far as she was concerned, the rash of sightings was just another outbreak of millennial disease. One person claimed to have seen the giant boomerang, and the rest had probably heard the claims, then gotten excited and imagined seeing the same object. If there were so many spaceships out there, carrying all these aliens and snatching all these poor earthlings, where was the proof?

"Where's the evidence?" she asked Freddie. "Show me a damned alien, for God's sake."

As it turned out, no more evidence was forthcoming from the woman with the missing time that night in Pennsylvania. After the first session with Laura, she called and said she'd changed her mind. She would not be returning for another session.

Laura went on with her studies. She continued reading about UFO sightings and other paranormal events; she also continued performing the spirit detachments and the occasional exorcism. She and Freddie were still experimenting with the Ouija board, trying to contact beings from other realities.

Then, one night late that summer, Laura had a stunning experience. This was 16 August 1993. Laura and her family had eaten dinner. It was getting late. Lewis was inside; Laura was in the backyard with three of her children, swimming in the family's above-ground pool and staring up at the sky. There was a meteor shower that week, and Laura and the kids were hoping to relax in the pool and see some shooting stars.

As Laura would later describe it, they had been staring at the sky for just a short while when suddenly an enormous black boomerang-shaped object appeared directly above their house and over the pool. It was low in the sky, perhaps ten feet above the roof of the house. It moved slowly. It made no sound.

"Mom, look at that!" the children cried. "What is it?"

Laura didn't know what to say.

"A flock of geese," she said, grasping at any explanation. "Flying south for the winter."

Then came the second boomerang.

This one was on a path about fifty feet to the west of the first object, again flying low, just above the house. Floating in the water, Laura studied the object carefully. She looked for flapping wings, listened for the telltale honking, but saw and heard nothing that suggested a flock of geese. This was a single, solid object, with a black, metallic surface. On its burnished exterior, she could see the reflection of the lights from the family pool.

Slowly it passed over them, the houses beyond, the middle school down the street. Then, it disappeared into the night. The children were beside themselves. They were yelling. Laura did not know what to say. When Lewis came outside to find out what all the shouting was about, Laura clung to her original statement and told her husband that they'd just seen two flocks of geese.

Laura knew that was impossible. No, these had not been birds of any kind. She could not erase what she had seen with her own eyes.

But what exactly had she seen?

In the days to come, Laura narrowed it down to two possibilities: either she had become infected with her own case of millennial disease or UFOs were an undeniable, inescapable, objective reality.

Laura did her best to put such thoughts aside. What good did it do to think about any of that? The face at the window, the dream of the woods, those presences she had sensed in her bedroom time and again. And of course, the night when she had dreamed that bright lights were streaming through her bedroom window and then awoken later to discover that she had been walking outside in the dark.

Laura had pushed these connections away for so long. That was why she had resisted Freddie's theories. It was why she'd fought against the evidence before her. It was all too real.

THE AUTHOR, MUCH TO HIS SURPRISE, MEETS THE GOLDEN BARBARIAN

My encounters with Laura Knight began a year and a half after her alleged sighting of the giant flying boomerangs.

I had never heard of dark entities or spirit detachments. I did not know that anyone around Tampa Bay actually claimed to be performing exorcisms. I certainly had not foreseen the day when I would be called upon to write, with a straight face, a sentence that ended with the words "giant flying boomerangs."

I met Laura for the first time on the afternoon of Saturday, 25 February

1995 at the east branch of the Clearwater Library. She and I were there for the meeting of a local chapter of the Mutual UFO Network, better known as MUFON, an organization that investigates reports of UFOs and alien abductions. I had not been aware that there was any such chapter in Tampa Bay, much less that it had enough members for them to congregate en masse at the public library. I wanted to know more, so I went.

This was in the early stages of the latest national obsession with all things UFO-related. The *X-Files* was only in its second season, the so-called alien autopsy video was not yet airing on the Fox network, and the only person I knew personally who had seen a UFO—or at least, who had admitted such a thing to me—was my former hairdresser.

Still, the congregants at the library were excited that Saturday. They knew that a groundswell of interest in other worlds and other intelligences was gaining momentum around the country; they sensed that they were in the first wave of a profound shift in the public's willingness to consider the possibility that alien visitations might just be a verifiable fact of life on this planet. After years of being derided, these people were finally getting some attention and respect.

To say that Laura made an impression that day is an understatement. When it was her turn to speak, she instantly seized control of the room. She had so much presence, she was almost radioactive. And hers was no ordinary presence. She was not about to be mistaken for a movie star; she was overweight and slightly mussed, and her clothes were almost defiantly unfashionable. She wore leggings that, as I recall, were a little too tight and a tunic adorned with amber beads and painted gold spirals. I took one look at her and said to myself, "I bet she has a bust of Elvis in her living room."

Somehow, though, Laura used all these qualities to her advantage. She was too much, and knew it, and did not care; if anything, she reveled in her over-the-topness, which gave her tremendous freedom and power. Her eyes flashed; her hair flowed freely; her slightly crooked smile ignited the atmosphere around her.

In a short talk, apparently delivered without any notes, Laura gave an overview of her life, telling a little about her childhood, her work as an exorcist, her hypnosis session with the woman with the missing time, the night she and the kids saw the two ships above their swimming pool. She also spoke about some recent experiences with a spirit board, which as I understood it was similar to a Ouija board but more elaborate. Using this spirit board, she said, she and Freddie and some other friends had begun communicating with what she called "sixth-density beings" from the stars that make up the Cassiopeia constellation.

Laura's story was easily the wildest I heard that day. It didn't matter. She was smart, charming, completely real. She joked about herself, her kids, her husband, her family's decidedly off-beat riff on middle-class life. She even joked about these sixth-density beings, whatever they were. "The boys from Brazil," she called them, and the way she said it made me laugh, even though I had no clue what she was talking about.

She was giving a performance, and I was not the only one in the audience who enjoyed it. Cherie Diez, a *Times* photographer with whom I'd worked for many years, had come with me to the MUFON meeting. The two of us were searching for someone unusual to follow for the newspaper. After seeing and listening to Laura that day, Cherie and I believed that we had found a subject who exceeded our every expectation.

In between our work on other projects for the paper, we were drawn again and again to Laura's house in New Port Richey, hanging out for hours at a time with her and her family and friends. What we saw, every time we visited, was a woman leading a life on her own terms, defining herself every day. Laura's life was crammed with seemingly incongruous elements. She was a walking smorgasbord of the paranormal, yes. But she was also a mother of five, making dinner and doing the laundry. She was a glorious amalgamation, a mixture of Bette Midler, Father Damien, Donna Reed, and Agent Scully.

Laura defied all categories. She did not, would not fit into any box, including one that I had tried to stick her into that first day at the MUFON meeting. When I toured her home, I found no bust of Elvis in the living room. But on her mantel, above the fireplace, there was an eerie, almost ghostly ceramic pitcher bearing the likeness of Edward VIII. Laura's grandparents had bought it in 1937, just after Edward gave up the English throne to marry Wallis Simpson.

So much for my stereotyping.

Laura's house was one huge encyclopedia of her life, overflowing with things that testified to the breadth of her curiosity and interests. On the walls hung Victorian prints from her grandparents, a painting of Jesus, a map of the world, pieces of her children's artwork, oversized reproductions of tarot cards, *Star Trek* posters the kids had put up.

Laura's study was lined with shelves crammed with hundreds and hundreds of books. Scanning through just a few of the titles, I found *Angels and Aliens, The Bible as History, On the Dead Sea Scrolls, Alien Intelligence, Genesis Revisited, UFO Encounters and Beyond, Infinity and the Mind, Extra- Terrestrials Among Us*. One day, while I was talking to Laura in that same study, I asked her what she liked to read purely for fun, when she wasn't memorizing science textbooks or researching the paranormal. Her son, Jason—he was twelve at the time and liked sitting in on our interviews— started laughing and shaking his head.

"She reads puppy books," he said.

I didn't understand.

"You know," said Jason. "The man and woman fall in love, get together, and then have puppies."

He reached for a well-worn paperback from one of the shelves. It was *The Golden Barbarian*, a book with one of those covers where a woman with a heaving bosom surrenders to a man with rippling biceps.

Jason handed it over with a knowing grin.

"Check out page 193," he said, nodding meaningfully at me, one man to another.

These were the kinds of moments when I found it impossible to simply dismiss Laura and her life. It was one thing trying to get a handle on a woman who thought she was an exorcist and a psychic and a transmitter for long distance calls from enlightened aliens. But someone who was into these things, plus raising an adolescent son who knew where all the racy sections were in her romance novels? That person I could begin to understand. It helped me relate to her, even if I didn't subscribe to everything she believed.

Though some of her children occasionally were enrolled in the public schools for a semester or two, Laura still homeschooled them for the most part. She seemed to be doing a good job. Jason and his siblings—he was the middle child, and the only boy—were smart and well educated. They were constantly drawing, reading, playing the piano, inventing their own secret codes, working out math problems for fun; whenever I asked them anything about history or science or literature, they usually showed themselves to be far ahead of most other children their age.

In some ways, their lives were strange. Like their mother, at least a couple of the children claimed to have paranormal abilities; several years before the movie *Sixth Sense* came out, Jason told me, without a trace of a smile on his face, that he could see the spirits of dead people walking around him on the street. Yet for all these oddities, Jason and his siblings were still just kids. They complained about taking out the trash. They argued about who would get to sit in the front seat of the family van. They could watch TV for hours on end, sprawled across the furniture in front of the set like lazy jungle cats.

Aletheia and Anna, the two oldest girls—they were sixteen and thirteen when I met them—were embarrassed by their mother. This was not surprising. Virtually every teenage girl is appalled by her mom at one time or another. But in their case, Aletheia and Anna were appalled because their mother channeled communications from sixth-density beings with friends on Saturday nights.

"Mom," Aletheia would say, "can't you play bingo? Would you please sell Tupperware, for God's sake?"

As Cherie and I went on interviewing Laura, asking her to fill in the blanks from over the years, the children listened, adding their own details and impressions of what they had seen themselves. In many ways, they were Laura's witnesses. They had been on hand for much of what she described to us, and they corroborated her stories. They remembered seeing the boomerangs flying over the pool; they also had seen channeling sessions. Though the children were not allowed to attend the exorcisms, they knew about those sessions as well.

Lewis Martin, who was ten years older than Laura, said little about his wife's paranormal activities. Many times when Cherie and I visited the house, Lewis was not around. By this point he was working for a construction company, and he seemed to be gone much of the time, either off at his job or out fishing. Once, when we did talk, Lewis told me he had been raised in south Florida and had spent much of his childhood wandering the Everglades with his stepfather, hunting and exploring. He still loved the outdoors.

I liked Lewis. He was always polite and friendly—he had a big, calloused, he-man handshake—and he seemed to enjoy the kids. Like most children, Jason and his siblings craved their father's attention and adored it when he took them out in his pickup truck to go fishing. Still, as I watched Lewis puttering in the yard, I could not help but wonder what he made of the direction in which his wife was taking her life. I never heard him utter a word against her, but I also never saw him take much interest in Laura's activities. She would be in the study with Freddie and others, channeling with the Cassiopaeans, and often Lewis would be in the next room, eating a sandwich or watching TV. Sometimes when he came home he would not come inside immediately, but would sit in his truck in the driveway, listening to music on the radio.

Lewis's detachment was a relatively benign response to what was happening under his roof. I got a kick out of Laura and all her exotic endeavors, but I didn't have to live with all of it day in and day out. Just from my contact with her, I knew how exhausting she could be. It wasn't just the channeling and the spirit detachments. Laura was constantly reading another handful of books on Atlantis, and cataloging her dreams, and contemplating the nature of evil, and drawing up astrological charts, and writing massive treatises on vampires and aliens, and driving away to UFO conventions, and firing off e-mails about the latest alien sighting in Brazil.

Like so many married couples, Lewis and Laura were obviously leading parallel lives. Yet, at that point, I did not hear Laura complain about the marriage, either. Sometimes she seemed tired and distracted; occasionally she would call me sounding a little down. But that was all. Most of the time, she seemed too busy to be depressed. She moved in a constant whirlwind, driving the kids around, throwing another load of laundry into the dryer, reading up on crop circles, typing transcripts of the channeling sessions.

She was always blasting one kind of music or another on the stereo. She swooned to Beethoven, Brahms, countless operas and choral pieces, not to mention Pink Floyd; predictably, one of her favorites was *Dark Side of the Moon*. She loved to go to movies, to escape on excursions with Freddie and other friends, to brush her daughters' hair and laugh at Jason's imitations of Data, the android from *Star Trek: The Next Generation*. And she never lost her sense of humor.

Once, we stopped at a diner for breakfast. The waitress, taking Laura's order, asked if she wanted home fries or grits.

"Who's cooking the grits?" said Laura.

The waitress stopped writing and looked up from her pad.

"My brother," she said, smiling uncertainly.

"Was he born in Florida?" Laura asked.

"No."

"Then I'll take the home fries."

Laura was always hard to keep up with. Cherie and I followed along as best we could. We sat in on one of Laura's spirit detachments; we attended several of the channeling sessions she and Freddie were leading. In addition, we spoke with many of the people around Laura. We met the Pasco woman whose story of the missing time had so deeply shaken Laura; this woman's son, who had been in the car with her on the night in question, joined us for the interview.

Although both the woman and her son preferred not to be identified in print, they confirmed at least the basics of what Laura had told us. I also watched the videotape Freddie had shot on the night of this woman's hypnosis. It did not show the entire session, and much of what the woman said was hard to hear—she spoke very softly—but the tape did seem to show the session essentially as Laura and Freddie and the woman had described it.

We were never allowed to attend one of Laura's exorcisms. They seemed to happen infrequently, and Laura told us the sessions were too personal and too volatile to permit our presence or to let us speak to her subjects after the exorcisms had ended. Besides, she said she had always found the exorcisms disturbing and was trying to scale back on that part of her work. A year or so after we first met her, she stopped performing exorcisms entirely.

Our understanding of this particular part of Laura's story, in other words, was based almost entirely on Laura's descriptions, and her word. The only corroboration came from Freddie, who sometimes assisted Laura in these sessions.

From the start, we recognized the possibility that Laura could have lied to us about the exorcisms and many other things. She could have made up her memories of the reptilian face at the window, the dreams, the breaking glass. If she had wanted to do so—and it would have required the cooperation of not only her children, but many other people as well—she could have been staging an almost impossibly elaborate hoax on us for several years.

Neither Cherie nor I saw anything to indicate such a hoax. After spending several years in her company, we never found any evidence to suggest that Laura was some con artist faking her studies of the paranormal to gain money or attract publicity. Everything about her suggested someone who was trying her best to give a full and accurate account of her life.

Thousands of pages of notes, essays, and papers testified to the genuine depth of Laura's interest. She was clearly devoted to these questions long before we entered her life; she talked about the exorcisms and the channeling that first day at the MUFON meeting before she knew we were in the audience.

Once we sought her out, Laura repeatedly expressed ambivalence about her story appearing in the newspaper. At times, when she worried about how readers might react to her story, she even asked us to reconsider writing about her at all.

Money never appeared to be the driving force behind Laura's activities. She lived modestly, driving a used van and raising her kids in a house that was in constant need of repair. Laura showed scant interest in making money from her paranormal activities. While she did charge minimal fees for her sessions, they never amounted to much. Several years ago, when she made some transcripts of her channeling sessions for us, we paid her $100; since then, she has given us hundreds of more pages of these transcripts and has refused to accept a penny more for her trouble.

If she was out to make a buck, she was terrible at it.

I had missed it.

In all the time I was spending with Laura, and all the time I was thinking about her and trying to put together the pieces of her, I had overlooked one simple detail that had been available from the very beginning. A detail that should have told me so much about what was happening inside her.

The puppy books.

With everything else that was already on Laura's shelves, with all those science books and history books and volumes on the paranormal just waiting to be read, why on earth was she wasting a single second reading romance novels? Why were those books so important to her? What was she finding there that she could not get anywhere else?

It was right in front of me.

And I could not see it.

Laura turned on the tape recorder at 10:41 p.m.

"All right, everybody. The date is February third, 1996."

She and Freddie were seated around the spirit board at a table in the living room. Two fingers from Laura's right hand and two from Freddie's were extended to the center of the board and were resting lightly upon the planchette. Extending in a circle around the planchette, printed on the board, were the letters of the alphabet.

"Hello," said Laura, and the planchette began to move, veering from one letter to another. Speaking in a monotone, Laura called out the letters, one at a time, in an unbroken flow.

"W-O-R-D-S-M-E-A-N-L-I-T-T-L-E."

In the corner, one of Laura's friends—a woman named Susan Vitale— sat with a notebook and pen. As Laura announced the letters, Susan wrote them down. When Laura stopped, Susan looked at the page and read aloud what the letters actually said.

"Words mean little."

Other people were seated around the room. Cherie and I were there; so was Lewis this time. We were all there to watch, and listen, and learn whatever the Cassiopaeans—or whoever else was truly providing the answers— wanted to share with us.

"Okay," Laura asked them. "We have several questions tonight. Do you, first of all, have any particular messages for anyone here?"

The planchette moved.

"T-H-E-N-E-E-D-T-O-D-E-L-I-V-E-R-M-E-S-S-A-G-E-S-F-L-O-W-S-N-A-T-U-R-A-L-L-Y."

The stream of letters seemed to go on and on. Susan studied what she had written down, pausing for a moment to break the stream into words.

"The need to deliver messages flows naturally. There is no way to choreograph it by requesting a specific time for this procedure."

So they began. Laura and her friends posed their questions. The planchette journeyed across the board. The answers were written down, then recited aloud.

This night, the topics of discussion were varied. Laura and the others wanted to ask about a report they'd heard of some sort of giant spacecraft, a ship allegedly the size of Earth, sighted around the planet Saturn.

Complete nonsense, said the Cassiopaeans.

Their exact response, given in another stream of letters: "IT WAS ARTIFICIALLY CONSTRUCTED TALE."

Laura asked if a man she knew was controlled by aliens. Sometimes, came the answer. She asked about *el chupacabras*, a strange creature that had been reported recently in Puerto Rico, slaughtering animals and drinking their blood. Some people wondered if the creature was an alien. Well? said Laura.

The answer: "IT IS WHAT IT IS."

"Is there any possibility that this creature will attack human beings?"

"YOU DO NOT YET COMPLETELY UNDERSTAND THE MECHANICS OF . . . "

On and on it went. The planchette kept moving from one letter to the next. There were also punctuation marks on the board, such as a comma, a period and a set of quotation marks, and sometimes the planchette would move to these as well.

From my seat nearby, I watched the whole thing carefully, studying Laura's and Freddie's shoulders and arms, looking for signs that they were purposely pushing against the planchette. I saw none, but that proved nothing. I listened to the answers that Laura was calling out, letter by letter. Usually they came quickly, flowing together without interruption, Laura announcing them all in the same monotone.

Laura appeared to be lost in concentration, focused entirely on the board. Yet when someone else in the room spoke, in between the exchanges, she heard them and responded. Freddie appeared to have gone into some kind of trance. His eyes were half-closed; his breathing seemed to have slowed.

This was the fourth or fifth channeling session I had attended, and still I had no idea what was really happening. Were Laura and/or Freddie directing the planchette, either consciously or unconsciously? Or were the answers truly coming from another corner of the Milky Way? Even the question itself seemed ridiculous. All I could do was sit and watch and pay attention.

Laura and Freddie had been conducting these sessions since 1994. After years of experimenting with the spirit board—Laura had found the board in the paranormal section of a book distributor's catalog—they said they had finally made a connection to beings from another reality. These were the so-called Cassiopaeans. Or, as Laura usually called them, the CS. Now, Laura and Freddie held a running conversation with them every Saturday night.

After sitting in on the sessions, I still would have been hard-pressed to describe what these sixth-density entities were supposed to be and why they were so eager to hang out in New Port Richey, chatting away for hours with Laura and Freddie. All I knew was that they were supposed to exist on a higher plane than earthlings—sadly, we have only achieved third-density status—which explained why they could just pop into Laura's living room and share secrets from not just the past and present but also the future.

Laura wanted in on some of the secrets. In one session after the other, she asked the CS about her life, her past, the fate of the Earth, anything that popped into her head. She asked about history, science, religion. She asked about Bigfoot, Hitler, President Kennedy.

For months now, she had been asking the CS about her son, Jason.

Something strange had been happening with him, ever since he was a little boy. From three or four onward, Laura said, Jason had gone on about another life, separate from the one he was living now. He had details. He talked about a different house, a different family. He talked about a black dog named Samson, brothers and sisters, a special friend of his. Sometimes he would have long conversations with this friend. He would sit in the bathroom and talk on and on with her, as though she were with him. He called her Janie.

There was more. Jason knew how he had died in this other life. Years ago, under hypnosis, he had talked about that, too. He said he remembered being in a plane. He was flying the plane, he said, and a missile was coming at him, and then there was smoke, and then nothing.

Now Laura wanted the CS to help her understand. Why had Jason carried these memories of another family? Why did he believe he knew how to fly a plane?

The answers startled her. In a former life, the CS told her, Jason had been an air force pilot killed during the Vietnam War when his plane was shot down by a surface-to-air missile. Now, they said, he was remembering details from the crash and from the life that had preceded it.

Sometimes, as in this case, the responses that came off the board were simple and direct. Many other times, though, they were vague and confusing. There were many topics the CS simply refused to talk about, saying that to do so would interfere with humanity's free will. The CS, it turned out, were big on free will.

All of the responses, no matter how confusing, were audiotaped and written down. Eventually the exchanges were typed out into the transcripts. By this point, there were nearly one thousand pages of transcripts, and Laura pored through them all, looking for clues, connections, suggestions for where to direct her energies next. To listen to her talk about it all, it was obvious that she thought that maybe, just maybe, she had finally found the cosmic blueprints. Now she was trying to learn how to decipher them.

If this sounds endlessly fascinating, think again. Sometimes, yes, the answers coming from the board were interesting, even fun. On a couple of occasions, the CS addressed themselves to Cherie or me directly. One night, just as I was putting away my notebook and getting ready to make an exit, they told me to sit myself back down. They were polite about it, but firm.

"Please do not leave just yet, Mr. French," said the stream of letters coming from the board.

Laura paused. "Why?" she said.

"WE MAY HAVE SOME THINGS TO SAY TO HIM."

I sat back down. When a sixth-density being tells you to do something, you tend to listen. Still, I could not help but laugh.

What followed was encouraging, but not especially dramatic. The CS told me that I had been through some hard times, but that I had finally opened "a doorway to my subconscious" and learned how to examine "the metamorphosis of my being." Good things, they hinted, were just down the road.

"THERE ARE MANY CHANGES YET TO COME."

This did not seem particularly prescient on the part of the CS.

Much of the material coming out of the sessions was rather dull. The answers seemed to take forever, what with each word being spelled out one letter at a time, and they almost always seemed to concern chakras and electromagnetic wave bursts and other concepts that only Laura and Freddie appeared to understand. Many times, I sat in Laura's living room, stifling a yawn.

Personally, though, I found the tedium reassuring. To me, it actually gave the channeling sessions a bit of credibility. Why do we expect that aliens are going to be so interesting? Isn't it more likely, if we were forced to actually sit next to them at a party, that some of them might just bore us to tears, going on about the maintenance on their hyper drives and so forth? I'm serious. If the CS had been showering us with galactic news flashes, claiming to tell us how to cure cancer and live forever and find Jimmy Hoffa's body, it would have made me suspicious. To my mind, it would have increased the likelihood that Laura was orchestrating the whole thing, trying to show off. But week after week, the sessions plodded along, moving down the same impenetrable path.

"TOTAL TRUTH IS ELUSIVE," the CS announced one night.

"What are we supposed to do?" asked Laura.

"YOU WILL DO WHAT YOU WILL DO."

Typing the transcripts of the sessions was monotonous work, and yet Laura poured herself into it, often staying at her keyboard until well past midnight. Piece by piece, she said, she felt she was moving closer to some answers. By this time, Laura had abandoned any serious resistance to the notion of alien interference on Earth. She seemed ready to accept that UFOs were real and that many of the abduction reports were true.

After months of studying the Cassiopaean transcripts, Laura was talking about a battle being waged on this planet and others between forces of good and evil—a battle similar to the struggle between light and darkness that she had described seeing during the exorcisms. She said there appeared to be many different races of aliens from different parts of the galaxy. Some of them, like the CS, were interested only in furthering our understanding of the universe. Others were malevolent. Repeatedly Laura told me that these dark aliens were systematically feeding off the energy and even the flesh of humans.

"We are not at the top of the food chain," she said.

These dark aliens, she asserted, were the same lizard-like creatures who had haunted her childhood. As best I could put it together, her theory was that these aliens—"the Lizzies," she often called them—were threatened by her and wished to control or even destroy her.

As she asked the CS more and more about these subjects, Laura's theories about the Lizzies became more sinister. She said she had met a woman who talked of dreams in which she had been raped by alligator-like creatures; clearly the Lizzies. Laura saw them everywhere. She talked about them implanting devices inside people's bodies to monitor their movements. Other times she went on about zombie-like people whom the Lizzies manipulated; she said they stole or paralyzed these people's personalities, then used the empty shells that remained as spies or soldiers. She even sensed the Lizzies' presence behind violent outbursts occurring around the planet.

One day, that March of 1996, I was interviewing Laura at the house when Lewis walked in, talking about a shooting in Scotland. A gunman had burst into a school and opened fire, killing sixteen children and their teacher.

"This is exactly what I'm talking about," Laura said.

Lewis scoffed. Clearly, he did not buy all of his wife's theories.

"I'm usually even-tempered, but I could be implanted," he said, suddenly making his eyes bug out. "You don't know."

Laura ignored him. Lewis walked away.

After hearing all her theories about the Lizzies, I asked Laura if she thought they were also responsible for many of the alleged alien abductions. She said yes; either they carried out the abductions themselves or directed humanoid aliens to carry them out. These were "the grays," the little gray men with huge black eyes, described in so many people's abduction accounts.

What about Laura? Looking back on all those strange nighttime episodes in her past, did she think that she too had been abducted?

When I first brought this up, Laura would not answer. She had clearly thought about the possibility, but when my questions veered into this territory, she would become visibly uncomfortable. As time went on, she gradually seemed more ready to talk about it. She had worked up the courage to ask the CS, she said, and they had confirmed that indeed the Lizzies had taken her away repeatedly, from childhood onward.

Even so, she was not willing to linger on what precisely had happened.

In all my conversations with Laura, this was the only subject she shied away from. If I pressed her on these issues, she would squirm in her seat, grow pale, look away.

"I don't want to think about it," she would say, fighting back the tears.

As the months went by, it seemed increasingly obvious that this subject was at the core of whatever was going on with Laura. Cherie and I had still felt that Laura genuinely believed the things she was telling us.

Something had happened to her. But what was it? I was not closed to the notion that in fact Laura and others might have suffered through terrible encounters with extraterrestrials. I have never seen a UFO myself, but I have no trouble accepting the possibility of alien life.

A succession of men did move through Laura's childhood. After Laura's parents divorced, her mother had remarried four times; once, Laura says, one of her stepfathers kidnapped her for several days. I asked Laura if she had ever been abused by that stepfather or anyone else. She said no, absolutely not. When I asked for details of the kidnapping, she said she did not know. She had almost no memory of it, she said; it was all a blank.

Other possibilities occurred to me. I wondered if maybe Laura had imagined the face at the window and all the other strange episodes as a way of injecting drama into her life. Was it possible that she was bored, or lonely, or simply so desperate to find something to occupy her mind that she had created this huge fantasy? What if all of it—the exorcisms, the spirit detachments, the channeling with the CS—was just some massive, unruly play that her subconscious was constantly staging to keep things interesting?

Then, of course, there was the simplest explanation: What if Laura was a victim of some psychosis?

This was a possibility Laura repeatedly raised herself. "Sometimes I think I'm losing my mind," she said to me. "Is this what being mad is like? Because, you know, some really crazy people can really seem sane."

Every time she brought up this possibility, Laura dismissed it. She said that she had occasionally been to counselors and psychologists, as many of us have. But to her knowledge, she told me, she has never been diagnosed with any mental illness. Early on, I considered asking Laura to be evaluated by a psychiatrist, at the newspaper's expense. What if a doctor could put a name on whatever was happening with her? What if he or she told us that Laura was manic-depressive, delusional, even schizophrenic?

Ultimately, though, I never asked Laura to put herself under the microscope. It didn't feel right. The more time I spent with her, the less I wanted to try to force her into another box. Whatever was happening with her, there was something remarkable about the way it was playing itself out. She was raising her children, enjoying her friendships with Freddie and others, reading and learning all the time, exploring the reaches of her imagination.

The woman was leading a life. It wasn't a perfect life, not even close. But it was hers, and it was extraordinary, and I was not about to interfere.

Things were happening in front of me that I could not explain. Laura did things, little things, that I could not figure out. Like the letters that came off the board when she was channeling. Sometimes she recited them so fast they came out in a single flowing stream. How did she do that? If she was just making up the answers, or her subconscious was making them up, how did she compose them so quickly, without hesitation or interruption?

These were not just "yes" or "no" answers. Sometimes the answers were long and complicated. Some of them sounded like things Laura would say; I could imagine her thinking them up, and then breaking them down and calling them out in the individual letters. But other times, the answers didn't sound like Laura at all. They sounded like they came from someone else, someone who knew things it seemed unlikely Laura would know.

Either way, I could not understand how she sometimes managed to call out the letters so fast. I would listen to the letters pouring out, and I would try to hear the words hidden inside them, and my brain could not keep up. The letters melted together into one long nonstop blur.

Maybe it proved nothing. Maybe all these things showed was that Laura was smarter and quicker than anybody I'd ever come across.

Still, none of that prepared me for the trip to Punta Gorda.

It was Jason.

Laura was still thinking about her son's recollections of his former life, the brothers he'd then had, the plane he had been on when it was shot down. She was still asking the CS about it, trying to learn as much as possible. They had supplied her with a name.

Actually, they had supplied her with two names. It could have been a first and last name, or a first and middle name; there was no way to tell. For reasons that I will soon explain, I am not sharing those names here. Laura and her friends had taken the names and done some research of their own. They had found a record of an air force captain whose plane had crashed during the Vietnam War, in April 1969. This captain's first and middle names appeared to match the ones supplied by the CS.

Through the research, Laura learned that this air force captain had grown up in Punta Gorda, only a couple of hours or so south of Pasco County. Laura called the funeral home that had handled the captain's funeral and found a man there who knew the surviving family. He told Laura that two of the captain's sisters still lived in the area. With his help, a meeting was arranged between Laura and Jason and the two sisters.

One bright Saturday morning, Cherie and I followed Laura and Jason down to Punta Gorda. We met with the sisters at one of their homes. One was fifty-nine, the other sixty-three. In the most unusual social encounter I've witnessed, the sisters conducted themselves with remarkable warmth and grace. As we all sat in the living room, they shared their family history and allowed us to look through photo albums.

"That's our mother," said one.

"Our mother," said the other.

The sisters told us about their brother and their grief when his plane went down. They took us to the cemetery where their brother was buried. Jason stood and stared at the captain's tombstone. He had hardly said a word all morning. Now he said nothing.

What I remember from that day, even more than the image of Jason standing over that grave, are the details from the captain's life and how some of them meshed with the things that Laura said Jason had talked about as a boy. Jason, the only boy in his family, had mentioned having brothers. There had been seven children in the captain's family: four boys, three girls.

Jason had described a black dog he called Samson. The captain's family had owned a dog. A black chow, named Sambo.

And then there was Janie. In the middle of telling the sisters all the things that Jason used to say about this other life, Laura mentioned, almost in passing, the conversations he would have with his special friend Janie. One of the sisters—whose given name was not Janie—grew very still. That was what her dead brother used to call her, she said. The two of them had only been a couple of years apart, and they had been close. And like the other siblings, she said, he had referred to her as Janie.

"No one outside the family knew I had the nickname," she said.

Laura wasn't sure what to think.

To her, the meeting with the sisters lent credence to the possibility that Jason had been a pilot in a former life.

After Laura and Jason headed home to Pasco County, the captain's sisters were left to ponder the episode. Later, when I called one of the sisters to ask for their impressions, she dismissed the whole thing.

She and her sister had agreed to meet with Laura and Jason, she said, merely to see if there was any substance to the story. Afterward, she said, they had decided there was not. Yes, Laura and Jason had supplied some details that matched their brother's life. But many other details, she said, were wrong.

For instance, Laura had talked about how the captain had died while returning from a mission. She'd said the CS had told her that a surface-to air missile had hit the plane. But after Laura and Jason left, the sister had written the federal government under the Freedom of Information Act and obtained records of her brother's death. Those records, she said, showed that his plane had not been hit by a missile, that it had crashed on takeoff. Furthermore, she had interviewed a man who drove her brother's flight crew out to the plane that day; he confirmed that it had crashed on takeoff.

Something else: Laura said Jason had talked about being a pilot, and the CS had told her that the captain in question had been flying the plane when he was shot down. But the sister told me that her brother had never been a pilot; he operated reconnaissance equipment on the plane.

Now, she wanted no part of Laura's theories. She felt for Jason and wondered if Laura had planted these suggestions in his mind. As for the facts that did match, she thought they were possibly a coincidence; she also wondered if Laura could have researched the family long-distance, before the meeting. Either way, the sister did not want her brother's name or her family's name connected to the reincarnation story.

"I just don't believe a word of it," she told me.

I had no idea what to make of it.

Many of the details supplied by Laura did not fit. And yes, she could have engineered the whole thing. Still, I had seen the surprise on the sisters' faces when the nickname of Janie was first mentioned. If Janie was only a family nickname, how much work would it have taken for Laura to come up with it? In a town the size of Punta Gorda, wouldn't the captain's family have heard if someone was checking up on them so extensively?

I did not see the turn in the road, just ahead.

"LAURA, DEAR LAURA," THE E-MAIL READ.
"YOU ARE REAL. YOU ARE NOT AN IMAGINATION"

On 2 April 1996, Laura called me and announced that she was getting a divorce. "Lewis and I," she said, "are having a semi-amicable parting of the ways."

Up until that moment, Laura had never said anything that would have led me to believe she was on the verge of ending her marriage. Despite all my questions and all my prying, she had remained discreet in regard to her relationship with Lewis. In the weeks that followed, Laura told me what had gone wrong. She shared her long-standing feelings of isolation and alienation, her sense that she and Lewis had been distant for many years, her nagging suspicion that she had devoted her life to the wrong man. Though she said it was a mutual decision, I sensed that the final call was more hers than his.

She said all of the things people say when they get divorced. She said that Lewis didn't understand her, that she felt he undermined her, that the two of them had been squabbling, that she was worried about the children, that she had no idea how to pay her bills. She had tried to stick it out and make it work, she said, but it never did.

"I believed that if I just loved him long enough and hard enough, that he would wake up," she said.

There was more. Laura said that Lewis did not support her channeling and other paranormal pursuits. She said he seemed to have changed in ways that startled her, to have become more cold and distant.

She wondered, aloud, if the Lizzies had somehow replaced him or transformed him into one of the zombie-like creatures, as part of the campaign to keep track of her movements. It wasn't his fault, she told me.

"It's only because of his relationship with me," she said.

Lewis had moved out of the house and was gone. Though he stayed in contact with the children, I never saw him again. Later, I caught up with him by phone and talked with him about what had gone wrong. His version was not that different from Laura's. He said they had struggled financially over the years and eventually drifted apart. Despite their breakup, Lewis spoke respectfully of Laura. He said he believed that she is truly psychic and has the ability to channel conversations with entities. He tried to be supportive of her activities, but she had taken them to a point that clashed with his fundamentalist Christian beliefs.

"I tried to be tolerant," he said, "but it got kind of out of hand."

Lewis avoided criticizing Laura. He acknowledged that he had worried that some of the entities Laura was channeling might not be benevolent. He was not surprised to learn that Laura had wondered if the Lizzies were manipulating him; he had already heard as much. He didn't appreciate that she had suggested such a possibility. It hurt his feelings, he said.

I was not particularly surprised by Laura's suspicions that Lewis had been changed into some kind of zombie. Those were the terms under which she had come to see the world; that was her prism. In the past, I had heard born-again Christians who were having marital problems talk about how Satan had entered their spouses and was manipulating them. Was this so different? I took this to be simply Laura's way of saying that Lewis had become a stranger to her and that she no longer trusted him.

Still, Laura's decision was alarming. Not only was she getting a divorce, she was not asking for any child support. Lewis had recently lost his construction job, and she did not think he had any money to spare. What she wanted, and what she said Lewis had agreed to, was for her to take the house and the family van, both of which were paid for, plus half of their savings. I could not figure out how she would make it work. Laura had no job outside her paranormal activities, and they paid almost nothing; also, she said that the family's savings were not substantial. How would she pay the bills? Also, what was to stop Lewis from trying to gain custody of the children? What if he stood before a judge and testified about him and the children living with his wife's exorcisms and spirit detachments and conversations with sixth-density beings?

At this point, Laura was forty-four. She was in the poorest physical condition I'd seen her; knowing what she was going through emotionally, this was not surprising. She had five kids, ranging in age from six to seventeen, with all the drama and complications that usually come with children. She had two dogs and a house badly in need of repair. She almost never got out of the house, except to buy groceries or run the children around.

Usually, she spent her days and nights reading or typing away at her computer. As she asked the CS more and more about these subjects, Laura's theories about the Lizzies became more sinister. She admitted she was sleeping more than usual. She was gaining weight. When I called, she barely seemed to have the energy to hold the phone.

Before, Laura had always worked on overdrive, operating with enough energy for three people. Now everything inside her seemed to be shutting down. She was moving in slow motion. Laura said she did not regret her decision, that divorce was the right thing to do. Never once did she waver from this position. Still, she acknowledged that the whole thing had been gut-wrenching for everyone in her family. She worried about how to pay the bills and keep food in the refrigerator. She talked about how much the children were hurting and missing their father.

As the weeks passed, she seemed to be descending further and further. She was spinning increasingly savage pictures of the world around her.

"It seems to me," she said one day, "that there are two main types of people. There are predators, and there are prey."

She asked the CS about why she felt so alone and frustrated. They told her that she was carrying anger about many things from the past, not just things related to Lewis, but to the Lizzies and her childhood abductions. At one point, she went to see a psychiatrist. Afterward, she told me what had happened. She had given the psychiatrist her life history, told him about the face at the window and the other disturbing childhood episodes. She said that he had suggested she consider the possibility that she was traumatized as a child.

She did not agree; she said her recollections of the incidents were too vivid and real for her to have imagined them. Laura pressed the doctor for help. What should she do? How was she supposed to handle these memories that haunted her? He said she should try to stop thinking about them, learn to cordon off those areas of her mind. Laura didn't think it was possible. How could she cordon off something so important?

Laura went to see the psychiatrist only a few times. She said he'd told her she was healthy and did not need to come back.

The weeks passed, and her grief seemed to be growing. She wondered aloud if perhaps "dark forces" were punishing her for daring to see them and talk about them. She quoted ominous passages from the Bible, going on about Eve eating the apple from the tree of knowledge and her eyes filling with tears from "the bittersweet flood of knowing." And she was sending me e-mails that sounded like they came from the Bible, too.

Laura was writing about mountains erupting and seas boiling over and the skies lowering to sweep man away like so much dust. She was telling me how she had just been outside driving through New Port Richey and had crossed the Pithlachascotee River and seen its tranquil eddies and seen the canopy of oaks along the road and even seen a flowering jacaranda tree that had baptized her with blossoms—these were her words—that filtered from the clouds above to emerge into a benediction of sunlight. Yet none of these beautiful sights made her feel any better.

"Because, in all these things is death and decay," she wrote. "Everywhere you look, something is consuming something else."

Melodramatic, yes.

Still, anyone who's been through a divorce would have understood exactly what she meant.

That July, three months after the breakup of the marriage, Laura contacted me again with another piece of news. She had met a man, she said. Well, not met him exactly. Not in person. But she had been talking to him, over the computer, and she was ecstatic.

The Cassiopaeans had pointed her toward this man, she said. She could hardly believe it herself, but it was true. The CS had given her some instructions, and she had followed them, and they had taken her straight to him. Breathless, she told me all about him.

He was a physicist.

He lived in Poland.

They were in love.

It had begun, appropriately enough, with gravity.

Yes, gravity. The invisible force that draws two objects together. The attraction, expressed throughout the universe, between planets, stars, and other celestial bodies. One night a few weeks before, as Laura explained it to me, the CS kept going on about gravity. She and Freddie were channeling with them, and she was trying to talk to them about some other things. But the CS said they wanted to talk about "unstable gravity waves," whatever those were. They told her she needed to learn all about the subject.

"Okay," Laura replied. "Unstable gravity waves. I'll see what I can find."

The CS weren't done with the subject. A few moments later, they told her: "WE MEAN FOR YOU, LAURA, TO MEDITATE ABOUT UNSTABLE GRAVITY WAVES AS PART OF RESEARCH. UNSTA-

BLE GRAVITY WAVES UNLOCK AS YET UNKNOWN SECRETS OF QUANTUM PHYSICS TO MAKE THE PICTURE CRYSTAL CLEAR."

In the weeks that followed, the CS kept returning to the subject of gravity. Laura put together all the passages, along with some other sections related to physics, and posted it on the Internet, on a discussion list popular with UFO researchers, astronomers, other scientists. She wanted some help. Could anyone read this stuff and tell her what they thought it meant?

A few days later, she got an e-mail from a man who wanted to know some more about her research. He explained that he was a professor at the University of Wroclaw, in Poland, in the university's institute for theoretical physics. He said his name was Arkadiusz Jadczyk, but he told her to call him Ark. Over the next few days, Laura and Ark e-mailed back and forth. At first they were talking mostly about physics. It turned out that Ark had a Web site that was devoted to, among other things, gravity waves.

Laura called up the Web site, read through Ark's writings, began to get excited. They continued the e-mails, getting to know each other. Even over the computer, across the span of an ocean, Laura could feel an energy growing between them.

That was all it took. Within a few weeks, they were declaring their love for each other, sharing their life stories, comparing notes, flirting over the information superhighway. They almost couldn't believe it was happening.

"Laura, dear Laura," Ark wrote her in one e-mail. "You are real. You are not an imagination."

He was fifty-two, he said. He was married, but the marriage had been dead for years. Furthermore, he was a physicist who had spent his life studying time and space, the nature of consciousness, the fabric of reality—all the subjects that had consumed Laura since she was a girl. They exchanged photos. Laura sent several from different points in her life; Ark sent a portrait that showed a slender man with delicate features and thin white hair. He also sent her tapes of him singing to her, in Polish. When she played one for me, I didn't understand any of it, except for one word that he kept singing softly, over and over.

"Laura . . . Laura."

Soon she was talking about the two of them in eternal terms. She said they were conducting a "cosmic love affair." She was convinced that Ark was the man she'd dreamed about all those years before, the husband she'd seen killed by the Nazi soldiers in her vision. They were meant to be together, she said.

She was sure of it.

Ark's e-mails made it clear that he felt exactly the same. The man had it bad.

"Look what has happened," he wrote Laura late that August, barely more than a month after they'd begun their exchanges. "Impossible has happened. What we did during these forty days is impossible indeed. Like an explosion, like a flood. Like a fusion—but a controlled one."

I loved the fusion thing. The physicist, working it.

"You are right," he told her, still rolling. "Put it all in a book and nobody will believe it. We would not believe it. If not for the fact that the book is written by us. . . . Somehow we manage to have no fear of dreaming. Somehow our dreams are finding a way to materialize. Somehow the words that we speak with faith but without reasons to believe—somehow these words became true."

On and on he went.

"Each day is a new day. Each new day is awaited. We know how much yet is to be done. We know we have not even begun. And yet there is no return."

Ark seemed perfect for Laura. In fact, he seemed almost too good to be true. So I checked. I did not want to see Laura crushed into oblivion. I did not want to learn, six months down the line, that this soul mate of hers was actually a fourteen-year-old boy in Philadelphia, doing what any fourteen-year-old boy would be doing on the other end of the computer line. I asked one of the *Times*'s researchers to see if Arkadiusz Jadczyk was real.

Indeed he was; in 1995, he had even won something called a Humboldt Award, which if I understood correctly, was a respectable achievement in the world of physics. Laura had already told me about the Humboldt Award. When I found out it was true, I kept it to myself. I didn't want to offend her, letting her know that I'd felt it necessary to check up on Ark.

Laura was the happiest I had ever seen her. Suddenly she was taking better care of herself. She was swimming every night in the pool, working out at the gym, watching what she ate. She was losing weight, fast. But the transformation went deeper than that. Laura was feeling good about herself, her life, the future. She was laughing again, charging back into her work, playing the piano for the first time in months.

She told me that she and Ark were making plans for him to come to the United States as soon as possible. At first he would come to visit for just a few weeks, but then he would come back for good. Ark was going to find a teaching job somewhere over here. He and Laura were going to finalize their divorces. They were getting married.

Up to this point, the two of them had only talked through the computer and over the phone. What would happen when they finally met in person? What if Ark was not all Laura believed him to be? What if Laura was not the person Ark expected? What if all of it—the kids, the house, the channeling sessions—was just too much for him?

Soon we would know.

Ark flew into Tampa International Airport on Tuesday, 11 February 1997, one day before Laura's forty-fifth birthday. Cherie and I wanted to be there. We wanted to witness the precise moment when Ark and Laura laid eyes on each other for the first time, but Laura would have none of it. She would not disclose his flight number or his airline or even the day of his scheduled arrival. For the time being, she wanted Ark all to herself.

Who could blame her?

We were allowed an audience with Ark a few weeks later. We took him and Laura to dinner. Laura said he didn't eat much, so we chose a salad place on U.S. 19, Sweet Tomatoes, and stared at him over our lettuce. Ark looked just like his picture, only more pale and slender. His white hair was striking; his accent was beautiful; he could not have weighed more than 140 pounds. He was sweet and gentle. He had a quiet but persistent sense of humor.

That night, and every time we saw Ark and Laura together afterward, it was obvious that the two of them adored each other. They held hands, kissed, smiled constantly. Furthermore, Ark was comfortable with Laura's children. He liked them, and they seemed to enjoy him. As for Laura's channeling sessions, Ark relished them. If he thought there was anything strange about sitting around the spirit board, posing queries to disembodied entities, he showed no sign of it. He had many questions himself for the Cassiopaeans; he said he wanted their help with his research. The first time he sat down before the spirit board, he asked the CS about what lay ahead. He had read the transcripts and seen how they talked about him and Laura having a "predestined mission."

"My first question is," said Ark, "I want to understand what is this 'predestined mission,' what it consists of?"

"IT CONSISTS OF FOLLOWING THE PATH THAT HAS CONFRONTED YOU," came the reply. "WE DO NOT TELL YOU OF YOUR PREDESTINED MISSION, BECAUSE THEN IT IS NO LONGER 'PREDESTINED.' YOU LEARN BY EXPERIENCE, AND AS YOU SENSE, YOU ARE ON THE THRESHOLD OF A RATHER PROFOUND EXPERIENCE."

When Ark asked what they meant by a "profound experience," the CS declined to get too specific, saying merely that he was at a turning point. Laura kept asking questions, too. She wanted to know more about her future with Ark.

"I was just wondering," she said, "if our pathways are supposed to now be parallel or diverge."

"SEEMS TO US THAT YOUR PATHWAYS ARE INTERTWINING!"

"Well," said Laura, "I am tired; Ark is tired. So is there anything further you would like to tell us this evening?"

"COMBINE ENERGIES IN PURSUIT OF ANSWERS, AND THE REST FALLS INTO PLACE."

"You say 'Combine energies.' Is there any reason why this will facilitate the pursuit of answers?"

"COMPLEMENTARY SOULS."

That was how Laura and Ark saw themselves, too. The two of them were building more than a life together, they said. When they had found each other, they had entered a whole new universe of possibilities.

A couple of months later, Laura put Ark on the plane back to Poland. He already was talking about his return. Ark had a special backpack that he had worn on the plane when he flew over. It was adorned with an image of Batman; he'd found it somewhere in Europe. That was how he'd told Laura to recognize him at the airport when he arrived that day. He would be the guy, he told her, wearing the Batman backpack. Now he was leaving. But when he came back, he said, he would have the backpack on again.

Of course Ark would be returning to Laura; he would cross the Atlantic, again, with the assistance of the Caped Crusader—nothing could stop him.

"It's five after," said one of the guests, checking her watch. "It's time. It's time."

"All right," said Laura. "We're ready to get married here."

It was the afternoon of Saturday, 12 September 1998. They were all gathered at the house in New Port Richey, waiting for the ceremony to get under way in the living room. Laura's mother and brother were there, as were all of the children except Aletheia, who had to work, and Freddie and a handful of longtime friends.

The bride wore an embroidered, mustard-colored dress made of India cloth and a pearl choker that her intended had brought her from Brussels. The groom wore a black shirt and black pants that set off his hair. Neither wore socks or shoes.

They began with Laura sitting in a chair and Ark crouching before her to wash her bare feet. When he was done, they switched places, and Laura washed his feet. The ritual symbolized the marriage between heaven and earth. Then they stood and lit candles and listened as the woman who was presiding over the ceremony, a notary and a friend, gave a reading.

"I am the light that is over all things. I am all. . . . Split a piece of wood, and I am there. Pick up a stone, and you will find me there."

Then came the vows, and the confirmation of the vows, and the placement of the circles of gold upon their fingers. "With this ring, I thee wed," said Laura, staring into Ark's solemn face. "In love and truth, and with all my worldly goods, I thee endow."

Then the kiss, and the applause, and Ark with his arms wrapped tightly around his bride and his eyes drowning with tears. "Okay," said Laura, beaming afterward as they cut the cake. "What's next?"

EPILOGUE

After all this time, I cannot begin to tell you what is truly happening with Laura. I do know that she remains as intriguing as ever. From the moment I met her, she has made me consider possibilities that would not have occurred to me otherwise. She has forced me to see and think in new ways.

This is Laura's true gift, the only special ability of hers to which I can swear.

When I share Laura's story with people, they ask me what it means. I tell them I do not know. I cannot prove that sixth-density beings, hailing from a constellation in the sky, actually hooked her up with a second husband who was perfectly suited for her but who lived across the ocean.

All I know is, Laura is real, and Ark is real, and against all the odds, they found each other and are now married.

Isn't that enough?

I find it amazing that Laura has spent so much of her life pursuing aliens and dark entities, when in the end she caught hold of something far more elusive. We talk about love all the time, but how do we know it's real? We can't see it, can't nail it down, cannot begin to prove exactly what it is. Love is an idea, an invisible notion without form or substance, that we accept on faith. And yet we spend our lives chasing it. We crave it, long for it, cry ourselves to sleep over it. We do these things because we feel what love means inside us, and that is all we need to know that it is real.

When I go to see Laura and Ark these days, I think about these things. I see them together, and it reminds me that the invisible is sometimes within reach. They have been married for a year and a half now. They live in the house on Montana Avenue. They have renovated it and redecorated extensively. The walls in the living room have been painted an odd shade, vaguely purple; the windows are hung with curtains of leopard prints. One of Laura's friends, viewing the changes, has politely called Laura's taste "whimsical."

"I think it's pagan baroque," says Laura, grinning.

The kids are growing up. Laura's two oldest daughters have jobs now and have moved out. The three remaining children, including Jason, live at home. Their father, Lewis Martin, lives not far away, in Crystal River. He sees the children whenever he can. If he feels any bitterness toward his ex-wife, he did not show it when I last spoke with him. He told me he has moved on; he said he still believes in Laura and considers her "a seeker."

"I wish her no ill will."

Laura and Ark have gone on with their lives as well. Ark says he works as a contractor for Constellation Technology, a defense company in Largo. He works at home mostly, staring at his computer screen, working on mathematical equations and physics problems that I could not begin to explain. Laura works at the house as well. She is busy with the kids, assisting Ark with his research, branching into new directions with her work, which remains as provocative as ever. Though she no longer performs spirit detachments or exorcisms, Laura says she and Freddie still channel communications from the Cassiopaeans; Ark sits with them, posing questions about physics and other topics. Laura and Ark have also put together something called a "psychomantium" in Laura's study, which is basically a black felt tent that she lowers from the ceiling. As best I can understand it, Laura sits inside the darkened enclosure with a candle and a mirror. By staring into the mirror for extended periods of time, she hopes to someday see images from past lives or other realities.

In recent months, Laura and Ark have devoted a great deal of time to a sprawling Web site that discusses their lives, their theories, the channeling with the CS. Those who read through its contents will see that my descriptions of the channeling have only skimmed the surface of that subject.

Laura's curiosity remains as epic as ever. Not long ago, I noticed two piles of books—her current reading material—stacked precariously beside her chair in the living room. The titles included *The Atlas of Early Man*, *The Myth of the Eternal Return*, *Mysteries of the Alphabet*, *The Etruscans*, and *Subquantum Kinetics*. Not all of her selections were so intellectual. Wedged in the middle of the books was a copy of *Woman's World* magazine, which she was scanning for new diets.

Her desire to unlock the mysteries of the cosmos burns just as fiercely as when I first met her. Recently I asked what her goals were for the years ahead. She gave me her list.

"A," she told me, "change the universe.

"B, transcend space and time, which includes time travel into the future and into the past.

"Or, C, transition into another density and effect all of the above."

In the meantime, Laura and Ark have each other. The two of them talk for hours on end. They almost never go out, except when she wants to venture to Sam's Club to hunt for bargains. "We don't go anywhere," she says happily. "We don't do anything."

There is a different feeling now to Laura's life. It feels less scattered than before, less uncertain, immeasurably more calm. Inside the house, there is a palpable, tangible sense of contentment.

Recently I asked her what she has learned. Not so much about aliens or UFOs, but about her heart. Laura paused and thought for a moment.

"In my mind," she said, "life is an ongoing miracle. It really is a miracle. And the one thing I have learned just in the past few years is that if you don't see something miraculous in your life, if it seems dark or sad or it seems like a burden, the most miraculous thing you have is your ability to choose to be that miracle. I mean, to be it. I think once people choose to be a miracle, the universe reflects that back to them."

Some people would call this luck. Laura would not.

A few weeks ago, I joined Ark and Laura and a few of their friends for the last New Year's Eve of a thousand years. We ate miniature key lime pies, sipped champagne, sat in the living room with little, pointed hats on our heads.

Just before the clock struck twelve, we stepped out onto the front lawn and watched as Laura and Ark lit fireworks in the street. All around the neighborhood, other people were shooting off fireworks of their own. Laura and Ark were acting like school kids. They would run into the street, light one of the fuses, then run together back onto the lawn, laughing and holding hands.

At the stroke of midnight, cries and cheers rose from the houses and streets around us. The two lovers kissed as a blaze of explosions lit the sky, obscuring the stars burning in the blackness beyond.

Joe Mackall

By Force, Threat, or Deception

On Friday the thirteenth, just twelve days before his forty-second birthday, a birthday he swore he'd never see, Don pulled out of his parking space at a job he hated and turned into eastbound traffic. As he headed down Detroit Avenue to one of his favorite bars, he turned on his headlights to combat the disappearance of daylight, on one of those winter afternoons when darkness comes before supper, when evening subsumes late afternoon, when all that is known of daytime bows to the early night.

As he drove toward the Driftwood Inn through the rain and snow, mixed and falling, perhaps Don thought of ways to spend the paycheck neatly folded in his wallet, or of his dream of becoming a painter; or maybe he conjured up images of his past: of his time as a dance instructor at Arthur Murray's, guiding couples through the steps of the waltz or the gyrations of the jitterbug, or of his time in the service during the Korean War. Or maybe thoughts of his recent past crept into his mind with the stealth and skill of a cancer cell: of his leaving his kind wife and doomed marriage of twelve years, the look on the face of the ten-year-old daughter he loved as he drove away from their home, to his new home five miles away, with his belongings carefully packed in the trunk of his Lincoln Continental.

He had popped in the bar merely to have a drink and cash his check. Bars did that then. Maybe some still do. While he was in the bar, Don no doubt talked easily to strangers; he was friendly, well-liked by men and women. Especially women. They could always talk to him. And his dark brown hair, aquiline nose, easy manner and penchant for dressing above his means seemed to draw women to him. On this day maybe he bought a few drinks for friends, feeling that familiar working-class flush of Friday riches: riches tentative, hard won, well-deserved, riches here on Friday afternoon and gone on Monday morning.

When Don walked to his car, having stayed no more than an hour, just long enough to get out of the cold, have a warm drink, enjoy the reflection of himself in a barroom mirror, he made the mistake of letting strangers see his wad of money. As he braced against the light breeze blowing in off Lake Erie, two young men—two Hispanic kids, Spanish or Puerto Rican—surprised him. One pushed a gun in Don's back and forced him into his car.

The men wound up at the northwestern edge of Edgewater Park in Cleveland at a place called Perkins Beach, where the lake became part of the night. Lake Erie's latent waves crashed and fell against the rocky shore of Edgewater Park. The temperature hovered just above freezing. The older kid, the kid who did all the talking, got in the passenger seat; the other kid got in the back. The boy in back was only sixteen.

The punk sitting shotgun pointed a .38 in Don's face.

"Hand over the money or I'll kill you," the punk said.

Don lunged for the gun. The kid fired: two bullets in the neck, one in the side of the face, one in the temple.

For years this was the story the family believed. A convenient story. Ugly, but safe. Horrible, but ordinary. But it wasn't the whole truth.

Somehow I always knew much of what happened to my uncle had become a family fiction. Maybe it was the way the story never changed, as if one detail out of place would cause the entire narrative edifice to come tumbling down, resembling a collapsed cathedral, its glory betrayed by the sudden clutter of its bricks. It could have been the way my father, a former Cleveland homicide detective and my uncle's good friend, mysteriously lost interest in the case. He simply didn't want to know anything he didn't want to know.

I, however, have never been able to let it go. I've encouraged the family to talk about it. Not because I thought it would do any of us any good, but because aspects of my uncle's murder had been mired in mystery for so long that rumors and innuendo had begun to seep into holes of doubt. I needed to know more. For twenty-five years I have remained selfishly, seriously curious. I am now the age my uncle was when he died. I'm probably not even entitled to dig around in the ruins of my uncle's murder. We were not bound by blood but by marriage. He taught me how to play tennis; he talked to me often and always treated me well, assuring me that when it came to women, I wouldn't have a problem. As an awkward and unhappy teenager, I appreciated the apparent sincerity and wisdom of his words.

I know I loved him, and I'm hoping this love is enough to attempt to tell his story.

You're at Uncle Don's house not long after he and your aunt separated. You watch the maroon Lincoln Continental pull in the driveway. You see him kiss his ten-year-old daughter goodbye. (Was it the last time he ever saw her? She him?) You run through the kitchen and down the steps. When your aunt sees you she asks where you're going. You tell her you want to talk to Uncle Don. "You don't have to," she says, picking up a laundry basket filled with women-only whites. "Okay," you say, hearing something in her words you feel you should obey. You turn your back on the door that leads to him. You never see your uncle again.

The night after the murder, my uncle's smiling face from better times appeared boxed in the corner of the TV screen. The newscaster mispronounced his polysyllabic Polish surname. After a day or two his picture was replaced with an icon meant to represent murder in the abstract: a cartoon-like drawing of a gun superimposed on a chalk sketch of a body strewn on a street, a faceless, nameless body. It could have been anybody. Which it was. Which it wasn't.

In order for members of my family to get at what really happened twenty-five years ago this fall, we'd have to give up at least a modicum of the memory of the man we thought we knew. We'd have to take a fresh look at the man we called husband, brother-in-law, father, friend. The man I called Uncle Don. And, finally, we'd all have to learn a little something about a few strangers—strangers even to my uncle. We'd also have to get to know a guy named Alan G. Barnes.

You have appointed yourself the person who has to get at the truth. After 25 years, you still believe the truth is out there. In buried police reports and in the distant memories of aging detectives. In secret, stolen family moments. In the hidden history of people you claim to love. You want to tell your uncle's story. No matter what. Why is it so important that you know what happened? Who are you to believe you have a right to the truth—or even the facts?

On Friday the thirteenth, just twelve days before his forty-second birthday, a day he swore he'd never see, Don—whose father died at forty-one—pulls out from his parking space at Alan Packing and Rubber Co. and away from the steeple-shadow of the Methodist church on the corner, which must have hovered over him on this day the way the Catholic church had his entire life. As he turns into eastbound traffic and heads down Detroit Ave. to one of his favorite bars, he switches on his headlights and settles restlessly into the leather seats of his Lincoln.

As he drives toward the Driftwood Inn through the rain and snow, mixed and falling, perhaps Don calculates the division of his paycheck, wondering how much he'd have left after debts and other bills. Surely enough for the extra gas for the long, out-of-the-way drive to Perkins Beach.

Alan G. Barnes also felt the promise of Perkins, albeit in a more sinister way. Barnes must have been feeling the oncoming weight of his twentieth birthday, which at the time of his becoming a murderer was only three days away. Perhaps he foresaw his dimly lit future, which looked a lot like his present. He was nineteen years old, living in his parents' W. 87 St. Cleveland home; he had minimal education, no job, and a shared, fledgling criminal enterprise with a sixteen-year-old who would soon become his accomplice in a kidnapping and murder.

But Barnes had stumbled onto something interesting and potentially profitable back in August of 1974 when he'd assaulted his first victim; and it was then he must have begun noticing the population frequenting Perkins Beach. It was the same population that frequented other Cleveland hot spots like West 25th, West 32nd (where the gay bath houses sat), West 45th, West 65th. Barnes viewed the gays who congregated at these spots as easy marks. A lot of them were married. Even if they weren't married, they didn't want to report to the police that they had been cruising when robbed. A lot of people could not care less what befell homosexuals. They probably asked for it anyway. They were the perfect marks.

Some members of the Cleveland and Lakewood police departments even had a name for Barnes and those with a similar modus operandi: "tulip vultures." Barnes quickly became a tulip vulture extraordinaire. Although Barnes lived in Cleveland, the then sixty-four-year-old city of Lakewood began only thirty blocks from his house, and even in the early 1970s, the city was known as the "flower patch." Just five miles west of

Cleveland's downtown sat what was once a forest along Lake Erie, now a city fertile with homosexuals, mostly male. And near the border of Lakewood and Cleveland sat Perkins Beach, which already had a reputation as a lovers' lane, a place where gays could hook up, hang out and not be hassled by the police.

The border separating the two cities was symbolic as well as geographical, serving as a dividing line between decent living and decadence, moving up or going down. The Cleveland police were too busy with homicides (350 a year at that time) and other big-city crime; and neighboring Lakewood police had an arrangement with the city's large homosexual population, which in 1974 was just over twenty thousand "card-carrying homosexuals" in a city of around seventy thousand. The arrangement, simply stated, was: "We won't bother you guys, but don't lie to us. If you're cruising and get beat up, just say that. Don't make up a big story that's impossible for us to believe."

Perhaps because they were left alone by the police and didn't want to jeopardize that relationship, or their marriages, or their reputations, more than 90 percent of gay victims of crime never filed reports.

With all this in his favor, Barnes figured he was onto something good. He assumed that at five feet ten inches tall and 170 pounds, young and lithe, with brown hair and hazel eyes, the correct moves and the right clothes, he just might be able to make this work.

It's bad enough you have to pry into your uncle's life, but you soon learn that to discover what happened to him, you'll have to investigate a string of robberies committed by the murderer just prior to the murder. And in the robbery reports are the names of other victims. Were they all lured by the unspoken promises of Perkins Beach? Suddenly you're reading the names of others, names attached to men, men attached to lives and families. In at least one case you'll know more than his wife and family ever knew about a particular autumn day. You wonder if you know more than your aunt does. You worry about the talk you'll soon have to have with her.

Michael McEntee was ten years out of college. He had a wife and two young children, a good job in Cleveland, and an urge he couldn't control. At least he couldn't control the urge on November 1, 1974.

McEntee left downtown Cleveland at 1 p.m. and headed west. He later told the police he wanted to grab lunch at the Blue Fox, a restaurant that for a generation had served fine dinners and businessmen lunches on the boundary of Cleveland and Lakewood. But he needed some cash first, so he pulled up in the auto teller line at Cleveland Trust for some lunch money.

Enjoying a free hour, McEntee cranked up the car radio as he waited in line. He wasn't in line very long when a guy without a weapon jerked open the driver's door and pushed McEntee hard on the left shoulder so he'd move to the passenger seat. The perp got behind the wheel.

"Give me your wallet," he said.

The perp took McEntee's wallet. Disappointed by the few dollars he stole, the guy eventually forced McEntee to write several checks.

Detective Michael Flynn of the Lakewood Police Department couldn't understand why a guy looking to rob somebody would choose a car sitting in an auto teller line, where the car could easily be trapped.

"I remember talking to this guy [McEntee]," Flynn said twenty-five years later as he looked over the police report, running his fingers through his thinning gray hair. "I knew I was being hosed. I knew he had cruised somewhere. He had to have been at Perkins."

Flynn remembers McEntee making a composite of the suspect. He remembers him mentioning several times that he was married.

Detective Flynn, whose still handsome, angular face and mustache conjure images of former TV cops, knew it was time to ask the question he'd been holding back.

"Why did you pull off at Perkins Beach?"

McEntee wouldn't answer.

"Are you a homosexual?" Flynn asked, his experience telling him that crime at Perkins Beach always involved homosexuals.

"I'm a heterosexual," McEntee said. "I told you. I'm married."

At this time Flynn brought up the possibility of McEntee taking a polygraph test.

Flynn waited.

"One time. In college. A group of us from Ohio State went out and had a homosexual commit fellatio on us," McEntee said.

Flynn waited. He wanted to leave McEntee a respectable out.

"I'd like to change one thing in my story, and then I'll take a polygraph."

McEntee informed Flynn that the crime did initiate at Perkins Beach, not in an auto teller line.

McEntee left downtown Cleveland at 1:00 p.m. and headed west. He wanted to grab lunch at the Blue Fox, a restaurant that for a generation had served fine dinners and businessmen lunches on the boundary of Lakewood and Cleveland. Instead of going to lunch, however, McEntee decided to waste a little time at Perkins Beach, maybe catch a little shut eye before heading back to work. He drove his gray 1971 Camaro up the long road leading past Edgewater Park and into the more secluded Perkins Beach area.

He draped his suit jacket over the back of the passenger seat, undid his top shirt button, loosened his tie, leaned his back against the driver's door and stretched his legs across the Camaro's console. Finally, he dozed off.

Suddenly McEntee jerked awake. Some guy ripped open the driver's door and grabbed McEntee's arm with one hand and his tie with the other.

"Move over," the guy demanded.

McEntee scrambled to the passenger seat.

Barnes, clean-shaven and neatly dressed in brown from his zipper-down shirt to suede zippered boots, hurried behind the wheel and threw McEntee's suit jacket into his lap.

"Give me your wallet," Barnes said.

McEntee removed his wallet from his jacket and handed his money, eleven dollars, to Barnes. Barnes took the wallet, checked it out and handed it back.

"You got a checkbook, right?" Barnes asked. "Then write a check for fifty dollars. Where's the closest auto teller?"

McEntee told Barnes where he could cash the check.

With McEntee still in the passenger seat, Barnes left Perkins Beach and drove east along the Cleveland Shoreway. Frustrated by construction, Barnes turned and took an alternate route, pounding the Camaro over a dirt road filled with holes. As he drove, Barnes flipped through McEntee's checkbook.

"Is the balance in here right?" Barnes asked.

"No."

"Write another check for fifty dollars."

"Why?"

"Because of that," Barnes said as he pointed to another branch of Cleveland Trust bank.

McEntee wrote another check for fifty dollars.

"When can I get out of the car?" McEntee asked.

"In a couple of minutes. Write another one for two hundred dollars," Barnes said as the Camaro idled in the Cleveland Trust auto teller line. Barnes took both checks and edged up in line.

"It's dumb to have two checks because they'll only cash one of them," McEntee told Barnes, either because he was trying to win him over or because he was frightened of what might happen if the bank refused to cash the checks.

Barnes agreed, ripping the smaller check into tiny pieces and tossing the scraps in the car's ashtray.

Losing patience, Barnes suddenly began pounding on the horn and rocking the car back and forth as he tried to get out of line. When he managed to escape the line, Barnes darted to the front and parked right by the lobby.

When Barnes informed McEntee that they were going inside the bank to cash the check, McEntee figured this would be the best time to get away. He too got out of the car and walked in front of Barnes into the bank. "Look at the crowd," McEntee said when he opened the bank door.

"Get in the car," Barnes shouted. "Get back in the car or else!"

McEntee opened the car door as if to get in, but then he slammed the door and ran into the bank.

Barnes started the car and drove away, the dual white walls on the Camaro's front tires blurring in the afternoon. The police later found the car in the parking lot of a Cleveland bar.

"The only reason this guy filed a report is because the check was out there, and he knew he'd have to tell his wife something," Flynn said. "He had to come up with an explanation. If it was money only, we'd have never heard from him."

You recall your recent conversation with McEntee's wife. "My husband died four years ago," she said. "Cancer. He was only fifty-one. I don't think I want to talk about this over the phone. For all I know you could be the guy who did it. Anyway, I don't think I can tell you anything about your uncle's murder," she tells you. "All I know is that my husband was in line at an auto teller and the guy jumped in his car."

You thank her and tell her you will not call again. You hope you can keep your promise.

Over the next six weeks, Barnes picked up his pace. Shortly after the McEntee kidnapping and the bungled check-cashing scheme, Barnes kidnapped Thomas Walker on November 12 under similar circumstances. He abducted Michael J. Palmison on December 4 and Alan W. Rounds on December 11. All of these men were picked up in or around Perkins Beach. All of them had been taken "by force, threat or deception."

Don pushes the accelerator down as he picks up his speed, driving faster now, hard. As he drives toward Perkins, he passes apartment buildings built in English Tudor style, and cruises beneath the shade of the maples and oaks lining Clifton Blvd., which once was home to Cleveland's wealthy families of industry.

Although Don at times may have lived as if he were from a wealthy family, he was not. With only a high school education, he had worked as an elevator repairman, a street sweeper, a shipping clerk. For a time he even trafficked in cigarettes. Don would drive his Lincoln down to North Carolina where he'd pull up in front of a barn at 3:00 a.m. The barn door opened and he drove in. Immediately the door shut behind him and lights went on. Without much being said, three or four guys would load the Lincoln with one thousand cartons of cigarettes, ensuring that not a single carton showed above window level. Don would pay the sellers one dollar a carton in North Carolina, drive back to Ohio and sell them for two dollars a carton when cartons regularly sold for four dollars. The only tax that went unpaid was the Ohio tax, so it looked to be a good gig. Unfortunately, Don never had money in his hands for long. Instead of turning around with the one thousand dollars profit and going back for another cache, Don blew the money and had to borrow cash from friends and family in order to make another run, which was why the paycheck stub found in his wallet on the day of his death was for $282 for two weeks of work.

Don doesn't stay long at the Driftwood Inn, just long enough to get out of the cold, feel the wet heat of Cutty Sark, enjoy his reflection in a barroom mirror, and cash his check.

No minorities—no Spanish or Puerto Ricans—spotted a wad of money. Barnes waits miles away, eating chicken and holding a gun.

You once watched Uncle Don wash his wife's hair, carefully brushing it out, blowing it dry, gently foraging through it with his fingers as if searching for the secret of the static electricity he created. Her hair billowed. He was electric; he had the touch. As he brushed his wife's hair, he had everything in its place: brush here; gel there, comb here. Twice you playfully rearranged his tools. The second time that he told you not to move anything again, you heard something in his voice—anger, simple and clean—that you'd never heard before.

A guy named Allen Gump lived on Cleveland's west side and had an acquaintance named Barnes. Barnes and his minor sidekick Michael visited Gump often enough to know he owned just the help they needed to upgrade their business in a hurry without a cent of overhead. Gump owned a .38 blue-steel snub-nosed revolver. Barnes needed the gun, so he broke into his friend's house and took it.

On December 12, 1974, just about twenty-four hours before Barnes would become a murderer, he decided to step things up. Now he had a gun. All he needed was another so-called tulip ready to be picked.

Richard Wilkinson stopped his silver two-door 1972 Mercury XR7 at a red light near Perkins Beach. As he waited for the light to change, his passenger door flung open and Wilkinson stared into the two-inch barrel of a .38 caliber revolver.

"Freeze or I'll shoot you, you bitch," the gunman said, his hazel eyes flashing. "If you move I'll blow your balls off with this gun."

Barnes, with his hair slicked back and greasy under a black leather cap with a brim, a green field jacket and light-colored plaid pants, forced Wilkinson to drive to Perkins Beach.

You visit Perkins Beach, take pictures, time distances to get things right. On the way home you go out of your way to drive past your aunt's house. If you see her outside you'll stop and visit. See if she feels like talking about her dead husband. Surely a quarter of a century has eased the pain. After all, they were on their way to a divorce when he was killed, you tell yourself as you pass duplex after duplex. You see her outside. She's playing with her grandchildren in the rear of her narrow driveway. It's a beautiful summer afternoon. You keep driving.

When they arrived at Perkins, Barnes forced Wilkinson into the back seat. Barnes's accomplice sat in the passenger seat. The minor, referred to only as Michael, who stood no more than a few inches over five feet tall and weighed less than 140 pounds, wore a black sweater with blue stripes, shoulder-length brown hair parted on the left. He held the .38 Titan Tiger on Wilkinson while Barnes did the driving.

Barnes drove Michael and their victim to an apartment complex, where he stopped the car and got out to inspect the trunk. He reached into the trunk, produced a tire iron and got back in the car.

"You better come up with fifty dollars or we'll kill you," Barnes said, brandishing the weapon.

"I don't have any money," Wilkinson said.

Barnes then dragged him out of the back seat, smacked him on the head with the barrel of the gun and threw him into the trunk.

Barnes and the kid sped around enjoying the power and speed of the XR7. Every half hour or so, Barnes would pull the car over, open the trunk and crack Wilkinson in the head with the tire iron. By the time Barnes freed Wilkinson from the trunk, the young kid was gone and Wilkinson was forced back up front.

"I really just want to be friends," Barnes said as he held the .38 on Wilkinson. "You should come and see me. . . ."

After his bizarre comments about becoming friends, Barnes stopped the car in the parking lot of a dry cleaners and got out, telling Wilkinson to head west and to keep going.

Weeks before you were to make the sacrament of Confirmation at St. Bridget's Catholic Church, you asked Uncle Don if he would be your sponsor, somebody willing to stand for and with you as you became a soldier of Christ. Uncle Don said he'd love to, but that he could not. At the time he felt he was not a good Catholic. He wasn't even receiving Communion. He refused to be a hypocrite by playing the role of good soldier. He apologized for letting you down. You admired him for his honesty. You hoped you had the courage one day to follow his lead.

Just after 6:00 p.m. Don maneuvers his 1971 Lincoln into the entrance to Edgewater Park and moves slowly up the drive to Perkins Beach, where unbeknownst to him, Barnes waits, finishing take-out chicken and sipping a can of RC Cola.

Perhaps Don checks himself out in the rearview mirror, slips his glasses into their black case, nods in a knowing way that he looks good. Although he's still wearing his work clothes, light gray pants and matching work shirt with Houghton Elevator sewn over the right shirt pocket and his name stitched over the left, he looks fine, dapper even. His brown dress shoes ease up on the accelerator as he nears the portal to Perkins. The temperature this close to the lake is only a couple degrees above freezing; Don's lucky he wore his blue nylon work jacket.

He backs into a spot along the cul-de-sac, turns off his headlights, and then the engine. To his left and across a more inland section of the shoreline the lights of Cleveland shine through the oncoming darkness. He sees the Terminal Tower. Behind him sit leafless trees, and beyond the trees a black drop-off to the shallowest of the five Great Lakes. On the other side of the cul-de-sac stands a sixty-three-year-old statue of German composer Richard Wagner. Wagner's beret-topped head angles away from Perkins Beach; his coat looks as though it has been blown open, and he holds a sheaf of music in his left hand. Don gazes around casually, non-committally, perhaps clicking the ball point pen in his shirt pocket or fingering the yellow-handled pocket knife in his pants.

Barnes licks three chicken bones clean, throws them into the black plastic box they came in and drops the box to the ground. Another tulip. And this time Barnes is ready. He's tired of playing around.

When he sees the young man approaching his car, does Don's heart pick up speed? Does he quickly rehearse his lines or does he know the drill? Does he check his hair one last time, frustrated by the tinges of gray growing above the ears? Does he lower his power windows a bit to convey a welcome? Is this his first time, the time he's fantasized about, the time he's been forbidden to fantasize about? Forbidden himself to fantasize about? Does his conscience tingle with the electric knowledge you get when you know something's wrong and you do it anyway, as if you're moving through everything you are and know to enter another place, whose passage you'll only worry about once you're safely back from the other side? Is this why, when Barnes pulls out his gun and demands money, Don can't possibly give it to him? Can't possibly give in to him?

Surely Don knows the fantasy is over when the minor accomplice gets in the back seat and he's forced into the passenger seat. Barnes is once again behind the wheel, still sipping his pop.

From the passenger seat Don lunges for the gun. Barnes pulls the revolver's trigger six times; two of the six hit the firing pin but do not fire. Two bullets rip through Don's right upper chest and lodge in his back. Another hits the upper left side of the neck and exits from the right side of the back. The final bullet enters in front of Don's left ear and exits through the back of the same ear. In the confusion windows are busted, blood and glass sprinkle the black vinyl roof, the seats, the maroon carpet on the floor, the door panels. While Barnes fires, Don attempts to get out the passenger side of the car. Frightened, Barnes flees, drops the gun on the front seat. Don dies before he can get away; he dies lying half in, half out of his car, his right lung perforated, specks of gun powder in the wounds, massive internal hemorrhaging, seventy-five feet away from a police call box.

The lady at the Cuyahoga County Coroner's office warns you about one of the autopsy pictures. She says you don't have to pay for that one if you don't want to. You thank her but insist on seeing all seven of them. She says okay and hands them to you, back first, so the photographs face her. "What relation was he to you?" she asks. It should be a simple question but has gotten considerably more complicated. Story to storyteller? Subject to writer? Nephew to...? "He was my uncle," you tell her. "Three and a half years ago my daughter came through here," she tells you. "That was hard." "I'm sorry," you say. "You do what you have to do, huh?" When she says this you almost think you hear her ask, "Why are you doing this?"

Around 7:00 p.m. on December 13, 1974, Edward Chomiak drives west on the Shoreway. Although he had hoped he could make it to his destination without having to stop, he finally decides he'll have to pull over and relieve himself. This isn't the first time he hasn't been in complete control of his body; it had betrayed him years earlier with boyhood polio.

Looking for a secluded place, Chomiak finds a darkened drive where he can relieve himself privately and be back on his way. But then he notices something. Although it is already dark and the weather's becoming more miserable, a light attracts Chomiak's attention. Walking with difficulty, he moves closer toward the light until he can make out its source, which is a dome light shining in the evening in what appears to be an abandoned car. He looks toward the middle of the cul-de-sac, to the third tree west of the center. Getting closer, he sees that the driver's side window has been smashed or the glass blown out, something. Because of his lack of agility, he heads carefully toward a Ford Falcon parked across from the Lincoln, where a man in his twenties with dark curly hair and a slight beard sits alone.

"You better go call the police," Chomiak tells the curly-haired man. "I think there's a body by that car over there."

"I'll call from a gas station on Detroit Ave. And then I'll be back," the young man says before driving away.

It's almost 7:30 p.m. now. The police have still not arrived and the curly-haired young man has not returned. Chomiak assumes that the kid has taken off without ever calling the police, apparently not wanting to be associated with a crime at Perkins Beach.

Chomiak drives the short distance to Detroit Ave. to make the call. At 7:51 p.m. Det. Bob Shankland and Det. Jimmy Fuerst arrive. Shankland, muscular, with a reputation as a tough, brave and gutsy no-holes-barred kind of cop with reddish-brown hair, heads directly to the Lincoln, where he'll collect pop cans and soil samples. His partner, Fuerst, a fun-loving, well-liked, stocky guy gets Chomiak's story and then, noticing he's partially paralyzed, gently takes Chomiak by the arm and walks him over to the Lincoln to see if he can identify the body.

Although Chomiak remembers looking into the upturned and bloody face of the dead man, the police report it differently. The victim was found lying outside the passenger door, face down, feet together and pointing south, left arm under the body and the right arm outstretched along the right leg, head pointing north. No mention of his soul leaving his body, tumble-drifting down, above and across the lake, flying fast and safe to the far north beyond the water.

Chomiak, who still thinks of the dead man and says a prayer for him whenever he passes by this place, stares at the once-handsome now blood-smeared face of the stranger.

You take one look at the autopsy pictures. One. The woman with the dead daughter was right. You should have thought twice about acquiring the pic-

tures. The wounds, both entrance and exit, are confirmed. Chomiak's right
about the blood-smeared face. You glimpse Uncle Don through the facade of
the murdered man. Yes it's him. No it isn't. Both equal and separate truths.
You should have spent more time with the woman from the coroner's office, the
one with the dead daughter. You should have listened to her tale of love and
loss. You need to talk to your aunt, your deceased mother's closest sister. The
time has come.

In the middle of the front seat, strewn cold, were car keys, and next to the keys, hot and spent, rested the .38 blue-steel revolver, an Arminius Titan Tiger, serial number 023805. Because Gump had reported his gun stolen, the trail led easily to Barnes. He and his minor accomplice were arrested while sitting on a couch the day after the murder. Barnes confessed immediately.

Uncle Don was taken to St. John's Hospital where he was pronounced dead at 10:05 p.m. on Friday, December 13, 1974.

My aunt asked if we would mind keeping the Lincoln at our house for a time. Perhaps she asked because my father was not only my uncle's friend but an ex-homicide detective. At first it simply took up space in our driveway and in my imagination. Soon we investigated it, my father piecing together clues, explaining to his young sons the likelihoods and probabilities: the shards of glass told one part of the story, the blood another part, the smell—in its utter indescribability—yet another. Soon we sat behind the wheel. Fearing a dead battery, my dad and I began driving the car, leaving the pieces of glass and splotches of dried blood where they lay. High school friends flocked to the car the way they were expected to. Soon the car was gone, at least from the driveway.

Good friends of my aunt and uncle—friends who lived directly across the street from them—bought the Lincoln; my uncle's then ten-year-old daughter saw it every single morning she left for school, each day she went out to play.

You call your aunt and ask her if you can visit. You ask her if she's willing to
talk about Uncle Don. She says she will but that she will not do it over the
phone. "He was a free spirit; that's for sure," she says. You stop at a local deli
and pick up sliced turkey breast, Swiss cheese and a loaf of Italian bread, as is
a family custom—not the specifics, just the gesture. Her oldest sister is also in

*town. They both want to talk about their parents. How one came from Italy as
a twelve-year-old, about the hardships their lovely, strong and gentle mother,
your grandmother, endured. You love these stories and let them lull you away
from what you want to talk about. Soon they produce boxes and bags of pictures of the family and its extensions.*

*"The guy who killed Uncle Don got released from prison in 1989," you say
when a photo of Uncle Don comes up. "He served fifteen years. There wasn't
even a trial. He pled to a lesser offense of murder, aggravated robbery and
kidnapping."*

*You don't tell her that you located Barnes, that he's been living in the same
house for about the last seven years. That you tried to talk to him. That he's
living with at least two other men, including a chiropractor with a bad back.
You don't admit that your repeated phone calls enraged a guy running interference for Barnes. 'I know Alan. I'm friends with Alan. I will talk to Alan, but
if I were you I wouldn't hold my breath.' You don't tell her about the letter you
wrote him, asking about the murder that "rightly or wrongly" he was convicted
of committing, asking about that night in December, twenty-five years ago, for
information that only he can supply. You don't bother telling your aunt that the
guy who killed her husband never responded to your request for information.*

"That's horrible the way Don died," Aunt Manny, the elder aunt, says.
"Being shot and all like that."

*Uncle Don's wife is silent for a moment and it makes you want to turn and
run in shame. You know at that moment that you won't be able to ask her the
questions you came prepared to ask. You're sitting in her kitchen which looks
exactly the way it did twenty-five years ago. You remember one Saturday night,
probably 30 years ago now. Your aunt and uncle sit with your parents playing Pinochle in this very kitchen. Hand after hand. Cigarette after cigarette.
Drink after drink. Laughter. Friendship. You're in the living room watching
"Mannix." Never before or since have you felt so simply loved, so perfectly safe.
Your aunt's a good woman and an even better aunt. She's your godmother.
And in a generation and a religion that took godparenting seriously, she took it
more seriously than most.*

"Here's some pictures of Don," she says.

You take up one of him in tennis whites standing next to his Cadillac. Another where he's lounging on an army cot during the service; he's wearing his uniform and a huge smile. You wonder how many points of view it takes to tell anything about anybody.

"This is your grandpa," my aunt says to her oldest grandchild, whom she babysits a couple of days a week.

The boy, holding a stack of baseball cards in his fist, stops for a second and looks at the black-and-white picture. Of course the statement is as true as it is false. There is no doubt that the blood of the man is coursing through the body of the boy. Yes, that's his grandfather. No, it isn't the whole picture.

What do you do with all the circumstantial evidence? All the other pictures? All the rumors about the guys Uncle Don moved in with after he left his wife. A family member asking him, 'Why are you hanging out with these queers?' Uncle Don's response, 'Don't knock it if you haven't tried it.' And what about Perkins Beach? What about the tulip vultures? What about going miles out of his way on a miserable evening to sit in a dark park with a reputation as a homosexual hangout? What about the other strangers? Did he die because he couldn't live as an openly gay man? Would there have been less pressure if he had lived anywhere but Lakewood, anywhere other than "gay city"? Was his death ultimately caused by force, threat or deception? All three? Threats from whom? Who was deceived?

But who's the real person? How vain and egomaniacal is it to think you know? How foolish? How wrongheaded? Does loving somebody and being a writer give you a right to his story? You cannot tell your aunt what you've learned, and you hope she never reads this story.

In one photograph Uncle Don and Aunt Dee stand in front of the fireplace in their Christmas-tree lit living room in the early 1960s, not long after their wedding. Flowers adorn the wooden mantel, as do a bronze plate and a candle. Two snowmen stand sentry, flanking the flower arrangement. Two Christmas stockings—a few years away from being three—hang from the mantel. In the background, in front of a window covered with a soft, white cotton curtain, a saint with a crown of gold and a gown of white stands atop a corner cupboard with glass doors. Small, light blue designs decorate Uncle Don's white, short-sleeve shirt. He wears navy blue slacks with a thin black belt. Aunt Dee's green dress curves perfectly with her form; there's a gold pin above her left breast.

Uncle Don's arms are wrapped around his wife's waist. Her right hand holds his left wrist. My aunt's smile at his holding makes her beautiful. Uncle Don's smile rules and lines his face.

Their smiles appear to be evidence of something. Of something good. Something worth telling. They seem, at this captured moment in time, two people possessed of all the love that can possibly exist in a world where people are murdered.

Maureen Stanton

Good Guys

THE BEAUTIFUL PLANT

My brother Patrick and I speed down Route 9, a curvy, one-lane, luge track of a road, toward Buchanan, New York, where the Indian Point III Nuclear Generating Station rises from the east bank of the Hudson River, thirty-five miles north of Manhattan. Through a friend, Patrick and I have landed temporary jobs as painters for a refueling outage and "plant beautification" project.[1] To work here, Patrick and I must join the International Brotherhood of Painters and Allied Trades. For this, we need a Good Guy letter from a union member vouching for our character. I have no idea who has signed for us—our friend has arranged that—but someone is willing to say we are Good Guys. (Incidentally, the Good Guy letter is an actual form with the words "Good Guy Letter" printed across the top.)

We pass a baseball diamond along the Hudson, then turn into a sylvan glade enclosed in chain link. At the guard station, Patrick offers the name of our employer, NPS Energy Systems, then we cruise past hunks of rusting metal and neolithic concrete forms in wire-mesh pens to a four-story, L-shaped training building. From the parking lot, we see only a half-dozen modular buildings and two warehouses surrounded by woods. I'm amazed at how easy it is to hide a nuclear power plant.

---

1. For the previous few months, I'd been living in my mother's cottage on Cape Cod and writing a novel. I'd quit my career as a fund-raiser and was answering a customer service hotline for Papa Gino's, Inc., a chain of two hundred pizza joints. For twelve hours a week, I listened to gripes about rude clerks, cold pizza, late delivery, and once, a call from a patron who complained that he could not "stop burping and farting." The painting job is an infusion of much needed cash for Patrick, too, who for years has been squirreling around with various inventions.

Inside the training center, next to a mock control room that visitors peer into as if looking upon a nursery, is the windowless conference room where we will spend the next five days in Fitness for Duty training. Our group of trainees includes thirty construction workers—pipe fitters, electricians, insulators, carpenters, painters—and one executive who looks pink and priggish in his white shirt and tight tie. Patrick and I stand out too, with our uncallused hands, our fingernails evenly trimmed white quarter moons, and Patrick's fleece pullover, evidently not a masculine fabric like denim or the brown Carhartt jackets everyone wears. Patrick's hair is resolutely short, unlike the "mullet" that is popular here, clipped bangs and sideburns with long hair in back, a schizophrenic style that shouts, "I may look like a citizen, but I'm a rebel at heart."[2]

Patrick would blend more easily if he weren't with me. Of the nearly three hundred construction workers hired for the outage, only eight are female. "It's nice that your brother brought you into the trade," a sixtyish electrician says to me before class. Then adds, "I just don't think women belong in construction."

Our instructor, Jack, a thin, ruddy-faced retiree who trains part-time, begins by administering a psychological exam, a series of statements to which we must respond *strongly agree, strongly disagree*, or *neutral*. Jack hands out number two pencils and answer sheets with rows of tiny blank ovals and instructs us to select *neutral* as seldom as possible.[3] The problem is that some statements I agree with slightly, but not *strongly*. For example: "Threats never bother me." Well, idle threats don't bother me. Serious threats do. The fact is threats *sometimes* bother me. I'm momentarily stymied, but finally choose *strongly disagree*. Now I worry they will interpret my answer as demonstrating paranoia. Haven't I just implied that "Threats *always* bother me?" Perhaps I am being paranoid. I move on.

"The pomp and splendor of any big state ceremony are things which

---

2. See *The Mullet: Hairstyle of the Gods* by Barney Hoskyns and Mark Larson.
3. The test is a version of the Minnesota Multiphasic Personality Inventory, which evaluates characteristics including masculinity and femininity, cynicism (two types—misanthropic beliefs and interpersonal suspiciousness), college maladjustment, brooding, need for affection, ego inflation, and poignancy. The test measures dozens of other personality traits; I've only listed the ones for which I might register as abnormal.

should be preserved." I typically don't go for ceremonies, but who doesn't like a parade? I think I agree, but certainly not *strongly*. What choice do I have? "If plates are the least bit dirty, I feel too disgusted to eat." I do have standards, but I don't want to appear neurotic. I decide to *strongly disagree*. "I have disturbing thoughts that keep me awake at night." I've been an insomniac most of my life, and yes, *thoughts* keep me awake. Are they disturbing? Sometimes, otherwise they wouldn't keep me awake. I'm beginning to feel anxious. I can't respond to any of the statements without a full-scale debate, then I come across this: "I would feel out a decision over a long period of time rather than make a quick decision using logic and reason." Naturally, I can't decide how to respond.

Around me, the other trainees are turning in their exams. I am the last one finishing; even my brother is done. In a panic, I select *neutral* for the remaining statements. Afterward, Patrick says, "I think I figured out the pattern behind the questions," as if he's fooled the testers. But why would you have to fool the testers if you aren't insane?

Jack passes out loose-leaf binders that we use to follow his lessons on everything from radiation waste ("which is shipped to North Carolina to pay for schools for the children," he says proudly) to hazardous materials to industrial safety ("Do not drive a vehicle with inoperable brakes"). Periodically during his lectures, Jack says, "This is informational," which makes me wonder how *that* information is distinct from other information he conveys that somehow *isn't* informational.

Perhaps he is following procedure. Everything at the power plant must be done by an approved, numbered, catalogued Procedure written by the Procedure Writing Group. Complying with procedures is even a Procedure. For example, you might be required to *read* each step of a Procedure before proceeding. A second level allows you to merely *refer* to the Procedure, and the final level, subtitled "Information Use," allows you to perform an activity from memory. If a task cannot be done by the Procedure, you must initiate a Deviation Event Report. "I think of standard deviation as a gay person," Jack quips.

Next, we watch a film on hearing loss. A female narrator invites us into an Inner Ear, a small dim room with panels of buttons. The voice-over: "It's 7:05 a.m. Carl is about to enter a loud environment." Within seconds, Carl's ears fall off his head and plop on the floor like two shriveled apricots. A colleague picks up an ear and says, "I think you lost this!" I marvel; this is pedagogy.

The narrator explains the signs of hearing loss—tinnitus, a constant ringing in the ear—and the names of the inner ear bones, malleus, incus, stapes, like tiny gnomes with woodwind instruments making music out of air and vibrations in their orchestral chamber, the tympanic cavity. Aside from hearing loss, workers face other job hazards. We learn the difference between heat cramps, heat stress, and heatstroke. When the plant is operating, the temperature in the dome can reach 120 degrees Fahrenheit. We learn how to behave in confined spaces and how to prevent back injuries and electrical shock. We learn fire science, how *not* to start a fire, and of course, the Procedure for reporting a fire.

After several hours of reviewing occupational hazards, we learn about emergency evacuation. Naturally, the reasons for evacuation are categorized, beginning with NUE (notification of an unusual event), no release of radiation; an Alert, possible release of radiation; and a Site Area Emergency, during which a major function of the power plant fails. Topping the list is a General Emergency, when the core degrades, or "melts," as it did at Three Mile Island. (It was only *after* Three Mile Island that evacuation plans were required.) Jack outlines the evacuation route and I'm certain I could never escape. I'm not good with floor plans or dance steps, make Ys backwards, and sometimes mistake the letter F for the number five.

Jack gives us a quick rundown on bomb threats. If you happen to be the person who receives the threat, you are advised to ask the caller questions: *Where is the bomb? Why did you set the bomb? Are you part of some organization?* And my favorite: *What is your name?*

At the end of the day, we review the star system, not astronomically speaking, but acronymically. Stop. Think. Act. Review. We go over this endlessly until it becomes a bright shining constellation in our minds. "You wouldn't want to do something that would affect the configuration of the plant," Jack says. He gives an example involving a painter who hung up his jacket on an innocuous looking lever that turned out to be a switch that shut down a cooling pump. "He tripped the whole plant," Jack says, almost gleefully. Tripping the plant means that you do something that might cause the entire plant—a power source for New York City's subways, hospitals, police and fire stations, and rail lines—to cease operating.

Patrick and I find temporary housing at the U.S. Academy Motel in Highland Falls. Because of the hordes of out-of-state workers in town for the upcoming outage, this is the cheapest place we can find—$800 a month.[4] As the manager hands me the keys, I notice a box of petrified donuts on the counter and a perpetual motion machine, a contraption of balls and metal that moves back and forth mockingly. We have two rooms in our efficiency: a kitchen and bedroom. As Patrick and I walk through the kitchen, our shoes stick to the greasy linoleum so that each step we take sounds like Velcro being pulled apart. Near the stove, the linoleum buckles into a six-inch-high wavelet that I will trip over daily. The bedroom smells of toxic fibers from new carpet, and stale beer and cigarettes, but I don't dare open the jalousie windows, which are held in place by duct tape. The curtains, soiled and falling down, are pocked with cigarette burns, as are the bedspreads and furniture.

When I close the door to the bathroom, I see an insect exuvium in a tumbleweed of dust settled into the corner. I step in the shower stall and close the Plexiglass door, and a pink tile pops off the wall as if I have upset the building's structural integrity. I soon discover that the temperature of the water is completely unrelated to the position of the faucet. (In this hotel, there seems to be a shortage of *cold* water.) I attempt to adjust the scalding water throughout my shower anyway. All I require for sanity is the illusion of control.

At the Grand Union down the street, Patrick and I buy a rotisserie chicken, breakfast and lunch makings, and cleaning supplies. We sit on our beds eating plates of chicken dripping with grease, yet dry like jerky. We watch Homer Simpson spill coffee on the control panel at the Springfield nuclear power plant. *Jeopardy* follows, and this becomes our evening routine. After dinner, Patrick and I clean and scrub the efficiency, lay a bath mat in the shower stall. I'm amazed how a five-dollar-rubber mat and a can of Ajax can make me briefly cheerful. Uplifting, too, is Patrick's comment: "We've earned $200 already for doing practically nothing."

---

4. The plant is shut down every two and one-half to three years to replace spent fuel rods and complete repairs in "hot" areas. The outages draw hundreds of short-term workers, increasing Indian Point's employees from approximately eight hundred to about two thousand.

NEUTRONS, ELECTRONS, PROTONS

On the second day we take a health exam. Workers are lined up in a hall-way outside of the medical department, waiting to enter the waiting room in which only five people are allowed to wait. Those of us who enter thumb our noses at the rest in line as if admitted by a bouncer to a posh New York City nightclub. Inside, a technician escorts me to a bathroom where I attempt the anatomically improbable task of peeing into a tiny cup. My hands are wet with urine, as is the cup, but the water in the sink is shut off so that people cannot tamper with their samples. I dry the cup with a sinful amount of paper towels, worrying that the technician out-side the door is becoming suspicious. If you are suspected of foul play, you will be accompanied into the bathroom by a same-sex health department employee who will watch you pee.

Back in the classroom, Jack is discussing contamination. "You all know the movie where Cher was thrown into the shower," he says. Wasn't it Meryl Streep? Oh, what's the difference. We learn that radiation is a term for the energy that nearly all substances exude, and that indeed, radiation is floating around us, on land and in the heavens, in rocks and soil and building materials, from the sun and the stars, with levels increasing at higher altitudes. There is radiation in food, potassium specifically. Bananas have radiation. We study neutrons and electrons and protons, and I am back in sixth grade science class.[5] We learn what a Curie is (a measure of radioactive material) without learning about Marie, who coined the term "radioactive" a hundred years ago. Alpha radiation can be brushed off like dandruff. Beta penetrates your epidermis like lead paint. Neutron radia-tion penetrates skin and bones but, strangely, can be shielded by hydro-gen-rich substances: water and paraffin. Finally, there is gamma radiation, which can only be shielded by lead, steel, or concrete and water. Patrick and I are the only trainees furiously scribbling notes for the quizzes. We feel like geeks, but we can't help it; we've been to college.

We learn about the effects of radiation on the body, starting with a les-son in basic cell biology: nucleus, cytoplasm, membrane. "Man's gesta-tion period is nine months," Jack says, followed by words like mutation,

---

5. FIRST ATOM: "Hey, I lost an electron." SECOND ATOM: "Are you sure?" FIRST ATOM: "I'm positive!"

cell death, chromosomal damage. "Thirty-three percent of Americans will contract some form of cancer," he warns, assuring us that our chances of getting cancer from radiation exposure are "less than the chance of drawing an ace four times in a row from a full deck of cards." I've never been lucky at poker. Perhaps that bodes well.

Jack asks the class where on our bodies we might pick up radiation. People shout answers: hands, face, feet, arms. I raise my hand. I have something original to say. "If you're sitting down, you know, you might get some on you."

"You mean your butt?" Jack says. A big Italian man named Joe says, "I'll clean it off for her!" and the class howls. My brother smirks, not because Joe's comment is funny, but because we both know: I am an idiot.

RANDOM INSANITY

The next day, Jack mentions that a few people will be called to speak to the psychiatrist. He makes a big deal of insisting the names are randomly drawn, and then calls my name. I think: Interviewing *random* people would be an inefficient, scattershot approach to sleuthing around for nut jobs. I'm on to their ruse. I have been singled out based on some character flaw made glaringly obvious by the clever test, which my clever brother has managed to deceive. Standing in line in the hallway with two other possibly unbalanced people, I suddenly regret my checkered past, experimenting with an array of hallucinogens in high school, involvement in activist groups in college. In fact, background checkers from the Wackenhut Corporation have been busy digging up my past.[6] The application form (which asks you to list your aliases) requires six references—excluding family members—who have known you for five years and employment history. For ten years prior to this, I worked as a fund-raiser for environmental groups. Carol, one of my former coworkers, had this conversation with a Wackenhut investigator:

---

6. The Wackenhut Corporation operates in every state and fifty countries. Revenues for the most recent twelve-month period were $2.1 billion. Their investigations division promises to "utilize the latest approaches to tell you if you have employees who are stealing, using drugs, not doing their jobs, abusing authority, engaging in discrimination or sexual harassment, committing fraud—and who they are."

Wackenhut guy: "Can you provide a reference for Maureen Stanton?" Carol (in her lovely Scottish brogue): "Oh, Mo is the best development director we've ever had. She's excellent at strategic planning." Wackenhut guy: "How is she at parties?" Carol: "She's great with major donors and board members." Wackenhut guy: "When she goes to parties, does she drink a lot?" Carol (growing confused): "No, she doesn't drink a lot." Wackenhut guy: "Is she the kind of person who might take a bribe? To your knowledge, has she ever been addicted to drugs?"

I am summoned into an office to talk to the psychiatrist, a kindly looking, well-tailored older man behind a desk. "Do you know why you were selected?" he says. "No," I say, "but I'm pretty sure it wasn't random." He laughs, and explains that my test was kicked out because the responses that measure self-discipline fell outside the bell curve.

"Can you explain?" the psychiatrist says.

"I'm a writer," I say. "But nobody pays me to write, so I have to be disciplined with my limited time and resources." I tell him I am painting to make some quick money and because it doesn't tax me mentally. The shrink says his daughter, an artist, waitresses for the same reasons. My lucky day; he has not discovered my neuroses. Instead, we chat amicably for ten minutes, and smiling, he says, "Go on, get out of here. And get that book written!"

THE TRAILER WARREN

After five days of training, we are fingerprinted, photographed, and handed over to the contractors. From the training building, Patrick and I walk along a blacktopped strip that we think is a sidewalk until we notice bright yellow words stenciled on the asphalt: "Danger: High Voltage." We casually step off. Appearing not to be fools seems more pressing than possible electrocution. Down a fairly steep hill from the training center, a good eighth mile from the power plant, we come across a warren of trailers—contractor's offices—in the middle of which is a large corrugated aluminum building, like a rectangular Quonset hut.

The Quonset hut is divided into work areas for the insulators (industrial sewing machines and huge flat tables); the pipe fitters (welding stations cordoned off with translucent black sheeting), a shop for carpenters, and four small rooms for the painters. In the paint shack, each room is connected by huge swinging doors like those to a restaurant kitchen and lit by bare bulbs dangling from twenty-foot-high ceilings. The concrete floor is littered with cigarette butts, wrappers, and sandwich crusts.

The center room contains two Dumpster-sized gang boxes filled with brushes and rollers and sleeves and scrapers, and the desk of our general foreman, Arturo Castellanos, a quiet, fiftyish Peruvian with disarmingly attractive green eyes and a streak of white in his wavy black hair. Upon Arturo's desk is a large mirror with a plastic mock rococo frame to which he has taped newspaper photos of Mother Theresa, one with a large, blockletter caption: "Bless Her."

Patrick and I think we are about to paint, but alas, we must fill out employment paperwork for NPS.[7] Then we sit in the contractor's office and read through technical procedures collated in two four-inch-thick binders. We are given a full day and a half to do this, though nobody *reads* the procedures. Instead they slowly turn pages in a show of reading, and when the supervisor leaves, rest their heads on the table and sleep. We must sign off after "reading" each section, so I make a solid effort. This only lasts a half hour, though, because none of the information has anything whatsoever to do with my job.[8] I begin to despise the blue binders and the tedious procedures. I can find no information related to "coating," the euphemism for painting. I begin to flip pages without reading; I rest my head on the table; I long for a cigarette, though I don't smoke. Sitting in the trailer pretending to read those unreadable notebooks is torture, even at our base pay of $26.70 per hour. This requirement makes me wish for hard labor. Perhaps that is its true purpose.

ACTUAL WORK

Since my photo ID takes a few days to process, on my first day of actual work I am escorted by Hector, a middle-aged, paunchy yet suave

---

7. NPS's beneficiary form asks for "wife's name." I righteously cross out "wife" and write "spouse," though I have no name to scribble there.

8. For example, ISP 3.14, Revision O, Attachment 1, Title 5—1, 5.15.11 of the Electrical Work Practices and Procedures Book reads: "Intermediate voltage disconnecting potheads shall not be used to break or pick up load or to energize or de-energize feeder cable, feeder mains, transformers, regulators, or capacitators."

Argentinian. Hector has sole responsibility for my actions and must keep me in sight at all times. He must enter the power plant before me, exit behind me, and stand guard while I am in the ladies' room. (This is a written Procedure, of course.) That morning, Hector goes to the men's room and leaves me alone in the hallway with my bright green visitor badge. A manager passing by asks, "Where is your escort?" I point to the men's room. The man waits until Hector returns, scolds him, and informs us of the procedure for peeing if you are escorting someone of the opposite sex.[9]

Finally, my badge arrives and I am free to roam about the plant, feeling a bit giddy for the havoc I have the potential to create. A typical day goes something like this: We arrive around 5:45 a.m. and sit in the paint shack until 6:00 a.m., when we are officially on the clock. Then we get a fifteen minute break. When I ask everyone why we get a break *before* doing a lick of work, Angela, a thirteen-year veteran of Indian Point, says, "It's something the union negotiated."

En masse we walk down the hill to the plant, which is surrounded by a chain-link fence topped with a garland of razor wire. Across the Hudson, small but steep jagged mountains funnel the air, so it's often windy at the security entrance, where the plant, at sea level, dips its toes in the Hudson. The brackish river water is sucked into the plant's cooling system, then pumped downstream. Fish are channeled through a passageway and released into the river.

We enter the security building, pick up our badges and pass through an Explosive Detector and a metal detector.[10] We swipe our ID card

---

9. Hector must fill out a form to transfer me to a temporary escort, then reclaim me after. Security must fear that I, a possible subversive, will outwit Hector, locate the control room, and sabotage the plant. I must confess, every time I pass a panel of switches and knobs and flashing red buttons, I get an urge to reach out and push one.

10. Each employee steps into a portal and places her feet on two adhesive footprints—like those rubberized bathtub flowers popular years ago—and waits six seconds for a green light. This is a walk-through Explosive Vapor Detector, which operates twenty-four hours a day and can process six hundred people an hour. There are two at the security entrance. Three more will be added for the outage at a cost of about $350,000 per unit. Certain perfumes can cause the explosive detector to alarm. (A perfume can contain over a hun-

into a reader and punch in a PIN that unlocks a turnstile for eighteen seconds. We are warned: You must never let someone else pass through with you, though we find piggybacking is treated like a venial sin. Our first stop is the tool room to pick up disposable brushes and ear plugs, lime green miniature marshmallow-like foam bullets you squish into your ears to muffle the steady locomotive-like roar of the plant's huge turbines.

Except for the administration building, the plant is divided into elevation levels instead of floors, the highest being the 95 foot level inside the dome. The painters' staging area is on the 15 foot level, in a corner of a gymnasium-sized room that, except for walkways, is dense with pumps and valves and tangles of pipe of varying lengths and widths through which lubricants or boiling water and steam continuously pass.

At the staging area, we stand around waiting for Arturo to issue assignments, a process reminiscent of kids choosing up teams. In school, Patrick and I were either captains or chosen early, but here, to our dismay, we are routinely fingered last, along with the oldest painter, Henri Leblanc, a little French Canadian with white hair and pale blue eyes who looks like he is made of sky. Even his five o'clock shadow is pure white; he reminds me of angel food cake.

Once you get an assignment, you gather tools and paint, which takes another fifteen minutes.[11] By now, 7:00 a.m., we've been paid for an hour. At 9:00 a.m., we get a fifteen minute break. We paint until 11:30 a.m., then clean up for lunch. Lunch is officially thirty minutes, but by the time we pass through security and walk up the hill to the lunch trailers and repeat in reverse after, it's 1:00 p.m. We get our afternoon break at 2:30

---

dred ingredients, including acetophenone, also used in tear gas.) More sophisticated machines can differentiate benign substances. A Dualscan-85600 from Spyworld, Inc., can measure one part per trillion of an explosive vapor in the air. The increase in terrorist activity worldwide has spawned a competitive market for formerly classified explosive detecting technologies. One can order a Dualscan-85600 over the Internet.

11. Buckets, screens, rags, an assortment of brushes, rollers and sleeves, drop cloths, ladders, sandpaper, scrapers, drop lights and extension cords, dust pans and brushes, and bottles of Spray-Nine, an industrial cleaner, which, its label declares, kills HIV-1 virus.

p.m., then clean up for the day at 3:30 p.m. We punch out at 4:00 p.m. for a ten hour day, seven of which are actually spent painting.

THE LUNCH TRAILER

There is a politic to the lunch trailer that takes me a few days to intuit. The first morning, I boldly take a seat at a table toward the front of the crowded seventy-foot-long trailer, near the refrigerator and microwave and the bulletin board where employees pin flyers for pig roasts or used trucks. I'm sitting with a half-dozen sixtyish men. I notice a tacit unease and when I turn around, I see a fellow loitering behind me. He seems at a loss as to how to handle this strange woman who has taken *his* seat with *his* friends. For all I know, the man has been sitting in this seat since Indian Point's start-up in 1976. "Oh, this is your seat," I brilliantly surmise. "Keep it," the displaced man says unconvincingly.

"No, it's your place, I'll find another." I walk away as the man is razzed. *You're going to make the lady stand? Taking a seat from a woman. There's a real gentleman.* I cruise the alley between the columns of picnic tables in search of an empty seat. My objective is to blend, to *not* be noticed, a fairly impossible task if you are the only woman in a trailer of a hundred or so men, with the exception of Pamela Anderson Lee, who's on a five-by-seven-inch postcard strung to the ceiling, and the many nameless naked women on the walls at the far end of the trailer, one whose legs are spread and who has a coke bottle inserted into her vagina. (To the credit of some manager, this photo is removed quickly, but Pamela Lee remains, floating and swaying above our heads like a busty angel.)

My subsequent lunchroom blunder is not as bad, but only because there are no witnesses. I pause strategically and scan for empty tables. Joy! A vacant spot. I unpack my lunch and take a bite of egg, then realize I am sitting directly across from Floyd Grabowski and he is, in fact, the reason the table is empty. Floyd heralds my presence with a trumpeting of his large rubious nose, the contents of which he issues into a hanky, momentarily studies, and then stores in his back pocket. The nose blowing precipitates a tuberculoid coughing fit that generates expellations of a substance I have heard called "lung butter."

I examine Floyd, a man whose lifelong project of ruining his body is in its final stages. At six-foot-three and probably four hundred pounds, Floyd is the oldest Grabowski brother working at the plant, Duane and Earl being the other two. Together they weigh half a ton; there are bridges I imagine they cannot cross in unison, elevators they must take turns riding. Floyd's head, a good thirty-pounder, rests on a goitrous collar of flesh. He has a cartograph of veinlets on the landscape of his enormous face with an alcoholic's ruddy, hamburger-like complexion and red, watery eyes beneath which are puffy aprons of skin. I studiously avoid lunching with Floyd again, but a bond has been established between us, and we smile and nod whenever we pass each other. We are alike, Floyd and I: the ogled, the joked about, the outsiders.

Once a week after lunch we have a "tailgate," a meeting of all hands at which a manager reads to us from *Fatal Facts*, a publication of the U.S. Department of Labor. One day we hear of a worker who slipped on icy scaffolding and fell to his death. Another day this article:

> A crew of ironworkers and a crane operator were unloading a 20-ton steel slab from a low-boy trailer using a 50-ton crawler crane with 90-foot lattice boom. The operator was inexperienced on this crane and did not know the length of the boom. Further, no one had determined the load radius. During lifting, the load moved forward and to the right. The boom twisted under the load, swinging down, under, and to the right. Two employees standing 30 feet away apparently saw the boom begin to swing and ran. The boom struck one of the employees—an ironworker—on the head, causing instant death. Wire rope struck the other—a management trainee—causing internal injuries. He died two hours later at a local hospital.

The article is accompanied by a line drawing of the crane and outlines of the two bodies. Safety talks usually have a theme such as proper lifting or ladder safety, though one day a manager announces, "A woman jumped off the Bear Mountain Bridge, but they haven't found her body yet, so if you're down by the water you might keep your eye out for anything unusual." Different managers give the talks, so occasionally there is repetition. The week before Christmas, I heard the same memo three times, which I recall because of this curious advice: "Keep dangerous objects away from children—guns, knives, and ornaments."

From day to day, we don't know what our assignments will be. Usually, Arturo will say something like, "Get some black and follow me."[12] He'll point to a machine or pipes we are to paint and in the way of nuance, say, "Don't go crazy." Work is confusing at first. Some days we are told to "stretch" the job, and other days we move at a frenzied pace. Days we paint floors are hectic; pot-time for floor epoxy is forty-five minutes so we must move quickly before the paint hardens. My job one morning is to "cut in" which means that I must crab walk under pipes and machines to paint the juncture where the floor meets the wall. Once Part A and Part B of the floor epoxy are blended with a huge electric mixer, I spider along the base of the wall in a space about two feet high, inhaling vapors, sweating in stiff polyester coveralls, trying to stay ahead of Hector "rolling out" the floor. We finish the job and post "Wet Paint" signs and signs that read "Fumes: Do Not Linger," cordon off the area with caution tape, wash brushes, dispose of cans and thinners, and clean up in time for lunch.

After lunch that day, Patrick and I are assigned to paint a living room–sized section of floor underneath a snarl of pipes on the 15 foot level. Patrick gets a shop vac to prep the area. My job is holding the cord. I decide I've had enough of the "girl" jobs (sweeping, scraping, opening cans), so I untie a second shop vac.[13] My idea is to work twice as fast. (It takes Patrick and me a while to realize that this is *not* the *modus operandi*. We must pace ourselves to neither appear idle nor out-perform our fellow

---

12. Or Authority Green, Alaska Blue, Spectrum Yellow, Dark Red, Albert Orange. I often wondered about the Albert in Albert Orange. When I called the paint manufacturer, Keeler and Long, a representative said, "Do you mean *Alert* Orange?" though he admitted that they name colors specifically for Indian Point, so the label could have been a joke on some employee named Albert. "That happens," he said, "or it could have been a misprint." Now I wonder: Was it a misprint, or was it I who was not too albert when reading the can?

13. Equipment is tied down in case of an earthquake. The plant is designed to withstand a quake with a magnitude of 7.0 on the Modified Mercalli Scale (difficult to stand, hanging objects quiver). The largest quake in the vicinity of the plant was in October 1985, a 4.0 on the mms (standing automobiles rocked, windows rattled).

workers. "Slow down," Hector says to me one day. "You'll paint yourself out of a job.")

I plug in my vacuum cleaner but it doesn't start, and now Patrick's vacuum has quit. Turns out, I've blown a circuit. Strange, I muse. In a power plant that generates enough electricity to send commuter trains careening past the Bronx and sixty miles to Poughkeepsie every ten minutes, I can't run two vacuums off one outlet. Now Patrick and I must use a tiny house type vacuum cleaner plugged into a distant outlet, trailing an extension cord one hundred feet, thus creating a tripping hazard.

For the "plant beautification project," we paint everything: pipes and valves and snubber attachments; channel iron, angle iron, and electrical boxes; pumps and floors and walls. "Don't stand still or they'll paint you!" workers joke daily. The crew of forty painters is an anomaly, the multi-million-dollar beautification project a rare expenditure.[14] We paint pipes large enough to crawl through in the Rock Room, a subterranean grotto resembling the Bat Cave, its granite walls graffitied with dates and initials (I add mine). Patrick and I paint fist-sized bolts and flanges in the Zurn pit, a strange small cell we must swipe our badges to enter. We paint floors in the Havoc room, the Iodine Labyrinth Room, the Water Factory, the Polisher Building. One morning I paint dozens of valves of various sizes —silver dollars to dinner plates—bright orange like blooming flowers; they're almost pretty.

For a week, I paint in the electrical tunnel—a long winding corridor so narrow you can't help but rub bellies when you pass a coworker. It's windowless and dimly lit, but cool and quiet, relief from the constant thundering of the turbines. Various widths of piping run along the walls of the tunnel in between racks that house sprinkler spigots that we must prime, being extremely careful not to paint any moving parts, a serious transgression that could prevent the system from functioning. Hector painted a moving part once, which earned him a Deviation Event Report. The morning after, Arturo gathered all the painters and one by one we filed past Hector's besmirched slide bolt.

---

14. Shortly after my employment, the New York Power Authority sold Indian Point III to Entergy, a private energy company based in New Orleans, for $967 million, the highest purchase price of a nuclear asset in the industry to date. The plant was the largest single asset of the State of New York.

For two weeks Patrick and I are assigned to the Pump House, a small brick building atop a hill, inside the chain link fence but outside the main building, perched next to two water tanks three stories tall. Here we are sequestered, scraping floors and washing grime off the pumps before painting. To get hot water for cleaning, I must carry two buckets a hundred yards down the hill into the Primary Auxiliary Building (an oxymoron, I point out to a group of coworkers, who stare blankly), and fill the buckets from the showers in the ladies locker room inside the plant—the closest source of running water—then schlep the buckets back up the hill. In the building that houses the pumps necessary to extinguish fires should the core melt, I cannot fill a bucket of water to mop the floor.

LADY PAINTERS

After two months, Patrick, my confrere, trades his blue hard hat for the white ones worn by management, working as a materials expediter.[15] (Every time he passes the painters, they taunt him about the white hard hat.) So I am partnered with Angela, and thereafter we are referred to by our fellow workers as the "lady painters." My friendship with Angela develops slowly, in fifteen-minute increments sitting in the women's locker room before work. "It's been seven years since I took a punch in the face," she tells me our first day together. My chest goes numb imagining someone slamming his knuckles into Angela's heart-shaped, intelligent face, pretty despite a faint patina of *tristesse*. Angela broke the mold in the early '80s when women in the trades were more rare, enduring daily crucibles like a foreman assigning her to move fifty cans of paint from one side of the room to the other, then back again. Angela is a foreman now, though not immune to mistreatment.

One day, the union representative, Leo Lacognata, is discussing the sexual harassment policy with some workers—joking about the "three-foot rule." Leo turns and bear-hugs Angela. "Hey, is this three feet? Is this sexual harassment?" he says, pinning her against the building. Angela laughs as she pushes Leo off, trying to be a good sport. The men laugh. It's

15. Daily, Patrick must face surly construction supervisors demanding supplies. There is pressure to complete jobs on time, especially during the outage when the plant loses nearly a million dollars a day in revenue.

all a big joke, like when Leo positioned himself behind his young secretary bent over a desk and mock-humped her.

Shortly after, a manager announces at a tailgate meeting that the sexual harassment policy will be posted on the bulletin board. Angela asks him why the policy isn't distributed.

"If I hand them out, they'll just throw them away. If I read it, they'll fall asleep."

"So you'll wait for a lawsuit before you'll do anything?" Angela asks.

"Yes," the manager says.

The New York Power Authority, which owns Indian Point and eleven other power plants in the state, treats sexual harassment more seriously than NPS. When the secretaries complain about the stares and catcalls from construction workers on break in the plant cafeteria, a wall of green tarpaulins is erected to shield the women, a kind of crude containment.

ZOOMIES

A blue inflatable hard hat the size of a Volkswagen appears one day at the plant entrance blazoning the start of the refueling outage as it bobbles in the breeze. That morning, Bob Barrett, the highest ranking executive on site, pep talks employees. "It's been 342 days since our last Human Performance," he says. He means Human Performance *Error*. A running tab of days without a Human Performance Error is tallied on a dry-erase board in the cafeteria. But his *faux pas* characterizes the atmosphere inside the plant while it's operating; you don't see many people working, *per se*, aside from the janitorial staff. There are no lines of workers assembling motherboards, or mechanical arms and robots fabricating widgets. Energy, the plant's product, is invisible.

Occasionally men in ties with immaculate white hard hats pass through the plant, bigwigs from the New York Power Authority or inspectors from the Nuclear Regulatory Commission. They always smile at me. It seems to warm their hearts to see a woman in the trades, as if they are responsible for the laudable diversity that I represent. Or maybe they are amused by my too big overalls and slipping-down safety glasses (protective apparel is often unavailable in small enough sizes). Or perhaps those clean, tall executives were smiling because they saw me on the day I painted a railing and then promptly leaned against it, yellow stripes across my backside broadcasting my blunder.

When the outage is scheduled to start, plant capacity is gradually reduced to ninety percent, then seventy percent, and so on. One day I arrive and it's quiet and eerie like the hour after the villagers have slain a terrible groaning dragon. After four months of adjusting to the roar of the turbines, the awesome silence seems disturbing and wrong, yet a welcome relief. We can talk in normal voices. We can remove the miniature marsh-mallows from our ears. And now workers are everywhere: hundreds of construction workers, engineers, Health Physics workers who staff control points, and nuclear cleanup crews, a coterie of out-of-staters who travel between nuclear power plants during outages.

Angela and I switch to the night shift, 7:00 p.m. to 3:00 a.m., which is less hectic and cooler, especially as we work mostly in Radiologically Controlled Areas, "controlled" being the operative word. To enter a Radiologically Controlled Area, you must stop at a control point and pick up a Self-Reading Pocket Dosimeter, which resembles a small pen flash-light. When held up to a light, a hairline needle shows how many milli-rems of radiation you've picked up, known to workers as zoomies.[16] Next, a Health Physic hands you a ThermoLuminescent Dosimeter (TLD), assigned to you by a five-digit code. Roughly the size of a microcassette, the TLD clips onto your clothing and keeps a cumulative count of gam-ma (whole body) and beta (skin exposure) radiation.

You scan your badge into a small keypad, enter your social security number, the work permit number, the baseline reading on your pock-et dosimeter, and hit a "yes" button when the keypad screen asks you if you've read the work order, whether you have or not. You push through a revolving gate into a long, winding hall, ascend several sets of stairs, and access locked steel fire doors, a sequence akin to Agent 86 entering the headquarters of Control in the opening sequence of *Get Smart*.

Entering a Radiologically Controlled Area is like being in the lobby of a bank; penetrating Vessel Containment, the dome, is breaking into

---

16. A millirem is a measure of the biological effects of radiation absorbed in human tissue, or greatly simplified, dose. The maximum allowable Total Whole Body Dose at the plant is 1,500 millirems—less than the Nuclear Regulatory Commission's ceiling of 5,000. An average American might pick up 400 or so millirems a year from "background" radiation (rocks, soil, sun, foods, consumer products).

the vault—a steel-lined, four- to ten-foot-thick concrete shell purportedly strong enough to withstand the impact of a 727 jetliner. The reactor inside the dome is further shielded by a seven- to twelve-inch-thick carbon steel barrier. It's behind that shield that the nuclei of uranium atoms are splitting and splitting and splitting, like dominos falling, in a controlled chain reaction. It is there that the dragon is harnessed, where the Lilliputians have strung up Gulliver. A controlled chain reaction seems as oxymoronic as a beautiful nuclear power plant.

To access the dome, add to your gear a half-face respirator and a Merlin Gerin Alarming Electronic Dosimeter, which, at the push of a button, gives a digital readout of radiation dose. At a second control point, you don protective clothing, enter more codes, and unlock more turnstiles and steel doors. Finally, you step into what looks like the antechamber of a submarine, an air-locked passageway with heavy steel doors at either end that a helmsman-like employee opens and closes by slowly cranking a giant metal steering wheel, Charon ferrying souls across the river Styx. You walk up a set of stairs and there you are, staring up at a ceiling that looks, perhaps, like the Sistine Chapel before Michelangelo's paint job, bowl-like, blank except for huge flakes of cream-colored paint threatening to flutter down.

Our goal is to locate the site we are to paint and work quickly to minimize radiation exposure. Angela is a genius at locating the job sites on the work order, finding the right sections within the dome, which has several levels below the 95 foot and a labyrinth of hallways and concrete sarcophagi-like cubbyholes. One night we paint a small crane the height of a giraffe that stands on three gangly legs. A young pipe fitter says to me, "I see you got that thing all painted and looking beautiful."

"I wouldn't exactly call it beautiful," I reply. After all, we're surrounded by steel and concrete.

"*I* think it's beautiful," the pipe fitter says.

"Beauty is in the eye of the beholder," I say. I envy his ability to see pleasing images where I see ugliness, but after a few weeks of working in the dome, I too see a kind of beauty: The curve of the ceiling is smooth and sensual; the rectangular tank in the middle of the floor, slightly smaller than a backyard swimming pool, is filled with absolutely clear turquoise-hued water that cools the zirconium rods filled with uranium pellets. The water is perfectly still and deep, calming. The giant forty-foot crane that rotates every so often on a groove that circumnavigates the floor is enormous and powerful. Size impresses. I'm a person who dreams of living in a modest hut in Maine, but I can't help being awed by the grandeur of the power plant and its workings.

Or maybe it's the lure of danger that appeals to me, though the *mis-en-scene* inside the dome is more surreal than perilous: workers in silly looking, oversized yellow rubber boots, yellow surgeon caps, elbow-length rubber gloves, and slack white jumpsuits, faces the only visible skin, like Teletubbies. A constant metronomical beeping, like an EKG monitor or a submarine radar detector, creates a sense of encapsulation, free-floating twenty thousand leagues under the sea or lost in space. You can forget that land is just outside.

Outside, workers stroll around the cafeteria or the smoking area in shorts and muscle shirts, breeding a peculiar intimacy. Hairy bodies, pale flesh, flabby arms, bow legs, callused knees, freckled shoulders, birthmarks; we know each other a little better now, though not by name.

TRANSMOGRIFICATION

I learn more about physics from painting than I recall from my high school course: gravity, friction, viscosity. Different paints have different properties. "Watch out for the red," Angela says to me. "It walks." Like no other color, red appears everywhere you don't want it to be. Before I leave the gang box one day, I have dribbled red paint on the floor, stepped in it, trailed footsteps like telltale blood stains. That day Angela and I paint steel fire doors. The paint, no matter how thinly I apply it, puddles. I push and drag with my brush and roller, but the paint gathers itself and drips again. I wipe, brush, dab. "The paint is cold," Angela says, but I know it's a poor worker who blames her equipment.

In painting, you are attempting the impossible, trying to control or defy the substance's natural property: flow. It's a somewhat ridiculous endeavor, but satisfying when you succeed. Transformation by paint is immediate. Paint beautifies. Paint redeems. It cleans and camouflages and lies. I am never as fast as the fastest painters, but after several months I can flick my wrist in one fluid motion to create a perfect arc around a doorknob. Painting becomes a meditation, a quiet, steady motion that I get lost in, a wide-open space where I can think and dream, lying under a ganglion of pipes with a bucket of Alaska Blue. Painters call missed spots "holidays," as if you were absent while painting. It's the right word. Hypnotized by the repetitive act of brushing or rolling, your body takes over, your mind checks out. You're split in half as neatly as the nucleus of an atom.

My original plan was to work two months and pocket a few thousand, but I become addicted to the money, drawn into the plant like a fish from the Hudson. I adapt easily to different environments, a beneficial survival trait perhaps, but it means that I settle or rise to the environment around me. I begin to change on a cellular level, transmogrify into a creature I only half recognize. After two months I can lift hundred-pound bags of coal sand for the sandblast machine. I feel strong and agile crawling behind Angela on scaffolding and underneath pipes, in tight, dark corners, somehow forgetting about my fear of heights *and* confined spaces.

On break, I take puffs from Angela's cigarette, one of those feminine brands, long and thin, with a purple logo. The lure of blowing hot sluggish streams of smoke, something to do between assignments, to squelch the boredom, is overwhelming. There's a natural bond among the smokers: the raw addiction to nicotine; the quasi-sexual pleasure of sucking; the perception of being outré, banished from the air-conditioned cafeteria, corralled outside by an arbitrary yellow line; the fearlessness of mocking emphysema and cancer. One wants to be part of this group.

I begin to wear makeup, investing in a stock that is valued here: conventional femininity. When some guy makes a flip remark, I retort hastily instead of blushing. I stop using words that nobody understands, like *oxymoron*. The foreman, Arturo, observes, "You know a lot more than these guys, but you don't use it to belittle them. That's power." Restraint is power. Control. But that's an illusion. I've lost control. The half-life of this job is already longer than I imagined, and there's work for a small crew for months to come, years maybe. I keep postponing my end-date a week at a time to collect another fat paycheck. The problem is, I haven't written anything in months. I am a painter, I fear, no longer a writer.

Finally, I select a date to quit—my six month milestone—and stick to it.[17] On my last night, after my terminal body count for radiation, before I have punched out for the final time, Hector decorates my jeans Jackson

---

17. Patrick, having greater responsibility as a manager, sticks it out for another two months until the outage and his position officially end.

Pollock—style. He flicks blue and red across my pants, splashes yellow and white as I rotate, then brown and sea foam green. He dips a brush into aluminum paint, which has a consistency similar to mercury (it wiggles), and spatters the canvas of my clothing using his brush like a magic wand. I drive through the security gate, past the giant hard hat now half-sunk and barely recognizable, arrive home at 4:00 a.m., and fall into bed. The next morning, I discover that the epoxy has bled through my clothes. Splotches of blue and red, and faint yellow spots like old bruises stain my thighs. There's a patch of white in my hair that prematurely ages me, and on my arms, I have shiny, shimmering silver freckles.

Deborah Peterson Swift

Ballouville

It is through a post office window that Joan Gosselin beholds life in Ballou-ville. Dozens of times a day, her gaze is coaxed by the slam of a car door or the fleeting glimpse of a figure passing by. Handing out mail, she provides a symphony of small talk with choruses that echo throughout the day.

The Australian Laughing Thrush wails, the orange-beaked Zebra finches twitter and the fish tank filters bubble.

Everyone who lives in Ballouville—all 110 post office box holders—is bound to pass through Arthur Berube's pet store sooner or later. They have to if they want their mail from Gosselin.

So suffice it to say, Berube and Gosselin know quite a bit about every-one in town.

Today, the two are engaged in a gentle debate within the paneled walls of the tiny post office in this village, bisected by the picturesque Five Mile River.

Even on the busiest days, when a truck brings in fresh fish for the pet store or Social Security checks roll in, their jobs leave plenty of time for idle chatter. Still, it is obvious that this is not a topic that has crossed their counters before.

"Do you think people in Ballouville are poor?" the gentle-spoken Berube turns to Gosselin and asks.

He poses the question in a way that says he cannot believe there could be any answer but "no."

"You don't know the debt they have behind those envelopes," says Gosselin, who knows more than she is telling Berube at this moment.

Berube shrugs his shoulders and goes back to work.

The Hartfords and New Havens have not cornered the market on pov-erty in a state that is defined by its wealth.

Nine of the fifteen poorest communities in Connecticut have populations under twenty thousand, by some estimates. Eastern Connecticut has more than its fair share, with several towns poorer than Bridgeport, when measured by the personal income of their residents. The town of Killingly, hard against the Rhode Island border and home to Ballouville, is among them. And, residents here are losing ground. In 1991, the average Ballouville resident was earning about 48 percent of the state average, but seven years later, in 1998, that number had dropped even further, to 45 percent, IRS figures show.

"We call it poverty with a view," quips David Shumway, who is reminded daily that the northeast corner is a distant runner in today's sophisticated economic race. Now, as that so-called New Economy struggles to fend off a national recession and deal with the aftermath of the September 11 terrorist attacks in New York and Washington, Shumway fears that places like Ballouville will be among the first to lose their tenuous place-markers. Even in the height of the prosperous times during a single month in the summer of two thousand, his homeless shelter in the Danielson section of Killingly turned away eighty people because no beds were available. A year earlier for the same period, just five people were shut out. More and more, the people who do stay there have jobs.

Killingly is the industrial anchor of a predominantly rural county and has attracted new companies as the stalwart industries have departed. The region's average wages in July were the lowest in the state, however, and its unemployment rate was Connecticut's third highest, state labor department figures show. One-third of Killingly residents have no high school diploma, the town's dropout rate is nearly twice the state average and about thirteen percent of all births are to teenage mothers. Windham County has the highest percentage of asthma cases among children in the state, and there is but one dentist in the entire county who accepts Medicaid patients.

To tell the easily overlooked story of the rural working poor in a state of breathtaking wealth, *The Courant* visited Ballouville over the past year. Here, in one of the state's poorest villages, the average resident makes about fourteen thousand dollars annually, about forty-five percent of Connecticut's average, the IRS estimates.

In this section of Killingly there is a woman who can't stand long enough to grocery shop because her body is beaten down from a lifetime of cleaning houses.

There is a man who lost a leg at seventeen who stays up some nights thinking about how his life would have changed if only he had gotten that fifth number right on the Power Ball. With four correct numbers, he called the local IGA and made the clerk check how much he would have won—it was one hundred thousand dollars. What could have been. He has not been out to dinner in years. Once in awhile, his wife gets the two of them takeout fish and chips at the Golden Greek restaurant. Even then, they split an order.

There is one church, a Catholic one, that sees more funerals than weddings and only partly because it does not have a middle aisle, as most brides prefer. The other choice for weddings is a chapel up the road that is tucked behind a showroom for tombstones. It is run by the local gravedigger, Mervin Whipple, whose Christmas village has made the area famous.

The eighty-year-old priest, Sylva LeCours, has never uttered a word about money from the pulpit in the eighteen years he has preached at the Church of St. Anne.

"I feel that they have always been generous. You see, they're giving, as far as I can see, to the best of their ability."

One of those people is Lisa Bates. She has been dusting, vacuuming, and mopping the church every week for free for nearly twenty years, since she was nine.

The church is too strapped to hire a sexton or any staff. White-haired volunteers count the Sunday collection money, bill by bill, on LeCours' dining room table. Another volunteer writes the newsletter.

Across the street from the church, close enough so that they hear the amplified conversations of teenagers who hang out in the parking lot after supper, a couple paid less for their house than some people pay for an SUV—thirty-five thousand dollars. It's a duplex.

Edward Berube, the son of the aquarium owner, works the overnight shift, earning $8.42 an hour cleaning the bathrooms at the Mohegan Sun casino. Luckily his wife makes good money—almost eleven dollars an hour—at Wal-Mart, and his father gives him a break on the rent for his apartment. He is counting on his coin collection to finance his retirement. "I don't trust the stock market. At least I know the coins, they increase in value."

The younger Berube has worked since he dropped out of school at sixteen, but for the setbacks caused by back injuries and the closing of a curtain factory. He resists retraining programs and urgings from workers' compensation insurers to go back to school and learn a skill that would save his back.

He has never gone away on a vacation. He hopes to take his first this year with his second wife to Niagara Falls.

He is forty-seven.

Another resident had his remaining eleven rotting teeth removed and decided he'd be better off without them when he learned the cost of getting false ones. The only food he misses is corn on the cob.

He is fifty-four.

Yet, ask the residents of Ballouville if they are poor, and they turn as incredulous as Berube and his son. They are as accustomed to their thrifty lifestyles as they are to passing through a pet store to get their mail.

We get by. We are lucky. Wealth is not measured in quantity of dollars. You are only as poor as you choose to be.

Everyone has an answer to prove you wrong.

Masters of disguise, their numbers are hard to measure. They have jobs—there are plenty of jobs. Gosselin, at the post office, can name only three work-aged residents who do not work. They earn more money than the official poverty level, and because they live in areas with clean-running streams, deep green forests and neighbors who don't lock their doors, they do not associate themselves with the crime-ridden poverty they see portrayed on television.

"It's different than people hanging out of windows in the city," says Joan Macneil, director of outreach services at Quinnebaug Valley Community College in Killingly. "They still get out in the fresh air, they feel safe," she says. "They go without a lot. They learn to cope without it. It's not easy. They'd like to have those things," she says. "They just don't see themselves as what they see on TV as being poor."

The rural working poor are the ones who collect soda cans, survive on wood heat, fix a car for a buddy, cut firewood and work seven days a week before they will ask for help. They are the ones who figure out how to get by. They get rides from friends, drop off their children with their mothers, sleep on floors and drive big, awkward cars.

Poor is for city folk, who can't or don't want to work.

They disdain welfare and tell stories of pushing through their injuries to stay on the job. Still it is hard to find anyone in Ballouville who has not pulled a muscle, torn a rotator cuff, or destroyed a disc.

They are not perfect. Some use plastic to spend more money than they have. Some have been handcuffed, sold drugs, drank themselves into oblivion, divorced, had more children than they can afford.

But they are proud. They are proud of their jobs, proud of themselves, proud of their homes, proud of what little they have.

They manufacture buttons, bake hamburger rolls for fast-food chains, load Staples office furniture onto pallets, and pack bags of Doritos into cardboard boxes. They clean homes and unload trucks at Wal-Mart.

They do not want your sympathy.

MILL RATS

"It all comes for free. It all burns the same."

It's the early 1950s, and John Grobofski is a lanky sixteen-year-old but his arms do not tire easily as he pushes a broom across the oil-soaked pine floors at William Pryms Inc. The reckless summer days he spent swimming up a factory spillway running along his Ballouville backyard have made his skinny arms strong.

Water has been the lifeblood of his hometown's economy, and with so many rivers and streams pumping through its veins, Killingly benefited early from America's industrial revolution.

But the straight pins and other debris that slip underneath the stiff brushes of young John's broom attest to another revolution. The wool and cotton mills that built entire communities in Connecticut's northeast corner are leaving, and the days are passing when villages, like today's sports arenas, are named after textile companies. Curtaintown, USA, is in trouble.

Otherwise John would be on the second floor of the two-room Ballouville School instead of starting his factory career as third boy, about the lowest you can go.

His parents lost their jobs on a late summer day, when the sun tires early in the evening and thoughts darken toward the winter to come.

Sewing notions, not textiles, push the factory where John is working to help bring home the family income. But capitalism has never made concessions based on the trite notion that one generation should be spared the cruel fate of the previous one.

John and Elise. Elise and John. One name is rarely spoken without the other. In 1959 they are newlyweds but two years when Elsie gets a job at Pryms, too. She is an inspector.

The whispers spread from machine to machine like a fast-moving game of telephone. How could this work out, a wife telling her husband what to do? How will he react when she tells him that the holes in the square snaps are misaligned. The round ones are meant to be sewn on by hand, so they can be a little off, but if a square one is imprecise, it will break a sewing machine needle.

We never had no problem. She had her job, and I had mine.

John had his moments (every husband in every marriage does), but that had more to do with his special coffee and a late-night poker game than quality control.

How firm his arms are, bulking out of his short sleeves and wrapped around his daughter at the company picnic in 1965.

John and Elise's two kids, a boy and a girl, are nearly on top of their parents, as the photographer snaps the group shot. Later that blond boy will have to learn to live without an eye. When he grows up, he, too, will work at Pryms. One day on his regular shift a straight pin propels into his eye, head-on. He wasn't wearing safety glasses. Few workers did.

Now his back is wasted. It's the only time John Sr. swears in front of a lady. "He can't [expletive] walk." All this lost to the company.

But it's a good company.

"Nobody realized how good a job we had, till we had to go work somewhere else," John says.

The couple has no problem paying the twenty dollars weekly rent to John's parents, who live in the other side of the duplex.

They frame their twenty-five-year certificates from Pryms and hang them on either side of their wedding photo above the boxy contraption that helps heat the twelve rooms.

John talks about buying a furnace. The 1820 house has never had one nor any central heating system. Why bother? Elsie reasons. "We get by good without it."

By now, word has spread. Anyone who tears down a barn, yanks out a staircase or gives up on regluing the leg of a stool for the umpteenth time can toss the wooden waste in John's side yard. Pallets, two-by-fours, even doors, are haplessly tossed onto the impressive mound. The junk fuels the imaginations of the neighborhood kids who have assembled its pieces into bike ramps, backstops, forts.

For John it is simply fuel.

"It all comes for free," John says. "It all burns the same."

That is how John's house has always been heated, by someone else's throwaways.

We get by good.

By the late '80s, John and Elsie are at the top of their games—he was union president, loan officer for the credit union, mechanic; she continued to call the shots as an inspector.

But the lines they are running churn out relics. Zippers took a bite out of the snap business. And, cloth-covered belt buckles? When was the last time you saw a belt on a lady's dress?

The trail to cheap labor in the South is well-worn by 1990, and Pryms has no trouble following it. The company purchases a South Carolina sewing distributor in a last grab for a market that suffers as working women shove their Singers into closets. Pryms closes its doors and John and Elsie are laid off.

Once a monument to possibilities: first to wool production, and then to mill reuse, the factory is now a giant brick tomb, its shattered windows an epitaph to the death of manufacturing jobs.

John tosses slabs of the factory's sturdy pine floor into the bed of his pickup truck. He spent thirty-six years working that factory floor.

But how could he follow Pryms South? This is the only house he had ever known. His mother is fading. Alzheimer's is coming on, and pretty soon they will have to cover all the mirrors in the house to keep her from arguing with her reflection.

Alzheimer's, that's a helluva a disease.

This was her house. It is where she set the pies on the kitchen sill to cool. The men from the Ballouville curtain mill outside the back window would pause to sniff the air and know that Whoopie's wife was baking again. Thursday was pie day. Apple, blueberry, peach, and custard. Friday was cake day for Sunday dinner.

Now, Whoopie is gone, and it is John's turn to support the family.

Again.

You do what you have to do.

Plus, whom is he kidding? He is over fifty. There would be new machines, and he would need retraining. The company would save that for the young, ripe and fresh for the picking.

John Jr. does go South in 1990 with twenty-one other workers, bad eye and all. He has his kids to think about. Five back surgeries would follow young John, and Pryms would shut down its manufacturing in South Carolina seven years later anyway.

John wishes he could retire. He and Elsie have saved plenty. About one hundred dollars a week. They have enough money to buy vehicles and give loans to their grandchildren, but other numbers weren't adding up. How could he shell out $850 a month for health insurance? That was damn near half of his gross monthly income when he was working.

There would be Elsie's cancer to pay for. How many times, years later, would he sit at the kitchen table, the only light of the afternoon, a prayer candle always burning for Elsie atop the hot water heater and thank God for that insurance. But, until he gets a new job, the couple is taking a chance, and living without medical coverage.

Months pass, and John finds temporary work, carting and sorting construction debris. John hopes the guy will give him permanent work. He is making two hundred dollars a week. John was also free to cart away truckloads of soda and beer cans and pocket the return deposits.

When the woman at the credit union wonders aloud how he manages to keep producing the car loan payment, "I said don't worry about it, every time I need clothes I go down with the returnables."

The permanent job never pans out.

His mother moves over to their side of the house. They can't afford a nursing home. Instead of looking for another job, Elsie will stay home and take care of her mother-in-law.

John makes the rounds within a forty-mile radius in search of a job. His mother always wants to come along for the ride. Elsie comes, too. He goes to one company seventeen times.

Seventeen times.

We'll call you. We'll call you.

The secretary puts him off.

Finally John corners the personnel manager when he is unshielded by his secretary. John doesn't want to do it, but he is mad. There's Elsie and his mother, waiting in the car.

He needs money. But, even more than that, he needs a job. A working man needs a job.

"I pinned his ears right to the wall."

"He said, 'You want a job?'"

"And I said, 'Yeah, I want to come to the door everyday and look at you.'"

"I was nasty."

"I said you told me 'no' seventeen times, I know what the problem is, I'm fifty-five going on fifty-six years old. You want to discriminate? I'm not going to argue with you. Monday morning I'm going down and sign an age discrimination complaint."

John gets the job, but he is laid off before his health benefits kick in.

He fills out more applications, and pretty soon he starts lying when he reaches the section about injuries. At first, he told the truth.

John Grobofski is a man of integrity.

Then he fails a company physical when he tells the nurse he once had back surgery. Give him a chance, they will see . . .

"Next patient."

That is the end of honesty. There is nothing to lose, he figures. He doesn't have a job anyway. It takes a year and a half, but in early 1992, John finally gets a permanent job at U.S. Button Corp. in Putnam. He is making half of what he was earning at Pryms: $6.50 an hour.

He is doing the shake and bake.

Every minute or so, a tray about the size of a cookie sheet fills with "pills"—plastic tablets, essentially. Each tray has from 175 to 300 holes. For some trays, John has precisely twenty-eight seconds to lift the tray and roll the pills around until at least ninety percent of the holes are filled, like marbles on a Chinese checkers board.

For the three hundred holes, he gets two minutes. Then he places the tray under the press. Whump. It flattens the pills into buttons and punches them with holes.

John is frequently wiping sweat from his brow. The press is heated at about 350 degrees and on some summer days, the air temperature inside easily reaches one hundred degrees. There is no air conditioning, just thunderous fans blowing the dusty air. Whatever color he is working that shift, he will see on his handkerchief when he blows his nose later.

After John retires they will put in two or three automated shakers to reduce repetitive stress injuries, but most remain manual, and some workers say the new ones are too slow anyway.

Finally there is some daylight streaming into the plant. Windows were installed because the new owner didn't buy the old-school notion that workers would use the outdoor scenery as props for idle daydreaming.

John's workday is broken into three parts. First break, ten minutes. Sit in the vending room and pull out his stainless steel Thermos of "coffee." Lunch, twenty minutes. John always brings his own. Last break, five minutes. He finishes the last of his "coffee"—Kahlua and milk.

"You can't get drunk on it. It just gives you enough spirit to continue."

John's grin is sly, playful.

But it is good here, they let you go to the bathroom when you need to, as long as it doesn't become a habit.

John's quota is to fill between 400 and 450 trays a shift. His shoulder finally protests. The rotator cuff is torn, but John keeps working through the pain, pumped up with Advil and occasional cortisone shots.

"I worked a whole year without missing a day. You know why?"

The company offers a fifty dollars gift certificate and one day's pay to workers who have no absences for a year.

John wins.

One day, John comes home to Elsie and tells her that a coworker is asking around about a place to live. He's just been released from jail in nearby Brooklyn, but the time did him good. The other side of the house is empty. Let's give the guy a break. They could use the extra money. With no security deposit, no rent in advance, no haggling with utility companies, the setup is a magnet for questionable characters with bad credit, police records and tragic stories. John's home is fast becoming the last station for people who have run out of stops.

The first tenant spreads the word, and eventually, more tenants move in and the first one moves out. Today one lives in a bedroom, just off the living room on John's side of the house. Three others live in the other side of the duplex, where the smell of cigarettes and coffee dominate. The bedrooms frame a stark kitchen with a buckling counter, wooden cabinets painted purple, and an enamel Glenwood wood-burning range worthy of the "Antiques Roadshow." The tenants share a single bathroom, crowded with an electric portable heater. The living room is bisected by a clothesline, where clothes hang to dry.

Ballouville's priest, Sylva LeCours, could be speaking for John's tenants when he raises his head and upturned palms to the heavens, considering this shepherd in his flock.

"Oh John. Oh, what would I do without John."

Not even the most evil of connivers, like the tenant who fabricated a story about his mother's death to skip out on the rent, breaks John's constitution. Rent is fifty dollars a week, fifteen dollars for electricity. Must be able to stow your life belongings into a single room and must be willing to keep your bedroom door ajar when you sleep to let in the heat of the woodstoves.

Barbara Brodeur is one who fits the bill.

Puddles of slush dot the main street of Ballouville earlier this year as Barbara walks home to the rooming house, where she has been living eight years now. She knows it is an ancestral walk of sorts, this daily ritual of leaving the factory at the end of the overnight shift. Generations of mill workers have passed these stone and wood houses once fronted by proverbial picket fences as white and neat as a starched shirt.

"Mill rats. Anyone who worked most of their lives in the mills are mill rats. My daddy was a mill rat. My mom was a mill rat, and I am one."

It is so blessed cold and cloudy this morning. Barbara is tired, anxious for warmth. Her 1982 Mercury Cougar, the color of grape Kool-Aid, has given up on reverse. By parking at the church lot instead of at the rooming house she does not have to back up her car because there are no painted lines corralling vehicles there.

Her car is one hundred years newer than this wooden gothic church built on land donated by the owners of mills for the French Canadians who came down to work in them. But it has nearly reached antique status for automobiles. It took her only seven minutes to walk the half-mile to the church lot last night on her way to work. She was speeded up by the rain and sleet pelting her face. Her blond bangs cut straight across her forehead, and the little red riding hood she wears through the storm gives her a hint of youthful innocence.

This morning she is feeling all of her forty-seven years. There is a slight rise in the road that challenges her lungs, courtesy of Marlboro, and as always she carries the weight of guilt. She cannot forget all those years she partied as a teenage mom.

The rooming house is around the corner from the old stucco mill that started processing cotton in 1825. Once a gin mill, literally, when Leonard Ballou bought it, it was used for grinding the rye for distilling gin. Bored with being a schoolteacher, the ambitious Ballou and his father-in-law, Jabez Amesbury, turned the tiny mill into a three-story building. This is now empty, too.

No sign marks John's rooming house, but it is recognizable by the trio of rust-blotched drums out front and a hand-painted sign "Barrels. Clean Ones. Ten dollars." The collection of ceramic animals strewn about the front lawn is marred with the dents of passing time. One is headless. On the front porch are salvaged cardboard boxes filled with John's "firewood."

Arthur Berube at the Ballouville Aquarium knows that John will take surplus boxes off his hands. In the sun porch alone there are a dozen boxes, mostly crowded atop a ragged sofa. That is about six days of fuel for the three wood stoves that heat the house, the condition of which the computerized assessor's report in town hall describes succinctly: poor.

Since the stoves' heat does not reach to the far edges of the house, which holds John's bedroom, he sleeps on a twin bed pushed up against the kitchen's forty-five-year-old refrigerator that Elsie once painted to freshen up. Barbara is sitting on the bed's Mickey Mouse quilt that is as faded and torn as a favorite pair of jeans. She reviews her night's tally from assembling batteries for booster rockets: thirty-two batteries, nine of them did not pass inspection. The total is not bad, she figures for her first week on the job.

Andy Kiederling, another tenant, stirs a pot of spaghetti sauce bubbling atop a gas stove in the kitchen. He is making lasagna for the benefit he is holding Saturday at the VFW in nearby Putnam for a coworker at U.S. Button Corp. who has cancer. For months Andy has been persuading local businesses to donate raffle prizes. Among the premium prizes is a George Foreman grill.

On Saturday night when his coworker walks into the VFW hall, stunned and in tears about the outpouring of goodwill, Andy is the first one to hug him. Andy rubs the back of his friend's neck as he is surrounded by well-wishers. The fund-raiser brings in three thousand dollars.

Andy's arms are his storybook. They are covered with tattoos. There's one for Vietnam, there are the names of his four children, and blotched over are the names of two of his three ex-wives.

He tosses into the wood stove the plastic grocery bags that carried the IGA lasagna boxes. The stove is from another era and takes up a good portion of the living room. It devours so much of the house's garbage that John does not subscribe to trash pickup. Food scraps, even cigarette butts, are dumped into the hot embers.

The dry air in the house itches the throat and weighs heavy on the chest like a night spent smoking in a bar. The stoves save about five hundred dollars a month of winter fuel, but John swears he doesn't do it for the money. It gives him something to do.

Yank nails from the boards, saw them to size. Pile the wood into the boxes. Lug them to the garage. Carry them to the porch.

Get up four times a night, guided by the night light of a prayer candle to refill the stoves.

On some days, when John walks gingerly through the wood piles that are as unstable as a seesaw, he bends down and picks up a tongue-and-groove pine slab: the factory floor.

Something to do.

I get by good. I've got no problem.

"If you can hold off until the summer, we'll pick one [a transmission] up at the junkyard, and I'll put it in for you," Andy tries to reassure Barbara.

No vehicle means no job in this rural region of the state, where the transit service is recovering from near-bankruptcy. It was turning into a virtual taxi service, so spread apart were the riders it served on the rural back roads. The director is still trying to lure back the towns that withdrew from the regional transit district. Still there were no buses for third-shift workers such as Barbara, anyway.

Andy and Barbara are another generation of factory workers removed from John, who is sixty-four, yet in today's new economy, they earn less money than John did more than a decade ago. The other day John gave Barbara forty-seven dollars for blood pressure medicine since she has no health insurance and is making only $7.50 an hour assembling batteries. She had stopped taking her pills because she was broke, and the requisite physical for this job discovered that her blood pressure was up.

At her last job she accidentally broke a mold in one of the machines. Some of them cost eighty thousand dollars. "They were nice about it; they didn't charge me for it," she says. But soon she was assigned to the worst-running machines. "You catch on pretty fast that something's up."

For a time in the '80s, her tour of duty at factories—filling bottles with sweet-smelling stuff at Crabtree & Evelyn, mixing dyes at Belding Heminway—was pleasantly interrupted by a government job-training program.

By then she had escaped her first husband. They married when she was sixteen, and she dropped out of high school because she was pregnant. "The year she was born, they came out with the pill," says Barbara, who never had another child after her daughter was born in 1970.

Her husband beat her.

"I guess, of course, when you are that age, you think marriage will change 'em."

"God, how stupid was I."

One morning her husband's breathing signaled that he had finally passed out, his rage asleep. Barbara phoned her sister and mumbled through the awkwardness of a fat lip: come get me. She scribbled a note calling him every name in the book, pulled wires out from under the hood of his car, grabbed her daughter, and got the hell out of there.

For years, he hounded her, refused to pay child support.

"Oh yeah, I had him arrested all the time. He wouldn't pay support, I had him arrested, he'd pay for a little while, then he'd stop, had him arrested, and he always worked under the table so you couldn't attach his pay."

There are all kinds of ways for women to self-medicate themselves through the trauma of being abused by their husbands, the father of their children. Booze became Barbara's inept therapist. She moved to Thompson into an apartment that reeked of kerosene and had a kitchen with a bare wood floor.

The next party was as far as the girl could see.

She lives with that every day, even though her thirty-year-old daughter has a good job in computers, is in love with a guy who treats her like a queen, and shows no outward signs of resentment.

She lives with that every day.

A government job program, reminiscent of Roosevelt's WPA programs, paid her to tape oral histories of Thompson, where she was born. The town elders told her stories of factory overseers, of the first automobile, of her own family.

She delighted in the people she met, pored over ways to frame questions that solicited the most insightful responses.

This mill rat was using her brain. In her spare time she let her imagination carry her to more magical places than here and started writing fairy tales.

She got her GED and enrolled at Quinnebaug Valley Community College. A writing professor praised her stories.

She planned to continue.

But soon, her second marriage was falling apart.

"Second husband, second separation, second divorce. That was bad."

She moved to Florida and became a bartender. A twister destroyed the trailer park where she lived.

Back in Connecticut family members promised to get her a job, car, and shelter. She was doing the shake and bake at U.S. Button when she met John.

Whenever John brings Elsie to the hospital, Barbara stays with John's mother, who can no longer be left alone. And, when liquid food needs to be poured into a feeding tube connected to his mother's stomach, Barbara does that, too. It's the barter system of favors.

You do what you have to do.

Elsie is gone three years now, dead of throat cancer. She started smoking at thirteen.

John's mother passed on, too. It cost one thousand dollars more to bury her just eighteen months later. Same type of coffin as Elsie and everything.

Barbara and John head outside. John, wearing his shiny union jacket, is carrying a funnel and hopes that transmission fluid will revitalize the gears of Barbara's car. Andy grabs a piece of generic white bread, folds it in half and dips it in the spaghetti sauce. "Here, the old Italian way."

A mousy guy with the slight body of a teenage boy, Andy's fifty-four years show in the deep crevasses of wrinkles that cover his face. There is a hollowness about his cheeks because he has no teeth. He had the last eleven rotting ones pulled four years ago and has never bothered to get them replaced, especially after hearing the two thousand dollars price tag.

Andy likes to talk, and he won't sandpaper over the spots in his story that are as rough as his callused hands. His mother gave her son up to her own mother because she worked in a nightclub and was about to lose him to foster care.

He laughs like hell when he tells the story of the day his mother tried to call the president to get her son sent home from Vietnam. She liked to drink. Andy quit drinking four years ago. He volunteered to go to 'Nam. He's an only son and could not be forced to go.

"I figured it was my turn."

It was not an easy run.

The day after the My Lai massacre, his unit passed through.

"People here in the United States don't know what we went through."

Every weekday afternoon he tunes the television to TNT and plops down, often with John by his side, to watch "Tour of Duty," a realistic dramatic series about the Vietnam War.

Andy never told his mother he was wounded until she noticed a slight limp in his walk when he returned home in 1968. His biological father Andy knew by name only, and Andy does not see three of his four children. He has been ordered by a court to stay away.

"I was a violent person. Well, working third shift, coming home, my wife going to work, and taking care of the kids when they come home from school, I got tired and I got violent. My kids did something, I bopped them one. I grew up like that, and I don't think I grew up to be a bad person."

He got arrested for hitting his third wife, the mother of those three children. He was thirty-five when he married her. She had just turned eighteen. They hoped to get married at Mervin Whipple's chapel, which is down the road from the rooming house. With two divorces behind him, this Las Vegas-esque chapel was a more viable option than the Catholic Church.

But since Whipple is also the local gravedigger, Andy lost out to a funeral.

They tied the knot at the American Legion hall in Putnam. The first few years of marriage were perfect, he says, but his wife turned twenty-one, got a job, started going out drinking.

"It's nothing to brag about, I have to live with it the rest of my life. I've never, ever hit a woman in my life until one day I snapped and that was it," he says. "We stayed together three months, and then that was it. Once you split up, you're never going to get it back. So I live without it."

With each misstep Andy came back to John's place.

Every summer he works behind the counter at the Ballouville church's annual flea market and tag sale, and he spends his vacation time dressing up as an eighteen-century button salesman with a club that does encampments on town greens.

Today Andy knows that illiteracy is the biggest challenge in his life. In the Army a fellow soldier read him the questions for the basic training test.

But at his job setting up presses at U.S. Button, his dyslexia is becoming an issue. It has taken him twelve years there to get this far and he plans to fight against being reassigned back to machine operator. After the rent and child support for three children, he has ninety-nine dollars a week left, and he often fixes cars for friends to make extra money.

"I consider myself happy. Money to me is the root of all evil. You can't live with it and you can't live without it. Just like a good woman, you can't live with them and you can't live without 'em. Well I'm a proven fact that I can live without either one of 'em."

Barbara and John return, and a trail of cold air follows them into the kitchen. Andy has just finished putting the Kraft pizza cheese on the foil pan of lasagna. Barbara plops onto the bed, her yellow Panama Jack T-shirt visible through the opening of her long raincoat.

"I'm screwed."

The Band-Aid approach to the transmission has failed. Baby, the rooming house cat, uncurls from her half-moon sleeping position, gets up, stretches, and saunters over. Barbara pets her, going for under the chin, and coos to her. The conversation turns to the age of the cat, and John declares that Baby came the year before Elsie died. Andy and Barbara verbally jump him. And it is during this good-natured ribbing that this trio, glued together by time and circumstance, seems most like kin.

Barbara is smiling now. Andy's thin lips are parted in conversation. The question of the feline's age is never fully resolved, nor is the fate of Barbara's car, as John segues into stories of when Elsie was alive. Barbara sits back slightly and lights another cigarette.

John recalls going to Red Lobster or Hometown Buffet for special occasions. The grandchildren—one of them is a high school honor student who wants to be a doctor so he can cure cancer—loved the buffet. That was cheaper—$8.95, all-you-can-eat. But Elsie loved lobster.

Andy nods. He is settled in the recliner now, his knees pulled up toward his chest, his gaze fixed on John. Andy was often there during those special days—birthdays and holidays. The exaggerated lives playing out on the soap operas have become extraneous now as John continues, seated at the kitchen table and its familiar plastic tablecloth.

Snow is starting to fall outside.

In here a kitchen lit by the flickering light of a prayer candle, heated by a stove fueled with junk and anchored by memories, three people are snug and sheltered.

Philip Gerard

The Thirteenth Hour

The Wreck of the Sailboat Morning Dew
and a Child's Voice in the Dark

ACT I

This is how things go very wrong, how a safe journey is not all one thing but an accumulation of right decisions made consciously and sometimes unconsciously, and how calamity begins with a failure of imagination or a simple wrong turn late in the day or stubbornness or inattention or too much confidence or fatigue with luck running out, or more likely a cascade of small bad choices whose hidden sum is great and irrevocable disaster—and four lives that end in cold water.

On the day after Christmas, 1997, at the Lightkeeper's Marina in Little River, South Carolina, a forty-nine-year-old country music singer-songwriter named Michael Wayne Cornett stepped aboard his thirty-four-foot sailboat *Morning Dew* to begin their first and last voyage together. The boat was a popular model, a Cal 34, built for day-sailing and coastal cruising. You could identify the make and model by a glance at the dark blue sail cover, stitched with a big signature C logo, with the numerals 34 inside the curve of the C. Her white hull had fair lines, a sharp cutter bow, and a slight flaring bustle to the transom. A blue canvas dodger protected the front of the cockpit from seaspray and rain. Hung from lifelines on either side of the long cockpit, matching blue canvas spray panels announced the vessel's name in big white capital letters: *MORNING DEW*.

Cornett had bought the boat locally a month earlier and planned to sell it for a profit in Florida—an inverted proposition in itself, since so many boats come onto the market in Florida from the charter trade that the usual practice is to deliver a boat north for sale at Charleston or Annapolis. He and his brother, Harold, had spent the night on the boat, plotting with a pencil the route that would take them down the Intracoastal Waterway

(ICW) to Georgetown, Charleston, and ultimately Jacksonville, where he planned to meet his wife, Libby.

The Lightkeeper's Marina is large and luxurious, located in Coquina Harbor, a man-made basin scooped out of a natural slough with high land all around, just off the newly developed strip of Highway 17 between North Myrtle Beach and the no-longer-small town of Little River, on the North Carolina border. It is accessible from the ICW through a narrow, curving channel that has good water even at low tide, marked by a coni-cal ornamental lighthouse rising only as high as a telephone pole, banded by five broad horizontal black and white stripes, that shows an actual light but is not an official aid to navigation. The tourists love it. Boaters love it more, for it provides an unambiguous landmark to the entrance to the channel—not so important in sunshine, but very handy in fog, rain, or darkness, or when fatigue interferes with attention. The marina is ringed by condos that provide a high windbreak, protecting the boats moored therein from all but the most easterly winds, making it a safe haven even in hurricanes.

For a year, I kept a sailboat about the size of the *Morning Dew* at the same harbor and raced it on weekends with the fleet off Myrtle Beach. I came in and out of that channel dozens of times, in clear light and in squalls, always glad to see that quaint toy lighthouse, to feel the blustery wind suddenly calm inside the protection of the harbor.

Harbor in its original meaning held no nautical connotation at all—it referred to a place of shelter or lodging for travelers, a haven from weather, storm, and highwaymen, or else a refuge for the infirm—or the insane. The distance between the dangerous world and a safe harbor is sometimes an infinite space that cannot be crossed. And sometimes the space of the crossing is the most truly dangerous ground.

Mike Cornett was the talented, likable grandnephew of the famous Carter family, legendary in country music for classic hits like "Wildwood Flower" and "Will the Circle Be Unbroken," and the owner of Classic Recording Studio in Bristol, Tennessee. He was in the process of recording a new CD but had taken a break for a short holiday vacation. In one of his last songs, he sings of dying at sea, exhorting his loved ones not to grieve for him. Joining him for the voyage, in addition to his brother, Harold, were his two sons—Michael Paul, sixteen; and James Daniel, thirteen—

and a nephew, Bobby Lee Hurd Jr., fourteen. For the boys, the trip would be a Christmas vacation adventure.

Mike Cornett was a family man through and through. His social life revolved around Libby and the boys and assorted other relations. Libby Cornett homeschooled her sons, who considered each other his best friend.

Cornett's son Michael Paul—who went by Paul—intended to study marine biology at college soon. His brother James Daniel—who went by Daniel—aspired to become a lawyer. Their cousin Bobby Lee played baseball with skill and exuberance. All three boys loved outdoor adventures—hiking, caving, and rock climbing. They were rough and ready boys who didn't mind a little discomfort. That's what family and friends said about them to reporters afterward.

But I didn't know them, and the truth is that they were young men still in the act of becoming, still discovering whatever their lives would turn out to be. There's a family photo of the three of them together on a sofa, smirking and gangly, typical teenaged boys with mischief in their eyes. It's easy to sentimentalize them, also perfectly natural. They weren't yet old enough to make the kind of moral choices that would define them. Who knows what kind of men they would have become, what failures and disappointments would have tempered the joy of their lives, or whether they would have led blessed lives, made loving husbands and raised precious children of their own, succeeded beyond their wildest dreams, surprised even themselves with the mysterious and unexpectedly wonderful ways a life can unfold.

That's always the bitter pill to swallow when a young person dies violently—the unfairness, the sense of a process cut off in midsentence. There's no use in speculating about how all men must come to terms with their own flaws, that some of us wake up in middle age to find ourselves flabbier or less successful or not as tolerant as we had planned, to find that we drink too much or don't treat our wives with the tenderness they deserve, that we vote our prejudices and get lazy at times and aren't always the fine role model we would choose for our own children.

The three boys died, and therefore we can spare them the secret griefs of manhood, the exhausting challenges, the deep wounds of the heart. It's only fair, because they will also never know the soaring joy of being in love for life or the heartfelt pride of doing a difficult job well or the sweet, quiet fullness of heart that comes from looking back on a long life well lived.

They were boys out for an adventure, and we can all imagine that—the small Huck Finn thrill in the chest when they cast off the lines and felt the boat slide out into the channel that would take them south, beyond the compass of their hometown lives. And before that adventure was finished, it's possible that all three of the boys deliberately dared acts of self-sacrifice that elevated them to manhood ahead of their time and made them genuine heroes.

But that was later. Now to the voyage.

There was little apparent danger on their planned route. Cornett was an experienced sailor who had once lived aboard a sailboat and had chartered extensively in the Bahamas and the Florida Keys. They would motor along a well-marked channel, protected from the winter ocean seas and winds, never more than a few hundred yards from a safe shore, docking each night at a marina for hot showers and the comforts of shore-side restaurants. The boys had brought sleeping bags and would bunk in the forward V-berth—shaped like it sounds inside the sharp bow—and the main "saloon" or cabin, sheltered from the chill weather.

After a good night's rest, the boys, their father, and their uncle were in bed by 10:00 p.m. and rose next morning at 6:00, ate a hearty breakfast ashore at a nearby restaurant, then stopped at a chandlery and bought shotgun-shell signal flares and nautical charts covering the route down the ICW—but no offshore charts, nor chart for the Charleston Harbor approaches, which cost twelve dollars.

Cornett, his brother, and the boys prepared to shove off. But the diesel engine would not start.

It's important how a voyage begins. Even rational, grounded men become superstitious aboard a boat. A dead battery is a bad omen, and another man less wedded to his holiday plan might have postponed the voyage, even canceled it. Cornett and his crew, however, did the sensible thing: they went ashore again, bought a new starting battery, and hauled it back to the boat. In minutes they had the diesel chugging at idle, charging the house battery that ran the radio and lights. Harold tested the VHF radio and got the latest weather report from the National Oceanic and Atmospheric Administration broadcast on weather channel 2: a small-craft advisory was in effect for the next twenty-four hours.

You can leave harbor during a small-craft advisory—often the best sailing is found when the recreational powerboaters must head for shore. A deep-hulled sailboat is built for the sea in a way that flat-bottomed open sport-boats are not. Built to sail cocked over on its side, to take green water over the sharp bow, to duck into a wave and come up again like a cork, watertight as long as hatches remain battened down, ballasted by a lead or iron keel that hangs under the hull and harnesses gravity to keep the boat upright. But a keel means two other things: first, that shallow water is the enemy, submerged rocks a boat-killer; second, that when the hull is breached for any reason, a hell of a lot of weight is now using gravity to pull the boat to the bottom.

Also, a small-craft advisory often leads to a small-craft *warning*—wind and seas building—so it's prudent to peer into the future a little farther, to check the barometer to see if it is steady or falling. A falling barometer means stormy weather coming down on you. The faster it falls, the worse the coming storm. The *Morning Dew* had no barometer aboard. In any case, Cornett didn't plan to head offshore, and he could easily duck the boat into a safe haven if the weather kicked up.

They tested the running lights on the vessel—red port, green starboard, white behind, white steaming light at the front of the mast—and all worked fine.

Once again, they prepared to shove off.

But at the last minute, brother Harold got off the boat—he had planned to go, but now upon reflection decided to stay behind to tend to their father, who was in the hospital. By the next afternoon, his brother Mike would need his help, his strength, his judgment. Or maybe it all would have turned out the same.

But it was another bad omen. Whenever a crew member balks at a voyage, bails out at the last minute, many sensible skippers feel a little prickle of foreboding. When it happens on my boat, it puts me on edge, partly for the practical reason that it increases the burden on the other crew, and partly for the unsettling premonition it casts on the voyage. Once, on a passage from Charleston home to Wilmington, North Carolina—sailing the same waters as, but in the opposite direction from, the *Morning Dew*—one of my two crew had to bail out for personal reasons just before we put to sea. By the time we made Long Bay, fifty miles south of Cape Fear, my single crew and I were both exhausted from hand-steering through boisterous weather and dodging container ships in the dark of night.

At daylight on the second day he called me on deck with an urgent shout. The sea had turned gray and gelid, the sky weird and low and still. "Biblical," I noted in the logbook.

And a towering black waterspout—a waterborne tornado—had reared up on our port quarter.

I started the engine and we ran as fast as we could toward the one crack of daylight in the surly clouds far ahead. Through the binoculars, off our stern I could see debris and fish sucked into the vortex and whirling round inside the funnel, which was steadily gaining on us even at full throttle. I called the Coast Guard, alerted any other vessels in the area. We furled all sails; retrieved the "abandon ship bag" and stocked it with portable GPS, hand-held VHF radio, a gallon of water, flares, and a bag of snack food; buttoned up the boat; and waited for the spout to hit. "What do I do now?" my crew asked. He was, in addition to being a natural sailor, a talented amateur photographer.

"Take a picture of it."

So he shot the funnel, and the framed photo now hangs on my wall—a dark trophy of escape. At the last minute the waterspout fizzled—simply got sucked back into the purple glowering sky with a sound like a burst from a gas station air hose—*whoosh!* And it was gone, the sea blank and still. And we could have been under it. Instead, we motored without incident into the fairway of the Cape Fear shipping channel and enjoyed scalding cups of coffee and laughed off the tension. I just hate it when a crew member balks at a voyage.

Cornett and the boys left Harold ashore, waving from the dock. They did not recruit a replacement crew—probably there was no time, no one available. The hour was about 12:30 p.m. Just a few minutes later, Cornett docked the boat at the Myrtle Beach Yacht Club, where he bought 39.5 gallons of diesel fuel—enough to get them to Charleston and beyond. The *Morning Dew* passed the Little River Swing Bridge heading south a little after 1:00 p.m., logged by the bridge tender. By nightfall they were safely tied up at the Boat Shed Marina near Georgetown, a historic waterfront town twenty miles south of where they had started. The Boat Shed was closed for the holidays and has no record that the *Morning Dew* ever docked there, but she was spotted by a salvage master from Georgetown.

The following day, though they had planned to set out early for the long run down to Charleston, in fact, for reasons that eluded investigators—more battery trouble?—the boat did not get underway until well after noon, probably as late as 1:00 p.m. Crucial bad timing, for this left just five hours of daylight to make the forty-three miles into Charleston. Not possible. The cruising speed of a Cal 34 under power would scarcely exceed six or seven knots, even without a headwind or adverse current, meaning that in five hours the *Morning Dew* could make thirty miles, maybe a little more with luck and favorable current, before stopping for the night. Unless you're a professional pilot, you shouldn't dare to navigate the ICW at night—it's just too tricky, narrowing and shoaling and turning to follow a man-made channel that really just connects all the local natural channels. And the section north of Charleston is twisty and somewhat baffling even in daylight, winding through low-country marshes, spoil islands, and false channels.

For reasons that remain a mystery, an hour after leaving the dock, Cornett steered the boat, not into the southbound channel of the protected ICW, but out through the main shipping channel of Winyah Bay into the Atlantic Ocean.

This turn was a life-and-death decision, though Cornett almost certainly did not know it at the time. But why did he make that turn?

One answer is that, at eye-level from the deck of a boat, the junction of the ICW as it crosses Winyah Bay is confusing—though plainly marked on the chart. As the channel narrows, a skipper can steer to the north or the south of a spoil island. The southern fork leads to a hard right turn and into the continuation of the ICW; the northern fork to the shipping channel and the ocean. This is the answer favored by investigators: unfamiliar with the channel, Cornett simply made the wrong turn.

And in the decision points accumulating toward catastrophe, Cornett now made another fateful decision: once he became aware of his mistake, he did not turn around and retrace his route inshore.

Why not?

Before he had gone very far, he would have seen without a doubt that he had made a wrong turn. The ocean channel at Winyah Bay continues for seven miles, lined by channel markers, then widens out beyond Marsh Island, leaving a clear view of the final leg between two ruined rock jetties and the ocean ahead. That day the ocean would have seethed with rough motion, a ragged line of flashing white breakers demarcating the bar beyond which lay deep water. In the sudden opening from the sea, the prevailing northeast wind would have piped up gusty and chill. The surface would have roiled and heaved as tide and wind funneled water into the sluice of the channel. Steering would have become a challenge it had not been inside the protected waterway. A few seconds in the churning motion of the fairway would have told his body he was heading for the sea, the wilderness. He would have felt the heave in his stomach, the lurching motion in his legs. He had sailed open water before.

Whatever mistake he had made in reading the channel markers, whatever wrong turn he had taken through lack of local knowledge, before long Cornett would have seen his mistake for exactly what it was. Then, if indeed the turn was a mistake, he undoubtedly made a new decision: not to turn back into protected water

Did the boys grow excited at the prospect of a voyage "outside" in the ocean? Did he start to turn back but gave in to their enthusiasm for adventure? Or did he just decide he would lose too much time by turning around—he had gotten such a late start—and figure he could handle the forty-odd miles to a well-marked harbor?

Or was it not a mistake at all but a calculated decision to avoid the difficult Intracoastal channel altogether? The open sea is relatively easy to navigate at night, so long as you know what you are doing and have the right instruments—there's sea room and deep water, not tight channels and sandbars that rear up without warning. And Charleston Harbor is one of the best marked harbors on the Eastern seaboard. So maybe he made the turn on purpose—despite what investigators think. Maybe he wanted to be in Charleston in one more leg—not moored to whatever fishing dock he could find by nightfall, still ten miles out—figured that he would get there in the dark and find the fairway and by dawn would be watching the flags snap in the onshore breeze over Fort Sumter.

But Charleston Harbor has a ship-killing approach, as we shall see.

In the fatal story of the last voyage of the *Morning Dew*, this was the end of the first act: the players had gathered on a picturesque dock in Little River, motored out past a toy lighthouse, set the voyage in motion, and made a simple wrong turn toward the ocean instead of toward the safe Intracoastal channel on the far side of Winyah Bay. Or maybe a wrong turn on purpose, to make up for lost time, by a skipper with just enough experience not to be prudently afraid, pressing his luck. Whatever the reason, the *Morning Dew* headed out into a blank wilderness of wind and sea and weather, crossing a boundary marked by channel buoys and a gray surf line. For awhile she would live in that wilderness, but the need for refuge would turn her back into that dangerous zone between open water and safe harbor, to cross that treacherous middle ground in swollen seas and keening wind in the dead dark hours of the night.

ACT II

Captain Ronnie Campbell, the same salvage master who had noticed the *Morning Dew* docked at the Boat Shed Marina the previous night, was headed inshore in the Winyah-Georgetown channel aboard the salvage vessel *Prodigal Son* when he spotted the sailboat about 2:30 p.m. at channel marker no. 26. The buoys are marked in ascending order from the seabuoy inshore—in other words, there were twenty-five more navigation markers left to pass before heading out to sea, any of which, compared to the chart, would have indicated that the *Morning Dew* was no longer in the ICW. For one thing, heading south in the ICW, *red* nun buoys, daymarks, and flashers are all on the right. But heading seaward in a shipchannel, all the *green* markers are on the right.

Captain Campbell presumed the sailboat had missed the turn from the channel into the ICW—pleasure boaters sometimes did—and was concerned that it was headed offshore into deteriorating weather. Remember, the weather service had issued a small-craft advisory, forecasting winds of up to twenty knots—23.5 miles per hour—and six-foot seas. In fact, the weather got far worse, blowing a near gale.

As Captain Campbell tells it, all sails were furled. An adult wearing a rain jacket stood at the helm of the sailboat, and three boys, wearing summer clothes, played on the foredeck, hanging onto halyards at the mast. Captain Campbell hailed Cornett repeatedly on the radio as the *Morning Dew* motored seaward into rising winds and seas—but he got no response.

The autopilot aboard the *Morning Dew* was not in working order, according to the previous owner, so Cornett would have had no relief from the fatiguing chore of steering the boat in rough seas. Heading out to sea, he would have known that. The boys would not have been experienced enough to hand-steer in building seas and in darkness. The only other adult, Harold, had gotten off the boat before she sailed.

So the mystery opens, the first of many in this cascade of fatal choices.

No one knows what happened aboard the *Morning Dew* as the weather worsened, the sun disappeared in a blear of winter clouds, and cold and fatigue inevitably set in. Steering a sailboat by hand for long periods is sometimes boring, at best exhilarating, always fatiguing far beyond what most people expect—even veteran mariners are continually surprised at the toll taken by such a prolonged effort of concentration. In rough seas, at night, in cold, with invisible waves slamming into the hull without warning, slewing it off course and heeling it dangerously, it can be physically and emotionally exhausting—even under power.

Indeed, a sailboat is at its best while *sailing*—the sails balance the motion of the hull, helping the keel to bite, achieving control and stability, so long as the right sails are set and the boat is not overcanvassed. So arguably motoring in the open ocean would have been even more challenging, more fatiguing, more difficult in every way, than sailing with a reefed-down mainsail. The *Morning Dew* never raised her sails.

Probably neither Cornett nor the boys enjoyed any hot food on such a squally night. Maybe they snacked on junk food or sandwiches, sipped Cokes or water. Most likely some or all of them got seasick from the corkscrew motion of the wind-driven waves against the hull, balance wavering, stomach heaving with each motion of the boat, so that just making it through the night would have seemed like a blessed deliverance. They would have been soaked with rain and spray, cold to the bone—which always makes seasickness worse. Cornett was wearing two T-shirts, a sports shirt, a nylon jacket, a windbreaker, blue jeans, nylon foul-weather pants, jockey shorts, dress socks, and boat shoes. Likely he was already feeling the first effects of hypothermia.

At some point, the boys went below to sleep, or try to. We know this because of what two of them were wearing when they were found: boxer shorts. In the forward V-berth, the pitch and roll of the boat would have been most violent, the waves banging noisily against the hull, so they may have bunked in the main saloon, even on the cabin sole or floor, closer to the center of gravity, where motion was reduced, with just a thin shell of fiberglass between themselves and the salt ocean.

Charleston Harbor is a glorious place to sail into. The shipping fairway is broad and well marked, and there is deep water nearly everywhere inside the harbor, with the ramparts of Fort Sumter rising on the left and Sullivans Island on the right. The cityscape between them is stunning, antebellum houses and steeples rising above the battery where once Confederate cannon fired on Fort Sumter to start the Civil War. In this season, the Battery was aglow with Christmas lights, undoubtedly shimmeringly beautiful from the sea.

But there's a trick to entering the harbor.

The water off Charleston is shallow for a long ways offshore. Thus a deep shipping channel has been dredged from the boundary of the inner harbor more than two and a half miles out to sea, protected from silting by rock jetties defining the north and south edges of the channel. On a chart, the jetties form a funnel, with the wide mouth opening into the harbor and the narrow stem debouching into the fairway and the open sea. The jetties are mostly submerged at high tide, at midtide often awash just below the surface, and at low tide often lashed by breaking waves that conceal their black spines. Sailing southward to Charleston, you can see over the water and the low-country tidal marshes for many miles before you can safely turn right at a ninety-degree angle northwest into the fairway. You must sail far enough offshore to weather the jetty, keeping at least three miles out on a course of, say, 215 degrees from Georgetown, roughly southwest, diverging from the land for several miles to gain searoom, aiming for either the seabuoy or one of three pairs of bracketing, flashing buoys outside the jetty that signal the safety of the deep fairway.

It's a kind of optical illusion, worse at night, with the lighthouse on Sullivans Island and the beautiful lights of Charleston proper beckoning close across the water. For many miles, it looks like you can just turn and be safely moored within the hour. And of course all water is merely a surface to the eye— it looks the same whether it's two feet deep or a hundred fathoms deep. And at night, lights tend to flatten out, distorting your sense of distance. Sparkling city lights twenty miles off can seem to lie just ahead, and the rocking lighted buoy a hundred yards off the bow can appear as a ship miles away.

Cornett had no chart of the Charleston Harbor approaches. Either "11521: Charleston Harbor and Approaches" or "11523: Charleston Harbor Entrance" would have served as a graphic warning to ignore the optical illusion, to proceed against intuition and what your eye tells you to be true.

But even without a chart, you still have many chances to make a safe landfall.

If you turn right too soon, your depth-sounder will quickly shrill an alarm as the water shallows beneath your keel from about twenty to ten feet.

If you have prudently programmed your GPS with the latitude and longitude of the seabuoy, you can make your turn when it signals "arrival."

If you have the light list, you can take bearings off the ranges off Fort Sumter and the Charleston Lighthouse on Sullivans Island and triangulate a safe course.

Lacking any of the above, you can hail the Coast Guard or any commercial vessel on the VHF radio and ask for advice about proceeding into an unfamiliar harbor.

There are many ways to navigate accurately, and safety lies in redundancy. But the *Morning Dew* carried neither a depth-sounder nor a GPS. The flashing lights are marked on charts which weren't on board. The radio was down below in the cabin, inaccessible to the man in the cockpit.

Captain John Vigor, a seasoned offshore mariner writing in *Good Old Boat* magazine, defined five essentials for a successful yacht voyage. The first four are logical and obvious: a well-found ship, a good crew, adequate preparation and maintenance, and seamanship.

The *Morning Dew* had not been surveyed—examined stem to stern by a professional who tests the hull, rig, instruments, engine, and other onboard systems to determine if the vessel is sound, if all the gear works as advertised—an essential preliminary to buying a boat and taking her to sea. So she may or may not have been well-found, in the sense of being seaworthy in bad weather and responsive to her helm, with a reliable motor and serviceable sails. If the engine quit, she may have been at the mercy of tides and currents when it counted most.

Her crew were largely young and inexperienced—kids—more passengers than crew. They sailed shorthanded, with only the barest preparation.

The *Morning Dew* carried minimal equipment, and the dead battery and the inoperative autopilot surely signaled that maintenance was an issue.

Cornett's seamanship was established later in court, based on his long experience with sailing boats in open water. But by the time he most needed to call upon his best resources, in the middle of a black and squally night, with only a magnetic compass for navigation, after twelve hours at the helm, he would have been exhausted, cold, probably hungry, possibly seasick and somewhat dehydrated—almost surely mentally and physically impaired.

Vigor's fifth essential is what he calls the "black box":

Every boat possesses an imaginary black box, a sort of bank account in which points are kept. In times of emergency, when there is nothing more to be done in the way of sensible seamanship, the points in the black box can buy your way out of trouble. You have no control over how the points are spent, of course; they withdraw themselves when the time is appropriate. You do have control over how the points get into the box: you earn them. For every seamanlike act you perform, you get a point in the black box.

Not a bad paradigm for steering any enterprise, for living a successful life.

A chart of the Charleston Harbor approaches. A GPS. A depth-sounder. An experienced adult crew to replace Harold. The judgment to turn back and rectify an error in navigation, despite the time lost. The patience to spend one more night on the waterway before arriving in Charleston. Sleep and nourishment for the crew. A radio call in unfamiliar waters. All points that could have gone into the black box of the *Morning Dew.*

Those who do not go to sea imagine—wrongly—that safety lies in staying close to shore. Before setting out, Cornett had been questioned by Richard Porter, a sound engineer at his studio, about the wisdom of venturing on such a journey at this stormy season: "You're nuts," he told Cornett. "The winds of the North Atlantic are terrible this time of year." But as Porter related to the Charleston *Post and Courier* after the fact, "He laughed it off and said he planned to take the Intracoastal Waterway, and that if he was offshore, he wouldn't be more than a mile off."

If he was offshore. So the possibility had entered his mind, and his plan in that event was to hug the shore.

Yet seasoned sailors understand that being too close to land is what usually brings danger. Safety lies in staying beyond the crossing zone, the zone where water transforms by deadly invisible increments into land. The *Morning Dew* needed to be another mile and a half offshore, at least. To steer her away from the land on a dirty night at the end of an exhausting trick at the wheel would have required a cool reasoning skipper familiar with the charted area and willing to go against every powerful instinct that wanted to make harbor as soon as possible, to bring this miserable, exhausting night to an end. In the event, Cornett did not sail far enough *away* from the land—instead he hugged the shore on a parallel course, remained in the zone that was not quite open sea and not quite land, and, at sea, sometimes parallel lines do indeed intersect with great violence.

By the time she approached the glittering lights of Charleston, the black box on the *Morning Dew* was empty. Her points—and her luck—were overdrawn.

Thirteen hours into the journey, in pitch blackness, buffeted by thirty-knot winter winds and five-foot breaking seas and blasted by torrential rain, the *Morning Dew* shuddered onto the rock jetty at the north entrance to the Charleston sea channel and tore out her bottom, The sharp rocks gouged a ten-foot-long gash in her starboard underside and killed the *Morning Dew*.

That the catastrophic damage occurred to only one side of the hull may indicate that, at the last moment, Cornett saw or sensed he was running onto the jetty and tried to turn, too late—the boat was now open to the sea. Or maybe a breaking sea simply slewed her around, out of control. The boat must have grounded with terrific violence. Investigators believe Cornett was flung over the side on impact, for he was likely alone on deck and he was wearing no safety harness to tether him to the boat—an essential for offshore sailing, especially shorthanded. There is no other reasonable explanation of why he left the boat and died first, long before the boys. The water temperature was fifty-four degrees Fahrenheit.

The informal Coast Guard rule is 50-50-50: in 50-degree water, a person has a 50 percent chance of surviving for 50 minutes.

The vessel ran aground at low tide, when the rocks protruded nearly seven feet out of the water. But the waves were almost that high, and the *Morning Dew* must have ridden the crest of one right onto the rocky spine of the jetty. She hung there for several minutes or several hours, with the boys probably still on board, then the flooding tide shoved the boat over the submerged jetty, and she sank on the far side in ten to twelve feet of water—inside the funnel made by the jetties at the edge of the deep shipping channel. This is known from testing paint scrapings recovered from the rocks on the jetty. A diver later found a debris field marking the vessel's progress across the rocks: her ship's bell, stove, rubber carpeting, fragments of her hull.

In the jargon of the National Transportation Safety Board (NTSB), the *Morning Dew* suffered an "allision" with the jetty—"the action of dashing against or sticking with violence upon." The ominous curtain for the second act.

ACT III

At 2:17 a.m. on December 29, in the middle of a howling winter gale, a twenty-three-year-old Coast Guard petty officer at the Charleston Station named Eric J. Shelley heard a garbled call on VHF channel 16, the distress channel: "May . . . mayday, U.S. Coast Guard, come in!"

Though he might have been able to hear clearly only, "U.S. Coast Guard . . . " repeated twice, picked up by the high-site antenna tower at Mount Pleasant, at the entrance to Charleston Harbor.

The voice was excited, even frantic—the voice of a scared kid. Three seconds of panic. Three times Petty Officer Shelley tried to raise the caller on his radio, using all six of the Coast Guard's high-site antennas to reach the phantom caller, but he got no response. Four minutes later, a burst of static indicated an open microphone—as if someone were trying to call but the transmission wasn't coming through. Later an enhanced replay would make it clear that under the static was a voice—the same adolescent boy's voice that had called the original Mayday. Then the radio went silent.

Petty Officer Shelley again attempted to raise the caller, but again he got no response. The operations duty officer (ODO), a thirty-seven-year-old boatswain's mate first class named Michael J. Sass, was sleeping, and Petty Officer Shelley did not wake him. Though he could have replayed the tape of the original call to glean more information from it, he did not. He took no further action and went off duty at 6:00 a.m.

He later told investigators, "I didn't get a response, so I thought, well, it might have been they didn't need me anymore, or they were out of my range or something because it was a bad transmission." He testified under oath that he thought the call might have been a hoax.

In the immediate aftermath, the Coast Guard denied receiving any distress calls on the night of December 28–29. For almost three months, it would keep secret the fact that a tape had been made of such a call, then reveal the secret in a manner that would strike Libby Cornett as unnecessarily cruel.

Petty Officer Shelley had already been on radio duty more than eight hours that night, with four more to go till the end of his shift—typical for an overworked "coastie," who might log eighty hours in a week's duty. When the call came in, he was actually away from his radio, getting a cup of coffee some seventeen feet away and outside the door to the communications center—too far away to clearly make out the message.

His training had consisted of a ten-week telecommunications school enhanced by a self-paced three- to four-week course in radio watchstanding. He qualified to stand watch alone by passing a twenty- to thirty-minute oral exam. The exam covered the technical aspects of working the radio and basic protocol for reporting and watchkeeping, but it did not include questions of judgment, such as when and whether to replay a distress call. Had he chosen to replay the message, he would have had to shut down the communications system to access a cumbersome and outdated analog recorder which actually *added* distorting noise to the message. Had he been seated at his console when the message came in, a radio direction finder might have told him immediately where the vessel was located—except that the outdated radio direction finder was positioned *behind* him, was not equipped to pinpoint a location but merely to provide a line of position which could extend many miles in two opposite directions, and in any case—since it rarely functioned properly—was turned off.

Meanwhile an exhausted man and three teenaged boys were struggling for their lives in the frigid waters of the Atlantic within sight of the lovely Christmas lights of Charleston.

Almost exactly four hours after the garbled Mayday call, the 617-foot automobile carrier *Pearl Ace* was passing Buoy 22, well inside the large end of the funnel formed by the jetties, coming through the fairway into Charleston Harbor. The ship's boatswain was securing the Jacob's ladder on the starboard side, after taking on a harbor pilot to guide the giant ship into port, when he heard cries for help coming from the water far below. At once he notified the bridge, including the ship's master, the chief officer, and the pilot, Gerald Lucas. All three at once hurried out onto the wing, an outside extension of the bridge, to scan the waters on the starboard side. The chief officer lit up the sea lane with a hand-held signal light called an Aldis lamp, but they saw nothing. All three listened, but over the thrumming of the ship's engines and the plash of the bow wave, they heard no cries from anyone in the water.

On board the *Pearl Ace*, Lucas radioed the pilot boat *Palmetto State*, which had deposited him on board and now was heading into harbor, asking that she return and search the area around Buoy 22. And then he made a second call which would carry lasting legal and moral repercussions for everyone involved in the drama: he called the pilot dispatcher and requested that he notify the Coast Guard about the possible distress cries and report that the pilot boat was returning to make a search for persons in the water. By now it was 6:25 a.m.

Three minutes later, the pilot boat telephoned the Coast Guard and reached the same watchstander who had heard the original Mayday call, Petty Officer Shelley. Shelley replied, "Okay, Okay. I'll alert the station, and they'll determine if they want to get underway also." This time Shelly immediately reported the call to the ODO.

The U.S. Coast Guard, now a part of Homeland Security, has an ever-expanding list of missions. But since 1915, when the Revenue Cutter Service—an antismuggling and customs collection fleet—combined with the U.S. Life-Saving Service, its primary mission has been to aid mariners in distress. Indeed, every boat station conducts regular drills in search and rescue, called SAR, and "coasties"—bored with barracks routine and endless drill—usually live for the chance to respond to a real emergency, to put to sea in the thrill of a life-and-death race against the clock and chase down vessels in distress. They're good at it. Over the years they have performed amazing acts of heroic rescue and take great pride in saving lives.

Later, in the cold clarity of a courtroom, as lawyers attempted to untangle the fatal train of passive decisions taken by the Coast Guard, after some prodding, Petty Officer Shelley confirmed that he had expected his station to launch a search:

PLAINTIFF: Would you expect ODO Sass to respond to those cries for help from someone in the water?
SHELLEY: I wouldn't know what to expect.
PLAINTIFF: What has been your experience?
SHELLEY: Well, we usually dispatch for a distress call. We have never had another call of somebody calling for help in the water before.
PLAINTIFF: Well, that's about as distressful as it gets, isn't it?

So what happened next is a mystery, not just in the usual sense of lacking a clear official rationale, but in the deeper sense of running contrary to habit, training, impulse, and human nature: *The Coast Guard did not go out.*

A forty-one-foot Coast Guard powerboat was available and ready, and ODO Sass had complete authority to launch it, yet he did not. He later testified as to his reasoning: "At the time, since they were going to have a boat right there and get back to us, I didn't personally feel a need to take it any further."

The Coast Guard has the authority to direct any vessel in U.S. waters to act under its orders. So from that point on, the *Palmetto State* became legally the sole vessel in a Coast Guard search and rescue operation—despite the fact that its skipper had no training or experience in search and rescue.

It was dark, a chill wind blowing from the northeast at twenty-five knots. In about ten minutes, the pilot boat was approaching Buoy 22. The first order of business was to find out if someone was clinging to the buoy. Then the pilot boat would sweep down-channel to Buoy 2, where the channel passes close to old Confederate Fort Moultrie on Sullivans Island, and on to Buoy 130, where the channel cuts into the ICW inside the harbor.

After searching for about twenty minutes, the *Palmetto State* gave up the search. The pilot dispatcher told the Coast Guard, "Well, the pilot boat's out there, and they don't see anything and they haven't heard anything, so they're going to come on back." The pilots assumed the Coast Guard would take up the search; otherwise they would have not given up so soon. "We'd have stayed and stayed and stayed," said the president of the Charleston Branch Harbor Pilots Association, Whitemarsh S. Smith III. The pilot boat passed less than a quarter of a mile from the wreck of the *Morning Dew*, whose mast protruded at a cockeyed angle from twelve feet of water—invisible in the darkness.

The *Palmetto State* quit her search at 6:48 a.m. All the boys would remain alive in the water for at least three, possibly four, more hours.

But even now, ODO Sass did not send out a Coast Guard search boat.

In his testimony, Richard Dein, a court-recognized expert in Coast Guard search and rescue, cast this decision—or non-decision—as a practically negligent one: "The normal progression of events in the SAR system is that you go out and look for something. If you don't find it, you don't diminish your efforts—you increase the efforts. And he didn't do that."

It was the dim wintry twilight before sunrise, and it was still not too late to save somebody.

For it wasn't until almost 11:00 a.m. when the first body was found— about 1,250 yards from Buoy 22. A couple walking along the beach of Sullivans Island near Fort Moultrie spied a boy floating in the churning surf as the wind whipped it into whitecaps: Bobby Lee Hurd. With the help of another beach-roaming couple, they managed to pull him out of the water. The boy had no pulse, and one of them tried CPR to revive him while others went for help. A National Park Service officer arrived and called 911. Before long, two police officers and paramedics arrived and worked on the boy. They intubated him with a carbon dioxide detection device that showed the boy was still producing carbon dioxide in his lungs. Bobby Lee was still alive, but barely. They could not revive him.

Nearby was a horseshoe life ring bearing the name *Morning Dew*. Evidently Bobby Lee had clung to it while swimming toward shore.

Ten minutes later, about a hundred yards west up the beach, one of the men, Hal Gaskins of Mount Pleasant, spotted another boy, rushed into chest-deep surf, and pulled him from the water, and again the paramedics tried CPR. The chief of the Sullivans Island Fire and Rescue Squad, Anthony Stith, asked the police to call the Coast Guard and request that a vessel and helicopter be dispatched to search for a boat. The National Park Service launched its own boat to begin a search, aided by local volunteers, ahead of the Coast Guard. All of this made the papers.

The lifeless boys—thirteen-year-old James Daniel Cornett and his cousin, fourteen-year-old Bobby Lee Hurd—were taken to the emergency room of East Cooper Regional Medical Center. There a team of doctors and nurses, including the coroner, Susan Chewning—herself a registered nurse—aggressively tried to revive them. But the boys could not be brought back and were pronounced dead.

At 1:00 p.m., the fire chief called the coroner to inform her that the body of a third boy, sixteen-year-old Michael Paul Cornett, had been found by a Coast Guard helicopter a mile to seaward of the sunken boat. He was wearing a life jacket, boxer shorts, and a pullover shirt. According to Dr. Sandra Conradi, formerly Chief Medical Examiner for Charleston County and a practicing forensic pathologist, before succumbing to hypothermia and asphyxia due to drowning, Paul could have survived for three to seven hours in that cold water. Since he was not struggling, as were his brother Daniel and cousin Bobby Lee Hurd as they swam toward the island, it's probable that he lived the longest.

What happened after the *Morning Dew* slammed into the jetty? The report of the NTSB, which launched a full-dress investigation of the sinking, concluded that the boat could have remained hung up on the jetty for hours, until the tide turned, possibly sinking as late as 9:00 a.m.

Could Have.

But it was a rough night, and the waves were slamming against the rocks, hammering at the stationary boat. The *Morning Dew* could have been carried across almost at once by the force of a wave train. That's how I imagine it: the boys jarred out of a seasick semisleep below, stumbling loggy and off balance up the companionway ladder to the cockpit, first astonished at the violence of the storm in the black night, then terrified by it, the boat pitching and heaving with each sea breaking aboard, the father gone, just vanished, into the seething water, the boys calling his name, clinging to each other, the oldest boy diving over the side on heroic impulse to find and save his father and being swept away, the two younger boys hanging on for life, then the youngest boy on board, Daniel, ducking into the black hole of the companionway, an act of daring and bravery with the water pouring into the dark cabin below, reaching for the radio by feel, depressing the mic and sending out his frantic Mayday, then as he tries again, the boat grabbed by tons of water and flung over the rocks, the boy scrambling out as the boat settles into the dark roiling water, then the two boys grabbing the horseshoe buoy off the rail, joining hands, jumping into the shock of frigid water together.

The NTSB determined that all four lived for some time after the sinking—perhaps as long as six hours; and that the cries heard in the water near Buoy 22 likely came from one or more of the crew of the *Morning Dew*—but which ones?

Probably either Daniel Cornett or Bobby Lee Hurd, or both. It was just before high tide. The voices came from exactly where the last of the incoming tide would have swept them, heading for Sullivans Island.

All three boys died some eight hours or more after the first distress call. At least two of them remained on board for an indeterminate time before the vessel scraped across the jetty and sank. None showed any signs of injury. Transit time for the Coast Guard vessel to the site of the wreck would have been only about twenty minutes. "Thus," concluded the NTSB Marine Accident Report, recovery of the children on the S/V *Morning Dew* would have easily occurred within two hours of the 0648 call (by 0848 hours [8:48 a.m.]) had a proper deployment been made and had the Coast Guard not terminated the search prior to daylight. Since all three boys were alive until between 1000 and 1100, they all would have been saved.

The sailboat was reported by the pilot boat *Sis* at 11:45 a.m.—the crew had sighted a mast sticking up out of the water near the south side of the north jetty, between Buoys 16 and 20—close to where the boatswain of the *Pearl Ace* had heard cries in the water more than five hours earlier.

Mike Cornett's body remained lost for almost a month before washing up on shore on January 23, 1998—also on the beach of Sullivans Island, a little northwest of the lighthouse.

The two boys found together on Sullivans Island were clearly trying to swim there and became exhausted. But did they, as Libby Cornett has always maintained, reach the island once safely and then venture back out into the channel in search of the other two? Chewning, the coroner, determined that at least one of the boys was alive more than eight hours after the boat ran onto the jetty—yet in theory he could not have survived that long in such cold water—so they might indeed have reached the island, rested awhile, and gone back into the water in search of their father and uncle, their brother and cousin.

I replay that scene in my mind, the boys swimming for their lives, reaching shore, flush with adrenaline, shivering uncontrollably from the frigid water, still reeling from the awful surprise of catastrophe, arms and legs rubbery from shock and fatigue, then *going back out there*.

Giving up their own salvation for the chance to save the others. Risking their lives in a magnificent act of love and courage. Just boys, not even men. Acting in the cold private dark as we all wish in our secret souls we would act. No witnesses to impress, no one but each other to answer to for their actions. Both swimming out again together, getting so far only and then giving out, trying to make it back against a tide that has turned strong against them, succumbing to cold, shock, and exhaustion only a few strokes from the beach.

And how did one of the boys, sixteen-year-old Paul, drown while wearing a life preserver? Why was he found so far from the other boys, and seaward of the boat? Did he, as some believe, remain near the boat to search for his father, then get swept out to sea on the outgoing ride, while the other boys struck out together to find help, then, discovering only a deserted beach, dutifully returned?

Or is that all wishful thinking, an attempt to make victims into heroes by allowing them the choice of how to die, in an act of self-sacrificing valor and not merely by being overwhelmed by the elements?

It's that dangerous middle ground again, the treacherous territory where one thing turns into another. It was either/or, but not both, not at the end. Yet for awhile it could have been both, heroism at the mercy of events that were out of their control. But ultimately it would be a terrible lie to call them merely victims if they behaved as heroes, just as it would be a self-serving lie to cast them as heroes if, in their final terrified hours, they scrambled to save themselves with no thought of the missing boy or the man they had relied on to guide them safely into harbor. The truth is absolute, yet unknowable, and we leave it where it belongs, unmolested in the eerie territory of crossing.

I have reimagined the fatal voyage of a good man and three good boys for many months—a voyage over home ground, through lovely waters—pondering each decision in a daisy chain of calamity, small choices that accumulated toward shipwreck and death. The choices occurred in the little spaces between one way of being and another, instinctive reactions to circumstances, and sensible reasons can be found for almost all of them.

Almost.

A crew member leaves the boat shorthanded—to care for an ailing father. How can you fault him? The voyage is delayed—prudently, to replace a dead battery. A skipper who should have known better turns his boat away from the safe channel and toward open water—perhaps in error, perhaps as a way of making up lost time, or maybe just to satisfy the longing for adventure in three boisterous teenaged boys. He's pushing his luck, and maybe at some instinctive level he knows this, but hey, it's only forty miles. He's been out there before—what can happen? A tired young petty officer standing radio watch half hears a faint, truncated message, mere nonsense, maybe—or maybe the desperate plea for help from a sinking ship. He is not near his radio but getting a cup of coffee to see him through the long hours left of tedious nighttime duty. He does not act—why not?

It is only a child's voice in the dark, after all. A hoax, maybe. Nothing at all, maybe. A few syllables and static and the voice does not answer back when called by one of the most powerful transmitting stations on the eastern seaboard. How close could such a voice be?

Yet the boatswain of the *Pearl Ace does* act—enlists his senior officers and the local harbor pilot, who hurry to the bridge wing to locate the voice in the water—another child's voice in the dark—then summons his colleagues on the pilot boat. Who call the Coast Guard.

The Coast Guard does not go out. Repeat: *The Coast Guard does not go out.* Maybe if they had. *Almost certainly* if they had, declared the court. Here sense and logic, even convenient, rationalizing logic, surrender to mystery. *What if? Why not? If not in that case, when? How much proof do you need of genuine distress before you send someone to the rescue? Why not check it out—where's the harm? Isn't it enough that the Mayday may be a maybe?*

All the maybes.

Each decision to act or not to act creating a radically different future for the four crew of the *Morning Dew* and the others whose lives will be indelibly altered—families riven by a violent grief, a grief fueled in part by outrage that the deaths were not inevitable, *that almost everybody could have been saved, almost to the last minute.*

Each decision taken in that no-man's-land of free will, where the consequences are already tallied on the bill but remain invisible until the future plays out. You have already made important things happen, have already prevented other important things from happening, yet for as far into the future as you can see with all your wisdom and experience and instinct, you cannot know what you have set in motion. You cannot know you have killed three boys as surely as if you had shot them down in cold blood.

That's the heart of it, I think, that at so many points the story could have turned out differently.

The voyage could have turned toward life. The boys could have had their holiday adventure. Mike Cornett might have sealed his own fate by his unlucky or reckless or merely mistaken turn into the ocean, but the fate of the three boys still hung in the balance, almost to the end. That's the maddening part. Had the Coast Guard duty officer sent out a boat after the first Mayday. Had the pilot boat passed a few yards closer to the boy in the water near Buoy 22, picked him up in the glaring beam of the

Aldis lamp. Had the *Pearl Ace* been steaming fifty yards closer to the boy in the water. Had the Coast Guard asked the pilots to keep on searching, to make another sweep. Had any of half a dozen people asked a certain question, made a timely radio call, felt any inkling at all that a deadly drama was unfolding within sight of the Christmas lights onshore. Where was that sixth sense that professionals count on, that prickly antenna of danger that alerts them that something is just not right?

The story goes on for years. It's a mystery of sorts, and it must be solved and ultimately judged.

Charleston Coast Guard Group Commander Manson Brown conducts a routine self-evaluation in which it is determined that "there are no systemic problems with the management of the Operations Center of Coast Guard Group Charleston" and the U.S. Coast Guard is blameless in the drowning deaths of Cornett and the three boys.

But the South Carolina Department of Natural Resources (SCDNR) has the real authority to investigate such accidents—treating each case as a crime in order to preserve crucial evidence until all parties are exonerated. To chief investigator Larry Pritchard, called in when the first two bodies washed up on Sullivans Island, the case quickly turns into an exercise in frustration: The Coast Guard is withholding crucial information.

He cannot reconstruct the tale without all the elements of the story, all the facts of the plot.

As Libby Cornett and Deirdre Lynn Hurd, mother of Bobby Lee Hurd, search for answers to the calamity, they become increasingly frustrated. Then their frustration turns to shock when Commander Brown himself flies to the Cornett home in Hiltons, Virginia, months after the sinking to play the tape of the distress call—the distress call which supposedly never came and of which no tape existed. As she listens to the spare, faint syllables, Libby immediately recognizes the voice of her thirteen-year-old son Daniel. It is a devastating moment, the confirmation of what she has long believed in her heart, and it leaves her shocked and breathless with the full impact of memory: the voice is real. It is her boy's. He is frightened and calling for help, and no one helped him.

A boating magazine files a Freedom of Information Act request to obtain the tape of the distress call. Senator Fritz Hollings and three other members of Congress eventually demand an investigation of the incident, and even as Commandant of the Coast Guard James M. Loy himself investigates the incident, the NTSB, the same agency that investigates commercial air disasters, launches an investigation of its own. What it finds is startling and deeply troubling: a pattern of slack oversight, routine negligence, and official complacency—aggravated by the Coast Guard's reliance on 1950s-era technology—with such dire implications for mariners and their families that it issues urgent advisories to the governors of all fifty states.

So the story of the voyage goes on and on, into the coroner's inquest and the investigations by the Coast Guard, the SCDNR, the NTSB, and the U.S. Congress. Its momentum carries it through a thirty-five million dollar federal lawsuit and appeal and a damning indictment of the actions of the Coast Guard at Group Charleston toward a rethinking of the entire culture of search and rescue.

The Coast Guard's remarkable defense at trial is worth noting: *Since it did not initiate a rescue attempt until after the boaters were dead, it could not be held liable for negligence in the rescue.*

Under the law, it turns out, the Coast Guard is not obligated to attempt to rescue mariners in distress—despite its unofficial motto: "We have to go out, but we don't have to come back."

U.S. District Judge David C. Norton doesn't buy the argument—the pilot boat became a proxy Coast Guard vessel as soon as it was directed to search near Buoy 22. So even if it didn't go out, the Coast Guard, in effect, went out. The judge is incensed that the government does not call a single live witness to answer the charge of negligence, relying instead on paper reports—a tactic he regards as arrogant and smug. He concludes: "As a result of the Coast Guard's reckless suspension of the search for the passengers of the *Morning Dew*, these children suffered horrific deaths in the cold waters of the Atlantic Ocean." He awards the families of the deceased a record nineteen million dollars.

"It was all so badly handled," Libby Cornett tells reporter Tony Bartelme of the Charleston *Post and Courier*, for the story is now a newspaper narrative, affecting public policy and full of "human interest" larger than mere local recognition—though all calamity is local for somebody, first, before its waves carry outward. "My boys might have been rescued."

Of the strange, insensitive, "duplicitous" decision to play the Mayday tape for Libby Cornett, Judge Norton writes,

Because of Commander Brown's actions, the last words that Ms. Cornett heard her son Daniel say were not, 'I love you, Mom,' as he left on his sailing adventure with his brother and father on December 27, 1997, but 'Mayd . . . Mayday, U.S. Coast Guard, come in.' It is patently obvious from witnessing Ms. Cornett at the trial of this case that these words will haunt her all the days of her life.

At the urging of the NTSB, the U.S. Coast Guard Auxiliary now uses the sinking of the *Morning Dew* as a case study to teach how to recognize and respond to mariners in distress, so the story has achieved some minor immortality as a lesson, a cautionary tale.

The battered *Morning Dew* herself is raised and accidentally sunk twice more by freelance salvage operators, further damaging the boat and spilling precious evidence into the sea, until at last she is raised competently by Joe Beasenburg of Towboat US, and finishes her story in a landfill.

The story churns up a wake of emotional wreckage among the families of the Cornetts and Bobby Lee Hurd. Libby Cornett, in the words of the judge who presided over her lawsuit, is left "lifeless" in the aftermath of the calamity, surviving each day with medication for depression and the help of friends and surviving family and her Christian faith, which must be sorely tested.

The Hurds, Bobby and Deirdre, withdraw from their social circle, sell the dream home they have recently acquired, because they cannot bear to live in it with the ghost of their son.

When I first began writing the story of the *Morning Dew*, I thought it was a tale about the Coast Guard, how a lone determined woman in her crushing grief made history by holding a government agency responsible to live up to its obligations, its duty, its promise. Now I see that is just a minor theme of the story, crucial for the peace of mind of the surviving family and ultimately good for any recreational sailor who finds himself in distress in waters patrolled by the Coast Guard, but still not the heart of the story.

Somehow the story is about rescue, about the arbitrary nature of salvation, how you cannot choose to be rescued but only do your best to be ready for it and to accept it if it comes, and that if you're smart you'll damn well do your best to rescue yourself. Which means, of course, filling up that black box every chance you get. Not just on your boat, either.

And the inverse of rescue is doom, so this story, this voyage, is also about the nature of doom—how it hardly ever starts out as doom but masquerades as a lark, luring us on toward the thrill of an offhand adventure, until by accident or design we make a false turn, then another, and finally have wandered far afield of our destination and don't even know we have blundered onto dangerous ground.

So ultimately for me, this voyage, this story, is about navigating that treacherous middle ground, the crossing ground that is neither deep sea nor dry land, but something in between, a transition zone where the weather is always worst and the seas steepest and the ship-killing rocks lurk invisible just beneath the waves like dragons' teeth ready to tear out your bottom, where you cannot always trust your eye or your heart and there exists that ever-present risk of *allision*, sticking with violence upon, in that dangerous space of decision between wilderness and safety, between one sure thing and another, between risk and reward.

Between: No longer where we were, not yet where we're going to be— with great good luck and reliable navigation.

And so in all the haunted hours daydreaming that luckless voyage alive again, a voyage over familiar sailing grounds where my own sharp flash-bulb memories mix with the blurry scenes I only imagine but that seem almost as real as my own memories, I do not follow the story ashore. My living imagination leaves me always stroking through the roiling dark cold water toward Buoy 22, watching in terror and desperate hope as the great thrumming black hull of the *Pearl Ace* slides past, tall as a factory, deck aglow with lights, disappearing down the fairway toward Fort Sumter. Off in the distance, the luminous thrashing of surf, the beckoning flash of a lighthouse, strings of colored holiday lights.

WORKS CITED

"Allision." *Oxford English Dictionary Online*. 2005. Oxford University Press. http://www.oed.com/.

Bartelme, Tony. "Family Voyage Deadly." *Post and Courier* [Charleston] 31 Dec. 1997: A1.

———. "Morning Dew Tried to Radio Coast Guard, Tape Reveals." *Post and Courier* [Charleston] 19 Mar. 1998: A1.

Cornett v. United States of America, 134 F. Supp. 2d 745 (U.S. Dist. 2001).

Post and Courier [Charleston]. "Coast Guard Must Provide More Answers in Tragedy." 20 Mar. 1998: 20.

————. "Errors Compound Tragedy." 23 Mar. 1998: A12.

United States. National Transportation Safety Board. *Marine Accident Report: Sinking of the Recreational Sailing Vessel* Morning Dew *at the Entrance to the Harbor of Charleston, South Carolina, December 29, 1997.* Springfield: National Technical Information Service, 1999.

Vigor, John. "Vigor's Black Box Theory." *Good Old Boat* July–Aug. 1999: 32.

Other sources consulted include numerous articles by the Charleston *Post and Courier* written by Tony Bartelme, Edward C. Fennell, Richard Green Jr., Terry Joyce, Rochelle Killingbeck, Schuyler Kropf, Elsa McDowell, Erik Neely, Steve Piacente, and unattributed staff; Associated Press articles by Bruce Smith and unattributed staff; articles from the *New York Times* written by Robert Hanley, Herb McCormick, and unattributed staff; articles from *Boat U.S. Magazine* by unattributed staff; "Case Study/Preventive SAR #1—*Morning Dew*" from the U.S. Coast Guard Auxiliary; "SSEE's Specialized Communications Expertise Aids NTSB in Improving Coast Guard Communication Center" by Leslie Spaulding of the Naval Surface Warfare Center, Carderock Division.

Gay Talese

A New Journalist's Suggestions for Daily Journalists

The following is an edited transcript of comments made by Gay Talese at the Nieman Narrative Journalism Conference at Harvard University in Cambridge, Massachusetts, on December 1, 2001.

I am a man who has never had a happier time in my life than when I was a reporter in the *New York Times* news room. I left the *New York Times* with a tear in my eye—more than a tear. I was thirty-two years old. I had been at the *Times* since I started at twenty-two, and I left not because of any disenchantment with the paper but rather because the limitations of daily journalism—space particularly and the time that one could devote to the indulgence of one's curiosity—made it somewhat frustrating to stay on a daily newspaper. I wanted to spend more time with people who were not necessarily newsworthy. I believed then—and I believe now even more than then—that the role of the nonfiction writer should be more with private people, insignificant people perhaps, but people whose lives represent a larger significance than their own lives.

The fiction writer, playwright, and novelist deal with private life. They deal with ordinary people and elevate these people into our consciousness and give them names and give them a place in life because of the power of the writer, the power of the word. The world of the nonfiction writer, the writer of biography, primarily has dealt with people in public life, names that are known to us. But the private life that I wanted to delve into as a young writer for the *New York Times* was the life of the person who would not be worthy of news coverage. I thought that if we could bring those people into the larger consciousness, they could help us understand the trends in all the lives around us.

My father was a tailor; my uncles were tailors. I believe a man who is a tailor or who is a doorman at a fine hotel gets the sense of the flow of life. It is a time in which a man who has a gift of observing can understand people. The men who entered my father's tailor shop—who could afford a fine suit and there weren't many of them—brought into that shop a sense of who they were, and my father was the man who measured them, who had a kind of relationship with them, who could understand a great deal about lives more broad than his own. He had come from a small village in southern Italy, but he was very fine with a needle and thread. He wanted to bring to the suits he made a sense of his own style. He had a great sense of caring about a perfect buttonhole, of measuring perfectly, of making a suit that would fit on the body and would elevate the presence. He was an artist with a needle and thread, and he didn't care if he would make a lot of money. Each suit was a work of art in his definition. And he was an observer.

We are the people of the underclass—people who went out and observed and were not observed. My father was an eavesdropping tailor. He knew a lot about the people who came into his shop. I grew up hearing about the lives of people, ordinary people, and I thought they were interesting. One of the people that I heard about was a man named Garet Garrett, a funny name. He was an editorial writer for the *New York Times*. He worked directly with the great Adolph Ochs, the patriarch of the *New York Times*, whose family still is in control of the newspaper. In his retirement Mr. Garrett would come to the Jersey shore and go to my father's shop to be measured. I was fourteen and in high school. I would eavesdrop on what Mr. Garrett was telling my father. My father learned the English language by reading the *New York Times*—particularly during World War II when my father's relatives back in Italy were all on the wrong side of the war. My father's brothers were fighting with Mussolini's army against the invading Allies in 1943. So I grew up with my father reading the *Times* with a certain sense of concern, being the only immigrant in the family and having his brothers shooting at the Americans and Canadians who were coming into Italy after the invasion of North Africa.

My father was trying to be patriotic, which he was on the surface, but in the evening after the door was closed and he'd turn on the shortwave radio, he would listen to the war news from Europe, particularly from Southern Italy. I was seeing in this little house of mine how major events affected us. Each day the *New York Times* had maps and arrows showing the armies getting closer and closer to my father's village and I could see a great sense of drama.

This is nonfiction; this is me. I was a kid going to Ocean City High School in New Jersey. I could hear Mr. Ochs referred to again and again by Mr. Garrett as Mr. Garrett was on a pedestal getting measured. My father would stitch and stitch and stitch all night making the perfect suit for what he thought was the perfect man. And I thought: I'm going to write my term paper on Mr. Ochs as he was described by Mr. Garrett. I started writing about Mr. Ochs for my English class. I got a B minus. I was very disappointed and so was my father.

About twenty-some years later, when I left the *New York Times* in 1965, the first thing I did was go back to the paper and write about some of those wonderful people, those characters who were in the city room and who were not news. The first person I wrote about was an obituary writer. He would wander around the city room with a little green cap, smoking a pipe in the days when you could smoke pipes. He would be thinking about death. He would be thinking about people who were about to die because he would interview them and tell them that he was going to update the files on these people, a sort of advance obituary. He made his living in this very distinguished way. The first thing I did when I went to *Esquire* from the *Times* was to write about Mr. Bad News, I called him. What was it like to be a man who interviewed people whose time on earth was worthy of space in the *New York Times* when they died?

Then I wrote about Clifton Daniel at the *Times* and about Harrison Salisbury, a great correspondent. I was seeing journalism as a great story, as being worthy of reporting. I wanted to move the realm of curiosity into the lives of people who were being ignored because they had something to say and their lives had something to represent, so I wrote about these people for *Esquire*. What I brought to that magazine was the fulfillment of my own desire to write about people who were generally ignored. A lot of this became the book, *The Kingdom and the Power*. But it all came from my being at the *New York Times* and seeing these people that were interesting and were not written about. The average city room character had not been written about, and it abounds in *The Kingdom and the Power*.

It all comes out of the tailoring background. As inquiring people, as curious people, we all bring parts of our ancestral experience to the way we see America, the way we see America represented.

I have a continuing quality of curiosity. I am sixty-nine years old, and I have as much of that curiosity as when I was twenty-two. Curiosity is not something that we are going to get from the Columbia School of Journalism or the University of Missouri or anywhere else. Curiosity comes from within us.

I will give you an example from the book on which I am now working. You let the story live and you let the characters live their lives. That's what I do in nonfiction: indulge my curiosity. I am interested in private lives, nonfiction as a creative form. Creative—not falsified—not making up names, using real names, not composite characters, no taking liberties with factual information, but getting to know your characters through research, trust, building relationships. You know them so well they are like part of your private life. I have a feeling of respect for these people, even though I have written about gangsters or pornographers in books like *Thy Neighbor's Wife*. But I saw the world as they see it. So curiosity is the beginning, seeing it as the son of a tailor. The diversity of a great newspaper allows for this kind of varied look at the larger world from writers who come from backgrounds as dissimilar as mine, people who have not had bookshelves in their homes, who have not gone to college.

I find a way to write with respect, a way to write the truth that is not insulting. That is where precise writing allows you to do things in telling the truth that sloppy writing will not allow you to do. I get this care for the language from reading the great fiction writers: F. Scott Fitzgerald, John O'Hara, Irwin Shaw, fine short story writers. They would write about girls in their summer dresses, the football player and his relationship with a woman. Carson McCullers wrote a little piece in *The New Yorker* about a jockey who wants to eat more than he can. She described in her short story, "The Jockey," how each time this man eats a lamb chop he seems to see its formation on the side of his ribs.

When I was a sports writer, I wanted that kind of detail. I couldn't make it up, but I wanted that kind of detail. Fiction writers were my idols, but I wanted to bring that sense of reality to my nonfiction. Even when I was a daily journalist, I wanted to write the news through people. I wanted to write about people. When I covered a fire, the people were talking across the tenements. There was a kind of unity to the neighborhood. It wasn't a major fire, but I wrote about the fire through the dialogue, the firemen, the dog barking, the hoses all over the street, and the blocked traffic. It was a scene. This two-bell fire became a feature story.

In 1999 I had spent eight years unable to finish a book that I am now finishing. I wanted to get to my own story, but I didn't know how to get into it. I wanted to write about John Wayne Bobbitt, the guy who lost his penis. He got no sympathy from anybody and his wife was now being treated as a virtuous woman because he got what he deserved. This was interesting. So I got to know John Bobbitt and I hung around with him for six months. I drove him around, got to know him, got to know his doctor, and eventually got to know his wife. I traced the knife to Ikea where she had bought it three years before. I got the woman who sold the knife. Later on I became interested in urology and in 1995 I went to a convention in Las Vegas where there were eleven thousand urologists, and one of them, of course, was the guy who put back the penis. I also got John Bobbitt to come to that convention because I found that urologists are mostly men. In fact there was only one female urologist in New York.

I cultivated her.

"Are you going to the convention?" I asked her. "I want you to meet John Bobbitt."

"Oh, I'd like to meet John Bobbitt," she said. "I don't think his penis will ever work again."

"He told me it would work," I said. This was three years after the severance. "If I can introduce you to him, could you see if you could get it to work?"

We went to this hotel where we were all staying at the Hilton. John Bobbitt did agree to come over. The lady doctor put on some pornography on the hotel television set to try to get him sufficiently tumescent. And I had the scene. It was a wonderful scene. This is crazy, but I was looking for interesting situations. Getting a lady doctor and John Bobbitt in the same room was one of them.

After that I got involved with a restaurant owner at 206 E. 63rd St., a location where every restaurant failed, because I am interested in failure. Failure is a learning experience. When I was a sports writer the locker room of a loser was always more interesting than the locker room of a winner. So here was John Bobbitt, who was a loser in every sense, losing his most important member; for five hours it was on the grass. From 1992 until 1999 I had invested eight years of my life on three subjects: the restaurant that was always failing and the history of its building, a redneck sheriff from Selma from my days in the civil rights movement, and the John Bobbitt story. I added my own life coming into the *New York Times*, but the organizational problems were enormous. The choreography of nonfiction if it is sprawling presents major control problems. You have to get all the steps, all the dancers in accord, if the book is going to hold up. And I had been eight years working, floundering, getting nowhere.

But in July of 1999, a Saturday, I happened to be watching a baseball game on television between the Yankees and the Mets. I had been a Yankee fan all my life because during World War II the Yankees trained near Ocean City because of gas rationing, so I got hooked on baseball as an eleven-year-old and remain hooked from then until now. Anyway I was watching baseball, and on that same Saturday was a highly advertised game between the United States national women's soccer team and the national team of China. I was channel surfing, and I was interested in this soccer game because I had seen a number of Gatorade commercials involving Mia Hamm, who was doing the commercials with Michael Jordan and was beating him at everything. I had never heard of her, but Mia Hamm was said to be the greatest soccer player in the United States, not only among women but among men. So when I saw the United States soccer match led by Mia Hamm, I started flipping between the baseball game and the soccer, trying to avoid work, so I could get my mind off of the miserable life that I was living.

I had never watched soccer in my life; like people of my age, I don't understand soccer. It's a foreign game. My father might have understood it, but for all the wonderful things that were imported from the old country, they did not import soccer. And here I am watching this game, and I'm not being very enthralled by it because I don't understand it. But I do know that there are ninety thousand people in the Rose Bowl watching it. They were enthusiastic. I don't know what they were making all the noise about, but they were clearly excited. I was interested because of the adversarial relationship between the United States and China. That relationship brought a kind of Cold War element to the game as great sports events sometimes do, as a Joe Louis v. Max Schmeling fight did years ago in the period of Nazi Germany.

So I saw this game as interesting on that level. These women from the People's Republic of China are athletes and they are against the United States and Mia Hamm. It wound up being a nothing-nothing game. But after the extra time they had a shootout of penalty kicks. One Chinese woman ended up missing the penalty kick, and the game was over. If

I were a sportswriter I would be in that locker room right now, and I wouldn't be talking to Mia Hamm—I would be talking to that woman who missed the kick. She has to get on that airplane in Los Angeles and go all the way back to China somewhere, twenty-some hours in the air, and she has to live with that. She has to go back to a China that is so eager to knock off the Americans, so angry at our meddlesome foreign policy. It struck me that this was the way to write about China. This woman is twenty-five years old and she lost; she screwed up. What is it like for a twenty-five-year-old woman to screw up in this Communist regime emerging as a world power with a certain sense of an adversarial relationship with the United States?

I thought: "Oh, the *New York Times* will have that tomorrow." But there was nothing in the paper about this woman who missed the kick. That week both *Newsweek* and *Time* had cover stories. This was the Women's World Cup. It was a big thing. But there was nothing about what I wanted to know. It was all about the American victory, and something about the Chinese and how they missed the kick, but nothing about that woman—number 13, missed the kick, little red uniform, didn't know how to shoot straight and missed it.

So at my age I have met a lot of people who are powerful in journalism, and I know a big honcho at Time-Warner, *Time*, *Sports Illustrated*, *Fortune*, all that. So I called him.

"Norman," I said. "In the article today there was nothing about the Chinese woman." So I sent him a fax, and I told him what I thought would be a good story.

I said, "If you write about this woman, she will tell you something about how the Chinese react to this woman, what the neighborhood said about her, what her mother had to deal with. This Women's World Cup was on television around the world. She is suddenly being watched by the world, and she misses. How do they deal with defeat? We are talking about women who are part of the great achievement of China's being a world power, and she is therefore part of this. She is young, and she's probably had a great-great grandmother who had bound feet. And now she is using soccer to represent the new China, but she misses the damn ball, and she now represents disappointment."

This woman is an insignificant nonstory because it wasn't in the *New*

York Times; it wasn't in *Newsweek*. But I thought she could be a real key to representing the story of China. And I told him that I would be glad to do that story.

They called me up, thanked me for my idea, and told me to keep sending ideas in the future because I have good ideas. But nothing happened. Nothing happened. So the summer passes, and I am not getting anywhere. I was celebrating my fortieth anniversary with my wife in Frankfurt. And I decided I was not going back to New York at the end of the week. I went to the airport and changed my ticket and went to Hong Kong. I went to get a ticket into Beijing, speaking not a word, knowing nobody. I checked into a good hotel because surely someone would speak English in the hotel. I asked the concierge. This is not like calling the public relations department of the New York Yankees for an interview with Derek Jeter. You can get that tomorrow. But here I am, over there, wanting to talk to someone who had missed a kick. It was not something to be very proud of.

It took me five months. I stayed in China five months looking for her. And you have to be pretty damn curious to stay in China for five months. But finally after five months I got to meet her. And I kept seeing her again and again through interpreters. I got to see her on the field, meet her teammates. I got to know them. Soon I had put a year in it. I got permission from the coach to go with them when they went to games. One of the places they went to was Taiwan. In the year 2000 the Chinese mainland team went to Taiwan, and I went with them. I wasn't on the team bus, but I was following them, and I was able to hang around. What I am talking around is the art of hanging around. This is the type of nonfiction that I indulge in, hanging around people. You don't necessarily interview them, but you become part of the atmosphere. That is what I gradually did, even in China.

I have been on that story for two years. And now not only has that story come together, but all that other stuff—John Wayne Bobbitt, the restaurant that doesn't work, the redneck sheriff in post-Selma, all that—is now the story of me trying to deal with reality, with all its misadventures, it's wrong turns but with an ever-energized quest to know something about the people who tend to be ignored. This has been my life-long experience from the time I was a kid on the *New York Times* until now when I stand before you battered and aged—well-tailored but battered and aged.

I am the same guy, the same guy who is interested in all those people. So the little girl who missed the kick is a featured figure in this book that I am doing; the redneck sheriff is a featured figure; the guy who couldn't get his act together in a restaurant is a featured figure; and Loraine and John Bobbitt also make more than one appearance. Mr. Garrett is in there, as is the trip to Alabama, my own odyssey into the Deep South—like my father's before me from Calabria in Southern Italy to America.

It's the continuation of American assimilation, the lasting change of America, and the growth of American education to the point where the journalism is far superior to what it once was. This is my life as a journalist, the son of a tailor who is curious about everyday people. It is all there in the book that I am writing.

Daniel W. Lehman

The Body Out There

The Stakes of Jon Krakauer's Adventure Narratives

Reading Jon Krakauer is like shouldering your way through tangled under-growth toward a stone-cold slab where a body cools.

You move carefully; you take your time. You think you've been here before: daredevils high on the mountain's icy face or deep in the Alaskan woods. They hurl themselves against the implacability of nature and are found wanting. Their bodies await you: you already know that. But there's something more here. Something you sense more than see. You part the branches and look for signs. The writer is out here somewhere: weighing himself against the scale of his task, testing his limits, carving his prose, working his ice ax into the fissures of history. And over there, over that rise, are the readers who have been wounded by his work.

THE IMPLICATIONS OF NONFICTION

> It was as if there was an unspoken agreement on the mountain to pretend that these desiccated remains weren't real—as if none of us dared to acknowledge what was at stake here. (*Into Thin Air* 107)

Jon Krakauer's task is to make these stakes real for his readers. Indeed, we read Krakauer not so much to find out what will happen to his heroes (we already know from the dust jackets of his books that they will die) as to ponder the lessons of their deaths and to breach the veil that normally separates the dead from the undead. Krakauer's winding narratives draw us toward the bodies in the snow or on the abandoned bus in the Alaskan wilderness; few readers can resist his invitation to a prolonged gaze at their horror.

Death always sells.

But *Into Thin Air*, Krakauer's account of the May 10, 1996, blizzard on Mt. Everest that killed eight climbers, and *Into the Wild*, his story of the Alaskan death of young adventurer Christopher McCandless, also are remarkable for Krakauer's almost unprecedented willingness to reveal and to second-guess the reporting methods that make his narratives possible. Certainly few best-selling thrillers have made such capital of their indeterminacy. The author discloses the manner by which conflicting evidence robs his stories of certainty, confesses the mistakes he has made as a reporter, and repeats the angry accusations of survivors who have been hurt by his narratives. It's as if both he and his subjects are risking it all for a payback that will either spell death or recovery. Krakauer's work thus grows from a conundrum unique to nonfiction: their power depends on a claim to tell the truth about death, even as their premises trouble the foundation on which truth lies.

These matters penetrate the heart of the nonfictional transaction and are far less typical of standard forms of fiction. The writer of nonfiction—particularly disaster narratives—gains the power and sanctity that a reader might assign to actual lives in exchange for the responsibility of reproducing those lives in text. While a reliable truth standard may be insufficient to build an unwavering distinction between fiction and nonfiction, the experience of reading the invented and the historical tale is anything but identical. Nonfiction is a form of communication that purports to reenact for the reader the play of actual characters and events across time. What counts is not so much whether the events are historically fixed, but that they also are available to and experienced by readers and subjects outside of the written history. Because both the author and her subjects engage in a contest for meaning in narrative drawn from historical experience, an author who makes a claim that her story is "true" is forced to negotiate her role in reconstructing and telling events. Jon Krakauer seems to understand that responsibility. Indeed, Krakauer shatters the false dichotomy that over the past few years too often has typified discussions about nonfiction. His work proves that scrupulous, in-depth reporting and self-probing memoir can join forces to produce compelling historical narrative.

> I felt increasingly uncomfortable in my role as a journalist. . . .
> When they signed up with Hall's expedition, none of them [the oth-
> er climbers] knew that a reporter would be in their midst—scrib-
> bling constantly, quietly recording their words and deeds in order
> to share their foibles with a potentially unsympathetic public. (*Into
> Thin Air* 137–38)

Because they write nonfiction reporters face the journalistic equivalent
of the Heisenberg Uncertainty Principle: the act of observing the real
life phenomenon invariably alters its conditions. That principle takes
on somewhat more ominous overtones when the phenomenon to be
observed is the death of another. Unlike a lesser reporter Krakauer seems
to understand the way he trades on the power of death to excite readers
and therefore reveals both his access to facts and his personal responsibility as a character and as a reporter. In *Into the Wild* Krakauer admits that
Christopher McCandless's disappearance and death in the Alaskan wilderness "struck a personal note that made a dispassionate rendering of the
tragedy impossible." Although he says he tried, "and largely succeeded, I
think," to minimize his presence, he offers the reader a direct warning not
to trust him as an impartial observer: "I interrupt McCandless's story with
fragments of a narrative drawn from my own youth," Krakauer says. "I do
so in the hope that my experience will throw some oblique light on the
enigma of Chris McCandless" (unpaginated author's note).

And on Everest Krakauer goes even further. He admits that he ignored
the advice of seasoned editors by writing the book so soon after a tragedy
in which he was involved. "I ignored it—mostly because what happened
on the mountain was gnawing my guts out," he confesses. "I thought that
writing the book might purge Everest from my life. It hasn't, of course"
(xii). Krakauer thus trades the distance of objectivity for the heat of grief
and regret. "I hoped something would be gained by spilling my soul in the
calamity's immediate aftermath, in the roil and torment of the moment,"
he writes. "I wanted my account to have a raw, ruthless sort of honesty
that seemed in danger of leaching away with the passage of time and the
dissipation of anguish" (xiii). Objectivity, it turns out, was never possible.
Krakauer's presence on the climbing expedition organized by Rob Hall's

Adventure Consultants not only affected his fellow climbers, but also may have caused Hall and other guides to take risks they would not normally take. One of those companions, Beck Weathers, later admitted in an interview cited by Krakauer that the reporter's presence "added a lot of stress." Specifically, Weathers said, "That somebody may have you written across the pages of some magazine as a buffoon and a clown has got to play upon your psyche as to how you perform, how hard you'll push. And I was concerned that it might drive people further than they wanted to go" (138).

Krakauer's book length narratives are further deepened and complicated because they grow from extended articles that Krakauer first published in *Outside* magazine. Krakauer's reporting assumes interlocking levels: the initial events, the process of reporting by which the events were first recounted, the effects of the initial narratives on magazine readers, and the way that the initial reading and response affected the narratives later published in Krakauer's books. Added to these layers are Krakauer's subsequent participation in *Outside* magazine online discussion groups about his articles, as well as his responses to several letters written to the magazine. One example of this multi-layering is that Krakauer alters his conclusion in *Into the Wild* about what caused Chris McCandless's death, deciding upon further research after the *Outside* article appeared that McCandless was tricked by a highly technical mistake in a guidebook to edible plants rather than by the more elementary mistake of confusing a wild pea for a wild potato as Krakauer had reported in *Outside* (192–93).

As another example, the publication of the magazine article prompted an eighty-year-old friend and would-be adoptive grandfather of McCandless, Ronald Franz, to contact Krakauer and to offer valuable insights and letters that became the primary sources for the book's "Anza-Borrego" chapter. In it, Krakauer extends the central theme of the book: that McCandless avoided any relationship that had potential for family closeness. The author relies on a long letter from McCandless to Franz to slip into McCandless's point of view. "McCandless was thrilled to be on his way north," Krakauer reports, "and he was relieved as well—relieved that he had again evaded the impending threat of human intimacy, of friendship, and all the messy emotional baggage that comes with it. He had fled the claustrophobic confines of his family" (55). One of Krakauer's sources for this omniscient reporting appears to be passages written by

McCandless in a letter to Franz that the elderly man showed to Krakauer after the *Outside* article but before publication of *Into the Wild*. "You are wrong if you think Joy emanates only or principally from human relationships," McCandless had written to Franz. "God has placed it all around us. It is in everything and anything we might experience. We just have to have the courage to turn against our habitual lifestyle and engage in unconventional living" (57). Because McCandless had rejected Franz's offer to adopt him as a grandson and had counseled the older man that "you do not need me or anyone else to bring this new kind of light into your life" (57), Krakauer was able to conclude that McCandless's solitary trip to Alaska freed him from all his "messy emotional baggage" (55). Krakauer's careful reporting made such conclusions possible, but, as we shall see, such conclusions produce reactions among readers that are not always under the author's control.

WOUNDED BY HIS WORK

Based on your written word, you certainly seem now to have the uncanny ability to know precisely what was going on in the minds and hearts of every individual on the expedition. Now that you are home, alive and well, you have judged the judgments of others, analyzed their intentions, behaviors, personalities and motivations. . . . All according to Jon Krakauer, who after sensing the doom brewing, scrambled back to his tent for his own safety and survival. (*Into Thin Air* 285)

Characters in nonfiction have a presence that cannot be managed by the text; therefore, the ability of the narrator to know and report on the motivations of characters can implicate the nonfiction author in ways that rarely are faced as directly by writers of omniscient fiction. In fiction an author feels free to relay the thoughts of characters and to reveal their motives; in nonfiction, by contrast, these decisions can be costly. For years reporters and editors have debated whether nonfiction can make use of after-the-fact scene reporting or omniscient narration—all the while treating these decisions as primarily *formal*, rather than primarily *social*, dilemmas. Jon Krakauer's work—because of its many levels and its uncommon amount of candor—allows readers to weigh the social ramifications of his textual decisions.

Most reporters would bury an angry letter such as the one Jon Krakauer received after his *Outside* article from Lisa Fischer-Luckenbach, the sister of a man killed on Everest. Scott Fischer was the leader and head guide of the Mountain Madness guided expedition, whose illness from hypothermia and cerebral edema on Everest the day of the ill-fated climb caused him to lag behind his team and was one of a long series of crucial circumstances that helped to bring about the Everest tragedy. That Krakauer chooses to reprint his sister's angry response to the *Outside* piece in *Into Thin Air* reveals a lot about both Krakauer and about the social responsibilities of nonfiction narrative. In *Outside* magazine Krakauer on two occasions had questioned Fischer's decisions in ways that came close to omniscient reporting. One was Krakauer's conclusion that, in trying to become established in the expedition business, Fischer "needed to get clients to the summit, especially a high-profile one like Sandy Hill Pittman, the Manhattan boulevardier-cum-writer who was filing daily diaries on an NBC World Wide Web site." In the magazine article Krakauer concluded from interviews with other clients that Fischer did nothing to stop his most experienced Sherpa guide, Lopsang Jangbu, from hauling Pittman up the mountain on a short rope and thus exhausting himself to the detriment of other clients when Fischer became ill. Additionally Krakauer had concluded that Fischer was partially to blame for allowing his top Russian guide, Anatoli Boukreev, to climb without oxygen, a decision that perhaps left Boukreev's energy depleted during the crisis. A careful reading of both the magazine article and the book shows that Krakauer appears to have ample reporting to back up his forays into omniscience, but the reaction they produced (including angry letters from both Lopsang and Boukreev) shows the ways that nonfiction writers risk bruising real-life readers with competing perspectives on similar events. (Indeed, the most recent edition of *Into Thin Air* contains a tortured account of Krakauer's interactions with Boukreev before the latter's death in a climbing accident. Their competing accounts of what happened on Everest became a long-running saga of "he said, she said" proportions.

The much longer narrative about Everest contained in *Into Thin Air* allowed Krakauer to expand on his observations and to provide more detailed documentation. For example, in the magazine article, Krakauer had said that "Fischer encouraged his clients to be independent, to move at their own pace, to go wherever they wanted, whenever they wanted" and suggested that the guide's attitude grew out of his "infectious, seat-of-the-pants approach to his own life [that] was reflected in his improvisational approach to guiding Everest." In the book Krakauer had space to write a much longer profile of Fischer that helps to explain how Krakauer was so certain of the sort of thought process that typified the Mountain Madness leader. "Hey, experience is overrated. It's not the altitude that's important, it's your attitude, bro'. You'll do fine," Krakauer recalls Fischer telling him about the Everest expedition. ". . . We've got the big E figured out, we've got it totally wired. These days, I'm telling you, we've built a yellow brick road to the summit" (66).

In addition to the influence that any reporter has on the events that he covers, and in addition to the wounds caused when writers report thought patterns and motivations, Krakauer tells the reader that several of his decisions on the Everest climb directly altered those events. Krakauer's misidentification of another hiker for New Zealand guide Andy Harris during the fatal snow squall meant that rescuers at first believed Harris was safe and delayed rescue efforts when Harris might have been saved. Moreover, Krakauer's misidentification caused the team to radio Harris's female companion in New Zealand, Fiona McPherson, and to inform her that Harris was safe when in fact he had lost his life. Together these misjudgments added up to a mistake that Krakauer says is "likely to haunt me the rest of my life" (88). During the period between the publication of the magazine article and the book, Krakauer learned he had compounded the mistake by reporting in *Outside* that Harris had plunged off a four thousand-foot drop into the Western Cym when, in fact, he had died from exposure much higher up the mountain. "I was stunned," Krakauer recalls in the book. "For two months I'd been telling people that Harris had walked off the edge of the South Col to his death, when he hadn't done that at all. My error had greatly and unnecessarily compounded the pain" of Fiona McPherson and Harris's family (220). Even though Krakauer directly was responsible for the rescue of fellow climber Beck Weathers from certain death and played an important role in the partially successful Everest rescue, the author Krakauer details the shortcomings of the character Krakauer with an honesty that is rare among contemporary journalists: "My actions—or failure to act—played a direct role in the death of Andy Harris. And while

Yasuko Namba (a fellow climber) lay dying on the South Col, I was a mere 350 yards away, huddled inside a tent, oblivious to her struggle, concerned only with my own safety," he reports in the book. "The stain this has left on my psyche is not the sort of thing that washes off after a few months of grief and guilt-ridden self-reproach" (271).

ABANDONMENT AND RECOVERY

I tied my sleeping bag to the end of one of the curtain rods and waved it for all I was worth. The plane banked sharply and headed straight at me. The pilot buzzed my tent three times in quick succession, dropping two boxes on each pass; then the airplane disappeared over a ridge, and I was alone. As silence again settled over the glacier, I felt abandoned, vulnerable, lost. I realized that I was sobbing. Embarrassed, I halted the blubbering by screaming obscenities until I grew hoarse. (*Into the Wild* 141)

While Jon Krakauer, the writer, had ample material about Jon Krakauer, the character, to mine for his Everest narrative, his account of Christopher McCandless's death in the Alaskan wilderness, invited the writer to inject himself in a more unusual way. As Krakauer discloses in the author's note cited near the beginning of this essay, the writer discards objectivity for an inter-subjective examination of McCandless that trades both on in-depth reporting and relentless self-examination. Can he explain what drove Chris McCandless to his death by writing a memoir of his own reckless assault on the Stikine Ice Cap of Alaska's Devil's Thumb some twenty years earlier? Krakauer tells us that, like McCandless, "figures of male authority aroused in me a confusing medley of corked fury and hunger to please" (134). Like McCandless Krakauer was obsessed with proving his character against nearly impossible physical challenges. "I was twenty-three, a year younger than Chris McCandless when he walked into the Alaska bush," Krakauer tells us. "My reasoning, if one can call it that, was inflamed by the scattershot passions of youth and a literary diet overly rich in the works of Nietzsche, Kerouac, and John Menlove Edwards" (135), a British rock climber and psychiatrist who committed suicide in 1958.

Krakauer's decision to render the McCandless story subjectively seems in retrospect to have been productive. Because he never was able to interview his young subject and because he had only limited letters and journals available from McCandless, Krakauer's interweaving of his own story with that of his subject adds depth to the narrative, insights into McCandless's relationship with his own father, and credibility to Krakauer's reporting voice. Yet beyond what Krakauer acknowledges in *Into the Wild*, a careful reading of Krakauer's work provides a pathway into Krakauer's blend of memoir and research as well as the risks that he has taken as a reporter.

Krakauer's writing—in his choice of subjects, in his unconventional methodology, indeed, even in his selection of the nonfiction genre—enacts a drama of risk and abandonment that forces competing alternatives of death or recovery. The risks that Krakauer takes as an adventurer and as a writer explain in large measure the extraordinary degree to which he implicates himself, particularly in *Into Thin Air*, as a reporter. The author, it seems, wishes to test himself at every turn—sometimes by taking physical risks, sometimes by writing manuscripts against the advice of others, always by pitting his talents against the expectations of his subjects and readers in the deeply implicating nonfictional transaction. Krakauer, himself, recognizes the link between his adventurism and his writing. In fact, he has explicitly rejected the advice of more timid associates who have counseled caution in physical challenges or discretion in matters of the pen.

"Some of the same people who warned me against writing hastily had also cautioned me against going to Everest in the first place," Krakauer tells his reader at the opening of *Into Thin Air*. "There were many, many fine reasons not to go, but attempting to climb Everest is an intrinsically irrational act—a triumph of desire over sensibility. Any person who would seriously consider it is almost by definition beyond the sway of reasoned argument" (xiii).

Applied to the extraordinarily personal Stikine Ice Cap episodes of *Into the Wild*, this sort of analysis illustrates why physical and emotional abandonment is so freighted for the isolated adventurer in the Krakauer narrative. Both McCandless and Krakauer, the author tells us, were haunted by their discovery of deep personality flaws in their fathers. Krakauer understands this link between the two young men but seems rather less aware of the manner by which he seeks recovery. *Into the Wild* culminates in a scene that reunites the surviving father of Chris McCandless with

Krakauer himself, whose own father is now gone. Krakauer seems to seek psychic recovery with his own father by reconciling the elder McCandless to his son's memory.

For this essay to prove that assertion, a careful reading of Christopher McCandless's flight from his father and family against the backdrop of Krakauer's own fragile family relationships is in order. Christopher McCandless became estranged from his father, Walter, in June of 1986, after learning that his father essentially had lived as a bigamist many years earlier and had fathered a child in his other marriage after Chris was born. Curiously Krakauer tells us that "two years passed before [Chris's] anger began to leak to the surface" (122), but it is rather clear that Chris's reaction to his father's deception surfaced almost immediately in a dramatic way. Prior to his discovering his father's transgressions, Chris's sister recalls that Chris had told his father "he was grateful for all the things Dad had done for him . . . how much he respected Dad for starting from nothing, working his way through college, busting his ass to support eight kids" (118). Yet, one month after learning of his father's other marriage in a visit to El Segundo, California, Chris wandered into the Mojave Desert, became lost, and nearly died of dehydration. He arrived at home thirty pounds underweight, reminding his sister, Carine, of "those paintings of Jesus on the cross" (118). When his father later counseled him "to be a little more careful and to keep us better informed of his whereabouts" (119), Chris bristled at his father. Although Krakauer doesn't say so, it is not much of a stretch to conclude the son believed that his father should have been the one to be "more careful" and should have kept the family "better informed of *his* whereabouts." Indeed, Chris's sister recalls during this period that Chris declared "the deception committed by Walt . . . made 'his entire childhood seem like a fiction'" (123).

In this context it seems clear that McCandless's Mojave Desert foray reenacted the abandonment he felt from his father when he learned of his father's other life. The sharp change in Chris's attitude toward his father corroborates this theory. Although Krakauer makes it clear that this discovery—reminiscent of, though even more dramatic than, Biff Loman's famous fictional discovery of Willy Loman's philandering in Boston—deeply affected McCandless, he qualifies the son's outrage by noting that Chris "didn't hold everyone to the same exacting standards" and "was temperamentally incapable of extending such lenity to his father" (122).

Krakauer seems here to pull his punches against the elder McCandless, perhaps because he knew how deeply the revelation would hurt the father and perhaps because of how closely the McCandless family's relationship mirrored that between Krakauer and his own father.

Like Chris, Krakauer virtually was estranged from his own father, particularly once he learned the "long-held family secret" that his father was a prescription drug addict and had attempted suicide (148–49). "[W]hen I noticed that this deity who asked only for perfection was himself less than perfect, that he was in fact not a deity at all—well, I wasn't able to shrug it off," Krakauer writes. "I was consumed instead by a blinding rage. The revelation that he was merely human, and frighteningly so, was beyond my power to forgive" (148). It is striking how much more anger Krakauer allows his own youthful character to articulate as contrasted to his rather sanguine description ("he was temperamentally incapable of extending such lenity") of Chris's anger. Krakauer thus deftly transfers most of the emotional weight of paternal transgression to his own dead father rather than to McCandless's living one—a move that seems to reveal Krakauer's desire not to wound further the elder McCandless.

"As a young man, I was unlike McCandless in many important regards; most notably I possessed neither his intellect nor his lofty ideals," Krakauer writes. "But I believe we were similarly affected by the skewed relationships we had with our fathers. And I suspect we had a similar intensity, a similar heedlessness, a similar agitation of the soul" (155). Both Chris McCandless and Krakauer, therefore, placed themselves repeatedly in risky situations that would reenact the abandonment of the father. For his part Krakauer recalls that on his Devil's Thumb expedition he felt "abandoned, vulnerable, lost" and that when he saw the lights of Petersburg, Alaska, from the mountain "I was overcome by a wrenching loneliness. I had never felt so alone, ever" (141, 152).

One of the more telling symbolic moments of the Stikine Ice Cap excursion is grounded in personal memoir that in turn illuminates Krakauer's reporting project. After the young Krakauer first fails to ascend Devil's Thumb, he accidentally burns an expensive nylon tent he had borrowed from his father. Krakauer recalls smoking a marijuana joint in a wallow of self-pity and burning the tent while trying to prepare oatmeal to cure a resulting case of the munchies. "For several minutes I sat dumbstruck, staring at the wreckage of the tent's once-graceful form amid the acrid scent of singed hair and melted nylon," Krakauer recalls. "You had to hand it to me. I thought: I had a knack for living up to the old man's worst expectations" (147). Ironically the scene prefigures another one twenty years later in *Into Thin Air*, after Krakauer has returned from Everest to the lowlands of Katmandu to wrestle with his memory of the failed expedition and his culpability in the death of his friends. Unable to relax he buys resinous marijuana from a street urchin and smokes a joint and a half until the room spins. "As I turned my head to the side, my ear brushed against a wet spot; tears, I realized, were running down my face and soaking the sheets," Krakauer writes. "I felt a gurgling, swelling bubble of hurt and shame roll up my spine from somewhere deep inside. Erupting out of my nose and mouth in a flood of snot, the first sob was followed by another, then another and another" (269–70).

The final scene of *Into the Wild* unites the reporting and memoir strands in an event that seems designed to close the gap between the elder and younger McCandless. Krakauer arranges for Walter McCandless and Chris's mother, Billie, to be helicoptered to the scene of Chris's death in the Alaskan wilderness. Billie is "calm and centered" as she prepares to visit her son's death site, but Chris's father is "distracted, irritable, edgy" (201). After the helicopter ride the elder McCandless is scowling and testy as he and his wife explore the abandoned bus where their son died. Walt hangs a brass plaque inside the door of the bus while Billie leaves a first-aid kit with a note urging anyone who finds it "to call your parents as soon as possible" (120). Our last glimpse of the father offers the reader the hope that Walter McCandless can begin to make peace with his son's death. "Walt, in a reflective mood, has had little to say," Krakauer reports, "but he appears more at ease than he has in many days. 'I didn't know how I was going to react to this,' he admits. 'But now I'm glad I came.' . . . This brief visit, he says, has given him a slightly better understanding of why his boy came into this country. There is much about Chris that still baffles him and always will, but now he is a little less baffled. And for that small solace he is grateful" (203). Although his own father is dead, Krakauer takes faith from the symbolic reunification of father and son, merging memoir and reporting in a scene of reconciliation that joins the reporter and Chris McCandless. And the "small solace" that Walt McCandless drew comfort from that day has appeared to survive the publication of *Into the Wild*, at least in Krakauer's opinion. "Walt, Billie, and Carine have each told me that they think *Into the Wild* is an honest, well-told book, but I know its publication has been very hard for them," Krakauer told an online questioner in an *Outside* magazine forum in February, 1996. "I have immense respect for the McCandlesses and remain exceedingly grateful for their generosity and magnanimity."

Jon Krakauer is too complex a reporter and a man to have exorcized his demons with the graceful ending of *Into the Wild*; his even more complex and tortured *Into Thin Air* now proves that fact. Perhaps in an echo of his developing relationship with McCandless's parents, Krakauer recently disclosed in an interview with writer Mark Bryant on the first anniversary of the Everest tragedy that he has found some solace in contacts with Ron and Mary Harris. They are the parents of the Everest hiker Andy Harris, for whose death Krakauer feels responsible. "I've opened up my research to them, and Ron's read everything about Everest that he can . . ." Krakauer told Bryant. "[They] want to know every detail of what happened to Andy, even though there's not a lot of detail to be had. And so we have things to share. They don't hold me responsible, and yet they understand why I feel as I do. Ron says, and I concur, that we now have an unusual bond."

For a writer who obviously broods over human relationships and persists in testing their limits, it is somehow fitting that Krakauer has chosen a narrative form—literary nonfiction about death and trauma—that constantly pits him against readers and subjects in a struggle over meaning and that ultimately offers some hope for reconciliation after honest discovery. He seems to understand that one pathway into the writing of fact depends on both scrupulous reporting and painful self-discovery. His is a shifting, multi-leveled world, a world without obvious answers, a passage through tangled undergrowth. In that world, however, the possibility of truth will gleam like a high peak in the first light of morning.

WORKS CITED

Bryant, Mark. "Everest a Year Later: False Summit." *Outside* May 1997: http:// www.outsidemag.com/magazine/0597/9705krakauer.html.
Krakauer, Jon. "Death of an Innocent." *Outside* Jan. 1993: http://outsidemag.com/ magazine/0193/9301-ldea.html.
———. *Into the Wild*. New York: Anchor, 1996.

————. *Into Thin Air: A Personal Account of the Mount Everest Disaster.* New York: Villard, 1997.

————. "Into Thin Air." *Outside* Sept. 1996: http://outsidemag.com/0996/9609feev.html.

————. "*Outside* Online Guests: Jon Krakauer: Into the Wild." *Outside* 19 Feb. 1996: http://outsidemag.com/disc/guest/krakauer/qa0219bonesteel.html.

Andrea Lorenz

When You Weren't There

How Reporters Recreate Scenes for Narrative

The setting was a funeral on a cool, windy day. The pallbearers took up four rows. Writer Tom French described clothes, pictures, flowers, and streets lined with news crews. The choir sang a song, which French named, and the pastor asked a question, which French put in quotes: "How could God have let this happen?" The sermon continued. "From outside," French wrote, "the people could hear a sparrow chirping." This scene appeared in French's narrative series, "Angels and Demons," which won a Pulitzer Prize.

The question is do we care if Tom French was there at the funeral? French probably couldn't have been in that room because the reporters had to wait outside. And if French wasn't there at all, how could he have known it was a sparrow? Some might say, "French damn well better have been there."

The truth is that the funeral was years before French even started reporting. French had recreated the scene. He stood inside the church. He interviewed people who attended. Someone had an audiotape of the service. On the tape French heard weeping and birds singing. He sent the tape to a bird specialist, who said the sounds came from sparrows.

Unable to rely on their own eyes and ears, reporters look to witnesses and documentation, both paper and electronic, to create a setting so real it's like fiction. Interviews with eleven journalists who recreated scenes elicited four common attributes that were present to ensure accuracy: access, source cooperation, trust between reporter and source, and a harmony of source accounts. Because of the small sample size of the analysis, the results cannot be generalized. However, among the eleven journalists, any variation of the four attributes resulted in an interrupted narrative, unless the writers found tools to smooth the story.

ACCESS TO INFORMATION

Obtaining the cooperation of parties holding key information is helpful when reporting any story. But access is essential in narrative reporting, when reporters forgo the traditional news form in favor of literary tools. While reporting "Out of Nowhere: Inside the Pentagon on 9/11," Earl Swift of the *Virginian-Pilot* had a source who gave him a floor plan of the Pentagon. "I charted where everybody sat and where everybody was at the exact moment that the plane hit and what route they took to get to the door," Swift said. "Without that floor plan, it would have been way vague and a completely different story." The maps and diagrams Swift created in his reporting were extensive. But none appeared in the story, and the readers never knew about all that hard work.

Maura Lerner of the *Star Tribune* in Minneapolis had a similarly open experience with the military. She reconstructed an injured soldier's surgery and her return home in a coma. With the soldier's permission the military hospitals gave Lerner the soldier's medical records. The nurses' and doctors' notes contained the information necessary to reconstruct the chronology of events. "Good thing," Lerner said, "because the initial newspaper reports about the soldier were wrong." The records were the backbone of the narrative, which she supplemented with details from extensive interviews with doctors, nurses, and the soldier's family.

Another instance of access to records was Tom Farragher's experience reporting the murder of a priest in prison. Farragher of the *Boston Globe* obtained prison records of the incident and correspondence between the priest and his lawyers. But the priest's sister didn't want Farragher to see the letters between her and her brother. Farragher was still able to recreate the key scene of his murder, but the reconstruction of the priest's life in prison would have been enhanced by the correspondence with his sister. Access to information means more than obtaining a file. Like French and the funeral, Farragher visited the prison where the priest was killed to experience smells and sounds for himself.

Keith McKnight and Ed Meyer used complete records of a boating accident they recreated for the *Akron Beacon Journal*. They did not rely on newspaper reports because some details turned out to be false.[1] The records allowed them to recreate the physical effects of the crash on the victims and the boat's infrastructure. McKnight wrote this section without attribution. But the recreation was incomplete because of the problems Meyer had accessing sources.

SOURCE COOPERATION

Two of the three people on the boat were killed in the accident. The only survivor refused to participate. Meyer tried to contact him, but the accident had been detrimental to the survivor's career and personal life. The resulting narrative had few details about what happened in the boat before and immediately after the crash. As a result, McKnight used traditional news-style attribution in the narrative.

Eric Adler of the *Kansas City Star* found that in order to recreate cheerleading tryouts when he was reporting on an overweight cheerleader, he had to track down each girl who tried out, as well as the coach. "You've got to talk to them all," Adler said. He had the total cooperation of the squad and the cheerleader's family. The day was memorable to her family because on the night of the tryouts her father committed a crime that would later put him in jail. Recreating a less significant day would have been tougher.

---

1. Maura Lerner of the *Star Tribune* also found inaccurate information in previous newspaper accounts about her subject. Can reporters rely on newspaper accounts as an accurate memory of the event? Steve Paul of the *Kansas City Star* must rely on Star reports from 1941 about Ernest Hemingway's visit to Kansas City. "If he says Hemingway said something, I guess I believe him," Paul said. The reporter said it rained that day, and Paul did check it out with weather reports. But "was the rain beating against the screen at the same moment I have Hemingway saying something that the article also said? I don't know," Paul said. Walt Harrington said newspaper articles are considered documentary pieces of information. "We will trust that even though that has all the problems of accuracy we're worried about today." Harrington points out that reporters question sources' memories more than they question newspaper articles. In the end reporters must judge each instance on a case by case basis. Paul resolves his conflict by asking "What can I say? How can I say it? How do I know what I know?"

Finding out someone in your family has cancer is also a memorable moment. But Jeremiah Tucker of the *Joplin Globe* in Missouri had trouble recreating the scene for a narrative he wrote about a dying woman. He couldn't find the chaplain or the physician who were present when the woman's family heard she had cancer. He based the scene on accounts from the family members, but they could not remember the conversation. The resulting narrative included no dialogue and only vague details because his sources, although fully cooperative, had faulty memories.

Military sources are "a reporter's dream" to work with when recreating scenes, Earl Swift found when he interviewed Pentagon workers. "These were very smart, detail-driven people with a meticulous nature," Swift said. "They're all personnel experts, which was even better because they're completely anal." Swift was fortunate because not only was he given total access to military records, but his sources were all willing to talk with him, if only to get a story into the media that they felt had been neglected. He trusted these sources as reliable witnesses, and they trusted him. This is not always the case.

TRUST BETWEEN SOURCE AND REPORTER

Ken Fuson had absolutely no trust in the title character of his narrative series, "The Truth about Bob," that he wrote for the *Des Moines Register*. "It's hard to reconstruct scenes with somebody who will agree to anything," Fuson said. "He's a notorious liar." In fact, the series was about how Bob conned a few Iowans into opening their homes and lives to him. Fuson remembers thinking "Jeez, am I going out on a limb here?" about a scene he reconstructed involving Bob and only one other person. "But the other woman was so specific I believed her," Fuson said. "So I thought I'd go with this is how it happened. I went over it with her several times."

Meyer and McKnight had the opposite problem with trust when recreating the boating accident. Not only would a key witness not participate, the sources who agreed to talk with Meyer did not fully trust him. The team was under pressure to complete the story quickly without spending too much money, so Meyer had to do interviews in the span of a couple days, and one key witness did not agree to an interview until just days before publication. This lack of trust played a role in the high level of traditional attribution used.

Over time Roy Peter Clark built up a high level of trust between him and a source for the series, "Three Little Words," in the *St. Petersburg Times*. Clark described the turmoil a family experienced when they found out their father and husband was gay and HIV positive. "I had a woman as my main character who was willing to tell me everything," Clark said. "And who was willing to answer all of my questions, including some amazingly intimate ones that I'm amazed I had the courage to ask." This trust, in addition to extensive reporting—such as visiting Brazil to recreate the deceased character's trips—allowed recreations whose accuracy Clark is confident of.

Eric Adler relies on internal dialogue in his narratives. "That's how characters are made," he said. "I think internal dialogue can bring you greater truth than memory of external dialogue. Thoughts are often more active than mouths." He gets this dialogue through extensive interviews and trust. "Just for a simple line, you get a half-hour interview. The story doesn't go into that history, but I know it as I'm writing." One hour of reporting made Adler comfortable enough to say that the overweight cheerleader had always thought another cheerleader beautiful, "with legs like a giraffe's." To get a teenage girl to talk about her inner feelings regarding her weight and to share insults by her peers, Adler had to spend hours with the source to build up trust.

SOURCE DISAGREEMENT

What happens when everyone agrees to interviews, but they don't agree with each other's accounts? It would be nice if every story involved Swift's military sources, who by nature constantly check their watches and internally note details. Swift recreated a meeting that was going on when a plane hit the Pentagon. "They all agreed, but they were sitting at different places around the table. Will had remembered McNair stand up and say 'What the hell was that?' McNair remembered seeing Marilyn's expression changing just as Will stood up and said 'What the hell was that?' So it was kind of cool that I had so many recollections to hear."

Again Meyer and McKnight's sources were less than perfect. McKnight wanted to write how the boat sounded when it hit the dock: "Was it a thump or a thud?" Besides the one survivor who refused to talk, there were two witnesses within earshot of the crash. One said it was a thump.

But the woman who was first on the scene couldn't recall hearing a sound at all. "When it hit, it made some sort of sound to draw her attention to it," McKnight said. "She was out back waiting for her husband and son to come home. She ran down to the water's edge." But the woman could not remember a sound. McKnight decided to attribute the thump to the man who remembered.

"I found in instances like this where there's trauma involved, very often people remember different things," McKnight said. "As time goes on their memory might become enhanced, and you have to guard against that. I know we fiddled around with the attribution then, putting it squarely in his lap, saying this is what he remembers. And it has nothing to do with libel—it has to do with accuracy."

Reporters must be able to trust not only the source but the source's memory. And that's tough. Walt Harrington said it's "not that we believe the subjects are lying, but because we really, really understand now that trusting memory is a faulty thing." People don't intentionally remember events wrong. "We fill in blanks," Harrington said. "We alter things over time to shape where we have gone in the interim. So we employ all sorts of techniques to ensure what we're remembering is correct." Reporters might make details vague enough so that all sources agree. If disagreements cannot be resolved the scene might be omitted from the narrative.

Adler compromised between sources who disagreed. Someone said a pair of shoes was red, another person said purple. "Can we agree it was sneakers?" Adler asked. So he went with sneakers. Discrepancies call for the reporter to go back and forth between sources as Adler did. When trying to find a consensus between the main character and his wife in her narrative series for the *Plain Dealer* in Cleveland, Andrea Simakis talked to the two separately. "If they didn't correspond, I went back and said, 'Bob said this,'" Simakis explained. "And Mary would say, 'No, it didn't go that way.' I wrote Bob in prison, and he said, 'Oh, perhaps she's right.' I tried to get them together, as close as possible to the actual conversation to where they'd say, 'I agree with that.'"

"That's how these things work," Fuson said. "You go back and forth to people like ten times. If you get two to three people agreeing to something, that's good." When agreement is impossible without harming the accuracy, reporters have a couple choices: omission or attribution.

When a discrepancy among sources came up when Farragher was

reporting a narrative series on two brothers and their weddings, he and his cowriter decided to leave the scene out. "Three of four people in the family said that after Eric came out and said he was gay at a restaurant in Harvard," Farragher said, "his father went home that day and was so upset he was lying on the floor in the living room and pounding his fists."

The father denied the scene happened. Farragher was pretty sure the story was accurate because the other three witnesses described it in detail. It was a pretty dramatic moment that would have added to the story. But because the main character disagreed, they left it out. "To use it, you'd have to go through some sort of torturous attribution. It just wasn't worth it to interrupt the flow." Had he left the scene in the story, Farragher said he would have told the scene from the viewpoint of the father and then the three witnesses.

Simakis did just that. The central conflict of her narrative series involved differing accounts of the same fight. The man who ended up going to jail for the fight said he was provoked. A witness for the defense supported the man's claim. But the prosecution's witness said the man attacked multiple times without warning. Obviously Simakis could not recreate the scene without making clear the discrepancy between the two accounts.

"The places where everybody agreed the same thing happened, I reported as fact," Simakis said. "Things they disagreed about, I telegraphed within the text. The lawyers and editors were very uncomfortable with it, but it was a pivotal scene." Simakis compromised with nervous editors and lawyers by attributing information. But instead of using the traditional attribution "he said," as McKnight and Meyer used, Simakis indicated within the narrative that the two accounts were conflicting.

Harrington was reporting an article about Carl Bernstein for the *Washington Post* when two sources disagreed. One of Bernstein's friends said Bernstein was angry and hurt when someone did not invite him to a birthday party. Bernstein said he had thought the situation funny, not hurtful. Harrington went back to Bernstein's friend, who again confirmed it. Then Harrington interviewed Bernstein, who again denied it. "If Carl had said to me, 'Yeah I was angry and hurt,' I would have said he was," Harrington said. "What I wrote was a much more journalistic line: 'A close friend of Carl's said he was angry and hurt. Carl said he wasn't.'"

Harrington said he triangulated the information to a point when all relevant parties agreed. "When Carl didn't confirm it, when he continually denied it, I can't assume he was lying," he said. "I can only assume that there's ambiguity." If there's disagreement among sources, and the reporter cannot resolve the differences, the story must reflect the ambiguity. "Pretty traditional sourcing," Harrington said.

More than ten years ago Roy Peter Clark recreated a scene when a husband and wife told their children that their dad had AIDS. Clark faced ambiguity about the location. "I heard them debate it. And guess what standard I applied? Majority rules." Today, Clark would have done it differently.

"It's so hard to pin things down when people are relying on their memories, especially, and conflicting memories, that you lose the ambiguity as a reality in human existence," Clark explained. Tying details together in a neat package is not real life. Sit down with any family and ask about a significant event, Clark said. Not one person will remember the same details. By talking to everyone who knew the man, Clark completed what he perceives to be a good character portrayal, even though Clark himself had never met the man.

"I know him in a way better than his wife, his children, his friends knew him," Clark said. "And the reason I could say it is that I came to know him through all of the different ways that they knew him. Which is another reason to embrace the ambiguity. Because that's the way families are. It's more accurate." Including discrepancies in memory within the narrative reveals something about human experience with trauma. It reflects life. And that's the purpose of accuracy.

TEST

Roy Peter Clark offered a three-pronged test that reporters should put stories through before publication. The first is accuracy. "Have I worked hard enough? Have I checked it out enough to have confidence in the material?" To produce an accurate scene reconstruction reporters employ whatever tool necessary to ensure they have it right.

"It's dangerous turf," Swift said. "And you have to go in knowing that. The number one rule, take no liberties. Take every precaution. I don't hesitate to read pieces of my narrative back to subjects. Because it's those details that will kill you. One little detail that's wrong ruins the whole damn thing."

And not only fact errors render a story inaccurate. Simakis portrayed a man's character as someone who did not drink or fight. This judgment was the crux of the story's theme: a man received an unjust punishment. Simakis was nervous about whether she had the character right. Was she being duped? "I talked to his friends, his family, boss, and they all said he never fought. I spent an incredible amount of time talking to everyone I could find, everyone who had ever known him and asked them, was he ever tipsy? What does he do at a party? I also spent time around him when he was under stress, and I never saw him drink. It was actually just creepy." In the story readers never see the reporting that went into the character description Simakis formed. But she was confident in its accuracy. "That's why it took so long to report. I had to make sure he was the man he was presenting to me."

Another tool used for accurate scene reconstructions is sharing the scene with the sources involved. Most reporters interviewed were reluctant to say they allowed sources to read the scene before publication, but they admitted to doing it. Others prefaced the statement with "journalism professors won't approve, but . . ." Clark shared drafts with his central character because he was dealing with intimate details about her life. He shared medical accounts with a physician source because he wanted to make sure he didn't say anything "wrong or stupid" in the story about AIDS. Earl Swift, an opponent of both editor's boxes and any level of attribution within the narrative, reads drafts to sources. Other reporters did not offer drafts but went over quotes and facts with sources to ensure accuracy.

The second question Clark said to ask is "Will the truth of this story (with a small *t*) stand up against the toughest prosecutorial editing?" An editor challenges information before readers see the story. "You should be able to defend anything you've got in your story in terms of accuracy through the interrogation of a good editor," said Harrington. "They should never trust that their writer got that information correct."

In Farragher's case, his editor at the *Boston Globe* wanted direct quotes to be paraphrased in reconstructed scenes for the wedding article. One of the brothers wrote extensive journal entries, which were used to recreate scenes. Farragher checked with family members who witnessed a particular scene described in the brother's writing. Even though everyone agreed, the editor was not convinced. "We were pretty rigorous about what we could tell the reader what happened and what we would have to attribute," Farragher said.

In the narrative, The Lost Youth of Leech Lake, editors' questions led Larry Oakes of the *Star Tribune* to verify whether the boy who murdered his father also killed his dog as he alleged. "I mean, what if Darryl's got an overactive imagination?" Oakes said. "I didn't have any reason to disbelieve Darryl at that point, but I thought, verification's good." Police records did mention a dog's body found in the woods. The boy named the color of the dog, and the color corresponded with the dog in the reports. "But there are many, many other details that were left out because we couldn't feel completely confident, and there were others that stayed in after similar searches," Oakes said.

The third test Clark suggested is much more subjective. "What do we have to tell readers about what we know and how we know it to give the story credibility in their eyes?" Clark doubts readers question where particular information comes from. "I've never written a narrative where someone's written me a letter, an outraged message saying, 'Well how do you know that? How do you know she was thinking that?'" Clark said. "And I defy you to find somebody who's had that experience."

Yet Clark still approves of the movement of newspapers toward greater transparency in narrative journalism, especially when scenes are reconstructed. Harrington doubts there will ever be a standard for how much transparency is necessary for scene reconstructions or narrative pieces in general. He likened the prospect to how papers deal with unattributed sources. There are standards within each institution. They differ, and even if the standard is applied the only thing that clears the practice is if the information is correct. The same goes for scene reconstructions. Attribute or not, include editor's notes or footnotes, he said, but "is it right?" Always this question should be in the reporter's mind while he or she decides what level of transparency a story should use.

Traditional attribution, "he said he thought," or "he remembers he said," stumbles the reader. But a nagging question of how the reporter knows information can stumble the reader just as much. Harrington explained that when "the reader's reading along, and you drop in information that seems so unbelievable to them that they stop in the narrative and say, 'Wait a minute, how can he know that?'"

When the reader finds no answer to this question, credibility decreases. Fuson has no problem with scene reconstructions, but he wants to know where the information comes from. Otherwise he stops reading, and he feels that newspaper readers do the same. "You don't want to step on the narrative," he said. "But sometimes I think if you don't step on the narrative, you step on the credibility quotient of the narrative. It stops the narrative every bit as much as your attribution does."

Reporters and editors know the information they are presenting is true. "But for readers," Oakes said, "some attribution is necessary." He "sprinkled" attribution within the narrative "to keep reminding people that this was journalism and not just a writing project. We were confident that what we were describing was true because of all the research. But we didn't want our readers to be distracted by wondering where we were getting this stuff."

Narrative reporters use many of the same devices to divulge how they know something to the reader. Harrington pointed to the "ancient police beat story," which uses one general attribution. "According to police reports, *colon.*" A narrative reporter might say, "It is a night he will always remember." Then the following description is understood by readers to be the memory of one person. And instead of "he said he was thinking," Harrington said reporters use "and his mind wandered off to imagine what it would be like . . ." But when traditional newsroom editors insist on the "he says he remembers," type of attribution it hinders the narrative. "Well, you know, if you're going to be that strict about it," Harrington said, "I think there are severe limits for what you can do in terms of creating a story-like feel."

Earl Swift likens any attribution in narrative to a train derailment: "The first rule of narrative is you don't want to remind the reader that he or she is reading a newspaper story. Attribution indicates the reporter is getting a quote, and then the narrative's dead." Swift's narrative team at the *Pilot* generally uses no editor's explanations at the end of a story. "The amount of time devoted to making sure we have it right goes so far beyond what is involved in putting together most stories," he said. The editing addresses those concerns. "We CQ and we double-CQ and triple-CQ everything. Every factoid is combed over." Questions are resolved by the reporters and editors, so the conversation about accuracy does not come up in public.

Swift says the trust he has built with his editors and the public gives credibility to his work.

Fuson takes issue with this lack of transparency. Not even the reputation of Bob Woodward resolves his questions about where material comes from. "If there's a scene describing two people talking to each other, I want to know where it's coming from. If the reporter's not in the room, I want some idea where they got that so I can judge it for myself. That's really what you're doing with all the footnotes—establishing credibility. Why wouldn't they put in footnotes?" Fuson asked. "Why not use an editor's box when it increases credibility? Really, that's kind of what Woodward says, 'Trust me.' Well I don't."

"Woodward can do it because he's Woodward," said Harrington. But Woodward writes books. Newspapers, even if they are producing narrative, must still abide by the traditional standards. Whatever method for transparency reporters use, "I think it's a wholesome process that needs to happen," said Mark Kramer at the Nieman Conference of Narrative Journalism. Newsroom conventions of attribution must expand because of narrative, and conversely, narrative must accommodate newsroom standards of transparency. "Some writers have taken this call for play-by-play sourcing as doubting their integrity," Kramer said. "I'd rather think of the new custom as an institutional accommodation, a new way for papers to accept narrative writers."

Transparency doesn't require attribution or even an editor's note in some cases. Maura Lerner's reconstruction of the injured soldier's first days in the hospital came mostly from the soldier's mother. *Star Tribune* editor Laurie Hertzel explained that the decision to not use traditional attribution or an editor's box was based on a couple things.

First, "they were of fairly simple, ordinary moments, such as Jessica waking up in her hospital bed in Bethesda." The rest of the story was witnessed by the reporter and photographer, and Hertzel felt this was pretty obvious because readers were able to see photos taken by the newspaper in the hospital. That hint tipped off readers that most of the scenes were witnessed. The reconstructed scenes also included hints that the soldier did not remember what happened, so that most of the information came from the mother or doctors. Finally, the dialogue became longer as the story progressed, and Lerner said this should have signaled to readers that the longer dialogue was witnessed, and the shorter dialogue was recreated.[2]

Hertzel was also an editor for Oakes' narrative about American Indian teenagers. The second word of the narrative is "remembers," a traditional newspaper attribution. Oakes' scene had more at stake than Lerner's scenes. "Since he was reconstructing a murder," Hertzel said in an e-mail, "the question of how we knew what we wrote was crucial. Even though Darryl Headbird was serving forty years in prison for killing his father, we needed to let the reader know how we could write the details of the crime with such assurance."

Oakes' story had an editor's box, but the decision to include it was not based on scene reconstruction. Hertzel said Oakes' story was reported over several months and was investigative in nature. The narrative included controversial issues a tribe was dealing with. The box served to explain how much time and effort went into the project. Lerner's narrative was reported in just a few weeks. Reconstructing private moments in a hospital room does not have the same effect on people's lives or as much weight with a reader as reconstructing a murder. Using Hertzel's rationale, the more controversial or serious the narrative's topic, the more transparency is necessary.

The levity of an event does matter when considering how much transparency is needed for recreated scenes. And it comes down to how reporters and editors perceive the intelligence of their readers, Harrington said. Reporters leave hints readers should understand. "The lead to numerous features are 'When Susan Smith got up on her birthday last year, the first thing she thought was, I'm going to get flowers from Joe today.'" This sentence is accepted by readers and editors because it's uncontroversial and "anybody with a pea-sized brain will know that information came from Sue."

If the story states a person woke up hungry without attributing that information, and later in the story it is clear the person was interviewed,

---

2. Adler explains why dialogue in his recreated scenes is minimal:

> If you notice, in a lot of these pieces, the quotes are awfully short. That's because people will remember specific words . . . "Randy, stop it!" Her mother said it. Her brother said it. Can I say what she said after? You can imagine there's not just silence in between it and the next quote. But I can't verify anything beyond "Randy, stop it!" So that's what I write.

the reader will know that the reporter knew the source was hungry because the source said so. Fuson used this example to explain that unattributed information in newspapers, no matter the form of the story, creates doubts about credibility. "Let's say President Bush woke up and told his wife something, and I've made it clear they haven't been interviewed for the story," Fuson said. "Well, how do we know that? That's the difference." When readers might doubt the veracity of information, they need to know how reporters are doing their jobs.

It comes down to what sets off doubt in a reader? Swift's perspective is that the accuracy speaks for itself in the level of detail in the story, and the length of the narrative hints to the reader that this is not the typical feature story reported over a couple days. Tucker, who wrote the piece about the dying woman, said the prominence his narrative was given in a special pullout section signals to readers that substantial reporting and time went into the story.

TRANSPARENCY EVOLVES

Clark cites three reasons for the shift to greater transparency. First, scandal fatigue. Reporters in all genres have misused the trust of editors and readers. No one wants to give an award back, as Janet Cooke had to when her story about a composite character won the Pulitzer. Greater transparency is a way to avoid a scandal.

Oakes said scandal fatigue had a lot to do with the *Star Tribune*'s decision to use both an editor's note and attribution clues such as "remembers." "We had to assure readers in this age of Jayson Blair and the crises with confidence in journalism we weren't making this stuff up." While narrative has not been any more likely to have these types of scandals than other stories, narrative is affected by them. "The terrible part here isn't in the case of a minor mistake, which inevitably happens," Harrington said. "The terrible thing is when people take advantage of all these things, and when you ask them how they know something, they lie." Strong editing decreases instances of reporter dishonesty.

Another reason is technology. "One of the reasons newspapers have not been as transparent is they don't have enough space," Clark said. "Books can do it because there's plenty of room for footnoting." The Internet leaves no excuse for lack of space.

The third reason Clark calls Pulitzer envy. "So you have this great work, right? And you don't care how many people read it. There's only one thing you care about—the big P." Awards matter. "There's been a reluctance in recent years for juries to give awards to stories that they're not really sure about."

"That was discussed here," Simakis said about the editor's note attached to her story. "Oh, well you need it for contests. So it was lawyers, contests; readers were probably third." Steve Paul of the *Kansas City Star* is not concerned even if modes of transparency are added solely for contests. "I think some readers aren't going to care. But in this age of credibility, I think some readers do care. And why not do it? If it helps win a prize, so what?" Paul feels that not including some sort of attribution or editor's box allows those who don't do the extensive reporting necessary for reconstructed narrative to get away with laziness.

Farragher said prizes contributed to the detailed editor's box that delineated each scene in the marriage series. His cowriter was up for a Pulitzer the year before when no prize for feature writing was given, and they speculated it was because of a need for greater transparency. So prizes were on their minds. But that wasn't the only reason for an editor's box. "I thought it freed us from the need to attribute in a way that wouldn't be jarring to the reader, but in a way to let the reader know where everything was coming from," Farragher said.

Scene reconstructions are no less accurate than traditional newspaper articles. They are also not exempt from newsroom standards. In a way, it's common sense. Let people know reporting methods. And "people" includes editors, readers, and yes, prize judges. But even a fifty-inch editor's note won't mean a thing if one question is not answered. As Harrington asked, "At the same time, are you right?"

Walt Harrington

The Writer's Choice

This article, in a slightly altered form, originally served as the keynote address at the Association of Alternative Newsweeklies/Medill Alternative Journalism Writing Workshop at Northwestern University.

Once upon a time I knew a young woman who was smart and beautiful, talented and hardworking. She reported well and wrote gracefully. She was, like everybody I knew in those years, ragingly ambitious. On the day that this promising and engaging woman—Janet Cooke—would be forever banished from the *Washington Post* and American journalism for having made up her Pulitzer Prize-winning story about an eight-year-old heroin addict, I came to the *Post* newsroom early in the morning. The place was nearly empty when I sat down at Janet's desk to do what any aspiring literary *journalist* should do—report. I took out a pad and began jotting notes on what was before me:

- A bottle of pink Maalox.
- A snippet from a Jackson Browne song: "Nobody rides for free . . . nobody gives you any sympathy . . . nobody gets it like they want it to be . . . nobody, baby."
- These words: "There is no therapy for whatever ails a good reporter like the challenge of an *impossible assignment*"—with "impossible assignment" underlined.
- And this aphorism: "Some people know what they want long before they can have it."

As I had expected, at 12:24 p.m. on April 16, 1981—I know the time and the day because I also jotted them in my notes—two burly men arrived at Janet Cooke's desk, cleaned its top and its contents into cardboard boxes, and rolled them away on a metal dolly. The infamous Janet Cooke was gone.

Well, not exactly.

You are living with her ghost—and her descendants and ancestors in fakery. Jayson Blair of the *New York Times*, a most astonishingly brazen faker known to all of you because his crimes are recent and led not only to his downfall but to the sad downfall of Howell Raines and Gerald Boyd, Numbers 1 and 2 at the *Times*. Stephen Glass of the *New Republic*, who five years ago was caught making up not only quotes and scenic details but entire human beings, businesses, legislation, even products—a Monica Lewinsky inflatable doll that recited Walt Whitman's "Leaves of Grass." That took fakery *and* creativity. Michael Finkel, who invented a West African teenage slave for the pages of the *New York Times Magazine*. Patricia Smith and Mike Barnacle, fallen columnists of the *Boston Globe*.

In the scholarly world—the *Journal of the American Medical Association* admitted that med student Shetal Shah's account of an old Alaskan villager killing himself by walking out into the frozen Arctic was a fake. In book publishing the examples are nearly endless, depending on how you define "fake." Binjamin Wilkomirski's 1995 memoir, *Fragments*, in which Wilkomirski, as a child, watched his mother die in a Nazi concentration camp. Too bad he was actually Bruno Grosjean, a Christian raised in foster homes in Switzerland. The "rounding" of the "corners" to which author John Berendt admitted after the publication of his nonfiction bestseller *Midnight in the Garden of Good and Evil*, a Pulitzer finalist. In a strangely unconvincing defense, Berendt said, "This is not hard-nosed reporting, because clearly I made it up."[1]

Faking it for art's sake has a long tradition: Truman Capote's made-up scenes for *In Cold Blood*; John Hersey's then-unacknowledged creation of a single character carved from the lives of many World War II vets in his famous 1944 *Life* magazine piece "Joe Is Home Now"; George Orwell's recreation of multiple events as a single scene in *The Road to Wigan Pier*. And, let's be honest, newspapers of the nineteenth- and twentieth-centuries that were famous for never letting the facts get in the way of a good story.

Finally, perhaps most frightening, the rise of the personal memoir as

---

1. Doreen Carvajal, "The Truth Is Under Pressure in Publishing," *The New York Times*, February 24, 1998, B1.

a profitable book form in the last twenty years has fostered some of the most bizarre, through-the-looking-glass logic about what is and isn't *truth* in what's loosely called nonfiction. Frank McCourt remembering dialogue as a toddler in *Angela's Ashes*. Vivian Gornick acknowledging that scenes with her mother, described with absolute realism in her much-praised memoir *Fierce Attachments*, didn't take place, and that a conversation her mother had with a street person in New York didn't happen—but that's OK because Gornick knew what her mother *would have said* to that street person if she had run into him. Dave Barry, I'm not making this up!

Now you probably expect me to rant with moral indignation against the fakers and hoaxers and the grand thinkers who argue with a straight face that fact and fiction are indistinguishable and, therefore, any effort to mark their boundaries is itself a fiction, a fraud, a fake.

Not gonna do it.

Because the battle against the aggressive fakers—the Janet Cookes, Stephen Glasses, Michael Finkels, and Jayson Blairs—is hardly worth our time. They are liars who lie to get ahead. They lie out of weakness and fear because they know what they want before they've earned the right to have it. They want fame and glory, and they want it early and often and easy. We can understand such people. They are old-fashioned people. They lack character. Of course, there are still lessons for us.

Simply put, as reporters and writers we must resist our darker angels, not fall to temptation. Get old-time religion. Remember that recognition and respect should come to people for their achievements and that real achievements are hard-earned. A journalism student of mine a few years into the work world once told me that the most inspiring thing I had ever said to him was that I'd never written anything worth remembering in the first ten years of my career.

The truth is, people are weak and flawed, and some percentage of them—of you out there today—will cheat. Look to your left and to your right. Nope, you can't tell which of you are the cheaters. Not by the cut of your suit or the width of your smile or the style of your hair. But cheaters live among us. If you are one of them, stop it. Perhaps you have only a small chance of getting caught, but when you are caught, it will be 100 percent. And *you* will not get Jayson Blair's six-figure book deal. He took down the editors of the *New York Times*. You will take down the editor of the *Fort Worth Weekly*. You will just be gone.

The lesson for editors? Interrogate even your most trusted reporters. Follow the old adage of investigative reporting: Assume the best and look for the worst. Anyone who resents that interrogation has something to hide or is too immature to realize what's at stake. And what's at stake is your credibility, your paper's credibility, and journalism's credibility. Ultimately, if the weight of all the lies becomes too great and society becomes too cynical about our work, our freedom to make honest mistakes without fear of going to jail or being sued into the poorhouse—the real roots of our "free press"—is at stake, too. When you hype a quote, fake a source, pipe a scene, you aren't committing an individual act. You are committing a social act. You are ripping a small tear in the contract of trust that Americans indulgently grant the press.

Yet, as I said, that's the easy stuff. We can attack the militant liars with diligence. We know how to toughen our standards. We understand lying for gain. But the sweeping societal drift of our thinking about what is and is not a *fact* is a tougher nut. Consider the following examples:

- Reality TV shows that are not reality at all.
- Respected biographer Edmund Morris making himself a fictional character in *Dutch*, an otherwise conventional biography of Ronald Reagan, in pursuit, he said, of his art.
- Teachers of "creative nonfiction" who argue that fine nonfiction writers don't seek a shabby thing called "literal truth" but the higher-minded "essence of truth." So combining disparate scenes isn't lying but "composing" in pursuit of literature.
- The journalist who began teaching nonfiction to bright Ivy League students and was shocked at how unconcerned they were about, say, whether a person's hair color was correctly remembered as blond or brown. "What does it matter?" they asked.
- The respected, brilliant book editor who argues that taking notes or using a tape recorder actually undermines accuracy by making people change their behavior, therefore it's more accurate to report only from memory.
- The respected, brilliant book editor who says that if something happened recently in a person's life but it better serves the story by happening twenty years earlier, it's fine to change that particular event because the alteration is in service to the narrative—to the essence of the truth, I suppose.

- The respected, brilliant book editor who tells a writer he should never fabricate anything but instead "trust" the accuracy of his memory—a thinly veiled excuse, I believe, to make up whatever you want because who will know?
- The respected publishing lawyer who says you can pretty much make up what you want as long as you put a little disclaimer in the front of your book saying that some facts and details have been changed for dramatic purposes. The memoir writer Augusten Burroughs included the following note in his book *Dry*, "Certain episodes are imaginative re-creations, and those episodes are not intended to portray actual events," to which the *Washington Post* book critic Jonathan Yardley responded, "There is a word for that: fiction."[2]
- Compare Burroughs's view of veracity with that of the revered historian John Hope Franklin, who once told the *Washington Post*'s Linton Weeks that he had been at the Library of Congress checking his memories against documentary facts as research for his autobiography. Franklin told Weeks he had remembered hearing George Gershwin's orchestra play "Rhapsody in Blue" at a concert in 1928 but that old newspaper accounts had proved his memory wrong—the actual work was "Concerto in F." Weeks asked Franklin what he thought about books written solely on memory. Franklin's answer was simple: "I couldn't do that."

In a certain crowd—probably most of you here today—this debate over accuracy is comical. You, as journalists, are shabby literalists—and proud of it! Yet we can't let it go at that, because the people who think this way are not dumb. They are not all self-serving and greedy. They have been born and bred in a time when we have come to question everything that we think we know. In a time when we understand that, as Akira Kurosawa made us see in his 1950 movie *Rashomon*, that where one stands while observing an event deeply shapes what one sees. What assumptions and biases we bring to bear matter.

We now know that memories are malleable and shifting over time, as we re-remember our pasts to fit our presents. We do not necessarily shape-shift our memory out of malice or self-interest. It's just what we as

---

2. Terry Greene Sterling, "Confessions of a Memorist," August 1, 2003, http://www.salon.com/books/feature/archives/2003/08/01/gornick/index1.html.

humans do to make sense of ourselves in our worlds. We have rightly been made thoughtful and sensitive about the multiplicity of perspectives and the watery quality of memory. We are better off for thinking this way, better knowing that much of what we believe we believe, what we believe we have seen and heard and experienced, is not shared even by others who lived the same experiences. Yet when we extend that insight to say that "facts" do not matter because all is perception, we enter dangerous territory. I think of a time a group of journalism graduate students I knew were being lectured by a philosopher arguing many of these points.

"But what about the truth?" a student asked.

"Truth?" the philosopher said confidently. "After all, what is truth?"

That cowed the students into silence.

Well, truth was at least the table at which they sat. Truth was at least that you could rap it with your knuckles and sound waves would shoot through the room and sensation would rocket through your hand. Truth was at least that the rectangular shape of the table distributed the students in a defined manner. Truth was at least that the table was made of a certain kind of wood that came from a certain kind of tree in the forest. Truth was at least that a craftsman had taken that rough chunk of wood and, through the creativity of his mind and the mastery of his hand, sawed and shaved and sanded and finished it into a table. Truth was at least that beneath its solid existence lived millions of dancing molecules.

Truth may be many things—but it is not nothing at all.

When a tree falls in the woods and nobody hears it, it still makes noise. Words spoken *were* spoken whether or not we can reconstruct them correctly. Events occurred in a certain sequence whether or not we can discern it. A man scratched his head after speaking certain words and did not scratch his head after speaking other words. It was raining or it was not.

I love the novels of Cormac McCarthy, who writes: "this world [. . .] which seems to us a thing of stone and flower and blood is not a thing at all but is a tale [. . .] All is telling. Do not doubt it."[3] Well, if we are interested in human meaning, then what objects mean to us always matters. But life as people live it is not a "tale." A thousand people killed in a mud slide is not a "tale." It is mud-clogged lungs choking for air, crushed bones and skulls, unimaginable pain. It is dead mothers encased in muck cling-

---

3. Cormac McCarthy, *The Crossing* (New York: Alfred A. Knopf, 1994), 143.

ing to their children. That mud slide—and the world of stone and flower and blood—is a *thing*. Do not doubt it. Truth is a documentary, physical reality—as well as the meaning we make of that reality, the perceptions we have of it. It's not one or the other. It's both, entwined. We cannot know the "essence of truth" if we are cavalier about "literal truth."

That belief must be what defines us as journalists, and our credo must be: When accuracy and art conflict, accuracy wins.

All this debate is deeply relevant to those of us who champion what has come to be called "narrative journalism"—what has been variously called "new journalism," "literary journalism," and "intimate journalism." You know the drill—stories rooted in immersion reporting; that move through time; develop character; use real-life action, scene, dialogue, and detail to bring them to life; that have a narrative story arc and that aim to feel like short fiction—what two-time Pulitzer Prize-winner Jon Franklin has called the "true short story." An approach that for thirty-five years now has consciously borrowed the devices of the novel. We can't pretend away that some of our craft's famous liars were reaching for this form of journalism. Janet Cooke was, in newspaper parlance, a "feature writer."

It's not a discussion we should duck. Because being clear about the place and purpose of literary device versus the place and purpose of documentary reality in our work needs serious conversation. In the last few years at the National Writers Workshop conferences held around the country, I've found myself asking speakers and participants if they have ever felt under pressure to make their reporting conform to the needs of dramatic storytelling. Many of them do. H. G. Bissinger, the author of the scrupulously nonfiction books *Friday Night Lights* and *A Prayer for the City*, said a few years ago, "More and more, the public expects nonfiction books to [. . .] have that perfect, seamless storytelling quality. That's an impossibly high bar [. . .] If you're trying to get it right, you really do suffer with the facts you have. Believe me, I went through a lot of days of depression and self-doubt, but one thing I was not going to do is make it up."[4] But the pressure to have the perfect story—facts be damned—is increasingly real.

I once listened to a group of true crime writers talk about how they select book topics. Other than the commercial pressure to write about *rich* murdered people, they were overwhelmingly concerned about find-

---

4. Carvajal, "The Truth is Under Pressure in Publishing," B1.

ing a strong narrative story line, a hero, and a redemptive ending. In other words, the needs of the storytelling form—not a story's social significance—were dominating the stories they chose to tell. I fear that, as literary or narrative journalism has come to be seen as an outgrowth of fictional literary devices that make stories more compelling, we have forgotten that we are not only "storytellers" but the "tellers of stories." We have allowed literary device and framing to become ends in themselves.

The power inherent in novelistic storytelling is not only the power of plot and character and scene. Certainly it's true that drama, intrigue, and tension hold readers. That's good in itself. But the elements of story are not only tricks but tools of inquiry, devices that direct our vision to the many nuances of real life. There's a reason we still read Robert Penn Warren's book, *All the King's Men*. It isn't only because Warren can turn a nice phrase and because the book's plot is compelling and its characters fascinating. It's a brilliant novel because it captures the depth and breadth of human experience—passion, greed, decency, selfishness. It portrays Depression-era Louisiana politics in ways that ring true. And it does so by evoking the richness of lives and culture through not only intellect but through emotion and sensory experience—through the full array of human experience.

The novelist's eye for detail and attention to moral complexity is not just a bag of techniques. It is a way of seeing, a kind of theory of human behavior. When we inquire with what we think of as the needs of storytelling embedded in our search, we are actually attuning ourselves beforehand to that human richness so often missing in our journalism. When used properly, the novelist's eye opens our eyes and heads and hearts to the breadth of what we can and should be looking for in our reporting. It doesn't take us away from the truth, as some traditional journalists fear. It helps us better see and hear and touch and feel the truth before us.

But that powerful lens must be coupled with journalism's twin commitment to documentary reality—a table is a table. The early New Journalists who came out of journalism as opposed to fiction shared this commitment—Tom Wolfe and Gay Talese. The *New Yorker* writers Lillian Ross, John McPhee, Susan Sheehan, and Tracy Kidder have never been accused of playing loosely with the facts. Nor have the younger generation of journalistically-bred literary journalists—the *Washington Post*'s David Finkel, *Sports Illustrated*'s Gary Smith, the *Oregonian*'s Tom Hallman, the *New Yorker*'s Susan Orlean; book authors such as Bissinger, Richard Ben Cramer, and David Maraniss. These men and women are artists not because they make stuff up but because, when unraveling the lives of others, they imbue their inquiries and stories with their own constellation of experiences, values, intelligence, and commanding philosophical questions to unlock the stories within the people they are writing about. What distinguishes a literary journalist-artisan from a literary journalist-artist is that if one or a thousand other reporter-writers went out to do the same story, they would never tell as uniquely insightful a tale.

I suspect that most of these masters thought of what they were doing not only as art but also as popular ethnography. They are people who consciously (as in the case of Susan Sheehan who was influenced by Oscar Lewis) or unconsciously borrowed the mindset of the ethnographer who wants to understand, describe, and explain worlds foreign to him in their own terms while evoking, as documentary writers said as far back as the '30s, the "feeling of a living experience." That, too, is part of our tradition. As journalist Pete Hamill once said, "Writers are rememberers or nothing. That's why the tribe gives us that job." We aren't trying only to tell a good story. We're trying to chronicle and illuminate the world, take readers into the lives of people they would never meet, write stories that are mirrors in which readers can glimpse a piece of unexpected humanity in others and, perhaps, even in themselves. If you do not have this deep commitment, it will be far easier for you to fall prey to making it up.

This is hard work. It's not a fluke that old newspaper union requirements used to define a journeyman reporter as someone with seven years of experience. That's because you learn something in those years of covering fires, murders, airplane crashes, town carnivals, and cats stuck up in trees. You learn first that although philosophers can argue that all reality is socially constructed, in the flesh-and-blood world people have a very clear idea of truth and accuracy.

John Smyth, with a *Y*, doesn't spell his name the same way as John Smith, with an *I*—and he actually cares about the difference. You learn that getting his name wrong reveals a dangerous tendency in you: You are assuming you know what you don't know. Reporting at the grass roots teaches you how many unconscious assumptions you make about everything, how difficult it is simply to describe what we believe to be in front of us, and how little we know with confidence about anything—the spelling of a name, the genus of a plant, the type of clouds billowing overhead, the exact make and model of a certain car, the difference between baby blue and delft blue. And those are the easy challenges. The hard challenges are knowing what people *mean* when they say things, what their gestures and expressions *mean*, what the objects arrayed in their homes *mean* to them.

Fine literary journalists are always masters of their craft, as are all masters of their forms. The famous jazz musician Charlie Parker, who when asked how he had gotten so good, supposedly answered that he had practiced his musical scales every day, all day for ten years and then forgotten them. A fine furniture maker I knew said it took years to learn to cut tight dovetail joints perfectly without having to think about the work intensely. When he had mastered it, though, when it became second nature to him, he could spend his hours of cutting joints thinking about the larger matters of design and artistry. *Esquire* writer Mike Sager, a fine literary journalist who came out of the *Washington Post*, says this of our craft: "The key is to get your tools honed to such an extent that the tools do their job without too much thought. Then your head is freed to do its job. Master technique, and then listen to your heart."[5]

I've always been intrigued by what philosophers call "tacit knowledge," which is knowledge so ingrained that we no longer know how we came to know it—the way we learn to walk and then take mobility for granted, the way we learn to talk and then take language for granted. Perhaps it's no accident that so many of the unmasked liars in our craft were young. They wanted to be the Charlie Parker of journalism before they had mastered their scales, before their knowledge had become tacit.

So much to learn: How to spell names, yes. But we also learn to take nothing at face value, to check and recheck everything. As the old journalism adage goes: "You say your mother loves you—check it out." We learn that there is often a difference between what people remember and what actually happened, and we believe—true to our documentary heritage—that the difference matters, that it is often revelatory. We learn that it is almost impossible to write anything that makes everybody you write about happy. We learn to take criticism as a daily diet. We learn, sadly,

5. Walt Harrington, ed., *Intimate Journalism: The Art and Craft of Reporting Everyday Life* (Thousand Oaks, CA: Sage Publications, 1997), 243.

that our critics are too often correct—that we were wrong. We learn that we have power, that people we write about call us on the phone and cry or run into us at the supermarket and turn away. We learn that their daughters go to school with our daughters. We learn that we can hurt people's reputations in the eyes of not only their community but in the eyes of their children. We learn that people call our bosses and try to get us fired, that they hire lawyers and sue us for millions of dollars, and that judges don't have an intellectual's view of the relativity of facts. We become paranoid about never being found indisputably wrong and to take every detail, word, quote, and conclusion as seriously as death.

We learn that the complicated worlds we enter are next to impossible to recreate in words. It is humbling and exhilarating to realize this. It sets off a lifelong journey to figure out how to turn those thousands of pieces of life and shards of perception into stories that are true to the documentary facts, as they also evoke people's subjective experiences in ways that are accurate to them, that make perfect strangers want to read on, and that, ideally, teach those strangers something important about themselves. We ask strange questions others would never think to ask because we know the answers are necessary to create the flow, sensory texture, and physical atmospherics of our stories: What did the dying woman's room smell like? What does the icy wind feel like on the priest's face? What color was the old Chevy you used to drive? What was the taste of your mother's spaghetti sauce? What did the gunshot that killed your son sound like in the small room? And this is before you even begin to write—rendering scenes, selecting telling details, avoiding melodrama, shaping material without distorting it, aptly balancing the particular and the universal, imposing themes rightfully rooted in your reporting, structuring stories so insight emerges, action concludes, characters change, and tension is relieved. Seven years is not so long a time to learn all of this. But, if it were easy, everybody would be Tom Wolfe or Susan Orlean or David Finkel. They aren't. And most of us never will be. How do you live with that? Do you fake your way?

In the end—you can't escape it—it's a matter of character.

I teach a class in personal journalism. And just last week I was going through passages in my most recent book, *The Everlasting Stream*, a chronicle of my years of rabbit hunting with my father-in-law and his Kentucky country friends. I was trying to help my students understand how paragraphs that read omnisciently were actually sourced. I said that when I write that the wind was gusting at thirty miles an hour, I had gotten the National Weather Service reports for that day. When I write that there was a waxing crescent moon in the sky, I had an astronomer calculate what kind of moon was in the sky on that date. When I write that the green briar bushes have been munched by deer, I had taken a naturalist into the field to confirm this for me. Rain really was falling because I noted it on my pad or into my tape recorder. When I say the men and I lit up and smoked Arturo Fuente Curly Head Deluxe Maduro cigars, we really smoked that brand of cigar, at that moment, in that place. When I write that the men stood in the woods and talked about chicken hawks, Carl's old .22 rifle, and beagle pups lost to marauding coyotes, they actually talked about these things then—not later, not before. When I say the sky was stacked with cloud plateaus on the eastern horizon, it was. I know because I carried a compass on my watchband. When I describe what the innards of a rabbit look like as I am cleaning the dead animal with my knife, I have been through a necropsy of a rabbit with two veterinarian students who annotated a rabbit's plumbing for me.

When I write that the spring water is fifty-one degrees, I have measured it with a thermometer. When I write that on a visit to the White House, I sipped La Crema Reserve Chardonnay and ate smoked salmon mousse, I have checked old White House records through the Bush Presidential Library. When I write that a series of mountains in the Kentucky countryside rise 700, 800, and 900 feet, I have checked those elevations on soil conservation maps. When I write that I remember my father and myself, as a boy, riding in the car one night singing "The Red River Valley" as we drove through the dip in Ashland Road just past Virgil Gray's house, I have relied on my memory of that night and the song but checked with my father to learn that it was Virgil Gray who lived in the house. Then I drove two hours to visit Ashland Road to make sure there really was a dip in the road just past Virgil's home. There was.

My students were quiet when I stopped giving examples. Then one young woman asked incredulously, "Do other journalists do that, too?"

Well, yes. Think of Paul Hendrickson's chapter "Ode to an Instrument" in his Critics Book Circle Award–finalist book *Looking for the Light*, about the life of Depression-era documentary photographer Marion Post Wolcott. It describes the old Speech Graphic camera that Wolcott used. It's an artful chapter. But it's the in-artful substructure—the reporting—that Hendrickson leaves out that makes the artful possible. What he doesn't mention is that he went to the Smithsonian Institution and got copies of the original catalogues and publicity literature on the Speed Graphic. Then he bought an old Speed Graphic so he could examine it, hold it, run through its complicated mechanical routine, hear its clicks and whirs. Then he found an old photographer who had used a Speed Graphic in his youth. Watching and hearing the man talk about the camera with awe and respect, Hendrickson told me later, was "like poetry." Yet none of this laborious reporting is in his chapter. The hard work is hidden. Only the reporter knows what it took. To the reader, it all looks easy. It's not, although it is easy to fake.

And that's why—at the end of the day—it's your choice.

In what do you believe? To what are you committed?

It really is *your* choice.

Contributors' Notes

KIM BARNES is the author of two memoirs, *In the Wilderness: Coming of Age in Unknown Country* (finalist for the 1997 Pulitzer Prize) and *Hungry for the World*, as well as two novels, *Finding Caruso* and *A Country Called Home*. She is coeditor with Mary Clearman Blew of *Circle of Women: An Anthology of Contemporary Western Women Writers*, and with Claire Davis of *Kiss Tomorrow Hello: Notes from the Midlife Underground by Twenty-Five Women Over Forty*. Her essays, stories, and poems have appeared in a number of journals and anthologies, including *MORE Magazine*, *Fourth Genre*, the *Georgia Review*, *Shenandoah*, and the *Pushcart Prize* anthology. She teaches writing at the University of Idaho and lives with her husband, the poet Robert Wrigley, on Moscow Mountain.

ANN M. BAUER is the author of the novel, *A Wild Ride Up the Cupboards*, which was published by Scribner in 2005 and named one of the best books of the year by the *Washington Post*. She is a regular contributor to Salon.com and a frequent writer for many other publications, including *Hallmark* magazine, *Redbook*, the *Sun*, and the *New York Times*. She lives in Minneapolis with her husband and daughter and is working on her second novel.

SOPHIE BECK lives in San Francisco. Her work has appeared in *Film Quarterly*, *Post Road*, *Fourth Genre*, and elsewhere. She is coeditor of *The Normal School* and mom to two girls under three. She once bowled frozen turkeys on ice before thousands of onlookers between periods of a Thanksgiving hockey game. She fell over but also won a turkey.

R. GLENDON BRUNK's many friends and students honor him in death as they valued him in life—a gifted writer, teacher, friend, and iconoclast. Before his untimely death last year, Brunk had lived and worked in Alaska for most of the past thirty years. He was a champion dogsled racer and the author of *Yearning Wild*. Among many interests, Brunk created The Last Great Wilderness, a multimedia slide show designed to save the Arctic National Wildlife refuge from petroleum development and toured the country with it for three years. He taught writing and environmental literature at Prescott College in Arizona.

JILL CHRISTMAN's memoir, *Darkroom: A Family Exposure*, won the AWP Award Series in Creative Nonfiction and was published by the University of Georgia Press in 2002. Recent essays appearing in *River Teeth* and *Harpur Palate* have been nominated for a Pushcart Prize. Her work has also been published in *Brevity, Barrelhouse, Descant, Literary Mama, Mississippi Review, Wondertime*, and other journals and magazines. She teaches creative nonfiction in Ashland University's low-residency MFA program and at Ball State University where she is an associate professor of English.

STEVEN CHURCH's first book, *The Guinness Book of Me: a Memoir of Record*, won the 2006 Colorado Book Award and has recently been optioned for television by Fuse Entertainment. His essays and stories have been published in *River Teeth, Fourth Genre, North American Review, Colorado Review, Post Road, The Pinch, Avery, Salt Hill, Ecotone, Quarterly West, Matter, Quarter After Eight, Powells.com*, and others. His work has been nominated five times for a Pushcart Prize. He teaches creative nonfiction and literature in the MFA Program at Fresno State, where he is a founding editor of the new literary magazine, *The Normal School*.

TRACY DAUGHERTY is the author of four novels, a book of personal essays, and three short story collections, the latest of which is *Late in the Standoff* (SMU Press). He has received fellowships from the National Endowment for the Arts and the Guggenheim Foundation. His biography of Donald Barthelme, "Hiding Man," is forthcoming from St. Martin's Press. He is Distinguished Professor of English and Creative Writing at Oregon State University.

DAVID JAMES DUNCAN is the author of the novels *The River Why* and *The Brothers K*, the story collection *River Teeth*, and the nonfiction collections *My Story as Told by Water* and *God Laughs & Plays*. He lives with his family in western Montana, where he is working on a novel called *Eastern Western*.

TOM FEENEY is a metro reporter at the *Star-Ledger* in Newark, New Jersey.

TOM FRENCH will take the position of endowed chair at Indiana University's School of Journalism in the fall of 2009. He previously worked as a reporter with the *St. Petersburg Times*. His book, *Zoo Story* is forthcoming from Hyperion. He also teaches in the low-residency programs at Goucher and Poynter.

DIANA HUME GEORGE is the author or editor of ten books of creative nonfiction, poetry, and literary criticism. Her recent essay in *Creative Nonfiction*, "Watching My Mother Hallucinate," also appeared in the book *Silence Kills*, and was nominated for a Pushcart. She's taught at Penn State, Allegheny College, Davidson, and SUNY Buffalo, and in 2009 she'll be a visiting writer at Ohio University. George is on the core faculty of the MFA program in nonfiction at Goucher College, and she often teaches at Chautauqua, where she also codirects the Writers' Festival and is a contributing editor of the journal, *Chautauqua*.

PHILIP GERARD is the author of three novels and four books of nonfiction, as well as numerous essays, short stories, and documentary scripts. He chairs the Department of Creative Writing at University of North Carolina Wilmington and with his wife Jill coedits *Chautauqua*, the literary magazine of Chautauqua Institution in New York.

STEPHEN GUTIERREZ is the author of many short stories and essays appearing in fine magazines and of short plays that have been awarded prizes in the San Francisco Bay Area. He is a past Pushcart Prize nominee. His short story collection, *Elements*, won the Nilon Award sponsored by publisher FC2. He has a new book of stories, *Live from Fresno y Los*, forthcoming with Bear Star Press. He directs the creative writing program at Cal State University, East Bay.

JESSIE HARRIMAN, a West Virginia native, holds an MFA in nonfiction writing from the University of Iowa. Her essays have appeared in *Best American Spiritual Writing*, the *Oxford American, Ruminate, Geez Magazine*, and *Bellingham Review*, as well as a few other journals. She held the 2007–8 Milton Fellowship at *Image* and now teaches at the Oregon Extension with her husband Mike.

WALT HARRINGTON heads the Department of Journalism at the University of Illinois at Urbana-Champaign, where he teaches literary journalism. He is a former staff writer for the *Washington Post Magazine* and the author or editor of six books, including *Intimate Journalism: The Art and Craft of Reporting Everyday Life* and *The Everlasting Stream: A True Story of Rabbits, Guns, Friendship and Family*. A documentary film based on the latter book aired nationally on PBS last year.

STEVEN HARVEY is the author of three books of personal essays. *A Geometry of Lilies* was twice honored as a finalist in the Associated Writing Program's nonfiction contest before being published by the University of South Carolina Press. Since then he has published two books from the University of Georgia Press: *Lost in Translation* and *Bound for Shady Grove*. He has edited an anthology of essays written by men on middle age called *In a Dark Wood*, also from Georgia. He received his PhD in American literature from the University of Virginia and is a professor of English at Young Harris College as well as a member of the faculty in the Ashland University MFA program in creative writing.

MICHELLE HERMAN is the author, most recently, of the novel *Dog* and the essay collection *The Middle of Everything*. "Idolatry" is part of a second collection of personal essays with the working title *Dream Life*. She has taught at Ohio State for what seems like a thousand years. (And yes, all these many television seasons later, she has continued to watch "American Idol," with a mixture of pleasure, fascination, horror, and despair.)

BARBARA HURD is the author of *Walking the Wrack Line: On Tidal Shifts and What Remains* (2008); *Entering the Stone: On Caves and Feeling Through the Dark*, a Library Journal Best Natural History Book of the Year (2003); *The Singer's Temple* (2003); *Stirring the Mud: On Swamps, Bogs, and Human Imagination*, a *Los Angeles Times* Best Book of 2001 (2001); and *Objects in this Mirror* (1994). Her essays have appeared in numerous journals including *Best American Essays* 1999 and 2001, the *Yale Review*, the *Georgia Review*, *Orion*, *Audubon*, and others. The recipient of a 2002 NEA Fellowship for Creative Nonfiction, winner of the Sierra Club's National Nature Writing Award, and Pushcart Prizes in 2004 and 2007, she teaches creative writing at Frostburg State University in Frostburg, Maryland, and in the Stonecoast MFA program at the University of Southern Maine.

DIANA JOSEPH is the author of the short story collection *Happy or Otherwise* (Carnegie Mellon University Press 2003) and the memoir *I'm Sorry You Feel That Way: The Astonishing but True Story of a Daughter, Sister, Slut, Wife, Mother, and Friend to Man and Dog* (Putnam 2009). She teaches in the MFA program at Minnesota State University-Mankato.

TED KOOSER's essay, "Small Rooms in Time," was included by Susan Orlean in *Best American Essays* 2005. Since the original appearance of the essay in *River Teeth*, Ted served two years as U.S. Poet Laureate and won the Pulitzer Prize for Poetry.

DANIEL W. LEHMAN is author of *John Reed and the Writing of Revolution* and *Matters of Fact: Reading Nonfiction over the Edge*, coeditor of *River Teeth: A Journal of Nonfiction Narrative*, and series editor of the *River Teeth* Literary Nonfiction Book Prize series for the University of Nebraska Press. A former journalist, Lehman is working on a book about the artistic and ethical implications of character formation in nonfiction narratives. Lehman was a Fulbright Scholar at Stellenbosch University near Cape Town, South Africa, and has traveled widely and studied nonfiction in Southern Africa. He is Trustees' Distinguished Professor of English at Ashland University.

ANDREA LORENZ is a reporter at the *Austin American-Statesman*. She wrote "When You Weren't There: How Reporters Recreate Scenes for Narrative" to complete her master's degree at the Missouri School of Journalism.

MARGARET MACINNIS was, in August of 2008, a VCCA Fellow at Moulin à Nef in Auvillar, France. Her nonfiction has appeared in *Colorado Review*,

Crab Orchard Review, Gettysburg Review, Massachusetts Review, Mid-American Review, River Teeth, and elsewhere. A 2007 William Raney Nonfiction Scholar at Bread Loaf, she is the nonfiction editor at *Pebble Lake Review* and an editorial assistant at *Iowa Review.*

JOE MACKALL is the author of *Plain Secrets: An Outsider Among the Amish* (Beacon Press) and of the memoir, *The Last Street Before Cleveland: An Accidental Pilgrimage.* He is cofounder and coeditor of *River Teeth: A Journal of Nonfiction Narrative* and of the *River Teeth* Literary Book Prize Series. His work has appeared in many publications, including the *Washington Post,* as well as on National Public Radio's *Morning Edition.* He's working on a new book of nonfiction that will be published by Beacon Press in spring 2010.

TEDDY MACKER's recent work is forthcoming in *Antioch Review, Margie,* and *Court Green.* He lives on an old farm in Carpinteria, California.

NANCY MAIRS, though born by accident of war in Long Beach, California, grew up north of Boston. A poet and an essayist, she was awarded the 1984 Western States Book Award in poetry for *In All the Rooms of the Yellow House* (Confluence Press, 1984) and a National Endowment for the Arts Fellowship in 1991. Her first work of nonfiction, a collection of essays entitled *Plaintext: Deciphering a Woman's Life,* was published by the University of Arizona Press in 1986. Since then she has written a memoir, *Remembering the Bone House,* a spiritual autobiography, *Ordinary Time: Cycles in Marriage, Faith, and Renewal,* and three more books of essays, *Carnal Acts, Voice Lessons: On Becoming a (Woman) Writer,* and *Waist-High in the World: A Life Among the Nondisabled,* all available from Beacon Press. The work on her latest book from Beacon, *A Troubled Guest: Life and Death Stories,* was funded by a fellowship from the Soros Foundation's Project on Death in America.

LEE MARTIN is the author of the novels, *The Bright Forever,* a finalist for the 2006 Pulitzer Prize in Fiction; *River of Heaven;* and *Quakertown.* He has also published two memoirs, *From Our House* and *Turning Bones;* and a short story collection, *The Least You Need To Know.* His fiction and nonfiction have appeared in such places as *Harper's, Ms., Creative Nonfiction,* the *Georgia Review, Story, DoubleTake,* the *Kenyon Review, Fourth Genre, River Teeth,* the *Southern Review,* and *Glimmer Train.* He is the winner of the Mary McCarthy Prize in Short Fiction and fellowships from the National Endowment for the Arts and the Ohio Arts Council, as well as the 2006 Ohio State University Alumni Award for Distinguished Teaching. Since 2001 he has taught in the MFA Program at The Ohio State University where he is now professor of English and director of creative writing.

REBECCA MCCLANAHAN has published nine books, most recently *Deep Light: New and Selected Poems 1987–2007* and *The Riddle Song and Other Rememberings,* which won the 2005 Glasgow Award for nonfiction. Her work has appeared in *Best American Poetry, Best American Essays, Kenyon Review, Georgia Review,* and numerous anthologies; her awards include the Wood prize from *Poetry,* a Pushcart Prize, and the Carter award for the essay. She and her husband have recently celebrated their tenth year in New York and all signs (as in "Signs and Wonders") point to many more years in the city they have grown to love.

AMY MORGENSTERN holds a PhD in philosophy in the areas of ancient Greek philosophy, gender and queer theory, postmodern theory, and phenomenology. After nine years of working in academia, she left to pursue an MFA in multimedia conceptual art at the San Francisco Art Institute. Her work, comprising video, audio, text, and photography, operates at the limit between speech and speechlessness. It takes its departure from the idea that language is the seat of our humanity or inhumanity. Her most recent project is a video performance during which she plants herself in the earth at Pt. Reyes National Park for three hours over dusk.

CHRIS OFFUTT is the author of *Kentucky Straight, Out of the Woods, The Good Brother, The Same River Twice,* and *No Heroes.* His stories and essays have been published in *Esquire, GQ,* the *New York Times, Best American Short Stories,* and four appearances in *Best Stories of the South.* In 1996 *Granta* magazine selected him as one of the twenty best writers in the United States. He is the recipient of a Lannan Award, the Whiting Writer's award, a Guggenheim fellowship, an NEA grant, and a Literature Award from the American Academy of Arts and Letters for "prose that takes risks." His short fiction has twice been read on NPR's program *Selected Short Stories* and *All Things Considered*. He has also written screenplays, teleplays for HBO and TNT, and scripts for graphic novels. His work is excerpted in many textbooks, and his books are taught in colleges and high schools throughout the country. He has been a visiting professor at the University of Iowa, University of Montana, University of New Mexico, and Mercer University. Chris has many interests but no hobbies. He lives in Iowa and owns the Midwest's largest collection of rocks with holes in them.

SAM PICKERING has written twenty-one books and teaches English at the University of Connecticut. He has just returned from half a year in Australia where he spent his time roaming libraries and the outback and writing "A Tramp's Wallet," a manuscript describing his rambles.

SETH SAWYERS's work has appeared in *Fourth Genre, Crab Orchard Review, Ninth Letter, Fugue, Jabberwock Review,* and elsewhere. He is currently working on a memoir about growing up in the 1980s, deep in the western Maryland hills. "Fried Eggs" was his first publication, and he will always remember the call from *River Teeth*, a call he answered on a pay-as-you-go cell phone while working a one-week temp job, alphabetizing personnel files for a multinational corporation. He lives in Baltimore and teaches writing classes at the University of Maryland, Baltimore County. He has an MFA from Old Dominion University.

FLOYD SKLOOT's new memoir, *The Wink of the Zenith: The Shaping of a Writer's Life* was published by the University of Nebraska Press in fall 2008. His newest collection of poems, *The Snow's Music* appeared from LSU Press also in the fall 2008. His work will be included in the 2009 *Pushcart Prize* anthology, his third Pushcart appearance.

BRENT SPENCER is the author of a novel, *The Lost Son*, and a collection of short stories, *Are We Not Men?*, chosen by the editors of the *Village Voice Literary Supplement* as one of the twenty-five best books of the year. His short stories have appeared in the *Atlantic Monthly*, *American Literary Review*, *Epoch*, the *Missouri Review*, *GQ*, and elsewhere. His story "The True History," first published in *Prairie Schooner* (summer 2006), is included in the 2007 edition of *Best American Mystery Stories*, edited by Carl Hiaasen. He teaches fiction writing and screenwriting at Creighton University and is at work on a new novel.

MAUREEN STANTON's essays have appeared in *Fourth Genre*, *Creative Nonfiction*, the *Sun*, *Crab Orchard Review* and other journals and anthologies. Her nonfiction has received a National Endowment for the Arts Literature Fellowship, a Pushcart Prize, the Iowa Review award, the American Literary Review award, and been listed as "notable" in *Best American Essays* (1998, 2004, 2005). She teaches in the creative writing program at the University of Missouri in Columbia.

DEBORAH PETERSON SWIFT, a former staff writer for *Northeast* magazine who bicycled from Hartford to San Diego in 1996 and wrote about it for the *Hartford Courant*, headed West again in 2005 and this time settled there. She is Deputy Features editor at the *San Jose Mercury News* and when she is not editing stories about food, wine, and house tours in Silicon Valley, she is contemplating writing a book about the differences between living in the East and the West. (Think hanging out in the sun at a glorious farmer's market, waiting for the termite fumigator to finish spraying poison gas in your breathtakingly expensive condo). Deb is working on a screenplay about her mother's decision to die and exploring California with her writer-husband, Mike Swift. They share their time between Northern California and Truro on Cape Cod.

GAY TALESE was born in Ocean City, New Jersey, on February 7, 1932, to Italian immigrant parents. He attended the University of Alabama and after graduation was hired as a copyboy at the *New York Times*. After a brief stint in the Army, Talese returned to the *New York Times* in 1956 and worked there as a reporter until 1965. Since then he has written for numerous publications, including *Esquire*, the *New Yorker*, *Newsweek*, and *Harper's Magazine*. Talese has written eleven books. His most recent book is *A Writer's Life*, a memoir about the inner workings of a writer's life and the interplay between experience and writing. Talese lives with his wife, Nan, in New York City. He is working on a book about marriage for Knopf.

BRAD K. YOUNKIN: Before his untimely death, Brad K. Younkin taught English in Pasadena, California. He earned his MFA at Southern Illinois University at Carbondale. "The Speed of Memory" was his first published work.